ENCYCLOPEDIA OF WORLD CONSTITUTIONS

Volume I

ENCYCLOPEDIA OF WORLD CONSTITUTIONS

Volume I

(Afghanistan to France)

EDITED BY GERHARD ROBBERS

☑️®Facts On File
An imprint of Infobase Publishing

Encyclopedia of World Constitutions

Facts On File, Inc.
An imprint of Infobase Publishing
132 West 31st Street
New York NY 10001

Library of Congress Cataloging-in-Publication Data
Encyclopedia of world constitutions / edited by Gerhard Robbers.
p. cm.
Includes index.
ISBN 0-8160-6078-9
1. Constitutions. 2. Constitutional law. 3. Comparative law. I. Robbers, Gerhard.
K3157.E5E53 2006
342.02—dc22   2005028923

Facts On File books are available at special discounts when purchased in bulk quantities for businesses, associations, institutions, or sales promotions. Please call our Special Sales Department in New York at (212) 967-8800 or (800) 322-8755.

You can find Facts On File on the World Wide Web at http://www.factsonfile.com

Text design by Erika K. Arroyo
Cover design by Dorothy M. Preston

Printed in the United States of America

VB Hermitage 10 9 8 7 6 5 4 3 2 1

This book is printed on acid-free paper.

Contents

Contributors

General editor **Gerhard Robbers** is professor of law at the Institute for European Constitutional Law at the University of Trier, Germany, specializing in constitutional law, law of religion, and international public law. He also serves as judge at the court of appeals of Rhineland-Palatinate, Germany. He obtained a Dr. iur. utr. from the University of Freiburg and has published extensively in the field of law, including *An Introduction to German Law* (fourth edition, 2006) and *State and Church in the European Union* (second edition, 2005).

***

Kenneth Asamoa Acheampong is an associate professor of private law and public law, as well as the acting dean at the Faculty of Law, National University of Lesotho, in Roma. A barrister, he is also a solicitor of the Supreme Court of Ghana and has published several works on human rights, humanitarian law, constitutional law, jurisprudence, and public international law.

Roland Adjovi has been a legal officer at the International Criminal Tribunal for Rwanda since 2003 and, since 2000, a tutor for a distance learning French-language radio program on human rights. From 1998 to 1999 Adjovi lectured on public law and international law at the Université de Bouaké, Côte d'Ivoire, and from 2000 to 2002 on public law and international law at the Université de Paris II (Panthéon-Assas), France. Adjovi's areas of specialty are in constitutional law, international public law, human rights, and international and criminal law. He has written several publications, including reports on human rights practices in Benin and Côte d'Ivoire and on human rights law in Africa and a commentary on the jurisprudence of the International Criminal Tribunal for Rwanda in *African Yearbook of International Law* (2002 and 2004).

Mohamed A. Al Roken, Ph.D., is an associate professor of public law at the University of the United Arab Emirates and the national vice president of the Union Internationale des Avocats. He was also previously the chairman of the United Arab Emirates Jurists Association and a member of the International Association of Constitutional Law ([ACL).

Elvin Aliyev holds an LL.M. in international human rights law from the Raoul Wallenberg Institute of Human Rights and Humanitarian Law of Lund University, Sweden. Currently a staff member of the Secretariat of the European Committee for the Prevention of Torture and Inhuman or Degrading Treatment or Punishment, Aliyev specializes in civil and political rights, freedom of assembly and association, and the prohibition of torture.

Aurela Anastasi has been a professor of constitutional law and history of institutions at the University of Tirana since 1987. The head of the Public Law Department and of the Albania Constitutionalists Association, Anastasi has also practiced civil law and acted as an adviser to several Albanian nongovernmental organizations. Anastasi is the author of several publications, including the monograph *Political Institutions and Constitutional Law in Albania during 1912–1939* (1998) and two textbooks for the students of the Law Faculty: *History of Institutions* (2004) and *Constitutional Law* (2004). In addition Anastasi has written numerous articles, papers, and speeches on scientific national and international activities in constitutional law, history of law, law on religion, and constitutional history.

Anthony Hewton Angelo holds an LL.M. from Victoria University of Wellington, New Zealand. He is a professor of law, whose research interests are comparative law, conflict of laws, and Pacific law. He is a member of Wellington District Law Society, New Zealand Association for Comparative Law, Society of Public Teachers of Law, Australasian Law Teachers Association, and International Academy of Comparative Law. Angelo is a constitutional and legal adviser to many Pacific states.

Agúst Thor Árnason is a professor of law in the Faculty of Law and Social Sciences, University of Akureyri, Iceland. He is the director of the Icelandic Human Rights Center.

Ayodele Atsenuwa earned an LL.B. from the University of Ife (now Obafemi Awolowo University), Nigeria, in 1984; an LL.M. in criminology and criminal justice administration from the University of London, England, in 1987; and an LL.M. in law and development from the University of Warwick, England, in 1998. Currently an associate professor of public law at the Faculty of Law, University of Lagos, Nigeria, Atsenuwa has extensive teaching and research experience and has published works on public law, especially on human rights in Nigeria. Atsenuwa is a social activist involved with human nongovernmental work and has been director of the Legal Research and Resource Development Centre, a Nigerian human rights nongovernmental organization, since 1995.

Samir A. Awad holds a Ph.D. in political science from Columbia University, New York, and is chairman of the Political Science Department at Bir Zeit University, Palestine. He has been a researcher at the Palestinian Centre for Policy and Survey Research (2003) and then the director of the Palestinian Centre for Regional Studies. In both capacities Awad has been an observer of the legislation process.

Ringolds Balodis is an associate professor and head of the Department of Constitutional Law at the Faculty of Law, University of Latvia. He is the former director of the National and Religious Affairs Department in the Latvian Republic Ministry of Justice, president of the Latvian Association for Freedom of Religion (AFFOR), and head of the Board of Religious Affairs, Republic of Latvia.

Bernard Bekink holds a B.L.C., LL.B., and LL.M. in public law from the University of Pretoria, South Africa. He is currently in the process of completing an LL.D. in public law at the same university. A senior lecturer in public law and a practicing attorney of the High Courts of South Africa, Bekink specializes in public law and especially in constitutional and local government law. He has conducted various research projects on constitutional law matters and is also currently a vice chair of the International Bar Association's Public Law Committee.

Nathalie Bernard-Maugiron, Ph.D. in law, is a senior researcher at the Institut de recherche pour le développement in Cairo, Egypt, and a professor of public law and human rights law at the American University in Cairo. She works in constitutional law, personal-status law, and the judiciary in Egypt and the Arab world. She has worked for several international and national nongovernmental organizations.

Nadia Bernoussi earned an M.S. in public law from the University of Montpellier, France, in 1984 and a Ph.D. in public law from Rabat University, Morocco, in 1998. As a professor at the Ecole Nationale d'Administration since 1984, Bernoussi specializes in constitutional law.

Malte Beyer holds an LL.M. from the College of Europe, Bruges, Belgium, and is a J.D. candidate at the University of Trier, Germany.

Chacha Bhoke Murungu holds an LL.B. (Hons) from the University of Dar-es-Salaam, Tanzania, and an LL.M. from the University of Pretoria, South Africa. Bhoke Murungu has taught public international law and prepared a legal memorandum, "Joint Criminal Enterprise and Those Who Bear the Greatest Responsibility," for the defense team of the Special Court for Sierra Leone.

Sophie C. van Bijsterveld, Ph.D., is an associate professor of European and public international law at Tilburg University in the Netherlands. She is a member of the Dutch Council for Public Administration (Raad voor het openbaar bestuur), a member of the Advisory Panel on Freedom of Religion or Belief of the Office for Democratic Institutions and Human Rights of the Organisation for Security and Cooperation in Europe (ODIHR/OSCE), and a member of the board of the Dutch Association for Comparative Law.

Ann Black, B.A., BsocWk, LL.B. (Hons), LL.M., S.J.D., was admitted as a barrister to the Supreme Court of Queensland, Australia. She is a lecturer in law at the T. C. Beirne School of Law at the University of Queensland and a fellow of the Centre for Public, International and Comparative Law at the University of Queensland. Black is the coeditor of the *LAWASIA* journal.

Lasia Bloss, LL.M., received her LL.M. in European studies from the College of Europe in Bruges, Belgium, in 2001 and was an Emile-Noël fellow and teaching/research assistant to Professor Joseph H. H. Weiler at the Jean Monnet Center for International and Regional Economic Law and Justice at Harvard Law School and New York University School of Law from 2001 to 2003. Currently, she is working in the law department of the Foreign Ministry in Berlin, Germany, while finalizing her Ph.D. dissertation.

Michael Blumenstock is a researcher at the Institute for Legal Policy at the University of Trier, Germany. From 1994 to 2000 he completed law studies at the University of Trier, Germany, and the University of Sussex at Brighton, United Kingdom. He completed the first state exam in law in 2000 and the second state exam in law in 2002. Blumenstock's areas of work include constitutional law, expert commissions in particular, and international and European law.

Anja-Isabel Bohnen studied law at the University of Trier, Germany, and at the University of Málaga, Spain, from 1994 to 2001; from 2002 to 2004 she completed an obligatory two years' work in Trier (Germany), Spain, and Luxembourg; in November 2004 she passed her second state exam in law. Since 2005 she has been employed by the M. M. Warburg-Luxinvest S.A. in Luxembourg and has been working on a doctoral dissertation on constitutional law. Her areas of specialization are European law, international public law, constitutional law, and law of funds.

Bettina Bojarra, M.A., graduated from the Law Faculty of the University of Augsburg and then obtained a postgraduate degree from the European Master's Program in Human Rights and Democratization, a European Union initiative to create a pool of qualified human rights professionals in Europe. She has since worked for the European Parliament in Luxembourg. After a legal training program at the Regional Court of Appeal of Munich, Germany, she was admitted to the bar in 2005.

Christoffel Johannes Botha holds a B.A. (Hons) in international politics from the University of South Africa, an LL.B. from the University of Pretoria, and an LL.D. from the University of South Africa. Botha is currently a professor of public law and head of the Department of Public Law at the University of Pretoria, South Africa, and teaches and publishes in the fields of legal interpretation, constitutional law, media law, human rights law, and international humanitarian law. Botha has also written a textbook on interpretation of legislation (2005).

Alan Bronfman, Ph.D., is a professor of constitutional law at the Catholic University of Valparaiso, Chile. He is a member of the Political Science and Law Advisory Group for the National Research Fund.

Eulogi Broto Alonso is currently a judge in the province of Barcelona, Spain. He holds a Ph.D. from the University of Barcelona and a doctor license in canon law from the Catholic University of Leuven, Belgium. He has been a professor of state ecclesiastical law at the University of Barcelona (1997–2003), a notary at the Ecclesiastical Court of the Archdiocese of Barcelona (1993–1999), and a judge at the courts of Huesca in the province of Aragón, Spain (2000–2001 and 2001–2002). He has been a member of the Ilustre Colegio de Abogados de Sant Feliu de Llobregat, Barcelona, since 1998. He is an expert in and has worked on several publications about canon law, ecclesiastical law, matrimonial law, and religious freedom in Spain and other nations.

Vincenzo Buonomo holds an M.S. in international law and in European law and a Ph.D. in *utroque iure* (canon law and comparative law) from the Pontifical Lateran University (Vatican City). He is professor of international law and international organization at the Institute of Law, Pontifical Lateran University, and has published books and articles on international institutions, human rights law, and international law and cooperation. His areas of specialization include the role and activities of the Holy See and of the State of Vatican City in the international community. Professor Buonomo represents the Holy See at

the Commission for Democracy through the Law (Venice Commission) and at the Steering Committee for Human Rights of the Council of Europe and participates as legal adviser in the Delegations of the Holy See to the United Nations Bodies on Human Rights, Food and Agriculture Organisation (FAO), International Fund for Agricultural Development (IFAO), and World Food Programme (WFP). He is a member of the Advisory Panel of Experts on Freedom of Religion or Belief of the Office for Democratic Institutions and Human Rights of the Organisation for Security and Co-operation in Europe (OSCE).

Oerd Bylykbashi graduated in law in 1996 from the University of Tirana, Albania, and has been head of the Electoral Reform Unit in the Democratization Department of the Organisation for Security and Co-operation in Europe (OSCE) in Albania since 2001. Bylykbashi worked for the Albanian parliament as an expert for the 2002–2003 electoral reform and was cochairman of the Technical Expert Group of the assembly for the 2004 electoral reform.

Licia Califano has been a professor of constitutional law at the University of San Marino since 2003. Califano is a former professor of constitutional law in the Faculty of Law of the University of Urbino (2000–2001) and is a board member of the Ph.D. program in constitutional law at the Universities of Bologna, Genova, Parma, Salerno, Urbino, and Modena–Reggio Emilia, Italy. Her areas of interest include constitutional law, local government, and European Union law. She has published several works, including *Innovazione e conformità nel sistema regionale spagnolo* (1988), *Le commissioni parlamentari bicamerali nella crisi del bicameralismo italiano* (1993), *Saggi e materiali di diritto regionale* (with A. Barbera) (1997), *Argomenti di diritto costituzionale* (2000), and *Il contraddittorio nel processo costituzionale incidentale* (2003).

Jennifer Corrin Care, Ph.D., is the executive director of comparative law in the Centre for Public, International and Comparative Law and senior lecturer in law of evidence and South Pacific comparative law in the T. C. Beirne School of Law, University of Queensland, Australia. She was formerly an associate professor in the School of Law at the University of the South Pacific in Vanuatu, where she taught contract law, civil procedure, and dispute resolution. Between 1987 and 1996 Care practiced as principal in her own law firm in the Solomon Islands, and she has also practiced as a solicitor in England. In 1999 she was a visiting fellow at the Institute of Advanced Legal Studies, University of London, England. Care has published many works in the areas of court systems, civil procedure, customary law, human rights, land law, South Pacific law, and constitutional and contract law. These works include *Contract Law in the South Pacific* (2001), *Civil Procedure and Courts in the South Pacific* (2004), and *Civil Procedures of the South Pacific* (1998). She is coauthor of *Introduction to South Pacific Law* (1999) and *Proving*

Customary Law in the Common Law Courts of the South Pacific (2002).

Jesús María Casal Hernández is the dean and professor of constitutional law at the Law Faculty of the Andrés Bello Catholic University, a professor of human rights at the Center of Graduate Studies of the Central University of Venezuela, the vice president of the Venezuelan Association of Constitutional Law, and a member of the Andean Commission of Jurists. He graduated summa cum laude from the Andrés Bello Catholic University (1998). He is a specialist in administrative law at the Central University of Venezuela and received the juris doctor from Complutense University, Madrid, Spain. Casal Hernández was formerly a lawyer and subdirector of human rights at the Prosecutor General's Office and director of the Department of Studies and Representation of the Parliamentary Council Office of the Congress of the Republic.

Alma Chacón Hanson is a doctor in law and a professor of introduction to law at Venezuela's Central University and a professor of introduction to law and philosophy of law at Andrés Bello Catholic University. She previously was an investigative attorney in the Venezuelan Parliamentary Council Office, assessor attorney of the National Legislative Commission, assessor attorney of a National Assembly Citizen Participation Commission, and external assessor of the Venezuelan Parliamentary Council Office.

Juan Manuel Charry Urueña is a titular professor of constitutional theory in the Colegio Mayor de Nuestra Señora del Rosario, Bogotá, Colombia, and was dean of the School of Law from 2001 to 2003. A graduate of Colegio Mayor Nuestra Señora del Rosario, he specializes in constitutional law and political science.

Tsi-Yang Chen is a professor of law at the National Taipei University, Taiwan. Chen is a member of the Human Rights Advisory Committee, Presidential Office; an Executive Yuan member of the Petitions and Appeals Committee; Executive Board member of the Taiwan Law Society; Executive Board member of the Taiwan Administrative Law Society; executive director of the Constitutional Law and Administrative Law Committee; adviser of the Ministry of the Interior; and a member of the Petitions and Appeals Committee of the Ministry of the Interior. Chen's areas of expertise include constitutional law, administrative law, and environmental and technology law. Chen has published several works in the field of constitutional and administrative law.

Danwood Mzikenge Chirwa earned an LL.D. in the area of obligations of nonstate actors in relation to socioeconomic rights from the University of the Western Cape; his LL.M. from the University of Pretoria, South Africa; and his LL.B. (Hons) from the University of Malawi. He is currently a senior lecturer in law at the University of Cape Town, where he has taught human rights law and business law since January 2004. He was admitted to practice law in the High Court and Supreme Court of Malawi in 2001. Chirwa practiced law with the firm of Savjani & Company of Malawi from 2000 to 2002 and worked as a doctoral researcher in the SocioEconomic Rights Project of the Community Law Centre between 2002 and 2004. He has published widely in the field of socioeconomic rights, the horizontal application of human rights, children's rights, privatization, women's rights, and the protection of human rights under the Malawian constitution.

Chongko Choi is a professor of law at the College of Law, Seoul National University, South Korea. He studied law at Seoul National University from 1966 to 1972 and received a doctor of jurisprudence degree at Freiburg University in Germany in 1979. Choi was formerly a visiting professor at University of California–Berkeley and Harvard Law Schools and a visiting professor at University of Hawaii. In 2002 Choi was a distinguished visiting professor at Santa Clara University Law School, teaching East Asian law and comparative law. Since 2003 Choi has been a member of the Executive Committee of the International Association of Legal Philosophy and Social Philosophy (IVR) and the president of the Korean Association of Legal History and of the Korean Biographical Society. Choi has published more than 20 books on Korean law and jurisprudence. Choi's English titles include *Law and Justice in Korea: South and North* (2005) and *East Asian Jurisprudence* (2006).

Moshe Cohen-Eliya, Ph.D., is an associate professor of constitutional law at the Ramat-Gan Law School, Israel. He received both LL.B. and LL.D. degrees from the Hebrew University in Jerusalem, Israel, and has done his postdoctoral work at Harvard University.

Abdulai O. Conteh has been chief justice of Belize since 2000. Conteh has practiced and taught law in both the University and the Law School of Sierra Leone and has practiced law in Gambia. A member of Parliament in Sierra Leone from 1977 to 1992, Conteh served for several years as minister of foreign affairs of Sierra Leone. Conteh also served as minister of finance, attorney general, and minister of justice and was first vice president and minister of internal affairs. Conteh's areas of work include constitutional law, international public law, human rights, and the environment. Conteh is author of several articles on law, governance, democracy, and the environment and of the book *Constitution of Sierra Leone* (1991).

Pierre Delvolvé has been a professor at the University Panthéon-Assas-Paris II, France, since 1981. He received his doctor of law from the Faculty of Law of Paris in 1966. Delvolvé was president of the *concours d'agrégation de droit public* (the competition for France's highest teaching degree in public law) from 1999 to 2000. He is vice president of the Supreme Tribunal of Monaco. Delvolvé has published many articles and books, including *Le Système français de protection des administrés contre l'administration* (coauthored with Doyen Vedel) (1991), *Droit public de l'économie* (1998), and *Le droit administratif* (2002).

Ioana Dumitriu holds an M.A. from the Faculty of Law, University of Bucharest, Romania, and an M.A. from the French College of European Studies. Dumitriu has worked as an agent of the government for the European Court of Human Rights Department and has been the third secretary in the Romanian Ministry of Foreign Affairs since November 2003.

Satyabhoosun B. Domah is a Supreme Court judge in Mauritius and has published three books on Mauritian law: *The Essentials of the Mauritian Legal System* (1989), *The Theory and Practice of the Mauritian Law on Swindling* (1988), and *The Mauritian Road Traffic Offences* (1993). He holds a Ph.D. in comparative law from Aix-Marseille University, France, and an LL.M. from University College, London, England, and was called to the bar at Middle Temple, London. Domah is a fellow of the Institute of Advanced Legal Studies, University of London; a member of the Commonwealth Magistrates and Judges Association; and a lecturer in administrative law at the University of Technology, Mauritius, and in principles of legal and judicial administration at the University of Mauritius.

Inger Dübeck is a professor of law at the University of Copenhagen, Denmark. She received her J.D. at the University of Copenhagen in 1978. She was candidate in law at the Law Faculty of the University of Copenhagen, where she was also a senior lecturer in legal history (1977–1991). She was a professor in family law at Aarhus University, Denmark (1991–1999). In 1999 she returned to the University of Copenhagen, where she studies and teaches legal history. Dübeck is specialized in Danish and European legal history. Her spheres of interest are church law, law of personal status and rights, and women's law.

Achilles Emilianides is an advocate with the firm Achilles & Emile C. Emilianides, Cyprus, who specializes in constitutional law, human rights, and law and religion. He holds a degree in law from the Aristotelian University Thessaloniki, Greece; an LL.M. from the Leicester University, England; and postgraduate degrees from the Aristotelian University. He is also a researcher and a member of the Cyprus Institute of Mediterranean, European and International Research and a member of the Executive Board of the Human Rights Cyprus nongovernmental organization. Emilianides is coeditor of the *Cyprus Yearbook of International Relations*. His major publications include *The Constitution of Cyprus after the EU Accession* (2005), *The Constitutional Aspects of the Annan Plan for the Solution of the Cyprus Problem* (2003), and *The Parliamentary Co-Existence of Greeks and Turks in Cyprus* (2003). Further publications relate to ecclesiastical

law, history of law, constitutional law, constitutional history, European Union law, intellectual property law, competition law, and human rights law.

Petros Evangelides received a doctorate at the University of Berne and is currently an assistant at the University of Zurich.

Carolyn Evans is the deputy director at the Centre for Comparative Constitutional Studies, Faculty of Law, University of Melbourne, Australia, and a former stipendiary lecturer, Exeter College, Oxford University, England. She specializes in constitutional and international law, particularly in the area of religious freedom and institutional protection of human rights. Evans has several publications, including *Religious Freedom under the European Court of Human Rights* (2000), *Religion and International Law* (coedited) (1998), and *Mixed Blessings: Women, Laws and Religion in the Asia-Pacific Region* (coedited) (2006).

João Miguel Fernandes holds an LL.B. from Catholic University of Mozambique Law School, a master of arts in development management (M.A.D.M.) from the Institute of Development Research and Development Policy Ruhr-University Bochum, Germany, and a master of laws in human rights and democratization in Africa from the University of Pretoria, South Africa.

Edmund Amarkwei Foley received his LL.B. from the University of Ghana in 2000. He entered the Ghana School of Law, Accra, in the same year in the professional law course and was called to the Ghana Bar in 2002. In 2004 he graduated from the University of Pretoria, South Africa, with an LL.M. in human rights and democratization in Africa. Foley is currently an associate barrister and solicitor with the law firm Sam Okudzeto and Associates, based in Accra, Ghana, and the Commonwealth Human Rights Initiative (CHRI), Africa Office Coordinator for the "Enhancing Police Accountability in Ghana" project. Since 2004 he has been developing his expertise in human rights, conflict resolution, and constitutional law through research, notable among which was a working visit to Rwanda during the 10th anniversary of the genocide. During this period he also worked and studied human rights in the Middle East and Africa at the American University in Cairo (AUC), Egypt. He was involved with human rights advocacy training for Egyptian human rights lawyers and activists at the International Human Rights Law Outreach Project at the American University in Cairo.

Idi Gaparayi holds an LL.M. from both Harvard Law School and the University of Pretoria, South Africa. Formerly a lecturer of public law at the National University of Rwanda, Gaparayi is now a legal officer in chambers at the United Nations International Criminal Tribunal for the former Yugoslavia.

Vivianne Geraldes Ferreira earned her bachelor in law in 2002 and her master in civil law in 2005, at the University of São Paulo School of Law, Brazil. Associated with the Brazilian Bar Association since 2003, Geraldes Ferreira is a lawyer in São Paulo and specializes in civil and business law. She has done extensive research in the area of civil law and philosophy and theory of law, along with the relationship between fundamental rights and civil law, specifically with regard to contract law.

Dimitar Gochev is a former judge in the Constitutional Court of the Republic of Bulgaria and a judge at the Court of Arbitration, International Chamber of Commerce (ICC), Paris. He is the former vice president of the Supreme Court and the former president of the Commercial Department of the Supreme Court of Arbitration.

Miguel González Marcos is an associate with the Heinrich Böll Foundation and a lawyer admitted to the bar in the Republic of Panama, Minnesota, and New York. An attorney with Wolters Kluwer Financial Services, he previously was a professor of law at the University of Panama. Gonzáles received an LL.B. from the University of Panama; a Dr. iur. from the Johann Wolfgang Goethe Universität, Frankfurt, Germany; a J.D. from the State University of New York at Buffalo; and an LL.M. from New York University.

Raúl Jaime González Schmal is a professor of constitutional law at the Iberoamerican University of Mexico. He received his license to practice law at the Autonomous National University of Mexico (Universidad Nacional Autónoma de México), his master of law at the Iberoamerican University of Mexico City (Universidad Iberoamericana de la Ciudad de México), and is a doctoral candidate at the Distance Education University of Spain (Universidad de Educación a Distancia de España).

Bettina Gräf holds an M.A. in Islamic studies and in political science from the Free University and Humboldt University in Berlin, Germany. She has been assistant to the director of the Center for Modern Oriental Studies, Berlin, Germany, since 2003 and is currently working on her Ph.D. project: Production and Adoption of Fatawa in the Era of Electronic Media with Reference to the Works of Yusuf al-Qaradawi.

Marie-Carin von Gumppenberg is the head of Policy Studies Central Asia, Munich, Germany. Since obtaining her Ph.D. in political sciences, she has worked for the Organisation for Security and Cooperation in Europe (OSCE) in Bishkek, Kyrgyzstan, and Tashkent, Uzbekistan. Von Gumppenberg has many years of research and practical work in and on Central Asia, conducting evaluations and fact-finding missions. Her publications include *State- and Nation-Building in Kazakhstan* (2002), *Lexikon Zentralasien* (2004), and *Kyrgyzstan/Kazakhstan: Quarterly Risk Assessment, Fast Early Warning* (since 2002).

T. Jeremy Gunn holds a Ph.D. from Harvard University and is currently the director of the Program on Freedom of Religion and Belief, American Civil Liberties Union. He is also the Senior Fellow for Religion and Human Rights at Emory Law School. Gunn is the author of several works on religion and law.

Angelika Günzel received a doctorate in law from the University of Trier, Germany. Currently she is working as a law clerk at the District Court of Cologne, Germany. She was formerly a research assistant at the Jean-Monnet Chair of European Economic and Environmental Policy at the University of Trier, Germany, and at the Institute of Legal Policy in Trier.

Muluberhan Hagos is a High Court judge and an adjunct lecturer at the University of Asmara, Eritrea. He has an LL.M. in constitutional practice and fundamental rights from the Centre for Human Rights, Faculty of Law, University of Pretoria, South Africa, and an LL.B. and a diploma in law from the University of Asmara, Eritrea. Hagos has written several articles on fundamental and constitutional law in Eritrea and is in the process of publishing a book on constitutional development in Eritrea.

Susanne Hansen holds an M.A. in Eastern European studies from Copenhagen University, Denmark, and an M.A. in public administration from Roskilde University, Denmark. In her studies Hansen has primarily focused on the institutional structures, democracy, and rule of law in some former Soviet Union countries. Living many years in the former Soviet Union has enabled her to study these areas up close.

Seyed Mohammad Hashemi is a professor of public law and the director of the Public Law Group and International Law Group at the University Shahid Beheshti, Tehran, Iran. He received a doctorate in law from the Université de Paris Panthéon-Sorbonne, France, in 1975. Hashemi has published several books, including *Droit constitutionnel iranien,* volume 1, *Principes et fondements généraux du régime,* and volume 2, *Souveraineté et institutions politiques, droits de l'homme et libertés fondamentales, et droit du travail* (2001).

Boubacar Hassane earned a doctorate in law from the Université des Sciences Sociales, Toulouse, France, in 1996. Formerly a legal consultant at the United Nations Conference on Trade and Development (UNCTAD), Geneva, Switzerland, Hassane is currently a lecturer at Abdou Moumouni University, Niamey, Niger.

Liam Herrick holds both a B.C.L. and an LL.M. from University College, Cork, Ireland. Herrick is currently senior legislation and policy review officer of the Irish Human Rights Commission, where he advises the government on compliance with the human rights standards contained in the Irish Constitution and in international human rights law. Herrick has worked previously with the Irish Council for Civil Liberties, the Irish Law Reform Commission, and the Irish Department of Foreign Affairs.

Nico Horn, Ph.D., is the executive director of the Human Rights and Documentation Centre in the Faculty of Law, University of Namibia. Before moving to Unam, he was a state advocate prosecutor in the High Court of Namibia for seven years. Horn has published several books and articles on human rights and issues of morality. His special fields of interest are constitutional development in Namibia and the protection of minority rights. He is the editor of the *Namibian Online Human Rights Journal.*

Stepan Hulka holds a J.D. from the Faculty of Law, Charles University, Prague, Czech Republic; an LL.M. from the Masterprogramme at the Westfälische Wilhelms-Universität Münster, Germany; and a Ph.D. from the Faculty of Law, Charles University. Hulka is an administrator with the Legislative Department of the Senate of the Czech Parliament, in which he gives legal opinions on international public law and European Union law and drafts implementing legislation. He is also an executive editor of *Church Law Revue.*

Iván C. Ibán, Ph.D., has been a professor of state and church law at the University Complutense of Madrid, Spain, since 1989. He was a professor of canon law at the University of Cádiz, Spain, from 1983 to 1989. He is a member of the Executive Committee of the European Consortium for State and Church Research. His areas of work include constitutional law, canon law, and state and church relations.

Amina Ibrahim holds an LL.M. in international law of war and the use of force and international human rights law from the School of Oriental and African Studies, University of London, England, and is currently a case manager at the Office of the Prosecutor for the United Nations International Criminal Tribunal of Rwanda, based in Arusha, Tanzania.

Sibel Inceoğlu, formerly an associate professor of constitutional law at the University of Marmara, Turkey, is currently a member of the Human Rights Commission of the City of Istanbul. Inceoğlu specializes in constitutional law and human rights law and has published *Right to Die* (1998) and *Right to Fair Trial* (2002), both in Turkish.

Djemshid Khadjiev graduated with honors from the International Law Department of the Turkmen State University. He received an LL.M. in international human rights law from the Central European University in Budapest, Hungary. After working as the staff attorney at the American Bar Association's Central and East-European Law Initiative, Khadjiev is currently a legal adviser at the

Organisation for Security and Cooperation in Europe (OSCE) center in Ashgabat.

Hamid Khan is a senior advocate of the Supreme Court of Pakistan, the chairman of the Executive Committee of the Pakistan Bar Council, and a visiting professor at Punjab University Law College, Lahore, Pakistan. He earned a B.A. from Government College, Lahore, Pakistan, in 1964; an LL.B. from University Law College, University of the Punjab, Lahore, in 1966; an M.A. in history from the University of the Punjab, Lahore (1968); and an LL.M. from the College of Law, University of Illinois, Champaign, Illinois. Khan is the author of *Constitutional and Political History of Pakistan* (2001) and *Eighth Amendment: Constitutional and Political Crises in Pakistan* (1994).

Magnus Killander holds an M.A. in human rights and democratization from the University of Padua, Italy, and an LL.M. from Lund University, Sweden. Killander is currently an LL.D. candidate at the Centre for Human Rights, University of Pretoria, South Africa.

Kithure Kindiki, Ph.D., was previously a lecturer of constitutional and international law at Moi University, Eldoret, Kenya, and is currently a lecturer of public international law at the University of Nairobi, Kenya. Kindiki specializes in public international law, human rights law, and constitutional law. Kindiki has published several works, including articles in *Human Rights Law in Africa* (2004), *East African Journal of Human Rights* (2004), *Yearbook of International Humanitarian Law* (2001), and *Zambia Law Journal* (2003).

Edward C. King has been the executive director of the National Senior Citizens Law Center (NSCLC), the only U.S. national organization focused on legal issues that affect elderly and disabled low-income people, since January 2002 and has been associated with the organization more than eight years. In addition to his work with the center and as deputy director and chief of litigation of Micronesian Legal Services Corporation (1972–1976), his public interest law background includes service as directing attorney of the University of Detroit Law School Center for Urban Law and Housing from 1970 to 1972. Before moving to public interest law, he worked in private practice engaged in corporate and business law from 1964 to 1970.

Merilin Kiviorg is a Ph.D. candidate at the University of Oxford, England, and a lecturer in public international law and European Community law at the University of Tartu, Estonia. Kiviorg is a fellow of the Constitutional Law Institute, Estonian Law Center Foundation. Kiviorg's areas of work are public international law, constitutional law, human rights, and law on religion. Kiviorg has been an adviser to the Ministry of Internal Affairs Department of Religious Affairs, Legal Chancellor and Office of the

President, Estonia. Her publications include articles in *Rechtstheorie: Zeitschrift für Logik, Methodenlehre, Kybernetik und Soziologie des Rechts* (2001) and *Church Autonomy: A Comparative Survey* (2001).

Andreas Kley is a professor of public law, constitutional history, and philosophy of law at the University of Zurich, Switzerland, and has several publications in law and constitutional history. He received a Dr. rer. publ. and the *habilitation* (highest academic degree) from the University of Sankt Gallen, Switzerland.

John C. Knechtle is a professor of law and the director of international programs at Florida Coastal School of Law. He teaches constitutional law, international law, comparative law, and comparative constitutional law. He received his B.A. from Wheaton College and a J.D. from Emory University School of Law, where he was the editor in chief of *International Law Journal*. He also studied at the Institut d'Études Européenes, Vrije Universiteit Brussel, in Brussels, Belgium. Professor Knechtle is the cofounder and president of the American and Caribbean Law Initiative (ACLI), a consortium of five U.S. and three Caribbean law schools dedicated to the development of law, legal institutions, and collaborative relationships in the Caribbean basin.

Jolanta Kuznecoviene is the head of the Department of Sociology at Vytautas Magnus University, Lithuania. She holds a Ph.D. in philosophy from Saint Petersburg University. Kuznecoviene has published several works, including chapters in *State and Church in the European Union* (2005), *Law and Religion in Post-Communist Europe* (2003), *Diritto e religione nell'Europa post-comunista* (2004), and *Cirkev a stat v Litve // Štat a cirkev v postsocialistickej Europe II: Ustav prie vztahy štatu a cirkvi* (2004) and articles in *European Journal for State and Church Research* (1999) and *Politines sistemos* (1995).

Eric L. Kwa is currently a lecturer in law at the University of Papua New Guinea Law School. Kwa also holds a Ph.D. from the Auckland University Law School, New Zealand. Kwa's areas of work include constitutional and administrative law, local government law, environmental law, natural resources law, and customary or traditional law. Kwa has been actively involved in research in these areas over a period of 10 years and is a practicing lawyer, as well as a consultant to the Papua New Guinea government and international organizations. Kwa's publications include *Constitutional Law of Papua New Guinea* (2001), *Twenty Years of the Papua New Guinea Constitution* (2001), *Development of Administrative Law in Papua New Guinea* (2000), and *Judicial Scrutiny of the Electoral Process in a Developing Democratic State* (2003).

Jean-Pierre Lay learned a J.D. from the Université Jean Moulin Lyon III, Lyon, France, and is a lecturer in public law at the Université Paris XII (Val-de-Marne), France. He has published several works in the areas of administrative law, fiscal law, and constitutional law.

Aristides R. Lima, LL.M., has been the Speaker of the National Assembly of Cape Verde since 2001. Formerly he was a legal adviser of the president of the republic and director in the Ministry of Justice of Cape Verde. Lima's specialties are constitutional law and international public law. Lima's publications include *Political Reform in Cape Verde: From Paternalism to State Modernization* (in Portuguese) (1992), *The Constitutional Position of the Head of State in Germany and Cape Verde: A Comparative Study* (in Portuguese) (2004), and *Constitution, Democracy and Human Rights* (2004).

Azza Kamel Maghur earned a B.A. in law from the Faculty of Law, Gar Yunis University, Benghazi, Libya, in 1985 and an LL.M. from the Université de Paris I, (Panthéon-Sorbonne), France, in 1988. Fluent in Arabic, French, and English, Maghur is senior partner at Maghur & Partners, Attorneys-at-Law; a member of the Tripoli bar; and a lawyer before the Libyan Supreme Court. Maghur was a lecturer in the High College of Administration and Finance in Tripoli in 1992–1993 and at the Faculty of Law El Fateh (Tripoli) University in 1996. She has written several articles and is a member of the Lawyers Syndicate.

André Mbata B. Mangu is a professor of public law at the University of Kinshasa, Democratic Republic of Congo, and of constitutional and public international law at the University of South Africa. He is also a resident research fellow at the Africa Institute of South Africa. Mangu was formerly a public law lecturer at the University of Kinshasa, a public law lecturer at the University of the North (South Africa), and a judge at the Peace Tribunal of Kinshasa-Nd'jili. Mangu's areas of work include constitutional law, public international law, and international human rights law. His publications include *Nationalisme, panafricanisme et reconstruction africaine* (2005); many chapters in books and articles in journals, including *Netherlands Quarterly of Human Rights* (2005), *Stellenbosch Law Review* (2004), *South African Yearbook of International Law* (2004), and *Indian Journal of International Law* (2004).

Ngo Due Manh is the director general of the Center for Information, Library and Research Service and head of the Legislative Research Service Division of the National Assembly Office, Vietnam. He holds a J.D. with honors and a Ph.D. in jurisprudence from Moscow State University, Russia. Manh was a Fulbright Fellow and an LL.M. graduate from the Georgetown University Law Center. He has actively participated in working sessions with government agencies in drafting new laws and regulations that resulted in promulgation of the Land Law, the Civil Code, the Law on Organization of the Government, and the Law on Organization of the People's Councils and the People's Committees. He has also published many articles on Vietnamese laws in foreign and Vietnamese law publications.

Alhagi Marong is a legal officer at the Chambers Support Section of the United Nations International Criminal Tribunal for Rwanda (ICTR), Arusha, Tanzania. Marong has been a barrister and solicitor of the Supreme Court of The Gambia since 1993 and is a former senior state counsel, Attorney General's Chambers, Banjul, The Gambia. He has taught at the Department of Law, American University of Armenia, and worked as co-director for Africa programs at the Environmental Law Institute in Washington, D.C. He earned an LL.B. (Hons) from the University of Sierra Leone, 1992; a B.L. from Sierra Leone Law School, 1993; an LL.M. from McGill University, Canada, 1997; and a D.C.L from McGill University, 2003.

Leonardo Martins, Ph.D., LL.M., is a professor at the Federal University of Mato Grosso do Sul, Brasil, where he teaches constitutional law; he is also a professor at the Humboldt University, Berlin, Germany, where he teaches Brazilian law. He has studied law at the University of São Paulo, Brasil, and earned the doctor iuris at the Humboldt University.

Thulani Rudolf Maseko holds a B.A. and an LL.B. from the University of Swaziland. He also holds an LL.M. in human rights and democratisation from the University of Pretoria, South Africa, and wrote a dissertation on the writing of a democratic constitution in Africa with reference to Swaziland and Uganda. He is an attorney of the courts of Swaziland and the secretary general of Lawyers for Human Rights, a professional organization focusing on the promotion and protection of human rights. He is also the head of the Secretariat of the National Constitutional Assembly (NCA), a broad-based organization of civil society and political parties whose objective is to campaign for the promulgation of a constitution with a justiciable bill of rights founded on the free and democratic will of the people of Swaziland, written under an enabling political environment.

John David McClean earned his doctorate from the University of Oxford, England. He is an emeritus professor of law at the University of Sheffield, England, and as a result of holding national office in the Established Church of England, he has worked with a number of parliamentary committees. McClean is an expert on civil aviation law and general editor of the standard text, *Shawcross and Beaumont on Air Law*. As a private international lawyer, he regularly works as an adviser to the Commonwealth Secretariat in matters that relate to international cooperation in promoting civil justice and combatting international organized crime.

Michael McNamara holds a B.C.L. from the University College Cork, National University of Ireland. He has worked on human rights for the Organisation for Security and Cooperation in Europe (OSCE), including its Election Support Team to Afghanistan in 2004. His main areas of expertise are freedom of religion or belief and electoral issues. McNamara was also a legal officer with the Electoral Complaints Commission of Afghanistan.

Florentín Meléndez holds doctor of law and master of human rights degrees from Complutense University, Madrid, Spain, and a licenciatura in judicial sciences from the Faculty of Law, University of El Salvador. He has conducted various studies on human rights and humanitarian law at the International Institute of Human Rights (Strasbourg, France), at the Inter-American Institute of Human Rights (San José, Costa Rica), and at the Human Rights and Humanitarian Law Institute, Faculty of Law, American University (Washington, D.C.). Meléndez is currently a member of the Inter-American Commission on Human Rights of the Organization of American States (OAS) (Comisión Interamericana de Derechos Humanos de la Organización de los Estados Americanos [OEA]). He is the author of several publications on human rights, international law, and constitutional law.

Jörg Menzel holds a Dr. jur. degree from the University of Bonn, Germany. Menzel is currently a senior legal adviser to the Senate of the Kingdom of Cambodia. His specialties are constitutional law, administrative and public international law, and legal development in Southeast Asia and the South Pacific.

Valeria Merino Dirani is a lawyer who has worked to further democracy and transparency initiatives in Latin America for more than 15 years. Since 1999 she has been the executive director of Corporación Latinoamericana para el Desarrollo (CLD), Transparency International's (TI's) national chapter in Ecuador. Merino Dirani has helped to establish a network of TI chapters in Latin America. In 1995, she was appointed a member of the Council of the United Nations University and served as the university's vice president. She has been a pro bono adviser to several committees of Congress and public entities in Ecuador and has participated in numerous programs aimed at reforming aspects of the public sector, including public procurement. Through the CLD, she was a strong advocate for Ecuador's recently passed freedom of information law. Merino Dirani has been on the Board of TI since the 2004 Annual Membership Meeting, held in Nairobi, Kenya.

Rakeb Messele, formerly a legal researcher with the Ethiopian Women Lawyers Association (EWLA) and a Counter-Trafficking Programme coordinator for the International Organization for Migration, is currently a board chairwoman of EWLA and a country program coordinator and senior project manager of Children's Legal Defense Center of the African Child Policy Forum.

Paul Henri Meyers, a doctor of law, is a member of parliament in Luxembourg. He is an honorary president of the Employers Pension Fund and an honorary vice president of the Council of State of Luxembourg. He is also a member of the Chamber of Deputies and president of the Parliamentary Commission for the Institutions and Constitutional Revision and member of the Committee of the Regions.

Ugo Mifsud Bonnici was president of the Republic of Malta from 1994 to 1999 and is currently a member of the Council of Europe Commission for Democracy. He studied law at Malta University and graduated with an LL.D. in 1955. In 1956 Mifsud Bonnici began practicing law at the Superior and Appeals Courts in Malta, in civil, criminal, and commercial law. As Maltese civil law is based on the French Code Napoléon and public law is based on English law, Mifsud Bonnici acquired a practical grasp of both legal systems. Mifsud Bonnici became a member of the House of Representatives in 1966 and is responsible for passing the following laws through the house: the Education Law (1988), the Law for the Protection of the Environment (1990), the National Archives Act (1990), the Broadcasting Law (1991), the Law Transferring Church Property to the State (1992), and the Law for the Protection of Health and Safety at Work (1994). Mifsud Bonnici has published several works, including *The President's Manual* (1997), *How Malta Became a Republic* (1999), and *An Introduction to Comparative Law* (2004).

Neđjo Milićević is president of the Constitutional Court of the Federation of Bosnia and Herzegovina. He also is a professor at the Faculty of Law in Sarajevo, Bosnia and Herzegovina. In 1971 Milićević received a master's degree in legal sciences at the Faculty of Law in Sarajevo, and in 1978 the doctor's degree in legal sciences at the Faculty of Law in Ljubljana, Slovenia. Since 1979 he has been a professor at the Faculties of Law in Sarajevo and in Mostar, Bosnia and Herzegovina. From 1990 until 1997 he was a judge of the Constitutional Court of Bosnia and Herzegovina; since 2002 he has been a judge of the Constitutional Court of the Federation of Bosnia and Herzegovina and until October 2004 its vice president. Milićević is a contributor to several legal textbooks, to *Commercial and Labour Law* and *Local Self-Government in Bosnia-Herzegovina,* and has written commentary on the Constitution of the Federation of Bosnia and Herzegovina and of the Constitution of the Serb Republic. He is the author of *Commentary to the European Chart on Local Self-Government.*

Mohamed Moghram received an undergraduate degree in law from Sana'a University, Yemen, in 1984; an LL.M. from the American University, Washington, D.C., in 1998; and a Ph.D. in law from Pune University, India (1999). Moghram is an assistant professor of public law at the Faculty of Shariah Law, Sana'a University. He was a national legal expert for a United Nations Development Programme (UNDP) project on transparency and accountability in the public sector in the Arab region as well as a local expert on the Yemen Judiciary Support Program founded by the Dutch government. Moghram was also a team leader of the Justice Sector responsible for input to the Yemen Common Country Assessment (CCA) Report funded by the UNDP. Currently, he is the legal and constitutional expert for Yeoman Ward International, New Zealand, on the Civil Service Modernization Project–Yemen.

Sanaty Mohamed holds diplomas in environmental law and in public administration law from the University of Fianarantsoa, Madagascar, and has received an LL.M. in human rights and democratization in Africa from the University of Pretoria, South Africa. She had been working for the International Committee of the Red Cross from 2003 to 2005. Mohamed's main areas of work are human rights and humanitarian law in Africa.

George William Mugwanya earned an LL.D., summa cum laude, from Notre Dame University, Indiana; an LL.M., with distinction, from the University of Pretoria, South Africa; and an LL.B., with honors from Makerere University, Kampala, Uganda. Mugwanya is an advocate of Uganda's Courts of Judicature and was formerly a senior lecturer at the Faculty of Law, Makerere University. Mugwanya's specialties are international law and comparative constitutional law. He is an appeals counsel at the Office of the Prosecutor, United Nations International Criminal Tribunal for Rwanda, and is the author of many works, including *Human Rights in Africa: Enhancing Human Rights through the African Regional Human Rights System* (2003); chapters in *Constitution-Making and Democratization in Africa* (2001) and *Human Rights Law in Africa* (2004); and articles in *Netherlands Quarterly of Human Rights* (2001) and in *East African Journal of Peace & Human Rights* (2001).

Abraham Mwansa received an LL.M. from the University of Pretoria, South Africa, and an LL.B. from the University of Zambia. Mwansa is currently a principal advocate for the Legal Resources Foundation Zambia. His undergraduate research was on the myth of representative democracy in Zambia, and his master's degree research was on election politics and the New Partnership for Africa's Development (NEPAD), comparing the 2001 elections in Zambia and Uganda. Mwansa has been a human rights activist for more than seven years for the Legal Resources Foundation, a human rights nongovernmental organization.

Myint Zan holds both a B.A. and an LL.B. from Rangoon University, Burma; an LL.M. from the University of Michigan; and a M.Int.Law from Australian National University. Myint Zan is currently a lecturer at the Faculty of Social Science, Universty Malaysia Sarawak (UNIMAS), Sarawak, Malaysia. Myint Zan has written numerous academic journal articles and chapters in books on Burmese law and legal history, international law, human rights, and comparative law in publications based in

Australia, Germany, Malaysia, Singapore, the United States, and New Zealand.

Amarjit Narang is a professor of political science, coordinator of human rights education, and coordinator of consumer rights programs at Indira Gandhi National Open University, New Delhi, India. He is also the general secretary for the Centre for Development Studies and Action. He holds a Ph.D. in political science, an M.A. in political science, and a B.A. in political science and history from the University of Delhi.

Juan G. Navarro Floria is a lawyer and professor of civil law and Argentine ecclesiastical law at the Pontificia Universidad Católica Argentina in Buenos Aires. He is the president of the Consorcio Latinoamericano de Libertad Religiosa and founder and member of the Instituto de Derecho Eclesiástico and the Consejo Argentino para la Libertad Religiosa. He is also the former adviser and *chef de cabinet* of the Secretariat of Religious Affairs of the Argentine Republic and is currently a member of the Asociación Argentina de Derecho Constitucional.

Johanna Nelles holds a law degree from the Law Faculty of the University of Heidelberg, Germany, and an M.A. from the European Master's Program in Human Rights and Democratization, a European Union initiative to create a pool of qualified human rights professionals in Europe. She has since worked for the United Nations Economic and Social Commission for Asia and the Pacific, in Bangkok, Thailand, as well as the German Institute for Human Rights and is currently working for the Green Party in the German parliament.

Joakim Nergelius earned an LL.M. from Lund University, Sweden, in 1987 and an LL.D. from Lund University in 1996. Nergelius has been an associate professor and worked in the European Union civil service in the Court of Justice and the Committee of Regions. Nergelius is currently a professor at Örebro University, Sweden. Nergelius's published works include *Konstitutionellt rättighetsskydd—Svensk rätt i ett komparativt perspektiv* (1996); *Amsterdamfördraget och EU: s institutionella maktbalans* (1998), edited with Ulf Bernitz; *General Principles on European Community Law* (2000); and *Challenges of Multi-Level Constitutionalism* (2004), edited with Pasquale Policastro.

Katja Niethammer holds an M.A. from the Free University of Berlin, Germany. She has been a researcher for the German Institute for International and Security Affairs Middle East and Africa Research Group since 2004 and was previously a researcher at the Institute for Islamic Studies, Free University of Berlin, and coordinator for social and cultural history at the Middle East Interdisciplinary Center.

Martin Nsibirwa holds an LL.M. in human rights and democratization in Africa from the Centre for Human Rights, Faculty of Law, University of Pretoria, South Africa, where he is currently a program manager. He specializes in women's and children's rights and the democratization in Africa.

Gregor Obenaus is *chef de cabinet* of the princely House of Liechtenstein. He studied law at the Universities of Vienna and Innsbruck, Austria, and received an M.A. in European studies at the College of Europe, Bruges, Belgium. Obenaus was formerly a legal adviser in the cabinet of the chancellor of the Austrian Federal Republic (2000–2004), a diplomat in the Ministry of Foreign Affairs (1998–2000), and a legal adviser in the Constitutional Department of the Federal Chancellery (1995–1998). He is the author of several works, including *Austrian Participation in the Nomination of Members of Several Bodies and Institutes of the European Union* (2006), *Commentary to the Law on Animal Protection* (2005), and *Requirements of the Community Law for the Austrian Law-Making Process* (1999).

Emre Öktem is an associate professor of public international law at the University of Galatasaray, Istanbul, Turkey, and has been the assistant in constitutional law at the Istanbul University. Öktem is a member of the Advisory Panel of Experts on Freedom of Religion or Belief, Office for Democratic Institutions and Human Rights, Organization for the Security and Cooperation in Europe.

Valerio Onida is a professor of constitutional law at the University of Milan, Italy, and is the former president of the Italian Constitutional Court. He was previously a professor of constitutional law and public law at the Universities of Verona, Sassari, Pavia, and Bologna, Italy.

Bruce L. Ottley is a professor of law at DePaul University College of Law, Chicago, Illinois. He was formerly a lecturer and senior lecturer at the University of Papua New Guinea and district court magistrate at the National Capitol District Court, Papua New Guinea.

Valbona Pajo holds an M.A. in public law and a law degree from the University of Tirana, Albania, and is currently a visiting lecturer in constitutional law of the Law Faculty, Tirana University. Pajo has also been working as a staff member in the Organisation for Security and Cooperation in Europe (OSCE) office in Albania at the Democratization Department, Elections Unit, since 2003.

Un Jong Pak, Ph.D., was professor of law at Ewha Woman's University and is currently a professor of legal philosophy at Seoul National University, Republic of Korea. She was formerly president of the Korean Association of Legal Philosophy and a member of International Bioethics Committee of the United Nations Educational, Scientific and Cultural Organisation (UNESCO).

Ruxandra Pasoi received an M.A. in human rights from Central European University, Budapest, Hungary, in 2000. She is an assistant professor of public international law at the Ecological University of Bucharest, Romania; deputy director of the European Court of Human Rights Department of the Romanian Ministry of Foreign Affairs; and a human rights trainer at the National Institute of Magistracy. Pasoi's areas of expertise are public international law, human rights, and refugee law.

Donald E. Paterson, J.S.D. (Yale University), is an emeritus professor of law at the University of the South Pacific. He was formerly professor of law and professor of public administration as well as deputy vice chancellor at the University of the South Pacific.

Nickolay L. Peshin, Ph.D., was formerly a researcher at the Institute of Legislation and Comparative Law of the government of Russia. Peshin was a consultant and deputy director of the Russian Foundation for Legal Reform (1998–2004). Since 2002 Peshin has been a docent for constitutional and municipal law at the M. V. Lomonosov Moscow State University, Russia.

Lourens du Plessis is a professor of public law at the University of Stellenbosch, South Africa, and has published widely on issues of constitutional interpretation and constitutional theory. He received a B. Jur. et Comm., a B.Phil. and an LL.D. from the North-West University, Potchefstroom, South Africa, and a B.A. (Hons) from the University of Stellenbosch. Du Plessis teaches statutory and constitutional interpretation and comparative constitutionalism and chaired the technical committee responsible for drafting South Africa's first bill of rights in the transitional constitution of 1993.

Roman Podoprigora, Ph.D., was formerly an associate professor at the Kazakh State National University and is currently a professor and department chair at the Adilet Law School, Kazakhstan.

Vardan Poghosyan holds an M.A. in political science from Bonn University, Germany, and is currently a Legal Advice Project coordinator in Armenia in the German Agency for Technical Cooperation.

Latchezar Popov is a barrister at law. He serves as a chairman of the board of directors of the Rule of Law Institute, Bulgaria, a nongovernmental organization established in 1995 that has begun working closely with the Ministry of Interior on a variety of projects. Popov is president of Advocates Europe; his specialty is human rights. Popov is a licensed mediator and trainer from San Diego, California, National Conflict Resolution Center.

Richard Potz has been a professor of law of religion at the University of Vienna, Austria, since 1981 and is currently the head of the Institute for Legal Philosophy, Law of Religion and Culture, at the University of Vienna. He is also a member of the European Consortium for Church and State Research, Madrid, Spain. His areas of work include law on religion, law and culture, legal history, human rights, religious law, and Christian-Muslim dialogue. Potz has published numerous articles and books, including *Religionsrecht* (2003) and *Kulturrecht* (2004).

Ofa Pouono holds an LL.B. and a P.D.L.P. from the University of the South Pacific and an LL.M. with a specialty in maritime law from the University of Queensland. Pouono was appointed as an assistant Crown counsel, and later as an acting senior Crown counsel, of the Crown Law Department. A commissioner for oaths, Pouono has a private law practice as a barrister and solicitor of the Supreme Court in Tonga.

Martha Prieto Valdés is a professor of state theory and the law, philosophy of law, general constitutional and comparative law, and Cuban constitutional law, is chair of constitutional law, and is president of the scientific council of the Faculty of Law, at Havana University, Cuba. She is adviser to several national organs. Prieto Valdés has undertaken many years of research about state and local organizations, rights and guarantees of Cuban citizens, and themes of legal philosophy. She has also written many publications about Cuban constitutional law and theory of law.

Emmanuel Kwabena Quansah holds an LL.B. (Hons) and an LL.M. from the University of London, England, and an LL.D. from the University of South Africa. Quansah is a barrister in England and Ghana, as well as an attorney in Botswana. Quansah is an associate professor of law at the University of Botswana and specializes in family law, succession law, law of evidence, company law, and legal institutions. His publications include *The Botswana Law of Evidence* (2004), *Introduction to Family Law in Botswana* (2002), *Family and Succession Law of Botswana* (2002), and *Introduction to the Botswana Legal System* (2001).

Michael Rahe holds an Ass. iur. and has studied law at University of Trier, Germany, and Lancaster University, England. Rahe is currently an assistant and J.D. candidate at the Institute of European Constitutional Law, University of Trier.

Mianko Ramaroson holds an LL.M. in human rights and democratization in Africa from the University of Pretoria, South Africa, where she is currently a candidate for the LL.D. Her specialty is human rights law as it relates to human immunodeficiency virus/acquired immunodeficiency syndrome (HIV/AIDS).

Victor V. Ramraj, Ph.D., is an associate professor in the Faculty of Law, National University of Singapore (NUS), and has qualifications in both law (LL.B., University of Toronto, Canada, 1993) and philosophy (B.A., McGill,

Canada, 1989; M.A., Toronto, 1990, Ph.D., Toronto, 1998). He is a member of the Law Society of Upper Canada (Ontario). Before joining NUS, he served as a judicial law clerk at the Federal Court of Appeal in Ottawa and as a litigation lawyer in Toronto. He is the coauthor/editor of three books and numerous journal articles on criminal law, constitutional law, and anti-terrorism law and policy and has presented papers to audiences in Canada, Hong Kong, India, Iran, Ireland, the Philippines, Singapore, South Africa, Sweden, the United Kingdom, and the United States.

Barbara Randazzo holds a Ph.D. in constitutional law from the University of Milan, Italy, where she is currently an associate professor of public law, an assistant researcher at the Constitutional Court of the Italian Republic, and a lawyer.

Hartmut Rank graduated from the University of Potsdam, Faculty of Law, Germany, in 2003, after his studies in law and languages in Germany and the Russian Federation. During his studies, he also worked with Russian nongovernmental organizations as well as with the German delegation to the Council of Europe. Currently, he is enrolled at the German University of Administrative Sciences, Speyer. In 2006 he will be admitted to the bar. As a member of the German Society for Eastern European Studies, he is especially involved with legal questions of the region. He has also been seconded as an observer to several Organisation for Security and Cooperation in Europe (OSCE) election observation missions in post-Soviet countries, including Armenia and Ukraine.

Martin Risso Ferrand is a professor of constitutional law and dean of the School of Law of the Catholic University of Uruguay. He is also a member of the Directive Board of the World Association of Jesuit Schools of Law.

Jaqueline Robinson López is an English major at the Universidad Nacional Autónoma de México. She specializes in Spanish-to-English translation, mainly in the cultural-academic fields. Her translations include the book *Guadalupe* and the international bilingual magazine *Museos de México y del Mundo*.

Tim Rogan is a student in the Faculty of Law, University of Melbourne, Australia.

Johan Shamsuddin Sabaruddin is a lecturer in law at the University of Malaya, Malaysia. He holds an LL.B. (Hons) from the University of Malaya and an LL.M. from the University of London, England. Sabaruddin's specialties are constitutional law, law and society, the Malaysian legal system, and Malaysian constitutional law.

Solomon Sacco holds a bachelor of laws degree with honors from the University of Zimbabwe and is currently a staff development fellow in the Legal Aid and Advice Scheme at the Faculty of Law of the University of Zimbabwe. Sacco is the winner of the University of Zimbabwe Book Prize for 1999 and 2000. Sacco's specialties are development law, human rights, labor law, media law, access to justice, land reform, and intellectual property.

Ludmila Samoila holds a diploma in international law from the State University of Moldova, as well as an LL.M. in European and comparative law from the Maastricht University, the Netherlands. Samoila was formerly a legal consultant of the nongovernmental organization Legal Clinic and a legal assistant at the law firm Brodsky, Uscov, Looper, Reed and Partners. She is currently a human rights assistant at the Organization for Security and Cooperation in Europe Mission to Moldova.

Salvador Sánchez González holds an LL.B. from the Universidad Santa María La Antigua, Panama. He is a lawyer admitted to practice in the Republic of Panama and a professor at the Universidad Santa María La Antigua, School of Law. Sánchez González is also the former director for the Admission of Complaints at the Panamanian Ombudsman Office and the current secretary for government, human rights, and indigenous issues of the Panamanian National Assembly.

Balázs Schanda earned a degree in legal and political sciences at Eötvös Loránd University, Budapest, Hungary. He holds a licenciate in canon law and a Ph.D. in legal sciences. He serves at the Constitutional Court of the Republic of Hungary as a senior counseler and as an assistant professor at Pázmány Péter Catholic University and Eötvös Loránd University, Budapest, Hungary.

Martin Scheinin, Ph.D., a former professor of law at the University of Helsinki, Finland, and visiting scholar at the University of Toronto, Canada, is currently a professor of constitutional and international law at Åbo Akademi University, Finland, where he is director of the Institute for Human Rights. He is also a member of the Executive Committee of the International Association of Constitutional Law.

Christine Schmidt-König, Dr. iur., holds a *maîtrise* and master of law from the University Nancy, France, and an LL.M. from the University of Trier, Germany. Schmidt-König is currently an assistant at the Institute for European Constitutional Law at the University of Trier and lecturer for French law and French legal language at the Universities of Trier and Darmstadt, Germany.

Branko Smerdel is a professor of constitutional law and comparative government at the University of Zagreb Law Faculty, Croatia; chair in constitutional law; and editor in chief of *Collected Works of the Zagreb Law School*. Researching and teaching since 1973, Smerdel specializes in constitutional law, comparative government and politics, federalism, the European constitution, and legal English. Smerdel participated in drafting the Croatian Constitution in 1990 and its major revision in 2000 and has been involved in a number of statutes related to elections and human rights. Smerdel is an adviser to the Committee on the Constitution and Standing Rules of the Croatian Parliament. Smerdel's publications include *Ministerial Responsibility in Parliamentary Government* (1977), *Evolution of Presidential Government in the US: Congressional Veto* (1986), *Organization of Government* (1988), *American Theories of Federalism* (1989), *Constitutional Law* (1992, 1995, 1998, and 2006), *Constitutional Choice in European Union* (2003), and *English for Lawyers* (2005).

Marek Šmid, Ph.D., is the deputy director of the International Law Department, Ministry of Foreign Affairs of the Slovak Republic; the vice dean and head of the Department of International Law and European Law, Faculty of Law, University of Trnava, Slovakia; a member of the Attorney Chamber of the Slovak Republic; the vice president of the Slovak Society for International Law; and the conciliator pursuant to Article 2 of the Annex V to the United Nations Convention on the Law of the Sea.

José de Sousa e Brito is a justice (emeritus) of the Constitutional Court, Lisbon, Portugal, and a professor at Universidade Nova, Lisbon. Formerly a visiting professor at the University of Munich, president of the European Consortium of Church and State Research, and president of the Committee for the Reform of the Law of Religious Liberty of Portugal, Sousa e Brito is currently the Portuguese expert at the Committee of Experts for the Development of Human Rights of the Council of Europe. His specialties are philosophy of law, criminal law, constitutional law, and law on religion.

Igor Spirovski is a judge of the Constitutional Court of the Republic of Macedonia, the former secretary general of the Parliament and of the Constitutional Court, a former member of the Venice Commission of the Council of Europe, and a current member of the Council of the International Association of Constitutional Law. He is the author of numerous scholarly articles in the field of constitutional law, notably works on parliamentarism, constitutional justice, separation of powers, European Union law, public administration, and human rights, and has published works in the United States, France, Germany, Poland, Mexico, Portugal, Spain, Greece, and Macedonia.

Philippos C. Spyropoulos, LL.M., Ph.D., is a professor of constitutional law at the University of Athens, Greece. He is a former secretary-general of the Ministry to the Prime Minister and of the Ministry of Justice.

Lovro Šturm, Ph.D., is the minister of justice of the Republic of Slovenia and a professor of public law at the University of Ljubljana. Šturm was previously a judge and president of the Constitutional Court and minister of education.

Demba Sy is professor of public law, specializing in administrative law and constitutional law, at the University of Dakar, Senegal. His current positions are thesis director (*curateur aux thèses*) at the Faculty of Jurisprudence and Political Science (since 1995), coordinator of graduate studies (*Troisièmes Cycles*) at the Faculty of Jurisprudence and Political Science (since 1995), and director of the Laboratory for Law Studies and Political Studies of the faculty (LEJPO) (since 1994). He was also a member of the Reform Commission of the Senegalese Constitution in 2000.

Lidiya Syvko, holds an LL.M. in international law from National Taras Shevchenko University, Kiev, Ukraine. She is currently an assistant at the Faculty of Law of that university.

Eiichiro Takahata is an assistant professor of constitutional law at Nihon University, Japan. Takahata's specialties are constitutional law, comparative constitutional law, and law on religion. Takahata's publications include articles in *Comparative Law* (1998), *Nihon Hougaku* (2000), and *The Religious Law* (2000).

Norman Taku holds an LL.B. (Hons) from the University of Buea, Cameroon, and an LL.M. in human rights and constitutional practice from the University of Pretoria, South Africa. Taku is currently an assistant director at the Centre for Human Rights, Faculty of Law, University of Pretoria. Taku is responsible for the overall management and administration of the master of laws (LL.M.) degree program in human rights and democratization in Africa, a regional cooperation initiative involving six other African universities. In addition he is the coeditor of the French translation of the *Compendium of Key Human Rights Documents of the African Union* (2006).

Laurentiu D. Tanase holds a D.E.A. in sociology of religion from the Marc Bloch University in Strasbourg, France, and a D.E.A. from Robert Schuman University in Strasbourg, Institute for High European Studies. He also holds a Ph.D. in sociology of religions, Marc Bloch University, Faculty of Protestant Theology. Tanase has been a university titular lector at the University of Bucharest, Bulgaria, Faculty of Orthodox Theology, Board of Sociology of Religions, since 2002. He was secretary of state for religious affairs, Romanian Ministry of Culture and Religious Affairs from 2001 to 2004.

Ingvill Thorson Plesner earned a Cand. polit. in social science and public law from the University of Oslo, Norway, in 1998 and is currently a research fellow at the Norwegian Center for Human Rights, Faculty of Law, University of Oslo. In addition to receiving a degree in public law, including Norwegian constitutional law, from the University of Oslo, Thorson Plesner has been working with constitutional law in relation to her work in Norwegian public ministries (senior executive officer at the Norwegian Ministry for Research, Education and Church Affairs, 1999–2002; senior executive officer at the Norwegian Ministry for Cultural Affairs, 2002–2003) and her Ph.D. dissertation on freedom of religion or belief and state relations to religion.

Rik Torfs is a professor of canon law and the religion-state relationship at the University of Leuven, Belgium. His specialties are law on religion, canon law, and constitutional law. Torfs is also a columnist and writer and an adviser to several national governments, churches and religious groups, and international organizations. The editor in chief of the *European Journal for Church and State Research,* he is the author of 10 books and 300 articles.

Dahmène Touchent was *chargé d'enseignement* (responsible for teaching and evaluation) for economics and law at the European Institute of Corporatism (INEE, Paris) and has been *chargé d'enseignement* for labor law and commercial law at the University of Paris XIII (Nord), France, since 2002 and manager of the Algerian legal Web site Lexalgeria. Touchent's areas of work include constitutional law, international public law, consumer law, European law on sale, and francophone African law.

David Usupashvili, formerly an assistant professor of constitutional law at Tbilisi State University, chief legal adviser of the president of Georgia, member of the State Constitutional Commission of Georgia, president of the Young Lawyers Association of Georgia, and member of the Disciplinary Council of Judiciary of Georgia, is currently a senior legal and policy adviser at the Center for Institutional Reform and the Informal Sector (IRIS), Georgia.

Carlos Valderrama Adriansén, Ph.D., was formerly a professor of commercial law at Lima University, Peru, and is currently a professor in ecclesiastic law of the state at Catholic University of Peru, Lima. He is also president of the Institute of Ecclesiastic Law of Peru (IDEC) and past president of the Latin American Consortium of Religious Freedom.

Leo Valladares Lanza, Ph.D., has been a professor of philosophy of law and constitutional law at the Universidad Nacional Autónoma de Honduras since 1972. He was an adviser to the National Constitutional Assembly, which created the current constitution in 1982, and is a member and the former president of the Inter-American Commission on Human Rights. He was also a national commissioner of human rights in Honduras (1992–2002).

Johan van der Vyver has been the I. T. Cohen Professor of International Law and Human Rights at Emory University since 1995. He is a former professor of law at the University of the Witwatersrand, Johannesburg, South Africa. Van der Vyver is an expert on human rights law and has been involved in the promotion of human rights in South Africa. He also served as a fellow in the Human Rights Program of the Carter Center from 1995 to 1998. He is the author of more than 200 law review articles, popular notes, chapters in books, book reviews on human rights, and works on a variety of other subjects. He holds a B.Com. (1954), LL.B. (1956, Hons), and B.A. (1965) from Potchefstroom University for Christian Higher Education, South Africa; a doctor legum, University of Pretoria, South Africa (1974); diploma of the international and comparative law of human rights of the International Institute of Human Rights (Strasbourg, France, 1986); a doctor legum (honoris causa), University of Zululand, South Africa (1993); and a doctor legum (honoris causa), Potchefstroom University for Christian Higher Education (2003).

Olivera Vučić holds an M.A. and a Ph.D. in law from the Faculty of Law, University of Belgrade, Serbia-Montenegro, where she is currently the vice dean and an associate professor of constitutional law. Vučić has written several books, including *Collective Head of State* (1985), *Austrian Constitutional Court—the Safeguard of the Federation and Constitution* (1995), and *Constitutional Amendments and Validity* (2005).

Florian Wegelein, Dr. iur., LL.M., a former lecturer of German and European law at Tbilisi State University in Georgia, is currently a freelance consultant for European and international law in Göttingen, Germany. Wegelein's specialties are European and international public law, and environmental law. Wegelein has undertaken many years of research and practical work and is an adviser to national and international organizations. Wegelein's publications include *Marine Scientific Research* (2005) and *Organic Law of Georgia* (2003).

Richard Whitecross, Ph.D., is a lawyer and anthropologist. He completed a thesis on the Zhabdrung's legacy: state transformation, law, and social values in contemporary Bhutan (2002) and was a postdoctoral fellow at Economic and Social Research Council (ESRC), United Kingdom, the following year. He is currently an ESRC research fellow in socio-legal studies, School for Social and Political Studies, University of Edinburgh, United Kingdom.

Michael Wiener, LL.M., completed a law degree (second state exam) after studying law at the University of Trier, Germany, University of Lausanne, Switzerland, and the University of London, United Kingdom with scholarships from Cusanuswerk, Mobilité européenne, and the British Chevening Scholarship Scheme. He is currently a Ph.D. researcher on the mandate of the United Nations Special Rapporteur on Freedom of Religion or Belief.

Oliver Windgätter, Ref. iur., graduated with a concentration in Anglo-American law studies from the Institute for Foreign Law Studies, University of Trier, Germany. Windgätter has been a researcher at the Institute for Legal Policy at the University of Trier since 2003. His specialties are constitutional law (federalism) and European and international law.

José Woehrling has been a professor of public law at the Université de Montréal (Québec, Canada) since 1971. He specializes in Canadian and comparative constitutional law, international public law, law on religion, and law on human rights (in which he has many years of research and practical experience). He also is an adviser to several national governments and international organizations. Woehrling has published several books, including *Appartenances, institutions et citoyenneté* (2005) with Pierre Noreau and *Les Constitutions du Canada et du Québec: Du Régime français à nos jour* (1994) and *Demain, le Québec . . . Choix politiques et constitutionnels d'un pays en devenir* (1994), with Jacques-Yvan Morin. His other publications relate to Canadian and comparative constitutional law, international law, and law on human rights.

Krzysztof Wójtowicz, Ph.D., is a professor of law at the University of Wrocław, Poland, and head of the Department of International and European Law and director of the Center of Postgraduate Studies in Law and Economics of the European Union. He is also vice rector for research and foreign cooperation of the University of Wrocław.

Po Jen Yap is an advocate and solicitor of the Supreme Court of Singapore. He is currently pursuing a master of laws degree at Harvard University on a Kathryn Aguirre Worth Endowment for Faculty Enrichment scholarship. He has published on constitutional and international law.

Larissa Zabel holds a law degree from the University of Trier, Germany, specializing in European Union and international public law, and an LL.M. from the University of New South Wales, Australia. She was admitted to the bar in Germany in 2004.

Zhang Shoudong is an associate professor of law at the Law School of China, University of Political Science and Law (CUPL), and teaches and researches Chinese legal history and comparative constitutional law. Author of articles on Chinese legal tradition, Zhang Shoudong is also the translator of books on jurisprudence and law.

Zhou Qingfeng is a lecturer of constitutional law at the Law School of China, University of Political Science and Law (CUPL). Zhou is also a columnist on constitutionalism and human rights.

Preface

Easily accessible and ready at hand, *Encyclopedia of World Constitutions* gives a comprehensive overview of the constitutions of the world. The entries follow a common structure, making the systems easily comparable. All nation-states are covered, as are special and disputed territories. The authors are from all over the world. A large majority of articles are written by specialists in the respective country. All authors are outstanding legal and political experts; very often they hold or have held high offices in their country.

The articles concentrate on information most important for the understanding of the constitutional system, while covering all areas of predominant interest. As far as necessary for this purpose, reference is also made to constitutions of subdivisions of countries with federal structures. Suggestions for further reading attached to each article provide more detailed sources of information. This section includes Web addresses for the English text of the relevant constitutional document. The glossary explains special terms that help in understanding a particular constitution.

The following people and institutions to whom I am greatly indebted deserve special appreciation, in addition to all the many authors, for their assistance and contribution to this work: Claudia Lehnen, Michael Rahe, Florian Geyer, Gerhild Scholzen-Wiedmann, Christine Schmidt-König, Sylvia Lutz, Miriam Reinartz, Klaus Brokamp, and Maria Concepción Medina González from the Institute for European Constitutional Law at the University of Trier; Oliver Windgätter from the Institute for Legal Policy at the University of Trier; Sharon Zinns, Jessica Day, and Nancy R. Daspit from Emory Law School, Atlanta; Christof Heyns and Magnus Killander from the Centre for Human Rights, Faculty of Law, at the University of Pretoria; the Friedrich Ebert Foundation; the Konrad Adenauer Foundation; Barry Youngerman; and Claudia Schaab from Facts On File.

— Gerhard Robbers

Introduction

A constitution represents the legal fundamentals of a country. It outlines the rules that are fundamental for governing the community. Today, most countries of the world have one central document in which all or most of these rules are laid down. In a few countries, such as Austria, Israel, or the United Kingdom, several documents taken together form the constitution. Sometimes, constitutional documents, be they one or more, are combined with other sources of constitutional law, such as custom or even religious rules. In any case, the idea that a country should have a constitution has been adopted throughout the world. Whatever differences or similarities between constitutions there may be, it is obvious that, at least in constitutional law, common ideas are at work in most of the world. There is hardly a country in the world that does not explicitly claim to be a democracy, which respects the rule of law and fundamental rights. At least in theory, these ideas have been accepted throughout the world.

Constitutions differ. They are long or short, stable or easily changed. Government institutions as established by the constitutions vary in structure and powers. Mostly, however, constitutions give an idea of the very identity of a country. Usually, no other law of a given legal system may contradict the constitution of a specific country. All other laws and legal rules must comply with what the constitution says.

Constitutions should direct the facts of life, the actions of governments. They do not always do so. Sometimes, constitutions are seen as mere symbols of the independence and sovereignty of the nation, not primarily as a source of law. In some countries, constitutions are strong, and they are implemented in fact. In other countries, the respect for the constitution is weak. In such cases there may well be a convincing constitution, nicely worded, and in perfect harmony with what can be regarded as the Good and the Just. Nevertheless, the actual situation in that country may well be intolerable. Constitutions can be misused as mere propaganda, deceiving people and deceiving the world, but even then, constitutions may serve as yardsticks for reformers to cite.

Constitutions develop. Most constitutions contain explicit provisions for amendment or renewal. Usually, these provisions differ from the normal process of legislation and make the change of the constitution more difficult. This difference reflects the predominant importance of the constitution within the legal system, stressing the idea of continuity and identity of the community. Many constitutions go a step further in protecting identity by excluding the possibility of amending certain provisions that are held basic for this constitutional identity, such as the rule of law and democracy or a reference to religious belief. On the other hand, no wording of a constitution can escape interpretation. Even if the words remain the same, the understanding of what these words mean develops during time. The text of a constitution can be interpreted narrowly or generously, and what equality or freedom means differs from generation to generation, from country to country, and from culture to culture.

Constitutions live in language. Whoever wants to understand constitutions needs to speak the language in which they are written or must find translations. Translation of legal texts is a highly difficult task. It is not enough to find a word for a word, but the words must also fit into the legal structure of the country. Terminology varies, and sometimes the same word means a different thing in a different context. This variability may become obvious in the field of human rights or fundamental rights.

Fundamental rights are those rights of the individual that are the basis of his or her legal position in a community. Most of them are the human rights of every human being. The right to life, to freedom and equality; the freedom of belief and worship; free speech and prohibition of slavery are rights of everybody, and thus they are human rights. Many constitutions acknowledge that these rights are based in human dignity. Other fundamental rights are restricted to citizens or nationals of a certain country. The right to vote in elections, equal access to public office, and often also rights such as freedom of assembly and association are linked to membership in a specific political or economic system, and they are thus restricted to those belonging to this system.

Fundamental rights have developed over time. Some have early roots dating back to ancient times. In general, three generations of rights and freedoms are distinguished according to the time of their development. The first generation entails those fundamental rights often called liberal, classic, or civil, which are found in the early constitutions of the 18th and 19th centuries. These are guarantees such as freedom and equality; freedom of speech, assembly, and association; the right to own property; the freedom of the press; or habeas corpus—the right not to be jailed arbitrarily or without a decision by an impartial judge. These rights were developed in the era of liberalism especially in the later 18th and in the 19th century, in which the protection of the individual from government interference was seen to be paramount.

The second generation of fundamental rights turned to the social needs of the individuals. In the 19th and early 20th centuries there was a growing and widespread impression that the liberal fundamental rights were not enough to secure a proper life for the individual. Only those who owned property would profit from the protection of property; only those who had work opportunities would really enjoy their freedom of profession. Social rights were added to meet such needs such as the right to work, the right to strike, and the right to form trade unions. Many constitutions included protections for the family and for mothers, and guaranteed a minimal standard of living. Rights to education, housing, and health protection are characteristic of these second-generation fundamental rights.

The third generation of fundamental rights refers to groups and peoples. Whereas the first and second generations of fundamental rights predominantly care for the individual, the third generation of fundamental rights takes into account social coherence, traditions, and cultures. These third-generation fundamental rights protect minorities and preserve a diversity of languages, religions, and cultures. They provide for a right to sustainable development of developing countries and peoples.

Fundamental rights have developed in history as concrete answers to concrete problems. When governments have acted arbitrarily or subdued the people, demands emerged to limit government power. From here, habeas corpus rights against arbitrary arrests emerged, as did protection of property against unfair expropriation. However, governments have not always been seen as a threat. They have positive functions in providing the people with safety and with the necessary means of life. Accordingly, fundamental rights have developed in specific cases to answer specific needs: for education, minimal standards of living, or protection against others. These specific answers to specific problems have soon developed into a broad system of rights and freedoms forming a basis of communal life.

Differences between various constitutions as to which fundamental rights are guaranteed often reflect the specific needs of the specific country in a specific time. Very often, when a new need arises, constitutions are not amended, but jurisprudence, the courts, and public opinion interpret existing constitutional law in a way that includes new answers to new questions. In other constitutions, however, new needs may well lead to the introduction of an explicit new fundamental right.

One of the striking current developments is the extension of fundamental rights from a mere governmental perspective to a broad application within society. A first and primary function of fundamental rights was to structure the relationship between the individual and the government. Fundamental rights did not give direct answers to ways individuals should relate to each other. Today, in many constitutional systems, fundamental rights also give directives of the ways individuals should treat each other.

Constitutions tell about political participation of people. The systems vary considerably. Some countries have strong systems of a direct democracy in which the people decide directly by way of referendums about specific questions such as projects of laws or other issues. However, indirect representation prevails. People elect representatives, who then decide about specific questions. Many election systems provide for a decision between individually competing candidates. Then, the one who receives more votes would win the office; this constitutes the "first-past-the-post principle" or the principle of "the winner takes it all." Many other constitutions, however, provide for a proportional representation. In these systems political parties or other entities establish lists of candidates, and these lists are voted on by the electors. The number of votes a list wins in the elections decides the number of candidates who are elected from that list. Many constitutions provide for necessary representation of minorities by reserving seats in parliament or other offices for a certain part of the population.

Constitutions relate to religion. Religion is a central topic of constitutions throughout the world. Some sort of separation between churches or other religious communities and the state is predominant. That separation may be radically or moderately expressed. It can be hostile in order to push away religion, or it can be friendly to let religion have the freedom to flourish. As it usually does, much depends on practice. There are a number of constitutions declaring a certain religion or confession to be the religion of the state, the predominant religion, or a church to be the people's church. Others define themselves explicitly as Islamic republics or refer to Christianity. These explicit identities as secular or religious do not necessarily lead to unequal treatment of other religions or even to a loss of religious freedom.

Constitutions constitute identity and they represent the identity of their country. They do so in their text and they do so in the way they are implemented. Understanding a constitution is a step to understanding a people.

— Gerhard Robbers

Entries A to F

AFGHANISTAN

At-a-Glance

OFFICIAL NAME
Islamic Republic of Afghanistan

CAPITAL
Kabul

POPULATION
28,513,677 (July 2004 est.)

SIZE
250,001 sq. mi. (647,500 sq. km)

LANGUAGES
Official languages: Pashtu and Dari. Other languages: Uzbek, Turkmen, 30 minor languages

RELIGIONS
Sunni Muslim 80%, Shia Muslim 19%, other 1%

NATIONAL OR ETHNIC COMPOSITION
Pashtun 42%, Tajik 27%, Hazara 9%, Uzbek 9%, Aimak 4%, Turkmen 3%, Baloch 2%, other 4%

DATE OF INDEPENDENCE OR CREATION
August 19, 1919 (from U.K. control over Afghan foreign affairs)

TYPE OF GOVERNMENT
Transitional, Islamic republic

TYPE OF STATE
Unitary state

TYPE OF LEGISLATURE
Bicameral parliament envisaged by the constitution

DATE OF CONSTITUTION
January 4, 2004 (approved by constitutional Loya Jirga)

DATE OF LAST AMENDMENT
No amendment

The new constitution, as adopted on January 4, 2004, defines Afghanistan as a unitary Islamic republic, in which "no law can be contrary to the beliefs and provisions of the sacred religion of Islam and the values of [the] Constitution."

Afghanistan is made up of 34 administrative provinces, which according to the constitution will each have a provincial council. The constitution provides that "the government, while preserving the principle of centralism, shall delegate certain authorities to local administration units for the purpose of expediting and promoting economic, social, and cultural affairs, and increasing the participation of people in the development of the nation."

The justice system in Afghanistan is a combination of traditional and formal mechanisms, the formal justice system weakened by years of wars and civil unrest. During that time, traditional mechanisms served as the main judicial authority and in most parts of the country was the only one.

The 2004 constitution abolished the monarchy (which was still in effect under the 1964 constitution of King Zahir Shah) and established a strong presidential form of government, albeit with important powers reserved for the national assembly.

The religion of Afghanistan is defined by the constitution as "the sacred religion of Islam." Followers of other religions are free to perform their religious rites within the limits of the law. However, according to the constitution, no law can be contrary to Islam and the values of the constitution.

Although the economic outlook has improved significantly since the fall of the Taliban in 2001, as a result of over $2 billion in international assistance and a huge increase in opium production, Afghanistan remains extremely poor and highly dependent on foreign aid.

The president is commander in chief of the armed forces of Afghanistan. However, at the time of writing, armed factions continue to operate in many parts of the county; the process of disarmament, demobilization, and reintegration (DDR), supported by the United Nations (UN) and the international community, was progressing slowly.

CONSTITUTIONAL HISTORY

Afghanistan's history as a country spans little more than two centuries, although the countries and its peoples have contributed to the greatness of many great Central Asian empires.

In 328 B.C.E., Alexander the Great entered the territory of present-day Afghanistan, then part of the Persian Empire. Invasions by the Scythians and Gokturks followed in succeeding centuries. In 642 C.E., Arabs invaded the entire region and introduced Islam. Arab rule quickly gave way to that of the Islamized Persians, who controlled the area until conquered by the Ghaznavid Empire in 998. The Ghaznavid dynasty, which was Sunni, was defeated in 1146 by the Ghurids (Ghor); both empires spread Islamic rule into India. Various princes and Seljuk rulers attempted to rule parts of the country until Shah Muhammad II of the Khwarezmid Empire conquered all of Persia in 1205.

Between 1220 and 1223, the country was invaded by Genghiz Khan. One of his descendents, Timur, annexed the area in the early 1380s, and his reign ushered in the golden Timurid era, which saw a flourishing of the arts in northern Afghanistan and Central Asia. With the rise of the Mughal Empire, Kabul became the capital of an Afghan principality; when the empire conquered most of India, Afghanistan became merely a peripheral part of the empire.

In 1774, with European forces, especially British, eroding the influence of the Mughals on the Indian subcontinent, the kingdom of Afghanistan was founded by the Pashtun tribal leader Ahmad Shah Durrani. Soon, a long period of confrontation began with the British in the south, who feared Afghanistan might ally itself with the expanding Russian Empire to the north.

After several local wars, from 1878 to 1880, Afghanistan became more or less a protectorate of the British Empire. In 1893, the British drew Afghanistan's eastern boundaries along the so-called Durand Line, leaving half the Pashtun population stranded in British India, in what today is Pakistan.

Various British-backed reform initiatives provoked widespread resistance. The country remained precariously unstable for decades.

In 1964, King Zahir Shah promulgated a liberal constitution providing for a two-chamber legislature, to which the king appointed one-third of the deputies. The people elected another third, and the rest were selected indirectly by provincial assemblies. Although Zahir Shah's reform efforts had few lasting positive impacts, they allowed for the growth of unofficial extremist parties on both the Left and the Right, including the communist People's Democratic Party of Afghanistan (PDPA), which had close ideological ties to the Soviet Union, and militant Muslim parties.

The kingdom was abolished in 1973 when the former prime minister, Mohammed Daoud Khan, a cousin of the king, seized power in a military coup on July 17. Zahir Shah fled the country. Daoud issued a new constitution calling for a presidential republic and a one-party system of government; he declared himself president and prime minister. His attempts to carry out economic and social reforms met with little success, and a new constitution promulgated in February 1977 failed to quell chronic political instability. As disillusionment set in, on April 27, 1978, the PDPA initiated a bloody coup, which resulted in the overthrow and murder of Daoud and most of his family.

The new government, aided by thousands of Soviet military and civil advisers, implemented a radical socialist and modernizing agenda. Within a few months the government issued a series of decrees reforming landownership, abolishing usury, banning forced marriages, giving women the vote, replacing traditional religious/cultural laws with secular laws, and banning tribal courts. The overnight revolution plunged the rural majority of the population into disarray.

A great backlash against these reforms resulted among members of the traditional patriotic establishments and Muslim and tribal leaders. Some resorted to violence and sabotage of the country's industry and infrastructure. The government of Afghanistan responded to the attacks with heavy-handed intervention by the army. The government arrested, exiled, and executed many mujahideen, "holy Muslim warriors."

By the end of 1979, the Afghan army was overwhelmed by the resistance. Party leaders called in the Soviet Union, which sent tens of thousands of troops and backed a second communist coup. On December 25, 1979, the Soviet army entered Kabul, starting a 10-year war against the mujahideen resistance. Pakistan, Saudi Arabia, and the United States assisted in financing the opposition groups in support of their common "anticommunist" stance. Among the wealthy Saudis who helped finance the mujahideen was Osama bin Laden.

The Soviet Union withdrew its troops in February 1989 but continued to aid the government, led by Mohammed Najibullah. Aid from the United States and Saudi Arabia to the mujahideen also continued. After the collapse of the Soviet Union, the Najibullah government was overthrown on April 18, 1992, when General Abdul Rashid Dostum changed allegiances and delivered Najibullah to the mujahideen.

An Islamic State of Afghanistan was declared. Almost at once, fighting broke out among the various militias, which had coexisted uneasily during the Soviet occupation. An interim president was installed and was replaced two months later by Burhanuddin Rabbani, a founder of the country's Islamic political movement. Fighting among rival factions intensified.

In reaction to the prevalence of anarchy and warlords in the country and the lack of Pashtun representation in the Kabul government, a movement of religious scholars, many of them former mujahideen, arose, with heavy support from Pakistani military and political forces. The Taliban took control of 90 percent of the country by 1998, limiting the opposition to a small, largely Tajik corner in the northeast and the Panjshir valley. The opposition formed the Northern Alliance under Rabbani, which continued to receive diplomatic recognition in the United Nations as the government of Afghanistan.

In response to the September 11, 2001, terrorist attacks, the United States and its coalition allies launched a successful attack to oust the Taliban government, which had sheltered the al-Qaeda movement of Osama bin Laden, the apparent organizer of the attacks. The Bonn Agreement, sponsored by the United Nations, was signed on December 5, 2001, by representatives of several different anti-Taliban factions and political groups. It established a roadmap and timetable for establishing peace and security, rebuilding the country, reestablishing key institutions, and protecting human rights. The agreement formally put all mujahideen, Afghan armed forces, and armed groups in the country under the command and control of a 30-member interim authority under the Pashtun leader, Hamid Karzai.

An Emergency Loya Jirga (grand council) in June 2002 confirmed the interim authority as the Afghan Transitional Authority (ATA), and Hamid Karzai assumed the position of transitional president. In January 2004, the constitutional Loya Jirga adopted a constitution consolidating political power in the presidency. On October 9, 2004, Karzai was elected as president. The national assembly was inaugurated on December 19, 2005.

FORM AND IMPACT OF THE CONSTITUTION

Afghanistan has a written constitution, adopted by the constitutional Loya Jirga on January 4, 2004, which defines Afghanistan as a unitary Islamic republic in which "no law can be contrary to the beliefs and provisions of the sacred religion of Islam and the values of this constitution." It is unclear how the apparent contradictions might be resolved between traditional Afghan Islamic beliefs, on the one hand, and the values of the constitution, with its human rights protections, on the other.

BASIC ORGANIZATIONAL STRUCTURE

Afghanistan is made up of 34 provinces, each endowed by the constitution with a provincial council formed by "free, direct, secret ballot, and general elections by the residents of the province for a period of four years in accordance with law." The number and boundaries of the provinces themselves are established by law, in this case

a presidential decree. The constitution provides that the provincial councils will "take part in securing the developmental targets of the state and improving its affairs in a way stated in the law, and give advice on important issues falling within the domain of the respective province." However, the role provided for the provincial councils in the 2005 Law of Provincial Councils is largely consultative.

The constitution also provides for district councils to be elected in the same manner as the provincial councils but is silent as to their role other than to elect members of the Meshrano Jirga (House of Elders).

In practice, local government is strong in Afghanistan, with many matters decided by traditional local councils, called jirgas or shuras. The concept of a nation state and its functions is still in the early stages of development. Particularly in remote and rural areas, the state is not thought of as the primary dispensary power, in judicial as in other matters. The delegation of power to the state still must be negotiated with the local power structures such as tribes, *shuras,* or *jirgas.*

LEADING CONSTITUTIONAL PRINCIPLES

The constitution establishes a strong presidential form of government, albeit with important powers reserved for the national assembly.

The president, who is head of state, is assisted by two vice-presidents, whom the president must nominate when running for office. The president has wide-ranging powers, including supervising the implementation of the constitution, determining the fundamental policies of the state, acting as commander in chief, declaring war or a state of emergency, and appointing judges and high-ranking officials in the judiciary, the police, and the armed forces.

Members of the administration are appointed by the president and are subject to approval by the bicameral national assembly, which consists of the House of People (Wolesi Jirga) and the House of Elders (Meshrano Jirga). The national assembly adopts laws and legislative decrees (and can override the president's veto), but no law or decree can be enforced unless it is approved by both houses.

CONSTITUTIONAL BODIES

The predominant bodies provided for in the constitution are the president, assisted by two vice presidents; the cabinet; the national assembly; the Loya Jirga; and the judiciary.

The judiciary remains in an embryonic stage, with the supreme court yet to be reformed to align it with constitutional requirements.

The President

Apart from his or her role as head of state, the president has wide-ranging powers, including supervising the implementation of the constitution; determining the fundamental policies of the state; acting as commander in chief; appointing judges and other high-ranking officials in the judiciary, the police, and the armed forces; and declaring war or a state of emergency. The president also appoints the cabinet members, subject to approval by the national assembly. The president additionally has the power to call a national referendum on important political, social, or economic issues.

In case of resignation, impeachment, or death of the president or of a serious illness that hinders the president's performance, a vice president undertakes the duties and authorities of the president. Impeachment requires the support of a Loya Jirga, which then refers the case to a special court. An election for a new president must be held within a period of three months.

The president is elected for a five-year term and can be re-elected only once. In presidential elections, if none of the candidates receives more than 50 percent of the votes in the first round, a runoff is held between the two top candidates. The runoff must be held within two weeks of the announcement of results of the first round.

The president must be at least 40 years of age, a citizen of Afghanistan born of Afghan parents, and a Muslim. A president must not be a citizen of another country or have been convicted of crimes against humanity or criminal acts.

The Cabinet

Cabinet ministers are appointed by the president, subject to approval by the national assembly; they may or may not be members of the national assembly. A member of the national assembly who is appointed cabinet minister must be replaced by another person in accordance with the provisions of law.

The constitution defines the cabinet's duties as follows: to execute the provisions of the constitution, other laws, and final orders of the courts and to protect the independence, defend the territorial integrity, and safeguard the interests and dignity of Afghanistan in the international community. The cabinet is also responsible for maintaining public law and order, eliminating administrative corruption, preparing the budget, regulating financial affairs, protecting the public wealth, and devising and implementing programs for social, cultural, economic, and technological progress. At the end of the fiscal year it must report to the national assembly about the tasks accomplished and the main plans for the new fiscal year. It must present the budget to the Wolesi Jirga each year. Only the cabinet can initiate budgetary and financial bills.

The National Assembly

The bicameral national assembly consists of the Wolesi Jirga (House of People) and the Meshrano Jirga (House of Elders). The national assembly adopts laws and legislative decrees, which are then endorsed by the president. No law or decree can be enforced unless it is approved by both houses.

The national assembly has the following powers: ratification, modification, or abrogation of laws and/or legislative decrees; approval of plans for economic, social, cultural, and technological development; approval of the state budget; permission for obtaining and granting loans; creation and modification of administrative units; and ratification or abrogation of international treaties and agreements.

The Wolesi Jirga is directly elected every five years. There is a constitutional requirement that at least two female delegates must be elected from each province.

Members of the Meshrano Jirga are indirectly elected or appointed. Each provincial council sends one of its members to the house for a period of four years. The district councils within each province send one of their members for a period of three years. The president appoints the remaining one-third of the members from among experts and experienced personalities; he or she must include two representatives of the disabled and two representatives from the Kochis (nomad). Half of the appointees must be women.

Members of the national assembly, as the president, must not have been convicted by a court of committing a crime against humanity or any crime or have been sentenced to deprivation of his or her civil rights. Members of the Wolesi Jirga must be 25 years old at the date of candidacy, and members of the Meshrano Jirga must be 35 years old at the date of candidacy or appointment.

The Lawmaking Process

According to the constitution, laws must be approved by both houses of the national assembly and approved and endorsed by the president. If the president rejects the bill, he or she can send the document with justifiable reasons back to the Wolesi Jirga within 15 days of its submission. If the president does not send it back within 15 days, or if the Wolesi Jirga approves the bill again with a majority of two-thirds of those voting, the bill is considered endorsed.

Either the cabinet or members of the national assembly can introduce proposed laws. It also appears that the Supreme Court can initiate bills for the regulation of judicial affairs. In budgetary and financial matters, however, the cabinet has exclusive power to introduce bills. Cabinet bills are submitted first to the Wolesi Jirga.

Bills relating to budgetary and financial affairs or to the taking or giving of loans are considered passed if the Wolesi Jirga does not approve or reject them within one month. The bill is submitted to the Meshrano Jirga after its approval by the Wolesi Jirga. The Meshrano Jirga decides on the draft within a period of 15 days.

If the decision of one house is rejected by another house, a combined committee composed of equal members of each house is formed to resolve the disagreement. The decision of the committee is binding after its approval by the president. If the combined committee cannot resolve the disagreement, the bill is considered void.

Loya Jirga

According to the constitution, the Loya Jirga (Pashtu for grand council) is "the highest manifestation of the people of Afghanistan." The Loya Jirga is a traditional forum, unique to Afghanistan, in which tribal elders from the country's various ethnic groups meet together to settle intertribal disputes, discuss social reforms, and, most recently, approve a new constitution.

A Loya Jirga, as defined in the constitution, consists of members of the national assembly and chairpersons of the provincial and district councils. Ministers, the chief justice, and members of the Supreme Court can participate in the sessions of the Loya Jirga without the right to vote.

A Loya Jirga is convened to make decisions on issues related to independence, national sovereignty, territorial integrity, and the supreme interests of the country. It is also convened to amend the provisions of the constitution or to prosecute the president. Decisions of the Loya Jirga are ordinarily determined by a majority of the members present.

The Judiciary

The judicial branch consists of the Supreme Court (Stera Mahkama), High Courts, and Appeals Courts.

The Supreme Court is composed of nine members appointed by the president with the approval of the Wolesi Jirga for a period of up to 10 years. The head of the Supreme Court is also appointed by the president. Members of the Supreme Court are required to have a higher education in law or in Islamic jurisprudence and to have sufficient expertise and experience in the judicial system of Afghanistan.

The constitution precludes the transfer of any case from the jurisdiction of the judicial branch to any other organ of the state. At the time of writing, the judiciary had yet to be reshaped to conform to the new constitutional requirements. The judiciary currently operates with minimal training.

THE ELECTION PROCESS

The president is elected by a majority of more than 50 percent of the votes cast. If none of the candidates wins a majority in the first round, a runoff is held between the two top candidates within two weeks of the announcement of results of the first round. In the runoff, the candidate who gets the majority of votes is elected president.

Parliamentary Elections

Elections to the Parliament took place on September 18, 2005. The Decree on the Election Law of 2005 foresees multimember constituencies in each province and a Single Non-Transferable Vote (SNTV) system, which would favor independent candidates over political parties.

POLITICAL PARTIES

Citizens of Afghanistan have the right to form political parties, provided that the program and charter of the party are not contrary to the provisions and values of Islam or of the constitution; the organizational structure and financial sources of the party are made public; the party does not have military or paramilitary aims and structures; and the party is not affiliated to foreign political parties or sources.

Political parties are required by the Political Parties Law to register with the Ministry of Justice, which has an established office for registration. The process of registration is governed by a separate regulation. Article 6 of the Political Parties Law lays out a number of factors that exclude parties from registration, including pursuit of objectives opposed to the principles of Islam and incitement to ethnic, racial, religious, or sectarian violence. They are also prohibited from having military wings or affiliations with armed forces.

Parties are also required, by the same law, to register their assets with the Ministry of Finance and provide documentation from the Ministry of Finance certifying their assets.

CITIZENSHIP

Beyond providing that citizens may not be deprived of their Afghan citizenship, the constitution does not regulate the matter further.

According to the law on citizenship, Afghan citizenship is acquired if a person has one parent who is an Afghan citizen, regardless of where he or she is born. Persons born of foreign parents in Afghanistan also acquire Afghan citizenship if one of their parents was born and continuously lived in Afghanistan or if they themselves continuously lived in Afghanistan, until reaching the age of 18.

In slightly unusual provisions of the law, foundlings born in Afghanistan and persons who have entered Afghanistan from foreign countries, who have concealed their original citizenship, who have bought property reserved for Afghans, who own herds, or who have engaged in trade or agriculture shall also be considered citizens.

FUNDAMENTAL RIGHTS

The constitution contains several provisions enunciating basic political, civil, economic, and social rights. It guarantees rule of law, incorporating the presumption of innocence and the right to legal counsel, and defines crime as a personal action, stating that the resulting penalties cannot affect another person. The constitution prohibits torture and "punishment contrary to human integrity." While the right to life is enshrined in the constitution, it also allows for the imposition of the death penalty.

The constitution also contains a range of political rights protections, including the right to elect and to be elected, the right to freedom of expression (Article 34), the right to form social organizations and political parties subject to certain restrictions, and the right to demonstrate.

In addition to prohibitions on discrimination and provisions for the equal rights and duties of women and men before the law, the constitution includes provisions requiring specified levels of women's representation in both houses of the Parliament.

The right to education is also enunciated; education up to a secondary level is guaranteed.

The right to work is provided for in the constitution, and forced labor is forbidden. The right to form social organizations for the purpose of securing material or spiritual aims, in accordance with the provisions of law, is guaranteed to every individual.

The constitution pledges the state to abide by the United Nations (UN) Charter, international treaties, international conventions to which Afghanistan is a signatory, and the Universal Declaration of Human Rights. Afghanistan has ratified the International Covenant on Civil and Political Rights, the Convention on the Elimination of Racial Discrimination, and the Convention on the Elimination of all forms of Discrimination against Women. It has also signed the International Covenant on Economic Social and Cultural Rights (ICESCR); the Convention against Torture and Other Forms of Cruel, Inhuman or Degrading Treatment or Punishment (CAT); the Convention on the Rights of the Child (CRC); and the Rome Statute of the International Criminal Court (ICC).

Impact and Functions of Fundamental Rights

Despite these legal provisions on political, civil, economic, and social rights, their implementation has yet to be ensured. The constitution does not adequately address the role of Islamic law and its relationship to human rights protections.

Since the adoption of the constitution, the Supreme Court has remained very proactive in stressing the Islamic nature of the state, which it appears to give precedence over the other values of the constitution, such as the protection of human rights. This has led the court at various times to ban the broadcast of female singers on national television as being contrary to the teachings of Islam, without weighing the impact on freedom of expression, guaranteed in the constitution. The court also intervened in the 2004 presidential elections, calling for the disqualification of a candidate who, it claimed, espoused values contrary to Islam.

The Independent Human Rights Commission of Afghanistan, established in the Bonn Agreement, also has a constitutional status. However, it does not have a constitutional mandate to address issues of past war crimes and serious human rights abuses.

At the time of writing, there has still been no process of transitional justice. Members of armed factions alleged to be responsible for human rights abuses have not been made accountable and continue to act with impunity in some areas.

Although the constitution contains provisions that people who have been convicted by a court for committing a crime, specifically a crime against humanity, are prohibited from holding public office, no one has been tried by a competent court for crimes committed during the years of conflict in the country. Indeed, persons reputed to have led armed factions alleged to be responsible for human rights abuses were able to register as candidates in the 2004 presidential elections and 2005 Wolesi Jirga and Provincial Council elections.

ECONOMY AND ECONOMIC RIGHTS

The constitution "encourages and protects private capital investments and enterprises based on the market economy and guarantees their protection in accordance with the provisions of law." The state constitution also provides that the state shall "formulate and implement effective programs for development of industries, growth of production, increase of public living standards, and support to craftsmanship," and "design and implement within its financial resources effective programs for development of agriculture and animal husbandry, improving the economic, social and living conditions of farmers and herders, and the settlement and living conditions of nomads."

The state is obliged to "adopt necessary measures for housing and the distribution of public estates to deserving citizens in accordance within its financial resources and the law."

Minerals and other underground resources are properties of the state, and foreign individuals do not have the right to own immovable property in Afghanistan.

RELIGIOUS COMMUNITIES

The state religion as defined by the constitution is "the sacred religion of Islam." Followers of other religions are free to perform their rites within the limits of the law. However, according to the constitution, no law can be contrary to Islam.

It is estimated that 84 percent of the population is Sunni Muslim. Approximately 15 percent is Shía Muslim, the majority of whom are ethnic Hazaras. Other religious groups, including Sikhs, Hindus, and Jews, make up less than 1 percent of the population.

Traditionally, Sunni Islam of the Hanafi school of jurisprudence has been the dominant religion. Relations between the different branches of Islam in the country have been difficult. Historically, the minority Shiites faced discrimination from the majority Sunni population. However, the new constitution does not grant preferential status to the Hanafi school, nor does it make specific reference to Sharia law. The constitution also grants that Shia law will be applied to cases dealing with personal matters involving Shiites; there is no separate law applying to non-Muslims.

MILITARY DEFENSE AND STATE OF EMERGENCY

The president is commander in chief of the armed forces and has responsibility for declaring war, issuing a cease-fire, or sending contingents of the armed forces to foreign countries, which requires the approval of the national assembly. The president is also responsible for appointing and dismissing or accepting the retirement or resignation of officers of the armed forces.

The powers of the president, as defined by the constitution, also include "taking the required decisions in defense of territorial integrity and in protecting independence."

The president is also responsible for declaring a state of emergency in some or all parts of the country with the approval of the national assembly "if due to war, threat of war, serious rebellion, natural disasters, or similar situation, the protection of the independence or survival of the nation becomes impossible by following the [non-emergency] provisions of this constitution." If the state of emergency continues for more than two months, the approval of the national assembly is required for its extension. During the state of emergency, the president, in consultations with the heads of the national assembly and the chief justice, may transfer some authorities of the national assembly to the cabinet.

With the consent of the heads of the Parliament and the Supreme Court, the president may also suspend or restrict the right to unarmed demonstrations during a state of emergency. Internment may be introduced, and the state may inspect correspondence and communications and enter and inspect private residences without a warrant.

If the presidential term of office and/or the legislative period ends during a state of emergency, new elections are postponed, and the existing terms are extended for up to four months. If the state of emergency continues for more than four months, a Loya Jirga is summoned by the president for further decisions. After the termination of the state of emergency, the delayed elections are held. Immediately after termination of the state of emergency, the emergency measures adopted shall be considered invalid.

AMENDMENTS TO THE CONSTITUTION

The provisions regarding adherence to Islam and the regime of the Islamic republic cannot be amended. Any amendments of the fundamental rights of the people "are permitted only in order to make them more effective."

Proposals to amend other provisions of the constitution can be made by the president or by the majority of the national assembly. A commission composed of members of the government, national assembly, and supreme court is then established by a presidential decree, and the commission prepares a draft of the amendments. A Loya Jirga shall be convened by the decree of the president.

If the Loya Jirga approves an amendment by a majority of two-thirds of its members, it goes into force after endorsement by the president. The constitution may not be amended during the state of emergency.

PRIMARY SOURCES

Constitution in English (unofficial translation). Available online. URL: http://www.oefre.unibe.ch/law/icl/af00000_.html. Accessed on June 17, 2006.
Constitution in English and Dari: http://www.jemb.org/eng/legislation. Accessed on June 17, 2006.

SECONDARY SOURCES

Afghan Constitution Resource Page (various documents, concepts, and papers). Available online. URL: http://www.cic.nyu.edu/. Accessed on September 12, 2005.
Khaled M. Abou El Fadl et al. *Democracy and Islam in the New Constitution of Afghanistan.* New York: Rand Corporation NBN, 2003.

Michael McNamara

ALBANIA

At-a-Glance

OFFICIAL NAME
Republic of Albania

CAPITAL
Tirana

POPULATION
3,581,655 (July 2006 est.)

SIZE
11,100 sq. mi. (28,748 sq. km)

LANGUAGES
Albanian

RELIGIONS
Muslim 38.8%, Christian 35.4% (consisting of Roman Catholic 16.8%, Orthodox 16.1%, Protestant 0.6%), other 25.8%

NATIONAL OR ETHNIC COMPOSITION
Albanian 95%, Greek 3%, other 2% (Vlach, Roma and Sinti, Serb, Bulgarian)

DATE OF INDEPENDENCE OR CREATION
November 28, 1912

TYPE OF GOVERNMENT
Emerging democracy

TYPE OF STATE
Unitary state

TYPE OF LEGISLATURE
Unicameral parliament

DATE OF CONSTITUTION
November 22, 1998

DATE OF LAST AMENDMENT
No amendment

Albania is a parliamentary republic based on the rule of law with a separation and balancing of legislative, executive, and judicial powers. It is organized as a unitary and indivisible state. The constitution is the highest law in the Republic of Albania. The independence of the state and the integrity of the territory, dignity of the individual, human rights and freedoms, social justice, constitutional order, pluralism, and national identity and inheritance are the bases of the state, which has the duty of respecting and protecting them. The same applies to religious coexistence, as well as coexistence with and understanding of minorities.

The president is head of state and represents the unity of the people. The central political figure is the prime minister as head of the executive power. Governance is based on a system of free, equal, general, and periodic elections. A pluralistic political party system has intense political impact.

Freedom of conscience and religion is guaranteed. Albania is a secular state, with no official religion. The economic system is based on private and public property, as well as on a market economy and free economic activity. The armed forces maintain their neutrality in political issues and are subject to civilian control. No foreign military force may be stationed in or pass through Albanian territory, and no Albanian military force may be sent abroad, except by a law approved by a majority of all members of the Assembly.

CONSTITUTIONAL HISTORY

The Organic Statute of Albania, dated October 4, 1914, is regarded as the first Albanian constitution. It was endorsed by the International Control Commission, composed of representatives of the great European powers at the time, which was set up after the declaration of independence on November 28, 1912. The constitution declared Albania to be an "autonomous, sovereign, and inheritable principality" under the guarantee of the great powers. The powers appointed a German prince, Wilhelm of Wied, as head of state.

After World War I (1914–18), the country became a theater of hostilities. Albania experienced difficult times, and four constitutions were adopted in 19 years. These were the 1920 Statute of Lushnje, the 1922 Statute of the Albanian State, the 1925 Fundamental Statute of the Republic of Albania, and the 1928 Fundamental Statute of the Albanian Kingdom. Albania changed its governing system twice from a monarchy to a republic and vice versa. The royal crowns of Albania and Italy were joined as a result of the invasion of Albania by Italy on April 7, 1939.

After World War II (1939–45), a Constitutional Assembly was elected in December 1945. The following year it drafted and adopted a constitution for the new People's Republic of Albania. In 1976, another constitution, which deepened the communist nature of the state, was adopted and declared Albania "A Socialist People's Republic."

The 1990s saw many democratic changes based on various limited constitutional laws. The most important of these was adopted in 1991 by the first pluralist parliament. It was entitled "On the Main Constitutional Provisions." This law was supplemented by a series of other constitutional laws passed between 1991 and 1994. An attempt to introduce a comprehensive constitution failed to win a majority of votes in a referendum held in November 1994. The current constitution was adopted in 1998 by the Albanian legislative body and was ratified in a general referendum.

FORM AND IMPACT OF THE CONSTITUTION

Albania has a written constitution, codified in a single document called *Kushtetuta;* it has precedence over all other national laws. The provisions of the constitution are directly applicable, except when the constitution provides otherwise. The Republic of Albania accepts various international laws as binding. Any international agreement that has been ratified by the Assembly and published in the *Official Journal* becomes an integral part of the internal juridical system. Such agreements have precedence over any national laws that are not compatible with it.

BASIC ORGANIZATIONAL STRUCTURE

Albania is a unitary and indivisible state. Its administrative divisions consist of 12 regions (*qarqe,* singular *qark*) and 384 municipalities and communes. Local government in the Republic of Albania is founded on the principle of decentralization of power and subsidiarity and is exercised according to the principle of local self-government.

LEADING CONSTITUTIONAL PRINCIPLES

Albania's system of government is a parliamentary democracy. There are separation and balance of executive, legislative, and judicial powers. The judiciary is independent.

The Albanian constitutional system is defined by a number of leading principles: Albania is a democracy, a republic, a social state, based on the rule of law; the sovereignty belongs to the people, who exercise it through their representatives or directly. Rule of law is of decisive impact. All state actions impairing the rights of the people must have a legal basis. Further principles, such as religious neutrality, are implicitly contained in the constitution.

CONSTITUTIONAL BODIES

The most important constitutional bodies provided for in the constitution are the Assembly, the Council of Ministers, the president, the Constitutional Court, the judiciary, and organs of local self-government.

The Assembly (Parliament)

The Albanian Assembly is the central representative organ of the people. It is a legislative body that is comprised of 140 deputies. One hundred are elected in single-member constituencies with an approximately equal number of voters; 40 deputies are elected from multiname lists of parties or party coalitions according to their respective order on each party's list.

The Assembly is elected for a four-year term. Its mandate is extended only in the case of war and only for as long as the war continues.

The Assembly elects and discharges its Speaker, who directs the work according to the rules of procedure. The highest civil employee of the Assembly is the secretary general.

Political parties, coalitions of parties, and voters may present candidates for deputy. Deputies represent the people and are not bound by any obligatory mandate from their party or any other side.

The Lawmaking Process
Laws can be proposed by the Council of Ministers, any deputy, or a group of at least 20,000 electors. A draft law is voted three times: once in principle, then article by article, and then in its entirety. The constitution specifies cases in which a qualified majority is required to approve a law. Once the Assembly approves the law, the president of the republic promulgates it by a decree. A law enters into force with the passage of no fewer than 15 days after its publication in the *Official Journal.*

In case of extraordinary measures, dire necessity, and emergency, a law may enter into force immediately upon its publication in the *Official Journal,* but only if the Assembly decides so by a majority of all its members and the president of the republic consents.

The president of the republic has the right to veto a law only once. A law vetoed by the president can be passed again by the Assembly.

The Council of Ministers

The Council of Ministers consists of the prime minister, deputy prime minister, and the ministers. The prime minister is appointed by the president on the recommendation of the party or coalition of parties that has the majority of seats in the Assembly. The Council of Ministers defines the principal directions of state policy. It issues decisions and instructions. Members of the Council of Ministers enjoy the immunity of deputies.

The President

The president is head of state and represents the "unity of the people." Only an Albanian citizen by birth who has been resident in Albania for the last 10 years and who has reached the age of 40 may be elected president.

The president is elected by secret vote and without debate by the Assembly, by a majority of three-fifths of all its members. Candidates for president are nominated by groups of at least 20 deputies. The president is elected for a five-year term and can be reelected only once. Failure to elect a president leads to dissolving of the Assembly and early elections.

Among the president's duties are addressing the Assembly, granting pardons according to law, granting citizenship, signing international agreements, and setting the date of elections.

The president of the republic, in the exercise of his or her powers, issues decrees. The president may not exercise other powers besides those recognized expressly in the constitution and granted by laws issued in compliance with it.

The Constitutional Court

The Constitutional Court guarantees respect for the constitution and makes final interpretations of it. The court is subject only to the constitution. The Constitutional Court is composed of nine members, who are appointed by the president of the republic with the consent of the Assembly for nine-year terms, without the right to be reappointed.

The Judiciary

Judicial power is exercised by the High Court, by the courts of appeal, and by courts of first instance, which are established by law. The Assembly may establish by law courts for a particular field but cannot establish extraordinary courts.

Being a judge is incompatible with holding any other state, political, or private office or business. Judges are independent and subject only to the constitution and the laws. They issue decisions in the name of the republic. Judicial terms are unlimited, and pay and other benefits cannot be lowered.

THE ELECTION PROCESS

All Albanians who have reached the age of 18, even on the date of elections, have the right to vote and be elected. However, citizens who have been declared mentally incompetent by a final court decision do not have the right to vote. Convicts who are serving a sentence enjoy the right to vote but not the right to be elected to office. The vote is personal, equal, free, and secret.

The elections to the Assembly are based on a mixed member proportional system. Voters have the right to vote directly for a candidate in a single-member constituency and for a political party. The electoral system allocates 100 seats through the first-past-the-post vote and 40 through the proportional vote for political parties, aiming at an overall proportional distribution of seats in the Assembly based on the overall proportional vote for political parties. A legal threshold of 2.5 percent for single political parties and 4 percent for party coalitions must be met in order to gain representation in the Assembly.

Local government officials such as mayors and council members are also directly elected. Mayors, who are executive officers, are elected through a first-past-the-post vote. Councils, which are representative bodies, are elected in a proportional system. No legal threshold exists for parties seeking council seats.

The Central Election Commission

The Central Election Commission is a seven-member permanent constitutional body that prepares, supervises, directs, and verifies all aspects of elections and declares election results. The mandate of its members is seven years.

POLITICAL PARTIES

Albania has a pluralistic system of political parties. Political parties are created freely, and their organization must conform to democratic principles. The laws bans any political parties or other organizations whose program and activity are based on totalitarian methods; that incite and support racial, religious, or ethnic hatred; that use violence to take power or influence state policies; or that have a secret character. The sources of political party revenues as well as their expenses must always be made public.

ALGERIA

At-a-Glance

OFFICIAL NAME
Democratic and Popular Republic of Algeria

CAPITAL
Algiers

POPULATION
32,818,500 (2005 est.)

SIZE
919,590 sq. mi. (2,381,741 sq. km)

LANGUAGES
Arabic (official), French, Berber (national)

RELIGIONS
Sunni Muslim (state religion) 99%, Christian and Jewish 1%

NATIONAL OR ETHNIC COMPOSITION
Arab-Berber 99%, European less than 1%

DATE OF INDEPENDENCE OR CREATION
July 3, 1962

TYPE OF GOVERNMENT
Presidential democracy

TYPE OF STATE
Unitary state

TYPE OF LEGISLATURE
Bicameral parliament

DATE OF CONSTITUTION
November 22, 1976

DATE OF LAST AMENDMENT
April 10, 2002

Algeria is a presidential democracy based on the rule of law with a clear division of executive, legislative, and judicial powers. It is divided into 48 *wilaya* or governorates, each headed by a *wali* or governor appointed by the president. The constitution of Algeria guarantees the inviolability of the human person and freedom of conscience and protects the free exercise of beliefs, with reservation that they do not disturb the public order.

Freedom of opinion, expression, the press, publication, assembly, and association are also guaranteed within the conditions defined by the law. The Algerian constitution guarantees the inviolability of the home; the secrecy of correspondence; and the right to move freely within the country, to leave it, and to establish a domicile within the limits established by the law.

The president of Algeria is the head of state and the guarantor of national independence, of the integrity of the territory, of the execution of treaties, and of respect for the constitution and the laws. The president watches over the regular functioning of the constitutional authorities and assures the continuity of the state. The president

of Algeria represents the executive power and is assisted by a cabinet directed by a prime minister.

The economic system can be described as a social market economy. The military is subject to the civil government in terms of law and fact. By constitutional law, Algeria is obliged to contribute to world peace.

CONSTITUTIONAL HISTORY

The native Berber population of Algeria has been under the rule of foreign occupants for much of the last 3,000 years. The Phoenicians (1000 B.C.E.) and the Roman Republic (200 B.C.E.) were the most important of these until the entry of the Arabs in the eighth century C.E. Algeria became part of the Ottoman Empire under Khair ad-Din and his brother, Aruj, in the early 16th century, the latter making its coast a base for pirate corsairs. The French invaded Algiers in 1830 and quickly conquered the country.

Algerians began their revolt against France on November 1, 1954. A referendum held in Algeria on July 1,

1962, backed independence. France declared Algeria independent two days later.

The first legislative election took place on September 20, 1962. The main objective of the assembly, elected for only one year, was to promulgate the fundamental law of the country: the constitution of September 10, 1963.

From 1965 to 1976, a Council of Revolution was instituted as the head of the Algerian state. By the Ordinance of July 10, 1965, it held the sovereign authority. A new constitution was promulgated in November 22, 1976, which instituted a single house called the National People's Assembly entrusted with the legislative power. The first assembly was elected in February 1977 for a five-year term and renewed by elections in 1982 and 1987.

The constitutional revision of February 28, 1989, established the separation of the legislative, executive, and judicial powers (Art. 92).

When the assembly reached the end of its term, its reelection was interrupted by the resignation of the president of the republic, which left a juridical vacuum. Transitional structures were established—a High Council of State and National Consultative Council, then a National Transitional Council—until a revised constitution was issued on November 28, 1996. The new document instituted a bicameral parliament, consisting of a National People's Assembly (380 members) and a Council of the Nation (144 members).

On April 15, 1999, Algeria held democratic presidential elections, which were won by Abdelaziz Bouteflika, who again won the presidential elections in April 2004.

FORM AND IMPACT OF THE CONSTITUTION

Algeria has a written constitution, codified in a single document, that takes precedence over all other national law. International law must be in accordance with the constitution to be applicable within Algeria.

Treaties enter into force only after their ratification, and provided they are applied by the other party. Treaties ratified by the president and approved by the Chamber of Deputies have higher authority than that of laws.

BASIC ORGANIZATIONAL STRUCTURE

The Algerian territorial structure is made up of three levels: 48 wilayas (departments), 567 dairates (underdepartments), and 1,540 municipalities.

At the central level, there are ministries, organized into general directorates in accordance with the French administrative model. At the intermediate level each of the 48 wilayas is headed by a wali (prefect), who is appointed by the president.

The wali is the representative of the central government and works with an Executive Council composed of representatives of every ministry. Each of the 48 wilayas has its own Popular Assembly made up of 30 representatives elected every five years. The wilayas enjoy financial autonomy. Their responsibilities include the territorial organization of state services; the regulation of agriculture, tourism, school systems, road networks, and medium-size industries; and all activities related to private sector development.

At the local level, each municipality is headed by a president elected to a five-year term and a Popular Assembly made up of 10 to 80 members elected every five years. The municipality is responsible for local administration, economics, finances, social and cultural activities, and planning.

LEADING CONSTITUTIONAL PRINCIPLES

Algeria's system of government is that of a presidential republic with a separation of the executive, legislative, and judicial powers, based on checks and balances. The judiciary is independent and includes a constitutional court.

The state is based on the principles of democratic organization and of social justice. At the same time that it promotes political and civil rights, Algeria endeavors to guarantee the social, economic, and cultural rights of its citizens.

Islam is the official state religion. However, the Algerian constitution does not allow the exploitation of religion or race for political purposes. It states in Article 42 that "a political party cannot be founded on a religious, linguistic, racial, sex, corporatist or regional basis."

The preamble of the Algerian constitution says that the constitution is "the fundamental law which guarantees individual and collective rights and liberties, protects the principle of the people's free choice and gives legitimacy to the exercise of powers. It helps to ensure the legal protection and control of the public authorities in a society in which lawfulness and man's progress prevail in all their dimensions."

The preamble to the constitution commits Algeria to promote world peace; to consolidate national unity; to remain faithful to the human values that constitute the common heritage of peoples; to support human dignity, justice, and liberty; and to work for peace, progress, and free cooperation among nations. The constitution obliges Algeria to take an active part in Maghreb (North Africa) integration.

CONSTITUTIONAL BODIES

The predominant bodies provided for in the constitution are the president; the prime minister and cabinet ministers; the parliament, formed by the Chamber of Deputies and the Chamber of Advisors; and the judiciary.

The President

The president is the head of state of the Republic of Algeria. The president appoints and dismisses the prime minister, who is the head of the executive government. The president promulgates the laws. The president also represents Algeria in international affairs, ratifies treaties, and declares war and concludes peace with the approval of the parliament. The president directs the general policy of the nation, defines its fundamental options, and informs the national parliament accordingly. The president formally appoints and dismisses the highest civil servants and soldiers. The president has the right to pardon criminal offenders in the name of the republic.

The president is the guarantor of national independence, of the integrity of the territory, and of respect for the constitution and the laws as well as the execution of treaties. The president watches over the regular functioning of the constitutional public powers and assures the continuity of the state.

The president is elected for five years by universal, free, direct, and secret suffrage; elections are held within the last 30 days of the previous term of office. A candidate for the presidency must be an Algerian who does not carry any other nationality, who is of the Muslim religion, and whose spouse has Algerian nationality without previous interruption. The candidate must be at least 40 years old and enjoy all civil and political rights. Candidates can be nominated in one of two ways: either by 600 elected officials (local and national) or by popular petition of at least 75,000 registered voters.

The term of the presidential office is five years. A president may serve only one term.

The Executive Administration

The executive administration or cabinet puts into effect the general policy of the nation in conformity with the directions and options defined by the president of the republic. The cabinet is responsible to the president of the republic for its conduct.

The president appoints the prime minister, who is the head of the cabinet, and on the suggestion of the prime minister appoints the other ministers. The president presides over the cabinet.

The president dismisses the cabinet or any of its members on his or her own initiative or on the recommendation of the prime minister. The prime minister distributes the functions among the other members in accordance with the provisions of the constitution.

The prime minister submits the administration's program and policies for approval by the parliament and may adapt the program in light of parliamentary debate. In a case when the parliament refuses to approve the program, the prime minister presents the resignation of

the cabinet to the president of the republic. The latter then chooses a new prime minister in accordance with legal procedures. If the National People's Assembly's approval is not obtained, the assembly is dissolved by law.

The prime minister may ask the assembly for a vote of confidence. If the motion of confidence is rejected, the prime minister and the cabinet resign. In this case, the president of the republic may decide to dissolve the assembly and call new general elections, which must be held within a maximum of three months.

The Parliament

The legislative power is exercised by a parliament consisting of two chambers, the National People's Assembly and the Council of the Nation. The parliament is sovereign to draft and approve laws.

The National People's Assembly is elected for a period of five years by universal, free, direct, and secret suffrage. Candidates must be at least 28 years old and Algerian by birth or naturalized for at least five years. Independent candidates must have collected at least 400 voter signatures to be eligible. Both men and women are eligible to run. The president of the people's assembly is elected for the term of the legislative body.

The Council of the Nation is composed of senators, whose numbers cannot exceed half the number of the members of the assembly. Senators serve for six years; half of the seats are renewed every three years.

The members of the Council of the Nation are chosen indirectly. Two-thirds are elected by and from among the members of the provincial and municipal assemblies and the People's Wilaya Assemblies. The remaining one-third are designated by the president of the republic from among personalities of national standing and qualified persons in the scientific, cultural, professional, economic, and social fields. The Council of the Nation chooses a president after each three-year election.

Deputies and members of the Council of the Nation enjoy parliamentary immunity during the period of their mandate. No member can be arrested or prosecuted for the duration of his or her mandate for a crime or misdemeanor unless the National People's Assembly or the Council of the Nation decides by the majority of its members to lift the immunity. However, an arrest is permitted if the member is apprehended during a crime; even then, the National People's Assembly or the Council of the Nation must be informed without delay.

The Lawmaking Process

The cabinet and any 20 deputies have the right to initiate laws. Draft laws are presented in the cabinet after review by the Council of State, a regulating body of the judiciary responsible for ensuring respect for the law. The bill is then submitted to the bureau of the National People's Assembly by the prime minister.

To be adopted, any draft law or law proposal must be debated successively by the National People's Assembly and the Council of the Nation. The Council of the Nation needs a three-quarters majority of its members to adopt a bill. In case there is a disagreement between the chambers, a committee with equal representation of the two meets at the request of the prime minister to propose a compromise version of the disputed provisions. The revised text is submitted by the prime minister to be adopted by the two chambers and cannot be further amended without the agreement of the cabinet. In case the disagreement persists, the bill is withdrawn.

The parliament legislates in the domains that the constitution assigns to it, such as the fundamental rights and duties of individuals and public freedoms in particular, as well as general rules concerning personal and family status, in particular marriage, divorce, and inheritance, and basic legislation concerning citizenship.

The president of the republic promulgates all constitutional, organic, or ordinary laws and ensures their publication in the *official journal of the Algerian Republic* within a maximal period of 15 days counting from the transmission by the president of the national parliament. During this period, the president of the republic may return the bill to the national parliament for a second reading. If the bill is adopted by the national parliament with a majority of two-thirds of its members, the law must be promulgated and published within a second period of 15 days.

The president of the republic can legislate by ordinance in case the National People's Assembly is suspended or in the period between sessions of the parliament. The president of the republic must submit the texts of such enacted ordinances to be approved by each of the two chambers of the parliament in its next session. Ordinances not adopted by the parliament become void. The president of the republic may also legislate by ordinance during a state of exception.

The president may also ratify armistice and peace agreements, alliance and union treaties, treaties related to state borders, and treaties involving expenses not provided for in the state budget but only after explicit approval by each of the chambers of the parliament.

The Judiciary

The judiciary in Algeria is independent of the executive and legislative branches and is a powerful factor in legal life. Magistrates are nominated by decree of the president upon the recommendation of the Superior Judicial Council.

The Superior Judicial Council serves as the administrative authority of the judiciary. The council is presided over by the president of the republic and is composed of senior jurors. The minister of justice serves as vice president. The current judicial system has civil, criminal, and administrative departments.

At the base of the Algerian judicial structure are the first-degree courts or jurisdictions of common right, which are qualified for all litigation relating to civil, commercial, or social matters. There are 48 courts of appeal for appeals against judgments given in courts of first resort.

The Supreme Court has the highest jurisdiction. It hears only appeals in cases of incompetence or abuse of power; violation or substantial omission of the rules of procedure; or defect, insufficiency, or contradictions of reasons of a judgment.

Special administrative courts have jurisdiction of common right for administrative cases. The law of May 30, 1998, instituted a Council of State to regulate administrative judicial activity. It ensures consistent administrative jurisprudence through the country.

The Court of Auditors reviews the public purses, local authorities, and public services.

THE ELECTION PROCESS

All Algerians over the age of 18 have the right to vote in the elections. "Suffrage is universal, free, direct, and secret." Citizens who have been naturalized for more than five years can also vote, as can Algerians living abroad who have registered in their embassy or consulate and have received their electoral card.

A Presidential and Legislative Elections National Observer has been established to control the electoral process. This body includes personalities known for their independence. The Constitutional Council reviews the validity of presidential candidate filings and the results of elections.

Parliamentary Elections

Any 18-year-old Algerian enjoying civil rights is entitled to vote in the elections. A candidate to the Chamber of Deputies must be an Algerian by birth and 23 years of age. Persons convicted of a crime entailing an unsuspended sentence of imprisonment in excess of three months cannot run for office. Guardianship, undischarged bankruptcy, insanity, and active service in the armed or security forces also disqualify a person for office.

Candidates can advertise in the press and other media. Campaigning is allowed for only the two weeks preceding the election.

No military or security forces may be present in the polling stations during voting without special permission, and voters may not carry arms.

POLITICAL PARTIES

Algeria has a "pluralistic system" of political parties. The Law Relative to Political Associations of July 1989 recognized the existence of political parties.

The 1989 law also prohibited associations formed exclusively on regional, ethnic, or religious grounds. However, the two parties that polled highest in the 1990 and 1991 elections were the Islamic Salvation Front and the Rassemblement pour la Culture et la Démocratie of the Berber Kabylie region. In December 1991, the Islamic Front won the first round of multiparty elections. The second round of elections was canceled after the military coup of January 11, 1992. On December 7, 1996, President Liamine Zeroual banned political parties that are formed on the basis of religion or language.

CITIZENSHIP

Algerian citizenship is primarily acquired by birth. The principles of *ius sanguinis* and *ius soli* are applied.

FUNDAMENTAL RIGHTS

The Algerian constitution guarantees the inviolability of the human person and freedom of conscience and protects the free exercise of beliefs, provided they do not disturb the public order. Freedom of opinion, expression, the press, publication, assembly, and association is also guaranteed and exercised within the conditions defined by law.

The constitution also guarantees the inviolability of the home, the secrecy of correspondence, the right to move freely within the country or to leave it, and the right to establish one's domicile within the limits established by the law. Article 29 provides a general equal treatment clause, which guarantees that all citizens are equal before the law.

Limitations to Fundamental Rights

The fundamental rights specified in the constitution are not without limits. The constitution itself lays down such possible limitations in the interest of the public or of the rights of others. Article 57 states, "The law may forbid or limit the right to strike in the field of national defense and security or in any public service or activity of vital interest for the community." On the other hand, no fundamental right may be disregarded completely. Each limit to a fundamental right faces limits itself.

ECONOMY

The Algerian constitution does not specify any specific economic system. However, it does explicitly state that public property belongs to the national collectivity. Such property includes mines, quarries, energy resources, and the mineral, natural, and biological resources found in the country's national forests, waters, and maritime areas. Such public properties also include rail, maritime, and air transport; mail and telecommunications; and other properties defined by the law.

RELIGIOUS COMMUNITIES

Freedom of religion or belief is guaranteed as a human right. Islam is the state religion. The constitution provides for the free exercise of other religions that do not disturb the public order, and the government generally observes and enforces this right.

The government controls and subsidizes mosques and pays the salaries of prayer leaders. The law provides that only personnel appointed by the government may lead activities in mosques.

MILITARY DEFENSE AND STATE OF EMERGENCY

In case of imminent peril menacing the institutions of the republic or the security and independence of the country, or obstructing the regular functioning of state powers, the president of the republic may take exceptional measures necessitated by the circumstances, such as declaring a state of emergency, after consultation with the prime minister and the president of the national parliament.

AMENDMENTS TO THE CONSTITUTION

Only the president of the republic has the right to propose constitutional revisions. They must then be approved by both houses of parliament, following the same procedure as ordinary laws. If it is passed, an amendment is submitted to a referendum to be approved by the people within 50 days.

Constitutional revision may not infringe on the republican nature of the state, the democratic order based on the multiparty system, Islam as the religion of the state, Arabic as the national and official language, fundamental liberties and citizen's rights, and the integrity of the national territory.

Three-quarters of the members of the two chambers of the parliament meeting together can propose a constitutional revision and present it to the president of the republic, who can submit it to a referendum.

A constitutional revision, approved by the people, is promulgated by the president of the republic.

PRIMARY SOURCES

Constitution in English. Available online. URL: http://www.chr.up.ac.za/hr_docs/constitutions/docs/AlgeriaC(rev).doc. Accessed on August 18, 2005.

Constitution in French. Available online. URL: http://www.droit.mjustice.dz/CONSTITUTION.pdf. Accessed on September 6, 2005.

Constitution in Arabic. Available online. URL: http://www.droit.mjustice.dz/portailarabe/doustour.pdf. Accessed on July 20, 2005.

SECONDARY SOURCES

Bekhechi Mohamed Abdelwahab, *Constitution algérienne de 1976 et le droit international.* Alger: Office des publications universitaires, 1989.

Bureau of Public Affairs, U.S. Department of State, "Background Note and Country Reports on Human Rights Practices and International Religious Freedom Report 2004." Available online. URL: http://www.state.gov/. Accessed on August 7, 2005.

Francois Borella, *Droit public économique de l'Algérie.* Alger, Impr. Officielle, 1967.

Mohand Issad, *Droit international prive: tome II, Les règles de conflits.* Paris: Éditions Publisud, 1986.

Ahmed Lourdjane, *Le code civil algérien.* Paris: Éditions L'Harmattan, 1985.

Ahmed Mahiou, *Cours d'institutions administratives: Troisième semestre de la licence en droit,* 3d ed. Alger: Office des publications universitaires, 1981.

———. *Etudes de droit public Algérien.* Alger: Office des publications universitaires, 1984.

Mohamed Mentalecheta, *L'Arbitrage commercial en droit algérien,* 2d ed. Alger: Office des publications universitaires, 1986.

Ahmed Rahmani, *Les Biens publics en droit algérien.* Alger: Les Editions internationales, 1996.

Hélène Vandevelde, *Cours d'histoire du droit musulman et des institutions musulmanes: Troisième semestre de la licence en droit.* Alger: Office des publications universitaires, 1983.

Dahmène Touchent

ANDORRA

At-a-Glance

OFFICIAL NAME
Principality of Andorra

CAPITAL
Andorra la Vella

POPULATION
71,201 (July 2006 est.)

SIZE
180 sq. mi. (468 sq. km)

LANGUAGES
Catalan

RELIGIONS
Catholic 90% (active attendees 50%), Protestant 2%, Muslim 3%, Jewish 0.5%, Jehovah's Witnesses 0.5%, atheist 1%, unaffiliated or other 3%

NATIONAL OR ETHNIC COMPOSITION
Andorran 37.92%, Spanish 38.82%, French 10.02%, Portuguese 6.4%, other 6.8%

DATE OF INDEPENDENCE OR CREATION
Documented with the same borders as today since 839 C.E. It became a feudal territory on its own, subjected to the persons of the two coprinces in 1278. Modern independence since 1993.

TYPE OF GOVERNMENT
Parliamentary coprincipality

TYPE OF STATE
Democratic and social independent coprincipality

TYPE OF LEGISLATURE
Unicameral parliament

DATE OF CONSTITUTION
March 14, 1993

DATE OF LAST AMENDMENT
None

A small country in the heart of the Pyrenees between France and Spain, Andorra is a parliamentary co-principality in which sovereignty lies in a democratic parliament chosen by universal suffrage by the Andorran people. Andorra is a democratic, independent, and social state based on the rule of law, with a clear division of executive, legislative, and judicial powers. The two heads of state, who serve by personal right, are the bishop of the Catholic Diocese of Urgell (in Catalonia, Spain) and the president of the French Republic. Apart from their representative functions, the coprinces retain a degree of governing power.

The constitution proclaims that the action of the Andorran state is inspired by the principles of respect and promotion of liberty, equality, justice, and tolerance. It provides far-reaching guarantees to protect human rights and the dignity of the person. The constitution has become the centerpiece of the modern Andorran identity, as the text that gave the country international recognition.

The central political figure is the head of government (*cap de govern*), who derives his or her powers from parliament (Consell General). Free, equal, and direct elections of members of parliament are guaranteed. A pluralistic system of political parties has emerged.

Religious freedom and freedom of worship are guaranteed, subject only to the limitations prescribed by law if necessary in the interest of public safety, order, health, morals, or protection of the fundamental rights and freedoms of others. Religious communities are separated from the state, but the Roman Catholic Church has a preeminent historic position, and its relations with the state are legally well defined by a system of cooperation as defined in Article 11.3 of the constitution.

The economic system can be described as a social market economy. No military exists in Andorra.

CONSTITUTIONAL HISTORY

Andorra emerged in the ninth century C.E. as a fief of the County of Urgelland; its current borders go back to the year 839 C.E. Andorra fell under the sovereignty of the bishop of Urgell in the 11th century. With the *pariatges* or treaties of 1278 and 1288, the lordship rights of the bishop of Urgell were shared with the count of Foix (in present-day France), under homage to the king of Aragon and count of Barcelona.

The treaties, signed by Pere of Urtx, bishop of Urgell, and Bernat III, count of Foix, in the presence of the count of Barcelona and ratified by the pope, were based on the idea of equality in lordship. However, they also guaranteed the formal homage of the count to the bishop. The 1278 document provided for shared participation in the payment of tribute, the naming of judges, and military service; the 1288 agreement specified that each coprince should name a public notary and barred the construction of fortresses by either of the princes without license from the other. The two treaties are considered to be the most fundamental documents and sources of Andorra's history and its juridical-political system. Their spirit survived until the current constitution took force in 1993.

With the treaties in force, the internal life of Andorra continued to evolve. In 1419, the Land's Council (Consell de Terra) was created as an organ of representation and administration for the valley. It was the predecessor of the current parliament.

In 1589, Henry of Navarre, count of Foix, succeeded to the throne of France as Henry IV. In 1607 he formally attached his sovereign rights over Andorra as count of Foix to the Crown of France. As count of Foix the king of France would also become coprince of Andorra.

Early in the 11th century the bishop of Urgell had given these lands in fief to the Caboet house. The rights of the Caboet house later passed to the Castellbó counts and from them to the counts of Foix. France's Crown received the rights via Henry, and afterward they passed to the French Republic. Thus the president of the French Republic became coprince of Andorra.

The fact that one of the colords of Andorra was a king of another state gave further prestige to his acts, but it turned the valleys into an enclave with an unusual status. Toward 1715 the bishop of Urgell began to use the title of "Princeps Supremus Vallis Andorre." As the enclave's two lords (formerly a bishop and a count) now used the titles of king and prince, it became only a matter of time for the old feudal domain to be identified with the idea of sovereignty. This became easier once the Kingdom of Aragon–County of Barcelona (the former ultimate sovereign of Andorra) disappeared and was partitioned between Spain and France.

From the 18th century, the Lands Council became the mainstay of Andorra's independence and neutrality as it began to follow the concepts and practices of a government. In 1758 the council ordered that the tacitly structured Andorran laws and customs be compiled and written down.

The second half of the 19th century and the beginning of the 20th were difficult and violent as modern liberal ideas spread in a formally feudal state. New economic interests provoked numerous public quarrels; there were continuous confrontations between the two coprinces. However, during World War II (1939–45) the constitutional role of the bishop of Urgell stood in the way of the occupation of Andorra by German troops after their occupation of France. Thus, the existence of two coprinces has been the key to preserving the integrity, neutrality, and independence of the country.

In 1946, universal suffrage for men 25 years of age, originally introduced in 1933, was restored after having been abolished by Marshal Pétain in 1941. In the 1970s the rights of active and passive suffrage were also recognized for women. In January 1981 an "institutional reform process" began, leading to the emergence of the government of Andorra the following year.

On March 1989, the Law of the Rights of the Human Person was approved; it stated that "fundamental rights, as defined in the Universal Declaration of Human Rights of 1948, are included in the legal system of the Principality." On March 14, 1993, the Andorran people approved the first constitution in the country's history. The same year Andorra was admitted as a member of the United Nations. It joined the European Convention for the Protection of Human Rights and Fundamental Freedoms in 1996. Andorra has not asked for membership in the European Union but maintains diplomatic and other ties.

The legitimacy of the succession of the president of the French Republic to a personal title of nobility was long questioned. The referendum and constitution of 1993 completely legitimized this situation.

FORM AND IMPACT OF THE CONSTITUTION

Andorra has a written constitution, codified in a single, relatively short document, officially called the Constitution of the Principality of Andorra; it takes precedence over all other national laws and customs. The constitution cites the Universal Declaration of Human Rights; international laws must be in accordance with both documents to be applicable within Andorra. There are other unwritten norms that have binding force in Andorran private law, such as custom or Roman and medieval canon law (*ius commune*). The law of the European Union does not affect Andorra, but certain bilateral treaties have binding force.

BASIC ORGANIZATIONAL STRUCTURE

Andorra is divided into seven parishes (*parròquies*), territorial entities with some legislative power over local administration and regulations. The parishes are represented and administrated by the *comuns,* public corporations with legal status. Their ruling bodies are elected democratically, and they are entitled to lodge appeals of unconstitutionality. The parishes differ considerably from each other in economic strength but have identical administrative competences.

LEADING CONSTITUTIONAL PRINCIPLES

The political system of Andorra is a parliamentary coprincipality. Government is based on parliamentary democracy, with a strong division between the executive and legislative branches; there is an independent judicial power. The constitutional system is defined by several leading principles: Andorra is a democratic, independent, and social state abiding by the rule of law. The constitution proclaims that the Andorran state is inspired by the principles of respect for and promotion of real and effective liberty, equality, justice, and tolerance, and the protection of human rights and dignity. All state actions impairing the rights of people must have a basis in a "qualified parliamentary law" (*llei qualificada*) requiring a greater majority than other laws. Integrity and neutrality are two of Andorra's main principles. Further principles expressly mentioned in the constitution are hierarchy and transparency of norms, nonretroactivity of unfavorable or restrictive norms, security of the judicial system, accountability of public institutions, and prohibition of arbitrary acts. The constitution, as the highest law, binds all public institutions as well as individuals. Any kind of discrimination is forbidden.

Treaties and international agreements cannot be amended or repealed by law. Article 44.1 of the constitution states that the coprinces are the symbols and guarantees of the independence and continuity of Andorra and provides for the maintenance of the traditional parity in relations with the neighboring states.

CONSTITUTIONAL BODIES

The main bodies provided for in the constitution are the coprinces; the parliament, or Consell General, and its president, the *síndic general;* the *govern,* or administration, with its head and his or her ministers; the comuns, the representative organs of the parishes; and the judiciary, including the Constitutional Court.

The Coprinces

In accordance with the institutional tradition of Andorra, the coprinces are jointly and indivisibly heads of the state and its highest representatives. Dating from the treaties or *pariatges* of the 13th century, the coprinces are by personal and exclusive right the bishop of Urgell and the president of the French Republic. Their powers are equal and derive from the constitution, and each of them swears or affirms to exercise his or her functions in accordance with the constitution.

Apart from their function as heads of state, they also exercise some powers, such as proclaiming the consent of the Andorran state to adopt and honor international obligations and treaties. By acts of free will, they may jointly exercise the prerogative of pardon, create and structure appropriate services for performing their duties, appoint some Consell members and half the members of the Constitutional Court, make preliminary judgments as to the constitutionality of norms prior to their ratification, and participate in negotiating treaties affecting relations with neighboring states concerning internal security and defense, diplomatic or consular functions, and judiciary or penal cooperation.

Each coprince appoints a personal representative in Andorra, who is immune from court actions. The acts of the coprinces are under the responsibility of those who countersign them.

As heads of state, the coprinces arbitrate and moderate the functioning of public authorities and institutions and are kept regularly informed of affairs of state. They issue the call for general elections and referendums, sign the decrees of dissolution of the Consell, accredit diplomatic representatives to foreign states, appoint state officeholders, and sanction and enact laws and international treaties and ordain their publication. Foreign envoys present credentials to both of them.

In case of vacancy of one of the coprinces, the constitution recognizes the succession mechanisms provided for in their respective legal systems (canon law and French public law), so as not to interrupt the functioning of Andorran institutions.

The Consell General (Parliament)

The Consell General is the central representative organ of the Andorran people; it expresses a mixed and apportioned representation of the national population and the seven parishes. It exercises legislative powers, approves the budget of the state, and controls the political action of the government. It is composed of deputies elected for four-year terms by free, equal, and direct suffrage of all Andorrans.

The Consell General consists of a minimum of 28 and a maximum of 42 members, half of whom are elected in an equal number by each of the seven parishes and the other half elected on the basis of a national single constituency.

Resolutions of the Consell General require a quorum of half the deputies and take effect when approved by the simple majority of those present. Special majorities are required for certain matters, including regulations on fundamental rights.

The Síndic General

The *síndic general* is the chair of the Consell General. The *síndic general* may not exercise the office for more than two consecutive full terms and chairs sessions of parliament.

The *Govern* (Administration)

The *govern* (administration or cabinet) consists of the *cap de govern* and the ministers. The administration carries out the national and international policy of Andorra and is vested with statutory powers under the laws and the general principles of the legal system. Its actions and decisions are subject to judicial control. Members of the cabinet cannot be members of the Consell General and cannot exercise any other public office not derived from the cabinet. The *cap de govern* may not hold office for more than two consecutive terms.

The cabinet ceases to function upon the dissolution of the Consell General; the resignation, death, or permanent disability of the *cap de govern;* the approval of a motion of censure or the lack of approval in a vote of confidence.

The *Comuns*

The *comuns* are the corporations that represent the interests of the parishes or *parròquies.* They approve and carry out the communal budget, develop public policies within their territory, and manage and administer all parish properties of any kind. The *comuns* function under the principle of self-government and are presided over by a *cònsol.* The parishes are divided into Quarts and Veïnats, which are represented in the Consell del Comú.

The Lawmaking Process

The Consell General and the *Govern* have the right to propose a law. Any three *comuns* can combine to present private members' bills to the Consell General, as can 10 percent of the electoral roll. Once a bill has been passed by the Consell General, the *Síndic General* presents it to the coprinces so that they may sanction it, enact it, and publish it in the official bulletin.

The Judiciary

The judiciary is independent of the administration. Because of the paucity of legislation in some areas, it is a powerful factor in legal life.

There is a Constitutional Court (Tribunal Constitutional) as highest interpreter of the constitution and the highest protector of fundamental rights. It consists of four magistrates who serve for a period of eight years. The court ranks above the Supreme Court (Tribunal Superior de Justícia d'Andorra), which consists of eight magistrates and a president. The judiciary is divided into three different branches: civil, criminal, and administrative and fiscal.

THE ELECTION PROCESS

All Andorrans over 18, in full command of their faculties, have both the right to vote and the right to stand for election.

POLITICAL PARTIES

Andorra has a pluralistic system of political parties, dominated by the Social-Democratic Party and the Andorran Liberal Party. All Andorrans have the right to create political parties, which must have democratic structures and engage in lawful activities. Political parties can be banned, suspended, or dissolved only by a decision of the judicial organs.

CITIZENSHIP

Andorran citizenship is quite restrictive because of the small size of the country, and it is primarily acquired by birth when one of the parents is an Andorran citizen. It can also be acquired by birth within Andorra by foreigners who are legal residents or who were themselves born in Andorra. Adoption confers Andorran nationality, but three years of residence is required after marriage. Nationality can also be acquired by residence. In 2004 the required residence period was reduced from 25 to 20 years. Only 10 years of residence is required if the applicant has studied in Andorra and 15 years if grandparents were from Andorra.

FUNDAMENTAL RIGHTS

The constitution, in chapter III of its second title, defines fundamental rights as of basic importance. It guarantees the traditional set of human rights and civil liberties.

Taking human dignity as its starting point, the constitution has some introductory articles on equality and liberty and guarantees numerous specific rights. The basic rights bind all public authorities as directly enforceable law.

Article 8 protects the right to life; it specifies full protection of all phases of life, prohibiting abortion, euthanasia, and the death penalty.

Impact and Functions of Fundamental Rights

For the Andorran constitution, human rights are the axis on which all legal thinking turns. The fundamental rights represent a constitutional decision in favor of certain values, and thus they are of direct application to the interpretation of all laws.

Limitations to Fundamental Rights

The fundamental rights of religious freedom, freedom of expression, inviolability of dwelling and communication, right to assemble, right to associate, and right to property contain constitutionally defined limitations, but they may never be completely disregarded. Fundamental rights cannot be limited by ordinary law; any limitations require a qualified law. There is an exceptional procedure of appeal before the Constitutional Court against acts of public authorities that may violate the essential contents of fundamental rights. Aliens legally resident in Andorra have complete protection of fundamental rights, but such rights may be limited during a state of alarm or suspended in a state of emergency.

ECONOMY

The Andorran constitution does not specify any economic system, but the state may intervene in the functioning of the economic, commercial, labor, and financial systems to ensure the balanced development of society and the general welfare, within the framework of a market economy system. The constitution protects the freedom of private property, the right of enterprise, the right to and freedom of profession, the right to health protection, and the obligation of the state to guarantee a system of social security. The state is obliged to ensure a reasonable use of the soil and to keep the ecological balance. It must also defend decent housing and consumers' rights.

RELIGIOUS COMMUNITIES

Freedom of religion and worship is guaranteed as a human right, and no one is bound to state his or her ideology, religion, or belief. Religious freedom also involves rights for religious communities, with traditional limitations. The state and religious communities are separate, and there is no established state church.

The constitution expressly mentions the Roman Catholic Church, however, and guarantees relations of special cooperation in accordance with the Andorran tradition. The bishop of Urgell, the diocesan bishop governing the Catholic Church in Andorra, is also one of the heads of the state. The constitution recognizes the full legal powers of Roman Catholic Church bodies in accordance with canon law. Development laws grant the Catholic Church a special position, notwithstanding the constitutional provision that all public authorities must remain strictly neutral in their relations with religious communities and that all religions must be treated equally.

MILITARY DEFENSE AND STATE OF EMERGENCY

There is no army in Andorra. The defense of the country is coordinated with France and Spain. The police forces are presumed to be able to cope successfully with all emerging difficulties. Therefore, no military service is provided for legally.

A state of alarm can be declared by the *Govern* in case of natural disaster, for a term of 15 days, upon notifying the Consell General. The right to move freely about or enter and leave the country as well as the right to private property may be limited. A state of emergency can be declared by the *Govern* for a term of 30 days, with the authorization of the Consell General, in cases in which the normal functioning of democratic life is interrupted. People can be detained for up to 48 hours, and the administration can suspend freedom of expression, the inviolability of dwellings and communication, the right to meet and assemble, the rights of workers and employers, and the right to move about and leave the country.

Further extension of states of alarm and emergency requires the approval of the Consell General.

AMENDMENTS TO THE CONSTITUTION

The constitution can be changed only with the joint initiative of the two coprinces or at the request of one-third of parliament. A majority of two-thirds of the members is required to pass any amendment. It must be ratified in a referendum and sanctioned by the two coprinces in order to go into force. The constitution does not specify any matters that may not be amended, except that the coprinces must approve any change or new constitution that deposes them.

PRIMARY SOURCES
Basic Law in English. Available online: URL: www.consell. ad/micg/webconsell.nsf. Accessed on June 17, 2006.
Basic Law in Catalan (original document). Available online: URL: http: www.consell.ad/micg/webconsell. nsf. Accessed on June 17, 2006.

SECONDARY SOURCES
Bertrand Bélinguier, *La condition juridique des vallées d'Andorre*. Paris: Edicion Pedone, 1970.
Eulogi Broto, *Church and State Relations and Right of Religious Freedom in Andorra. European Journal for Church and State Research*, 9 (2002), 10 (2003).
Leuven: Ed. Peeters; Pere Figareda i Cairol, *Las instituciones del Pincipado de Andorra en el nuevo marco constitucional*. Barcelona: Ed. Civitas/Institut d'Estudis Andorrans (IEA), 1996.
Antoni Fiter i Rossell, *Manual Digest*. Andorra: Ed. Consell General, 2000.

Josep Maria Font i Rius and Ramon Gubern, "Perfil esquemático de historia constitucional andorrana." In *Les problèmes actuels des vallées d'Andorre*. París: Ed. Pédone-Publications de l'Institut d'Etudes Politiques de Toulouse, 1970.

Nemesi Marqués, *La reforma de les institucions d'Andorra (1975–1981)*. Lleida: Ed. Virgili & Pagés, 1989.

Andorra en el ámbito jurídico europeo. Madrid: Ed. Marcial Pons-Jefatura del Estado Andorranol. Copríncipe Episcopal, 1996.

Laura Roman, *El nou estat andorrà*. Andorra: IEA, 1999.

Àlvar Valls, *La nova Constitució d'Andorra*. Andorra la Vella: Ed. Premsa andorrana, 1993.

Karl Zemanek, *L'estatut Internacional d'Andorra*. Andorra la Vella: Edicion Casa de la Vall, 1981.

Eulogi Broto

ANGOLA

At-a-Glance

OFFICIAL NAME
Republic of Angola

CAPITAL
Luanda

POPULATION
12,127,071 (July 2006 est.)

SIZE
481,354 sq. mi. (1,246,700 sq. km)

LANGUAGES
Mainly Portuguese as official language; also
Ovimbundu, Kimbundu, and Bakongo

RELIGIONS
Roman Catholic 68%, various Protestants 20%,
indigenous beliefs 12%

NATIONAL OR ETHNIC COMPOSITION
Ovimbundu 37%, Bakongo 13%, mixed racial 2%,
European 1%, other 47%

DATE OF INDEPENDENCE OR CREATION
November 11, 1975

TYPE OF GOVERNMENT
Republic

TYPE OF STATE
Unitary state

TYPE OF LEGISLATURE
Unicameral parliament

DATE OF CONSTITUTION
November 11, 1975

DATE OF LAST AMENDMENT
August 26, 1992

Angola is a multiparty democratic state based on the principles of the rule of law and the protection of internationally recognized fundamental rights. There is clear division among the executive, legislative, and judicial powers although significant overlap of the branches of the government does occur. The country is organized as a unitary state, with a strong central government and 18 less powerful provinces. Provision has been made to oversee constitutional compliance by the creation of a separate Constitutional Court.

The president of the republic of Angola is both head of state and head of the administration. The office of a prime minister has also been established with the primary function of directing and coordinating the general activities of the ruling administration. The central figure, however, is the president, who possesses wide-ranging powers and functions. The national parliament consists of a unicameral National Assembly with 223 members elected through a system of proportional representation. Sovereignty of the state is vested in the people, who exercise political power through their right to periodic universal suffrage.

With the enactment of radical constitutional changes in 1992, explicit provisions calling for a multiparty state and a free market economy were added. The constitution furthermore protects religious freedom; it requires a secular state and specifies the separation between the government and religious organizations.

Angola has a fast-growing economy, funded mainly from rich oil reserves, but the economy is largely in disarray because of many years of political instability due to civil war. The constitution provides for national defense, with the overall objective of guaranteeing national independence, territorial integrity, and the freedom and security of the Angolan population.

CONSTITUTIONAL HISTORY

The recent constitutional history of Angola can be traced back to 1482 when Portuguese seamen landed along the northern coast. Although Dutch people occupied the territory briefly after 1641, Brazilian-based Portuguese forces retook the capital, Luanda, in late 1648. From that year, the territory remained a colony of Portugal until independence.

During the latter part of the 20th century, decolonization built up strong momentum in Africa. In Angola, three independence movements emerged: the Popular Movement for the Liberation of Angola (MPLA), the National Union for the Total Independence of Angola (UNITA), and the National Front for the Liberation of Angola (FNLA). These movements fought together against the Portuguese occupation.

In 1974 a coup d'état in Portugal resulted in a new military government. This new government agreed in the Alvor Accords to end Portugal's occupation of Angola and hand over power to a coalition government that comprised the three independence movements. However, ideological differences among the movements led to armed conflict. UNITA and the FNLA formed a coalition against the MPLA and attempted to take control of the capital city, Luanda. The internal struggle was further complicated by the intervention of armed forces from South Africa on behalf of UNITA, from Zaire for the FNLA, and from Cuba for the MPLA. The MPLA remained in control of the capital and on November 11, 1975, declared independence. The movement subsequently proclaimed itself to be the government. It adopted a constitution that proclaimed a Marxist-Leninist ideology and a one-party state.

Civil war overwhelmed the new Angolan state for decades after independence. Various attempts were made to resolve the conflict and to stabilize the region, including the Lusaka Peace Accord of 1984 and the Bicesse Accord of 1991. In 1990 a process of democratization began when the MPLA government proposed major constitutional reforms, which were instituted in 1992. Political parties were legalized, including UNITA, and communism was rejected in favor of democratic socialism. After the reforms were established, a general election was held in 1992. The MPLA leader, José Eduardo dos Santos, obtained 49 percent of the vote against the UNITA leader Dr. Jonas Savimbi's 40 percent. Dr. Savimbi, however, called the election fraudulent, and the parties resumed civil war. In 1994 the parties agreed to disarm according to the terms of the Lusaka Protocol, but peace again collapsed in 1997 when a government of unity and national reconciliation was formed without Dr. Savimbi. The United Nations imposed sanctions against UNITA.

In 1999 the MPLA launched a massive offensive against UNITA and captured vast territories. In February 2002 Dr. Savimbi was killed in combat; his death ironically lead to a cease-fire and disarmament negotiations. During November 2003, both UNITA and the MPLA government declared that all outstanding issues had been resolved and proposed national elections to take place in 2005.

FORM AND IMPACT OF THE CONSTITUTION

With the 1992 constitutional reforms, the Angolan state was transformed from a one-party Marxist-Leninist system to a nominally multiparty democracy. The constitution establishes the broad outlines of the new governmental structure and delineates the rights and duties of all citizens. It consists of a single written document, which explicitly enshrines the principles of international law. The finer details of government are mainly based on ordinances, decrees, and decisions issued by the president of the republic and the cabinet ministers and also through legislation produced by the National Assembly and approved by the president. Generally speaking, the unicameral parliament is subordinate to the executive authority of the state, and the office of the president is the most influential position. The constitution remains fundamentally important in a political sense as it influences and impacts all aspects of the government and the legal system, but it enjoys no special status, and its provisions are generally supplemented by other national laws.

BASIC ORGANIZATIONAL STRUCTURE

Apart from its national territory, Angola is divided into 18 provinces, approximately 164 municipal areas, and many smaller communes, neighborhoods, and villages. The state has created various local government agencies and administrative bodies, which function in accord with the constitution and the law. The powers and functions of these bodies have been significantly decentralized in order to implement the administration's goals at the lowest levels of the government. Each province is headed by a provincial governor appointed by the president of the republic. These governors are the representatives of the national government in each province. Their general duty is to oversee and ensure the effective functioning of local administrative bodies.

LEADING CONSTITUTIONAL PRINCIPLES

The Republic of Angola is constituted as a sovereign, independent nation whose primary objective is to build a free and democratic society. The state is based on the principles of the rule of law, national unity, and protection of basic rights and freedoms of the person. Government authority and sovereignty are vested in the people of Angola, who are constitutionally permitted to organize themselves in many political parties and to exercise political power through regularly held, free, and fair elections. There is a clear division of powers among the executive, legislative, and judicial institutions. The state is unitary in form and has a secular nature.

CONSTITUTIONAL BODIES

The three branches of the Angolan state are divided into five separate constitutional bodies: the president, the Council of the Republic, the National Assembly, the administration (the cabinet), and the judiciary.

The President

The first and most important body is the office of the president of the republic. The president is both head of state, symbolizing national unity, and head of the national executive branch. The president is also the commander in chief of the armed forces. He or she defines the country's political policy, and political power is concentrated in the presidency. The president is directly elected by an absolute majority of voting citizens for a fixed term of five years. The president's various powers and functions are specifically enumerated in the constitution and other laws. It is, for example, the privilege of the president to appoint the prime minister, the other ministers, and the judges of the Supreme Court. In the exercise of his or her political powers, the president issues presidential decrees that must be published in the official government gazette, the *Diário da República*.

The Council of the Republic

The Council of the Republic serves as the political consultative body for the president; it functions as a quasi cabinet. The president presides over the Council of the Republic, which includes ex-officio members such as the president of the National Assembly, the prime minister, the president of the Constitutional Court, the attorney general, the former president of the republic, and the leaders of the political parties represented in the National People's Assembly, as well as 10 citizens appointed by the president of the republic.

The National Assembly

National legislative authority is vested in a unicameral National Assembly consisting of 223 seats. The assembly functions as the national representative body of the people. Representatives are elected for four-year terms in accordance with proportional representation. Members of the assembly have the right to question the administration on its performance, and the members of the administration are accountable in terms of the constitu-

tion and the law. In essence, the National Assembly is the highest legislative organ of the state with the power to amend the constitution and to approve laws on all other matters. The assembly has a president chosen by the parties or coalitions represented in it. Normally, the assembly functions with a simple majority of members present.

The Lawmaking Process
Members of the National Assembly, parliamentary groups, and the cabinet have the right to propose legislation. In general, laws are adopted by a simple majority of the members present.

The Administration

The constitution provides for a national administration as the highest public executive body in the state apart from the presidency. It meets in a Council of Ministers and discharges its duties through executive laws or decrees. The administration is politically accountable to the president of the republic and the National Assembly, and it is composed in accordance with an executive law. The members of the administration may not be members of the National Assembly as the system provides for direct separation of powers.

The Judiciary

The constitution provides for judicial bodies in the form of courts that function as sovereign bodies subject only to the law. The constitution mandates the courts to ensure compliance with the law and more specifically the constitution. Specifically, the constitution provides for a Constitutional Court, a Supreme Court (Tribunal da Relação), provincial and municipal courts, and such other courts as may be established by law. A High Council of the Judicial Bench is established to manage and discipline the judiciary; it is presided over by the president of the Supreme Court. The Constitutional Court, which has not yet been established, is to adjudicate over constitutional matters only and should consist of seven judges. Finally, the constitution provides for an attorney general and a judicial procurator to oversee and control criminal prosecution and the public administration, respectively.

THE ELECTION PROCESS AND POLITICAL PARTICIPATION

Universal suffrage is only for citizens, who must be over the age of 18. All adult citizens have the right and duty to take part in public life, to vote, and to stand for election. The electoral process is not specifically regulated by the constitution but is conducted according to various other national laws.

POLITICAL PARTIES

Before 1992, only the ruling MPLA party was constitutionally authorized, but the constitutional changes of that year provided for multiparty democracy and legalized various other parties including the rival UNITA. Many parties are active on the political playing field, but the MPLA remains dominant, and there are few practical opportunities for the opposition. Still, the authorization of different political parties not only allows for better public participation and representation but also ensures a truly democratic and pluralistic Angolan future.

CITIZENSHIP

Broad principles regarding citizenship are not included in the text of the constitution. Instead, they are prescribed by other laws.

FUNDAMENTAL RIGHTS

The Angolan constitution specifically protects various internationally accepted fundamental human rights.

Impact and Functions of Fundamental Rights

The constitution determines that all citizens are equal under the law and that the state has an obligation to respect and protect the person, human dignity, life, a healthy environment, due process of law, and free movement. The state must also protect against cruel, inhuman, or degrading treatment or punishment. Family life is regarded as the basic nucleus of social organization. Although the current constitution tends to stress primarily liberal rights, some social rights are also included.

Limitations to Fundamental Rights

Fundamental rights are not regarded as absolute, and limitations may be lawful if they are in accordance with the constitution and the law. The constitution is silent on when and under what circumstances rights may be limited, as such details are to be found in other national laws.

ECONOMY

On paper, Angola is a relative rich country with an estimated gross domestic product of $23 billion in 2004. Although the economy is growing fast, it remains in disarray because of the civil war that ravaged the country for nearly a quarter of a century, corruption, and public mismanagement. The country survives mainly on oil production; other national resources include diamonds, iron ore, uranium, gold, granite, and copper. Various agricultural products and sectors are also important, such as bananas, sugarcane, coffee, corn, tobacco, livestock, and fisheries. Subsistence agriculture is the main livelihood of the majority of the population. Most foodstuffs are, however, imported since the agricultural and fishing resources are underexploited because of factors associated with the civil war. Despite the abundant natural resources, the output per capita remains among the lowest in the world. According to the constitution, it is the responsibility of the state to guide the development of the nation's economy, as all natural resources are constitutionally proclaimed to be the property of the state, to be managed and exploited for the benefit of the nation.

RELIGIOUS COMMUNITIES

Freedom of religion or belief is specifically protected under Angola's new constitutional system. There is no official state religion that is prescribed, and the people can practice their own religions freely. The state is secular in nature, and a direct separation between the state and churches is maintained. The constitution also places a duty on the state to respect religion and places of worship.

MILITARY DEFENSE AND STATE OF EMERGENCY

Angola is protected by national armed forces. The armed forces are headed by a chief of staff who is accountable to a civilian minister of defense. A special presidential guard (Casa Militar) is also provided, answering directly to the office of the president. Military service is mandatory and cannot be refused; no conscientious objections are possible. Only the president of the republic in cooperation with the National Assembly can declare a state of siege or emergency. Detailed requirements before such a state is declared are prescribed by law. During states of emergency, the president and the rest of the civil government structures continue to rule. It is, however, specifically determined in the constitution that during a state of siege or emergency, no amendment of the constitution may be made.

AMENDMENTS TO THE CONSTITUTION

In comparison with many other constitutions in the world, the Angolan constitution is fairly easy to amend. The constitution determines that the National Assembly may review or amend the constitution through a decision of a two-thirds majority of the members present, which is a relatively weak quorum. Any 10 or more members of the assembly or the president of the republic may propose amendments to the constitution. Amendments may be made at any time except during a state of siege or emergency. The president has no veto over a constitutional amendment if the amendment procedure was carried out in accordance with the law. Finally, the constitution requires that any amendment conform to certain criteria such as a guarantee of fundamental human rights protection, the rule of law, political pluralism, direct suffrage, a secular state, and the independence of the courts.

PRIMARY SOURCES

Constitution in English. Available online. URL: http://www.oefre.uniba.ch/law/icl/a00000_.html. Accessed on June 17, 2006.

SECONDARY SOURCES

A. P. Blaustein and G. H. Flanz, eds. *Constitutions of the Countries of the World: Angola.* New York: Oceana, 1992.

R. M. Byrnes, "Angola-Government and Politics." In *Angola—a Country Study,* edited by T. Colleto. Washington, D.C.: Library of Congress, Federal Research Division, 1991.

H. Campbell, "Peace, Democracy and Elections in Angola." *Southern Africa Political and Economic Monthly* 5, no. 12 (1992): 8–11.

Christof Heyns, ed., *Human Rights Law in Africa.* Vol. 2. Leiden: Martinus Nijhoff, 2004.

J. Kirsten and M. Bester, "Political-Constitutional Change in Angola and Mozambique since Independence: A Comparative Perspective." *Politeia* 16, no. 2 (1997): 50–59;

Report by U.S. State Department. Available online. URL: http://www.state.gov/r/pa/ei/bgn/6619.htm. Accessed on August 23, 2005.

Bernard Bekink

ANTIGUA AND BARBUDA

At-a-Glance

OFFICIAL NAME
Antigua and Barbuda

CAPITAL
Saint John's (Antigua)

POPULATION
68,722 (2005 est.)

SIZE
171 sq. mi. (443 sq. km)

LANGUAGES
English (official), local dialects

RELIGIONS
Anglican 45%, Protestant 42% (Moravian 12%, Methodist 9.1%, Seventh Day Adventist 8.8%), Roman Catholic 10.8%, Jehovah's Witness 1.2%, Rastafarian 0.8%, other 0.2%

NATIONAL OR ETHNIC COMPOSITION
Black African origin 82.4%, white 12%, mulatto 3.5%, British 1.3%, Portuguese, Lebanese, Syrian 0.8%

DATE OF INDEPENDENCE OR CREATION
November 1, 1981

TYPE OF GOVERNMENT
Constitutional monarchy

TYPE OF STATE
Unitary democratic state

TYPE OF LEGISLATURE
Bicameral parliament

DATE OF CONSTITUTION
November 1, 1981

DATE OF LAST AMENDMENT
No amendment

The islands of Antigua and Barbuda form a constitutional monarchy with the British monarch, who is the nominal head of state, represented by a governor-general. The governor-general is appointed by the monarch on the advice of the prime minister. Under the 1981 constitution, the political system is a parliamentary democracy. Antigua and Barbuda has a multiparty political system with a long history of hard-fought elections, three of which have resulted in peaceful changes of government.

The judicial branch is relatively independent of the other two branches even though the magistrates are appointed by the office of the attorney general in the executive branch.

The constitution of 1981 was promulgated simultaneously with the country's formal independence from Britain. It provides a basis for possible territorial acquisitions, expands upon fundamental human rights, recognizes and guarantees the rights of opposition parties in government, and provides Barbuda with a large measure of internal self-government.

The constitution sets forth the rights of citizens, ascribing fundamental rights to each person regardless of race, place of origin, political opinions or affiliations, color, creed, or sex. It further extends these rights to persons born out of wedlock, an important provision in that legitimate and illegitimate persons did not have equal legal status under colonial rule.

CONSTITUTIONAL HISTORY

Antigua was visited in 1493 by Christopher Columbus, who named it after the Church of Santa Maria de la Antigua in Sevilla (Seville), Spain. The island was colonized by English settlers in 1632 and remained a British possession for centuries, although it was raided by the French in 1666. Initially tobacco was grown, but in the later 17th century, sugarcane was found to be more profitable. Antigua became one of the most lucrative of Britain's colonies in the Caribbean.

The nearby island of Barbuda was colonized in 1678. In 1685 the Crown granted the island to the Codrington family, who governed it until 1870. Barbuda became part of Antigua in 1860. It reverted to the Crown in the late

19th century, and its administration became so closely re-lated to that of Antigua that Barbuda eventually became a dependency of the larger neighboring island.

The Leeward Islands colony, of which the islands were a part, was defederated in 1956, and in 1958, Antigua joined the West Indies Federation. When the federation was dissolved in 1962, Antigua persevered with discussions of alternative forms of federation. Provision was made in the West Indies Act of 1967 for Antigua to assume a status of association with the United Kingdom, which took effect on February 27 that year. As an associated state, Antigua was fully self-governing in all internal affairs, while the United Kingdom retained responsibility for external affairs and defense.

By the 1970s, Antigua had developed an independence movement, particularly during the administration of Prime Minister George Walter, who wanted complete independence and opposed the British plan of a federation of islands. Walter lost the 1976 elections to Vere Bird, who favored regional integration. In 1978, Antigua reversed its position and announced it wanted independence. The autonomy talks were complicated by the fact that Barbuda believed that it had been economically shortchanged by the larger island and wanted to secede. Eventually, on November 1, 1981, Antigua and Barbuda achieved independence with Vere Bird as the first prime minister. The state obtained United Nations and British Commonwealth membership and joined the Organization of East Caribbean States. Bird's party won again in 1984 and 1989 by overwhelming margins, giving the prime minister firm control of the islands' government.

During elections in March 1994, power passed from Vere Bird to his son, Lester Bird, but remained within the Antigua Labor Party, which won 11 of the 17 parliamentary seats. The United Progressive Party won the 2004 elections, and Baldwin Spencer became prime minister, thus removing from power the longest-serving elected government in the Caribbean.

FORM AND IMPACT OF THE CONSTITUTION

Antigua and Barbuda has a written constitution, codified in a single document. The Constitution of Antigua and Barbuda of November 1, 1981, is the supreme law of the state; it declares void any legal provision inconsistent with it. International law is not explicitly regulated within the constitutional body.

BASIC ORGANIZATIONAL STRUCTURE

The unitary state of Antigua and Barbuda is divided into six parishes (Saint George, Saint John, Saint Mary, Saint Paul, Saint Peter, and Saint Philip) and two dependen-

cies, Barbuda and Redonda, which have a certain degree of autonomy. The constitution provides for a Constituencies Boundaries Commission, which, when called upon, has the task of reviewing the number and the boundaries of the constituencies and reporting accordingly to the Speaker of parliament.

In order to quell secessionist sentiment in Barbuda, the writers of the constitution included provisions for Barbudan internal self-government, constitutionally protecting the 1976 Barbuda Local Government Act. The elected Council for Barbuda is the organ of local self-government. It has the power to draft resolutions covering community issues or domestic affairs. In the areas of defense and foreign affairs, however, Barbuda remains under the aegis of the national government. The Barbuda Council consists of nine elected members, one Barbudan representative to the national parliament, and several government-appointed councilors. Council elections are held every two years.

LEADING CONSTITUTIONAL PRINCIPLES

Antigua and Barbuda is a unitary sovereign democratic state within the Commonwealth of Nations. Its system of government is a constitutional monarchy acknowledging the king or queen of the United Kingdom as the official head of state, represented by an appointed governor-general who exercises the executive authority on behalf of the monarch. The legislative, executive, and judicial branches are distinct and independent; none of these branches may delegate the exercise of their proper functions. Holders of public office must take an oath to observe and comply with the constitution and the laws and to bear true allegiance to Her Majesty Queen Elizabeth II.

CONSTITUTIONAL BODIES

The main bodies provided for in the constitution are the parliament, consisting of the House of Representatives and the Senate; the governor-general; the prime minister and cabinet ministers; the judiciary; the supervisor of elections; and the director of audit.

The Parliament

The legislature is the bicameral parliament consisting of a 17-member House of Representatives elected by popular vote for a five-year term and an appointed Senate of 17 members. Antigua has 16 seats in the House, and Barbuda one. Of the senators, 11 are appointed by the prime minister, four by the parliamentary opposition leader, one by the Barbuda Council, and one by the governor-general. In this way, the opposition, the leader of which is recognized constitutionally, is ensured a voice in government. In practice, the major figures in parliament and the executive government are members of the House of Representatives. The constitution provides for two standing committees, the Advisory Committee on the Prerogative of Mercy and the Public Accounts Committee. Parliament is free to set up more nonstanding committees.

The Lawmaking Process

To become laws, bills must be passed by the Senate and the House of Representatives and assented to by the governor-general on behalf of her majesty. After assent is given, the bill must be published in the *Official Gazette* to enter into effect.

The Governor-General, the Prime Minister, and Cabinet Ministers

The executive authority of Antigua and Barbuda is vested in her majesty, the queen of England. In practice, it is exercised on behalf of her majesty by the governor-general, either directly or through officers subordinate to him or her. The governor-general appoints the prime minister, usually the leader of the political party that commands the support of the majority in the house. The executive branch is derived from the legislative branch. As leader of the majority party of the House of Representatives, the prime minister appoints other members of parliament as cabinet ministers. The prime minister and the cabinet are responsible to the parliament. The governor-general in principle acts in accordance with the advice of the cabinet or a minister acting under the general authority of the cabinet. The prime minister has to keep the governor-general regularly and fully informed.

The Supervisor of Elections

The governor-general appoints a supervisor of elections by notice published in the *Official Gazette*. The supervisor of elections exercises such functions, powers, and duties as may be provided by law for the elections.

The Director of Audit and Public Accounts Committee

The constitutional bodies in charge of oversight of public finances are the office of the director of audit and the Public Accounts Committee. The director of audit enjoys full functional and administrative independence in the performance of his or her duties.

The Judiciary

The judiciary, which is part of the eastern Caribbean legal system, is independent. There is an intraisland court of appeals for Antigua and five other former British colonies in the Lesser Antilles. The judiciary consists of the Magistrate's Court for minor offenses and the High Court for major offenses. To proceed beyond the High Court, a case

must pass to the Eastern Caribbean States Supreme Court, the members of which are appointed by the Organization of Eastern Caribbean States. Jurisprudence is based on the English common law system. The Eastern Caribbean Supreme Court is based in Saint Lucia; one judge of the Supreme Court is a resident of the islands of Antigua and Barbuda and presides over the Court of Summary Jurisdiction.

Any person who alleges that any provision of the constitution has been or is being contravened can, if he or she has a relevant interest, apply to the High Court. The right to apply for a declaration and remedies is additional to any other legal action in respect of the same matter. There is a possibility of appeal to the Court of Appeals and, further, to the Privy Council in Britain.

THE ELECTION PROCESS

Citizens of Antigua and Barbuda of at least 18 years old are eligible to vote in universal suffrage. Any person who at the date of his or her election is a citizen of the age of 21 years or more, who has resided in Antigua and Barbuda for a period of 12 months immediately preceding the date of election, and who is able to speak and read the English language is, in principle, qualified to be elected as a member of the House of Representatives.

POLITICAL PARTIES

Antigua and Barbuda's political system emerged from British political tradition and the development of trade-union activism. Antigua shifted from a one-party to a two-party system after 1967. In 1971, the Progressive Labor Movement (PLM) won a majority of seats in the House of Representatives in the general election, ending the Antigua Labor Party's (ALP's) continuous dominance in national politics. The ALP regained control of the government in the 1976 general election.

Elections to the House of Representatives were held on March 23, 2004. The ALP under Lester Bryant Bird won only four seats, while Baldwin Spencer's United Progressive Party (UPP, a coalition of three opposition parties: United National Democratic Party [UNDP], Antigua Caribbean Liberation Movement [ACLM], and PLM) became the strongest faction. The Barbuda People's Movement (BPM) under Thomas H. Frank did not win any seats.

CITIZENSHIP

Citizenship of Antigua and Barbuda is obtained by birth or by naturalization. Every person born in Antigua who was on October 31, 1981, a citizen of the United Kingdom or its colonies was proclaimed a citizen on November 1, 1981. The same rule applies to any person born outside

Antigua, any one of whose parents or grandparents was born therein or was registered or naturalized while resident in Antigua. The constitution provides for the concept of dual citizenship; a citizen cannot be denied an Antiguan passport on grounds of being entitled to apply for some other country's nationality.

FUNDAMENTAL RIGHTS

The constitution establishes the fundamental rights of all persons, regardless of race, place of origin, political opinions or affiliations, color, creed, or sex, but subject to respect for the rights and freedoms of others, and for the public interest. The right to life is guaranteed: No person shall be deprived of his or her life intentionally, save in execution of the sentence of a court in respect of a crime of treason or murder of which he or her has been convicted.

In addition, the constitution acknowledges the right to personal liberty, protection from slavery and forced labor, protection from inhuman treatment, protection of freedom of movement, protection from deprivation of property, protection of persons or property from arbitrary search or entry, protection of freedom of conscience, protection of freedom of expression including freedom of the press, freedom of assembly and association, and protection from discrimination on the grounds of race, sex, or other characteristics.

ECONOMY

The constitution protects the right to private property. No property of any description shall be compulsorily taken except for public use in accordance with the provisions of the law; fair compensation must be paid within a reasonable time.

Antigua and Barbuda's economy is service-based; tourism and financial and government services represent the key sources of employment and income.

RELIGIOUS COMMUNITIES

The constitution provides for freedom of religion, and the government generally respects this right in practice. The government at all levels strives to protect this right in full and does not tolerate its abuse, either by governmental or by private actors. The government is secular and does not interfere with an individual's right to worship. Christian holy days, such as Good Friday, White Monday, and Christmas, are national holidays. Relations among the various religious communities are generally amicable. The Antigua Christian Council, an interdenominational group, conducts activities to promote greater mutual understanding and tolerance among adherents of different denominations within the Christian faith.

MILITARY DEFENSE AND STATE OF EMERGENCY

The islands maintain the Royal Antigua and Barbuda Defense Force, including the Coast Guard. In addition, the constitution acknowledges a Police Service Commission in charge of administering a professional police force.

The governor-general can declare a state of emergency for a period of seven days during a session of parliament and for a maximum of 21 days or, in specified cases, for a period of three months, unless parliament in the meantime has passed a declaration of a state of emergency. Parliament has the right to do so on its own initiative. A vote for a state of emergency requires a simple majority in each of the two parliamentary chambers. The assumption of emergency powers is taken in the case of war (periods of 12 months renewable) or if there is a vote of two-thirds of the members of each chamber declaring that the democratic institutions of Antigua and Barbuda are facing a threat of subversion (hostile action from outside or as a result of a natural disaster).

AMENDMENTS TO THE CONSTITUTION

Parliament may alter any of the provisions of the constitution. Depending on the particular article being amended, a majority of two-thirds or three-quarters of members is required. Further requirements are detailed in Article 47 of the constitution.

PRIMARY SOURCES
Constitution in English. Available online. URL: http://www.georgetown.edu/pdba/Constitutions/Antigua/ab81.html. Accessed on August 16, 2005.

SECONDARY SOURCES
Antigua and Barbuda Foreign Policy and Government Guide. Washington, D.C.: International Business Publications, 2004.
The Antigua and Barbuda Research Group, *A Strategic Assessment of Antigua and Barbuda.* Strategic Planning Series, San Diego: Icon Group International, 2000.
Margaret DeMerieux, *Fundamental Rights in Commonwealth Caribbean Constitutions.* Bridgetown, Barbados: Faculty of Law Library, University of the West Indies, 1992.
Antigua and Barbuda Country Study Guide. World Country Study Guide Library, Washington, D.C.: International Business Publications, 2003.
Velma Newton, *Commonwealth Caribbean Constitutions: Dynamic or Stagnant?* Bridgetown, Barbados: Faculty of Law Library, University of the West Indies, 1987.

Lasia Bloß

ARGENTINA

At-a-Glance

OFFICIAL NAME
Argentine Republic

CAPITAL
Buenos Aires

POPULATION
39,537,943 (2005 est.)

SIZE
1,077,924 sq. mi. (2,791,810 sq. km)

LANGUAGES
Spanish

RELIGIONS
Catholic 80%, Protestant 9%, Jewish 1%, other 3%, nonbelievers 7%

NATIONAL OR ETHNIC COMPOSITION
Argentine 95.6%, other South American natives (largely Paraguayan, Bolivian, Chilean, and Uruguayan) 2.8%, other (largely Italian and Spanish) 1.6%

DATE OF INDEPENDENCE OR CREATION
May 25, 1810

TYPE OF GOVERNMENT
Presidential democracy

TYPE OF STATE
Federal state

TYPE OF LEGISLATURE
Bicameral parliament

DATE OF CONSTITUTION
May 1, 1853

DATE OF LAST AMENDMENT
August 22, 1994

The Argentine Republic is a republican democracy and presidential state. Its constitutional system is similar to that of the United States. Argentina is a federal state composed of 24 autonomous provinces and a federal district, although it also has a strong central government, which comprises an executive power managed by a president, a bicameral legislative power (Senate and Chamber of Deputies), and an independent judicial power. The president, elected by the citizens by direct vote, is simultaneously the chief of state and chief of the administration. Each province has its own constitution and its own government. The federal constitution and several international treaties that possess constitutional rank guarantee the fulfillment of human rights. Civil rights are equal for all inhabitants, Argentines or foreigners. The country promotes immigration, which has contributed to the development of its diversified population. Although the Catholic Church holds a special status and legal recognition, ample religious liberty exists.

CONSTITUTIONAL HISTORY

The Argentine Republic became independent after the fragmentation of the Spanish Empire in America, early in the 19th century. Its present territory was part of the thinly populated Virreinato del Río de La Plata, the capital of which was Buenos Aires, where the split with the Spanish Crown started on May 25, 1810. Independence was formally declared on July 9, 1816. In the meantime, the existing cities became the nuclei of several of the present provinces, although others formed independent nations such as Uruguay, Paraguay, and Bolivia in the following years.

After independence, the Provincias Unidas del Río de La Plata, today's Argentina, constituted a confederation, but it was exposed to four decades of civil war. There were failed attempts at constitutional organization in 1817, 1819, and 1826. In 1852 several provinces defeated the governor of Buenos Aires, Juan Manuel de Rosas, and a federal system was imposed. A Constitutional Congress adopted a constitution in 1853. In 1859 the province of Buenos Aires, which had refused to join the federation, was reunited with the nation, prompting the revision of the constitution the following year, which produced its final text. The 1853–60 constitution was based on the ideas of the jurist Juan Bautista Alberdi and shaped according to the model of the constitution of the United States of America, taking into account other national models.

The national constitution survived without incident until 1930. By then, substantial European immigration had contributed to the modern Argentinean social profile and led to important economic development. Between 1930 and 1932 a military revolution produced a suspension of the constitutional government; this occurred again between 1943 and 1946. In 1946, Colonel Juan D. Perón was democratically elected president, but he went on to govern in an authoritarian and demagogic way. He introduced important economic and social changes of nationalist orientation. In 1949, the constitution was amended through questionable procedures in order to permit the reelection of Perón.

The 1949 constitution was abrogated in 1956 by a revolution that ousted Perón. In 1957, a constitutional convention reestablished the 1853 constitution with some changes, recognizing the rights of workers and promoting social security. The military government of 1966–73 produced a modified constitution in 1972, which remained in force during the democratic government of 1973–76. A new military dictatorship in 1976–83 suspended parts of the constitution, which went back in force in 1983. In 1994 the constitution was modified once again to include new rights and guarantees and to update the provisions concerning governmental structure. An independent judicial power survived under the military governments (1930–32, 1943–46, 1955–58, 1962, 1966–73, and 1976–83), but the national congress and provincial legislatures remained closed; the president of the nation (or a Junta Militar) exercised the legislative power and appointed the governors of the provinces.

Argentina, Brazil, Paraguay, Uruguay, and, in part, Chile and Bolivia are members of MERCOSUR (Mercado Común del Sur; Common Market of the South), an economic integration agreement aimed at developing closer economic ties among these states. The 1994 constitutional reform authorizes Congress to approve integration treaties that delegate competences and jurisdiction to supranational organizations.

FORM AND IMPACT OF THE CONSTITUTION

The Argentine Republic has a written constitution, codified in one single document. International treaties and concordats with the Holy See, the leading body of the Roman Catholic Church, take precedence over any norm of internal law with the exception of the constitution. Since 1994, Argentina has signed the main international human-rights treaties such as the International Covenant on Cultural, Social, and Economic Rights; the Covenant on Political and Civil Rights; and the American Convention on Human Rights. These treaties have constitutional status and complement the statement of rights and guarantees in the national constitution. Not only the Supreme Court, but also any federal or provincial judge can declare laws or other rules unconstitutional and thus prevent their application in concrete cases. Even during the military dictatorships, judges declared laws or dispositions of those governments unconstitutional in order to implement the rights contained in the constitution.

The rights and guarantees held in the constitution have been for the most part respected, even during the military governments. After several decades of institutional instability during the 20th century, a great consensus concerning those institutions now exists since the reestablishment of democratic institutions in 1983.

BASIC ORGANIZATIONAL STRUCTURE

The Argentine Republic is composed of 24 provinces and one autonomous city, Buenos Aires, which is also the capital city of the nation. Some provinces were formed before the founding of the nation, while others were created during the 20th century out of territories that were incorporated into the nation after its founding. All provinces have equal rights, but they are very different in size, population, wealth, and economic development. The provinces have their own institutions and adopt their own constitutions without intervention of the federal government. They retain all powers not delegated to the federal government by the constitution; however, this delegation is very extensive.

Among other responsibilities, the provinces regulate health care and primary and secondary education under a legal framework created by the national congress. Most taxes are collected on the national level; portions are then distributed among the provinces. The financial and economic dependence of many provinces on the federal government limits their autonomy, although the provinces control natural resources in their territories. The federal government has exclusive authority in many fields such as foreign affairs, defense and military matters, and citizenship.

The provinces can conclude treaties among themselves and can create "regions" encompassing several provinces for optimal social and economic development. Since the 1994 constitutional reform the provinces can also conclude international covenants with the knowledge of the Congress. These treaties must be compatible with national foreign policy.

Each province has the duty to organize municipal governments. The municipalities are small territorial units, with local governments elected by the inhabitants directly. Usually, foreign residents have the right to vote in these elections.

LEADING CONSTITUTIONAL PRINCIPLES

Argentina is a presidential republic. It has a strong division of powers among the executive, legislative, and judicial branches; powers are based on a system of checks and balances. The judicial power is independent, and the Supreme Court also functions as a constitutional court. Article 1 of the constitution states that "the Argentine Nation adopts for its government the federal, republican, representative form." Each province must adopt a constitution under the republican representative system according to the principles, statements, and guarantees of the national constitution. Representative government means that the citizens democratically choose their representatives to form the executive and the legislative power.

In a relatively new departure that has not yet been effectively applied, the constitution authorizes semidirect forms of democracy as well. These include the citizens' ability to introduce bills to the Chamber of Deputies, in matters other than constitutional reform, international treaties, taxes, budgets, and criminal law. Congress can also submit bills or other matters to popular referendum.

The principle of republican government means that Argentina does not allow a monarchy and that there must be periodic rotation in government power. The ideology behind the constitution is liberal, emphasizing the protection of individual rights. The introduction to the constitution cites the goal of "ensuring justice," "promoting the general welfare, and securing the blessings of liberty to ourselves, to our posterity, and to all men in the world who wish to dwell on Argentine soil." Subsequent reform has introduced guarantees of social rights for families, workers, and consumers, including the right to live in a healthy environment. It has also given constitutional standing to international treaties that protect human rights of the first and second generations.

The state is secular, although in the framework of extensive freedom of worship, it offers special recognition to the Catholic Church.

The constitution foresees and authorizes the integration of the Argentine Republic with other states, particularly those of Latin America.

CONSTITUTIONAL BODIES

The main constitutional organs are the president of the nation, who exercises the executive power with the aid of the cabinet of ministers or federal administration; the Congress, made up of the Chamber of Deputies and the Senate, and the judiciary including the Supreme Court of Justice. Other organs also have constitutional rank, such as the general auditing office, the defender of the people (ombudsperson), and the office of the chief public prosecutor.

The President (and the Vice President) of the Nation

The executive power is individual, and it is exercised by a citizen holding the office of the "president of the Argentine nation." The president is elected together with a vice president, who can replace the president, permanently in case of death, renunciation, or dismissal or temporarily in case of illness or absence from the country. The vice president does not exercise executive powers independently. As president of the Senate, he or she can participate in debates but cannot vote. The president and the vice president are elected for a period of four years and can be reelected only for a single consecutive period. They are elected directly by popular vote. Candidates for president or vice president must be at least 30 years old and Argentine citizens.

According to the constitution, the president "is the commander in chief of the nation, leader of the government and political head of the general administration of the country." The president is the supreme commander of the armed forces. The president also appoints federal judges and members of the Supreme Court, with the agreement of the Senate, and appoints ambassadors and higher officers of the armed forces.

The president participates in the legislative activity in several ways. He or she can propose bills to the Congress; most laws passed in recent decades have originated as projects of the executive. When Congress passes a bill, the president can either promulgate and publish it as law or veto it. The president has also the power to adjust laws but only in such a way as "not to alter its spirit" by means of exceptions.

In principle, the president cannot dictate laws. However, since the 1994 constitutional reform, the president has the power to issue decrees with the force of law, except in electoral, tax, and those penal matters that concern political parties. This power is supposed to be used only in exceptional cases in the face of urgent necessity. Such "urgency and necessity decrees" are supposed to be communicated to Congress for ratification or modification. However, no law to regulate this procedure has yet been passed, and presidents have become accustomed to abusing this power and to issuing such decrees even in cases lacking any real necessity or urgency.

The president also conducts foreign affairs and can sign international treaties that must then be approved by Congress. According to the constitution, the president cannot leave the country without the permission of Congress. However, in practice, Congress passes a law every year authorizing such trips whenever the president deems them necessary.

The Federal Administration

While executive power in Argentina is exercised by one person—the president—the constitution provides for cabinet ministers to assist the president and to validate presidential acts by countersigning them.

The number of cabinet ministers and their individual functions are provided for by law. While serving as ministers, they cannot also be senators or deputies. They have the right to participate in congressional sessions, without voting, although this right is rarely used.

The president appoints a cabinet chief, whose function is the "general administration of the country." This function includes collecting national taxes and administering the national budget, appointing those public officials not appointed by the president, and reporting to Congress every month concerning the most important governmental issues. In theory, the cabinet chief is a special link between the president and the rest of the executive branch. In practice, the chief is treated as any other cabinet minister is.

The cabinet ministers and the cabinet chief are appointed by the president without the consent of Congress or any other body, and they can be removed freely by the president. In theory, they can also be removed by Congress in a procedure called political trial (Juicio Político). However, this has never happened.

The Congress

The legislative power is exercised by Congress, composed of the Chamber of Deputies and the Senate.

The deputies are directly elected by the people in the provinces and in the city of Buenos Aires, whom they represent. At present, there are 256 deputies. Each province or district is allocated seats in proportion to its population, although the law establishes a minimum of five deputies per province, with the result of overrepresentation of the provinces that have fewer inhabitants.

To be elected as a deputy, a candidate must be at least 25 years old, must have been a citizen for four years, and must be born in the province or have been a resident there for two years. The deputies are elected for four years and can be reelected. The Chamber of Deputies changes half of its members every two years, so there is at least one legislative election within each presidential term.

The Senate comprises three senators per province and three for the city of Buenos Aires, all elected by direct vote. In each constituency, the party that receives most votes gets two senators, and the runner-up party gets the third. The senators are elected for a period of six years and can be reelected with no limits. The senators' chamber changes 33 percent of its members every two years.

The two chambers are in principle equal and have equal prerogatives, but each has unique functions. Only the Chamber of Deputies can introduce legislation related to tax matters and to the recruitment of troops. This chamber also can impeach the president, the vice president, cabinet ministers, or judges of the Supreme Court. The Senate, however, is responsible for distributing national taxes; approving appointments of judges, military leaders, and ambassadors; and actually trying a president, vice president, cabinet ministers, or a Supreme Court judge who has been impeached by the Chamber of Deputies.

The deputies and senators enjoy immunity as soon as they are elected, and they can be neither indicted nor interrogated judicially because of their opinions. They cannot be arrested unless they are caught performing a criminal act.

Neither the governors of provinces nor members of Roman Catholic religious orders can be elected to Congress. The latter prohibition is widely regarded to be outdated and to lack justification.

The legislative powers of Congress are very extensive. It can pass and modify provisions in the Civil Code, the Code of Commerce, or the Penal Code, as well as laws regulating mining, labor, social security, taxes, and political parties.

The Lawmaking Process

In general, a bill can be introduced in either chamber by one or more members of Congress or by the administration. All laws have to be approved in both chambers. If the introducing chamber approves the law, it remits the project to the other chamber to consider it and submit it to a vote.

If one of the chambers rejects a project approved by the other, that project cannot be reintroduced during the same year. If the project is partially rejected or amended, it is returned to the original chamber to approve or reject the changes. When both chambers reach agreement, the bill is forwarded to the president for approval, promulgation, and publication. The president can veto the law and return it to the Congress. If both chambers insist on the project with a two-thirds majority of votes, the bill becomes law despite the president's opposition.

The Defender of the People (Ombudsperson) and the General Auditing Office of the Nation

The Defender of the People is an independent body charged with defending and protecting human rights and other rights, guarantees, and interests enumerated in the constitution and laws, against governmental acts and omissions. It also reviews the exercise of public administrative functions. The Defender of the People is appointed by a two-thirds majority of the members present in each of the two chambers and serves a five-year term of office.

The 1994 constitutional reform created another organ of control within the legislative branch that functions autonomously, the General Auditing Office of the Nation. The general auditor is appointed on recommendation of the largest opposition party in Congress. The office audits and controls all the functions of the executive branch.

The Judiciary

The judiciary is an independent power exercised by a Supreme Court of Justice and lower courts located in the federal capital and in the provinces. The nine judges of the Supreme Court are appointed by the president with the consent of two-thirds of the members of the Senate. Each lower-court judge is also appointed by the president with the consent of the Senate, but he or she must choose from a list of three candidates nominated by the Judicial Council. The Judicial Council is composed of members of Congress, judges, lawyers, and academics. Its functions are to nominate judges (other than for the Supreme Court) by means of public competition, to supervise the administration of the judiciary, and to discipline and even dismiss judges.

All judges remain in office until age 75 unless their actions are contrary to their duty or to good behavior. Their remuneration cannot be reduced. When judges reach 75 years old, they can be reappointed by the Senate for a period of five years that can be renewed indefinitely. Supreme Court judges can be removed by means of political trial only (impeachment), with the Chamber of Deputies acting as the accusing party and the Senate as a court of judgment; in both cases, a two-thirds majority is required.

The Supreme Court has exclusive and original jurisdiction in several matters, such as disputes among provinces. It also hears appeals in matters governed by federal laws. All federal judges have authority to hear cases governed by federal laws. Since 1853, the constitution has provided for juries in criminal trials, but such juries have never been established. Each province has its own Supreme Court or Upper Court, chambers of appeals, and courts of first instance, with varying jurisdictions.

Any federal or provincial judge at any level can declare a law or other norm such as a regulation unconstitutional in the specific case under review, and the law or norm is not applied. Nevertheless, the law remains in force because a statement of unconstitutionality is only valid for the case to which it has been applied. Decisions of the Supreme Court are not formally binding in the future on lower courts. However, such decisions have "moral" and factual relevance; the criteria that the court establishes in federal matters are in fact followed by the other courts. There is no "constitutional court" in Argentina other than the Supreme Court of Justice. In this respect, Argentina follows the model of the judiciary system of the United States.

The Office of the Public Prosecutor

The Office of the Public Prosecutor is an independent body established to defend lawfulness and the general interests of society in coordination with the other authorities of the republic. It is composed of a national chief prosecutor, a national chief public defender, and other members that the law may establish.

THE ELECTION PROCESS

All citizens over 18 years of age have the right to vote for and to be elected to public office. This right does not apply to mentally impaired persons, those who have been sentenced to prison, and soldiers of the armed forces.

Foreigners who have permanent residence can also vote in some provincial and municipal elections. The electoral registers are controlled by the judicial branch. Voting is compulsory; this requirement was first established by a law (in 1912) and in 1994 was added to the constitution.

The judiciary has refused to allow conscientious objection to the compulsory vote. It considers election to be an essential institution of democracy; in any case, those who do not desire to participate can submit blank ballots. The failure to vote is sanctioned by fines, which have not actually been enforced.

Voting is secret, with penal sanctions for those who reveal their vote at the time of the election. It is also a crime to hinder the liberty of the voting process in any way.

Electoral procedures, regulated by law, impose multiple controls on political parties. In general, elections in Argentina are thought to be free of fraud. Only recognized political parties can present candidate lists. Independent candidates can only run in municipal elections.

Candidate lists are required by law to include at least one-third women; for every two male candidates there must be at least one female candidate. Since this requirement was implemented, female representation has increased notably in legislative bodies, especially in Congress, although their representation does not yet equal that of their male counterparts.

POLITICAL PARTIES

The constitution explicitly affirms that political parties are "fundamental institutions in the democratic system." It guarantees their free and democratic organization, their representation of minorities, and their right to communicate their ideas publicly.

There are political parties that act only on the local level, as well as national political parties. To be recognized on the national level, a party must first be recognized in at least five districts or provinces. To be recognized as a local political party, it must in elections represent at least 4 percent of the voters in that locality. The parties are legal and political entities, and they function under the control of the judiciary. They can form confederations and alliances, which may be permanent or transitory, for a single election. The governing bodies of the parties and the candidates they present for public elections must be chosen in internal elections regulated by the judiciary. The parties are funded through contributions from their members and from the state, which is obliged by the constitution to work with them. The state contribution is proportional to the number of votes obtained by the party in the elections. The law provides for mechanisms to keep party finances transparent, but the rules have turned out to be difficult to implement.

There is a pluralistic party system in Argentina. Throughout its history, political parties have played a prominent role. In 1946, the Justicialista party was founded by Colonel Juan D. Perón; it has been the dominant party in the country ever since. Occasionally, other parties or alliances of parties have won elections against the Justicialista party, such as the Unión Cívica Radical, founded in 1891, which has politically liberal but economically nationalist tendencies. However, no non-Justicialista administration has been able to complete a full term in office. As a consequence, internal disputes within the Justicialista party have been very important for national elections.

The Justicialista party lacks a clear ideological identity, but it is clearly populist and demagogic in tone. Socialists are divided among several parties and have been represented in parliament. They have, however, never controlled the government. Provincial parties are generally conservative; they tend to control provincial governments. Groups of provincial parties have at times joined with other conservative parties to become a third electoral force on the national level behind the Justicialista party and the Unión Cívica Radical. However, their heterogeneous nature has prevented them form forming a strong party at the national level. In recent years, the party system has experienced a severe crisis, and the identities of the various parties have become uncertain.

CITIZENSHIP

All persons born in Argentine territory have the right to citizenship according to the principle of the *ius soli*. Children of Argentine citizens who are born abroad can adopt Argentine citizenship and acquire the same rights as native Argentines. From its inception, Argentina has welcomed immigration. The constitution guarantees foreigners the same civil rights as citizens. They are not eligible to hold a number of offices, but they can vote in municipal and provincial elections. Foreigners of at least 18 years old and without a criminal record may acquire citizenship after residing in the country for two years. The procedure is simple and is carried out before the federal judiciary. The period of residence can be shorter if the applicant has rendered notable services to the republic or has married an Argentine citizen. Citizenship cannot be denied on racial, religious, political, or ideological grounds. The constitution exempts nationalized foreigners from military service for 10 years after they have obtained citizenship.

FUNDAMENTAL RIGHTS

The constitution guarantees extensive fundamental rights. Its first chapter includes the recognition of political and civil rights.

The 1949 constitution, in force until 1955, proclaimed a long list of social rights for the family, workers, children, the elderly, and others. The 1957 constitutional reform incorporated the essential components of these social rights and added guarantees such as the right to strike, the right to form unions, and protection of employment.

International human rights treaties such as the International Covenant on Civil and Political Rights; the International Covenant on Cultural, Social, and Economic Rights; and the American Convention on Human Rights form part of national law.

Impact and Functions of Fundamental Rights

All the social, civil, and fundamental rights receive very broad constitutional protection. Today, fundamental rights in general are protected.

Limitations to Fundamental Rights

Fundamental rights are regularly guaranteed in accordance with the laws that regulate their exercise. They thus find their limits in the laws. Congress may not, however, confer either on the national executive or on the provincial legislatures or the provincial governors powers whereby the lives, the honor, or the property of Argentines will be at the mercy of governments or any person whatsoever.

ECONOMY

The constitution tends to be liberal in economic matters. The right of private property is extensively guaranteed, as are other economic liberties such as navigation, industry, and commerce. These liberties have generally been respected.

Nevertheless, especially between 1940 and 1990 many economic interventionist laws were passed, and the state was actively involved in the production of goods and services through public enterprises. This trend partially modified the liberal model that had predominated since 1853. In the 1990s, an abrupt change of economic rules was introduced in favor of liberalization. In an effort to promote an open economy, all public enterprises and state agencies that controlled economic activity were quickly dismantled. This new form of action, or of inaction, of the state in the economy caused a serious crisis in 2001 and resulted in substantial backward movement of the country's development indicators.

The 1994 constitutional reform explicitly permitted economic integration, especially with states of Latin America.

RELIGIOUS COMMUNITIES

At the time of independence, the Catholic Church was the only organized religion in the country, and it had a strong social presence. The first constitutional projects declared the Catholic faith as the religion of the state. The 1853 constitution did away with this and recognized extensive freedom of worship, after much debate in the constitutional convention. At the same time, the constitution recognized the privileged position of the Catholic Church, stating in Article 2 that "the federal government supports Catholic worship." It also gave the federal government the right of patronage that had previously belonged to the kings of Spain. This meant that the government could intervene in the appointment of bishops, the income of religious orders, and other matters. For these reasons, the president was required to be Catholic. In 1966, Argentina signed an agreement with the Holy See that gave extensive freedom and autonomy to the Catholic Church and removed the right of patronage from the state. The 1994 constitutional reform formalized these changes and removed the requirement that the president be Catholic. At present, no religious condition is required for any public office. Article 2 of the national constitution is still in force, but the economic contribution from the state to the Catholic Church is very small. In the Argentine republic there is now substantial separation between church and state.

Religious liberty is very extensive in Argentina, although there is no formal religious equality. The Catholic Church is recognized as a "public legal person," while other religions are considered private legal persons that act in the framework of freedom of association. These religions have to register with an office of the federal government. There are a great variety of churches, such as the Christian Orthodox churches, mainly Greek, Russian, Antiochian, and Armenian. Also present are Anglicans; Protestants and Evangelicals of different denominations; important groups of Sunni and Shiite Muslims; Jewish communities; Buddhists; Umbanda and Afro Brazilian groups; the Church of Jesus Christ of the Latter Day Saints; Jehovah's Witnesses; and other groups. All religions are tax exempt. Many of them maintain schools at different levels, and they receive subsidies from the state. The armed forces, the police corps, and most of the prisons and hospitals have Catholic chaplains only, but ministers of other religions are permitted when they are required.

Individual religious liberty is extensively guaranteed, and it has been recognized by the courts in several disputes. Religious discrimination is always prohibited and is punished severely. Thanks to cultural traditions, the main Catholic festivals are official holidays; the law also recognizes the more important Muslim and Jewish religious festivals as holidays.

The right to conscientious objection has been recognized by law in matters of military service, and for medical doctors and nurses. It is also applied by the courts in matters of labor, transfusions of blood, reverence to the flag or national symbols, oaths in diverse situations, and other matters.

Domestic law as well as international treaties with constitutional status recognize the parental right to choose a religious education for children. Religion can be taught after school hours or within the school curricula in religious schools. In some provinces the Catholic religion is taught as a subject in public schools, though attendance is voluntary.

MILITARY DEFENSE AND STATE OF EMERGENCY

The armed forces are a federal institution. The provinces have only corps of police to maintain local and internal order; they do not have their own militias. The president of the nation is the commander in chief of the armed forces in war and peacetime. The national armed forces participate regularly in peaceful operations under the flag of the United Nations, as "blue helmets." Between 1930 and 1983, the armed forces had an active party in national politics. Since the nation restored democracy, the armed forces have been subordinate to the civil authorities.

The constitution imposes on all citizens the duty of "being armed in defense of the country" in case of need. Until 1994, military service for one year was compulsory for all male citizens after the age of 18. Since then a voluntary military service has been established for males and females. In case of necessity, the Congress could reintroduce military service. Were that to occur, the law provides for the recognition of conscientious objection and the introduction of a civil service substitute of equal duration. In case of "interior commotion," the Congress can declare a state of siege with martial law, either throughout the country or just in a specific location. The president can also declare a state of siege in circumstances of external attack with the approval of Congress. This state of emergency implies the suspension of some constitutional guarantees. However, even then the executive cannot exercise judicial functions; it can only make arrests and transfer prisoners to another location, unless they prefer to leave Argentine territory.

The Congress, and in specific cases the president, has the power to intervene in the provinces, temporarily replacing provincial authorities with federal personnel. This procedure is used in situations of serious crisis in a province, although at times the national government has abused this right and replaced provincial governments on grounds of political opposition.

AMENDMENTS TO THE CONSTITUTION

The Argentine constitution requires a special procedure for amendments. The Congress must declare the need for a reform by a two-thirds majority of all its members, specifying the issues needing reform; the reform is prepared by an elected constituent convention meeting especially for that purpose. Historically, constitutional reform has been minimal because it was very difficult to obtain the needed majorities. Many authors agree that the constitution, especially its first articles, contains certain features that are "written in stone" and can never be altered. This applies to the principles of a federal state and a republican government and to the guarantee of civil rights. Congress can, with a two-thirds majority of all its members, offer constitutional status to international treaties on human rights, as it did in the case of the Pan-American Convention on Forced Disappearance of Persons. The 1994 constitutional reform included a clause specifying that any act against the constitution or any modification carried out by acts of force against the institutional order and the democratic system will not enter into force and that all citizens have the right to resist them. Anyone who commits such acts or usurps functions of the constitutional authorities is to be punished, and such crimes are not subject to amnesty.

PRIMARY SOURCES

Constitution in English. Available online. URLs: http://www.hrcr.org/docs/Argentine_Const/argentine1994.html; http://www.chanrobles.com/argentina.htm. Accessed on September 13, 2005.

Constitution in Spanish. Available online. URL: http://www.aadconst.org/documentos/docum/docum.php. Accessed on September 13, 2005.

SECONDARY SOURCES

Constitución de la Nación Argentina, texto oficial según ley 24.430, 5th ed. Buenos Aires: Editiorial Universitaria de Buenos Aires, 2001.

Constitución de la Nación Argentina 1994: Incluye la Ley no. 24,309, Declaración de la Necesidad de la Reforma de la Constitución Nacional. Buenos Aires: Santillana, 1994.

Ernesto Nicolás Kozameh, et al., *Guide to the Argentine Executive, Legislative and Judicial System.* Available online. URL: htt://www.llrx.com/. Accessed on August 26, 2005.

United Nations, "Core Document Forming Part of the Reports of States Parties: Argentina" (HRI/CORE/1/Add.74), 1 July 1996, Available online. URL: http://www.unhchr.ch/tbs/doc.nsf. Accessed on September 7, 2005.

Juan G. Navarro Floria

ARMENIA

At-a-Glance

OFFICIAL NAME
Republic of Armenia

CAPITAL
Yerevan

POPULATION
3,100,000 (2005 est.)

SIZE
11,506 sq. mi. (29,800 sq. km)

LANGUAGES
Armenian

RELIGIONS
Armenian Orthodox 94%, other Christian 4%, Yezidi
(Zoroastrian/animist) 2%

NATIONAL OR ETHNIC COMPOSITION
Armenian 96%, Kurd, Yezid, Russian, Jewish,
Assyrian, and Greek 4%

DATE OF INDEPENDENCE OR CREATION
September 21, 1991

TYPE OF GOVERNMENT
Mixed presidential-parliamentary democracy

TYPE OF STATE
Unitary state

TYPE OF LEGISLATURE
Unicameral parliament

DATE OF CONSTITUTION
July 5, 1995

DATE OF LAST AMENDMENT
November 27, 2005

Armenia is, according to Article 1 of the constitution, a sovereign, democratic, and social state based on the rule of law. It is a unitary state. Although the constitution provides for guarantees of human rights, in practice there are substantial barriers to the effective protection of these rights.

Despite the proclamation of the principle of separation of power, political power is concentrated in the presidency. The president is the central political figure who puts together and dismisses the administration. The administration is also responsible to the National Assembly, but the latter has substantially less authority than the president.

Armenia has a market economy with equal legal protection for all forms of property. The constitution guarantees freedom of economic activity and free economic competition. By its constitution, Armenia is obliged to conduct its foreign policy in accordance with the norms of international law, with the aim of establishing good neighborly and mutually beneficial relations with all states.

CONSTITUTIONAL HISTORY

One of the world's oldest civilizations, Armenia, over the centuries, has been conquered by the Greeks, Romans, Persians, Byzantines, Mongols, Arabs, Ottoman Turks, and Russians. After the collapse of the Russian Empire, an independent republic was established in May 1918, which survived only until November 1920 when it was annexed by the Communist Soviet Army. The first independent Republic of Armenia did not manage to adopt a constitution. The first Soviet Armenian constitution was adopted on February 3, 1922. On March 12, 1922, the Soviets joined Georgia, Armenia, and Azerbaijan to form the Transcaucasian Soviet Socialist Republic, which became part of the Soviet Union, the Union of Soviet Socialist Republics (USSR). In 1936, after reorganization, Armenia became a separate constituent republic of the USSR. The second and third Soviet Armenian constitutions were adopted in 1937 and 1978, modeled on the Soviet constitutions of 1936 and 1977, respectively.

Armenia gained its independence from the Soviet Union in September 1991. Work on the constitution only began in October 1992, although the Constitutional Commission of the parliament had been established in November 1990. The constitution-building process, dominated by the president and his party, lasted over three years. The draft constitution was approved by the parliament in May 1995 and was adopted on July 5, 1995, by referendum.

FORM AND IMPACT OF THE CONSTITUTION

Armenia has a written constitution, codified in a single document that takes precedence over all other national law. International law must be in accordance with the constitution to be applicable within Armenia. International treaties that have been ratified are a constituent part of the legal system of Armenia. The norms of these treaties prevail over the ordinary laws of Armenia.

The impact of the constitution is not comprehensive because of the persisting imperial and Soviet legacies and the authoritarian practices of the successive administrations. None of the elections held since 1995 has met international standards. The right of citizens to change their government has been severely restricted in practice. The elections were marked by abuses of state power, fraud, and harassment of the opposition. Basic civil rights are frequently violated.

BASIC ORGANIZATIONAL STRUCTURE

Armenia is a unitary state. The administrative territorial units are the provinces and communities. The provinces are governed by the national administration, which appoints and removes the governors of the provinces, who implement the central government's regional policy and coordinate the regional activities of the national executive branch.

Local self-government is exercised in urban and rural communities through bodies such as the Council of Elders and the leader of the community, who are all elected by universal suffrage for terms of four years.

Armenia's system of government is characterized by features typical of both parliamentary and presidential systems. For example, the administration is responsible to parliament; yet the president is elected by universal suffrage. The main feature of this system, which has been called a semipresidential government, is the dualistic structure of executive power. This dualism can accommodate a great variety of patterns of distribution of power between the president and the prime minister.

In principle, semipresidential governments are of two varieties: premier-presidential and president-parlia-mentary. Armenia clearly belongs to the president-parliamentary category, which is characterized by the dual responsibility of the administration: The administration depends upon the ongoing confidence of both the president and the National Assembly. This type of regime does not provide for a clear line of authority over the administration since the constitution permits either the president or the parliamentary majority to dismiss the administration. Besides, the popularly elected president can dissolve the National Assembly; that prerogative puts the president in a very strong position vis-à-vis the parliament, especially during the formation of the administration. The strong constitutional position of the president and the poorly institutionalized party system allow the president, in practice, to dominate governmental power. The system functions as a superpresidential system with a premier fully subordinated to the president.

LEADING CONSTITUTIONAL PRINCIPLES

The leading constitutional principles are set forth in Chapter 1 of the constitution. The key principles are the sovereignty of the state, democracy, the rule of law, the social state, and the division of power. However, the principle of the division of power is distorted in the constitution by extensive powers of the president over the legislative, executive, and judicial branches. This has resulted in the dominance of the president in the political system; it has left the legislature powerless to hold the executive to account and has precluded the development of an independent judiciary.

CONSTITUTIONAL BODIES

The basic bodies provided for in the constitution are the president of the republic; the parliament, called the National Assembly; the administration; and the Constitutional Court.

The President of the Republic

The president is the head of state. The president's main functions are laid down in Article 49 of the constitution, according to which he or she shall uphold the constitution and ensure the normal functioning of the legislative, executive, and judicial authorities. The president of the republic shall also be the guarantor of the independence, territorial integrity, and security of the republic.

The 17 sections of Article 55 of the constitution provide the president with extensive powers, including the power to appoint and dismiss the prime minister and, at the proposal of the latter, the members of the administration and to dissolve the National Assembly. The president has extensive appointment powers, covering civil servants and judges.

The president is elected by direct universal suffrage for a five-year term. The same person may not be elected for the post of the president of the republic for more than two consecutive terms.

The Administration

Executive power in the Republic of Armenia is vested in the administration, which is composed of the prime minister and the ministers. The administration's organization and rules of operation are determined by law, based on recommendations of the administration. Decisions of the administration are signed by the prime minister. Because of the president's organizational powers with respect to the administration (especially the right to appoint and dismiss the prime minister) and the president's authority in the areas of foreign, defense, and security policy, the president is generally the dominant figure in Armenian politics.

The National Assembly (Parliament)

The legislative power is vested in the National Assembly; all its powers are determined by the constitution. The National Assembly is a legislative body; it also approves the administration's program and can bring down the administration with a no-confidence vote. The body also adopts the state budget and has some supervisory powers in relation to the administration.

The Lawmaking Process

The main function of the National Assembly is the passing of laws. The right to initiate legislation in the National Assembly belongs to the deputies and the administration. The president has a veto right over legislation, which can be overridden by an absolute majority of the deputies. In order to make the lawmaking process effective, the constitution gives the administration the right to require urgent consideration of its proposals and to force a vote of confidence in conjunction with its proposed bills.

The Judiciary

Although Armenia's constitution enshrines the principle of an independent judiciary, the president wields control over all judicial appointments. The Council of Justice drafts annual lists of judges and prosecutors fit to be appointed or promoted, and it submits those lists to the president for approval. It may also subject any judge to disciplinary action and recommend removal of a judge from office in cases provided for by law.

The Constitutional Court is composed of nine members, five of whom are appointed by the National Assembly and four by the president of the republic. The Constitutional Court decides on the constitutionality of normative acts, on election disputes, and on the suspension or prohibition of a political party in cases prescribed by law. Citizens have the right to constitutional complaints.

THE ELECTION PROCESS

All Armenians over the age of 18 have the right to vote in elections. Citizens who are recognized as incapable by a court or have been duly convicted of a crime and are serving a sentence cannot vote or be elected. Any person who has attained the age of 25, been a citizen of the Republic of Armenia for the preceding five years, permanently resided in the republic for the preceding five years, and has the right to vote may be elected as a deputy to the National Assembly. Every person who has attained the age of 35, been a citizen of the Republic of Armenia for the preceding 10 years, permanently resided in the republic for the preceding 10 years, and has the right to vote is eligible for the presidency.

POLITICAL PARTIES

Armenia has a pluralistic political party system. The multiparty system is a basic structure of the constitutional order. Its constitutional function is to promote the formulation and expression of the political will of the people. Political parties can only be banned by a decision of the Constitutional Court.

CITIZENSHIP

Armenian citizenship is primarily acquired by birth. This means that a child acquires Armenian citizenship if one of his or her parents is an Armenian citizen. It is of no relevance where a child is born. A citizen of the Republic of Armenia may not simultaneously be a citizen of another state.

FUNDAMENTAL RIGHTS

The fundamental rights are set forth in the second chapter of the constitution, which follows the chapter on the foundations of the state and precedes the provisions on the state's organization. This structure reflects the constitution makers' new attitude to human rights, which were now considered fundamental values that should be protected by the state. Article 6 of the constitution states that its norms are applicable directly; thus the legislature, the executive, and the judiciary are bound by those fundamental rights and freedoms.

The constitution enshrines both liberal and social rights. The constitution guarantees the traditional set of liberal human rights and civil liberties and states in Article 42 that the rights and freedoms set forth in the constitution are not exhaustive and shall not be construed to exclude other universally accepted human and civil rights and freedoms. Thus this clause opens the door to considering as constitutionally guaranteed rights those universally accepted rights that are not explicitly enshrined in the constitution.

The constitution lacks a differentiated approach to liberal and social rights. A specific feature of liberal rights are that they are directly enforceable. On the other hand, many social rights are organically related to the existing economic structure of the state and thus do not directly entail personal rights to individuals. Social rights typically include the right to housing, free medical assistance, social security, and preservation of health. Because the norms of the Armenian constitution are supposed to be directly applicable, this undifferentiated approach to liberal and social rights will create difficulties when these norms are interpreted by the Constitutional Court.

Impact and Functions of Fundamental Rights

In practice, the impact of fundamental rights is limited. The barriers to the effective protection of fundamental rights stem mainly from the absence of an effective system of checks and balances. The judiciary is weak and far from fulfilling its role as a guarantor of law. A fundamental flaw of the constitution is the absence of the right of the citizen to apply to the Constitutional Court with a complaint. As a consequence, the provisions on fundamental rights do not decisively impact ordinary legislation.

Limitations to Fundamental Rights

Limitations to fundamental rights are specified in Article 43, according to which the fundamental rights and freedoms in a democratic society may only be restricted by law, if necessary, for public security, public order, public health, and morality, or the rights, freedoms, honor, and reputation of others. This article provides for constraints to limitations (the so-called limitation limits): They can be established only by law and are subject to the principle of proportionality.

ECONOMY

The Armenian constitution does not provide for a specific economic system. However, the constitution states certain basic principles that frame the economic system: the free development and equal legal protection of all forms of property, the freedom of economic activity and free economic competition, the freedom of choice of one's place of work, and the right to form associations. The principle of the social state requires the state to combine market freedom with balanced social policy.

RELIGIOUS COMMUNITIES

Freedom of thought, conscience, and religion are guaranteed by the constitution. Freedom of religion also incorporates the freedom of religious communities. There is no established state church. About 94 percent of Armenians belong to the Christian Orthodox Armenian Apostolic Church.

In line with the conditions for membership in the Council of Europe, Armenia is committed to ensuring freedom from discrimination also for new religious communities, of which about 50 are officially registered.

MILITARY DEFENSE AND STATE OF EMERGENCY

The guarantor of the independence, territorial integrity, and security of the republic is the president, who is the commander in chief of the armed forces and appoints the staff to its highest command. The administration has responsibility for ensuring implementation of defense and national security policies.

In the event of an armed attack, immediate danger to the republic, or a declaration of war by the National Assembly, the president is mandated to declare a state of martial law and may call for a general or partial mobilization. In the event of an imminent danger to the constitutional order, and upon consultations with the president of the National Assembly and the prime minister, the president is mandated to take measures appropriate to the situation and to address the people on the matter.

In Armenia, general conscription requires all men over the age of 18 to do basic military service of 24 months. Conscientious objectors can file petitions to be excluded from military service and perform service in social institutions instead.

AMENDMENTS TO THE CONSTITUTION

The constitution can be changed only by a referendum. Amendments can be initiated by the president or the National Assembly. They are considered to have been passed if they receive more than 50 percent of the votes cast and not less than one-third of the number of registered voters. Certain fundamental provisions are not subject to change at all. Article 114 says, "Articles 1, 2 and 114 of the constitution may not be amended." These refer to the essential identity of the constitution—sovereignty of the state, democracy, rule of law, social state, and sovereignty of the people.

PRIMARY SOURCES
The Constitution of the Republic of Armenia. Yerevan: Mkhitar Gosh, 1996.
Constitution in Armenian. Available online. URLs: http://www.parliament.am/parliament.php?id=constitution&lang=arm. Accessed on July 16, 2005.
Constitution in English. Available online. URL: http://www.parliament.am/parliament.php?id=constitution&lang=eng. Accessed on August 31, 2005.

SECONDARY SOURCES

Elizabeth F. Defeis, "Constitution Building in Armenia: A Nation Once Again." *Parker School Journal of East European Law* 2, no. 1 (1995): 153–200.

Henrik M. Khachatryan, *The First Constitution of the Republic of Armenia*. Yerevan, Armenia: Hayagitak Printing Office, 1998.

Vardan Poghosyan

AUSTRALIA

At-a-Glance

OFFICIAL NAME
Commonwealth of Australia

CAPITAL
Canberra

POPULATION
20,090,437 (July 2005)

SIZE
2,969,907 sq. mi. (7,692,024 sq. km)

LANGUAGES
English 79.1%, Chinese 2.1%, Italian 1.9%, other 11.1%, unspecified 5.8% (2001 census)

RELIGIONS
Catholic 26.4%, Anglican 20.5%, other Christian 20.5%, Buddhist 1.9%, Muslim 1.5%, other 1.2%, unspecified 12.7%, none 15.3% (2001 census)

NATIONAL OR ETHNIC COMPOSITION
Approximately 91% of European descent (mainly

English and Irish but also Greek, Italian, German, Dutch, and other), Asian 7%, Aboriginal 2%

DATE OF INDEPENDENCE OR CREATION
January 1, 1901

TYPE OF GOVERNMENT
Parliamentary democracy and constitutional monarchy

TYPE OF STATE
Federal state

TYPE OF LEGISLATURE
Bicameral parliament

DATE OF CONSTITUTION
January 1, 1901

DATE OF LAST AMENDMENT
May 21, 1977

Australia is a parliamentary democracy with strong historical and constitutional ties to the United Kingdom. The Australian constitution was created as a means of federating the six British colonies that existed on the territory of Australia in the late 19th century. Since its enactment in 1901, the constitution has proved stable and has rarely been modified. The system of government in Australia is based largely on the Westminster system of parliamentary democracy and constitutional monarchy. The federal system in Australia, however, is derived largely from the American model, as is the concept of a court with the power to invalidate legislation on the basis of unconstitutionality. This court, the High Court of Australia, has the ultimate authority to interpret and apply the provisions of the Australian constitution, and it has done so in a manner that has increased the power and significance of the Commonwealth government in relation to the states. A tradition of the separation of powers and respect for the rule of law has ensured that the decisions of the High Court

in constitutional matters have always been respected, even when they have dealt with areas of great controversy.

CONSTITUTIONAL HISTORY

For at least 40,000 years Australia was inhabited by its indigenous people, who lived in accordance with customary indigenous laws. This organization precluded the need for a formal or written constitution. While early white settlers and the British legal system assumed that indigenous Australians had no legal system, it is now clear that sophisticated legal, social, and religious obligations existed in indigenous societies. This condition has been recognized by the Australian legal system in recent decades, and this recognition has given rise to some acknowledgment of Aboriginal land rights but has not led to any more comprehensive recognition of the preexisting legal or constitutional order.

The British officially established the colony of New South Wales on January 26, 1788. New South Wales was the first Australian colony and originally spanned the entire eastern half of the continent before dividing into five separate colonies during the first six decades of the 19th century. Van Diemen's Land (now Tasmania) separated in 1825, South Australia in 1836, Victoria in 1850, and Queensland in 1859. Western Australia was founded independently in 1829.

In the late 19th century, there was a move toward federation between the colonies. Although there were some advances toward a federation, or greater cooperation, in the 1840s and 1850s, the movement did not gain momentum until near the end of the century. Several constitutional conventions were held during the 1890s to debate the issue of federation and the form that a new constitution might take. The first of these was the largely unsuccessful National Australasian Convention held in Sydney in 1891. Its membership was made up of colonial parliamentarians, and it failed to capture the popular imagination or to develop political momentum. In 1897, a convention made up of elected members was held, and it prepared a draft constitution. The draft was circulated for public and parliamentary comment, and large numbers of suggestions were made. The convention met a number of times before completing the draft and presenting it to the people by referendum. The referendum passed in Victoria, South Australia, and Tasmania but failed in New South Wales. After redrafting, another referendum was held, and the draft was approved by all four of these colonies and Queensland, which had, by this stage, decided to join the move to federation. Western Australia decided to join the federation only months before the constitution went into force.

Despite strong local participation in the drafting of the constitution, its final legal form was ultimately determined by a British parliamentary law. The British Colonial Office had made a number of suggestions for changes to the constitution during its drafting period, and the British Parliament made a small number of changes to the final draft before enacting it. The act, and thus the federated Commonwealth of Australia, went into effect on January 1, 1901.

There is a provision in the constitution for the creation of new states, but the six original states (New South Wales, Victoria, Queensland, South Australia, Western Australia, and Tasmania) remain the only states in Australia. The states have their own constitutions as well as certain rights and powers under the Commonwealth constitution that can only be removed by referendum. There are also a number of Australian territories that have some degree of self-government. The two most important of these are the Australian Capital Territory and the Northern Territory. The Northern Territory, which was part of South Australia at the time of federation, became a territory of the Commonwealth pursuant to Section 111 of the constitution in 1911. While the Northern Territory was granted a degree of autonomy by the 1978 Northern Territory (Self-Government) Act, it remains subject to Commonwealth legislative oversight. The Australian Capital Territory was surrendered to the federal government by New South Wales in 1909 and was anointed the seat of government in accordance with Section 125. The Australian Capital Territory was granted the same limited autonomy as the Northern Territory in 1988.

FORM AND IMPACT OF THE CONSTITUTION

The Commonwealth constitution is a single written document, although each of the states also has its own constitution. These state constitutions are, in most respects, subordinate to the Commonwealth constitution. The Commonwealth constitution consists of 128 articles and has proved stable and enduring since its enactment in 1901.

The Commonwealth constitution has had a considerable impact on Australian political life. The constitution created a new level of government (the Commonwealth or federal government), a new head of state (the governor-general), and a new court with the power to interpret and apply the constitution (the High Court of Australia). Over time, the influence of the Commonwealth government has grown since the High Court's expansive interpretations of the Commonwealth's powers. The rulings of the court, although sometimes controversial, are inevitably accepted and acted upon by the government. This has been the case even when the decisions have undermined important government policies, such as the nationalization of the banking system or the banning of the Communist Party.

While the written constitution is very important in terms of the structure and operation of the federal government, there are also conventions that underlie the constitution. It is impossible to understand the government's real workings, particularly of the executive arm of government, without reference to these conventions. Under Section 61 of the constitution, the executive power of the Commonwealth government resides in the governor-general, who is appointed by the queen. Under the constitution, the governor-general also has other significant powers and duties, which include commanding the armed forces, assenting to acts of Parliament (or refusing to do so), suspending Parliament, and appointing ministers. While the powers of the governor-general seem broad, convention ensures that the holder of the office is, in most cases, a figurehead whose power is more symbolic than real. In almost all cases, the governor-general exercises constitutional powers only on the advice of cabinet ministers. It is now very difficult to imagine a situation in which the governor-general could refuse to assent to legislation duly passed by Parliament or to act independently in commanding the armed forces. Thus, while the constitution designates the governor-general as the most powerful member of the executive, the political reality is that the prime minister and the cabinet are the most influential actors in the executive government under normal circumstances. The superiority of the prime minister is reinforced by his or her control over the appointment or dismissal of the governor-general. While the constitution gives the power to appoint the governor-general to the queen, it is now clear that she may exercise that power only on the advice of the Australian prime minister, who also has the power to advise her majesty to dismiss the governor-general.

There are limited exceptions to the rule that the governor-general acts only on advice. The governor-general retains narrow discretion over a small number of matters described as the "reserve powers," which may be invoked and exercised independently of advice in the extraordinary circumstance of a constitutional crisis. The reserve powers of the governor-general include the power to dismiss the prime minister in very limited circumstances. This occurred in 1975 when Sir John Kerr dismissed the Whitlam administration from office after the administration failed to convince Parliament to pass legislation granting it sufficient funds for the ordinary services of government. The dismissal of the Whitlam administration and the installation of the leader of the opposition as interim prime minister until elections were called continue to be a source of controversy among both constitutional lawyers and the public. The controversy surrounding this event has helped to ensure that governors-general are very cautious in their use of the reserve powers.

Another area of executive power that is not clearly defined by the constitution is the impact of international law obligations in the Australian legal system. The constitution does not delineate a particular relationship between international and domestic law. It is accepted that the executive arm of the Commonwealth government has the power to enter into treaties without parliamentary input or approval, as this was a traditional prerogative of the Crown. While Parliament currently exercises some oversight with regard to the treaty process through the Joint Standing Committee on Treaties, the committee only has the power to make recommendations, not to bind the executive. Once a treaty has been entered into, the Commonwealth Parliament has the power to enact legislation to ensure Australian compliance with its international obligations. This power is derived from a provision in the constitution that gives the Commonwealth Parliament power over external affairs and has allowed the Commonwealth to enact legislation in areas, such as human rights and environmental protection, in which it does not seem to otherwise have legislative power.

The details of the relationship between international and domestic law has been left to the courts to develop. It is clear that in Australia law treaties are not incorporated into domestic law upon ratification. Rather, they must be transformed into domestic law by an act of Parliament. This probably also holds true for customary international law, although the relevant case law is less clear. This process

has allowed Australia to ratify certain important treaties, such as the International Covenant on Civil and Political Rights and the Genocide Convention, without implementing them into domestic legislation. This system has led to some criticism of the Australian position by international human-rights-treaty bodies, although the government claims that Australia fulfills its international obligations without the need for specific legislation in all cases. Even if the government were to breach international law, it would be impossible for an individual to bring a case in Australia to enforce those international obligations directly. Some indirect role for international law has been recognized by the courts, however, which allows international law to be used in the interpretation of ambiguous legislation and in the development of the common law. In the Dietrich case, for example, the High Court refused to allow an unrepresented criminal defendant to rely directly on the provisions of the International Covenant on Civil and Political Rights regarding fair trials, but it held that the common law of fair trials had developed (in part as a result of the influence of international law) to create a right to legal counsel in serious criminal cases. Despite a number of examples in which international law has been influential in the development of common law or statutory protection of rights, international law has not had as strong an impact in Australia as in many other states.

BASIC ORGANIZATIONAL STRUCTURE

Australia has a federal system of government consisting of six states (Queensland, New South Wales, Victoria, Tasmania, South Australia, and Western Australia) and a Commonwealth government. It also has a number of self-governing territories that are subject to legislative oversight by the Commonwealth Parliament but that function with a high degree of independence. The most politically important of these territories are the Northern Territory and the Australian Capital Territory. The latter is the seat of the Commonwealth government. Local governments, which are subordinate to the respective state governments, exist in each state, but their power derives from statute; they are not mentioned in the Commonwealth constitution. A referendum to entrench local government in the constitution was rejected in 1988. Local governments in Australia are less powerful than their counterparts in many parts of the world and tend to control mainly service matters, such as garbage collection and planning permits. Their role in areas such as education or health is very limited.

The Commonwealth constitution lists a small number of legislative powers that are exclusive to the Commonwealth and a longer list of powers held concurrently with the state legislatures. All other legislative powers are assumed to remain with the states. It was believed by some of the drafters that limiting the list of powers that the Commonwealth possessed would make it the weaker federal partner. The High Court originally interpreted the Commonwealth's powers in a limited fashion to ensure that the traditional powers of the states were not undermined. From the 1920s on, however, the High Court has taken a more expansive view of Commonwealth power, leading to a significant increase in the areas over which the Commonwealth has jurisdiction. In instances of conflict between Commonwealth and state laws, the Commonwealth laws prevail. The High Court has the authority to determine the existence and extent of any alleged conflict between the two laws.

The other important change to the federal balance of powers since 1901 is that the Commonwealth has gained more control over revenues. Particularly important in this regard is that income tax has shifted from primarily a state matter to an exclusively federal matter. Under the constitution, the Commonwealth already had exclusive control of customs and excise taxes. The Commonwealth can use its control of the bulk of the revenue to give conditional grants to the states or direct, conditional grants of money to institutions, such as universities. Using this influence, it has taken control of many areas, such as tertiary education, over which it has no formal, constitutional power. This vertical fiscal imbalance has been the greatest cause of centralization in the Australian constitutional system. It was partially alleviated by a goods and services tax imposed by the Commonwealth, the revenues of which are distributed to the states unconditionally. This system has increased state revenues and control over financial resources but has not eliminated the significant fiscal imbalance between the two levels of government.

LEADING CONSTITUTIONAL PRINCIPLES

Australia is a constitutional monarchy. The current monarch of the United Kingdom is also the monarch of Australia. The queen or the king, acting through the representative the governor-general, is the Australian head of state. While Australians profess a strong belief in republicanism when polled, a referendum in 1999 that sought to change the head of state from the queen to an Australian head of state selected by Parliament was defeated.

The Australian constitution originally derived its authority and legitimacy from the assent of the British Parliament, and it remains a theoretical possibility that the Parliament of the United Kingdom could unilaterally amend the Australian constitution. Many writers and judges now, however, source the ultimate legitimacy and authority of the constitution in the will of the Australian people. This is the case despite the fact that the constitution does not expressly bind the Australian people and their government in any overarching social contract. While the preamble to the constitution codifies the agreement between the original colonies "to unite in one in-dissoluble federal union," there is a conspicuous lack of general sentiment expressed in the document as to how relations between citizen and state are to be conducted. Of particular note in this regard is the lack of a bill of rights in the constitution.

The political philosophy that underlies the constitution and Australian political life is one of liberal democracy, respect for the rule of law, and representative government. The model of Westminster parliamentary democracy, developed in the United Kingdom, has broadly been adopted in Australia.

The constitution implicitly enshrines a separation of powers among the legislature, the executive, and the judiciary, but the separation in Australia is not strict. In the tradition of Westminster-style responsible government, members of the executive are required also to be members of the legislature. This means that the lines between executive and legislative power become blurred. The Parliament, for example, can delegate considerable legislative power to the executive. The executive then uses this power to create delegated legislation in a wide variety of areas. The separation between the legislative and executive arms of government on the one hand and the judiciary on the other is more closely observed. It is unconstitutional to grant Commonwealth judicial power to any person or body other than a Commonwealth court set up under Chapter III of the constitution or a state court. There is no strict requirement that state governments adhere to a separation of powers, although the principles of separation are broadly adhered to in the states.

Australia's constitutionalism is underscored by concurrent commitments to democracy and to federalism. Conflicts can arise from the interaction between democracy and federalism. For instance, the constitution provides that the Senate is to be a states' house, composed of members from the six states. The constitution provides elsewhere that Parliament can make laws for the representation of the territories. An interpretation of the constitution that denies residents of territories representation in the upper house of Parliament would be difficult to reconcile with a commitment to democracy. On the other hand, federalist principles hold that the Senate was conceived as a states' house, and its composition should reflect that to the exclusion of the territories. The High Court has settled the issue, and the territories are now represented in the Senate, but the dispute illustrates the tension that can exist between democratic and federal principles.

CONSTITUTIONAL BODIES

The constitution establishes several principal organs of Australia's parliamentary democracy, including the Commonwealth Parliament, the governor-general, and the High Court. The framework of the Australian government is erected by the constitution, but much of the detail can only be understood by reference to convention. The Westminster system of responsible government is fundamental to the workings of the Australian government, but the framers, concerned with allowing flexibility within the democratic framework to meet future contingencies, decided not to codify many aspects of government, such as the role of the prime minister and the cabinet. This situation also reflected the British tradition of a largely unwritten constitution, particularly with regard to the workings of the executive.

The Parliament

Chapter I of the constitution establishes the Commonwealth Parliament, comprising the House of Representatives, the Senate, and the governor-general as the queen's representative. The Commonwealth Parliament is vested with legislative power over a finite list of subjects. The Commonwealth exercises exclusive legislative power in relation to a number of subjects and shares power to make laws with respect to a number of other matters with state legislatures. The legislature controls the supply of public funds to government.

The Parliament is directly elected by the people and must be dissolved and reelected at intervals of no longer than three years. Early elections may be called (effectively at the discretion of the prime minister) if the Senate has twice rejected the same piece of legislation that has twice passed the House of Representatives. In 2004, Australia elected its 43rd federal parliament in the 103 years since the first sitting. This averages to a parliamentary duration of two and a half years. The constitution prescribes no specific electoral process or method of voting. The only requirement is that the Parliament be "directly elected by the people," but this probably does not equal a requirement of universal suffrage, and it certainly does not amount to a right to vote for individual electors. Despite the lack of constitutional protection for voting rights, the right to vote in Australia is now very widespread and includes most people over the age of 18. Voting in Australia is compulsory by statutory provision.

The lower house of Australia's bicameral legislature, known as the House of Representatives, comprises 150 sitting members. Each member is the sole representative of a single electorate; changes in population size and distribution necessitate alterations in the number of members of the House of Representatives from time to time. These redistributions are undertaken by an independent statutory body, which is not subject to political influence or pressure. The House of Representatives may introduce bills on any subject within the constitutional power of the Commonwealth, as well as proposals for constitutional amendment by referendum.

The upper house of the legislature is known as the Senate and is composed of 76 sitting members. The constitution requires that states be equally represented in the Senate. At present, each state elects 12 senators, and each territory elects two senators. The Senate is vested with the same legislative power as the House, with the exception that the Senate cannot introduce financial legislation. By convention, most important legislation is introduced in the House of Representatives.

The Lawmaking Process

Australia's legislative process is bicameral. In order to become law, legislation must be passed both by the House of Representatives and by the Senate and must receive royal assent. The use of different voting systems for election to the two houses of Parliament means that the administration will rarely enjoy a majority in the Senate. Since legislation must pass through both houses before it can become law, the Senate plays a prominent role in the scrutiny and the occasional veto of the administration's legislative program. The Senate has established a series of committees with oversight responsibility over various areas of legislative and executive activity. These committees have proved relatively effective at holding administrations accountable.

The Executive

The executive power of the Commonwealth is nominally vested in the governor-general. On its face, the constitution installs the governor-general as the most powerful figure in government: His or her assent is required for legislation to become law, and he or she is the commander in chief of Australia's defense forces. The governor-general appoints cabinet ministers, may dismiss cabinet ministers, and retains the power to dissolve or suspend the Parliament. The constitution contains only limited prescriptions for the executive government and on its face vests wide power in the governor-general. In practice, however, the office of the governor-general is largely symbolic, and its attendant powers are exercised only by the Australian executive government.

The executive branch is outlined in Chapter II of the constitution. It is in practice constituted by the prime minister and the cabinet, neither of which is mentioned in the text. They develop policy and exercise the most important executive powers. The governor-general's role is limited to giving assent, which gives effect to cabinet decisions. Most aspects of executive government are conducted according to convention rather than to the text of the constitution.

The prime minister is by convention the leader of the party with the majority of seats in the House of Representatives; he or she wields more power than any other actor in the executive branch. Cabinet ministers are appointed from within the Parliament. The constitution prohibits any person who is not a member of Parliament to hold a position as a minister for more than three months. In practice, all ministers are members of Parliament.

In reality, the executive exercises a significant degree of control over Parliament and the legislative process. The prime minister and the cabinet are the leaders of the party or coalition of parties that, by virtue of its majority in the House of Representatives, forms the administration. As such, they usually control the passage of bills through the House. They do not always enjoy the same advantage of numbers in the Senate.

The High Court

Chapter III of the constitution outlines the process for establishing a federal judiciary. Despite the opposition of the colonial superior courts, the framers of the constitution made a provision for the establishment of a Federal Supreme Court. That court was inaugurated as the High Court of Australia in 1903. The High Court exercises both original jurisdiction and appellate jurisdiction. The original jurisdiction of the court encompasses review of actions and decisions taken by the government, including the constitutionality of legislative and executive actions. The appellate jurisdiction of the court extends to the decisions of State Supreme Courts and inferior federal courts, but it is exercisable only where the court itself grants special leave. The High Court is the ultimate court of appeal in Australia, and while there remains an avenue of appeal to the Privy Council in England, that avenue is now open to appellants only in the unlikely event that the High Court grants its assent.

A strong culture of judicial independence and integrity has developed in Australia. The courts have been fastidious in maintaining this culture and are especially protective of the separation between the judicial and administrative arms of government.

Justices of the High Court are appointed by the governor-general on the advice of the prime minister, as are other federal judges. Judicial appointments were initially for life, but a constitutional amendment in 1977 imposed a mandatory retirement age of 70. Judges can be removed from office by resolution of a joint session of Parliament on the grounds of "proved misbehavior or incapacity." This provision has never been invoked, and there is considerable uncertainty as to what constitutes "proved misbehavior" and "incapacity."

The High Court's most important and most contentious function has been adjudicating the constitutional validity of Commonwealth legislative enactments. There is no specific provision of the constitution that authorizes the court to carry out this function. The Australian constitution, however, was framed more than 100 years after the United States Supreme Court confirmed that it had the power to invalidate unconstitutional laws, and it was assumed by the Australian constitutional framers that the High Court would exercise the same authority. The court has proceeded on that basis and has regularly declared legislation dealing with a wide variety of matters to be unconstitutional. Some key cases from the court's history demonstrate the variety and significance of the work undertaken by the court.

The court's decision in the Engineer's case (1920) has been described as a watershed moment in the federal division of power in Australia and in the court's approach to interpreting the constitution. The court overturned two doctrines of interpretation that had been invoked to preserve the states' powers as they existed before federation. This laid the groundwork for the expansion of the power of the Commonwealth government at the expense of the states.

In the Uniform Tax case (1942), the High Court confirmed that the Commonwealth government has the power to levy income taxes nationally and that the Commonwealth imposition of income tax has priority to state levies of income tax. This made it politically impossible for the states to raise income taxes themselves because to do so would place a significant additional tax burden on their own constituencies. While the taxation measures were initially justified as wartime measures, they later became permanent.

The Tasmanian Dam case (1983) effected a considerable expansion in the legislative power of the Commonwealth government. The court ruled that the Commonwealth's power to make laws with respect to external affairs allowed it to prevent the damming of a river in a World Heritage Area on the basis that the proposed action was inconsistent with a treaty to which Australia was a signatory. The effect of the decision was to authorize the Commonwealth government to make laws to implement international treaty obligations. Given the increased use of treaties in areas such as rights, health, and the environment (areas traditionally considered to be in the province of states under the constitution), the decision gave rise to a significant increase in potential Commonwealth power.

The decision in Mabo (No. 2) (1992) was perhaps the most significant and controversial in the High Court's history. It also demonstrates the important role that the court plays as both an appellate and a constitutional court. The court rejected the notion that Australia had been nobody's land when Europeans arrived, an idea that had served as the basis for British claims of sovereignty over the continent. On the contrary, native title had existed prior to British rule and survived in some circumstances. The decision was an affirmation of the Aboriginal people's traditional ownership of Australian land. The declaration that native title existed, despite that title's fragility, was an important development. This decision, and a later ruling that pastoral leases do not necessarily extinguish native title, led to the court's being subjected to intense media and political scrutiny, including calls by some politicians for the appointment of more conservative judges to the court.

The decision in Mabo (No. 2) was arguably the high-water mark of an approach to constitutional interpretation that was disapprovingly described by some as "judicial activism." Different compositions of the court have led to different approaches at other times, but criticism of the court at various stages in Australia's history is, if nothing else, testament to the impact it has had and continues to have on Australia's constitutionalism.

The other federal courts set up under Chapter III of the constitution are the Federal Court (which has similar jurisdiction to that of the High Court), the Family Court (which has jurisdiction over family law issues), and the Federal Magistrates Court (which primarily has jurisdiction over migration matters and minor family law matters).

Each state also has its own court system. As a general rule, the highest court is called the Supreme Court, which often has a division that deals only with appeals. The State Supreme Courts have general jurisdiction over serious criminal and civil matters. There are also commonly a county or intermediate court and a Magistrates Court, which deal with more trivial legal matters. Appointment to any of these courts requires legal qualifications and generally some period of time in legal practice. While traditionally only barristers (who may plead in open court) were appointed to the courts, an increasing number of solicitors (other lawyers) and even a small number of academics have been appointed in recent years.

The States

Chapter V of the constitution states that the federating colonies continue as states in the newly created Commonwealth. The states' prior constitutions and laws are preserved; this provision has had a minor restrictive effect on Commonwealth power. In general, states are restricted in their fields of activity. For instance, they cannot raise naval or military forces and cannot coin money. The primary constitutional constraint on state powers, however, is the provision in Section 109 that state laws that conflict with Commonwealth laws shall be invalid "to the extent of the inconsistency." Section 109 has led to the invalidation of state laws in a number of areas.

The constitution also requires that full faith and credit be afforded throughout the nation to all laws, public records, and judicial proceedings of any of the states. There is no provision for the secession of states from the federation. Indeed, the covering clauses to the constitution describe the federation as "indissoluble."

The states broadly reproduce the judicial, legislative, and executive arrangements of the Commonwealth. With the exception of Queensland (which has a unicameral parliament), the state parliaments are bicameral. Each state has a governor as the nominal head of the executive. The system of responsible government exists at the state level, and the administration is led by a premier who is the leader of the party that commands control of the lower house of parliament.

THE ELECTION PROCESS AND POLITICAL PARTICIPATION

The constitution mandates that members of the Commonwealth Parliament be "directly chosen by the people." Australia was one of the first democracies to extend voting rights to women. Australia achieved adult suffrage by 1908, except for the Aboriginal people, who were denied equal voting rights until 1962. Voting entitlements

are set out in the Electoral Act of 1918. The entitlement to vote in federal elections is afforded to citizens, and to British subjects who were on the electoral roll prior to 1984 who are 18 years or older (in the past British subjects always had the right to vote in Australian elections). The 1918 act denies the right to vote to persons of unsound mind, criminals serving penal sentences of five years or longer, and those found guilty of treason and are unpardoned.

Eligibility to stand for Parliament is provided for by statute and the constitution. The general conditions are set out in the 1918 Electoral Act, but eligibility is also subject to a number of disqualifications set out in the constitution. For example, Section 163 of the act provides that persons eligible to vote are eligible to stand for Parliament. However, the constitution prohibits concurrent membership in both houses of Parliament. Citizens and subjects of foreign powers are ineligible for election to Parliament; nor can anyone who is convicted of treason or a serious crime or is bankrupt be elected. The holder of any paid office under the Crown is ineligible for Parliament, as is any person who has a direct pecuniary interest in any agreement with the Commonwealth Public Service.

No methods of voting or electoral processes are prescribed by the constitution. Voting is compulsory by statute. Elections for the House of Representatives are conducted by using a system of compulsory voting in single-member districts. Senate elections employ proportional representation with multimember districts. The constitution does require that the House of Representatives employ a scheme of single-member districts and that Senators represent multimember districts.

The constitution also requires that the number of members in the lower house be, as nearly as practicable, twice the number of members in the upper house. This requirement is known as "the nexus." States are guaranteed an equal number of senators and no fewer than five members of the House of Representatives. Currently, each state elects 12 senators. The High Court has held that the Parliament may provide for the election of senators representing the territories. Presently, the Northern Territory and the Australian Capital Territory each elect two members to the Senate. As a result of constitutional requirements, the Senate is malapportioned. Tasmania—with a population of about 400,000—elects as many representatives to the Senate as Victoria, whose population approximates 4 million. This means that some 33,000 votes will secure a Tasmanian candidate a seat in the Senate, whereas more than 10 times that number of votes is required to secure a seat for a Victorian candidate.

POLITICAL PARTIES

Australia is a pluralistic, democratic society. Two major political blocs have dominated Australian politics for many decades: the conservative coalition led by the Liberal Party of Australia on the Right and the Australian Labor Party on the Left. One or the other of these parties has governed at the Commonwealth level since World War I (1914–18). Minor parties, however, have often held the balance of power in the Senate, which has given them a good deal of influence over the government's legislative agenda. Influential minor parties have included the Democratic Labor Party (a splinter group from the Australian Labor Party that effectively kept Labor out of office for many years by splitting its voter base), the Democrats, the Australian Greens, and the One Nation party. These parties span the political spectrum from the left-wing, progressive Greens party, to the right-wing, nationalistic One Nation party.

There has only been one attempt to ban a political party in Australia, that by Prime Minister Robert Menzies to ban the Communist Party during the cold war. The High Court ultimately found that this action was unconstitutional on the basis that the Commonwealth Parliament had no constitutional power in this area. This left open the possibility that the states could ban a political party. Prime Minister Menzies also attempted to amend the constitution to ban the party, but the referendum lost by a very narrow margin. It is likely that any attempt to ban a political party now would fall foul of the implied constitutional freedom of political speech.

Political parties are regulated by law; in order to be registered as a party, certain minimal standards must be met. The Electoral Act provides two ways to qualify: A party that has at least one member sitting in the Commonwealth Parliament and has a written constitution setting out its aims can register; alternatively, a party must have 500 members, as well as a written constitution.

CITIZENSHIP

Citizenship is not discussed in the constitution. The definition of a citizen is set out in the Australian Citizenship Act 1948. This act has been amended many times. The lack of importance given to the concept of citizenship in Australia can be seen in the fact that the term *Australian citizen* only appeared in 1948.

Until 1987, Australian citizens were automatically British subjects as well, reflecting the country's historic association with the United Kingdom and the Australian sense of identity. After 1987, Australians became solely Australian citizens. Prior to 1986, people became Australian citizens automatically if they were born in Australia. Now, an Australian-born potential citizen must show that at least one parent is a citizen or a permanent resident or that he or she has been resident for 10 years. People can become Australian citizens by adoption, descent, and grant. Citizenship can be lost under law but only in very limited circumstances. Very few Australian laws distinguish between citizens and noncitizens, apart from electoral and immigration laws.

FUNDAMENTAL RIGHTS

Australia is one of the few developed countries that have refused to adopt a bill of rights in either constitutional or statutory form. There are references to only a small number of express rights in the Commonwealth constitution, such as freedom of religion, freedom of movement between states, the right to a jury trial for indictable offenses, the right to compensation for deprivation of property, and nondiscrimination between residents of states. Even such rights as there are in the constitution have often been read in a restrictive manner by the High Court. Thus, while there is a right to a jury trial for indictable offenses, the court has said that the government has the right to determine on indictment whether an offense is triable by jury.

The High Court has also held that there are certain implied rights that can be determined from the structure and nature of the constitution itself. The most important of these is an implied freedom of political communication that limits the ability of governments to restrict free speech. This freedom was used to strike down government legislation that sought to limit political advertising.

The Australian Capital Territory in 2004 enacted a Human Rights Act, giving at least limited protection to civil and political rights in the territory. While there is no comprehensive bill of rights in any other state, there are a number of statutes that serve to protect particular rights. These are particularly common in the area of discrimination, which both state and Commonwealth laws prohibit on the basis of such characteristics as race, religion, gender, and age. Power to deal with complaints about the breach of certain human rights is given to the Human Rights and Equal Opportunity Commission at the Commonwealth level. The commission has limited power to deal with individual complaints and does not have the power to make enforceable decisions, but it does play a role in scrutinizing legislation for rights compliance, public education, interventions in court cases, and investigations and reporting on serious rights problems such as the detention of asylum seekers or the removal of Aboriginal children from their parents.

While Australia is a party to all of the key United Nations treaties on human rights, whether civil, political, economic, social, or cultural, these treaties are not directly enforceable domestically unless they are enacted in legislation. Most of these treaties have not been domestically implemented and thus remain unenforceable in Australia.

Impact and Functions of Fundamental Rights

While there is little in the way of formal protection of rights at either the state or Commonwealth level, most rights are reasonably well respected in practice. Important areas of concern include the treatment of asylum seekers, who can be indefinitely detained, and recognition of the rights of the indigenous people.

Limitations to Fundamental Rights

There is no explicit, commonly accepted theory of how fundamental rights should be limited. In determining whether statutory limitations on constitutional rights are acceptable, the High Court often adopts a test asking whether the limitations are "appropriate and adapted" to achieving a legitimate, democratic end. Specific statutory protection of rights generally includes specific circumstances under which the rights can be limited.

ECONOMY

The Commonwealth constitution does not require any particular form of economy, but it does deal with a number of economic issues. The most important of these is the distribution of revenue between the Commonwealth and state governments. Both levels of government have the power to raise taxes, but through a combination of Commonwealth acts and constitutional interpretation, the Commonwealth government has taken control of income taxation, the most important tax revenue. The constitution also grants exclusive power to the Commonwealth government to collect customs and excise taxes, and several state taxes have been struck down on the basis that they were in reality excise taxes. This combination of factors has led to the Commonwealth's gaining control over most of the lucrative sources of revenue, even though the states retain responsibility for the most expensive government functions, such as schools and hospitals. This fiscal imbalance has allowed the Commonwealth to exercise a high degree of control over areas that are theoretically under state control. The constitution permits the Commonwealth to make "tied" grants to the states, that is, grants that are conditional on the money's being spent in particular ways. This device has allowed the Commonwealth to influence policy in many areas not specified in the constitution.

The constitution also requires that "trade, commerce, and intercourse between the states" be free. While the interpretation of this section has been very controversial and has generated more case law than any other section in the constitution, it is now settled that what the section prohibits is protectionist barriers between states. The elimination of internal barriers between the colonies of Australia was one of the motivating factors in the decision to become a federation, and this provision has prevented the reemergence of internally protectionist markets. States continue to be allowed to impose constraints or regulation on goods entering from other states as long as these can be shown to be for genuine, nonprotective purposes. While this had led to controversy in application in a number of cases (for example, environmental

protections), trade between Australian states is now free of protectionism in most respects.

The constitutional assignment to the Commonwealth of power over customs and excise taxes was meant to ensure that the new country would have a single external tariff (customs) and that the states would not be able to distort that external tariff through the imposition of excise duties. The constitution does not, however, require any particular policy in regard to the use of the excise power. Different Commonwealth governments have pursued policies ranging from highly protectionist to the current broadly free trade, low-tariff approach.

RELIGIOUS COMMUNITIES

Freedom of religion is one of the few rights protected in the Commonwealth constitution. Under Section 116, the Commonwealth government is prohibited from making a law that interferes with religious freedom or that establishes a state church. While Section 116 was based on the First Amendment to the United States Constitution, it has been interpreted very differently and in a manner that gives less protection to religious freedom than its American counterpart. It is most unlikely that a Commonwealth law will be held to breach religious freedom unless it expressly singles out particular religions for regulation. In no case has the Commonwealth government been found to breach the constitutional prohibition on interfering with religious freedom.

The constitutional separation of church and state in Australia has not been interpreted particularly strictly by the High Court. The Commonwealth government can, therefore, fund private religious schools or religious groups that provide social benefits, such as employment schemes or rehabilitation. Such funding has increased in recent years. While this money predominantly goes to Christian groups of various denominations (as these are still the most numerically strong groups in Australia), money is also provided for other religions, for instance, for Jewish and Muslim schools. Australia also appointed a bishop of the Church of England (Dr. Peter Hollingsworth) as governor-general in 2001. While this caused some political disquiet in terms of separation of church and state in theory, it was widely agreed that the appointment did not breach the nonestablishment clause of the constitution.

While the states are not subject to Section 116 of the constitution, in practice religious freedom tends to be well respected. There is no real possibility that any of the states would set up an established church, even though this is permitted in theory. People of a wide variety of religious backgrounds practice their faith in Australia without interference from the government, although some increased religious animosity has been reported since September 11, 2001.

MILITARY DEFENSE AND STATE OF EMERGENCY

The military is under the control of the civilian Commonwealth government and has a long tradition of independence and neutrality in political affairs, although this has been under some strain in recent years. Even during wartime and in a state of emergency, the military is under the command of the civilian government, although the powers of both the government and the military increase during such times.

The Commonwealth Parliament is vested with the power to make laws with respect to defense by Section 51 (vi) of the constitution. The scope of this power is potentially very wide. In interpreting Section 51 (vi), the High Court has established that the defense power is greatly expanded during wartime and may override some of the constraints on the exercise of power expressed and implied in the constitution. The exigencies of war necessitate a strong central government, and to that end the Commonwealth government's wartime power is much wider than its power in peacetime. The federal division of powers between the Commonwealth and the states may be subordinated to the immediate imperatives of fighting a war. The expanded power of the federal government will not necessarily recede immediately upon war's end, although the legislative power does contract.

Military service is not compulsory today, but conscription is not prohibited by the constitution. At various times the government has instituted conscription, most controversially during the Vietnam War. The constitution allows for the conscription of noncitizen residents for the defense of the nation at war. Conscientious objection was recognized in Australia when conscription was in force, although it is not required by the constitution; in fact, the constitutional right to religious freedom has not been interpreted as giving rise to a right to conscientious objection.

AMENDMENTS TO THE CONSTITUTION

Amendments to the Commonwealth constitution are regulated by Section 128, which presents a number of hurdles that must be overcome before change is made. A proposal for a referendum must first be passed by both houses of Parliament or by one house twice. For political reasons, only the House of Representatives can use the latter option. After approval by the governor-general, the proposal must be passed by a majority of people in a majority of states. If the amendment affects the rights of a particular state, the proposal must pass in that state as well. In practice, the Australian people have been resistant to change and have approved only eight of 44 proposed amendments in more than 100 years—and a number of those dealt with relatively trivial issues, such as the retirement age of judges. The only referenda to pass have been those backed by both major political parties and both the Commonwealth and state governments. This phenomenon has led one Australian constitutional lawyer to describe Australia as the "frozen continent" of constitutional reform.

The procedures for changing state constitutions vary from state to state but are generally more flexible. Many state constitutions were originally simply acts of Parliament and could be amended by another act of Parliament. Now, however, a number of state constitutions have entrenched certain constitutional provisions, and amendments require either a parliamentary supermajority or a referendum. On the whole, however, the state constitutions have proved more flexible over time than the Commonwealth constitution.

PRIMARY SOURCES

Constitution in English. Available online. URL: http://www.aph.gov.au/senate/general/constitution/index.htm. Accessed on August 24, 2005.

SECONDARY SOURCES

Tony Blackshield and George William, *Australian Constitutional Law and Theory*. 3d ed. Annandale: Federation Press, 2002.

Tony Blackshield, Michael Coper, and George Williams, *The Oxford Companion to the High Court of Australia*. Sydney: Oxford University Press, 2001.

Peter Hanks, *Constitutional Law in Australia*. 2d ed. Sydney: LexisNexis Butterworths, 1996.

Sarah Joseph and Melissa Castan, *Federal Constitutional Law—a Contemporary Perspective*. 2d ed. Sydney: Lawbook Company, 2004.

Carolyn Evans
Tim Rogan

AUSTRIA

At-a-Glance

OFFICIAL NAME
Federal Republic of Austria

CAPITAL
Vienna

POPULATION
8,192,880 (July 2006 est.)

SIZE
32,385 sq. mi. (83,871 sq. km)

LANGUAGES
German; traditional minority languages: Slovenian, Croatian, Hungarian (official languages)

RELIGIONS
Catholic 73.7%, Protestant 4.7%, Muslim 4.2%, Christian Orthodox 2.2%, Jewish 0.1%, Jehovah's Witnesses 0.3%, other 1.1%, unaffiliated 12%, unspecified 1.7% (2001)

NATIONAL OR ETHNIC MINORITIES
Austrian 91.1%, Serbian-Croatian-Bosniac 4%, Turkish 1.6%, other 3.3% (2001)

DATE OF INDEPENDENCE OR CREATION
1156 (duchy with special privileges in the Holy Roman Empire); 1804 (empire); November 12, 1918 (republic)

TYPE OF GOVERNMENT
Parliamentary democracy

TYPE OF STATE
Federal state

TYPE OF LEGISLATURE
Bicameral parliament

DATE OF CONSTITUTION
October 11, 1920

DATE OF LAST AMENDMENT
No single date

Austria is a parliamentary democracy based on the rule of law; the separation of executive, legislative, and judicial powers (although there are some elements of concentrated power in parliament); and the protection of fundamental rights. Organized as a federation, Austria is made up of nine federal states and a strong central government. The constitutional law of the federation provides for far-reaching guarantees of human rights. If a violation of constitutional law occurs in an individual case, there are effective remedies enforceable by an independent system of specialized and centralized constitutional review. This includes a Constitutional Court that is organized outside the regular court system.

The federal president is the head of state. While he or she is not the chief executive, the presidential function is not merely representative; it is also part of a system of checks and balances. The president appoints the federal chancellor, who is in fact the central political figure, although formally the chancellor is only first among equals in the federal administration. The administration

must enjoy the confidence of the National Council as the representative body of the people; the council is shaped by free, equal, general, and direct elections. A pluralistic system of political parties is guaranteed by constitutional law and has intense political impact.

There is also a traditional system of "social partnership" that formed, for many years, a "side government" of employers' and employees' associations but has lost its importance in recent years. The system of social partnership is also primarily responsible for the prevailing concept of a social market economy.

Religious freedom is guaranteed; state and religious communities are institutionally separated.

CONSTITUTIONAL HISTORY

Starting in the 10th century C.E., Austria was part of the Holy Roman Empire of the German nation and was organized as a bulwark against invasion from the southeast. In

1156, Austria became a duchy, which in 1282 was handed over to the Habsburgs. After 1526, the Habsburgs added Bohemia and Hungary to their territories; they established a monarchical union of the Eastern Alpine, Danubian, and Carpathian regions. The union had, among other purposes, the aim of defending Europe against the Ottoman Turks. Members of the Habsburg dynasty ruled the Holy Roman Empire, with brief intermissions, from the 15th century until its dissolution in 1806.

In 1804, Austria established itself as an independent empire combining the Habsburg territories belonging to the Holy Roman Empire with the territories of the Hungarian kingdom. From 1815, Austria was one of the two leading members of the German Confederation (Deutscher Bund), a confederation of sovereign countries that replaced the Holy Roman Empire. The confederation lasted until 1866 when the other leading state, Prussia, defeated Austria. The new German Empire (Deutsches Reich) of 1870–71 excluded Austria.

Beginning with the revolution of 1848, Austria, as did other European countries, experienced a series of constitutional reforms followed by neoabsolutistic restoration. After the loss of dominant positions in Italy (1859) and Germany (1866), a period of constitutional experiments ended in the Ausgleich (compromise) with Hungary and the enactment of the so-called December Constitution in 1867.

Thus the Austrian Empire was transformed into the Austro-Hungarian Dual Monarchy, a union of two states with only a few common affairs. A similar solution in favor of the Czechs failed because of the opposition of German liberals and nationalists. In 1878, Austria occupied the Turkish provinces of Bosnia and Herzegovina. After their annexation in 1908, the idea of a Trialistic Monarchy was raised, turning the southern territories inhabited by people of Slavic descent into a third partner. One of the promoters of this concept was the heir designate to the Austrian throne, Archduke Francis Ferdinand, whose assassination by a young Serb nationalist on June 28, 1914, marked the beginning of World War I (1914–18).

The defeat in World War I led to the partitioning of the multinational Austro-Hungarian monarchy according to the national ambitions of the peoples. The German-speaking territories proclaimed the Republic of German-Austria and declared it a part of the new German republic. However, the peace treaty of Saint Germain of September 10, 1919, between Austria and the Allies barred Austria from joining Germany or from incorporating other German-speaking territories in Czechoslovakia and Italy.

On October 1, 1920, the Austrian Republic adopted a federal constitution, which concentrated political power in the parliament. An amendment in 1929 strengthened the position of the federal president so that the Austrian system of government now combined elements of parliamentary and presidential democracies.

Distrust between political groups grew after 1927, and on March 4, 1933, the administration declared the dissolution of parliament. On May 1, 1934, the constitution of 1920, as amended in 1929, was replaced by a new constitution based on a Christian Authoritarian Corporate system.

On March 12, 1938, German troops invaded Austria and incorporated it into the National Socialist German Reich. In a plebiscite four weeks later, the overwhelming majority of Austrians endorsed the union. In World War II (1939–45), Austrians not only served as soldiers in the Wehrmacht but also took part in the Nazi terror regime, which raised questions of Austria's portion in responsibility for its crimes.

In 1945, Austria was reestablished as an independent state under Allied control; unlike in Germany, one government was set up for all four occupied zones. After Stalin's death in 1953, the Soviets started negotiations with Austria that resulted in a state treaty with the four Allies, signed on May 15, 1955, by which Austria regained full sovereignty. According to an agreement with the Soviet Union, Austria adopted permanent neutrality in a federal constitutional law of October 26, 1955.

Since 1995, Austria has been a member state of the European Union (EU). While Austria started out on the EU's eastern border, as more states joined the union, Austria's geographic position was closer and closer to the center. This corresponds with Austria's traditional national identity as a link between East and West and its role as a bridge in the European integration process.

In May 2003, a Constitutional Convention was established in order to draft a new Austrian constitution.

FORM AND IMPACT OF THE CONSTITUTION

Austrian constitutional law is all written law, but it is not codified in a single document. Any legislation can be designated as a constitutional provision by a two-thirds majority vote of the National Council. One can find "constitutional law" in about 1,300 places spread over the entire legal order. The primary constitutional documents are the 1929 Federal Constitution (Bundes-Verfassungsgesetz) and the 1867 Basic Law on the General Rights of the Citizens.

Constitutional law takes precedence over all other national law, according to the theory of the hierarchy of norms. The general rules of international law are automatically part of Austrian federal law. International treaties must be transformed into Austrian legislation. The law of the European Union has precedence over the Austrian constitution as long as it does not contradict its fundamental principles.

BASIC ORGANIZATIONAL STRUCTURE

Austria is a federation made up of nine federal states, called Bundesländer. Each state has its own constitution and is essentially equal to all others from a constitutional point of view. The federal states do not have the right to leave the federation.

The constitution regulates the allocation of legislative and executive power between the federation and the federal states. The most important powers are allocated to the federation, which therefore dominates the system. However, the federal states enjoy residual powers in areas not expressly mentioned in the constitution. In recent times, further legislative powers have passed from the federal states to the federation by constitutional amendments because of their increasing supraregional importance. This has occurred, for example, in the areas of environmental law and animal rights.

Traditionally, local governments are strong in Austria. The local communities are entities incorporated into the states and the state administrative structure. However, local communities can make their own decisions on a number of issues of local interest. The citizens of the local communities elect the mayors and members of local political bodies.

FUNDAMENTAL CONSTITUTIONAL PRINCIPLES

The Austrian constitutional system is based on a number of fundamental principles. A substantial alteration of any of them would be considered a significant revision of the constitution. Constitutional amendments of such magnitude must be approved by a popular referendum according to Article 44, Section 2, of the 1929 constitution.

Articles 1 and 2 of the constitution explicitly refer to the democratic, republican, and federal principles. According to Article 1, Austria is a democratic republic whose authority emanates from the people. In principle the whole system rests on indirect democracy, combined with a constitutional guarantee of a pluralistic political party system; it is rounded out by certain features of direct democracy, such as popular initiative, public consultation, and referendum. Since its introduction in 1973, there have been 31 popular initiatives. The republican principle has rather limited meaning in Austria today. It simply conveys that there shall be no monarchy. According to Article 2 of the 1929 constitution, Austria also is a federal state. Therefore, the legislative and executive powers are divided between the federation and the federal states. The federal states have the opportunity to participate in legislation of the federation.

According to legal doctrine, three more principles are implicitly contained in the constitution. The first is the principle of the rule of law, which requires that all state actions have a legal basis and that the judiciary be independent. The second is the principle of separation of powers. The third implicit principle is the liberal principle, guaranteeing a system of liberal fundamental rights.

Although there is no explicit clause providing for a social state, certain standards of labor and social welfare law are in fact treated as fundamental laws in Austria.

Further structural principles are implicitly contained in the constitution, such as religious neutrality and a commitment to the concept that the state must support culture. This is of special importance because Austria often identifies itself by emphasizing its cultural traditions. Protection of the environment and of animals also is specified in constitutional law.

CONSTITUTIONAL BODIES

The predominant constitutional bodies are the National Council and the Federal Council, forming the legislative power, the Federal Assembly; the federal president; the federal administration; and the judiciary, including a separate Constitutional Court. A Board of Audit and a People's Advocates' Office are regarded as forming part of parliamentary control.

National Council (Nationalrat)

The Austrian National Council (Nationalrat) is the central representative organ on the federal level. In terms of the legislative process, the National Council and Federal Council may be regarded as two chambers of parliament, although the latter has a relatively weak position.

The members of the National Council have the right to put questions to the administration, and any federal minister may be called to appear before parliament. Upon the demand of five members, any question must be answered in the course of the same meeting.

Members of the National Council or the Federal Council cannot be subjected to any criminal prosecution, arrest, or limitation of their personal freedom, except with the permission of their council. The only exception to this privilege occurs when the delegate is arrested in the course of committing a crime.

The National Council consists of 183 deputies. Their term of office, the legislative term, is four years. The deputies are elected in a general, direct, free, equal, and secret balloting process.

A president, a second president, and a third president are elected by the National Council from among its members, forming a steering committee. They collectively take over the functions of head of state in case the federal president is temporarily disabled for more than 20 days.

Federal Council (Bundesrat)

In the Federal Council, the federal states participate in national legislation. The members are not elected directly by the people but are deputized by the parliaments of the federal states. Its composition, therefore, changes with every election in the federal states. Practically speaking, the influence of the federal states on policy on the federal level primarily comes to bear within the framework of the political parties.

Federal Assembly (Bundesversammlung)

The Federal Assembly is composed of the members of the two chambers of parliament. Its main functions are to witness the induction of the federal president into office, to impeach the federal president, and to declare war.

The Lawmaking Process

The right to introduce a bill can be exercised by the federal administration, by at least five members of the National Council, by the Federal Council, or by a popular initiative signed by at least 100,000 voters.

After the National Council has passed a bill, it is passed to the Federal Council, which in most cases has only a suspensive veto, which at most delays legislation. The Federal Council may raise objections, but if these are rejected by the National Council (a process that requires a higher number of deputies), the bill becomes law in any case. The Federal Council has an absolute veto in only two cases: when a constitutional provision would restrict the power of the federal states or when it would affect the functions of the Federal Council itself.

Once a bill has been passed by parliament, it must be countersigned by the federal chancellor and the responsible federal minister. To enter into force, the law needs the federal president's assent. It is a controversial question whether the signature of the federal president serves merely a notary function, or whether the president has the right, and the duty, to refuse signature in case of doubts concerning the constitutionality of the act.

The Board of Audit (Rechnungshof)

The Board of Audit, an auxiliary organ of the legislature, is an institution under a president elected by the National Council. Although the board can only make recommendations for improving the efficiency of the administration, its high standing in public opinion has given it great influence.

The People's Advocates' Office (Volksanwaltschaft)

The People's Advocates' Office was created in 1977 in imitation of the Scandinavian "ombudsman." It examines complaints filed by citizens or legal entities alleging improper administration on the federal level when there is no legal recourse available or all legal remedies have been exhausted. If it considers a complaint justified, it issues a recommendation to the competent administrative body, which must act according to the recommendation or explain its refusal to act.

The Federal President

The federal president is the head of state but not the head of the executive. The president represents the federal republic in international affairs.

The president is elected directly by the people for a period of six years; a reelection for a second term is allowed. To be elected, a candidate needs more than one-half of the valid votes cast. The two leading candidates enter a runoff if no one wins a majority in the first round.

The federal president may in principle act independently to appoint or dismiss the federal chancellor or the entire federal administration and may act to sign laws for promulgation. This is also the case in the president's function as supreme commander of the armed forces.

In other areas, the president can only act if asked by some other body, usually the federal administration. That is the case with dissolving the National Council; summoning the National Council; ordering referendums; appointing high-level civil servants, army officers, judges, and university professors; and granting pardon to criminal offenders.

Although the Austrian federal president, by law, has a relatively strong position, in political practice the president's functions are restricted. For that reason, in recent decades there have been widespread discussions about reforming the presidential office. In practice, a great part of the president's political impact depends on personal charisma.

The Federal Administration

The federal administration is the political nerve center of Austria. It consists of the federal chancellor (Bundeskanzler), the vice-chancellor (Vizekanzler), and the federal ministers.

The federal chancellor is the head of the administration. The chancellor is appointed by the federal president. By this decision, the federal president is free in terms of law but is politically bound because the federal administration must enjoy the confidence of the National Council. The other federal ministers are appointed by the federal president according to the federal chancellor's proposal.

The federal administration, as the whole executive branch, can act only on the basis of law. It has political responsibility toward the federal president, who may dismiss the federal chancellor or the entire federal government at any time, and to the National Council, which may pass a vote of no confidence at its discretion.

Although the federal chancellor has no formal legal power to set policy guidelines independently, the chancellor is generally the dominant figure in Austrian politics. Because the majority in parliament backs the administration and stands against the parliamentary minority, and also because of the influence of the media, there has been a development toward a "chancellor democracy" in recent decades.

The Judiciary

The judiciary in Austria is independent of the executive and legislative powers. All courts are federal institutions.

The ordinary court system for civil and criminal matters is organized into four levels. At the top of the pyramid is the Supreme Court (Oberster Gerichtshof) in Vienna. Various civil matters are designated to specific courts or panels of regular civil courts, namely, for commercial law and antitrust law, as well as for issues of labor and social welfare law. In these cases, informed lay judges are members of the panel.

Austria also has a long tradition of administrative adjudication, which has existed since the 1867 constitution. There is a Supreme Administrative Court that can be petitioned after exhausting all internal administrative appeals. In recent decades, the system has been expanded by introducing independent administrative authorities. These bodies are collegial. Their decisions may be reviewed by the Administrative Court only in instances of a special legal provision. In 1988, independent administrative panels were introduced in the federal states to provide two levels of judicial proceedings.

The Constitutional Court

Austria has a specific tradition of constitutional review from the 1867 constitution. Such review is handled by a unitary Constitutional Court outside the regular court system. This court can make decisions without necessarily deciding a specific case at issue, and its rulings have general effect. The system has been adopted by most European and Latin American countries, including the new Central and East European democracies.

The central task of the court is to examine the constitutionality of acts of parliament. It can also examine administrative acts, rule on jurisdictional disputes among state organs, resolve electoral disputes, and conduct impeachment trials. A constitutional complaint can be taken before the Constitutional Court by any person alleging that the state has infringed one of his or her fundamental rights.

The Constitutional Court is composed of a president, a vice president, 12 members, and six substitute members. The members are appointed by the federal president on the nominations of the federal administration, the National Council, and the Federal Council.

The major changes in the court's decision making since the early 1980s add up to a paradigm shift. Previously, the court restricted itself to a strict textual interpretation of the law. From that point on, the court departed from this judicial self-restraint until, at present, it shows a certain degree of judicial activism.

THE ELECTION PROCESS

All Austrians over the age of 18 have the right to vote in the election of the National Council, and every Austrian above the age of 21 may stand for election to the National Council.

The 183 seats are distributed among the 43 electoral districts according to population and the principle of proportional representation. The seats and votes that remain after distribution in the electoral districts are distributed on the state level but only to parties that won at least one district seat or at least 4 percent nationwide. Any further remaining seats or votes are then distributed on the federal level.

In 2004, four political parties were represented in the National Council.

POLITICAL PARTIES

Austria has a pluralistic political party system. In 1975, a constitutional provision explicitly established that political parties constitute essential components of the democratic system of Austria.

This provision requires political parties to specify the rights and duties of the members and show a desire to participate in the democratic legislative process. It does not mandate an internal democratic structure.

Parties that are represented in the National Council are financed by public funds. Parties not represented in the National Council only receive public funds in an election year if they won at least 1 percent of the votes in the last election.

There is no provision for banning a political party. However, courts and administrative bodies may decide whether a party has violated the prohibition of reviving Nazi or fascist ideology, if this question is raised in a specific proceeding.

Since the early 1990s, four parties have been represented in every National Council: two larger parties, the Austrian People's Party (Österreichische Volkspartei) and the Social Democratic Party (Sozialdemokratische Partei Österreichs), as well as two smaller parties, the Freedom Party (Freiheitliche Partei Österreichs) and the Green Alternative (Grüne Alternative).

CITIZENSHIP

Austrian citizenship is primarily acquired by birth under the principle of *ius sanguinis;* a child acquires Austrian citizenship if at least one parent is an Austrian citizen, no matter where he or she is born. The law provides for the possibilities of acquiring citizenship in special cases.

FUNDAMENTAL RIGHTS

Austrian fundamental rights are embodied in constitutional acts, such as the 1867 State Fundamental Law, or treaties under international law, such as the Treaty of Saint Germain. The relevant documents date from several historical epochs and display different understandings of fundamental rights. This makes Austrian fundamental rights guarantees unique. In 1958, the European Convention on Human Rights and Fundamental Freedoms became part of the constitutional system. As a result of the gradual development of rights in Austria, individual constitutional provisions overlap. In addition, certain guarantees of fundamental rights are laid down in special constitutional laws and in single constitutional provisions in ordinary statutory law, as is the case for the law on data protection.

All these provisions guarantee the traditional, classic set of human rights. Social rights, such as the right to work, education, and welfare, are somewhat underrepresented as the constitution lacks explicit clauses on those matters. However, the actual state powers specified in the constitution presuppose extensive state activities in the social realm. Whether social fundamental rights should be embodied in a new Austrian constitution is a crucial issue currently being debated by the constitutional convention.

Since the 1867 constitution, the Austrian system has distinguished between rights that apply to every human being and those rights reserved for Austrian citizens only. Because of the constitutional status of the European Convention on Human Rights and Fundamental Freedoms, a number of traditional citizens' rights have now become general, such as freedom of association and freedom of assembly.

Impact and Functions of Fundamental Rights

Although there is no explicit ranking of fundamental rights, the right to equal treatment can be viewed as the most important. The Constitutional Court must ensure that this principle is at the forefront of the complex modern society and determine its parameters.

While the term *equality before the law* suggests only that laws must be equally applied, it has become clear that lawmaking itself is bound by the principle of equality. Therefore, Austrian constitutional doctrine also speaks of an equality in law.

At present, the principle of equality is understood to mean objectivity and reasonableness in legal regulations. Organs of the executive branch may not make arbitrary decisions and must observe the principle of proportionality. The legislature must ensure that any legal differentiation is based on reasonable criteria and must also respect proportionality.

According to a modern understanding of fundamental rights, the state must promote conditions whereby fundamental rights can actually be exercised as far as possible. Whether an objective obligation of the state creates an enforceable claim or only a justification for state subsidies must be investigated in each individual, concrete case.

Limitations to Fundamental Rights

According to the 1867 State Fundamental Law, rights can be limited only when the restrictions are specified in the law explicitly, as they are in many cases. In contrast, the reservations found in the European Convention of Human Rights and Fundamental Freedoms are of a more practical nature, implying a process of weighing the legal merits of each case. The most important instrument available for such calculations is the principle of proportionality, the idea that the means applied must relate to the aims pursued. This principle implies a balancing of the legal and factual merits in every case. The least oppressive path must be taken in pursuing the aim intended. In other words, only pressing social needs can justify limiting the right in question.

Proportionality may be considered the unchallenged principle of the law of the European Union. It permeates the entire legal system.

ECONOMY

The constitution in Austria does not require a free market system. However, certain fundamental economic rights that allow free, private economic activities are guaranteed. They include freedom of property, acquisition, profession, and association. State authorities must not interfere in bargaining between trade unions and employer's associations. Such activities may only be restricted for public reasons, in accordance with the principle of proportionality.

With regard to labor law, Austria can be described as an extended welfare state. European Community Law limits the national legislators' margin of appreciation, including that of the constitutional legislator.

RELIGIOUS COMMUNITIES

Freedom of religion or belief is guaranteed as a human right. This guarantee also includes the rights of religious communities. Today, it is generally accepted in Austria that it is a primary responsibility of the state to support religious communities in order to protect the religious interests of the individual adherents.

The legal system regulating the relations between the state and religious communities is based on the principles of religious neutrality, equality, and self-determination. While there is no established state church, there are two categories of religious communities who enjoy special legal status. Certain churches and religious societies are recognized by ministerial order and have public law status. Other religious communities are registered with the state with private law status, according to a special law on religious associations. There are differences between these two categories of religious groups in various legal spheres, such as denominational religious instruction in schools and preferential treatment in tax law. The constitutionality of these differences is in dispute.

Today, 13 religious communities enjoy public law status. These include not only the larger groups such as Catholics, Protestants, Muslims, and Orthodox Christians but also smaller communities such as the Church of Jesus Christ of Latter-day Saints and the New Apostolic Church, Jews, and Buddhists.

MILITARY DEFENSE AND STATE OF EMERGENCY

The armed forces are established as a militia army. Men above the age of 18 must serve for nine months. Women have been allowed to volunteer since 1999. According to Article 9a of the 1929 constitution, nonmilitary service, lasting 12 months, is provided for conscientious objectors.

The armed forces are part of the executive branch according to the constitution. The federal president is commander in chief. The power of mobilization is divided between the federal president and the minister of defense; the latter needs prior authorization from the federal administration.

The armed forces are entrusted with the defense of the nation; the protection of constitutional institutions, democratic liberties, public order, and internal safety; and, finally, the rendering of aid in case of a natural disaster or extraordinary accident.

AMENDMENTS TO THE CONSTITUTION

Constitutional laws or constitutional provisions contained in simple laws can be passed by the National Council. A quorum of at least half the members is required, and the measure must win two-thirds of the votes cast. The approval of the Federal Council is required; in case such laws or provisions limit the lawmaking competence of the *Länder*. A complete revision of the constitution requires approval by a popular referendum.

PRIMARY SOURCES

Constitution in English. Available online. URL: http://www. ris.bka.gv.at/info/bvg_eng.pdf. Accessed on September 22, 2005.

Federal Constitution. Available online. URL: http://www. ris.bka.gv.at/bundesrecht/. Accessed on September 21, 2005.

SECONDARY SOURCES

Herbert Hausmaninger, *The Austrian Legal System*. 3d ed. Vienna: Manz, 2003.

Richard Potz

AZERBAIJAN

At-a-Glance

OFFICIAL NAME
Republic of Azerbaijan

CAPITAL
Baku

POPULATION
7,868,385 (July 2004 est.)

SIZE
33,436 sq. mi. (86,600 sq. km)

LANGUAGES
Azerbaijani (Azeri) 89%, Russian 3%, Armenian 2%, other 6%

RELIGIONS
Muslim 93.4%, Russian Orthodox 2.5%, Armenian Orthodox 2.3%, other 1.8%

NATIONAL OR ETHNIC COMPOSITION
Azerbaijani 90.6%, Lezgin 2.2%, Russian 1.8%, Armenian 1.5%, Talysh 1%, other (made up of Avars, Meskhetian Turks, Georgians, Ukrainians, and other nationalities) 2.9% (as of 1999)

DATE OF INDEPENDENCE OR CREATION
August 30, 1991

TYPE OF GOVERNMENT
Presidential republic

TYPE OF STATE
Unitary state

TYPE OF LEGISLATURE
Unicameral parliament

DATE OF CONSTITUTION
November 12, 1995

DATE OF LAST AMENDMENT
August 24, 2002

Azerbaijan is a democratic republic based on the rule of law with separation of state powers into the legislative, executive, and judicial branches. Although proclaimed a unitary republic by the constitution, Azerbaijan has an autonomous state on its territory—the Nakhchivan Autonomous Republic—which enjoys a relatively limited form of self-government. The constitution of 1995, which is the supreme law, declares that the principal aim of the state is to ensure human rights and fundamental freedoms. The rights and liberties set forth in the constitution have a direct binding effect; citizens may challenge any violation of constitutional provisions by lodging a complaint with the Constitutional Court.

The president is the head of state. The constitution vests vast executive functions with the president, who appoints and dismisses the prime minister and members of the cabinet. The parliament is formed on the basis of general, equal, free, and direct suffrage and represents the major political parties in the country.

The economy is based on free market interactions and diverse forms of ownership. The constitution guarantees religious freedom and states that all religions are equal before the law. Religion is separate from the state. The military is totally subordinate to the civil government. General conscription applies to all men over 18, but the constitution provides for alternative service. Under the constitution, Azerbaijan rejects war as a means to resolve international conflicts and intends to live in peace with all nations of the world.

CONSTITUTIONAL HISTORY

The first polity in the territory of Azerbaijan, called Manna, existed between the ninth and the sixth centuries B.C.E. It was followed by two other states—Aderbaygan (Atropatena) and the Caucasian Albania. The first Turk-speaking, ethnically Azerbaijani states appeared in the Middle Ages—the Shirvanshakhs, Qaragoyunlu, Aghgoyunlu, and finally Sefevi states. The latter existed for nearly 300 years until it disintegrated into several semi-independent khanates and sultanates in the 18th century. As a result of the various Russo-Persian wars of the 19th century, Azerbaijan was divided between Russia and Iran, with the latter gaining most of the country.

On May 28, 1918, after the revolutionary events of 1917 in Russia and the collapse of the Russian Empire, the Azerbaijan Democratic Republic was founded. For the first time, the country formed a parliament, which adopted the declaration of statehood. As the first parliamentary democracy in the Islamic world, the Azerbaijan Democratic Republic received de facto recognition by the Allies as an independent nation in January 1920. The parliament appointed the prime minister, who was vested with the power to govern the state. The Azerbaijan Democratic Republic became the first Muslim state to grant women suffrage. The first republic existed for only 23 months, until the end of 1920, when Bolshevik Russia's Red Army invaded and terminated independence. In 1922, the Soviet Socialist Republic of Azerbaijan "voluntarily" joined the Soviet Union. The constitution of the Azerbaijan Soviet Socialist Republic was adopted in 1925. It established a single-party system of governance with separation of state powers into the legislative, executive, and judicial branches. The constitutions of 1937 and 1978 had likewise a rather ideological nature and were aimed at preserving the core ideas and foundations of the Communist regime.

The Azerbaijan Soviet Socialist Republic ceased to exist at the collapse of the Soviet Union in 1991; on August 30 of that year, Azerbaijan declared its independence from the Soviet Union. The Constitutional Act on State Independence, dated October 18, 1991, established the foundations for the political and economic structure of the Third Republic—the Republic of Azerbaijan. The current constitution, which was developed in accordance with the fundamental principles and norms of international law, was adopted in 1995 by a referendum; it proclaims the country a democratic, secular, and unitary republic based on the rule of law.

FORM AND IMPACT OF THE CONSTITUTION

The Republic of Azerbaijan has a written constitution, codified in a single document. International treaties to which Azerbaijan is a party constitute an integral part of its legislative system. The constitution states that in the event of conflict between the normative legal acts forming part of the Azerbaijani legislative system and the provisions of international treaties to which Azerbaijan is a party, the international treaty provisions shall prevail. Only the constitution and statutes adopted by a referendum prevail over those treaties.

The constitution is first in the hierarchical scale of legislative components, followed by acts adopted by a referendum, laws, presidential decrees, decisions of the cabinet of ministers, and normative acts of the central executive bodies such as ministries and state committees.

BASIC ORGANIZATIONAL STRUCTURE

The constitution stipulates that Azerbaijan is a unitary republic. The territory of the republic is divided into more than 80 administrative districts (called *rayons*). The president appoints and dismisses the heads of local executive bodies, who implement the executive power in the respective *rayons* and major cities. The president also determines the responsibilities of the local executive bodies.

The Nakhchivan Autonomous Republic is an autonomous state within the Republic of Azerbaijan. The constitution vests legislative powers in the autonomous republic's parliament, or Ali Mejlis, while executive and judicial functions are vested in its cabinet of ministers and courts, respectively. The constitution and laws of the Republic of Azerbaijan, decrees of the president, and decisions of the cabinet of ministers of Azerbaijan have binding effect in the territory of the autonomous republic. Accordingly, the legislative system of the Nakhchivan Autonomous Republic, including its constitution, laws, and decisions of the cabinet of ministers, cannot contradict the respective components of the Azerbaijani legislative system. According to the constitution of Azerbaijan, the Ali Mejlis of the autonomous republic may adopt general legislation on economic and social development, such as its annual budget, tax issues, protection of the environment, and public health.

LEADING CONSTITUTIONAL PRINCIPLES

Azerbaijan is a democratic, constitutional, and secular republic where governance is based on the principle of division of powers; the legislative, executive, and judicial branches act jointly and are independent within the framework of their authority.

The supreme aim of the Azerbaijani state is to ensure human rights and fundamental freedoms. The state guarantees the rule of law as an expression of the people's will. Religion is separate from the state. All religions are deemed equal before the law, and there is no established state religion. Azerbaijan intends to remain faithful to universal human values, to live in peace and freedom with all the nations of the world, and to cooperate with them to that end.

CONSTITUTIONAL BODIES

The major constitutional bodies are the president; the cabinet of ministers, headed by the prime minister; the

National Assembly called the Milli Mejlis; and the judiciary, including the Constitutional Court.

The President

The president of the Republic of Azerbaijan is the head of state and the supreme commander in chief of the armed forces. According to the constitution, executive powers are vested not in the cabinet, but in the president, who determines economic and social policy. The president appoints and dismisses the prime minister in coordination with the Milli Mejlis; he or she also appoints members of the cabinet of ministers, the prosecutor general, and judges, except the judges of the Constitutional, Supreme, and Economic Courts. The president also signs and issues laws, concludes international treaties, declares states of emergency and martial law, settles citizenship questions, decides on granting of political asylum, and grants pardons.

The president is elected for a five-year term and can be reelected successively only once. A candidate for the presidency is considered elected if more than half of the voters who participated in the election voted for him or her.

The Cabinet of Ministers

The cabinet of ministers is answerable exclusively to the president. It is headed by the prime minister, who is appointed by the president. The latter determines the activities of the cabinet. All ministries and other central executive bodies report to the cabinet. The cabinet resigns on the day a new president takes office.

The Milli Mejlis (National Assembly)

The legislative power in Azerbaijan is exercised by the unicameral Milli Mejlis. It consists of 125 deputies elected on the basis of the majority of votes in single-member districts and general, equal, and direct suffrage by free, individual, and secret ballot. The term of office of the Milli Mejlis is five years.

The Milli Mejlis passes laws, approves the state budget and controls its implementation, and appoints the judges of the Constitutional, Supreme, and Economic Courts.

The Lawmaking Process

According to the constitution, the Milli Mejlis has authority to adopt general legislation in a variety of areas. Once passed by the Milli Mejlis, a law is submitted to the president for signing. The president can reject the law and return it to the Milli Mejlis together with his or her own proposals. Parliament can override the president's objection by a qualified majority. However, the president has absolute veto power with respect to constitutional laws, which introduce additions to the constitution of Azerbaijan.

The Judiciary

According to the constitution, judicial power in Azerbaijan is exercised only by courts of law and on the basis of due process. The judicial system consists of first instance courts, appellate courts, and a Supreme Court, which functions as the court of final appeal; it is the last instance in civil, criminal, and other cases.

The Constitutional Court decides whether laws, presidential decrees, court decisions, and other normative legal acts conform to the constitution and settles disputes over the authorities of the legislative, executive, and judicial branches. Relevant state authorities as well as individuals may directly appeal to the Constitutional Court.

THE ELECTION PROCESS

All Azerbaijani citizens have the right both to vote and to be elected to government bodies. The voting age is 18.

POLITICAL PARTIES

Azerbaijan has a pluralistic system of political parties. A party can be banned only by a court decision.

CITIZENSHIP

A person born to an Azerbaijani citizen or in the territory of Azerbaijan shall be a citizen of the Republic of Azerbaijan. A person is considered an Azerbaijani citizen if one of his or her parents is an Azerbaijani citizen.

Under no circumstances may a citizen of the Republic of Azerbaijan be deprived of Azerbaijani citizenship.

FUNDAMENTAL RIGHTS

The Republic of Azerbaijan is a party to all the major multilateral human rights treaties, including the European Convention on Human Rights. According to the constitution, the rights and freedoms enumerated therein are to be exercised in accordance with international treaties. Thus, in the sphere of human rights (and only in that sphere), international treaties take precedence over the constitution.

The constitution declares the protection and promotion of human rights and fundamental freedoms to be the supreme aim of the state. It further obliges the legislative, executive, and judicial branches to observe and protect the human rights and freedoms it enumerates.

The constitution guarantees the full set of universally recognized human rights and civil freedoms. Article 25 guarantees everyone's equality before the law and prohibits any forms of discrimination. Articles 44 and 45 provide for the right to preserve one's national and ethnic identity and to use one's native language, including the right to receive education in one's native language.

Impact and Functions of Fundamental Rights

The basic rights set forth in the constitution are directly applicable; therefore, citizens may challenge in court any decisions, acts, or omissions that infringe on the rights and freedoms established by the constitution. Moreover, provisions of international treaties to which Azerbaijan is a party may be cited in the courts.

Limitations to Fundamental Rights

According to the constitution, the implementation of certain rights and freedoms can be partially or temporarily limited (while taking into account Azerbaijan's international obligations) upon a declaration of war, martial law, or state of emergency; or in the interests of national security, public safety, or the economic well-being of the country; or for the prevention of disorder or crime. The limitations must be proportionate to the legitimate aim pursued. The population shall be notified in advance of the limitations on their rights and freedoms.

ECONOMY

According to the constitution, the state is to create favorable conditions for the development of the economy, based on market relationships and diverse forms of ownership. It must guarantee free enterprise and prevent monopolies and unfair competition. The constitution guarantees the right of everyone to engage in all kinds of economic activity either alone or jointly with others, provided such activities do not contradict the law.

RELIGIOUS COMMUNITIES

The constitution guarantees the right to freedom of religion or belief. Everyone is free to define his or her attitude toward religion, to profess any religion alone or in community with others, and to express and disseminate his or her beliefs. Yet the law prohibits foreign citizens and stateless persons from engaging in religious propaganda. Additionally, dissemination and propaganda of religions that violate human dignity and contradict the principles of humanity are banned.

Religion and religious communities are separated from the state in Azerbaijan, and the state does not interfere in the activities of religious communities. All religions and religious communities are equal before the law, and there is no established state religion.

The state educational system is secular.

MILITARY DEFENSE AND STATE OF EMERGENCY

The constitution states that the Republic of Azerbaijan rejects war as a means of encroaching upon other states' independence or settling international conflicts. The armed forces have the sole purpose of ensuring the country's safety and defense.

In Azerbaijan, the military is totally subordinate to the civil government. The president of the republic is the supreme commander in chief of the armed forces.

General conscription applies to all men of 18 to 37 years of age. Women between the ages of 19 and 40 years can volunteer. The duration of active military service is 18 months. According to the constitution, active military service can be replaced by alternative service if serving in the military runs counter to a person's convictions.

Azerbaijan has acceded to the Nuclear Non-Proliferation Treaty as a nonnuclear weapons state and participates in the North Atlantic Treaty Organization's (NATO's) Partnership for Peace.

AMENDMENTS TO THE CONSTITUTION

Changes in the text of the constitution can be made only through referendum. Certain fundamental provisions are not subject to change at all. Proposals aimed at the destruction of any of the rights and freedoms set forth in the constitution or at their limitation to a greater extent than is provided for in international treaties to which Azerbaijan is a party cannot be put to nationwide vote.

PRIMARY SOURCES
Constitution in English. Available online. URL: http://www.president.az/s30_government/_government_e.html. Accessed on September 23, 2005.
Constitution in Azerbaijani. Available online. URL: http://www.president.az/s30_government/_government_a.html. Accessed on September 18, 2005.

SECONDARY SOURCES
Glenn E. Curtis, *Armenia, Azerbaijan and Georgia.* Washington, D.C.: United States Government Printing Office, 1995.
Edmund Herzig, *The New Caucasus: Armenia, Azerbaijan and Georgia.* London: The Royal Institute of International Affairs, 1999.
Organization for Security and Co-operation in Europe (OSCE), Available online. URL: http://www.osce.org/. Accessed on August 3, 2005.
United Nations, "Core Document Forming Part of the Reports of States Parties: Azerbaijan" (HRI/CORE/1/Add.117), 27 February 2002. Available online. URL: http://www.unhchr.ch/tbs/doc.nsf. Accessed on August 30, 2005.

Elvin Aliyev

BAHAMAS

At-a-Glance

OFFICIAL NAME
Commonwealth of the Bahamas

CAPITAL
Nassau

POPULATION
301,790 (2005 est.)

SIZE
5,358 sq. mi. (13,878 sq. km)

LANGUAGES
English

RELIGIONS
Baptist 32%, Anglican 20%, Roman Catholic 19%, Methodist 6%, Church of God 6%, other Protestant 12%, none or unknown 3%, other 2%

NATIONAL OR ETHNIC COMPOSITION
Black 85%, white 12%, Asian and Hispanic 3%

DATE OF INDEPENDENCE OR CREATION
July 10, 1973

TYPE OF GOVERNMENT
Constitutional parliamentary democracy

TYPE OF STATE
Centralist state

TYPE OF LEGISLATURE
Bicameral parliament

DATE OF CONSTITUTION
June 20, 1973

DATE OF LAST AMENDMENT
None

The Bahamas is a parliamentary democracy and a constitutional monarchy within the British Commonwealth of Nations. The executive, judicial, and legislative powers are separated. The country is organized centrally. Fundamental rights and freedoms enjoy constitutional protection, and effective measures exist to provide redress for their violation.

The executive head of state is the British monarch, represented by an appointed governor-general. Political power is effectively exercised by the cabinet, headed by the prime minister. The cabinet relies on parliamentary support. The members of the House of Assembly are elected by popular vote, whereas the members of the Senate are appointed by the governor-general. The party system is pluralistic.

The constitution grants freedom of conscience. The state is not affiliated to any religious group. The constitution protects the enjoyment of private property.

CONSTITUTIONAL HISTORY

Constitutional history in the Bahamas begins in 1647 when the islands, already an English colony, were granted by the English king, Charles I, to a group of Protestant settlers from England and Bermuda, called the Company of the Adventurers for the Plantation of Eleutheira. The system of self-government provided for by the royal order was so revolutionary that one can say it establishes the first republic in the Western Hemisphere: All free men of the settlement were to be represented in a Senate. An elected governor and 12 elected counselors were to take care of the daily affairs of the government of the colony. Freedom of religion was granted.

A group of about 70 settlers arrived on one of the then-uninhabited islands in about 1648. Internal disagreements caused the company to split up, and a major group settled on another island.

At the end of the 17th century, British-sponsored privateers used the numerous mostly uninhabited islands and islets of the archipelago as their favorite hideout. The pirates even proclaimed their own republic, with no laws or government except a magistrate.

To fight the buccaneers, Britain installed a royal governor in 1718. In 1729, a bicameral legislature was instituted to complete the government of the colony. This system of government persisted for almost 250 years.

During this period, the franchise was based on property, effectively reducing the electorate to a small group of wealthy white male landowners and merchants. This became even more true after the 1780s, when, after the American War of Independence, thousands of English loyalists moved to the Bahamas, taking with them their slaves of African descent to work cotton plantations. Universal suffrage was not introduced until 1969.

As a result of the century-long exclusion from the electoral process, political awareness among the black majority did not arise until the 1950s. In 1953, the first Bahamian political party, the Progressive Liberal Party (PLP), was formed by blacks who were discontented with the policies of the governing elite and the concentration of wealth in the hands of a few white Bahamians.

In the 1960s, gradual steps toward independence were taken. A new constitution replaced the rule of the royal governors with a premier and a cabinet in 1964. Internal self-government was gained under the 1969 constitution. The Bahamas became fully independent from Great Britain in July 1973.

The predominant figure in the transition and early independence periods was Lynden O. Pindling, leader of the PLP and the country's first black prime minister. He remained in office until 1992.

FORM AND IMPACT OF THE CONSTITUTION

The constitution is set out in the Bahamas Independence Order 1973. It is the supreme law of the Bahamas and prevails over any other law made by Parliament.

BASIC ORGANIZATIONAL STRUCTURE

The Bahamas is organized centrally. The country is divided into 21 districts. These local entities are administered by the national minister of local affairs, who appoints commissioners for the districts.

LEADING CONSTITUTIONAL PRINCIPLES

The Bahamas is a parliamentary democracy and a constitutional monarchy under the British Crown. The country forms part of the Commonwealth of Nations. There is clear division of power among the legislative, the executive, and the judicial powers and an adequate system of constitutional checks and balances exists. The judiciary is independent. The constitution protects individual fundamental rights.

CONSTITUTIONAL BODIES

Constitutional bodies are the governor-general, the Parliament, and the cabinet of the Bahamas.

The British Monarch and the Governor-General

The executive head of state is the British monarch, represented by a governor-general appointed by the monarch. The governor-general appoints the prime minister, the ministers, and the senators and exercises the power of pardon. In most cases, the governor-general is obliged to act on the advice of the cabinet. The governor-general's duty to act on constitutional advice is not legally enforceable.

The Cabinet of the Bahamas

The cabinet of the Bahamas, headed by the prime minister, has responsibility for the general direction and control of the government. In practice, the prime minister is the most powerful political figure in the executive. The governor-general appoints as prime minister that member of the House of Assembly who commands the support of the majority of the members. The other ministers are appointed from among the members of either house of Parliament. The cabinet is collectively responsible for its policies to Parliament and may be dismissed from office by a vote of no confidence.

The Parliament of the Bahamas

The Parliament of the Bahamas is based on the Westminster model. It is composed of the British monarch, the House of Assembly, and the Senate.

There are 38 elected members in the House of Assembly, elected from districts of equal population.

The Senate consists of 16 members, all appointed by the governor-general. Nine are appointed on the advice of the prime minister, four on the advice of the leader of the opposition, and three on the advice of the prime minister after consultation of the leader of the opposition. The Parliament's term of office ends after five years.

The Lawmaking Process

Laws are made by both houses of Parliament. General legislative bills may be introduced in either house by any member. To pass, they require the approval of a majority of votes in both houses. The House of Assembly may, however, ultimately override the rejection of a bill by the Senate. To go into effect, the governor-general's formal assent on behalf of the Crown is required.

Bills on issues of public finance may only be introduced to the House of Assembly.

The Judiciary

The legal system of the Bahamas follows the British model and is adversarial in both criminal and civil cases. The judiciary is independent of the legislative and the executive branches.

The judiciary is composed of a Supreme Court and a Court of Appeal. The constitution confers on the Supreme Court original jurisdiction to hear civil and criminal matters, as well as cases of violations of fundamental rights and freedoms. It can hear only certain constitutional issues concerning the membership in the House of Assembly or the Senate. The Supreme Court's decisions may be appealed to the Court of Appeal. The court of last instance is the Judicial Committee of the Privy Council in London.

THE ELECTION PROCESS

Generally, every Bahamian aged 21 or older is eligible to run for office as a member of Parliament. Candidates must have resided in the Bahamas for at least one year immediately before the election. Prisoners under death sentence and members of the police or the armed forces are not eligible to stand.

Further details on the electoral process are specified in the electoral law. At present, there is full general adult suffrage for all citizens aged 18 or older. Seats are won by a majority of votes in each district. Voters participate in the political process directly when voting on constitutional amendments in a popular referendum.

POLITICAL PARTIES

The party system is pluralistic. The electoral system favors larger major parties; as a result, there are only two political parties in the Bahamas, the Progressive Liberal Party and the Free National Movement.

CITIZENSHIP

Every person born on Bahamian territory to Bahamian parents or born abroad to a father who has Bahamian citizenship automatically attains citizenship. Others may apply for citizenship under certain conditions—children born to foreign parents in the Bahamas, children born abroad to a mother with Bahamian citizenship, or women married to Bahamian men.

FUNDAMENTAL RIGHTS

Individual fundamental rights are protected under Chapter III of the constitution. The rights granted are mainly the classic liberal rights. Protection is given to life, liberty, and the security of the person; to freedom of conscience, expression, assembly, and association; all are ensured by the protection of the law. Protection from discrimination on grounds of race, origin, color, religion, or sex is strongly emphasized. Redress for violations of fundamental rights may be sought in the Supreme Court without prejudice to any other legal action.

Fundamental rights are limited by the rights and freedoms of others or the public interest. Generally, funda-

mental rights and freedoms are respected by Bahamian public authorities.

ECONOMY

The country's economy is market based. The constitution provides for the protection of property as a fundamental right in Section 27.

RELIGIOUS COMMUNITIES

The constitution grants freedom of conscience, religious belief, and observance. There is no established or official state religion. Religious communities have the same rights and obligations as most legal entities.

MILITARY DEFENSE AND STATE OF EMERGENCY

The Bahamas has a small army made up of volunteers. There is no conscription. The army is under the control of civilian authority.

The governor-general has the power to declare a state of public emergency. The proclamation is generally valid for 14 days and may be extended to a maximal period of six months. It may be revoked by the House of Assembly.

AMENDMENTS TO THE CONSTITUTION

Amendments to essential provisions of the constitution, such as guarantees of fundamental rights or matters relating to the cabinet or the judiciary, require the approval of three-fourths of all the members of each house of Parliament. All other provisions may be altered with the approval of two-thirds of all the members of each house. In addition, any amendment to the constitution must be approved by a majority of the electors in a popular referendum.

PRIMARY SOURCES
Constitution in English. Available online. URL: http://www.georgetown.edu/pdba/Constitutions/Bahamas/bah73.html. Accessed on September 17, 2005.

SECONDARY SOURCES
Order for the Company of Adventurers for the Plantation of the Islands of Eleutheira. Available online. URL: http://www.jabezcorner.com/Grand_Bahama/1647_articles.htm (accessed June 21, 2005). Accessed on September 8, 2005.

Larissa Zabel

BAHRAIN

At-a-Glance

OFFICIAL NAME
Kingdom of Bahrain

CAPITAL
Manama

POPULATION
677,886, including 235,108 nonnationals (July 2004 est.)

SIZE
280 sq. mi. (712 sq. km)

LANGUAGES
Arabic

RELIGIONS
Predominantly Muslim (est. Shia 70%, Sunni 30%), Jewish, Christian, and Hindu minorities

NATIONAL OR ETHNIC COMPOSITION
Bahraini 63%, Asian 19%, other Arab 10%, Iranian 8%

DATE OF INDEPENDENCE OR CREATION
August 15, 1971 (from U.K.)

TYPE OF GOVERNMENT
Constitutional hereditary monarchy

TYPE OF STATE
Unitary state

TYPE OF LEGISLATURE
Bicameral parliament

DATE OF CONSTITUTION
December 6, 1973

DATE OF LAST AMENDMENT
February 14, 2002

After almost three decades during which Bahrain's constitution had been suspended, the ruler of Bahrain promulgated a thoroughly amended constitution on February 14, 2002. In 2001, a general referendum had approved the National Action Charter, a document specifying some of the planned amendments. Nonetheless, the status of the constitution of 2002 remains politically contested. While the government views the constitutional amendments as legitimized by the referendum, opposition groups have questioned the procedural legality of this process. Moreover, these groups also raise objections regarding the contents of some amendments, most notably the bicameral nature of the parliament, the National Assembly. The constitution of 2002 has introduced an appointed Consultative Council (*majlis ash-shura*) as an upper house, complementing the elected Chamber of Deputies (*majlis an-nuwwab*). The ongoing political debate on this issue may well result in further amendments.

The 2002 constitution explicitly bases the political system on both the Islamic concept of consultation (*shura*) and "the whole human heritage in both East and West."

It transforms the "State of Bahrain" into the "Kingdom of Bahrain," thus elevating the *amir* to a king. It provides for a separation of powers among the legislative, executive, and judicial branches. Universal suffrage for all Bahrainis, male and female, is guaranteed.

As head of state, the king appoints the prime minister and the cabinet. Although not stipulated in the constitution, in practice, ministers holding central portfolios (defense, foreign affairs, interior, oil) are chosen from the ranks of the ruling family.

Political and civil rights are guaranteed without discrimination on the basis of origin, language, religion, creed, or sex, except in matters concerning personal status such as marriage or inheritance. Civil rights may effectively be limited when their expression violates fundamental religious beliefs or endangers national unity. The constitution also guarantees social and economic rights within an overall free market economy.

Islam is the state religion, but non-Muslim minorities, including nonmonotheistic ones, are free to practice, maintain places of worship, and display religious symbols.

CONSTITUTIONAL HISTORY

The islands' ruling family, the Al Khalifa, who originated in the interior of Arabia, established themselves on the Gulf archipelago of Bahrain in the late 18th century. From the beginning of the 19th century, Bahrain was under British domination. In the 1930s, calls for popular participation and constitutionalism surfaced, taking on an anticolonial tone by the 1950s. Only when independence from the United Kingdom was achieved in 1971 was a first constitution drafted. Late that year, spurred at least in part by Iranian claims on Bahraini territory, the then-*amir,* Shaykh Issa b. Salman Al Khalifa, decided to introduce a constitution "on democratic principles." Subsequently, he ordered the formation of a 40-man constituent assembly, of which 22 members were elected by a general if exclusively male vote. The constitution, promulgated on December 6, 1973, established a system with a separation of powers, but the executive remained dominant as the legislative power was "vested in the Amir and the (unicameral) National Assembly." Roughly two-thirds of its members were elected by universal male suffrage. Ministers were considered ex officio members.

After a conflict over a drastic security bill proposed by the government, the *amir* dissolved the National Assembly on August 26, 1975, thus effectively suspending the constitution after only two years. Demands to resume constitutional and parliamentary life were frequently raised, notably in several popular petitions during the 1990s. In 1992, the government attempted to counter these demands by establishing an appointed consultative council, but violent protests began in 1994. After rising to power upon his father's death in 1999, Shaykh Hamad b. Issa Al Khalifa embarked on a far-reaching reform program. An appointed committee was charged with drafting a "National Action Charter." In an attempt to establish a new contract between the ruler and the ruled, the document proposed to reinstate constitutional life, expand public participation, and hold free elections. The charter included a call to transform the State of Bahrain into the Kingdom of Bahrain and a proposal for a bicameral legislature. The National Action Charter was accepted in a popular referendum on February 14, 2001, by 98.4 percent of the votes. One year later, on February 14, 2002, the ruler promulgated the amended constitution without further referendum.

FORM AND IMPACT OF THE CONSTITUTION

The constitution is contained in a written document. International law must be transformed into national law in order to be applicable within the country.

BASIC ORGANIZATIONAL STRUCTURE

Bahrain is subdivided into five governorates (*muhafazat*) and 12 municipalities (*manatiq* or *baladiyyat*). Municipal council members are elected, but the main legislative and administrative functions are assigned to the central government.

LEADING CONSTITUTIONAL PRINCIPLES

Bahrain is a hereditary monarchy based on the Islamic heritage of counsel (*shura*) and popular participation. Primogeniture within the ruling family is specified. The Islamic Sharia is "a," not "the" principal source of government. According to Article 1 of the constitution, "the system of government is democratic, sovereignty being in the hands of the people, the source of all powers," but other constitutional articles show a concentration of power with the king. The separation of powers is not very rigid. Article 32 states: "Legislative authority is vested in the King and the National Assembly in accordance with the constitution. Executive authority is vested in the King together with the Council of Ministers and Ministers, and judicial rulings are issued in his name."

CONSTITUTIONAL BODIES

The main bodies are the king, the Council of Ministers, the bicameral National Assembly, and the judiciary, including the Constitutional Court. A financial control office charged with budget supervision has also been established.

The King

The king is the head of state and exercises his powers directly and through his ministers. He appoints and dismisses the prime minister, the ministers, and the higher judges. He is the supreme commander of the Defense Force. The king may propose laws and amendments to the constitution, and he may order a popular referendum on important laws.

The Council of Ministers

While the king is part of the executive authority and can choose to chair any cabinet session, the day-to-day business of the administration rests with the Council of Ministers. Among them, the prime minister enjoys a privileged position; unlike any other cabinet minister, the prime minister can not be subjected to a vote of no confidence. The National Assembly can, however, decide by a two-thirds majority that cooperation with the prime minister is not possible. The king will then either dismiss the prime minister or dissolve the Chamber of Deputies.

The National Assembly

The National Assembly consists of the Consultative Chamber (*majlis ash-shura*) and the Chamber of Deputies (*majlis an-nuwwab*). Each chamber has 40 members. The term of office is four years.

Members of the Consultative Chamber are appointed by the king. The chamber has the same legislative power as the Chamber of Deputies but with fewer supervisory powers. The Chamber of Deputies is elected by free, direct, general, and secret ballot. In addition to its legislative functions, the Chamber of Deputies is entrusted with the governmental supervision.

The Lawmaking Process

Bills are presented by the Council of Ministers to both chambers. Members of either chamber may send proposals to the Council of Ministers, but they cannot themselves draft bills. For a bill to become law, it must be approved by both chambers. If the king returns a draft without approval, it must be reapproved by two-thirds of the National Assembly in order to become law.

The Judiciary

The legal system is based on a mix of British common law and Sharia law, the latter reflecting the one Shiite and two Sunni schools present in Bahrain. The judiciary is organized into two branches, civil law courts and Sharia courts. Only issues related to the personal status of Muslims are within the jurisdiction of the Sharia courts.

The 2002 constitution established a Constitutional Court. Its president and six members are appointed by royal decree. Any legislator, member of the Council of Ministers, or—conditional on relevance in another law case—individual can challenge the constitutionality of laws in the Constitutional Court. Any convictions issued under a law that has been found unconstitutional are automatically null and void.

THE ELECTION PROCESS

All Bahraini men and women over the age of 21 are allowed to vote. Citizens of the other Gulf Cooperation Council states (Saudi Arabia, Kuwait, Qatar, Oman, and the United Arab Emirates) may vote only when they have dual nationality. The minimal age to stand for elections is 30 years.

POLITICAL SOCIETIES

While political parties remain illegal, political societies are allowed to function as parties in most respects. They field candidates for election and act as parliamentary blocs.

CITIZENSHIP

Bahraini citizenship is either acquired by descent from a Bahraini father or granted by merit. The transmission of citizenship through female descent is currently debated. The granting of Bahraini citizenship to military and police staff of foreign origin is politically controversial.

FUNDAMENTAL RIGHTS

Civil liberties include safeguards against illegal searches, arrests, detention, forced confession, and physical and psychological torture, as well as the rights to trial, freedom of conscience, freedom of speech, academic freedom, freedom of the press, privacy of homes, freedom to form associations and trade unions and hold public assembly with prior notification. Social and economic goals are also stated in the constitution, as the state aims to provide education, social security and insurance, housing for the poor, and medical care. The state undertakes to guarantee job opportunities for citizens and fair work conditions.

Impact and Functions of Fundamental Rights

Since the civil and social rights guaranteed in the 2002 constitution are a fairly recent development, a number of laws predating the constitution that limit those rights are still in effect. Amendments to these prereform laws (the penal code, the law on public gatherings, and others) are still being debated in the National Assembly. Stability in government institutions and in society as a whole must be achieved for these rights to be fully exercised.

Limitations to Fundamental Rights

The constitution stipulates that guaranteed freedoms cannot be limited; however, limitations are allowed when national unity is endangered, a situation that remains rather ill defined. Shiites complain of discrimination, especially with regard to job opportunities in the armed forces.

ECONOMY

The constitution guarantees the right to private ownership and freedom of capital. At the same time, it obliges the state to work toward social justice. Natural resources, such as oil and gas, are considered state property. The state aims to foster economic development and works toward the establishment of a unified market for states of the Gulf Cooperation Council. Protection of the environment and wildlife is another stated goal.

RELIGIOUS COMMUNITIES

Islam is the state religion. Jews, Christians, and (exceptionally for the region) nonmonotheistic minorities such as Hindus are free to practice their religion, maintain places of worship, and display religious symbols.

MILITARY DEFENSE AND STATE OF EMERGENCY

The organization of the armed forces is not detailed in the constitution. No general conscription exists. The king is the supreme commander of the Defense Force, which, according to Article 33, "is directly linked to the king, and maintains the necessary secrecy in its affairs." Wars of aggression are forbidden. Defensive war and martial law are declared by royal decree and then presented to the National Assembly, which must consent.

AMENDMENTS TO THE CONSTITUTION

A majority vote of two-thirds of the members of both parliamentary chambers, fully assembled, is required to pass any amendment to the constitution. The state religion, the system of constitutional monarchy, civil liberties and equality, and the bicameral system cannot be amended.

PRIMARY SOURCES

Constitution in English. Available online. URL: http://www.bahrain.gov.bh/pdfs/constitutione.pdf. Accessed on June 17, 2006.
Constitution in Arabic. Available online. URL: http://www.bahrain.gov.bh/pdfs/constitution.pdf. Accessed on July 24, 2005.

SECONDARY SOURCES

Michael Herb, "Princes and Parliaments in the Arab World." *Middle East Journal* 58, no. 3 (summer 2004): 367–384.
Hassan Ali Radhi, *Judiciary and Arbitration in Bahrain: A Historical and Analytical Study*. London and New York: Kluwer Law International, 2003.

Katja Niethammer

BANGLADESH

At-a-Glance

OFFICIAL NAME
People's Republic of Bangladesh

CAPITAL
Dhaka

POPULATION
144,319,630 (July 2005, est.)

SIZE
55,813 sq. mi. (147,570 sq. km)

LANGUAGES
Bangla (only official language), English, Urdu

RELIGIONS
Muslim 88.3%, Hindu 10.5%, Buddhist 0.6%,
Christian 0.3%, other 0.3%

NATIONAL OR ETHNIC COMPOSITION
Bengalian 98%, tribal groups, non-Bengali Muslim

DATE OF INDEPENDENCE OR CREATION
December 16, 1971

TYPE OF GOVERNMENT
Parliamentary democracy

TYPE OF STATE
Unitary state

TYPE OF LEGISLATURE
Unicameral parliament

DATE OF CONSTITUTION
November 4, 1972

DATE OF LAST AMENDMENT
May 16, 2004

Bangladesh is a parliamentary democracy based on nationalism, democracy, socialism, and Islam. The legislative and executive are divided; the judiciary is independent in the higher courts but forms part of the executive in the lower courts. Bangladesh is a unitary state with a tendency toward decentralization. The country is subdivided into administrative divisions.

The constitution contains a large section on human rights, but their enforcement has not always been guaranteed. The Supreme Court has jurisdiction over violations of fundamental rights, but the exercise of this jurisdiction is limited by a vast backlog of cases.

The president is the ceremonial head of state; executive power rests with the prime minister, who is selected by the president. The president receives advice from the prime minister in almost all matters. The unicameral parliament is composed of members who are elected by universal suffrage.

Although Islam is the state religion, other religious organizations are allowed to exercise their faith. The economy is socialist with an ever-increasing proportion of private businesses.

CONSTITUTIONAL HISTORY

Bangladesh is a relatively young country, having attained independence only in 1972, but it has a rich and diverse cultural and legal history. It is located to the east of today's India in an area formerly known as East Bengal.

In about 300 B.C.E. Bengal formed the eastern part of the Mauryan Empire, the first great Indian empire, which stretched over almost the entire subcontinent. Bengal was only loosely attached to the succeeding Indian empires, and in about 750 C.E., it won independence under a Buddhist dynasty, which was then replaced by Hindu rulers. In 1203, the last Hindu ruler was overthrown by Muslims who owed allegiance to the Pathan Empire, a state to the northwest of Bengal ruled by Sunni Muslims. Bengal paid tribute in the form of war elephants. After some decades of independence in the 14th and 15th centuries, Bengal was incorporated into the Mughal Empire, the most powerful state in India and Pakistan in the 16th and 17th centuries. Under the Mughals, Bengal's integration into the subcontinent began. However, because of its remoteness from

75

the center and poor lines of communication, the region retained some independence.

In the mid-17th century, the British East India Company established a trading outpost in Bengal and began gaining influence. In 1757, the British gained formal control over Bengal in exchange for an annual tribute to the Mughal emperor.

In the 19th century, Indians launched several rebellions against the British. The most severe, which occurred in 1858, led to the formal transfer of power from the East India Company to the British Crown and the incorporation of Bengal into India. The administration installed by the British was made up mostly of Hindus; Muslim Bengalis were not allowed to join the military.

As early as 1875, the Muslim leader Sir Syed Amad Khan proposed a two-nation theory to improve the status of Muslims in India. At first, Muslims were discouraged from joining the Indian National Congress (INC) that was founded by Hindus in 1885. Eventually, Muslims succeeded in installing a voting system in the INC, based on religious affiliation. In 1906, Aga Khan founded the Muslim League. Attempts at cooperation between the INC and the Muslim League failed because the Government Act of 1919, which provided for separate electorates, assured a Muslim majority in only one province. In Bengal, which was clearly Muslim, Hindus still controlled the provincial government.

After World War II (1939–45), general elections in 1946 resulted in a major victory for the Muslim League in Bengal. The state then threw its support behind the establishment of an independent Pakistan, which the British government opposed. When the British tried to pass power to the INC in British India, the Muslim League threatened to declare independence anyway. In 1947, Britain decided on independence for two states. Their original plan included an option for Bengal to obtain independence on its own. But Nehru opposed this plan, and in the end, Bengal was given the choice of joining either Pakistan or India. The Bengal legislative assembly voted to be incorporated into Pakistan as long as the state was not divided. The Hindu-dominated western part of Bengal, however, decided to split off and be incorporated into India. After bloody struggles, when, on August 15, 1947, the two countries gained independence, the Hindu-majority areas joined India, and East Bengal joined Pakistan.

Under the 1935 Government of India Act, all of Pakistan was ruled by a strong governor-general, who appointed the governors of each province. East Bengal soon was given a government of the Urdu-speaking minority (Urdu is the dominant language of today's Pakistan). The struggle in the province increased when the Muslim League clashed with other Muslim parties in elections and strikes after the elections. In 1956, the Pakistani constitution was adopted, and East Bengal became East Pakistan. However, unrest and political turmoil did not cease; in fact, political instability became a major feature of both sections of the Pakistan state.

The constitution established that although East Pakistan held 56 percent of the population, West and East Pakistan must be represented equally in parliament. This led to the underrepresentation of the east.

East Pakistanis felt that they were subordinated to West Pakistan. Only two Bengalis were part of the Pakistani government in the early 1950s, and in the military there were few Bengalis, as they had been deemed a nonmartial race under British rule and thus were never allowed to join the army.

In 1962, a new constitution was enacted for Pakistan, but it was suspended so soon that, practically, it never had effect. The frictions between East and West led to the founding of the East Pakistan Awami Muslim League to promote Bengali interests, later called the Awami League. From the 1960s, this party sought autonomy for East Pakistan. In the national elections of 1970–71, the Awami League won almost all East Pakistani seats for the national assembly and was by far the strongest power in the joint parliament. Talks were opened on constitutional amendments and changes in government, but they eventually failed. The Pakistani president suspended parliament indefinitely, and unrest followed in East Pakistan. On March 26, 1971, after brutal repression from the Pakistani military, the East proclaimed its independence as the People's Republic of Bangladesh. Because of refugee pressure along India's borders, India intervened, and on December 16, 1971, the Pakistani forces surrendered.

On November 4, 1972, Bangladesh adopted its constitution, which is still in force today. The constitution established a secular, nationalist, democratic, and socialist Bangladesh and was modeled on the Indian constitution, although omitting India's federalism. It created a strong executive prime minister and a ceremonial head of state, the president.

The nationalization of manufacturing and trading, begun after independence from Pakistan, became an enormous burden for the government because the economic situation was deteriorating rapidly. In 1974, the president declared a state of emergency and had the constitution amended to limit legislative and judiciary powers as well as to establish a strong president. A one-party system was instituted. In August 1975, the president and his family were assassinated.

An era of military coups and martial law administrations followed. In 1977, the constitution was amended to abolish secularism and introduce Islam as the sole basis for state policy. The one-party system was abolished. Only in the mid-1980s were the political agenda liberalized and attempts at decentralization undertaken. In 1986, the constitution was amended to confirm previous actions under martial law. After this amendment, martial law was lifted. In 1988, the constitution was further amended to proclaim Islam as the state religion. Opposition parties fought the government and the present system of a strong president. Violence and demonstrations then led to the resignation of the president.

In 1991, free elections were held, and the electorate approved of several constitutional amendments reestablishing the parliamentary system and reducing the president to a ceremonial role. This new start was followed by opposition attacks on the government and civil unrest in many parts of the country. In 1996, a constitutional amendment introduced a new constitutional body—the "nonparty caretaker government," which was to assume office during elections. Nevertheless, the situation in Bangladesh had not stabilized by the first years of the 21st century.

FORM AND IMPACT OF THE CONSTITUTION

Bangladesh has a single written constitution. It is the supreme law of the state, and all national laws derive their validity from it. According to Article 7 of the constitution, any law inconsistent with it is void. The constitution also provides for voiding all laws that are not in conformity with the fundamental rights enumerated in Articles 26–47. Its importance is further derived from the fact that it is the founding document of an independent Bangladesh and therefore the result of centuries of struggle for independence. The constitution has been repeatedly changed and amended during its more than 30 years of existence.

BASIC ORGANIZATIONAL STRUCTURE

Bangladesh is a unitary state, but for administrative purposes, it is subdivided into several levels (six divisions, 64 districts, 464 subdistricts, and 4,451 unions). Since the 1980s, the governments of Bangladesh have tried to decentralize authority by strengthening local bodies. Parliament has given elected local governments powers of taxation and responsibilities for public services, economic development, and the maintenance of public order. The most important local body is the *union parishad,* the members of which are elected and represent the views of the villages under its jurisdiction.

LEADING CONSTITUTIONAL PRINCIPLES

Bangladesh is a parliamentary democracy based on nationalism, socialism, and, since a constitutional amendment in 1977, Islam. Since 1988, Islam has been the state religion (Article 2A), but other religions can be practiced in "peace and harmony." The constitution contains a section on fundamental principles of state policy and a separate section on fundamental rights. The fundamental principles include the participation of women, the promotion of local government, free education, and separation of the judiciary and executive. These principles cannot be enforced by court rulings. The constitution attempts to achieve socialism through the means of democracy. Socialism, according to the constitution, means economic and social justice.

CONSTITUTIONAL BODIES

The Bangladeshi constitution provides for the following main constitutional bodies: the president, the prime minister and cabinet, a special government body called "Non-Party Caretaker Government," the unicameral parliament, and the judiciary, consisting of a Supreme Court and subordinate courts.

The President

The president is the constitutional head of state of the People's Republic of Bangladesh. Constitutionally, the president has discretion in the appointment of the prime minister and the chief justice and the authority to administer mercy and grant pardons. The president also formally appoints the cabinet ministers after the prime minister has chosen the candidates and is commander in chief of the military. The president takes precedence over all other citizens. All actions of the executive are to be expressed in the name of the president.

The president has a rather ceremonial position; he or she is obliged to follow the advice of the prime minister in all matters not related to those mentioned earlier. Whether or not advice was given cannot be challenged in courts. The executive power therefore rests with the prime minister.

The president is elected for a five-year term by parliament and can hold office for a maximum of two terms, even nonconsecutively. Candidates for the presidency must be 35 years of age or older. The president can be removed from office by parliament through an impeachment process or on grounds of incapacity.

The Prime Minister and the Cabinet

The prime minister is the key executive figure in Bangladesh. All executive power is to be exercised by or on the authority of the prime minister. The prime minister is appointed by the president and must be a member of parliament. The president is obliged to select a member who appears to have a majority in parliament. Thus the president regularly selects from among the winning party in parliamentary elections.

The prime minister is the head of the cabinet and determines the number of ministers, ministers of state, and deputy ministers. At least 90 percent of the cabinet should consist of members of parliament; the remainder can be chosen from among independent persons who are not disqualified from running for parliament. The cabinet is collectively responsible to parliament.

The prime minister can ask the president to dismiss any of the cabinet ministers at any time, and the cabinet is deemed to have resigned when the prime minister resigns from office or ceases to be a member of parliament. If parliament gives a no-confidence vote, the prime minister may ask the president to dissolve parliament. The president then has the choice either to choose a new prime minister or to dissolve parliament.

The House of the Nation (Parliament)

The Bangladeshi parliament (House of the Nation) is the central legislative organ in the People's Republic. It is a unicameral body with 300 seats. The most recent constitutional amendment, in effect since May 2004, enlarged the body on a preexisting provision with an additional 45 seats, which are all reserved for women. These 45 seats are to be filled in proportion to the representation of parties in parliament. Members of parliament enjoy immunity for actions in parliament. The majority in parliament often takes the form of a coalition, as many parties are elected to parliament.

Parliament is summoned and dissolved by the president. Its legislative powers are limited only by the constitution. Parliament has power over taxation and must approve the budget.

Every person over 25 years of age who is not disqualified by constitutional provisions is eligible to run for parliament. Members of parliament are elected by universal suffrage from single constituencies in a "first-past-the-post" system. They serve for a period of five years. Members of parliament lose their seats if they leave the party that nominated them or vote against that party in parliament.

The Lawmaking Process

Every bill passed in parliament must be presented to the president for assent. If the bill is not returned within 15 days, it is deemed to have received assent. If the president returns the bill with a message detailing concerns and requesting reconsideration, parliament deliberates and votes again. This time, a majority of the total members of parliament must vote in favor. It is then returned to the president, who then must assent to it. The president does not have the right to veto any bills concerning financial issues such as taxes or borrowing.

The Nonparty Caretaker Government

After political turmoil in the mid-1990s and national boycotts by opposition parties, parliament enacted the 13th constitutional amendment that established a neutral body to conduct parliamentary elections: the nonparty caretaker government. It comes into existence when parliament is dissolved and ceases to exist once the new prime minister has entered office.

The nonparty caretaker government is headed by the chief adviser, who is either the immediate former chief justice or another former chief justice, and consists of not more than 10 advisers who cannot be members of political parties. They are appointed by, and responsible to, the president and perform the administrative duties of government but do not make policy decisions.

The purposes of the caretaker government are to ensure fair elections and to prevent the executive from influencing the election process.

The Judiciary

The Bangladeshi constitution contains a large section on the judiciary and proclaims freedom of the judiciary from the executive power. It consists of the Supreme Court, the higher courts, and lower courts. While the Supreme Court and higher courts have displayed a certain degree of independence, the lower courts are still controlled by the executive and deemed part of it. The highest court in the country is the Supreme Court, which comprises an Appellate Division and a High Court Division. The Supreme Court is the guardian of the constitution, and its decisions are binding on all lower courts.

The Appellate Division is headed by the chief justice, who is appointed by the president. It hears appeals from decisions of the High Court Division on questions of constitutional interpretation, capital cases, and cases that the Appellate Division grants leave to appeal. The president can refer any matter of importance to the Appellate Division for deliberation and an advisory opinion.

The High Court Division not only has jurisdiction over decisions of subordinate courts in civil and criminal matters but also has original jurisdiction. Especially in questions of fundamental rights, the High Court Division can, upon application of an aggrieved person, issue orders and directions. It also has the constitutional right to transfer cases from lower courts to its own jurisdiction.

Lower courts exist on division, district, subdistrict, union, and local levels, with magistrates and judges appointed by the president.

In 2001, the Appellate Division of the Supreme Court affirmed a High Court Division order to the government of 1997 to separate the judiciary from the executive. While the judgment has not yet been implemented, the Supreme Court has granted extensions, as the government has shown itself willing to cooperate. The Supreme Court expects a timeline of six to seven years for full implementation.

In addition to the court system, there is an informal system of justice that takes care of approximately two-thirds of all cases on the local level. The disputes are decided by members of the local government.

THE ELECTION PROCESS

All Bangladeshis over the age of 18 have the right to vote in elections. Parliamentary elections follow the first-past-the-post system.

POLITICAL PARTIES

Bangladesh has had a pluralistic party system from its inception. However, strong presidents and military interventions assured that up until the 1990s, there was a tendency for powerful single parties to dominate parliamentary elections.

In 1975, a formal one-party system was created by a constitutional amendment, but by 1978, restrictions on parties were removed. Up to the present, opposition parties in parliament tend to distrust the ruling parties, with resulting strikes and civil unrest.

There are no explicit provisions on political parties in the constitution.

CITIZENSHIP

The constitution contains no provisions on citizenship, but it includes references to citizenship laws enacted in 1972 and 1978. Bangladeshi citizenship is primarily acquired by birth in the country or to a Bangladeshi father abroad. As Bangladesh, with approximately 2,500 inhabitants per square mile, has the highest population density in the world, immigration was never as common as emigration. Under the 1978 Citizenship Act, foreign women can obtain Bangladeshi citizenship if they are married to a Bangladeshi and have resided in Bangladesh for a minimum of two years. Any other person can obtain citizenship after five years of residence. Dual citizenship is prohibited.

FUNDAMENTAL RIGHTS

Part III of the constitution, directly following the fundamental principles of state policy, is a section of 23 articles on fundamental rights. These fundamental rights can be enforced by the Supreme Court. Any provisions in a law found to be not in accordance with fundamental rights are considered void. The fundamental rights section includes all classic human rights. The constitution differentiates between citizens' rights and universal rights that apply to citizens and noncitizens alike.

Citizens' rights include equality before the law; prohibition of discrimination; equal opportunity in public employment; freedom of assembly, movement, association, thought, speech, and conscience; freedom of profession; freedom of religion; and protection of privacy. Fundamental rights awarded to all persons include the right to life and personal liberty, habeas corpus, and prohibition of forced labor.

Impact and Functions of Fundamental Rights

According to all major human rights groups, the enforcement of fundamental rights remains weak today in Ban-

gladesh. The long periods of martial law that started in the mid-1970s and continued until the mid-1980s undermined many fundamental rights. The executive still influences the press and media, thereby inhibiting freedom of speech.

Limitations to Fundamental Rights

Most fundamental rights are not without limits. The constitution imposes several direct limits on certain of them. For example, the prohibition of forced labor can be suspended by any law for public purposes. Various other fundamental rights can be limited for reasons such as morality, decency, public order, or public interest.

ECONOMY

The constitution calls the state the People's Republic of Bangladesh and calls it a socialist country. Therefore, a fundamental principle of state policy is that the people own or control all instruments and means of production and distribution (Article 13). However, this article also allows private ownership.

Shortly after independence and the proclamation of the constitution in the mid-1970s, the difficulties of public ownership became apparent. With the economy slumping, private ownership began to be promoted, and it has since increased. But with changing governments, policies have also changed, and many important areas of the economy remain under government control.

RELIGIOUS COMMUNITIES

Under the heavily contested eighth constitutional amendment, Islam became the state religion of Bangladesh in 1988. However, the constitution grants freedom of religion to all religious communities that practice their faith peacefully. The first constitution stated that Bangladesh was a secular state, but this was repealed in 1977 when Islam was proclaimed the solitary base of the state.

Bangladeshis have a long record of amicable relations among faiths. Religious organizations are not required to register with government agencies and can build houses of worship, travel freely, and proselytize. However, if they receive foreign financial aid, they must register with the Nongovernmental Organizations Affairs Bureau, which can deny and cancel the registration and block foreign financial aid to religious communities.

The government supports Muslim, Hindu, Buddhist, and Christian houses of worship with grants. Religious education is part of the curriculum of government schools. Parents have the right to have their children taught their own religion.

MILITARY DEFENSE AND STATE OF EMERGENCY

The armed forces of Bangladesh are divided into the army, navy, and air force, with the president as commander in chief. Bangladesh has never known conscription, but the Bangladesh Army Act provides for its possible introduction. Persons can enter the military from the age of 16 onward. The army of 110,000 is a defensive military. The navy and air force are each made up of 7,000 people. Since its independence, Bangladesh has not engaged in any wars. The military has been called upon to provide assistance during catastrophes and internal struggles, especially during the regularly occurring flooding of the country during the monsoon.

The constitution makes only marginal provisions for the military, mainly declaring the president to be commander in chief and specifying parliament's budgetary role. Most military policy and regulation is left to acts of parliament.

Bangladesh's military takes an active part in United Nations Peace Keeping Missions; Bangladeshi service members have done duty in many areas of conflict around the world.

A state of emergency can be proclaimed by the president and is valid for up to 120 days, if parliament does not prolong it. The proclamation can be issued in advance of the emergency if there is imminent external or internal danger. The state of emergency permits the suspension of freedom of movement, assembly, association, thought, conscience and speech, and profession, as well as property rights. The president can suspend the judicial enforcement of fundamental rights for the duration.

AMENDMENTS TO THE CONSTITUTION

The Bangladeshi constitution has been changed several times since its enactment.

Amendments or revisions of the constitution require a two-thirds majority of the total members of parliament. The president has no veto power. Any amendment to Article 8 (the fundamental principles of state policy), Article 48 (on presidential elections), Article 56 (on the appointment of the prime minister and cabinet ministers), and Article 142 (on amendments) has to be referred by parliament to a popular referendum.

PRIMARY SOURCES

Constitution in English. Available online. URL: http://www.pmo.gov.bd/constitution/index.htm. Accessed on August 17, 2005.
Bangladeshi Constitution (bilingual edition), *The Constitution of the People's Republic of Bangladesh.* Dhake: Ministry of Law, Justice and Parliamentary Affairs, 2000.

SECONDARY SOURCES

A. K. M. Shamsul Huda, *The Constitution of Bangladesh.* Chittagong: Rita Court, 1997.
Mahmudul Islam, *Constitutional Law of Bangladesh.* 2d ed. Dhaka: Mullick Brothers, 2002.
Library of Congress Country Study (early 1990s): Available online. URL: http://lcweb2.loc.gov/frd/cs/bdtoc.html. Accessed on September 13, 2005.

Oliver Windgätter

BARBADOS

At-a-Glance

OFFICIAL NAME
Barbados

CAPITAL
Bridgetown

POPULATION
279,254 (July 2005 est.)

SIZE
166 sq. mi. (431 sq. km)

LANGUAGES
English

RELIGIONS
Protestant 67% (Anglican 40%, Pentecostal 8%, Methodist 7%, other 12%), Roman Catholic 4%, unaffiliated or other 29%

NATIONAL OR ETHNIC COMPOSITION
African descent 90%, white 4%, Asian or mixed 6%

DATE OF INDEPENDENCE OR CREATION
November 30, 1966

TYPE OF GOVERNMENT
Parliamentary democracy

TYPE OF STATE
Centralist state

TYPE OF LEGISLATURE
Bicameral parliament

DATE OF CONSTITUTION
November 22, 1966

DATE OF LAST AMENDMENT
None

Barbados is a parliamentary democracy and a constitutional monarchy within the British Commonwealth of Nations. There is a clear division of powers among the executive, the judiciary, and the legislature. The country is organized centrally. Fundamental rights and freedoms enjoy constitutional protection, and effective measures for redress for their violation exist.

The head of state is the British monarch, represented by an appointed governor-general. Political power is exercised by the cabinet, headed by the prime minister. The cabinet relies on parliamentary support. In Parliament, the members of the House of Assembly are elected by popular vote, and the members of the Senate are appointed by the governor-general. The party system is pluralistic.

Freedom of conscience is granted. The state and religious communities are separated. The constitution protects the enjoyment of private property.

CONSTITUTIONAL HISTORY

Although Barbados was a British colony for centuries, the country has a long parliamentary and constitutional history.

The island was settled in 1627 by the British. Production of sugarcane on large plantations operated with African slaves began in the 1640s. In 1639, the island's freeholders formed a House of Burgesses, later to become the House of Assembly; it was only the third representative assembly anywhere in the British Empire.

During Britain's civil wars in the 17th century, Barbados supported the Crown and declared itself independent from Britain. Invaded by a fleet sent by Oliver Cromwell, Barbados had to sign the Charta of Barbados in 1652. Although originally a document of surrender, the Charta was the basis for a considerable measure of local self-governance for centuries. Under the document, executive power was vested in an appointed governor, representing the British monarch. Laws were made by the House of Assembly, in which every parish of the island was equally represented. The House of Assembly retained the right to pass all money bills, including the governor's pay, an effective tool to exert control over the colonial administration.

The franchise was based on property, reducing the electorate to a small group of wealthy male landowners. As a result, the majority of the population of African descent was excluded from the electoral process even after slavery was abolished in 1834–38. An executive committee to support the governor with functions similar to those of a cabinet was formed in 1881.

Political organization among the black population started in the 1920s. In 1951, universal adult suffrage was introduced, and in 1954, Sir Grantley Adams became the country's first black premier.

From 1958 until 1962, Barbados formed part of the West Indies Federation, which comprised 10 British island colonies in the Caribbean. In 1964, the executive committee was abolished in favor of ministerial government by a cabinet. In 1966, Barbados gained full independence from Great Britain.

Discussions on turning the country into a republic have flared up regularly since the 1970s. A Constitutional Review Commission recommended in 1998 that the country's system of government should be a parliamentary republic with a president as head of state. In January 2005, the Barbadian prime minister announced a referendum on the matter that has not yet taken place.

FORM AND IMPACT OF THE CONSTITUTION

The constitution of Barbados is set out in the Barbados Independence Order 1966. The constitution is the supreme law and prevails over any other law made by Parliament.

BASIC ORGANIZATIONAL STRUCTURE

Barbados is organized centrally. All the country's affairs are administered by the central government and statutory boards. There is no local government.

LEADING CONSTITUTIONAL PRINCIPLES

Barbados is a parliamentary democracy within the British Commonwealth of Nations. At least at present, the country is a constitutional monarchy under the British Crown. Legislative, executive, and judiciary powers are separated, and there is an adequate system of constitutional checks and balances. The judiciary is independent.

CONSTITUTIONAL BODIES

Constitutional bodies are the monarch and governor-general, the cabinet, Parliament, and the judiciary.

The British Monarch and the Governor-General

The head of state is the British monarch, represented by an appointed governor-general, who exercises the executive powers on the advice of the cabinet through appointed officials. In practice, the principal political power lies with the prime minister and the cabinet. However, the governor-general's duty to act on constitutional advice is not legally enforceable.

The Forde Constitutional Review Commission recommended in 1998 that if Barbados should become a republic, the head of state should be a president with Barbadian citizenship, inheriting the present functions and powers of the governor-general. This president should be elected by an Electoral College composed of both houses of Parliament.

The Cabinet

According to the constitution, the cabinet of Barbados, headed by the prime minister, advises the governor-general on the exercise of the executive authority. In practice, however, the prime minister is the most powerful political figure in the executive. The governor-general appoints as prime minister the member of the House of Assembly who commands the support of the majority of that house. The other ministers are appointed from among the members of either house of Parliament.

The cabinet is collectively responsible for its policies to Parliament and may be voted out of office by a vote of no confidence.

The Parliament

The Parliament of Barbados is based on the Westminster model. It is composed of the British monarch and the two houses of Parliament—the House of Assembly and the Senate. The House of Assembly has 30 members who are elected in general elections, providing equal representation for the citizens of each constituency.

The Senate consists of 21 members, all appointed by the governor-general. Twelve are appointed on the advice of the prime minister, two on the advice of the leader of the opposition, and seven at the governor-general's discretion to represent religious, economic, social, or any other interest the governor-general deems appropriate.

The Parliament's term of office is five years.

The Lawmaking Process
Laws are made by Parliament. Bills may be introduced by any member of either house. Passage requires the approval of a majority of votes in both the House of Assembly and the Senate. However, the House of Assembly can ultimately override the Senate's rejection. Money bills containing solely financial provisions can only be introduced in the House of Assembly and may be passed with-

out the Senate's consent. For a bill to go into force, the governor-general's formal assent on behalf of the Crown is required.

The Judiciary

The legal system is based on the British adversarial system in both civil and criminal cases. The judiciary is independent of the executive and the legislative.

The constitution provides for a Supreme Court of Judicature; composed of a High Court and a Court of Appeal. Each of these courts has four judges, with the chief justice presiding in both.

The High Court is the court of original jurisdiction for civil and criminal matters as well as for individual allegations of violations of fundamental rights and freedoms. There is no further constitutional jurisdiction. The High Court's decisions may be appealed in the Court of Appeal.

The court of last instance used to be the Judicial Committee of the Privy Council in London. It has now been replaced by the Caribbean Court of Justice of the Caricom Single Market and Economy (CSME).

Important rulings of the Judicial Committee in recent years concerned the consistency of the death sentence with the constitution of Barbados. At present, a number of cases are pending with the Inter-American Commission on Human Rights challenging the mandatory death sentence for murder without provision for extenuating circumstances.

THE ELECTORAL PROCESS

Any person aged 21 or older is eligible to stand for office as a member of Parliament. Ministers of religion may not run for the House of Assembly, and holders of certain public offices in the judiciary and the executive may not serve in either house of Parliament.

Further details on the electoral process are specified in the electoral law. All citizens aged 18 or older may vote. Constituencies are won by majority of votes.

POLITICAL PARTIES

The party system is pluralistic. However, the electoral system favors major parties, and, as a result, there are only three political parties in Barbados. The two larger parties represented in Parliament are the Barbados Labour Party (BLP) and the Democratic Labour Party (DLP).

CITIZENSHIP

Citizenship is acquired by any person born on Barbadian territory or to a father who is a citizen of Barbados. Women can become citizens by marriage.

FUNDAMENTAL RIGHTS

Chapter III of the constitution provides for the protection of individual rights. It provides protection for life, liberty, and security; for the privacy of an individual's home; against deprivation of property without compensation; and for protection of the law. Additionally, it secures freedom of conscience, of expression, and of assembly and association. Fundamental rights can be limited to protect the rights and freedoms of others or the public interest. Generally, fundamental rights and freedoms are respected by public authorities.

Redress for violations of fundamental rights may be sought in the High Court without prejudice to any other legal action.

ECONOMY

The economy is market based.

The constitution provides for the protection of property as a fundamental right. Deprivation of property is strictly limited and may not be exercised without compensation. Any person claiming such compensation must be given access to the High Court for the determination of his or her rights and the amount of compensation.

RELIGIOUS COMMUNITIES

Freedom of conscience is granted as a fundamental right and the government strives to protect this right. The constitution offers no special protection for any religious community. Ministers of religion are not eligible to become members of the House of Assembly.

MILITARY DEFENSE AND STATE OF EMERGENCY

Barbados has a small army made up of volunteers. The army is responsive to civilian authority. Besides being responsible for national security, the Barbados Defense Force assists the police forces regularly in times of emergency, the sugar harvest, or any other special need.

The power to declare a state of public emergency is vested in the governor-general. The proclamation of a state of emergency is generally valid for one month and may be extended to a period of up to six months. It may be revoked by the House of Assembly.

AMENDMENTS TO THE CONSTITUTION

Amendments to most sections of the constitution require a majority of two-thirds of all the members of each house of Parliament. Amendments establishing new forms of association with any other part of the Commonwealth of Nations require only a simple majority of votes of all members of both houses.

PRIMARY SOURCES
Constitution in English. Available online. URL: http://www.georgetown.edu/pdba/Constitutions/Barbados/barbados66.html. Accessed on September 29, 2005.

SECONDARY SOURCES
Neil Sammonds, "Accountability of the Security Forces in Barbados." In *A Need to Know: The Struggle for Democratic, Civilian Oversight of the Security Sector in British Commonwealth Countries.* London: University of London, Institute of Commonwealth Studies, 2000. Available online. URL: http://www.cpsu.org.uk/downloads/NEED2.pdf. Accessed on April 27, 2005.

Larissa Zabel

BELARUS

At-a-Glance

OFFICIAL NAME
Republic of Belarus

CAPITAL
Minsk

POPULATION
9,950,900 (2005 est.)

SIZE
80,155 sq. mi. (207,600 sq. km)

LANGUAGES
Belarusian, Russian

RELIGIONS
Eastern Orthodox 70%, Roman Catholic 20%, unaffiliated or other 10%

NATIONAL OR ETHNIC COMPOSITION
Belarusian 81.2%, Russian 11.4%, Polish 3.9%, Ukrainian 2.4%, other 1.1%

DATE OF INDEPENDENCE OR CREATION
August 25, 1991

TYPE OF GOVERNMENT
Presidential republic

TYPE OF STATE
Republic

TYPE OF LEGISLATURE
Bicameral parliament

DATE OF CONSTITUTION
March 30, 1994; fundamentally revised by a national referendum November 24, 1996; effective from November 27, 1996; at a national referendum on October 17, 2004, the constitution was changed again when the electorate (allegedly) supported lifting the two-term limit on the presidency.

DATE OF LAST AMENDMENT
October 17, 2004

Belarus is a social state based on democracy and the rule of law; fundamental human rights are acknowledged. Democracy, the rule of law, and human rights have traditionally not existed in Belarus. They have yet to be implemented in all layers of the society.

The country is organized as a unitary republic with a very strong president from whom most political power radiates. According to the constitution, power is divided; it provides for free elections held on the basis of universal, equal, and direct suffrage by secret ballot.

Religious freedom is guaranteed. The constitution does not prescribe any particular economic system, but many features of the old planned economy still exist. The military is subordinated to the president, who is the commander in chief in peace and wartime.

Belarus pledges to make its territory neutral and nuclear-free.

CONSTITUTIONAL HISTORY

The earliest state institutions appeared on the territory of Belarus in the seventh to the ninth century C.E. In the 13th century, the Belarusian principalities participated in the formation of the Grand Duchy of Lithuania.

Starting in 1468, various legal codes were written; because of many inconsistencies in the courts, the grand duke called for a consistent general law, which went into force in 1530. Between 1772 and 1795, Belarus was gradually incorporated into the empire, where there were generally no limits to the czar's authority.

The first Russian Constitution (1906) maintained that autocracy since the powers of the parliament were limited and the ministers were exclusively responsible to the czar.

After a short period of independence from 1918 to 1919, the territory of Belarus was gradually incorporated into the Soviet Union as the Belarusian Soviet Socialist Republic (BSSR).

In the Soviet era, the BSSR saw four different constitutions, each of which was based on the ideology of Marxism-Leninism. As a result of turbulent events in the Soviet Union, BSSR proclaimed its independence on August 25, 1991; subsequently its name was changed to the Republic of Belarus.

In March 1994, Belarus approved a new constitution, which contained provisions for a separation of powers and effective mechanisms of checks and balances. Democracy, protection of human rights, a constitutional court, and a presidential office were also established.

In June 1994, the first presidential elections were held. Alexander G. Lukashenka, who campaigned against corruption and advocated closer ties to Russia and more state control, received 85 percent of the votes in the second round.

Though Lukashenka was elected with an overwhelming majority, conflicts with different parts of the political establishment soon emerged. The Constitutional Court soon found that several of the president's decrees were unconstitutional and, consequently, were invalid. The president reacted by issuing a decree at the end of 1995 obliging the government and local authorities to disregard the court's rulings. This decree was also declared unconstitutional.

The president's relationship to both the pre- and postindependence parliament was also problematic, and Lukashenka twice used national referendums to resolve those conflicts. In both cases the people supported the president, but the November 1996 referendum was very controversial. Lukashenka proposed amendments to the constitution that were so comprehensive that the Constitutional Court considered it to be a new constitutional draft. The court consequently stated that such amendments could not be subject to a referendum because a new constitution cannot be adopted through a plebiscite. Nevertheless, more than 70 percent of the electorate supported the president.

In October 2004, the constitution was changed again as a result of a national referendum, in which the electorate allegedly supported the president's wish to run for a third term, and as such the two-term limit on presidency was abolished.

The amended constitution seems to be influenced by several sources. There are provisions from the American, French, and Soviet constitutions.

FORM AND IMPACT OF THE CONSTITUTION

The constitution is one written document that has supreme legal force. In case of discrepancy between a law, decree, or ordinance and the constitution, the constitution is to prevail.

Though the constitution is relatively new, it has had a major impact because of its differences from the Soviet model. The changes adopted in 1996 have also had a significant impact, since they turned Belarus from a parliamentary to a presidential state, where the president has extensive powers.

BASIC ORGANIZATIONAL STRUCTURE

Belarus is a unitary state, arranged in three tiers: regions, districts, and cities. Local administration is based on local councils and on local executive and administrative authorities. The citizens elect the local councils for a four-year term.

The chairs of the local executive and administrative authorities are appointed and dismissed by the president. Other subnational officials are appointed either by the corresponding legislative bodies or by the head of the local or regional executive branch.

LEADING CONSTITUTIONAL PRINCIPLES

Belarus is defined as a unitary republic and a democratic and social state, based on the rule of law. Furthermore, Belarus pledges to be a neutral and nuclear-free state. The constitution recognizes universal principles of international law and provides that the country ensure that its legislation complies with such principles. It is also stated in the constitution that Belarus recognizes the values common to all humankind.

The constitution stipulates the division of powers, but not consistently. Checks and balances among the branches of government have been supplanted by the domination of the executive.

CONSTITUTIONAL BODIES

The most important body is the presidency. Others are the administration or Council of Ministers, the two chambers of the National Assembly or parliament, and the judiciary, which are all subordinate to the president.

The President

The president is the head of state and the guarantor of stability in the country. The president has a constitutional right to convene and dissolve the parliament and to issue decrees that have the force of laws. The president appoints all significant officeholders both in the central government and in the regions. The president is outside the framework of the separation of powers and coordinates and mediates among the other branches of state power. The president enjoys immunity, and the law protects his or her honor and dignity.

The president is elected directly by the people for a term of five years. The president may be impeached by a two-thirds vote of the deputies in both chambers, and both chambers must act within one month of each other.

The Council of Ministers (The Administration)

The Council of Ministers consists of the prime minister, two vice–prime ministers, and other ministers. The president with the consent of the House of Representatives appoints the prime minister. The Council of Ministers is accountable to the president and responsible to the parliament.

The National Assembly (The Parliament)

The National Assembly is the representative and legislative body. It consists of two chambers, the House of Representatives (the lower chamber) and the Council of the Republic (the upper chamber), which represent the various territories.

Both chambers are elected at the same time for four years. Their sessions begin and end at fixed dates, and they meet for 170 days each year.

The Lawmaking Process

Legislative initiative belongs to the president, the deputies of the two chambers of parliament, the Council of Ministers, and a bloc of a minimum of 50,000 eligible voters. However, only the president and the Council of Ministers have the right to introduce draft laws to the House of Representatives that involve a decrease of state funds or an increase in expenditures.

The Judiciary

The constitution states that judges shall be independent and subordinate to law alone. However, appointment of most judges is under presidential control, and so is dismissal from some of the important judicial posts.

The Constitutional Court

The Constitutional Court, which supervises the constitutionality of all enforceable enactments, can only examine cases on recommendation of the president, the chambers of parliament, the Supreme Court, the Supreme Economic Court, or the Council of Ministers.

The Constitutional Court consists of 12 judges. The president appoints the chairperson and five members, and the Council of the Republic elects the additional six members. Judges serve a term of 11 years.

THE ELECTION PROCESS AND POLITICAL PARTICIPATION

Citizens over the age of 18 are eligible to vote in elections.

Presidential elections and elections to the lower chamber of parliament are free and held on the basis of universal, equal, and direct suffrage by secret ballot. Elections to the upper chamber are partly indirect; in addition, eight of its members are appointed by the president.

Citizens who are at least 35 years old and who have been residents in Belarus for at least 10 years prior to the election may be elected president. To be nominated, candidates need a minimum of 100,000 signatures of eligible voters.

Citizens who are at least 21 years old may be elected to the House of Representatives. One deputy is elected from each of 110 constituencies. Candidates can be nominated by political parties, labor collectives, or citizens.

Citizens who are at least 30 years old and who have been living in the respective region at least five years prior to the election may be elected to the Council of the Republic. The council consists of 64 deputies. Eight are appointed by the president, and eight are chosen from every region and from the capital by deputies of local councils; all members must be approved by the president's representatives in the regions.

Other Forms of Political Participation

It is possible to hold referendums on the national and on the local level, and citizens also have the right to hold rallies, assemblies, marches, demonstrations, and pickets.

POLITICAL PARTIES

Belarus is a pluralistic state where the diversity of political institutions, ideologies, and views is acknowledged.

Political parties need to register with the authorities. There are 17 registered political parties. A few of them support the current regime, while the majority are in the opposition. In general, they enjoy little popular support and have few members. It is possible to ban parties, but this has only happened once.

CITIZENSHIP

Citizenship is primarily acquired by birth. A child born to Belarusian parents becomes a Belarusian citizen, regardless of his or her place of birth.

FUNDAMENTAL RIGHTS

According to the constitution, the people of Belarus adhere to the values common to all humankind. Article 2 states that the supreme goal and value of society and the state are to guarantee the individual his or her rights. The constitution enunciates a long list of fundamental rights and a number of duties.

Belarus is a social state, and thus many social rights are granted to the citizens.

Functions and Impact of Fundamental Rights

Everyone has the right to appeal to international organizations to defend his or her rights, provided all internal state means of legal defense have been exhausted.

Limitations to Fundamental Rights

The constitution provides that restrictions on personal rights and liberties shall be permitted only in the instances specified in law, in the interest of national security, public order, or the protection of the morals and health of the population or the rights and liberties of other persons. No one may enjoy advantages and privileges that are contrary to the law.

ECONOMY

The constitution does not prescribe any particular economic system. Property can be private as well as state owned, but some natural resources can only be state owned. After independence, the privatization of state enterprises began, but from 1995, the political agenda changed, and the process has since dramatically slowed. Nationalization of property is only permitted in case of public need.

The National Bank is under direct governmental supervision, and the president has the right to appoint and dismiss the chairperson and the entire board. The president has dismissed the chairperson only once.

RELIGIOUS COMMUNITIES

Religions and faiths are equal before the law, and everyone is guaranteed freedom of belief. The law states, however, that unregistered religious activity is illegal.

The authority responsible for registration had by January 2002 registered 26 different denominations. They included the traditional Belarusian religious groups, several nontraditional groups, and a few Eastern religious groups.

MILITARY DEFENSE AND STATE OF EMERGENCY

The constitution expects Belarus to defend its independence, territory, and constitutional system and to safeguard law and order. Every citizen is responsible for defending the country. Men are required to perform 18 months of military service from the age of 18. The president is the commander in chief, and he or she also appoints the heads of the Security Council. The president can impose martial law, announce mobilization, and declare a state of emergency.

The powers of parliament may be extended in the event of war.

AMENDMENTS TO THE CONSTITUTION

Only the president or a minimum of 150,000 citizens can initiate changes to the constitution. The issues in question must be debated and approved twice by at least two-thirds of both chambers of parliament, which must act with at least a three-month interval between the two votes in each house.

Sections one, two, four, and eight, which concern the principles of the constitutional system, can be amended only by a referendum. The constitution cannot be changed during a state of emergency or during the last six months of the term of the House of Representatives.

PRIMARY SOURCES
Constitution in English. Available online. URL: http://www. belarus.net/costitut/constitution_e.htm. Accessed on September 20, 2005.
Constitution in Russian. Available online. URL: http://www.belarus.net/conendru.htm. Accessed on August 19, 2005.

SECONDARY SOURCES
Elena Korosteleva, Colin W. Lawson, Rosalind J. Marsh, eds. *Contemporary Belarus between Democracy and Dictatorship*. London: Routledge, 2002.
Anton Matusevich, "On the State of Legislation in the Republic of Belarus: Politics and Law." *Belarusian Journal of International Politics* 1 (1997): 2–6.
Alexander Danilovich, "Understanding Politics in Belarus, 2001." Available online. URL: www.demstar.dk/papers/Belarus.pdf. Accessed on August 2, 2005.

Susanne Hansen

BELGIUM

At-a-Glance

OFFICIAL NAME
Kingdom of Belgium

CAPITAL
Brussels

POPULATION
10,309,700 (2005 est.)

SIZE
11,799 sq. mi. (30,559 sq. km)

LANGUAGES
Dutch, French, German

RELIGIONS
Roman Catholic 70%, Protestant 1%, Muslim 4%, nonbelievers and small religious groups 25%

NATIONAL OR ETHNIC COMPOSITION
Dutch-speaking region 57.81%, French-speaking region 31.95%, bilingual region of Brussels-Capital 9.56%, German-speaking region 0.68%

DATE OF INDEPENDENCE
November 18, 1830

TYPE OF GOVERNMENT
Parliamentary monarchy

TYPE OF STATE
Federal state that grew out of a unitary decentralized state

TYPE OF LEGISLATURE
Bicameral parliament (federal), asymmetric regional structures

DATE OF CONSTITUTION
February 7, 1831

DATE OF LAST AMENDMENT
March 26, 2005

Belgium is a parliamentary democracy based on the rule of law with a division of executive, legislative, and judicial powers. At the same time, it is a constitutional monarchy. Belgium has three communities: the French, the Flemish, and the German. It is divided into three regions (the Walloon Region, the Flemish Region, the Brussels-Capital Region). The constitution offers adequate guarantees for the protection of human rights. There is a Court of Arbitration that determines whether legislation is in compliance with the allocation of powers provided under the constitution and its enabling laws.

The king is the head of state. The monarchy is the living symbol of the continuity of the nation. The real power lies with the administration, which is responsible to Parliament. Democratic elections are compulsory for all citizens 18 years old and older. Belgium has a pluralistic system of political parties. As no political party extends across all the linguistic communities, there are no parties operating on the entire territory of Belgium.

Religious freedom is guaranteed. The state and religious communities are mutually independent. The economic system is a social market economy, with strong but slowly weakening trade unions. The military is entirely subject to the civil government.

CONSTITUTIONAL HISTORY

The Kingdom of Belgium was created in 1830; yet its roots go much deeper. In the late Middle Ages, present-day Belgium was divided into various autonomous counties, principalities, and cities. In the 15th century, the dukes of Burgundy undertook a successful centralization policy, which led to the creation of the 17 provinces covering the current Belgium, the Netherlands, Luxembourg, and parts of northern France. The 17 provinces were linked by dynastic bonds but also by common political institutions.

Mary of Burgundy (1457–82) married Maximilian of Austria, putting the realm under the Habsburg dynasty. The Habsburg Holy Roman Emperor Charles V (1500–58) maintained the centralization policy started by the dukes of Burgundy. His son, Philip II (1527–98), ruled the provinces from Spain, pursuing an absolutist policy at a time of political and religious instability. His unconditional support of the Roman Catholic Church provoked the northern, Protestant part of the 17 provinces to revolt. As a result of the Union of Utrecht (January 1579), an independent state was proclaimed in the north—the Seven United Provinces. The intelligentsia from the south left for the north. This, together with a blockade of the crucial port of Antwerp, led to a deep economic crisis in what was left of the 17 provinces, more or less corresponding with the current Belgium. Political autonomy decreased. Various foreign rulers occupied the country, including the Austrians (1714–94) and the French (1795–1814). At the Convention of Vienna in 1815, Prussia and England wanted to create a barrier against French imperialism by reunifying the old 17 provinces together with the prince-bishopric of Liège. This led to the creation of the United Kingdom of the Netherlands (1814–30), governed by the Dutch king, William I.

The industrial and economic policies conducted by this king were efficient, but in various other fields, William I was less successful. In order to create a spirit of national unity, the king tried to unify the education system under the state and to build a Catholic Church free of foreign control. The powerful Roman Catholic Church opposed both reforms.

Liberals were also disappointed with the king. William I promoted the use of Dutch language, making it mandatory in the administration and to some extent even in the schools of the southern provinces. The liberals did not appreciate this policy, as many of them belonged to the French-speaking upper middle classes; they also opposed the constitution of 1815, which endowed the king with very broad powers. The king considered himself to be vested with all powers that were not formally attributed to some other body.

Ultimately, the king created an almost unanimous feeling of discontent in the south.

Since peaceful opposition was of no avail, a revolution broke out. The September riots of 1830 led to the proclamation of Belgian independence on November 18 of that year. After the first elections, in which only 1 percent of the Belgian population was entitled to vote, the National Congress finalized a draft text for the Belgian constitution. Although the new constitution was influenced by older documents, including the 1815 United Kingdom of the Netherlands constitution and the French constitutions of 1791 and 1830, it was seen as quite innovative. Tolerant liberals and open-minded Catholics found it a very balanced document. Belgium became a constitutional monarchy, with a king who had to accept the responsibility of his government ministers before parliament. Rights and liberties were clearly specified.

The system of parliamentary monarchy introduced in Belgium soon appealed to other nations in Europe. Between 1837 and 1866, the Belgian constitution was more or less copied by other constituent assemblies, such as those of Spain (1837), Greece (1844 and 1864), Luxembourg (1848), Prussia (1850), and Romania (1866). It was a source of inspiration for many other countries.

Today, the 1831 constitution still exists. However, it has undergone some important changes, especially concerning democratic standards and federalism. The first two revisions of the constitution (1893, 1920–21) turned the liberal constitution of 1831 into a really democratic one. In 1831, only persons paying at least a certain amount of taxes were allowed to vote. The 1920–21 revision of the constitution formalized universal adult male suffrage, ratifying a condition that had existed de facto since 1919. The constitution explicitly provided that the right to vote could be extended to women by a two-thirds vote in the parliament. This was done in 1948.

In 1831, Belgium was a unitary state. Since 1970, the country has gradually become a federal state. The fourth state reform of 1992–93 finally stabilized this centrifugal process. The federal character of the state is now solemnly proclaimed in the amended Article 1 of the constitution: "Belgium is a federal state, composed of the communities and the regions."

Belgium is a member state of the European Union and a member of the North Atlantic Treaty Organization (NATO).

FORM AND IMPACT OF THE CONSTITUTION

Belgium has a written constitution, codified in a single document, made and modified by a constituent assembly that uses a procedure more formal and more difficult than the procedure used to pass ordinary federal laws. The constitution is a solemn, rather inflexible set of rules that are the supreme law of the land.

The highest lawmaking authorities are those at the international level. Internally, there are three levels of norm-making authorities. In descending order, they are the constitution-making level, the legislative level, and the executive level.

The constitutionality and the legality of all norms can be reviewed by courts or tribunals or by administrative agencies, with but one exception: the constitution itself. Where fundamental rights and freedoms are concerned, the courts and tribunals must test the legality of a norm in the formal constitution in light of international treaties to which Belgium has adhered.

The Belgian constitution, in the substantive meaning of the word, is not to be found in toto in the text bearing the title of *constitution*, nor is every article of the written constitution truly a fundamental and general rule, concerned with the institution and powers of the state or the rights of the individual. The substantive constitution has many rules originating in other sources than the constituent assembly.

The substantive constitution includes most articles of the formal constitution but also of decrees on legislation passed prior to the 1831 constitution, certain federal acts, and custom or unwritten rules.

BASIC ORGANIZATIONAL STRUCTURE

Belgium is a federal state with a parliamentary system. The country comprises communities and regions. The communities and regions have partly overlapping territories, though their authority covers different subject matters. Moreover, each has its own institutions.

The constitution acknowledges the existence of three communities: the French community, the Flemish community, and the German-speaking community. If *communautarisation* (the creation of the communities) was principally a response to Flemish aspirations, *regionalisation,* the creation of the regions, sought to meet the desire for economic autonomy of the Walloons. Three regions exist: the Walloon region, the Flemish region, and the Brussels-Capital region.

The double set of federated entities has created a complex institutional framework. Each community and each region has a legislative body, called a council, and an administration, called the executive. Yet, instead of six councils and executives, there are in fact only five. In Flanders, the councils and executives of the Flemish community and the Flemish region, though not legally merged, are organized and managed as one entity.

Contrary to the situation in most federal states, the communities and regions in Belgium are not empowered to create the rules concerning their own institutions. They cannot have a constitution of their own. The rules that determine the composition and operation of their institutions are provided for in the federal constitution and in the double and ordinary majority legislation implementing the constitution.

Each of the two types of federal unit has its own exclusive powers. The powers of the communities relate to cultural matters such as education, aspects of health care and social assistance, language, cooperation between the communities, and international cooperation. The regions have broad powers in the economic area, including environment, rural development, housing, nature conservation, water policy, economic affairs, energy policy, public works and transport, and employment policy.

The constitution also recognizes and guarantees the existence of 10 provinces and of an undefined number of municipalities. All these are territorial subdivisions with a political structure that participates in the main functions of the state. They have the power to issue legislation, to shape their own policies in the light of the local general welfare, to raise taxes, and to approve their own budget.

LEADING CONSTITUTIONAL PRINCIPLES

Belgium's system of government is a parliamentary monarchy. There is a strong division of the executive, legislative, and judicial powers, based on checks and balances.

The decision of the National Congress in 1831 to make Belgium a hereditary monarchy was a pragmatic and political choice. On the one hand, a hereditary monarch seemed to allow a more perfect parliamentary system, and on the other hand, a judicious choice of a monarch would make the new state more acceptable to the powers of the time. The parliamentary regime rests upon the principle of periodic free elections to form an assembly competent to create legislation and with the power to control the executive.

The rule of law also is a leading principle. The written constitution sets out and limits the power of the state and of all authorities within the state. The Belgians were of the opinion that people build a state because they need such a social structure. Consequently, the state should be their protector and their servant. In that regard, the first article of the constitution, dealing with the institutions and the powers of the state, clearly states that all powers emanate from the people and must be exercised in the manner established by the constitution.

Other important principles are the equality of all Belgians before the law and the guarantee of individual liberty. The constitution contains a well-elaborated bill of rights that is not limited to Belgians but is extended to all foreigners who find themselves on Belgian territory.

CONSTITUTIONAL BODIES

The main bodies provided for in the constitution are the king, the federal administration, and the Parliament. The Court of Arbitration also plays a vital role. The lawmaking process and the judiciary are worked out in detail.

The King

The king is the head of state. Because the king himself is inviolable and unaccountable, he appoints ministers and state secretaries who are responsible for his acts. Consequently, the constitutional notion of the king refers both to the person of the king himself and to the responsible ministers and state secretaries. The executive has therefore a dualistic structure.

The monarchy is hereditary in the line of natural legitimate heirs of King Leopold I, in order of primogeniture. Since the 1991 revision of the constitution, the succession of the throne has been extended to female descendants.

The king cannot act independently and has no personal power. He exercises all his powers together with the ministers. However, the fact that the king has no personal power does not mean that he has no political influence. That influence can only apply insofar as it is accepted by the ministers and through them by Parliament. The king exercises his political influence most of all during the process of forming a new federal government and through his consultations.

Historically, Belgian kings often saw their role as active participants in politics. For example, King Leopold III found himself in open conflict with his ministers before and during World War II (1938–45). On July 16, 1951, he abdicated under heavy political and social pressure.

King Baudouin, in 1990, refused to sign a liberal law on abortion. To solve the constitutional problem that resulted, Baudouin was declared to be in a state of incapacity. The ministers meeting in council, under their own responsibility, exercised the powers of the king and signed the new law, and the king resumed his functions.

In general, the evolution of Belgium toward a federal state resulted in an increased role for the monarchy, which now functions as a link between the federal entities and a counterbalance to centrifugal tendencies.

The Federal Government

The federal government (administration) is the political nerve center of Belgium. Regional structures are becoming increasingly important, but the federal government remains the dominant factor.

The king appoints the ministers and state secretaries. De facto, he accepts the candidates proposed by the coalition partners in the administration. King Baudouin (1930–93, king since 1951) sometimes refused to appoint ministers he disliked personally. His successor, Albert II, discontinued this debatable tradition.

Since 1970, the constitution requires a balanced composition of the Council of Ministers. With the possible exception of the prime minister, the Council of Ministers is composed of an equal number of French-speaking and Dutch-speaking ministers.

The federal administration is based upon a parliamentary majority. In normal circumstances, the king decides who will form the new administration, most of the time the same person as the future prime minister. However, he does not exercise that role after a "constructive motion of no confidence," when the House of Representatives withdraws its confidence in a "constructive way," by directly appointing a successor to the prime minister at the same time as the no-confidence vote, or within a period of three days after a motion of confidence has been rejected.

The constitution does not provide a solution when this successor fails to form a new administration. However, parliamentary elections are the most likely result.

The Federal Parliament

The federal Parliament has two branches, the House of Representatives and the Senate.

The House of Representatives is composed through direct elections, for a maximal period of four years. The number of members is fixed at 150. The House of Representatives exercises general political control over all the decisions of the federal government. It also plays a key role in the process of legislation, sometimes together with the Senate. The constitution splits federal subject matter into three parts: those in the sole competence of the House of Representatives, those that are equally within the competence of the two houses and require an identical procedure and decision in both, and those in the competence of the House of Representatives but that the Senate may discuss and seek to amend.

The Senate has four categories of members: (1) senators appointed by and from within the councils of the three communities (Flemish, French, and German), (2) senators elected by each language group (Flemish and French), (3) senators co-opted by the senators representing the Flemish or the French citizens, and finally (4) senators by law, namely, the children of the king, or, if the king has no children, the descendants of the reigning branch of the royal family. Currently, the Senate is seen primarily as a place for deeper reflection on issues of importance to the country.

The Lawmaking Process

The initiative for legislation lies with the administration and with each member of the two houses. Once a bill is introduced by the administration, Parliament cannot refuse to discuss it. Each house can refuse to discuss a private member's bill but does so very rarely, for instance, when the proposed text is manifestly unconstitutional.

In case a bill is adopted, the government transmits it to the king, who signs it, sanctions it, and promulgates it as a statute.

The Court of Arbitration

The Court of Arbitration, a constitutional court, was created during the 1980 constitutional revision. The establishment of a constitutional court was an important innovation in Belgian constitutional law. Even in 1980, the innate mistrust of a "government by judges" did not disappear entirely, and the court's jurisdiction was limited to conflicts of power between the various legislatures. This was even reflected in the name given to the court, Court of Arbitration.

The court's jurisdiction was extended during the third state reform in 1988–89. The court was now empowered to review whether legislative norms (federal statutes and decrees, and ordinances of communities and regions) conformed to three constitutionally guaranteed fundamental rights: the principles of equality and nondiscrimination and the right to and freedom of education.

The Judiciary

The judiciary in Belgium is independent of the executive and legislative branches and is a powerful factor in legal life. The Belgian judicial organization is built on two main principles: that there should be a court or tribunal for every dispute and that the ordinary courts and tribunals are competent for all disputes about individual rights.

The ordinary courts and tribunals are organized according to the principles of specialization and territorial justice. In this system, the Cour de Cassation (court of final appeal) is the Supreme Court.

In the realm of administrative courts and tribunals, the highest and most important court is the Council of State, created only in 1946.

THE ELECTION PROCESS AND POLITICAL PARTICIPATION

All representative assemblies are composed through elections organized according to the same principles: universal suffrage in single-member districts, compulsory voting, publicity (transparency), periodic and free elections, secrecy of the vote, and proportionality.

Citizens of the European Union who do not have Belgian nationality but live in Belgium can take part in the elections and in elections for the European parliament, after registration as voters. Starting in 2006, non–European Union residents will also be able to vote in municipal elections.

In the elections, seats are distributed among the districts in proportion to population. Candidates are elected by votes cast for them or for their party via proportional representation.

POLITICAL PARTIES

Belgium has a pluralistic system of political parties. They play an important part in the public life of the country, even though they are not mentioned in the constitution and are merely de facto associations having no legal personality. They receive funding from the state in proportion to their electoral strength.

Since usually no party is able to secure an absolute majority in elections, coalition governments are required. The process of forming an administration after general elections is mainly the result of negotiations among parties. The parties and their leaders, and not the electorate, have the final say. In particular, the growing linguistic and community division of political parties has resulted in an increasing number of parties and in the need to form coalitions across these divides.

CITIZENSHIP

Belgian citizenship is primarily acquired by birth. A person whose father or mother, on the date of birth, is a Belgian national becomes a Belgian citizen, even if that person is born outside Belgium.

Obtaining Belgian citizenship for foreigners living in Belgium has become increasingly easy.

FUNDAMENTAL RIGHTS

Fundamental rights are very important in the Belgian constitution. Their prominent presence in 1831 was one of its main attractions. These rights derive from the following principles:

All human beings are born persons at law. This means that they never can be made into mere objects of law or human actions. This is the reason why slavery, under whatever name or in whatever form, is prohibited.

The recognition of every human as a person is the first step in the recognition of human dignity. This dignity entails further that he or she is entitled to certain care and attention from the society in which he or she lives. This care finds expression in specific rights such as the social, economic, and cultural rights mentioned in the constitution, but also in the right of equal treatment.

Equality is also a key notion. The constitution says that the Belgians are equal before the law. This does not mean that the treatment is materially equal. While equals will be dealt with equally, those who are unequal will be subject of a different legal approach.

Of utmost importance is the principle of legality: A lower norm should always rest upon a higher norm, and a lower norm should never be inconsistent with a higher norm. Since all authorities function under the law, they all have to conform to these highest norms in whatever they do.

A further key idea is the presumption of freedom. The individual is allowed to do everything that is not explicitly forbidden by law.

Finally, there is a ban on preventive measures. This principle is recognized by an unwritten rule with constitutional authority. Preventive measures are interventions by the authorities aimed at preventing the exercise of freedoms by a general rule (e.g., by forbidding all public processions).

The importance of fundamental rights cannot be overestimated. They have a defensive function; yet they also involve the right to participate in the democratic political process. Moreover, they are also an important source of emancipation.

Yet, fundamental rights and freedom are not absolute. They have both natural and legal limits. Three natural limits can be evoked: Rights have no effect outside the context of human existence and activity; they cannot be used in opposition to their reason of existence; the very existence of other persons who have the same personal freedom also constitutes a natural border.

ECONOMY

The Belgian constitution does not specify an economic system. Taken as a whole, the Belgian economic system can be described as a social market economy. The constitution provides for a right to education and guarantees socioeconomic fundamental rights. Some of these socioeconomic fundamental rights are specified in ordinary legislation, such as the right to social relief and assistance.

RELIGIOUS COMMUNITIES

Freedom of religion and belief is constitutionally recognized in Belgium. There is no established church, but the state maintains privileged relationships with six recognized religious groups (Catholics, Protestants, Anglicans, Jews, Muslims, and Orthodox Christians) as well as with nonconfessional humanists. In principle, the salaries and pensions of their ministers are paid for by the state. Separation is not the best way to describe the actual relationships between religion and state; mutual independence gives a better idea. This characterization emphasizes not only freedom but also the notion of accepting each other's existence.

The independence and self-determination of the religious communities are very important. However, in recent years, secular judges have played a greater role in religious administration. They can rule whether a challenged decision by a religious body was made by the right church authority and in accordance with correct internal procedure.

MILITARY DEFENSE AND STATE OF EMERGENCY

The armed forces fall under the competence of the federal government. In matters of national defense, the executive power plays a predominant role, subject to the ordinary procedures of political supervision. The king has the power to command the armed forces, declare war, and conclude peace treaties as well as treaties of alliance and commerce.

Generally, Parliament can intervene only after the decisions have been made. Nevertheless, a prior decision of Parliament is necessary in some cases. It determines the method of recruiting for the army and determines its size.

No foreign troops can be admitted to the service of the state, nor can they occupy or pass through its territory, except by virtue of a law. In pursuance of this provision, a law of 1962 provides that armies of countries that, as is Belgium, are part of NATO may be stationed on Belgian territory or may pass through it. The military always remains subject to civil government, whatever the political or military circumstances.

Compulsory military service no longer exists. When it did, conscientious objection was allowed, with alternative service required, a system that led to some problems with Jehovah's Witnesses.

AMENDMENTS TO THE CONSTITUTION

The constitution forbids all revisions in time of war or periods when the two houses of Parliament cannot converse freely on federal territory. Revision of the article concerning the status and powers of the king is forbidden during times when the king cannot exercise his authority by himself. Otherwise, revision is possible. The constitution provides a somewhat long amendment procedure, requiring the cooperation of two consecutive parliaments and the approval of the text by a two-thirds majority in both houses.

The process has three phases: (1) a statement of revision by the three branches of the federal legislature (House of Representatives, Senate, and king), enumerating the articles of the constitution they think should be revised; (2) the regularly scheduled elections that follow the statement of revision, which allow the voters to elect candidates who represent their views concerning the revision; and (3) the work of the constituent assembly, which is free to revise the constitution or not and to decide the wording of the modifications, within the limits enumerated in the statement of revision.

PRIMARY SOURCES

Constitution in English. Available online. URL: http://www.fed-parl.be/constitution_uk.html. Accessed on August 23, 2005.
Constitution in Dutch. Available online. URL: http://www.senate.be/doc/const_nl.html. Accessed on July 31, 2005.
Constitution in French. Available online. URL: http://www.senate.be/doc/const_fr.html. Accessed on July 26, 2005.
Constitution in German. Available online. URL: http://www.senate.be/doc/const_de.html. Accessed on July 29, 2005.

SECONDARY SOURCES

André Alen, ed., *Treatise on Belgian Constitutional Law.* Deventer and Boston: Kluwer Law and Taxation, 1992.
Godelieve Craenen, ed., *The Institutions of Federal Belgium: An Introduction to Belgian Public Law.* Leuven and Leusden: Acco, 2001.

Rik Torfs

BELIZE

At-a-Glance

OFFICIAL NAME
Belize

CAPITAL
Belmopan City

POPULATION
272,945 (2004 est.)

SIZE
8,867 sq. mi. (22,966 sq. km)

LANGUAGES
English (official), Spanish, Mayan, Garifuna (Carib), Creole

RELIGIONS
Roman Catholic 49.6%, Protestant (Anglican 5.3%, Methodist 3.5%, Mennonite 4.1%, Seventh-Day Adventist 5.2%, Pentecostal 7.4%, Jehovah's Witnesses 1.5%) 27%, none 9.4%, other 14%

NATIONAL OR ETHNIC COMPOSITION
Mestizo 48.7%, Creole 24.9%, Maya 10.6%, Garifuna 6.1%, with minority groups of North Americans, Europeans, Chinese, and East Indians

DATE OF INDEPENDENCE OR CREATION
September 21, 1981

TYPE OF GOVERNMENT
Constitutional monarchy with parliamentary democracy

TYPE OF STATE
Unitary state

TYPE OF LEGISLATURE
Bicameral parliament

DATE OF CONSTITUTION
September 21, 1981

DATE OF LAST AMENDMENT
December 31, 2001

Belize is a constitutional monarchy with Queen Elizabeth II of the United Kingdom as titular head of state, represented locally by a Belizean governor-general. The country enjoys a parliamentary democracy based on the rule of law with a clear division of executive, legislative, and judicial powers and with a recognized leader of the opposition.

Belize has a written constitution, which is expressly recognized as the supreme law; any other law inconsistent with it is, to the extent of the inconsistency, null and void. The governor-general's functions are mostly representative and ceremonial; the governor-general assents to all laws passed by the National Assembly of Belize.

The central figure in the administration of Belize is the prime minister, who is the leader of the political party that commands the support of the majority of the members of the House of Representatives.

The cabinet consists of the prime minister and other cabinet ministers, who are appointed by the governor-general acting on the advice of the prime minister. It is the principal executive instrument of policy, responsible for the general direction and control of the government of Belize. Cabinet ministers must be members of the House of Representatives or the Senate.

Periodic elections, usually every five years, are held for membership of the House of Representatives. These elections are free, general, and direct on the basis of a pluralistic system of political parties. The Senate, which together with the House of Representatives constitutes the legislature of Belize, is composed of appointed members.

Religious freedom is guaranteed, and state and religious institutions are separated. The economic system can be described as a developing market economy. The military and the police are subject to the civil government by law and in fact.

CONSTITUTIONAL HISTORY

The country that is today known as Belize was, during the classic Maya period (300–900 C.E.), part of the Maya Empire with a flourishing Maya Indian civilization.

The advent of a European presence in the area, after the Spanish expansion into the New World in the 1500s, was the beginning of modern Belize. English buccaneers used the coastal waters around the area to prey on Spanish shipping; they subsequently established settlements in the Belize River valley to engage in logging, after buccaneering was abolished in 1667.

The settlements grew and expanded without any formalization of their legal status. The first attempt to constitute some formal governance for the area was Burnaby's Code in 1765. The code was named after Admiral Burnaby, the then commander in chief of Jamaica, who visited the area to ensure that the settlers were allowed to cut timber. The simple regulations introduced by the code were intended to maintain some sort of order.

On September 10, 1798, the Baymen, as the settlers came to be known, together with their African slaves who had been taken in to help cut log wood and timber, beat back Spanish attempts to overrun the settlements at the Battle of Saint George's Caye. By the end of the 18th century, a rudimentary system of government existed in the Bay Settlement. This consisted of a paid superintendent; a bench of seven magistrates elected annually who acted in both a judicial and executive capacity; and a public meeting as a legislative body. A supreme court was established in 1819, and a legislative assembly met for the first time in January 1854 with 21 members, of whom 18 were elected and three nominated by the superintendent. In 1862, Britain declared British Honduras, as the settlement began to be formally known, a Crown Colony.

Constitutional self-government was achieved in 1964 with George Price as the premier. In 1973, the country's name was officially changed to Belize, and the capital moved from Belize City to Belmopan.

After a Constitutional Conference in London in April 1981, Belize formally became independent and a member of the Commonwealth on September 21 of that year. It later was admitted to the United Nations.

Belize is also a member of the Caribbean Economic Community (CARICOM), a treaty arrangement designed to foster and enhance regional cooperation and development. Two important institutions in this regard are in the process of implementation and establishment, namely, the CARICOM Single Market and Economy (CSME) and the Caribbean Court of Justice (CCJ).

FORM AND IMPACT OF THE CONSTITUTION

Belize has a written constitution contained in a single document called the Belize Constitution. The constitution takes precedence over all other national law, and any such law inconsistent with it must yield. Although the constitution in its substantive provisions is silent concerning international law, the preamble does state that "the people of Belize . . . require policies of state . . . which protect the environment, which promote international peace, se-

curity and cooperation among nations, the establishment of a just and equitable international economic and social order in the world with respect for international law and treaty obligations in the dealings among nations." In order to be applicable in Belize, international law must be in accord with the constitution; treaties must be incorporated into law by an act of the National Assembly. Generally, laws in Belize do comply with the constitution, as its principles and provisions loom large during consideration of the bills and later application of the law.

BASIC ORGANIZATION STRUCTURE

Belize is a unitary state with a central form of government. It is divided into six districts: Belize, Cayo, Corozal, Orange Walk, Stann Creek, and Toledo. It has a representative form of local government. Two cities have elected councils and mayors—Belize and Belmopan. There are also elected Town Boards, mayors for the major towns, and Village Councils with elected chairpersons. Local government is not mentioned in the constitution; it is regulated by various acts.

LEADING CONSTITUTIONAL PRINCIPLES

The system of government is based on the principle of parliamentary democracy along the British Westminster model. The constitution provides for a division between the executive and legislative bodies, but the Westminster style of parliamentary democracy results, in practice, in majority support for the executive in the legislature. The judicial powers are separate and are vested in an independent judiciary.

The Belize constitution is characterized by a number of leading principles: Belize is a sovereign democratic state with a constitutional monarchy in whom all executive powers are vested; it is based on the rule of law. Executive powers are, in practice, carried out by a prime minister with the assistance of a cabinet of ministers.

The constitution is expressly declared to be the supreme law. The rule of law is therefore fundamental. A leading principle of the constitution is its protection of fundamental rights and freedoms. All state actions or legislative measures must generally conform with and not derogate from these rights and freedoms, except to the limited extent permitted by the constitution itself. Part of the structure of the constitution is the freedom of religion, which makes Belize a secular state.

CONSTITUTIONAL BODIES

The principal bodies provided for in the constitution are the governor-general, the prime minister and the cabinet ministers, the legislature, the judiciary, and the Public Service Commission.

The Governor-General

The governor-general is her majesty's representative in Belize; the holder of the office must be a citizen of Belize. The office, although largely ceremonial, involves some important functions such as appointing the prime minister, who is the leader of the political party that commands the majority of the members of the House of Representatives. The governor-general also appoints the judges of both the Supreme Court and the Court of Appeals; in the case of the chief justice and the justices of the Court of Appeals, he or she follows the advice of the prime minister after consultation with the leader of the opposition.

Executive authority in Belize is vested in her majesty the queen and is exercised on her behalf by the governor-general, in practice by the prime minister and other ministers of the administration. The prime minister is required to keep the governor-general fully informed of the general conduct of the government. There are provisions for acting governor-general and deputy to the governor-general, but there is no provision on the removal of the governor-general, who is said to hold office during her majesty's pleasure.

The Prime Minister and the Cabinet

The Belize constitution vests executive authority in her majesty the queen of England. It is exercised on her behalf by the governor-general either directly or through subordinate officers. The National Assembly does have some powers to confer executive authority on persons other than the governor-general, but this provision has never been put into effect.

The office of prime minister looms large in the exercise of executive or administrative powers. Although most appointments to important public offices are formally made by the governor-general, these appointments are made on the advice of the prime minister. For some appointments, such as the chief justice, justices of the Court of Appeal, and the chair of the Public Services Commission, the governor-general also consults the leader of the opposition.

The prime minister's functions are not explicitly stated in the constitution, but he or she is effectively the head of the executive branch. The prime minister together with other ministers compose the cabinet; together, they act as the principal executive instrument. The prime minister advises the governor-general on the appointment to the offices of ministers and ministers of state from among members of the House of Representatives and the Senate.

The prime minister is appointed by the governor-general; he or she must be a member of the House of Representatives and the leader of the political party that commands the support of the majority of its members. The prime minister can be removed from office within seven days of a successful resolution of no confidence in the House of Representatives, unless the minister resigns or asks the governor-general to dissolve the National Assembly. Any minister's office becomes vacant if the holder ceases to be a member of the House of Representatives other than by dissolution of the National Assembly. In the case of a cabinet minister, the governor-general can keep him or her in office on the advice of the prime minister.

The Lawmaking Process

The National Assembly, the legislature of Belize, is composed of the House of Representatives and the Senate; it has the power to make laws for the peace, order, and good government of the country. Bills must be proposed by the Senate and the House of Representatives and then assented to by the governor-general, after which they become acts.

The Judiciary

The judiciary is independent of the administration and forms a separate branch of the government. The highest court for Belize is still Her Majesty's Privy Council in London, which hears both civil and criminal cases on appeal.

The Court of Appeal is the next court below the Privy Council, and all appeals from the Supreme Court go to the Court of Appeal. The Supreme Court has unlimited original jurisdiction to hear and determine any civil or criminal proceedings under any law. This in practice means that the Supreme Court hears constitutional cases as well. In this connection, it has decided important cases involving fundamental human rights such as the protection of property, the right not to be deported without due process of law, and the right of an unmarried woman not to be discriminated against on the grounds of her pregnancy. These decisions were upheld by the Court of Appeal.

The Public Service Commission

The Public Service Commission is provided for in Chapter VIII of the constitution. It comprises a chairperson and 18 other members, including some ex-officio members. The chair and non–ex-officio members are appointed by the governor-general, acting on the advice of the prime minister, after consultation of the leader of the opposition.

The commission is responsible for the appointment of persons to hold or act in offices in the public service and exercises disciplinary control over public officers, including those in the military service.

THE ELECTION PROCESS

The minimal voting age is 18. General elections for the House of Representatives are held at periodic intervals of not longer than five years. The prime minister can ask the governor-general to dissolve the National Assembly and determine the date of general elections. Every Belizean over the age of 18 and resident in Belize for at least one year immediately before the date of nomination is entitled to stand for elections.

POLITICAL PARTIES

Belize has a pluralistic system of political parties that compete vigorously to form the government. The right to associate, and to form or belong to a political party, is guaranteed as a fundamental right by the constitution. There is no power to prohibit or ban political parties except those whose membership is restricted on grounds of race or color.

CITIZENSHIP

Belizean citizenship is primarily acquired by birth. This means that every person born in Belize immediately before Independence Day (September 21, 1981) automatically became a citizen on that day; persons naturalized under the British Nationality Act 1948 while resident in Belize also became citizens of Belize on Independence Day. Persons born outside Belize are also Belizean citizens if a parent or grandparent was a citizen of Belize upon independence.

Every person born in Belize after Independence Day is a citizen at the date of birth, provided neither parent is a diplomat accredited to Belize or neither parent is a citizen of a country with which Belize is at war and the birth occurred in a place under the occupation of that country.

Citizenship can also be acquired by registration, for example, by any person who is married to a Belizean citizen or by persons continuously resident in Belize for five years immediately before the date of application for registration. The constitution allows a Belizean citizen to have dual nationality.

FUNDAMENTAL RIGHTS

The constitution provides in Chapter II for the protection of fundamental rights and freedoms. It guarantees the traditional set of liberal human rights, and civil liberties in addition to some social rights, such as the right to work and the right to privacy and family life.

The constitution first recognizes the entitlement of individuals to fundamental rights and freedoms and then proceeds to guarantee various specific rights and freedoms. The fundamental rights and freedom set out in the constitution have binding force for the legislature, the executive, and all public authorities.

Section 3 sets out the fundamental rights and freedoms of the individual guaranteed by the constitution, Section 4 provides for the protection of the right to life, and Section 5 protects the right to personal liberty. Finally, Section 6 protects the equality of every person before the law and every person's entitlement without any discrimination to the equal protection of the law.

Impact and Functions of Fundamental Rights

The fundamental rights and freedoms provided for and guaranteed in the constitution occupy a central place in the governance of Belize and underpin the supremacy of the constitution itself. Therefore, in the interpretation and application of every law, the rights and freedoms specified in the constitution are always borne in mind. However, these rights more readily apply in the relationship between the individual and government and persons or institutions who could be said to exercise governmental functions or powers. These rights and freedoms do not readily apply in relationships among private persons, who, depending on the right in question, may have a private law remedy in contract or tort. The Supreme Court is given an original jurisdiction to hear and determine any alleged violation of the fundamental rights and freedoms.

Limitations to Fundamental Rights and Freedoms

The constitution recognizes limitations on the various enumerated rights and freedoms; these are designed only to ensure that the enjoyment of the stated rights and freedoms by any person does not prejudice the rights and freedoms of others or the public interest.

THE ECONOMY

The Belize constitution does not specify a particular economic system. However, the second preambular paragraph states that the people of Belize respect the principles of social justice and believe that the operation of the economic system must result in the community's material resources' being so distributed as to subserve the common good. It also states that there should be adequate means of livelihood for all and that labor should not be exploited or forced by economic necessity to operate in inhumane conditions. The constitution, however, explicitly guarantees freedom of property, the freedom of occupation or profession or trade, and the right to form associations. The equal protection of the law for all and the equality of every person before the law also guarantee the sanctity of contracts. Belize is a developing country with an economic system that can be described as a free market economy.

RELIGIOUS COMMUNITIES

Freedom of religion or conscience is expressly recognized and protected as a fundamental human right; it involves rights for "every recognized religious community." There is no established state church or religion, but there is a collaborative relationship between the government and various religious denominations and groups in the field of education. The state pays most of the salaries of teachers in schools run by these denominations and groups. However, public authorities observe neutrality in their relationship with religious communities. Persons attending educational institutions or in detention or serving in armed forces are not required to take part in any religious ceremony, observance, or instructions that do not relate to their own religions.

MILITARY DEFENSE AND STATE OF EMERGENCY

The constitution provides for the appointment of the commandant of the Belize defense force (by the governor-general with the advice of the prime minister) but is otherwise silent on the composition, maintenance, and deployment of armed forces in Belize. Such details are provided for in the Defence Act. The defense force is charged with defending Belize, supporting civil authorities in the maintenance of order, and performing such other duties as may be defined by the governor-general. It is, however, clear that the constitution considers the armed forces to be under the authority of the civil government.

There is no conscription in Belize nor requirement for military service. Military service is by voluntary enlistment in periodic recruitment campaigns by the military. The issue of conscientious objection does not arise in Belize as all members of the armed forces are voluntary recruits. No one under 18 years may enlist in the military.

The constitution provides for a "period of public emergency." This is stated to exist in three situations: (1) when Belize is engaged in any war, (2) when there is a proclamation by the governor-general that a state of public emergency exists, or (3) when there is in force a resolution by the National Assembly declaring that the democratic institutions in Belize are threatened by subversion. A proclamation of a period of public emergency may be made as a consequence of such events as earthquakes, hurricanes, floods, or other natural disasters.

A period of public emergency is limited in duration, though it is subject to renewal. The governor-general is empowered to make regulations for the period and purpose of the public emergency. The regulations or orders made thereunder may amend or suspend the operation of any law except the constitution itself. Even in the latter case, however, such emergency regulations cannot be found to violate fundamental constitutional rights and freedoms. Therefore, a period of public emergency can undermine some of those rights.

The National Assembly plays a major role in declaring, continuing, or revoking such a period; as such, an emergency will never result in a change of administration or institution. The proclamation may authorize any person or authority (including the military) to make orders and rules for the emergency.

AMENDMENTS TO THE CONSTITUTION

The Belize constitution itself states how any of its provisions can be amended or altered by the National Assembly. It stipulates certain safeguards that make it difficult to change certain provisions, including the amendment process, fundamental rights and freedoms, the judiciary, and provisions relating to the legislature, its dissolution, and general elections.

Any bill to alter these provisions must be supported by not less than three-quarters of all members of the House of Representatives and shall not be submitted to the governor-general for assent before 90 days have passed after the first introduction of that bill into the house and before the proceedings on the second reading of it in the house have started. Any other provision of the constitution can be altered by the House of Representatives by a vote of at least two-thirds of all members on its final reading.

Every bill proposing an amendment of any section of the constitution must be accompanied by a certificate signed by the Speaker of the house certifying that the provisions of the constitution on alteration have been complied with before it is submitted to the governor-general for assent.

The Referendum Act of 1999 provides that any proposed alteration of the constitution that derogates from the fundamental rights and freedoms guaranteed therein must be submitted to a referendum.

PRIMARY SOURCES
Constitution in English. Available online. URL: http://www.georgetown.edu/pdba/Constitutions/Belize/belize81.html. Accessed on July 17, 2005.
Constitution of Belize, Chapter 4 of the Laws of Belize, rev. ed., 2000. Available online. URL: http://www.BelizeLaw.org. Accessed on August 7, 2005.

SECONDARY SOURCES
Nigel Bolland, *Colonization and Resistance in Belize*. Belize: Cubola, 2003.
Narda Dobson, *A History of Belize*. London: Crown Copy Right, Longman, 1973.

Abdulai Osman Conteh

BENIN

At-a-Glance

OFFICIAL NAME
Republic of Benin

CAPITAL
Porto-Novo

POPULATION
7,460,025 (2005 est.)

SIZE
44,310 sq. mi. (114,763 sq. km)

LANGUAGES
French (official language), Baatonu, Basa, Dendi, Ditammari, Fon, Fulfulde, Gen, Gulmacema, Gun, Hausa, Nateni, Waama, Yoruba, and many others

RELIGIONS
Traditional 50%, Christian 30%, Muslim 20%

NATIONAL OR ETHNIC COMPOSITION
Aja, Waci, Gen, Xuéda, Xwla, Ayizo, Toli and Fon (south), Yoruba and Gun (Eastern South), Maxi and

Yoruba (center), Batumbu, Dendi, Mokole, Fulbe, Cenka, Hausa, Betammaribe, Waaba, Bebelbe, Natemba, Yowa, and Lekpa (north)

DATE OF INDEPENDENCE OR CREATION
August 1, 1960

TYPE OF GOVERNMENT
Presidential democracy

TYPE OF STATE
Unitary state

TYPE OF LEGISLATURE
Unicameral parliament

DATE OF CONSTITUTION
December 11, 1990

DATE OF LAST AMENDMENT
No amendment

Benin is a unitary democratic state. Its constitution guarantees a wide range of human rights. In 1989, an uprising of the population in which different social groups went on strike forced the government to adopt major political changes, principal among which was the introduction of democracy. The government abandoned the one-party system and called for a national conference, which took place in February 1990 with the participation of all social groups (*forces vives de la nation*) to discuss the new system. The conference called for drafting a new constitution to embed the principles and processes expected of a democratic state. The new constitution was adopted by referendum on December 11, 1990, and is still operative. This constitution establishes a multiparty system with a presidential regime and an independent judiciary. State and religion are separated. There is a market economy.

CONSTITUTIONAL HISTORY

In 1894, after King Gbèhanzin was defeated by French troops, Danhomè (Dahomey) became a French colony. On September 29, 1958, Danhomè voted to remain in the French Community, and on February 15, 1959, the Territorial Assembly adopted the first constitution. On August 1, 1960, the Republic of Danhomè became independent, and the Territorial Assembly adopted the second constitution. In 1963, a military coup d'état headed off an imminent civil war, and a third constitution was adopted by referendum on January 5, 1964. After several additional military coups, a fourth constitution was adopted by referendum on March 31, 1968. Another coup in 1969 installed a military council, which proclaimed yet another constitution on May 7, 1970, which was suspended by another military coup on October 26, 1972.

The country adopted the Marxist-Leninist form of government in 1974 and changed its name to the People's Republic of Benin the following year. On November 30, 1975, a constitutional commission was set up to draft the country's sixth constitution, which was adopted by the National Council on September 9, 1977. In 1989, after multiple strikes and a general social crisis, the government called for a National Conference to discuss the political future. The conference decided to rescind the constitution, put in place a transitional government, and set up a commission to draft a new constitution. The draft produced by the commission was adopted by referendum on December 2, 1990. The act, including the constitution, was published on December 11, 1990. The conference also changed the name of the country to the Republic of Benin. This last constitution includes the African Charter on Human and Peoples' Rights as an annex so that any citizen or resident of the Republic of Benin may seek redress in the courts in case of violation of his or her rights as recognized in the regional human rights system.

FORM AND IMPACT OF THE CONSTITUTION

The constitution is composed of 160 articles, including the African Charter on Human and Peoples' Rights as an annex. It establishes that international law prevails over national law, subject to the principle of reciprocity in international relations, meaning that Benin fulfills its international obligations as long as its treaty partner acts accordingly.

BASIC ORGANIZATIONAL STRUCTURE

The constitution sets up a presidential regime, with some checks and balances. The state is unitary, and there are 12 regions.

LEADING CONSTITUTIONAL PRINCIPLES

In the constitution, there are two leading principles. One is the protection of human rights, established by Articles 7 to 40 and by the African Charter on Human and Peoples' Rights. A Constitutional Court is established with a primary responsibility to ensure such protection. The second principle is democracy combined with the rule of law. The Republic of Benin is governed by institutions established by the constitution, and the citizens are required to disobey any regime that is in violation of the constitution. This principle is reinforced by the African principle of prohibition of unconstitutional change of regime or government.

CONSTITUTIONAL BODIES

The main constitutional bodies are the president, the executive government, the National Assembly, the Constitutional Court, and the rest of the judiciary.

The President

The president is the head of state. He or she is elected by the citizens for a term of five years and can be reelected only once. The president exercises executive power and shares the initiative for legislation with the members of the National Assembly. A presidential candidate must be a citizen of Benin who has lived in the country for the previous 10 years, of good moral standing, between the ages of 40 and 70, and in good health. The Constitutional Court has the jurisdiction to ensure that those conditions are met.

The Executive Government

The executive government is appointed by the president after consulting the National Assembly. The president is the head of government. The president appoints a cabinet minister to coordinate the action of the executive, with informal approval of the National Assembly.

The National Assembly

The National Assembly has legislative power. It shares the initiative for legislation with the president, adopts legislation, and exercises control over the actions of the executive. It is composed of deputies elected for a term of four years. The number of deputies, as established by legislation, is currently 83.

The Constitutional Court

The Constitutional Court must ensure that any law adopted by the National Assembly is in conformity with the constitution and that human rights are respected by the state and individuals. It is composed of seven judges, three appointed by the president of the republic and four by the Bureau of the National Assembly, who serve for a term of five years, renewable only once. The Constitutional Court was set up in June 1993.

The Lawmaking Process

The National Assembly meets twice a year for its ordinary sessions, which last not more than three months each. The right to introduce legislation is shared by the president of the republic and the deputies, but only the deputies can vote on proposals. A simple majority is usually sufficient, except for laws on specific important matters, called organic legislation. Organic legislation, such as the rules for the functioning of the Constitutional Court, requires an absolute majority. The constitution prescribes the possible subject matter of laws.

The Judiciary

The independence of the judiciary is provided for in the constitution, which establishes a Supreme Court as well as additional courts and tribunals. The constitution also states that judges shall be guided only by the law. The Supreme Court is the highest Beninese court and is competent to hear all matters related to the administration, individuals, and national budget. It is also competent to hear matters related to local elections.

In 1999, a High Court of Justice was established in order to try the president of the republic and other members of the executive government when an alleged crime was committed in the pursuit of their functions. It is composed of the members of the Constitutional Court, except its president, six members of the National Assembly, and the president of the Supreme Court.

THE ELECTION PROCESS

All Beninese above 18 years of age have the right to vote. Candidates for elections, other than the presidential election, must be at least 25 years old. To stand for the presidential election, candidates must be at least 40 years old, but younger than 70.

POLITICAL PARTIES

Political parties are allowed as long as they are in conformity with the principles stated in the constitution, specifically concerning human rights and freedom.

CITIZENSHIP

The issue of citizenship is a matter of law. Nationality is acquired by birth or marriage. A child who has one Beninese parent is Beninese, unless he or she chooses not to accept the nationality.

FUNDAMENTAL RIGHTS

The constitution establishes a complex system of human rights protection. It addresses the gamut of political, civil, economic, social, and cultural rights and includes references to the African Charter on Human and Peoples' Rights, the Universal Declaration on Human Rights, and other international legal materials. Not only are these rights protected in the relationship between the state and the individual but also between individuals. The constitution also affirms the duties that are the counterparts to the rights. The individual has duties in relation to the state but also to the community and the family.

Impact and Function of Fundamental Freedoms

Human rights became central to the political and social struggle of the Beninese people, and most of the demands in 1989 related to the infringement of fundamental rights. The constitution highlights those rights and provides for judicial protection by the Constitutional Court.

Limitations to Human Rights and Fundamental Freedoms

The only limitation of human rights are duties placed upon the individual. Those duties are also protected by the Constitutional Court. The court's jurisprudence has clarified the impact of human rights, especially the impact of freedom.

ECONOMY

The constitution does not stipulate an economic system of choice but provides for the protection of economic rights.

RELIGIOUS COMMUNITIES

Freedom of religion or belief is recognized in the constitution, and there is separation between state and religion. The constitution calls Benin a secular state. The Constitutional Court acts as a human rights court to ensure that religious freedom is respected by the government and individuals.

MILITARY DEFENSE AND STATE OF EMERGENCY

The president of the republic is the head of the armed forces. Any soldier seeking to run in the presidential election must resign from the armed forces beforehand. Defending the state is an obligation of all citizens. There is compulsory military service, but the National Assembly has not adopted any legislation to implement this provision as yet. Considering the history of coups in Benin, the constitution states that a military coup is a breach of duty, is actionable as treason, and calls for civil disobedience in opposition to such coups. The constitution prohibits the president from requesting any external military assistance when faced with a civil crisis or war, except in case of a military coup.

The constitution also provides for a state of emergency, during which the president is granted full powers, subject to the control by the National Assembly, which is automatically called into an extraordinary session.

AMENDMENTS TO THE CONSTITUTION

Amending the constitution is a long and difficult process. The president of the republic and the members of the National Assembly have the initiative. After the proposal, whether from the president of the republic or the assembly, three-fourths of the assembly have to approve the amendment, which is then submitted to referendum; a referendum can be avoided if four-fifths of the members of the National Assembly approve the amendment. The form of the regime (republic) and secularism (*laïcité*) cannot be amended.

PRIMARY SOURCES

Constitution in English (summary). Available online. URL: http://www.chr.up.ac.za/hr_docs/constitutions/docs/BeninC(englishsummary)(rev).doc. Accessed on June 17, 2006.

BeninC(englishsummary)(rev).doc. Accessed on September 26, 2005.

Constitution in French. Available online. URLs: http://www.gouv.bj/en/textes_rapports/index_top.php. Accessed on September 16, 2005.

Government of the Republic of Benin. Available online. URL: http://www.gouv.bj. Accessed on August 6, 2005.

Legislative Elections of 2003: Available online. URL: http://www.legislatives2003.gouv.bj. Accessed on September 10, 2005.

SECONDARY SOURCES

Toudonou Johanes Athanase and L. Césaire Kpenonhou, *Constitution et textes constitutionnels de la République du Bénin depuis les origines dahoméennes.* Cotonou: Université nationale du Bénin, 1995.

Christof Hartmann, "Benin." In *Elections in Africa: A Data Handbook*, edited by Dieter Nohlen, Michael Krennerich, and Bernhard Thibaut, 79–102. London and Oxford: Oxford University Press, 1999.

Christoph Heyns, *Human Rights Law in Africa.* Vol. 2, *Domestic Human Rights Law in Africa.* Leiden: Martinus Nijhoff, 2004. Available online. URL: http://www.chr.up.ac.za.

Nathanael G. Mensah, *Droit constitutionnel et institutions politiques.* Vol. 3, *Evolution politique et constitutionnelle de la République populaire du Bénin.* Cotonou: République populaire du Bénin, Centre de formation administrative et de perfectionnement, 1982.

Kaga Tako Nabia, *Réflexion sur la pratique de la correctionnalisation judiciaire au Bénin.* Thèse/Maîtrise en sciences juridiques, Université nationale du Bénin, 1995.

C. A. Oputa, *Human Rights in the Political and Legal Culture of Nigeria.* Lagos: Nigerian Law Publications, 1988.

United Nations, "Core Document Forming Part of the Reports of States Parties: Benin." (HRI/CORE/1/Add.85.), 17 February 1998. Available online. URL: http://www.unhchr.ch/tbs/doc.nsf. Accessed on September 10, 2005.

Roland Adjovi

BHUTAN

At-a-Glance

OFFICIAL NAME
Kingdom of Bhutan

CAPITAL
Thimphu

POPULATION
2,185,569 (July 2004 est.)

SIZE
18,147 sq. mi. (47,000 sq. km)

LANGUAGES
Dzongkha (official), Sharchop, Nepali, Bumthapkha, Khengkha, and 14 other minority languages

RELIGIONS
Vajrayana Buddhism 75%, Hinduism 25%

NATIONAL OR ETHNIC COMPOSITION
Northern Bhutanese (Ngalong, Sharchop, and smaller groups) 65%, Lhotshampa (of Nepalese descent) 30%, indigenous or migrant tribes 5%

DATE OF INDEPENDENCE OR CREATION
Consolidation begun in 1616; monarchy established 1907

TYPE OF GOVERNMENT
Emerging parliamentary democracy

TYPE OF STATE
Constitutional monarchy

TYPE OF LEGISLATURE
Unicameral parliament

DATE OF CONSTITUTION
2005 draft awaiting referendum

DATE OF LAST AMENDMENT
No amendment

Bhutan is a traditional monarchy in the process of becoming a parliamentary democracy. King Jigme Singye Wangchuk (1972–) is head of state. The king transferred royal powers to an elected Council of Ministers by royal edict in 1998 and is no longer head of the administration. The chair of the Council of Ministers acts as head of the administration.

At present, there is no written constitution. In December 2001, the current king issued a royal edict declaring that Bhutan should have a written constitution. A draft was prepared by a 39-member committee and submitted to the king in October 2002. The draft constitution was launched publicly on March 26, 2005. A public referendum on the constitution was postponed to 2008.

CONSTITUTIONAL HISTORY

Until the 17th century, Bhutan was not a unified country. In 1616, the *zhabdrung*, Ngawang Namgyal (1596–1651),

arrived from Ralung in southern Tibet after a dispute over his succession. *Zhabdrung* is a title for that spiritual leader of Bhutan and means "at whose feet one submits." Following an active policy of consolidating his authority in Bhutan, the *zhabdrung* unified Bhutan under the Drukpa (a religious community) theocracy. The system of government introduced by the *zhabdrung* took its definitive form in the 1640s.

Political affairs were under the control of the *Desi* (the theocratic civil government), while the monks were organized along the lines of the Ralung monastery in Tibet under a head abbot, or *je khenpo* (the elected head of the state monastic body). This system of government, with separate persons responsible for religious and secular affairs, was and is known as the dual system. Bhutan itself was divided into three large regions, each with a governor and a head lama. At the lowest level, village elders were appointed to look after several villages each and transmit orders from the *dzong* (fortress/monastery) to the local people. Although this dual system of government remained in place until the monarchy was established in 1907, the system was significantly weakened by the late 18th century, and Bhutan experienced ongoing conflicts between vying lords during the 19th century.

The monarchy was established in 1907 when a political vacuum appeared after the death of *Zhabdrung* Jigme Chogyel in 1904. A petition to appoint Ugyen Wangchuk as king was submitted to the State Council and unanimously approved. Ugyen Wangchuk was appointed as hereditary king on December 17, 1907. During his reign, he focused on stabilizing the political situation. Under his successor, Jigme Wangchuk (1926–52), the administrative system of the kingdom was reformed with a move toward greater centralization. There were reforms designed to reduce the threat of insurrection by powerful officials, establish an accountable administrative cadre, and reduce the tax burden on the common people.

The next king, Jigme Dorje Wangchuk (1952–72), introduced wide political, social, and economic reforms, which have continued to shape contemporary Bhutan. In 1953, the king established a National Assembly with 150 members. In 1965, a Royal Advisory Council was created. Various categories of serfs and slaves were liberated and a major program of land reform undertaken. Understanding the importance of international recognition, especially after the occupation of Tibet by Chinese forces in 1950, Bhutan joined the Colombo Plan in 1962; having sought United Nations membership since 1948, Bhutan was finally admitted in 1971.

The fourth and current king, Jigme Singye Wangchuk (1972–   ), ascended the throne at age 17. Under his direction, the process of modernization and ongoing transformation of Bhutan has continued.

FORM AND IMPACT OF THE CONSTITUTION

At present, the kingdom is governed by constitutional practices that have been developed over the last century, notably since the reign of King Jigme Dorji Wangchuk. A draft written constitution has been prepared by a Constitutional Drafting Committee established in 2001 and was made public in March 2005. The king initiated the drafting process and will personally tour the kingdom to present the draft constitution to the people prior to its debate in the National Assembly.

BASIC ORGANIZATIONAL STRUCTURE

Bhutan is divided into 20 administrative districts called *dzongkhag*. The *dzongkhag* varies significantly in geo-

graphical area, population size, and economic strength. Each one is administered by a district administrator.

Each *dzongkhag* has its own district court; there are two subdistrict courts in two of the larger districts. In accordance with the move toward decentralization, Dzongkhag Development Committees (DYT) have been set up, with responsibility for planning and coordinating development. Below the Dzongkhag Development Committee, Gewog Development Committees (GYT) are responsible for the lowest administrative and development functions.

LEADING CONSTITUTIONAL PRINCIPLES

Bhutan is transforming itself from a traditional monarchy into a parliamentary democracy. There is an emphasis on ensuring a strong division of the executive, legislative, and judicial powers.

The constitutional system is defined by the notion of Tsa Wa Sum—the king, the people, and the nation. Bhutan stresses the importance of balancing change with traditional values, including a code of conduct called *driglam namzha*. These traditional elements are counterbalanced by an emphasis on the rule of law, accountability, efficiency, and transparency in the operation of the state. These principles will be recast in the new written constitution.

CONSTITUTIONAL BODIES

The main bodies are the king, the Royal Advisory Council, the cabinet, and the National Assembly. Below these are the district and local development committees. The judiciary is independent of both the executive and legislature.

The King

Until 1998, the king was both head of state and head of the administration. The monarchy was established in 1907 and has been responsible for promoting the ongoing political and economic transformation of Bhutan. The monarchy remains central to Bhutanese identity and is deeply cherished. A vote of confidence was held during the National Assembly in 1999 and was overwhelming in its support for the king. Although no longer head of the administration, the king retains immeasurable personal influence and authority.

The Royal Advisory Council

The Royal Advisory Council was formally constituted in 1965 as the highest advisory body. It is made up of nine members. Six counselors are elected by the National Assembly through secret ballots for each of the districts, two representatives are nominated by the monks, and there is one representative of the administration, who acts as ex-officio chair. The six elected counselors serve for three years; the monk body representatives serve for one year only. Election to the Royal Advisory Council automatically makes the counselors members of the National Assembly and the cabinet.

The Cabinet

The cabinet (Lhengay Zhungtshog) was originally created in 1968 by the National Assembly. Until 1998, the cabinet was presided over by the king and made up of representatives appointed by him. Since 1998, the cabinet (now Council of Ministers) is elected by secret ballot by the assemblies and exercises full executive powers. A chairperson is appointed from among the elected ministers, and the position rotates annually. The cabinet ministers head the various government ministries, and the chair is in effect head of the administration.

The National Assembly

Established in 1953, the National Assembly has 150 members: 105 elected representatives of the people, 10 from the Central Monk Body, and 35 nominated by the government. The National Assembly elects the Council of Ministers, approves the annual budget, and, as its main function, passes legislation drafted by the ministries. The members serve for three years.

The Lawmaking Process
According to the 2005 draft constitution, parliament will consist of the Druk Gyalpo (the king of Bhutan) and of two chambers: the National Assembly and the National Council. A bill passed by one chamber is submitted to the other chamber for approval. If parliament passes the bill, it enters into force with the assent of the king. If one chamber does not approve a bill but amends it or objects to it, this bill is returned to the other chamber for reconsideration. If the other chamber refuses to incorporate the amendments or objections, it submits it to the king, who arranges for a joint session of both chambers. The bill is deemed to have passed after a certain period without passing or returning by the other chamber. A joint sitting also takes place when the king does not grant assent. Upon deliberation and passing of the bill in a joint session, it is again submitted to the king for assent, whereupon assent shall be granted to the bill.

The District and Local Level Development Committees

In 1981, the District Development Committees were established, followed in 1991 by the creation of Block Development Committees. They represent the decentralization of administration in Bhutan and focus on planning and implementing development strategies.

The Judiciary

The judiciary gained full independence from the administration in the early 1990s. There are plans to create a Supreme Court, which will act as the Constitutional Court. At present, the highest court in Bhutan is the High Court of Justice. There are eight High Court judges presided over by the chief justice. The chief justice is chair of the Constitutional Drafting Committee. Below the High Court are 20 district courts and two subdistrict courts with general jurisdiction. In a recent electoral corruption case, the High Court upheld the sentences awarded by the Chukha district court to those offering and accepting bribes during recent elections to the Royal Advisory Council.

THE ELECTION PROCESS AND POLITICAL PARTICIPATION

Elections for local administrator in 199 of the 201 village blocks were held in November 2002. It was the first secret ballot election held with universal suffrage, with each adult over the age of 21 (male and female enjoying equal rights) eligible to vote, rather than a representative from each village household as in the past.

POLITICAL PARTIES

At present, there are no officially recognized political parties in Bhutan. The draft constitution incorporates provisions for the creation of political parties and for granting to the winning party in a general election the right to form the new administration. The party with the second highest number of votes will form the opposition.

CITIZENSHIP

Citizenship is primarily acquired by birth, provided both parents are Bhutanese. The Citizenship Act of 1985 sets out various conditions for the granting of naturalized citizenship or registration for those individuals permanently resident in Bhutan from 1958.

FUNDAMENTAL RIGHTS

There is no bill of rights currently in Bhutan. At present, the supreme laws stress the equality of all before the law, irrespective of social status or wealth. The draft constitution is believed to contain an explicit statement of the basic rights of Bhutanese citizens. These will include freedom of association, freedom of movement, and freedom of expression and religious belief. In effect, the draft constitution provides for the direct incorporation of basic human rights set out in the 1948 Declaration on Universal Human Rights.

Impact and Function of Fundamental Rights

Awareness of human rights and fundamental freedoms is developing through access to external media. Bhutan is a United Nations (UN) signatory and by implication supports human rights. In recent years, Bhutan has actively worked to implement the Conventions on the Elimination of Discrimination against Women and Children's Rights.

Limitations to Fundamental Rights

Since there currently is no bill of rights, no legal limitations apply.

ECONOMY

The Bhutanese state is the primary employer in the country and is heavily involved in its economic development. The district and local development committees are responsible for preparing five-year plans for their respective areas, which may include the promotion of the district and local economy.

RELIGIOUS COMMUNITIES

Because of its intertwined political and religious history and the continuing links between the Bhutanese state and the Druk Kagyu religion, Bhutan is officially a Buddhist kingdom. The Central Monk Body under the authority of the Je Khenpo, the head abbot, continues to receive state support in return for the religious activities performed by the monk body for the spiritual and material well-being of the kingdom. Freedom of religion is recognized; however, the state prohibits religious proselytizing.

MILITARY DEFENSE AND STATE OF EMERGENCY

The Bhutanese army and police force are accountable to the chief operations officer of the royal Bhutan army, who is appointed by the king.

A militia force of volunteers, including women, was trained prior to recent military action against Indian guerrilla camps in southern Bhutan in December 2003. There is no compulsory military service and thus no provision for conscientious objection.

AMENDMENTS TO THE CONSTITUTION

An unwritten constitution developed with the establishment of the National Assembly. All changes to the current unwritten constitution require approval by the National Assembly.

PRIMARY SOURCES

Constitution in English. Available online. URL: http://www.constitution.bt/. Accessed on August 4, 2005.
Draft Constitution in English: *Tsa Thrim Chhenmo*. Available online. URL: http://www.bhutannewsonline.com/draftconstitutionofbhtan.pdf. Accessed on August 27, 2005.

SECONDARY SOURCES

Francis Robinson, *The Cambridge Encyclopedia of India, Pakistan, Bangladesh, Sri Lanka, Nepal, Bhutan and the Maldives*. Cambridge: Cambridge University Press, 1989.
Leo E. Rose, *The Politics of Bhutan: South Asian Political Systems*. Ithaca, N.Y.: Cornell University Press, 1977.
Andrea Matles Savada, ed. *Bhutan—a Country Study*. Washington D.C.: Library of Congress, 1991.

Richard Whitecross

BOLIVIA

At-a-Glance

OFFICIAL NAME
Republic of Bolivia

CAPITAL
La Paz (seat of administration); Sucre (capital and seat of judiciary)

POPULATION
8,857,870 (2005 est.)

SIZE
424,164 sq. mi. (1,098,580 sq. km)

LANGUAGES
Spanish, Quechua, Aymara (all official)

RELIGIONS
Roman Catholic 95%, Protestant (Evangelical Methodist) 5%

NATIONAL OR ETHNIC COMPOSITION
Quechua 30%, Mestizo (mixed white and Amerindian ancestry) 30%, Aymara 25%, white 15%

DATE OF INDEPENDENCE OR CREATION
August 6, 1825 (from Spain)

TYPE OF GOVERNMENT
Presidential democracy

TYPE OF STATE
Unitary state

TYPE OF LEGISLATURE
Bicameral congress

DATE OF CONSTITUTION
February 2, 1967

DATE OF LAST AMENDMENT
July 6, 2005

Bolivia is a presidential democracy. It is a social and democratic state of law. The recent constitution provides for a rigid separation of executive, legislative, and judicial powers. Since its independence, Bolivia has had more than 190 administrations. Organized as a unitary state, it is made up of nine departments.

A characteristic feature of the Bolivian constitutional system is the right of the National Congress to resolve presidential elections if no candidate receives an absolute majority. The traditionally strong executive, however, tends to overshadow the congress, whose role is generally limited to debating and approving legislation initiated by the executive.

The constitution provides for far-reaching guarantees of human rights. A national plan of action for the promotion and protection of human rights was adopted in 1999 to ensure their effectiveness.

Congressional elections are by universal, direct, equal, individual, secret, free, and obligatory suffrage. Citizens can initiate legislation and referendums. A pluralistic system of political parties has evolved.

The constitution recognizes the Roman Catholic apostolic religion and guarantees freedom of religion or belief. The economic system can be described as a social market economy. According to the constitution, the armed forces are under civilian control.

CONSTITUTIONAL HISTORY

The first great Andean empire on the high plateau between the mountains had emerged by 600 C.E. This was the territory of the Tiahuanaco Empire near the southeastern side of Lake Titicaca. In the 15th century it became part of Tahuantinsuyu, the empire of the Quechua-speaking Incas.

The colonial period from 1532 to 1825 began with the arrival of Spanish conquistadors and ended with independence from Spain. The official capital city of La Plata, known today as Sucre, was founded in 1538–39. It was the first of several settlements and later became the center of the Audiencia de Charcas—all the Spanish colonies were governed by regional councils (*audiencias*), with combined administrative, executive, and judicial powers.

The exploitation of the large silver deposits in Charcas was initially under the authority of the viceroy of Lima. The viceroyalty encompassed the entire South American continent apart from the Portuguese colony of Brazil. In 1776, the territory of Charcas was transferred to the newly formed viceroyalty of Río de la Plata (today Argentina, Paraguay, Uruguay, and Bolivia). The *encomienda,* a trusteeship system that had been introduced to all the Spanish colonies by the Laws of Burgos (1512), was also applied here. The Spanish king was believed to be the natural leader, chosen by God, to govern America.

Spanish authority in the New World weakened during the European wars of the Napoleonic era (1798–1815). In La Plata, the first calls for independence arose as early as 1809, but it was 16 more years before this goal was realized. When Argentina became independent from Spain in 1810, the Audiencia de Charcas was transferred to the viceroyalty of Peru. The territory became a battleground between Argentinean republican forces and royalist troops from Peru, which itself became independent in 1821. In the end, Antonio José de Sucre, in command of Simón Bolívar's Colombian troops, defeated the last Spanish garrison. The future status of Upper Peru (as Bolivia was then known) was a delicate issue, involving local interests as well as those of Argentina and Peru. Sucre called together a General Assembly (Asamblea Deliberante) in La Plata. It adopted the declaration of independence for the provinces of Upper Peru and then constituted itself as the República Bolívar (1825, soon changed to Bolivia). The famous liberator himself ruled the country, but he left for Peru after five months. As his successor, Sucre became president.

Bolívar presented a draft constitution, as he had been asked to do, in 1826. It reflected his fear of the growing disorder in all the liberated countries of South America. With a lifetime presidency, an independent judiciary, a tricameral congress, and an electoral body, it vested wide-ranging powers in the executive. The president even had the right to nominate his successor. The final version of the constitution remained heavily weighted toward the executive. Bolívar's vision of a League of Hispanic-American States "united in heart" did not prevail. The Congress of Panama (1826), in which all these states should have been represented, was a fragmentary affair. In the names of both the country and its capital, however, the memory of the two famous liberators has been preserved.

Some of the leaders, or caudillos, who followed involved themselves in the internal struggles of Peru; others struggled to prevent the annexation of Bolivia. Frequent changes in regime were then often accompanied by changes of the constitution—more than a dozen between 1831 and 1880.

The 1831 constitution introduced a bicameral legislature. The president was given the power to dissolve congress, but the new constitution abolished the lifetime presidency and limited it to renewable four-year terms. In contrast, the actual power of the president, Andrés de Santa Cruz, increased. He was a Mestizo and the first native-born president. With the support of Bolívar, he had briefly been president of Peru (1826). During his rule, he established a short-lived confederation of Bolivia and Peru (1836–39).

As an exception to the general rule of instability, the 1880 constitution lasted for almost 58 years, although it was amended several times. The constitution of 1878 had introduced the power of congress to summon the ministers for questioning and strengthened the legislature in other ways as well. With the 1880 constitution, Bolivia achieved a functioning constitutional system of political parties, interest groups, and an active legislature.

In contrast to this political stability, significant territorial and social changes occurred. During the War of the Pacific with Chile (1879–83), Bolivia lost access to the seacoast. In the War of Acre (1903), it lost Amazonian territories to Brazil, and it lost land to Paraguay in the Chaco War (1932–35). The seacoast, officially ceded to Chile in exchange for transit rights to the harbor of Arica (1904), is still the subject of Bolivian claims.

In 1952, a revolutionary party seized control of the government. The Movimiento Nacionalista Revolucionario (MNR) introduced far-reaching economic and social policy changes, such as universal suffrage, nationalization of the mines, and agrarian reforms. Those were mostly included in the revised 1961 constitution before the army finally deposed the government in 1964.

The 1967 constitution was a partial return to the liberal tradition of the 1880 document. The military leader, General René Barrientos, who had seized the government, sought democratic legitimacy; in exchange, he was willing to adapt his more radical plans. According to the constitution, Bolivia was a unitary republic with a democratic and representative democracy. Sovereignty resided in the people. The strong executive tradition, however, continued to exist in practice. In 1974, for instance, it was declared that the constitution remained in force only insofar as it did not contradict the statute of government, a decree law. Bolivians suffered through several more military presidents, and political instability continued as late as 1982.

In 1994, the constitution was heavily amended. The 1995 codification introduced a Constitutional Tribunal and explicitly provided for the collective rights of indigenous people. For the first time in Bolivian history, an Aymara Indian had been elected as vice president. After ongoing protests and political violence, further changes in 2004 introduced some direct democratic elements, including citizens' legislative initiatives, a referendum, and a Constituent Assembly.

Bolivia today is a member state of the Organization of American States (OAS), which promotes the idea of inter-American cooperation.

FORM AND IMPACT OF THE CONSTITUTION

The constitution (Constitución Política del Estado) consists of a single written document and additional interpretative laws (*leyes interpretativas*). The constitution takes precedence over all other national law.

BASIC ORGANIZATIONAL STRUCTURE

Bolivia is a unitary state made up of nine departments. Senior departmental officials are still appointed by the central government. Departments and local communities have received greater autonomy under the laws on administrative decentralization and popular participation.

LEADING CONSTITUTIONAL PRINCIPLES

Article 1 reads: "Bolivia, free, independent, sovereign, multi-ethnic and culturally pluralistic, constituted as a unitary Republic, adopts for its government the democratic representative and participative form, founded in the unity and solidarity of all Bolivians." It further declares Bolivia as a "social and democratic state of law," built on liberty, equality, and justice.

Article 2 establishes the legal structure: "Sovereignty resides in the people; it is inalienable and imprescriptible; its exercise is delegated to the legislative, executive and judicial powers." Direct democracy, whereby people decide directly on the relevant issues by means of a referendum, is also applied.

The Bolivian constitution also defines a number of special directives, such as the economic and financial directive, the social directive, the agrarian and rural labor directive, and the cultural directive. They serve as directive principles to ensure fundamental rights as well as the orderly operation of government.

CONSTITUTIONAL BODIES

The predominant bodies are the president, the vice president, the bicameral parliament (Congreso Nacional), and the judiciary including the Constitutional Tribunal. A number of other bodies complete this list, such as the Cabinet (Consejo de Ministros), the Constituent Assembly (Asamblea Constituyente), and the Public Defender (Defensor del Pueblo).

The President and Vice President

Although the constitution establishes the division of powers, the presidential system as a whole gives great visibility and political power to the president.

The president of the republic is both the chief of state and the head of the executive. The president appoints and dismisses the ministers of state. Responsibilities reserved for the chief executive include issuing appropriate decrees and orders, negotiating and concluding treaties (which must be ratified by the National Congress), conducting foreign relations, and administering the national revenues (in accordance with the laws).

Every year, the president opens the session of congress before an assembly of both chambers. On this occasion the president makes a state of the nation address. The president of the republic must submit the national budget to the National Congress. The president may not leave the national territory without congressional assent.

The president is captain general of the armed forces. The forces of the national police are subordinate to the president through a minister of state. The president may designate the commander in chief of the armed forces and the commander general of the national police. The power of appointment enables the president to exercise control over the large number of public servants at all levels of government.

The president is elected by direct suffrage for a five-year term and cannot be reelected to a successive term, although he or she may run again after one term has passed. No active member of the armed forces or clergy is allowed to run for president.

The vice president also has a very strong position, as he or she is elected together with the president. The vice president is president of the Senate as well as president of the National Congress.

The National Congress (Congreso Nacional)

Congress is the legislative body. It consists of two chambers, the Chamber of Deputies and the Senate.

Congress rules on the lawfulness of the election of the president and the vice president and swears them in. An important power is the right to resolve elections in which the winning candidate did not receive an absolute majority of valid votes. The Bolivian system has therefore been called parliamentarized presidentialism. It is presidentialist because the president is elected for a fixed term and, even though chosen by congress, does not depend on its continuing confidence. It is parliamentarized because the president is chosen by the legislature on the basis of postelectoral bargaining when no candidate has received an absolute majority.

The legislature also appoints justices of the Supreme Court, approves international agreements, and passes the annual budget (which must be submitted by the executive in a timely fashion.

Any legislator may request an oral report from a cabinet minister (*petición de informe oral*). If dissatisfied with the replies, parliament may exercise the right of interpellation and censure the cabinet minister by an absolute majority. Traditionally, a censured minister must resign and be replaced by the president.

Both chambers have a five-year term. Senators or deputies must be at least 35 and must have fulfilled their military duties.

During congressional recesses, the constitution provides for a congressional commission (*comisión de congreso*) to be elected by the members of each chamber. If necessary, the commission can convene an extraordinary session of congress.

Chamber of Deputies (Cámara de Diputados)

The Chamber of Deputies is responsible for overseeing the ministers. It can also initiate legislation.

The Chamber of Deputies elects justices of the Supreme Court from a list submitted by the Senate; it approves the executive's requests for a declaration of a state of siege and transmits to the president of the republic a list of names from which the latter must select the heads of social and economic institutions in which the state participates.

The Chamber of Senators (Cámara de Senadores)

The Senate plays a role in approving certain appointments and in appointing and impeaching certain officials. It approves ambassadors and promotions in the armed forces every year. The Senate submits to the president a list of candidates for comptroller general, attorney general, and superintendent of the national banking system. It also hears accusations against members of the Supreme Court of Justice raised by the Chamber of Deputies.

The Lawmaking Process

A bill must be passed by the legislature and must be signed by the president to become a law. Besides members of parliament, the president and vice president and even individual citizens have the right to present bills to parliament for consideration. After it has been submitted, it may be approved, amended, or rejected.

Once the bill is passed in one chamber of parliament, it is forwarded to the other chamber. If the other chamber approves the bill, it is sent to the executive for promulgation.

If the bill has been amended, the initial chamber examines it again. Then the amended bill is either passed by an absolute majority or examined by the two chambers meeting in joint session. A bill that has been finally rejected by either chamber cannot be resubmitted during the same annual session.

If the executive disapproves, the executive returns the bill to the chamber that originated it. The latter meets with the other chamber in joint session, which can amend the bill according to the executive's wish or override the veto by a two-thirds majority.

The law is binding from the day of its publication, unless otherwise specified in the law itself. Besides the exceptions explicitly outlined by the constitution, laws do not have a retroactive effect. They can only be applied for the future.

The Judiciary

Bolivia follows the civil law system. Legislation is the primary source of law, as opposed to case law or jurisprudence. Judges are supposed to determine what the law says. If judges are merely regarded as the "voice of the law," this implies a limitation to their freedom of interpretation. In Bolivia, this limitation is expressed even with regard to the constitution; congress has the power to enact laws interpreting certain aspects of the constitution. However, this opportunity does not mean that the National Congress is generally responsible for constitutional interpretation.

Under the Bolivian constitution, the judicial branch is independent of other government branches. It consists of the Supreme Court, the Constitutional Tribunal, the Judicial Council, and other courts.

The Bolivian Supreme Court (Corte Suprema de Justicia de la Nación) is the highest court of appeal. District Superior Courts (Cortes Superiores de Distrito) are courts of appeal for each department into which the country is geographically divided. They deal with appeals from the lower courts (*juzgados de partido, juzgados de instrucción,* and *juzgados de contravención*). The Supreme Court consists of 12 justices called *ministros* and is divided into five chambers.

The Constitutional Tribunal (Tribunal Constitucional) was introduced in 1994 and began its work in 1999. It has exclusive jurisdiction over all constitutional questions. It is independent and subject only to the constitution. The tribunal consists of a president and six magistrates, who form a single chamber.

The importance of the tribunal arises from the fact that all exercise of state power must be in compliance with the constitution. The tribunal can declare acts of parliament void. Concerning fundamental rights, the tribunal reviews decisions on petitions of habeas corpus and *amparo*. Whereas *amparo* is a general procedural remedy against violations of fundamental rights, the remedy of habeas corpus is a specific one against arbitrary arrest.

In addition to the high legal and political impact some of the court's decisions have had, the tribunal has had positive repercussions for public opinion in Bolivia. An example is the decision to uphold civilian jurisdiction in a case involving alleged killings by army troops. Bolivia's military court system had asserted jurisdiction over the case.

The Council of Judicature (Consejo de la Judicatura) is the administrative and disciplinary body of the judicial power. The council selects candidates for judges to be appointed by congress or by the Supreme Court. It is composed of four councilors, plus the president of the Supreme Court, who also presides over the council.

Other Constitutional Bodies

A two-thirds parliamentary vote can convene a Constituent Assembly (Asamblea Constituyente). It has the sole purpose of reviewing the entire constitution. The Public Defender (Defensor del Pueblo) ensures the compliance of administrative activities with fundamental rights and guarantees.

THE ELECTION PROCESS AND POLITICAL PARTICIPATION

All Bolivians over the age of 18 have the right to vote in elections. Suffrage is universal, direct, equal, individual, secret, free, and obligatory and relies on a public counting of votes and on a system of proportional representation.

The constitution now stipulates that the people govern through their representatives and through a Constituent Assembly, citizen's legislative initiatives, and referenda. These direct democratic elements within the constitution are being applied. For example, the people have voted about the export of Bolivian natural gas.

Parliamentary Elections

The 27 Senate members are elected by proportional representation from party lists. The Senate is composed of three senators for each department. They are elected by universal and direct suffrage: two for the majority party and one for the minority, according to law.

The members in the Chamber of Deputies are elected from party lists but also from districts. Of a fixed number of 130 deputies, 68 are chosen in single-member districts according to a winner-take-all vote (first-past-the-post system). The remainder are chosen by party list on the basis of proportional representation in nine regional multimember districts. Every voter, therefore, has two votes. There is a 3 percent threshold for representation at the national level for the party lists.

In 2005, four major political parties were represented in the chamber.

Presidential Elections

Should presidential candidates fail to win an absolute majority of votes, the result is determined by a secret ballot in congress for the leading two candidates.

POLITICAL PARTIES

The Bolivian party system has evolved from a highly fragmented one to a moderate multiparty system. There is no single predominant party, nor are there alternating majorities. The historical problem of minority governments has almost been solved by the postelectoral bargaining in congress, which tends to ensure majority legislative support.

According to the constitution, representation of the people is exercised through political parties as well as citizens' groups and indigenous peoples (agrupaciones ciudadanas and pueblos indígenas). The legal personality of all these units is acknowledged. The right to become organized is guaranteed by the constitution and further regulated by law (Ley de Partidos Políticos).

CITIZENSHIP

Bolivian citizenship is generally acquired by birth. It is of no relevance where a child is born. Dual citizenship is recognized.

FUNDAMENTAL RIGHTS

The constitution defines fundamental rights and duties in Part One, Title One, almost at the start of the document. In doing so, the framers of the constitution emphasized the importance of these rights.

The constitution guarantees the classic set of individual civil liberties such as the rights to "life, health, and safety" as well as freedom of expression. It also protects collective activities such as freedom of assembly and freedom of religion. Moreover, the constitution guarantees social rights such as the right to work, to social security, and to education. All these rights have binding force for the legislature, the executive, and the judiciary in accordance with the laws that regulate their exercise.

The prohibition of servitude is taken as the starting point. A general equal-treatment clause is contained in Article 6, which prohibits discrimination on the basis of race, sex, language, religion, political or other opinion, origin, economic, or social condition. Paragraph 2 reads: "Human dignity and freedom of the person is inviolable. To respect them and protect them is a primary duty of the state."

Articles 7 and 8 generally enumerate a number of classic rights and duties, which have been further regulated by law. Title Two contains several specific guarantees, including the remedies of habeas corpus and amparo.

The constitution states that public officials are liable to pay compensation for damage caused by their abuse of certain powers in the absence of a declaration of a state of siege. Citizens also enjoy the right to demand information about themselves (habeas data).

Impact and Functions of Fundamental Rights

Fundamental rights in Bolivia represent protection for citizens against a state that has been subjected to frequent changes of administration. Certain constitutional provisions specifically address the armed forces, such as the crime of sedition.

In addition to the traditional set of human rights, there are special constitutional directives that serve as principles to ensure social rights. For example, the constitution recognizes the social, economic, and cultural rights of the indigenous peoples within the national territory and protects them. Some of the social rights provisions serve merely as symbols of the people's struggle for better living conditions rather than as effective protections.

Bolivia has ratified a number of international human right treaties that also have an impact on the protection of fundamental rights. A national plan of action for the promotion and protection of human rights was adopted in 1999. A public defender or ombudsperson oversees the protection of fundamental rights.

Limitations to Fundamental Rights

Fundamental rights are not without limits. Article 7 starts with a general limitation clause, and specific rights contain specific limitation clauses. There is no explicit principle of proportionality to limit the limitations. The constitution underlines that no explicit constitutional guarantee shall be taken as a denial of other rights and guarantees.

ECONOMY

The Bolivian constitution itself does not specify a specific economic system, but it contains several regulations in that sphere. It mandates that the economic system must aspire to principles of social justice in order to ensure to all inhabitants a life worthy of the human being. The private concentration of economic power is prohibited to the extent that it endangers the economic independence of the state. The issue of external economic power is not addressed in the constitution.

Private property is guaranteed as long as it is not used in a way prejudicial to the collective interest. Certain property is regarded to be national property, and the state is allowed to program economic development. According to the constitution, Bolivia is defined as a "social democratic state of law," built on liberty, equality, and justice. Labor is a duty and a right, and it constitutes the basis of the economic and social order. The economic system can generally be described as a social market economy.

RELIGIOUS COMMUNITIES

Freedom of religion or belief is guaranteed, as are rights for religious communities. The constitution recognizes and upholds the Roman Catholic apostolic religion, while also guaranteeing the public exercise of any other form of worship.

Clergy and ministers of any religious faith are forbidden to be president or vice president. They may run for the office of national representative if they resign their position at least 60 days before the election.

MILITARY DEFENSE AND STATE OF EMERGENCY

The constitution identifies three states affecting the country or a portion of its territory: peace, war, and siege.

The president of the republic may declare war with the assent of the National Congress. The president is captain general of the armed forces and directs operations in the event of war. There is a law governing the Supreme Council of National Defense.

In the case of a grave danger caused by "internal disturbance" (*conmoción interna*) or international war, the president, with the approval of the cabinet, may declare a state of siege. The executive may not prolong such a state of siege beyond 90 days nor declare another one within the same year, except with the consent of congress.

Even during war, the rights and guarantees granted by the constitution may not be suspended ipso facto or in a general fashion. The limits may be applied against specified persons charged on good grounds with conspiring against the public order. The administration must report the reasons for the declaration to congress at its next session.

Article 115 reads: "Neither Congress nor any other association shall grant to the executive extraordinary powers, the whole of the public power or give it supremacy by which the life, the honor and the property of the Bolivians shall be at the mercy of the government or any other person whatsoever."

The law requires all Bolivian men who have reached the age of 18 to serve in the armed forces for one year. When the annual intake into the armed forces cannot be made up on a voluntary basis, recruitment is compulsory. A voluntary premilitary service (*servicio premilitar*) for boys and girls between 15 and 19 years of age coexists alongside compulsory military service. Conscientious objection is not recognized.

AMENDMENTS TO THE CONSTITUTION

The same rules apply for amendments to the constitution itself and to laws interpreting the constitution. The amendment provisions may also be amended themselves. Amendments may be either partial or total.

A partial amendment can be made by ordinary law; it requires two separate enactments, in different legislative terms. The first enactment provides a specific reference to the need for amendment (Ley de Necesidad de Reformas). It includes a rough list of all the changes envisaged. The bill must be approved by two-thirds of the members present in both chambers of congress. It is then sent to the executive for promulgation. The executive shall not have the right to veto the law declaring the amendment.

The second enactment provides for the final approval of the proposed amendment. The matter is taken up in the first meetings of the legislative session of a new constitutional term. It must be approved by a two-thirds vote of the National Congress in each chamber, starting with the one in which the amendment was proposed. It then shall be sent to the executive for its promulgation without right of veto.

The constitution allows for the reform of the constitution as a whole. This is done exclusively by a Constituent Assembly, convoked by a special law (Ley Especial de Convocatoria). It must be approved by two-thirds of the members present in both chambers of congress. The executive shall not have the right to veto it.

The principles, guarantees, and rights affirmed by the constitution may not be altered by laws that regulate their exercise. They are enforced even in the absence of specific regulations.

A Constituent Assembly began its work in 2005.

PRIMARY SOURCES

Constitution in Spanish. Available online. URL: http://www.comunica.gov.bo/. Accessed on September 28, 2005.

Constitution in English: A. P. Blaustein and G. H. Flanz, *Constitutions of the Countries of the World.* Dobbs Ferry, N.Y.: Oceana, 1971– .

SECONDARY SOURCES

Donna Lee Van Cott, "A Political Analysis of Legal Pluralism in Bolivia and Colombia." *Journal of Latin American Studies* 32, no. 1 (2000): 207–234.

Eduardo Gamarra, *The System of Justice in Bolivia: An Institutional Analysis.* Miami: Center for the Administration of Justice, Florida International University, 1991.

Rex A. Hudson and Dennis M. Hanratty, eds. *Bolivia—a Country Study.* 3d ed. Washington, D.C.: Federal Research Division, Library of Congress, 1991. Available online. URL: http://lcweb2.loc.gov/frd/cs/cshome.html. Accessed on August 20, 2005.

Stefan Jost et al., eds. *La Constitución Política del Estado—Comentario Crítico.* 2d ed. La Paz, Bolivia: Fundación Konrad Adenauer, 2003.

Justice Studies Center of the Americas (JSCA), *Report on Judicial Systems in the Americas 2002–2003.* Santiago, Chile: JSCA, 2003.

Herbert S. Klein, *A Concise History of Bolivia.* Cambridge: Cambridge University Press, 2003.

El Libertador: Writings of Simon Bolivar. Oxford and New York: Oxford University Press, 2003.

Michael Rahe

BOSNIA AND HERZEGOVINA

At-a-Glance

OFFICIAL NAME
Bosnia and Herzegovina

CAPITAL
Sarajevo

POPULATION
3,600,000 (2005 est.)

SIZE
19,741 sq. mi. (51,129 sq. km)

LANGUAGES
Bosnian, Serbian, and Croatian

RELIGIONS
Muslim 42.8%, Orthodox 30.2%, Catholic 17.6%, other 9.4%

NATIONAL OR ETHNIC COMPOSITION
Bosniac (Muslim) 43.5%, Serbian 31.2%, Croatian 17.4%, Yugoslavian 5.5%, and other 2.4% (the Law on Protection of Rights of the Members of National Minorities specifically lists 17 national minorities—Albanian, Montenegrin, Czech, Italian, Jewish, Hungarian, Macedonian, German, Polish, Gypsian, Romanian, Russian, Ruthenian, Slovakian, Slovenian, Turkish, and Ukrainian)

DATE OF INDEPENDENCE OR CREATION
April 6, 1992

TYPE OF GOVERNMENT
Parliament democracy

TYPE OF STATE
Federal state

TYPE OF LEGISLATURE
Bicameral parliament

DATE OF CONSTITUTION
December 14, 1996

DATE OF LAST AMENDMENT
No amendments

At the very moment of becoming independent on April 1992, Bosnia and Herzegovina was caught up in a war that lasted almost four years, ending only with the implementation of the General Framework Agreement for Peace in Bosnia and Herzegovina in November 1995. Integral to this agreement is the Constitution of Bosnia and Herzegovina.

The constitution proclaims that Bosnia and Herzegovina is a democratic state, which operates under the rule of law, based on free and democratic elections. It belongs to a complex state community of parliamentary democracies, organized federally. It comprises two entities (the Federation of Bosnia and Herzegovina and the Republic of Srpska), each having its own constitution and very significant state powers. The federal institutions of Bosnia and Herzegovina do not have the jurisdictional scope that modern federally organized states generally have.

The state authority is based on the principle of separation of powers into legislative, executive, and judicial. The Constitution of Bosnia and Herzegovina gives special importance to human rights and basic freedoms. It emphasizes full respect for the international legal documents governing this area.

The function of chief of state is performed by a tri-nominal presidency, while legislative power rests with the Parliamentary Assembly. The members of these bodies are elected by citizens through direct elections, based on the pluralistic system of political organization. The executive power rests with the Council of Ministers, whose rights and responsibilities respond to a large degree to the legislative body. The position of the judicial power fully affirms its independence of the executive and legislative powers.

CONSTITUTIONAL HISTORY

The first historical sources on Bosnia and Herzegovina originate from the 10th century. The period from 1180 to 1553 C.E. is considered to be the period of development and strengthening of the medieval Bosnian state. Thereafter, until 1878, Bosnia and Herzegovina was under Turkish rule. That year, it became part of the Austro-Hungarian Monarchy as a "specific area" (*corpus separatum*). At the end of World War I (1914–18), Bosnia and Herzegovina became a part of the Kingdom of Serbs, Croats, and Slovenes (later the Kingdom of Yugoslavia). After World War II (1939–45), it became one of the six federal units of socialist Yugoslavia. It remained in that status until the dissolution of Yugoslavia and recognition of its independence in 1992.

A significant historical characteristic of Bosnia and Herzegovina is its territorial continuity—its borders have not changed significantly since the 17th century. They have been internationally confirmed on more than a few occasions (Karlovac Peace of 1699, Berlin Congress of 1878, [Saint Vitus Day] Constitution of 1921, and international recognition of the Federative People's Republic of Yugoslavia after the end of World War II).

In 1867, during the last years of the Turkish rule, a constitutional law was enacted for the Bosnian Vilayet (district), but it was never in fact applied. In 1910, a new Territorial Statute for Bosnia and Herzegovina was declared as the basic legal document for this "special area" within Austria-Hungary. Within the federative Yugoslavia created after World War II, federal units were formed with mutual equality and certain elements of statehood. On the basis of that, in 1946, a new Constitution of the People's Republic of Bosnia and Herzegovina was enacted, defining it as a "people's republic having the form of republican government." From that time until independence, the constitutional framework of Bosnia and Herzegovina gradually strengthened and fleshed out, especially after the beginning of the 1970s, when the new concept of federalism and statehood of the republics was emerging.

Bosnia and Herzegovina gained independence in 1992.

FORM AND IMPACT OF THE CONSTITUTION

Bosnia and Herzegovina has a written constitution in the form of one document. It is a short constitution with a preamble and 12 articles. Because of the complexity of the legal framework in Bosnia and Herzegovina, the two entities and 10 cantons also have their own written constitutions. In addition, the District Brcko has a statute that, in the hierarchy, falls between the constitutions of the two entities and those of the cantons. However, all of these constitutions, as well as all laws, must be in accordance with the Constitution of Bosnia and Herzegovina. The Constitutional Court of Bosnia and Herzegovina protects constitutionality, and its decisions are final and binding.

According to the Constitution of Bosnia and Herzegovina, the basic principles of international law are an integral part of the legal framework of the country. All civil enforcement agencies that apply legal regulations are required to operate in accordance with internationally recognized standards and with respect to the internationally recognized human rights and fundamental freedoms. Special emphasis is given to the European Convention for the Protection of Human Rights and Fundamental Freedoms and its Protocols, which have priority over all laws.

BASIC ORGANIZATIONAL STRUCTURE

Bosnia and Herzegovina is a complex state composed of two entities (the Federation of Bosnia and Herzegovina and the Republic of Srpska), each covering about half the state territory. The Constitution of Bosnia and Herzegovina divides jurisdiction between the state and the two entities and defines the status of the entities. The jurisdiction of the entities is greater in scope than the jurisdiction of the institutions of Bosnia and Herzegovina.

There are 10 cantons in the Federation of Bosnia and Herzegovina. They differ in size, number of inhabitants, and economic strength but enjoy equal constitutional treatment and legal powers. Taking into consideration their exclusive legal powers and the legal powers they share with the entities, the cantons participate significantly in the overall performance of state authority.

Brcko District has a status of a special territory, directly linked to the institutions of Bosnia and Herzegovina. The city of Mostar also enjoys special legal treatment. Although it was established in principle that the city of Mostar should have the legal powers of a municipality, it significantly differs from other municipalities on the organizational level.

LEADING CONSTITUTIONAL PRINCIPLES

Considering the legal and constitutional framework, the state beyond doubt is a federation, although the constitution does not state that explicitly. One of its entities is itself called a federation, although it does not fulfill even the most basic legal requirements of such a complex form of governmental structure. The name was given prior to the peace agreement that established the constitutional structure. Bosnia and Herzegovina is a republic (although that is not explicitly stated in the constitution), with a parliamentary system.

The preamble of the constitution proclaims the following principles: respect for human dignity, liberty, and equality; dedication to peace, justice, tolerance, and reconciliation; commitment to sovereignty, territorial integrity, and political independence of the state; protection of private property and promotion of a market economy; full respect for international humanitarian law; and conviction that democratic governmental institutions and fair procedures best produce peaceful relations within a pluralist society. The rule of law and the principle of separation of powers, resting on the free will of the people expressed by democratic elections, are of key importance for the realization of these principles.

CONSTITUTIONAL BODIES

The Constitution of Bosnia and Herzegovina foresees the following governing bodies: Parliamentary Assembly, presidency, Council of Ministers, Constitutional Court, and Central Bank.

The Parliamentary Assembly

The Parliamentary Assembly is a representative body having constitutional and legislative powers. Its composition and decision-making process express the principle of national sovereignty, equality of all three constituent peoples (Bosniacs, Serbs, and Croats), and the complex structure of the state. The Parliamentary Assembly has two chambers: the House of Peoples and the House of Representatives. The House of Peoples has 15 members—five Bosniacs and five Croats (elected in the Council of Peoples of the Federation's Parliament and only from the territory of that entity) and five Serbs (selected by the National Assembly of the Republika Srpska and only from the territory of that entity). The House of Representatives has 42 members who are elected directly by the voters. Two-thirds of the mandates are elected from the territory of the federation and one-third from the territory of the Republika Srpska.

The Parliamentary Assembly has legislative and budgetary powers. It also has the power to decide on constitutional matters, to participate in decision making with respect to foreign policy, and to control the Council of Ministers. It has authority over matters needed to complete its duties or matters for which it has agreement of the two entities.

The decision-making process of the Parliamentary Assembly is very complex. Nine members of the House of Peoples compose a quorum, provided that at least three Bosniac, three Croat, and three Serb members are present. A majority of all members elected to the House of Representatives also constitute a quorum. All decisions in both chambers are brought about by the majority of those present and voting, provided that the majority includes at least one-third of the votes from the territory of each entity.

The Lawmaking Process

The constitution prescribes that all bills require the approval of both chambers by a majority of those present and voting in each. The delegates and members are mandated to try to win approval from at least one-third of the votes of delegates or members from each entity. If this is not achieved, the chair and deputy chairs meet as a commission and attempt to obtain approval within three days of the vote. If those efforts fail, decisions are made by a majority of those present and voting, provided that the dissenting votes do not include two-thirds or more of the delegates or members elected from either entity.

A proposed decision of the Parliamentary Assembly may be declared to be destructive of a vital interest of the Bosniac, Croat, or Serb people by a majority of, as appropriate, the Bosniac, Croat, or Serb delegates selected in the assembly. Such a proposed decision requires for approval in the House of Peoples a majority of the Bosniac, Croat, and Serb delegates present and voting.

When a majority of the Bosniac, Croat, or Serb delegates objects to the declaration of such a decision as destructive for the vital interest of one of the three constituent peoples, the chair of the House of Peoples convenes a Joint Commission comprising three delegates, one each selected by the Bosniac, Croat, or Serb delegates, to resolve the issue. If the commission fails to do so within five days, the matter is referred to the Constitutional Court, which reviews it for procedural regularity in an expedited process.

Decisions of the Parliamentary Assembly do not take effect before publication. Both chambers publish a complete record of their deliberations and in general deliberate publicly.

The Presidency

The presidency of Bosnia and Herzegovina is a collective chief of state; it carries executive powers within the framework of the jurisdiction of the institutions of Bosnia and Herzegovina. Its members are directly elected for a term of four years with the possibility of reelection for an additional consecutive term. The presidency consists of three members: one Bosniac, one Croat, and one Serb. The presidency has the function of expressing and securing the interests and the equality of all three constituent peoples. Each voter votes for one seat in the presidency; members of the Bosniac and Croat peoples are elected from the territory of the Federation of Bosnia and Herzegovina, and the Serb member is directly elected from the territory of the Republika Srpska. The members of the presidency appoint the chairperson among themselves, and this function rotates at prescribed intervals.

The presidency is responsible for conducting foreign policy; appointing ambassadors and other international representatives of Bosnia and Herzegovina; representing Bosnia and Herzegovina locally and internationally; negotiating, executing, or opposing international agreements; and, with the consent of the Parliamentary Assembly, ratifying such agreements. The presidency executes the decisions of the assembly and proposes the annual budget to the assembly, upon recommendation of the Council of Ministers. Each member of the presidency, ex officio, is also a civilian commander of the armed forces.

The constitution explicitly provides that the presidency must try to adopt its decisions by consensus, but it also provides for the possibility that decisions can be adopted by two members of the presidency when all efforts to reach consensus have failed. In that case, a dissenting member of the presidency may declare that decision destructive of a vital interest of the entity from which this member was elected. Such a decision is then referred to the National Assembly of the Republika Srpska or to the Bosniac or the Croat delegates of the House of Peoples of the federation, depending on which member made the declaration. If the declaration of opposition is confirmed by a two-thirds majority in the respective body, the challenged presidency's decision will not take effect.

The Council of Ministers

The Council of Ministers is an executive body having the function of an administration. Its mandate is four years. The president nominates the chair of the Council of Ministers, who takes office upon the approval of the House of Representatives of the Parliamentary Assembly. The elected chair is granted power to nominate ministers. The chair and the ministers assume power together upon approval of the House of Representatives. During the nomination process, special attention is given to representation from the entities, and no more than two-thirds of all ministers can be appointed from the territory of the federation. Also, a minister and his or her deputy cannot be from the same constituent people.

The Council of Ministers is responsible for conducting politics and policies within the competency of the institutions of Bosnia and Herzegovina.

The Constitutional Court

The Constitutional Court of Bosnia and Herzegovina has nine members—four elected by the Parliament of the Federation of Bosnia and Herzegovina, two elected by the National Assembly of the Republika Srpska, and three internationals elected through a process determined by the Parliamentary Assembly. The Constitutional Court has jurisdiction over the constitutionality of the entities' constitutions and laws. It can also decide on any dispute that arises between the institutions of Bosnia and Herzegovina and the entities or between entities and can determine the constitutionality of any decision of the entities to set up relations with neighboring states. In addition, the Constitutional Court has appellate jurisdiction over constitutional issues arising from a judgment of any court. All decisions are issued by the majority of the court's members.

In Bosnia and Herzegovina, there are also Constitutional Courts on the level of the entity. The jurisdiction of the Constitutional Court of the Federation of Bosnia and Herzegovina is to determine the constitutionality of the cantonal constitutions and the laws and regulations of the entity and the cantons. It also decides matters with respect to issues arising between bodies of the entity and matters between these bodies and the canton, city, or municipality, and it secures legal protection for local self-government.

The Constitutional Court of the Republika Srpska has jurisdiction to decide constitutional matters of that entity, including jurisdictional conflicts among various state bodies. It also rules on whether the general documents of political parties conform to the entity's constitution and laws.

Juridical power in Bosnia and Herzegovina is predominantly within the jurisdictional domain of the entities, each entity having its own Constitutional Court. However, since 2003, there is also a Court of Bosnia and Herzegovina, the jurisdiction of which is becoming increasingly more significant, specifically in criminal cases. The general characteristic of the judicial power is its complete separation from legislative and executive powers. All questions relating to the independence of the judiciary are within the jurisdiction of the courts and Prosecutor's Council of Bosnia and Herzegovina. This applies to the election of judges, their compensation, and disciplinary matters. Judges serve until the age of 70.

The Central Bank

The Central Bank has exclusive authority for issuing of currency and for monetary policy throughout Bosnia and Herzegovina. It is run by a governing board consisting of five members nominated by the presidency of Bosnia and Herzegovina for a period of six years. The board members elect the governor of the Central Bank from among themselves.

THE ELECTION PROCESS

The Constitution of Bosnia and Herzegovina pays special attention to voting rights and specifies in detail the way central state bodies are elected. The legitimacy and the legality of these bodies are based on the basic and equal right to vote, expressed by direct and secret voting in free, fair, and democratic elections. All citizens of Bosnia and Herzegovina who are at least 18 years of age have the right to vote. However, taking into consideration the extreme consequences of the war in Bosnia and Herzegovina, the constitution explicitly provides that no one serving a sentence handed down by the International Tribunal for the Former Yugoslavia and no one indicted by the tribunal who has failed to appear before it can be a candidate or hold any public office in the territory of Bosnia and Herzegovina.

POLITICAL PARTIES

Bosnia and Herzegovina has a pluralistic political system, based on the basic human freedom of each person to associate freely with others. Political parties are a primary factor of public life and a key subject of the election system.

CITIZENSHIP

There are two types of citizenship, one of Bosnia and Herzegovina and once of each entity. All citizens of either entity are thereby citizens of Bosnia and Herzegovina. The constitution provides that no person can be deprived of citizenship arbitrarily so as to leave him or her stateless. Citizens of Bosnia and Herzegovina may hold the citizenship of another country, provided that there is a bilateral agreement on that issue. A citizen of Bosnia and Herzegovina abroad enjoys the protection of Bosnia and Herzegovina.

FUNDAMENTAL RIGHTS

The Constitution of Bosnia and Herzegovina enumerates 13 human rights and basic freedoms (Article II) and 16 international legal documents on human rights applicable in this state. Among the latter is the European Convention for the Protection of Human Rights and Fundamental Freedoms (and its Protocols), which applies directly and has legal priority over all other laws. Taken as a whole, these include civil, political, economic, social, and cultural rights.

Proclaiming that Bosnia and Herzegovina and both entities shall ensure the highest level of internationally recognized human rights and fundamental freedoms, the constitution emphasizes the responsibility of all courts, agencies, government institutions, and instrumentalities operated by or within the entities to apply and conform with the human rights and fundamental freedoms referred to in the constitution. Discrimination on any basis is specifically forbidden. No amendment to the constitution may eliminate or diminish any of the rights and freedoms listed in Article II of the constitution or alter existing provisions.

ECONOMY

The preamble of the constitution states among its principles the desire to promote general welfare and economic growth through the protection of private property and the promotion of a market economy. The right to property is explicitly guaranteed. On the basis of this principle, all people retain freedom of movement of persons, goods, services, and capital throughout Bosnia and Herzegovina. According to the constitution, the International Pact on Economic, Social, and Cultural Rights counts among the documents that are included within the legal system of Bosnia and Herzegovina. This treaty not only requires application and respect by all of those in power but also serves as an inspiration for constitutional decisions.

RELIGIOUS COMMUNITIES

The constitution lists freedom of thought, conscience, and religion as basic freedoms. The freedom to express one's religion publicly or privately in accordance with the free will of the believer is guaranteed; no one may force anyone to reveal or alter religious beliefs. Public expression of religion can only be limited where prescribed by law and in accordance with international standards, if that is necessary in the interest of public security, public morals, or the protection of the rights and freedoms of others.

All religious communities are equal in rights and obligations. They have full freedom of religious activity, provided they do not spread intolerance and prejudice against other religious communities and citizens and that their activities are not contrary to the constitutional system.

Religious communities are separate from the state. The state cannot establish a state religion or a state religious community of any kind.

MILITARY DEFENSE AND STATE OF EMERGENCY

As a result of the peace agreement, there are armed forces on the entities' level; they are obligated to function in accordance with the principles in the constitution of Bosnia and Herzegovina. There is an obligation to serve in the military, but a person can raise conscientious objections and be excused, provided the person completes an alternative service of a clearly civil nature.

All armed forces must act consistently with the sovereignty and territorial integrity of Bosnia and Herzegovina. Neither entity can threaten or use force against the other entity. The armed forces of one entity can under no circumstances enter into or stay within the territory of the other entity, without the consent of its government and presidency of Bosnia and Herzegovina. Each member of the presidency, by virtue of the office, has civilian command authority over its armed forces.

There is a standing committee with responsibility to coordinate the activities of the armed forces in Bosnia and Herzegovina. It includes the members of the presidency of Bosnia and Herzegovina, who in turn choose the members.

The Constitution of Bosnia and Herzegovina does not address potential states of emergency. Such provisions can be found in the constitutions of the entities.

AMENDMENTS TO THE CONSTITUTION

As far as amendments go, the Constitution of Bosnia and Herzegovina belongs to the category of strict constitutions.

An amendment requires approval by both chambers of the Parliamentary Assembly of Bosnia and Herzegovina, including a two-thirds majority of those present and voting in the House of Representatives. In the House of Peoples, it can be adopted by the majority of the members present and voting, but there must be a quorum of at least nine members—three Bosniacs, three Croats, and three Serbs. However, should it be argued that the amendment affects the "vital interests" of one of the constituent peoples, then it must be approved by majorities of the Bosniac, Serb, and Croat members present and voting.

PRIMARY SOURCES

Constitution in English. Available online. URL: http://www.ohr.int/dpa/default.asp?contend_id=372. Accessed on August 25, 2005.

Constitution in Bosnian: *Ustav Bosne i Hercegovine.* Available online. URL: http://www.fbihvlada.gov.ba/bosanski/bosna/index.html. Accessed on August 2, 2005.

SECONDARY SOURCES

Bureau of Public Affairs, U.S. Department of State, "Background Note and Country Reports on Human Rights Practices and International Religious Freedom Report 2004." Available online. URL: http://www.state.gov/. Accessed on September 16, 2005.

Neđjo Milićević, *"Veliki drustveni znacaj ustavnih amandmana" Revija slobodne misli 99,* no. 38/02 (2002): 5–14.

Office of the High Representative, Laws of Bosnia and Herzegovina. Available online. URL: http://www.ohr.int/ohr-dept/legal/laws-of-bih/default.asp?content_id=31549. Accessed on August 29, 2005.

Kasim Trnka and Neđjo Milicevic, *Komentar Ustava Federacije Bosne i Hercegovine.* Sarajevo: Centar za promociju civilnog društva, 2004.

Kasim Trnka, *Ustavno pravo.* Sarajevo: Univerzitetska knjiga, 2000.

Neđjo Milićević

BOTSWANA

At-a-Glance

OFFICIAL NAME
Republic of Botswana

CAPITAL
Gaborone

POPULATION
1,639,833 (July 2006 est.)

SIZE
224,607 sq. mi. (581,730 sq. km)

LANGUAGES
Setswana (national), English (official)

RELIGION
Over 60% Christian (main denominations Roman Catholic, Anglican, Zion, Lutheran, and Methodist)

NATIONAL OR ETHNIC COMPOSITION
The Tswana people (Bakwena, Bangwato, and Bangwaketse) traditionally half or more of the country's population; small Asian and European population

DATE OF INDEPENDENCE OR CREATION
September 30, 1966

TYPE OF GOVERNMENT
Multiparty parliamentary democracy

TYPE OF STATE
Unitary state

TYPE OF LEGISLATURE
Unicameral parliament with a House of Chiefs

DATE OF CONSTITUTION
September 30, 1966

DATE OF LAST AMENDMENT
August 8, 2005

Botswana is a multiparty democracy. The 1966 constitution of Botswana provides for a republican form of government headed by a president, with three main organs of government, namely, the legislature, the executive, and the judiciary. The legislature, which comprises the National Assembly and the president, acting in consultation on tribal matters with the House of Chiefs, is the supreme legislative authority in Botswana. The executive branch consists of the cabinet, headed by the president. It is responsible for initiating and directing national policy; controlling government ministries and departments, which are headed by ministers and are staffed by civil servants; and overseeing parastatal corporations that provide certain national services. The judiciary administers and interprets the law of the land and is independent of both the executive and the legislature.

Religious freedom is guaranteed by the constitution, and state and religion are separated. The economic system may be described as a social market economy with strong encouragement of private enterprise through tax benefits. The military is subject to the civil government in law and in fact.

CONSTITUTIONAL HISTORY

In March 1885, Botswana was declared a British Protectorate by royal decree. Extensive territories belonging to Botswana's southern chiefdoms were incorporated into the then-British colony of South Africa under the name British Bechuanaland.

During the colonial period, various attempts were made to incorporate Bechuanaland into Southern Rhodesia and later into the Union of South Africa. The 1908 Act of Union that created the Union of South Africa provided that the union should grow by incorporating other territories, such as Bechuanaland, Lesotho, and Swaziland. However, the provision stated that this could only be done with the consent of the peoples of those territories. Bechuanaland chiefs, particularly Khama II of Bangwato, Bathoen I of Bangwaketse, Sebele I of the Bakwena, and later nationalist leaders vehemently opposed the idea of incorporation.

In 1961, a new constitution provided for an Advisory Executive Council; a representative Legislative Council of 34 members, 10 of whom were Africans; and an Advisory African Council. A judiciary was established, with a High Court comprising a chief justice and an assistant judge. The high commissioner and the resident commissioner were required to consult the Executive Council, although they were not bound by the council's decisions. Laws were made by the Legislative Council. The resident commissioner, however, reserved the right to enact or enforce any bill or motion not passed by the Legislative Council if he or she considered it necessary in the interest of public order, public faith, or good government. The African Council was to act as an electoral college, electing local candidates to the Legislative Council and advising the resident commissioner on tribal matters.

During 1963 and 1964, a series of constitutional discussions took place to determine proposals for internal self-government based on universal adult suffrage and a ministerial form of government. Early in 1964, the first census was conducted as a basis for delimitation of constituencies. By the end of the year, voters had been registered in all 31 of the new constituencies. In 1965, the country's capital was transferred from Mafeking, South Africa, to Gaborone in Bechuanaland. The first general elections were held in March 1965, and the Bechuanaland Democratic Party (now Botswana Democratic Party), led by Seretse Khama, won a landslide victory, taking 28 of the 31 contested seats. On September 30, 1966, after some 80 years of colonial rule, the Bechuanaland Protectorate became the independent Republic of Botswana.

FORM AND IMPACT OF THE CONSTITUTION

Botswana has a written constitution that takes precedence over all other national laws. Customary international law automatically forms part of domestic law that is subject to statutory modification or abrogation. As for municipal law, treaties and conventions form part of domestic law only if incorporated through national legislation.

BASIC ORGANIZATIONAL STRUCTURE

Botswana is a unitary state. For electoral purposes, it is divided into constituencies, each of which sends one member to the National Assembly. To ensure equitable representation, the Judicial Service Commission is required at intervals of not less than five years and not more than 10 years to appoint a Delimitation Commission to determine whether changes are needed. There are 406 district councils with elected councilors, but they have no fiscal autonomy and depend on the central government for revenue.

LEADING CONSTITUTIONAL PRINCIPLES

The Botswana constitution provides for a republican parliamentary form of government, headed by a president, with three main organs of government, namely, the executive, the legislature, and the judiciary. There is no preamble to the constitution with guiding principles. However, since independence, Botswana has been guided by four national principles: democracy, development, self-reliance, and unity. These principles are derived from the traditional culture of the Tswana people and, taken together, are designed to promote social harmony.

There is a strong respect for the rule of law, and government generally respects the human rights of its citizens. There is generally no governmental interference in the work of the independent judiciary. Fundamental rights, such as life, liberty, security of the person, and freedom of conscience, expression, assembly, and association, are guaranteed by the constitution and are uniformly upheld.

CONSTITUTIONAL BODIES

The most important bodies provided by the constitution are the executive, parliament (the legislature), the House of Chiefs, the judiciary, the Judicial Service Commission, and the Public Service Commission.

The Executive

The executive consists of the state president and cabinet ministers. The state president is the personification of the state. Legally, the president is head of the executive, commander in chief of the armed forces, and an ex-officio member of the legislature. The president has the power to dissolve parliament; select or dismiss the vice president, ministers, and assistant ministers; and exercise the prerogative of mercy. In international affairs, the president has the power to declare war, sign peace treaties, and recognize foreign states and governments. The president holds office for a period of 10 years.

The president normally acts on the advice of the cabinet, which is selected by the president from members of parliament. The cabinet at present consists of 14 ministers and three assistant ministers, all of whom run ministries and departments of government. Cabinet ministers, as members of parliament, participate in parliamentary debates, but they are normally bound by the ethic of collective responsibility. Ministers are responsible to the National Assembly, but the president may appoint or dismiss ministers without consulting the National Assembly or cabinet.

Parliament

Parliament is the supreme legislative authority in Botswana, but laws passed by parliament are subject to review by the judiciary to ascertain their constitutional validity. Parliament consists of the president and the National Assembly, and where tribal and customary matters are involved, it is obliged to act in consultation with the House of Chiefs. The president is a member of the National Assembly and has the power to address, summon, or dissolve it at any time. The president addresses the National Assembly at the opening of a new parliament every five years or whenever there is an important national issue. The president also addresses the last session of parliament after dissolving it to call a general election.

The main functions of parliament are to pass laws regulating the life of the nation, to scrutinize government policy and administration, and to monitor government expenditure. The National Assembly is a representative body elected by universal adult suffrage every five years. There are currently 57 seats in the National Assembly, and the quorum for meetings is one-third of members.

The House of Chiefs

Membership of the House of Chiefs consists of not fewer than 33 or more than 35 members, which shall be constituted as follows: (1) one person each for the time being performing the functions of a chief from 12 designated areas of the country, which may be fewer than 12 but not fewer than 10; (2) five persons appointed by the president; and (3) such number of persons, not being more than 20, as may be selected under the provisions of Section 78 of the constitution. They cannot engage actively in politics while serving in the house, but active participation in politics prior to being a member of the house shall not bar any person from being such a member.

The house sits whenever the executive government or National Assembly has referred a bill to it, whenever it has important business to transact, or at least once a year.

The Lawmaking Process

A bill presented to and approved by parliament is forwarded to the president for signature. The House of Chiefs does not have legislative or veto power. However, a draft of any National Assembly bill of tribal concern must first be referred to the House of Chiefs for advisory opinion.

The Judiciary

The judiciary is independent of the executive and parliament. The highest court in Botswana is the Court of Appeal, which consists of a president and such number of justices as may be prescribed by parliament; in addition, the chief justice and justices of the High Court (which is lower in the hierarchy than the Court of Appeal) also serve on the Court of Appeal. The court has primarily an appellate jurisdiction on all matters, civil, criminal, or constitutional. Many of its decisions have had significant legal and political impact. For example, its decision that certain sections of the Citizenship Act discriminated against women led to the amendment of the law to allow citizenship to be obtained through either the father or the mother of a child.

Other courts, such as the High Court, Magistrates Courts, and Customary Courts, deal with various matters before they reach the Court of Appeal.

Judicial Service Commission

The Judicial Service Commission advises the state president in the appointment of judicial officers. It is composed of the chief justice as chairperson, the chair of the Public Service Commission or the chair's nominee, a nominee from the Law Society, a nominee of the attorney general, and a nominee from the Court of Appeal.

Public Service Commission

The Public Service Commission is responsible for the appointment of persons to designated public offices. It is composed of a chairperson and not fewer than two or more than four other members. The commission is not subject to the direction or control of any other person or authority in the exercise of its functions under the constitution, though it must follow procedures established by law.

THE ELECTION PROCESS

All people of Botswana who have attained the age of 18 years are entitled to vote in elections, provided they have not been certified as insane or of unsound mind, are not under a death sentence, have not been declared insolvent in any part of the commonwealth, or are not under a sentence of imprisonment exceeding six months. The elections are conducted under the auspices of an Independent Electoral Commission, the chairperson of which is a High Court judge.

POLITICAL PARTIES

Botswana is a multiparty democracy. As of July 1998, there were 13 political parties, but some of them have since merged. The Botswana Democratic Party, the current ruling party, has dominated the political scene since independence.

CITIZENSHIP

Under the Citizenship Act of 1998, Botswana citizenship is primarily acquired by birth. A person born in Botswana shall be regarded as a citizen of Botswana if at the time of his or her birth his or her father or mother was a citizen of Botswana. A person born outside Botswana shall be a citizen by descent if at the time of his or her birth his or her father or mother was a citizen of Botswana. Citizenship can also be acquired by registration, for example, if a person is adopted, or by naturalization. Any person who is a citizen of Botswana and also a citizen of another country loses Botswana citizenship at the age of 21 years, unless such a person has renounced the other citizenship.

FUNDAMENTAL RIGHTS

Chapter II of the Botswana constitution gives protection to the fundamental rights and freedoms of the individual. Section 3 of that chapter, for example, provides that every person in Botswana (regardless of his or her race, place of origin, political opinions, color, creed, or sex) has the right to all of the following rights and freedoms: life, liberty, and security of person; protection of the law; protection of the privacy of home and other property, and from deprivation of property without compensation; freedom of conscience, of expression, of assembly, and association.

The constitution elaborates on these rights and the circumstances under which they can be lawfully abrogated. Some of the elaborations include protection from discrimination, protection from unlawful arrest or detention, right to a fair hearing in any court of law, and freedom from the imposition of torture or inhuman or degrading punishment.

Impact and Function of Fundamental Rights

The human rights record of Botswana is very good. In 2003, for instance, there were no reports of arbitrary or unlawful deprivation of life committed by the government or its agents and no reports of politically motivated disappearances. The courts vigorously uphold the guaranteed freedoms, and where these are violated, they declare such actions unconstitutional and apply the appropriate remedy.

Limitations to Fundamental Rights

There are two cardinal areas of limitations on fundamental rights.

Bill of Rights provisions are subject to such limitations as will ensure that their enjoyment does not prejudice the rights and freedoms of others or the public interest. The constitution does not define clearly what constitutes public interest. In a number of cases, the government makes that determination; an individual who is aggrieved by such a decision may challenge it in court.

Second, any law made during a declared emergency cannot be held to be inconsistent with or in contravention of the provisions of the constitution dealing with personal liberties. This limitation arises, for example, at times of war or natural disaster such as earthquake, flood, or outbreak of serious infectious disease.

ECONOMY

The Botswana constitution does not prescribe any type of economic system. However, there are provisions in the constitution that may influence the type of economic system that is pursued, such as protection of private property, prohibitions on the deprivation of property without compensation, and freedom of association. Accordingly, since Botswana's independence, the government has pursued a market-oriented economic policy with strong encouragement for private enterprise through tax incentives.

RELIGIOUS COMMUNITIES

Freedom of religion is guaranteed under freedom of conscience, assembly, and association. Botswana is a secular state, and as such there is no established state church. However, all religious denominations are registrable under the Societies Act.

MILITARY DEFENSE AND STATE OF EMERGENCY

The Botswana defense force is a creature of statute and is charged with the defense of Botswana and with such other duties as may from time to time be determined by the president. Membership in the defense force is voluntary, and there is no conscription. The defense force is subject to civil government. The president is the commander in chief and appoints the force commander. The president may at any time order the whole or part of the force to be employed outside Botswana. The president has the constitutional power to declare a state of emergency during which the president can deploy the force within Botswana, as the president sees fit.

AMENDMENTS TO THE CONSTITUTION

The constitution may be amended by parliament, in some cases subject to the approval of the electorate.

PRIMARY SOURCES
Constitution in English (extracts). Available online. URL: http://www.chr.up.ac.za/hr_docs/constitutions/docs/Botswana(summary)(rev).doc. Accessed on August 12, 2005.

SECONDARY SOURCES
Charles Manga Fombad, "The Constitutional Protection against Discrimination in Botswana." *International and Comparative Law Quarterly* 53, pt. 1 (2004): 139–170.
Christoph Heyns, *Human Rights Law in Africa*. Vol. 2, *Domestic Human Rights Law in Africa*. Leiden: Martinus Nijhoff, 2004.
Daniel Ntanda Nsereko, *Constitutional Law of Botswana*. Gaborone: Pula Press, 2002.
Kenneth E. Obeng, *Botswana Institutions of Democracy and Government of Botswana*. Gaborone: Associated Press, 2001.

Emmanuel Kwabena Quansah

BRAZIL

At-a-Glance

OFFICIAL NAME
Federal Republic of Brazil

CAPITAL
Brasília

POPULATION
179,284,871 (2004)

SIZE
3,287,357 sq. mi. (8,514,215 sq. km)

LANGUAGES
Portuguese

RELIGIONS
Catholic 73%, Protestant 15%, Spiritism/Kardecism 1.3%, Afro-Brazilian Umbanda and Candomblé 0.31%, Buddhism 0.12%, unaffiliated or other 9.2%

NATIONAL OR ETHNIC COMPOSITION
White 53%, Mulatto 38%, black 6.2%, Asian 0.44%, Native Indian 0.43%, undeclared 0.71%

DATE OF INDEPENDENCE OR CREATION
September 7, 1822

TYPE OF GOVERNMENT
Presidential

TYPE OF STATE
Federal state

TYPE OF LEGISLATURE
Bicameral congress

DATE OF CONSTITUTION
October 5, 1988

DATE OF LAST AMENDMENT
March 3, 2006

Brazil has a democratic and presidential system of government based on the rule of law, with a clear division of executive, legislative, and judicial powers. Organized as a federation, Brazil is made up of a central government and 27 federal states including the federal district. The federal constitution guarantees many human and social rights. Most of them have a purely political or programmatic character with only limited legal impact. However, the so-called public freedoms, such as the freedom of speech, can at any time be protected against state action by a judicial writ.

The president is the directly elected head of state and government. The president can participate in the lawmaking process, as every law requires presidential assent. The members of the National Congress are also elected directly. A pluralistic system of political parties is guaranteed.

Religious freedom is guaranteed, and the state and the religious communities are strictly separate. The economic system can be described as a market economy. There is a constitutional principle of the social function of property, which introduces a social element into the interpretation of civil law. However, this has not been sufficient to achieve the social constitutional goal of developing a free and equal society based on solidarity. The military is subject to the civil government. Brazil undertakes to respect and promote several principles of public international law, such as world peace, self-determination of peoples, and repudiation of terrorism and racism.

CONSTITUTIONAL HISTORY

Brazil was proclaimed an independent political entity by Crown Prince Dom Pedro I on September 7, 1822, after being a Portuguese colony since its discovery in the year 1500. The decisive fact in the process of independence was the arrival, in 1808, of the Portuguese royal family, who were escaping from the invasion of Portugal by Napoléon. The government was transferred to the city of Rio de Janeiro, which became the capital of the empire.

The first type of government was, therefore, a hereditary monarchy but also a constitutional and representative one, according to Article 3 of the first Brazilian constitution established by Dom Pedro in 1824. One of the most important provisions in that constitution was, in Article 3, the definition of Roman Catholicism as the official religion of the empire. Any other religion was tolerated only as a "domestic cult, or private in places with that destination, without any external configuration of a temple." The constitution granted "moderator" power upon the emperor, who had final say on all conflicts involving the exercise of the other three powers, the legislative, executive, and judicial.

The monarchy survived for 77 years, falling largely as a result of the collapse of the slave-based economy after the abolition of slavery in 1888. Republican ideals, imported by young members of the Brazilian elite who had studied in Europe, seeped into the Brazilian political scene at the end of the 1880s, leading to the proclamation of the Federal Republic on November 15, 1889. The first republican constitution was enacted in 1891. It consolidated the separation of powers and harmony between them, extinguished the moderator power, and catalogued a series of fundamental rights for Brazilian citizens, defined as anyone born on Brazilian territory. The constitution called for equal protection of the law, although beggars and illiterates were excluded from suffrage. Finally, it must be noted that the choice of a federative form of state and a presidential regime occurred under the influence of the model of the United States of America. Even the name Republic of the United States of Brazil reveals the source of inspiration for the revolutionary republicans.

The First or Old Republic, the period from 1889 to 1930, ended with the "hegemony crisis." The state of São Paulo, representing the coffee monoculture, and the cattle power state of Minas Gerais had until then shared a monopoly of presidential power. A new populist, authoritarian president now emerged out of Rio Grande do Sul. The Getúlio Vargas era (1930–45) had begun. In an attempted constitutionalist revolution in 1932, the State of São Paulo lost a struggle against practically all the other federal states, which remained loyal to Getúlio Vargas's central government. In 1934, the new Constitution of the Republic of the United States of Brazil was promulgated; it consolidated the 1891 constitution's liberal democratic achievements while attending to the particularities of the political situation after the revolution in 1932.

In 1937, at a time when fascism and Nazism were triumphant in continental Europe, Getúlio Vargas imposed the "New State" Constitution, revoking the democratic document of 1934. Basic public liberties, such as freedom of the press and freedom of speech, existed now entirely at the discretion of the state. A far-reaching mechanism of state repression of all democratic manifestations was created. In 1938, for example, a department of information and press was created with constitutional support. It was responsible for widespread censorship and the persecution of opponents of the new totalitarian regime.

Concomitantly with the defeat of fascism in Europe, democracy was restored in Brazil. Bereft of political support and having completely changed from support of fascism-Nazism to collaboration with the Allied countries in the persecution of war criminals, Vargas adapted himself to the new era of democratic reconstruction and strategically gave up power. Direct elections were held, and a new Brazilian constitution was promulgated on September 18, 1946.

The new constitution did not follow the classic liberal model. On the contrary, it guaranteed, besides classic fundamental rights, many others rights and specific duties. This was a constitution with a strong social nature establishing programmatic norms, as had occurred two decades before in the German Weimar Republic (1918–33).

This new (fifth) constitutional period also had a relatively short life and was marked with enormous initial (1945–54) and final (1961–64) instabilities. Getúlio Vargas was again, in 1951, the president of the republic but this time elected in direct elections. However, when his new totalitarian plans were frustrated, after he again claimed popular support to dissolve parliament, he committed suicide in 1954.

Brazil enjoyed a period of stability and progress under Juscelino Kubitscheck (1956–60). The period ended with another populist president with authoritarian aims, Jânio da Silva Quadros, who resigned the presidency in 1961 because of "hidden forces," as he called them. Since his replacement, the demagoguic socialist vice president João Goulart, belonged to a different party, serious political instability resulted, aggravated by an intensification of the cold war. On March 31, 1964, parts of the Brazilian military performed a coup d'état, which they themselves called a revolution, relying on substantial but not open support from the United States of America.

The military imposed the 1967 constitution. It changed the country's name to the Federal Republic of Brazil, thus demonstrating the nationalist orientation of the military, which was increasingly opposed to the growing U.S. influence in Latin America. The 1967 constitution provided for the so-called institutional acts that curbed individual rights and the rule of law. This reached its peak with Institutional Act No. 5 in 1969, which dissolved parliament. The military remained in power until the voluntary handover during the 1980s.

The 1980s were characterized by the return to democracy, aided by movements such as the *diretas já* (direct elections now) campaign. Political amnesty was granted to exiles, enabling their return to Brazil. However, the *diretas já* campaign was frustrated by parliamentary representatives who represented the old regime. Direct elections to the presidency did not come about until 1989, although the governors of the federal states were directly elected in 1985. A new constitution, created at a National Constitutional Convention consisting of representatives from a broad cross section of Brazilian society, was promulgated on October 5, 1988. It consolidated this second era of redemocratization.

FORM AND IMPACT OF THE CONSTITUTION

Brazil has a written constitution, codified in a single document, that takes precedence over all other national law.

International law must be in accordance with the constitution to be applicable within Brazil. The constitution is the basis of a Brazilian democratic and constitutional state devoted to the rule of law.

The text of the constitution is a political program that synthesizes frequently antagonistic ideas. It has the nature of a commitment to all sections of society, as did the constitution of the German Weimar Republic. It represents a symbolic power of transformation of the state and society rather than a really normative power.

BASIC ORGANIZATIONAL STRUCTURE

Brazil is a federation made up of 27 federal states, including a federal capital district of Brasilia. Each of the states has a constitution modeled in part on the federal document but with an identity of its own. The states differ considerably in geographic area, population size, and economic strength, but they have equal legislative, administrative, and judicial powers.

The explicit federal nature of the constitution has not defeated a strong tendency toward centralization. The distribution of legislative powers between the union and the states confirms the reality of a weak federalism. Articles 8 to 42 reserve few exclusive powers to the states. The union does have exclusive legislative powers (such as in criminal and procedural law), while the states have merely residual powers.

The municipalities also have relative autonomy, although they are not considered federation entities. In addition to autonomous public administrations (executive power), they have municipal chambers that are responsible for local law. They do not, however, have judicial powers. Article 30 allows the municipalities to "institute and collect taxes within their jurisdiction, as well as to apply their revenues . . . within the periods established by law." They also have powers to protect the local historic heritage. Matters that were traditionally part of the states' competence, such as education and, above all, public security, have also been assumed by the municipalities.

LEADING CONSTITUTIONAL PRINCIPLES

Besides the principle of federalism in Article 1 (also protected by Article 60), the separation of powers guaranteed in Article 2 is among the structural principles of the constitution; it is excluded from the possibility of amendment in Article 60. Article 1 lists the foundations of the federal republic to be sovereignty, citizenship, the dignity of the individual, the social value of work and of free enterprise, and political pluralism.

Of these, the principle of political pluralism has perhaps the broadest expression in practice. Since 1988, political parties have proliferated. With no legal minimal number of votes required, the new parties have won seats in national, state, and local legislatures. New laws have made access more difficult for new parties, which must collect a sufficient number of signatures in order to register. However, once registered, every political party has an equal right to participate in legislative elections.

Article 4 establishes the principles that govern Brazil's international relations: national independence, primacy of human rights, self-determination of peoples, nonintervention, equality among states, defense of peace, peaceful solution of conflicts, repudiation of terrorism and racism, cooperation among people for the progress of humankind, and granting of political asylum.

The repudiation of terror has an important influence on Brazil's legal system. In Title II, Chapter I, the constitution holds that "the law shall consider the practice of torture [or] terrorism . . . to be crimes not entitled to bail and to mercy or amnesty, and the principals, the accessories and those who, although able to avoid them, abstain from doing so, shall be held liable." This duty to protect the state against abuses is unique in Brazilian constitutional history. Regarding racism, Article 5 establishes that "the practice of racism is a crime not entitled to bail or to the statute of limitations, and subject to imprisonment, according to the law."

Regional integration is included as a programmatic norm in Article 4: "The Federal Republic of Brazil shall seek economic, political, social, and cultural integration of the peoples of Latin America, in order to form a Latin American community of nations." Such integration has been pursued, especially since the Treaty of Asunción, incorporated by Decree 350 of November 21, 1991, and by the development of MERCOSUR, the common market of Brazil, Paraguay, Argentina, and Uruguay.

CONSTITUTIONAL BODIES

The chief constitutional bodies are the president of the republic, who is simultaneously head of state and the administration, the National Congress, which is composed of the Chamber of Deputies and the Federal Senate, and the judiciary, including the Supreme Federal Court, which is responsible for safeguarding the constitution.

The President (Head of State and the Administration)

The Brazilian constitution has adopted the presidential system of government, whereby the president is both head of state and head of the administration. The president of the republic is also head of the federal public administration.

The president as head of state performs the typical functions of internal and foreign representation of the republic, such as the conclusion of international treaties and acts. The president is directly elected by the people for a fixed period of four years and can be reelected only once. The election is by universal suffrage and direct and secret ballot.

The 1988 Constitutional Convention provided an option for voters to determine the form and system of government by a plebiscite. Such a vote took place on April 21, 1993; it confirmed the Constitutional Convention's choice of a presidential republic.

The election takes place in two rounds so that the elected president attains an absolute majority of valid votes (not counting abstentions or invalid ballots). The second round is dropped if one candidate wins a majority in the first ballot; if not, the two candidates who receive the highest number of votes in the first round compete in the second. Voting is mandatory to ensure even greater legitimacy of the elected president. In case of impediment or a vacancy, the presidency is exercised successively by the vice president, the president of the Chamber of Deputies, the president of the Federal Senate and, finally, the chief justice of the Supreme Federal Court.

The president of the republic may be removed from office through impeachment and conviction, a mechanism imported from U.S. constitutional law. It is very effective and necessary in Brazil, which can still be considered an immature democracy, as the period of military dictatorship is fairly recent and constitutional history has oscillated between authoritarian periods and democratization or redemocratization.

The first president elected after the 1988 constitution, Fernando Collor de Mello, was the subject of the first impeachment procedure in Brazilian constitutional history. He was removed from office in 1992 after the decision of the National Congress. Under immense pressure from demonstrations with millions of people in all major urban centers, the National Congress exercised its radical constitutional power, a fact that made Brazilian citizens proud.

In cases of misuse of office, Articles 51 I, 52 I, and 85 provide that the competent body to initiate the legal proceedings and actually to try the president is the Federal Senate, with the chief justice of the Supreme Federal Court acting as its president. In the case of a common criminal offense, the competent body to affect the legal proceeding and trial is the Supreme Federal Court (Article 102 I). Should the president not take up the office, it can be declared vacant according to Article 78. This also happens if the president leaves the country, without authorization from the National Congress, for a period of more than 15 days. Finally, the president may resign without approval from the National Congress.

As head of the administration, the president defines government policies and appoints and dismisses the ministers of state (Article 84 I). The ministers' function is to assist the president in the higher management of the federal administration (Articles 76 and 84). They manage their areas within the federal administration and countersign the acts signed by the president in their areas (Article 87). The creation and structuring of ministries are provided by law (Article 88).

As head of the administration, the president of the republic has a special role in the lawmaking process. He or she can initiate legislation and must approve laws passed by the National Congress.

Finally, the presidency of the republic is the highest body of the direct federal public administration, which is constituted basically by the presidency and the ministries. Besides the ministries, there are bureaus, such as the secretariat of political affairs, the general secretariat, the secretariat of governmental communication, and the office of institutional security. The presidency of the republic is also constituted by other bodies that directly assist the president, namely, the Council of the Republic, the national defense council, the advocacy-general of the union, the special secretariat for urban development, and the office of the president of the republic.

The Congresso Nacional (National Congress)

The Brazilian legislative is genuinely bicameral; that is, there is no hierarchy of the two houses. The National Congress is made up of the Chamber of Deputies and the Federal Senate. The Chamber of Deputies represents the people, whereas the members of the Federal Senate represent their respective federal entities. Nevertheless, the constitution attributes a certain superiority to the Chamber of Deputies, which has the competence to start the lawmaking process in those cases in which the initiative is from bodies outside the legislative, such as the president of republic, the Supreme Federal Court, the Superior Court of Justice, or the citizens via a "popular initiative" (Articles 61, 64).

The National Congress exercises the legislative function of the union. It also controls state accounts, finances, and the budget (Articles 70). It also has some judicial functions, such as creating temporary committees and parliamentary inquiry committees (Article 58), which are very common in the Brazilian political scene.

The Câmara dos Deputados (Chamber of Deputies)

The Chamber of Deputies is formed by representatives of the people, elected by the proportional system in each state (Article 46). The legislative term of each deputy is four years, and multiple reelections are allowed.

A supplementary law has established the minimal number of eight and the maximal number of 70 deputies for each state. As a result, states such as São Paulo, which has more than 35 million inhabitants, are underrepresented compared to states such as Roraima, which has fewer than 1 million inhabitants. In order to be elected, a deputy in populous states such as São Paulo, Minas Gerais, Paraná, Bahia, or Pernambuco needs many more votes than a deputy in Roraima.

The Chamber of Deputies has the power to authorize legal proceedings against the president, vice president, or ministers of state by a two-thirds vote of its members. It also has the power to require the presentation of accounts by the president (Article 51).

The Senado Federal (Senate)

The Senate represents the federal states. Every state elects three senators, with two substitutes for each one, by a majority of voters in that state. The term of office is eight years. One-third and two-thirds of the representation of each state shall be renewed each four years, alternately.

The Senate has an extensive catalogue of exclusive powers established by Article 52. Among them there are to try the president and vice president of the republic for the crime of malversation (corruption) and to state the application of a law declared unconstitutional by final decision of the Federal Supreme Court.

The Lawmaking Process

The lawmaking process in Brazil is very complex. Normative acts can include amendments to the constitution, supplementary laws, ordinary laws, delegated laws, provisional measures, legislative decrees, and resolutions. Some of them do not even belong to the lawmaking process in its narrow sense, such as the provisional measure, which is within the exclusive competence of the president of the republic.

There are a common procedure for making ordinary laws, a brief procedure for ordinary laws with emergency character, and special procedures for amendments to the constitution, supplementary laws, and other normative acts listed in Article 59. Amendments require three-fifths of the members of parliament, whereas supplementary laws need an absolute majority.

The common procedure can be divided into three phases:

Initiative or presentation of the bill: The initiative may arise from bodies outside the legislature or either house of congress, in which case, the discussions begin, and the first vote is taken in that house.

Parliamentary vote: As soon as the bill is received by either or both houses, discussions and voting begin. Afterward, the bill is sent to the other house, which can approve it, reject it, or approve it with amendments. In the first case, the bill advances to the next phase, executive or presidential voting. In case of the rejection, the bill is dismissed. In case of the approval with amendments, they are to be voted once more by the house where the bill was first proposed. In this voting, the house may reject the amendments, and, in such case, the bill continues without the amendments of the reviewing house. The vote in both houses of parliament is carried out by simple majority.

Executive vote: The president of the republic may sanction or veto the bill as a whole or in part, but he or she must explain a veto. The president can veto the bill either as unconstitutional or as contrary to the national interest.

The veto can be rejected by the absolute majority of both houses. Once the bill has been sanctioned, the president of the republic promulgates the law and orders its publication.

The Judicial Power

The judiciary in Brazil is independent of the executive and legislative powers. Article 92 provides for a Federal Supreme Court, a Superior Court of Justice, federal regional courts and federal judges, labor courts and labor judges, electoral courts and electoral judges, military courts and military judges, and courts and judges of the states and of the federal district. This adds up to two superior courts, federal judicial bodies of the first instance and of appeal; three special judicial systems with their own superior courts, regional, and first instance courts; and finally the states' judiciaries organized in courts of appeal and judges of first instance.

Ordinary state and federal judges are admitted to the bench by means of a public examination, provided they have a law degree. The judges of the superior courts, known as ministers, are nominated pursuant to often complex quota rules, but they too must have law degrees.

The Federal Supreme Court is composed of 11 justices, chosen from among citizens over 35 years and under 65 years of age, with extensive legal knowledge and unblemished reputation. They are appointed by the president of the republic with the approval of the absolute majority of the federal Senate. The federal Supreme Court decides on the constitutionality of laws and on criminal offenses committed by superior bodies of the other powers, such as the president of the republic or ministers of state.

THE ELECTION PROCESS

The sovereignty of the people is exercised by universal and equal suffrage in a direct and secret ballot. It is mandatory for every literate Brazilian citizen over 18 and less than 70 years old to vote. Voting is optional for 16- and 17-year-old citizens, illiterate citizens, and citizens over 70 years old.

Direct elections are carried out every four years for the presidency of the republic, the state administrations, the Senate, the Chamber of Deputies, and the state Legislative Assemblies. Municipal elections and election for city councils also take place every four years, but not at the same time as the national and state elections.

Every literate Brazilian citizen who enjoys the full exercise of his or her political rights can stand for elections. However, in individual cases, these political rights can be cancelled by the electoral courts for a given period. Some offices have a minimal age requirement, such as 35 years for president of the republic.

Other forms of political participation are the plebiscite, the referendum, and the initiative of the people.

POLITICAL PARTIES

Brazil has a pluralistic system of political parties. Article 17 guarantees the freedom to create, consolidate, merge, and dissolve political parties as the final guarantee of the broad list of fundamental rights and guarantees. There is no explicit provision to prevent a political party from pursuing purposes that are harmful to the democratic regime.

The political parties have the nature of private legal entities. After acquiring corporate status under civil law, they must register their by-laws with the superior electoral court. They are granted wide autonomy to define their structure, organization, and functioning.

The political parties are entitled to free-of-charge access to radio and television in the periods before elections. The duration of their electoral advertisements depends upon their number of representatives in both chambers of the National Congress.

CITIZENSHIP

Brazilian citizenship is primarily acquired by birth in Brazilian territory. The principle of *ius soli* is applied. Also citizens are those born abroad of a Brazilian parent who is serving the Federal Republic of Brazil or is registered with a proper Brazilian authority. Those who live in Brazil before coming of age can choose Brazilian nationality at any time after having come of age.

Foreigners may naturalize, after they reside for over 15 uninterrupted years in Brazil, unless they are from a country where the official language is Portuguese. In that case, only one year of residence is necessary.

The law may not establish any distinction between born and naturalized Brazilians, except in the cases set forth in the Brazilian constitution, such as the reservation of certain public offices to those born Brazilian, for example, the president and vice president of the republic.

FUNDAMENTAL RIGHTS

Fundamental rights are guaranteed in the Brazilian constitution in the second title, which is divided into five chapters: individual and collective rights and duties, social rights, citizenship, political rights, and rights of political parties.

The constitutional text does not lend itself to easy reading. Article 5 of the first chapter of the second title consists of 77 items that list, on the one hand, classical public freedoms, such as freedom of speech, freedom of conscience and belief, freedom of social communication, the right to exercise one's profession, the right to property, and freedom of access to information. On the other hand, rights to material provision from the state are also established, such as the right of acknowledged poor people to register birth and death without charge. Finally, many procedural rights are included, among them novelties such as data protection and the injunction order, apart from the traditional writs of mandamus and habeas corpus. Even class action is assured as a fundamental right in this chapter.

According to Article 5, all persons are equal before the law without any distinction whatsoever; Brazilians and foreigners resident in Brazil are assured the inviolability of the right to life, liberty, equality, security, and property, among other rights. Nonresident foreigners are excluded from the list of those who are entitled to the rights of classical public freedoms. Then again, Article 6 assures the fundamental social rights in an impersonal manner and thus it can include, in principle, nonresident foreigners.

The second title guarantees as universal human rights the social rights of education, health, work, leisure, security, social security, protection of motherhood and childhood, assistance to the destitute, social rights of urban and rural workers, social rights to professional or union association, the right to strike, participation of workers and employers in collegiate bodies of government agencies, and the right of representation of employees in direct negotiation with employers.

Impact and Functions of Fundamental Rights

The tradition of fundamental rights in Brazil was based on North American influences, but since 1946, it has been guided more and more by the European continental experience. This reflects a desire to consolidate the classical public liberties with new personality rights and to assure the material resources to allow these rights to be exercised.

However, there is no explicit doctrine that allows judges to apply the fundamental rights. In Brazilian doctrine, fundamental rights immediately bind individuals, but the constitutional remedies assure jurisdictional protection only against state actions. Indeed, it is not clear how the immediate binding of individuals would work. Therefore, the principle is reduced to a political-programmatic intent.

Limitations to Fundamental Rights

Some fundamental rights are subject to legal reservation. For example, freedom of profession is conditioned by the compliance with the qualifications established by law. However, many others, such as freedom of speech, are guaranteed without any reservation whatsoever.

ECONOMY

The Brazilian constitution presents a clear program for a social market economy. The whole seventh title is devoted to the economic and financial system. It lays out general principles of economic activity, especially the commitment to the principle of private property and the principle of the social function of private property. Also mentioned are free competition, consumer protection,

protection of the environment, reduction of regional and social differences, and achievement of full employment.

RELIGIOUS COMMUNITIES

Freedom of religion or belief guaranteed as a human right, as are rights for religious communities. There is no established state church. All public authorities must remain strictly neutral in their relations with religious communities. Religions must be treated equally.

The constitution of 1988 also protects places of worship against aggression from individuals. It also provides for religious assistance in civil and military establishments of collective confinement.

The religious communities are organized pursuant to civil law, demonstrating the lack of a complete separation between religion and the state in Brazil. They enjoy tax exemption, which has led to the emergence of religious "empires." Evangelical organizations have acquired important television channels, which will eventually make the political, economic, and constitutional questions of media regulation even more complex. Representatives of the Afro-Brazilian religions feel cut off from access to television, the most overwhelming medium ever in Brazil. Constitutional law obliges the state to democratize the use of television, which is in practice almost entirely in the hands of private initiatives.

MILITARY DEFENSE AND STATE OF EMERGENCY

The armed forces are permanent and regular national institutions under the supreme authority of the president. They are mandated to defend the nation, guarantee the constitutional powers, and maintain law and order.

All men above 18 must perform basic military service for 12 months. In addition, there are professional soldiers. Women can volunteer. A conscientious objector can file a petition to be excluded from military service but may not always be permitted to do so. Article 143 states that "it is incumbent upon the armed forces, according to the law, to assign an alternative service to those who, in times of peace, after being enlisted, allege reasons of conscience, which shall be understood as reasons based on religious creed and philosophical or political belief for exemption from essentially military activities." A relevant law exists, but its application is discretionary and hence it is difficult for someone to be dismissed from mandatory military services by reason of religious creed or philosophical belief.

The constitution structures in great detail the "state of defense" and the "state of siege." The president may declare a state of defense to preserve or promptly reestab-lish, in certain and restricted locations, public order or social peace whenever threatened by serious and imminent institutional instability or when affected by major natural calamities. Before doing so, the president must hear the Council of the Republic and the Council of National Defense. The president may also, after hearing the Council of the Republic and the Council of National Defense, request that the National Congress authorize a state of siege, which entails suspension of even more rights. This is possible in the event of serious disturbance with national effects or if measures taken during the state of defense are evidently ineffective. This also applies to a declaration of a state of war in reaction to foreign armed aggression. Congress needs an absolute majority to declare a state of siege. Either state must be immediately ended when the reasons for them no longer apply.

AMENDMENTS TO THE CONSTITUTION

The constitution has been amended more than 40 times since its enactment in 1988 as a result of the relatively easy procedure involved. Amendments require a qualified majority of only three-fifths in both legislative houses in two readings.

However, no amendment is allowed that tends to abolish the federal form of the state; direct, secret, universal, and periodic elections; the separation of government branches; or individual rights and guarantees.

PRIMARY SOURCES

Constitution in English. Available online. URL: http://www. senado.gov.br/sf; http://www.oefre.unibe.ch/law/icl/ br00000_.html. Accessed on August 28, 2005.
Constitution in Portuguese. Available online. URL: https:// www.planalto.gov.br/. Accessed on July 30, 2005.

SECONDARY SOURCES

Abdo I. Baaklini, *The Brazilian Legislature and the Political System*. Westport, Conn.: Greenwood Press, 1992.
Rex A. Hudson, ed., *Brazil—a Country Study*. Washington, D.C.: Federal Research Division Library of Congress, 1997. Available online. URL: http://lcweb2.loc.gov/ frd/cs/brtoc.html. Accessed on August 16, 2005.
Robert M. Levine, *The History of Brazil*. New York: Palgrave Macmillan, 2003.
Marcelo Neves and Julian Thomas Hottinger, eds., *Federalism, Rule of Law and Multiculturalism in Brazil*. Basel: Helbing and Lichtenhaln, 2001.
Edilenice Passos, "Doing Legal Research in Brazil 2002." Available online. URL: http://www.llrx.com/features/ brazil2002.htm. Accessed on June 17, 2006.

Leonardo Martins

BRUNEI

At-a-Glance

OFFICIAL NAME
Negara Brunei Darussalam (The Nation of Brunei, Abode of Peace)

CAPITAL
Bandar Seri Begawan

POPULATION
365,000 (2005 est.)

SIZE
2,227 sq. mi. (5,769 sq. km)

LANGUAGES
Malay (official), English, Chinese

RELIGIONS
Muslim (official) 67%, Buddhist 13%, Christian 10%, indigenous beliefs and other 10%

NATIONAL OR ETHNIC COMPOSITION
Malay 68%, Chinese 15%, other indigenous 6%, other races 11%

DATE OF INDEPENDENCE OR CREATION
January 1, 1984

TYPE OF GOVERNMENT
Malay Islamic monarchy

TYPE OF STATE
Unitary state

TYPE OF LEGISLATURE
Appointed 21-person Legislative Council reconstituted on September 25, 2004

DATE OF CONSTITUTION
September 29, 1959

DATE OF LAST AMENDMENT
September 25, 2004

Brunei Darussalam is an independent Muslim Malay sultanate on the island of Borneo. Its ruler is the sultan of Brunei, who also holds the traditional Malay title of Yang di-Pertuan, meaning "king." As sultan, he is seen as God's representative on Earth, making him both head of state and head of the Islamic faith. The constitution of Brunei reflects this by giving to him supreme executive and religious authority. Although not required by the constitution, the current sultan is the nation's prime minister, finance minister, defense minister, and supreme commander of the armed forces. When the ministry of law was abolished in 1999, the sultan assumed responsibility for judicial administration as well. The judges and courts are regarded as operating independently and without state interference.

All legislation is currently enacted by royal proclamation of the sultan. This is because Part VI of the constitution, which provided for legislative powers to be exercised by a partially elected and partially appointed Legislative Council, had been suspended. In September 2004, the sultan reconstituted a modified version of the Legislative Council when he appointed 21 men to serve on it. However, the council has no powers independent of the sultan. Its role is to provide a forum for discussion of government programs and reforms.

The constitution allows the sultan to assume legislative powers when he has declared a state of emergency. In 1962, during a failed rebellion against the government, a state of emergency was declared; it has been regularly renewed every two years since that time. Accordingly, there have been no elections since 1962; therefore, there is little role for political parties to play in the sultanate. The sultan has indicated that there may be elections to the Legislative Council in the future.

Although there is no separation of powers in Brunei, there is a distinction between the state and the monarchy with separate financial regulations applying to each. The sultan is advised by the Council of Cabinet Ministers, all of whom are appointed by him and hold office at his pleasure. The operation of the Cabinet Council and the three other advisory councils is seen to reflect the traditional Malay processes of advice and consultation.

The constitution provides that Shafeite sect of Islam is the state religion but that other religions can be practiced in peace and harmony. The economic system is dependent on the country's natural oil and gas reserves.

CONSTITUTIONAL HISTORY

The Kingdom of Brunei is an ancient one. Brunei became a sultanate in the 14th century when its king converted to Islam and changed his name to Sultan Muhammad Shah in honor of the Prophet. The present sultan is his 29th descendant. Traditional Brunei Malay and Islamic practices continue to inform the concepts of constitutionalism in the sultanate. The nation's ideology—Melayu Islam Beraja (MIB), meaning Malay Islam Monarchy—is honored, and adherence to it is required. It is claimed that MIB's central tenets can be traced back in an unbroken line for five centuries.

Brunei became a protectorate of Great Britain in 1888 and a residency in 1905. The Residency Agreement acted as a de facto constitution. During the residency, the sultan remained the head of state but was bound to take advice from the British government on all matters not dealing with the Islamic religion. During this time, English common law and courts were introduced, and a civil service replaced the traditional roles of nobles and chiefs.

After a decade of negotiations, the residency ended in 1959, and Brunei gained internal self-rule, with Britain retaining responsibility for defense, foreign affairs, and internal security. Brunei's first written constitution began operation that year. It concentrated power in the hands of the sultan by giving him full executive authority but did provide for consultation with five advisory councils. There have been two major constitutional amendments since 1959. In 1971, the power of Great Britain was reduced to external affairs. In 1984, Brunei Darussalam became fully independent, and a system of ministerial cabinet government was introduced.

FORM AND IMPACT OF THE CONSTITUTION

Brunei has had a written constitution since 1959. It is contained in a single piece of legislation. As the supreme law of the country, it provides the constitutional framework for the nation but does not contain a bill of rights.

BASIC ORGANIZATIONAL STRUCTURE

Brunei is a unitary state with four administrative districts (daerah), each of which has a district officer responsible to the prime minister. A district is divided again into subdistricts (mukim), each of which is administered by an appointed headman (penghulu). The smallest administrative unit is the village (kampong). Since 1992, the village headmen (ketua kampong) are elected by secret ballot once their candidacy has been approved by government. They hold meetings with the minister of home affairs and meet formally once a month in consultative councils at both the kampong and the mukim level. In 1996, the first and, to date, the only General Assembly of Mukim and Village Consultative Councils was held. One thousand delegates participated. This was described as "grassroots democracy." The issues discussed were local government matters such as road improvement and maintenance of community halls.

LEADING CONSTITUTIONAL PRINCIPLES

The constitutional principles that govern Brunei are a fusion of traditional Brunei Malay concepts of governance and those derived from the British or Western system.

From traditional Malay concepts are drawn the principles supporting autocratic, divine, and absolute rule by the sultan. This rule is to be based on consultation with respected advisers and supported by a special relationship between ruler and subject. The sultan allows his subjects to have contact with him through meetings in villages, mosques, and workplaces. This is described by the government as living democracy. Democracy, in a Western form of representative government, has never operated in Brunei.

As the sultan is God's representative, the state promotes Islamic values and practices in all aspects of life in the sultanate.

From Britain and the West are derived principles of cabinet government, independence of the judiciary, and implied human rights. These rights must not be inconsistent with the interests and harmony of the state.

CONSTITUTIONAL BODIES

The bodies provided for in the constitution are the sultan (Yang di-Pertuan), the Council of Cabinet Ministers, the Privy Council, the Religious Council, the Council of Succession, and the Legislative Council.

The Sultan and Yang Di-Pertuan

The sultan (Yang di-Pertuan) is the head of state, head of government, and head of the religion of Islam. The position of sultan is hereditary and is for life. The sultan appoints and dismisses all members of the four advisory councils described in the following.

The Council of Cabinet Ministers

The Council of Cabinet Ministers provides advice to the sultan in the exercise of his powers and duties in governing the state. The constitution requires the prime minister to be a Brunei Malay who professes the Muslim religion of the Shafeite sect. Although the first cabinet was dominated by members of the royal family, this practice has not continued.

The Privy Council

The Privy Council advises the sultan on matters relating to amendment or revocation of the constitution, exercise of the royal prerogative of mercy, and conferral of Malay customary honors and titles. Its members must take an oath of secrecy.

The Religious Council

The Religious Council aids and advises the sultan on matters relating to Islam and is the highest authority in Brunei on Islamic law.

The Council of Succession

The Council of Succession determines the succession to the throne if the need arises. A Council of Regency can also be proclaimed when the sultan, at his accession to the throne, is under the age of 18 years.

The Lawmaking Process

Given the continued renewal of the state of emergency, the constitution gives power to the sultan to make any orders he considers desirable in the public interest. All laws are enacted as emergency orders. The legitimacy of the continuation of the state of emergency for more than 40 years has never been judicially considered.

The Judiciary

Details on the operation of the courts and the judiciary are not contained in the constitution but in separate legislation. In practice, the courts are considered to operate independently without executive interference, though the constitution does not provide for an independent judiciary.

There are two legal systems operating in Brunei. The civil system, which is derived from English common law, is administered through a hierarchy of secular common law courts. The final right of appeal from these courts for civil cases only is to the Judicial Committee of the Privy Council in London. Although a common-law country, Brunei does not have trial by jury. It uses the death penalty for serious offenses, such as murder, rape, and drug trafficking, and caning and imprisonment for other criminal offenses. The sultan appoints civil judges on renewable contracts.

The Islamic system has the Syariah Appeal Court as its highest court. It plays a supervisory role over lower Syariah courts. Syariah courts have jurisdiction over Muslims and deal with issues of marriage, divorce, custody, other aspects of family law, deceased's estates, Islamic trusts (*wakaf*), and offenses against Muslim morality and religious practice, such as nonattendance at Friday prayers. Islamic rules of evidence apply in these courts. The sultan appoints Syari'e judges on the advice of the president of the Religious Council.

THE ELECTION PROCESS

The only national election occurred in 1962. Subjects of the sultan who were over the age of 21 had the right to vote and stand for election to the 10 elected seats in the 21-member Legislative Council.

In 1989, the sultan announced he would consider introducing elections and a legislature "when I can see evidence of a genuine interest in politics on the part of the responsible majority of Bruneians." With the revival of the fully appointed Legislative Council in 2004, there have been calls for elected representatives to join the council. No schedule for possible future elections has been made public.

POLITICAL PARTIES

Brunei has one registered political party, the Brunei National Solidarity Party (PPKB). It has fewer than 100 members. To be registered, parties must pledge support to the sultan, the MIB ideology, and the existing system of government. Several political parties have been deregistered by the government since 1962. Members of the civil service and the armed forces are not allowed to join political parties.

CITIZENSHIP

Brunei citizenship is acquired by birth for those of the Malay race. Until 2002, citizenship could only be transmitted through the father, but it now extends to the children of female citizens who are married to foreigners. Otherwise, to attain Brunei citizenship, an individual must pass a test on Brunei Malay custom, culture, and language. Many of Brunei's Chinese are permanent residents who are entitled to live in the country but who do not enjoy the full privileges of citizenship, including the right to own land.

FUNDAMENTAL RIGHTS

The constitution does not specify or guarantee fundamental rights except for religious freedom. The rights that are enjoyed by the people of Brunei are implied rather than provided for expressly.

Impact and Functions of Fundamental Rights

In Brunei, fundamental rights operate with significant limitations. These limitations are seen as necessary to preserve the culture and cohesion of the nation.

Taking freedom of speech and expression as an example, this freedom is limited by censorship laws including the Local Newspapers (Amendment) Order of 2001. This gives the government complete control over the press, as all newspapers must apply to the minister of home affairs for annual publishing permits. The minister has sole discretionary power to grant permits, which is not subject to appeal or judicial review. The government has absolute power to bar the distribution of foreign publications in Brunei. The one local television channel is owned by the government. There are, however, no restrictions on Internet use.

Another example are the limitations on the right to form associations. Nongovernment organizations require government approval, and there are restrictions preventing Muslims from becoming members of service organizations such as Rotary and Lions. Trade unions are lawful, and there are three registered unions, but membership is very low.

ECONOMY

The constitution does not specify an economic system. Brunei's economy is heavily reliant on oil and gas revenues and income from the government's overseas investment. Islamic banking and financing operate in the sultanate. Citizens of Brunei pay no taxes and enjoy a generous welfare system.

RELIGIOUS COMMUNITIES

Islam is the state religion, and the Ministry of Religious Affairs promotes and controls its practice. There are religious police who can investigate any breach of Islamic law. Religious authorities from the ministry regularly conduct searches for alcoholic beverages and for food products that may not conform to *halal*, or lawful Islamic practices on food preparation.

Although other religions can be practiced, there are limitations. Censorship laws restrict information on non-Muslim religions. It is an offense to attempt to convert a Muslim to another religion. In schools, the teaching of any religion other than Islam is prohibited, while the teaching of Islam and MIB is compulsory.

MILITARY DEFENSE AND STATE OF EMERGENCY

The sultan is both minister of defense and supreme commander of the armed forces. There is no military conscription. Men over the age of 18 can volunteer to join the armed services.

Section 83 of the constitution provides that the sultan can declare a state of emergency when it appears to him that "public danger exists." It lasts for two years, but another declaration can then be issued. The sultan may make "any Orders whatsoever which he considers desirable in the public interest," including restrictions on fundamental freedoms and modifications, amendments, or suspensions of any written laws.

AMENDMENTS TO THE CONSTITUTION

The sultan may amend or revoke any of the provisions of the constitution. He is required to consult the Privy Council but is not obliged to act in accordance with that advice.

PRIMARY SOURCES
Constitution (1959, revised 1984) (Government of Brunei Darussalam Official Web site in English). Available online. URL: http://www.brunei.gov.bn/government/constitution. Accessed on June 17, 2006.

SECONDARY SOURCES
Ann Black, "Alternative Dispute Resolution in Brunei Darussalam: The Blending of Imported and Traditional Processes." *Bond Law Review* (2001): 305–334.
Carmelo V. Sison, ed., *Constitutional and Legal Systems of ASEAN Countries*. Manila: The Academy of ASEAN Law and Jurisprudence, 1990.

Ann Black

BULGARIA

At-a-Glance

OFFICIAL NAME
Republic of Bulgaria

CAPITAL
Sofia

POPULATION
7,801,273 (2005 est.)

SIZE
43,128 sq. mi. (111,700 sq. km)

LANGUAGES
Bulgarian

RELIGIONS
Eastern Orthodox 82.6%, Muslim 12.2%,
Jewish 0.1%, Catholic 1.7%, Protestant and other 3.4%

NATIONAL OR ETHNIC COMPOSITION
Bulgarians 83%, Turks 9.0%, Roma 3%, other 6%

DATE OF INDEPENDENCE OR CREATION
March 3, 1878

TYPE OF GOVERNMENT
Parliamentary republic

TYPE OF STATE
Unitary state

TYPE OF LEGISLATURE
Unicameral parliament

DATE OF CONSTITUTION
July 12, 1991

DATE OF LAST AMENDMENT
February 18, 2005

Bulgaria is a unitary state based on the rule of law. Fundamental rights are protected by the constitution. Bulgaria is a parliamentary democracy with a strong president. The executive power is primarily vested in the Council of Ministers, consisting of the prime minister and the cabinet ministers. The judiciary includes a Constitutional Court and is independent. Free economic initiative is guaranteed, as is freedom of religion. Eastern Orthodox Christianity is considered by the constitution to be the traditional religion of the Republic of Bulgaria.

CONSTITUTIONAL HISTORY

The Bulgarian state emerged in the second half of the seventh century C.E. In 681, a state treaty was signed between the Byzantine emperor, Constantine IV, and the Bulgarian khan, Asparouch, by which Byzantium recognized the Bulgarian state in the area north of the Balkan Mountains and around the Danube delta. Apart from the proto-Bulgarians, the area was home to the Seven Slav Tribes as well as a Thracian population. Asparouch signed a treaty giving the Slavs a degree of autonomy. Thus, Bulgaria became a recognized state with three main ethnic components—proto-Bulgarians, Slavs, and Thracians.

A hereditary monarch called the khan was the head of the state. The structure of the state mirrored the military organization; territorial units were headed by military leaders called Boils, who helped the khan govern the state in peace and war. The self-governing Slavs were ruled by tribal princes and councils of elders.

In 865, Khan Boris undertook a large-scale reform by imposing Christianity on his whole realm. His successor, Simeon, took the title *czar* from the Byzantine *Caesar*, imposed the language of his Slavic subjects as the official language, and adopted the recently created Cyrillic script. Within a short period, the major Byzantine religious and secular books were translated into this tongue, the first corpus of written literature in any Slavic tongue.

The Bulgarian state existed until 1018 when, during the reign of Emperor Vasilios II, the whole territory was annexed into Byzantium. In 1186, after an uprising, the Bulgarian state was restored under the kings of the Assenovtsi dynasty. The organization, structure, and state institutions of this second Bulgarian state generally followed the precedent established by its predecessor. In the 14th century, as a result of feudal processes, the country split into several smaller states, including the Tarnovo and Vidin Kingdoms.

In 1393, all these states were conquered by the Ottoman Turks and included in their newly created Ottoman Empire. Bulgaria remained under Ottoman rule for nearly 500 years.

In 1878, after the Russian-Turkish War (1877–78), the Berlin Treaty restored the Bulgarian state in two parts—Principality Bulgaria, still feudatory to the Ottoman Empire, and Eastern Roumelia, an autonomous province of the empire. In 1885, the two territories unilaterally declared their unification under the principality. In 1908, again unilaterally, the Bulgarian prince declared the independence of Bulgaria from the Ottoman Empire.

The history of written Bulgarian constitution began on April 16, 1879, when a Constituent Assembly adopted the Tarnovo constitution, so named for the medieval Bulgarian capital where the assembly met.

The Tarnovo constitution had all the positive characteristics of the liberal constitutions of 19th-century Europe. In compliance with the requirements of the Berlin Treaty, it defined the state as a parliamentary monarchy. A National Assembly held the legislative power; its members were elected by the general and equal vote of the male electorate. The monarch convened and dissolved the National Assembly. The administration was accountable to the head of the state. The supremacy of the constitution and the law was proclaimed, and separation of legislative, executive, and judicial powers was ensured. The political system was based on political pluralism and democracy. The principles of equality before the law, freedom of the individual, and freedom of the press were also proclaimed.

During World War II (1939–45), the country was allied with the Axis powers. After the war, the Soviet Army imposed Communist Party rule in Bulgaria. In 1946, a referendum voted to change the form of state to a republic. On December 4, 1947, a Great National Assembly adopted a new constitution.

The new constitution entirely abandoned the democratic principles of parliamentarism, although it formally endorsed direct elections, equality before the law, the inviolability of the home, and other freedoms. It imposed the communist principle of state regulation of economic life, based on the priority of state ownership. It also adopted a Soviet-style unification of power under the executive, contradictory to the principle of separation of powers.

Shortly after the adoption of the 1947 constitution, a fully Stalinist system was imposed on the state and society, resulting in a discrepancy between the formally declared freedoms and reality. Government was dominated by a parastate system of Communist Party bodies. The text of the 1947 constitution in fact did not correspond to the complete dominance of the Bulgarian Communist Party in the state and in the economic and public life.

The institutionalization of party power was established in the constitution of May 18, 1971. Article 1 stated that "the leading force in society and state is the Bulgarian Communist Party." The dominance of communist ideology was carried through the text. The proclaimed rights and freedoms were left without guarantees for their implementation, and the separation of powers was rejected. The principles of state regulation of all economic life, a planned economy, and state monopolies were upheld.

The collapse of communist power at the end of 1989 created an opportunity to establish a new constitutional order and to restore democratic principles. In January 1990, the National Assembly amended the 1971 constitution, abolishing Article 1 and a number of other provisions of an openly ideological nature. The assembly began preparing an entirely new constitution. On July 12, 1991, the seventh Great National Assembly adopted the new constitution, which is still in effect.

FORM AND IMPACT OF THE CONSTITUTION

The 1991 constitution is a single document. It contains 169 articles, grouped in 10 chapters and nine transitional and concluding provisions.

BASIC ORGANIZATIONAL STRUCTURE

Pursuant to the 1991 constitution, the Republic of Bulgaria is a united (unitary) state with local self-government. The possibility of creating autonomous territorial units is explicitly rejected. The territorial integrity of Bulgaria is inviolable. The structure of local self-government is detailed in a special chapter of the constitution.

LEADING CONSTITUTIONAL PRINCIPLES

Leading constitutional principles are stated in Chapter 1 of the constitution, which avers that Bulgaria is a republic with parliamentary rule, with all power vested in the people. Article 4 proclaims the principle of the supremacy of law. In order to underline the special place of the constitution in the legal system, its direct applicability is declared; the state authorities must apply its provisions with priority over any contradictory laws.

Another main constitutional principle is equality of all before the law. All people are declared to be born equal in dignity and rights; the constitution prohibits any limits on rights or privileges on the grounds of race, nationality, ethnicity, sex, origin, religion, education, convictions, political affiliation, personal and political situation, or condition of property.

The principle of political pluralism is also affirmed. The principle of the separation of powers into legislative, executive, and judicial branches is clearly defined by the constitution as it delineates the various functions and competencies of the constitutional bodies.

Religious freedom also is a main constitutional principle. Family, motherhood, and children enjoy special protection by the law.

CONSTITUTIONAL BODIES

The main constitutional bodies are the National Assembly as parliament, the president, the Council of Ministers, and the judiciary.

The National Assembly

The National Assembly (parliament) exercises the legislative power. It consists of 240 members elected directly by constituents for a term of four years. The parliament has only one chamber. It is headed by a chairperson elected by the members.

Parliament elects the prime minister and cabinet ministers. It has the power of parliamentary control and may pass a no confidence vote against the prime minister or the entire executive administration.

The parliament may be dissolved ahead of term by the president but only if there is no possibility of assembling a majority to support a new Council of Ministers.

The President

The president is the head of state and represents the state in international relations. The president is also the supreme commander in chief of the armed forces. The president is elected directly by the constituents for a term of five years.

The president personifies the unity of the nation. He or she can be a member of a political party but cannot participate in its leadership.

Although the president has no right of legislative initiative, he or she does have the power to veto laws adopted by the National Assembly or to refer them to the Constitutional Court for a ruling on their constitutionality. The president also publishes the laws in the *Official Journal.*

The president may appoint an interim executive government as an acting administration after having dissolved the parliament.

The Council of Ministers

The Council of Ministers formulates and carries out the domestic and foreign policy of Bulgaria. It is chaired by a prime minister and consists of the prime minister and the cabinet ministers.

The constitution gives the Council of Ministers a broad list of prerogatives in the field of executive power. The Council of Ministers is answerable only to the National Assembly, which can force its resignation by voting no confidence.

The Lawmaking Process

The Council of Ministers and every member of parliament have legislative initiative. Laws are adopted in two rounds of voting by simple majority; in order to become effective, they must be published in the *Official Journal.* The president has the power to return a bill for further debate. The new passage of such a bill requires a majority of more than half of all the members of the National Assembly.

The Judiciary

The Constitutional Court is a novelty for Bulgaria, appearing for the first time in the 1991 constitution. It ensures the supremacy of the constitution—the main element of the legal system. It rules on the constitutionality of laws or individual provisions of laws. When a law or provision is ruled unconstitutional by the court, it ceases to have effect. The Constitutional Court also gives binding interpretations of the text of the constitution.

The Constitutional Court may be called upon by one-fifth of the members of parliament, the president, the Council of Ministers, the Supreme Court of Cassation, the Supreme Administrative Court, and the Prosecutor in Chief. A citizen cannot directly address the Constitutional Court.

The judicial power is independent and has an independent budget. It includes three branches: courts, prosecution, and investigation.

Judges, prosecutors, and investigators are appointed and dismissed by the Supreme Judicial Council, an independent body. Half of the council members are elected by the National Assembly, and the other half by judges, prosecutors, and inquirers for terms of seven years.

An important achievement of the 1991 constitution was the restoration of judicial control of the executive authorities, which had been revoked after the 1947 constitution. The Supreme Administrative Court has been restored, with its power to decide claims of interested individuals and to revoke illegal executive actions. Administrative acts can be appealed, as can the actions of Council of Ministers and individual cabinet ministers.

THE ELECTION PROCESS

All elections and national and local referendums are held on the basis of universal, equal, and direct suffrage by secret ballot. Each citizen above the age of 18, with the exception of those placed under judicial indictment or serving a prison sentence, has the right to vote in elections and referendums.

Any Bulgarian citizen above the age of 21 who does not hold another citizenship is eligible for election to the National Assembly, provided he or she is not under judicial indictment and is not serving a prison sentence.

POLITICAL PARTIES

Bulgaria has a pluralistic system of political parties. Political parties must meet specific requirements: They must not claim that they are a state party or that their ideology is the state ideology. This is a retroactive rejection of the leading role of the Bulgarian Communist Party explicit in the previous constitution. Parties may not be formed on ethnic, racial, or religious grounds, and no party whose purpose is violent political change is allowed.

CITIZENSHIP

A Bulgarian citizen is anyone born of at least one parent holding Bulgarian citizenship or born on the territory of the Republic of Bulgaria and not entitled to any other citizenship. Citizenship can also be acquired by naturalization.

FUNDAMENTAL RIGHTS

The constitution of Bulgaria provides strong protections for fundamental rights. The preamble of the constitution holds liberty, equality, and the rights, dignity, and security of the individual as universal human values of the highest order. In its second chapter, the constitution guarantees the classic fundamental rights, including the right to life, personal freedom, and privacy, and freedom of conscience, of religion, and of dissemination of information. No one may be subjected to torture.

Impact and Functions of Fundamental Rights

In addition to ensuring rights and freedoms that limit government action, the Bulgarian constitution aims to protect certain institutions created by fundamental rights provisions. Thus, matrimony is defined as a free union between a man and a woman.

Fundamental rights also entail duties of the state. Thus, the state has to assist parents in raising their children; citizens have the right to social security, welfare assistance, and medical insurance. Everyone has the right to education.

The constitution also entails explicit duties of the people. Citizens must observe the constitution and the laws; they must defend the country, pay taxes, and assist the state and society in case of natural or other disasters.

The study and use of the Bulgarian language are a right and an obligation of every Bulgarian citizen.

Limitations to Fundamental Rights

A number of rights are guaranteed only under conditions established by law, such as parents' rights, the right to assembly, and protection from detainment. Some rights are granted under the condition that they are not practiced to the detriment of natural security, public order, public health and morals, or the rights and freedoms of others; among such rights are freedom of conscience and religion. Similar limits apply to the freedom to disseminate information and the right to choose a place of residence.

ECONOMY

The Bulgarian economy is based on free economic initiative. The right to property and inheritance and the freedom to choose an occupation are protected. Citizens have a right to work. The state has exclusive ownership over certain assets such as underground resources, beaches, waters, forests, and areas of natural importance. The state is obligated to establish and guarantee equal legal conditions for economic activity to all citizens and cooperative entities by preventing any abuse of monopoly status or unfair competition.

RELIGIOUS COMMUNITIES

Among the main constitutional principles is religious freedom. The constitution guarantees both the freedom of religion and the right to freedom of religious communities. Churches are independent and separate from the state, although the Eastern Orthodox religion is declared to be the traditional religion of the Republic of Bulgaria.

MILITARY DEFENSE AND STATE OF EMERGENCY

The president of the republic is the supreme commander in chief of the armed forces. The constitution states that defending the country is a duty and a matter of honor of every Bulgarian citizen. After a proclamation of war, martial law, or a state of emergency, the exercise of individual civil rights may be temporarily curtailed by law, except for certain fundamental rights such as the right to life or the right not to be subjected to torture.

AMENDMENTS TO THE CONSTITUTION

The initiative to amend the constitution belongs to one-quarter of the members of the National Assembly and to the president. A constitutional amendment requires a majority of three-quarters of all members of the National Assembly, in three separate ballots on three different days. A bill that has obtained less than three-quarters but more than two-thirds of the votes can be reintroduced; it then needs only a majority of two-thirds of the vote of all members.

A new constitution can only be adopted by a specially elected Grand National Assembly of 400 members. The same applies to any amendment of certain basic provisions of the current constitution, such as the form of the state structure or of government or the basic guarantee of fundamental rights. Restrictive procedural rules apply in this case; only the president or a full half of the members of the Grand National Assembly have the right to introduce such an amendment.

PRIMARY SOURCES

Constitution in English. Available online. URL: http://www.bild.net/constitut.htm. Accessed on September 7, 2005.

SECONDARY SOURCES

R. J. Crampton, *A Concise History of Bulgaria*. Cambridge: Cambridge University Press, 1997.

Glenn E. Curtis, *Bulgaria—a Country Study*. Area Handbook Series. Washington, D.C.: U.S. Government Printing Office, 1993.

United Nations, "Core Document Forming Part of the Reports of States Parties: Bulgaria" (HRI/CORE/1/Add.81), 3 July 1997. Available online. URL: http://www.unhchr.ch/tbs/doc.nsf. Accessed on August 25, 2005.

Latchezar Popov
Dimitar Gochev

BURKINA FASO

At-a-Glance

OFFICIAL NAME
Burkina Faso

CAPITAL
Ouagadougou

POPULATION
11,553,000 (2005 est.)

SIZE
106,000 sq. mi. (274,200 sq. km)

LANGUAGES
French (official), Moore, Dioula, others

RELIGIONS
Muslim 50%, Christian 10%, traditional beliefs 40%

NATIONAL OR ETHNIC COMPOSITION
63 ethnic groups among which are Mossi (almost half of the total population), Bobo, Mande, Lobi, Fulani, Gourounsi, and Senufo

DATE OF INDEPENDENCE OR CREATION
August 5, 1960

TYPE OF GOVERNMENT
Presidential democracy

TYPE OF STATE
Unitary state

TYPE OF LEGISLATURE
Unicameral parliament

DATE OF CONSTITUTION
June 11, 1991

DATE OF LAST AMENDMENT
January 22, 2002

Despite some growth, Burkina Faso is a relatively poor country with a largely illiterate, ethnically integrated population. Suffering from the massive return of migrant workers from neighboring Côte d'Ivoire, it maintains relative social stability in a society largely consisting of self-sufficient farmers.

The constitutional system is patterned after the French model. Democratic transition began in 1991 and is still not fully completed. Human rights are officially guaranteed but not always respected.

CONSTITUTIONAL HISTORY

Mossi kingdoms governed the area of what today is called Burkina Faso between the 11th and the 19th century with remarkable stability and religious and social cohesion. Given the fact that these kingdoms did not participate much in trans-Saharan commerce, it was neither touched by the slave trade nor the spread of Islam. The region was

surrounded by more powerful empires such as the one located in Mali.

When the French gained control over the region in the late 19th century against the competing British, they had to deal with the local ruler, the *mogho naba*, a king-magician. The French occupied the territory as of 1897. It became an autonomous colony under the name of Upper Volta as part of France's large possessions in western, sub-Saharan Africa. The French were able to build their colonial administration upon the existing Mossi structures and governed indirectly.

Burkina Faso did not see much development apart from a train line to the coast. Many of its people worked in cotton plantations in what today is Côte d'Ivoire or were used as soldiers in the two world wars (1914–18 and 1939–45).

The decolonization movement was built by these soldiers, Western-educated elites, and the traditional Mossi rulers. Burkina Faso was granted independence in 1960 along with other units of the French federation of colonies in this region. It became an independent country under the name of Upper Volta on August 5, 1960.

The first postindependence government quickly turned authoritarian. The country's subsequent history was largely a series of military coups.

The current president, Blaise Compaore, entered the political scene in 1983 when he helped free the rebel leader and erstwhile prime minister, Thomas Sankara, from prison. Sankara introduced left-wing revolutionary policies, fought against corruption and abuse of government funds, and renamed the country Burkina Faso, literally meaning "country of honorable people." Despite his popularity, he was assassinated in 1987, and Blaise Compaore, number two in his regime, became head of state.

Compaore began reforming his party and opening up the country to multiparty democracy. The opposition participated to a degree in preparing a new constitution for a Fourth Republic; it entered into force on June 11, 1991. The opposition boycotted the first presidential elections in December that year but participated in parliamentary elections the following year. Compaore and his ruling party won both elections.

FORM AND IMPACT OF THE CONSTITUTION

Burkina Faso has developed some constitutional habits in the ensuing years. The political process respects the institutions created by the constitution. Democratic competition for parliamentary elections is open and fair. However, it is not yet clear whether a transition to a democratic presidency is possible. In 2000, the constitution was amended to limit the president to two five-year terms.

Human rights are in principle respected. Severe violations do still take place, however. The judiciary appears to be functioning in principle, although judicial independence is limited in political cases.

BASIC ORGANIZATIONAL STRUCTURE

Burkina Faso is a unitary state. It is a presidential democracy based on the French model. The constitution provides for decentralization into substate entities, in particular, municipalities.

LEADING CONSTITUTIONAL PRINCIPLES

Modeled after the French example, Burkina Faso is a secular, democratic, unitary republic. It is founded on principles of democracy, the rule of law, and justice.

Its type of government is a presidential republic with separation of powers. The position of the president of the republic is strong. Unlike in the French model, the parliament (National Assembly) is unicameral.

The constitution complements fundamental rights by affirming civic duties.

The constitution provides for the transfer of sovereign powers to multinational African organizations.

CONSTITUTIONAL BODIES

The main constitutional bodies are the president; the executive administration; the National Assembly; the judiciary, including the High Court of Justice; the Constitutional Council; and the Social and Economic Council.

The President

The president is the most powerful figure in constitutional life in Burkina Faso. As head of state, the president is regarded as the guardian of the constitution and of the integrity, continuity, and sovereignty of the nation. He or she incarnates and assures national unity.

The president is directly elected for five years, with one reelection allowed. Candidates must be of Burkinabe nationality, Burkinabe descent, and at least 35 years of age. If no presidential candidate obtains more than 50 percent of the votes, the two best-placed candidates run in a second round, when a simple majority suffices. The president may not hold any other office.

The prime minister may substitute for the president in case of temporary incapacity. In case of vacancy or definite incapacity, the president is replaced by the president of the National Assembly.

The president appoints the prime minister and the executive administration and can demand resignation of the prime minister at any time. The president chairs the Council of Ministers. The president also appoints high officials in the civil administration and in the military.

The president promulgates laws passed by the National Assembly and can also send a law back for a second reading before promulgation. The constitution gives the president the authority to dissolve the National Assembly after consultation with the prime minister and the president of the National Assembly.

The Executive Administration

The executive administration is composed of the prime minister and the cabinet ministers. It is appointed by the president. It is responsible before the assembly. The executive government meets in the council of ministers, chaired by the president. The prime minister and the members of the executive administration may attend plenary and committee sessions of the National Assembly. Membership in the Council of Ministers is incompatible with holding any other office in public and private institutions. The executive government disposes of a broad regulatory power.

The National Assembly

Deputies are elected by universal suffrage for a five-year term with the possibility of reelection. The size of the assembly is determined by law (currently 111 members). Parliamentary activity is limited to two biannual sessions of 90 days maximum. The constitution provides for parliamentary immunity.

The National Assembly disposes of the lawmaking power. The division between parliamentary lawmaking power and governmental regulatory power is determined by a catalogue in the constitution.

The assembly enjoys the typical parliamentary means of controlling the administration. It can call a motion of censure at the demand of one-third of its members and requires a favorable vote of the majority of its members.

The Lawmaking Process

The executive administration regularly proposes laws. Draft laws may also be initiated by a popular petition signed by 15,000 voters.

Laws are voted by simple majority in the National Assembly. Organic laws on the function and the functioning of the institutions of government need the approval of the Constitutional Council before their entry into force.

The Judiciary

The judiciary is formally independent as a body, and the independence of individual judges is also constitutionally protected. The judiciary is responsible for guaranteeing respect for fundamental rights. It has ruled against the government in cases of flagrant human rights violations but not often enough to satisfy many critics.

There are separate branches for ordinary and administrative cases. A Cour de Cassation and a Conseil d'Etat (State Council) are at the apex of the two branches. A Cour de Comptes controls public finances.

The president of the republic is the guarantor of the independence of the judiciary. The president chairs the High Council of the Judiciary, which is in charge of all career matters within the judiciary.

The High Court of Justice

The High Court of Justice hears charges of high treason against the president of the republic and members of the executive government. It is made up by deputies from the National Assembly. The charges must first be approved by four-fifths of the members of the National Assembly in the case of the president and by two-thirds in the case of members of the executive government.

The Constitutional Council

A Constitutional Council reviews the constitutionality of laws and international treaties. It is composed of nine members and a president, who serve for seven years with the possibility of one renewal. The president of the republic appoints three members on his or her own advice and three more on the advice of the minister of justice; the president of the National Assembly appoints the final three members.

The council reviews the constitutionality of laws before their promulgation at the request of the president of the republic, the prime minister, the president of the National Assembly, or one-fifth of the members of the National Assembly. The council also decides disputes among the different institutions of the republic, as well as election disputes. The Constitutional Council also judges on the definitive incapacity of the president of the republic. It can outlaw political parties if they violate the constitutional prohibition of tribalist, regionalist, religious, or racist parties.

The Economic and Social Committee

The Economic and Social Committee is made up of representatives of societal associations. It is supposed to be consulted in all economic, social, and budgetary issues.

Its president is chosen by the president of the republic. The other 90 members are chosen by decree of the president. An organic law defines 31 groups of organizations from which the president has to choose. Among those are organizations representing different economic sectors, labor unions, artists organizations, organizations from the press and communications sector, women's organizations, but also representatives of traditional and customary authorities. Religious groups are not represented. Members need to show "good morals."

THE ELECTION PROCESS

Every Burkinabe citizen who are at least 18 years old may participate in elections. Foreigners may participate in local elections after 10 years of lawful residence, if they engage in legal occupations and have fulfilled their financial responsibilities. Elections are universal, direct, equal, and secret. Referenda can be called by the president of the republic on any draft law related to the national interest.

An Independent National Elections Commission watches over the elections to ensure that proper procedures are followed. It is composed of five members chosen by the government parties, five by opposition parties, and five by civil society associations—three of them religious communities. The commission's president must be one of the civil society members. Another body, the National Observatory of Elections, actually supervises each particular election. It is composed by one member of each party participating in the election, members from religious communities, traditional authorities, human rights organizations, labor unions, feminist organizations, and other nongovernmental organizations.

POLITICAL PARTIES

Burkina Faso has a multiparty system. The law provides for public funding of political campaigns. The right of a party to be in the opposition is explicitly recognized by the law.

The constitution bars political parties that are tribalist, regionalist, religious, or racist. Parties may be dissolved if they threaten to undermine public order, public peace, or moral, or if they field an illicit militia. Dissolution is decided by the executive administration meeting in the Council of Ministers and may be controlled by the Conseil d'Etat, the supreme administrative court.

There is an effective opposition. The presidential party currently has only 57 of the 111 seats in the National Assembly, with the remaining seats divided up between 13 parties.

CITIZENSHIP

Citizenship is acquired by descent from a Burkinabe father or mother, regardless of the country of birth. Naturalization is possible for those over 18 who have lived in the country for 10 years. A foreigner may register for citizenship six months after marriage to a Burkinabe citizen. Citizenship can be revoked if a crime against the institutions of the government has been committed.

FUNDAMENTAL RIGHTS

The constitution includes a catalogue of rights and civil duties. Fundamental rights include those of the first, second, and third generations (civil liberties, social rights, and cultural and environmental rights).

Impact and Functions of Fundamental Rights

The general human rights record is fair. National security laws permit surveillance and arrest without warrants. Police routinely ignore prescribed limits on detention, search, and seizure. Security forces commit abuses with impunity, including torture and occasional extrajudicial killing.

In 2002, more than 100 persons were found shot handcuffed within a period of three months. The administration explained this as part of an effort to crack down on banditry.

Human rights organizations and labor unions are an important element of civil society. They try to pressure the government to respect fundamental freedoms, but they are subject to occasional threats from government and nongovernment forces.

Women's rights are poorly enforced. Female genital mutilation is illegal but frequently practiced. There have been reports of recent crackdowns on the practice.

In 1998, a murder of an independent journalist allegedly involved people from the president's entourage. The judicial proceedings against the killing itself were ineffective for political reasons. However, since then, the government appears to have improved respect for freedom of the press. There is some self-censorship. Independent newspapers, radio stations, and one TV station exist.

The death penalty, without being formally abolished, is not applied. Freedom of assembly is constitutionally protected and generally respected, with required permits usually issued routinely. However, political demonstrations are sometimes violently suppressed or banned altogether.

Limitations of Fundamental Rights

Fundamental rights are guaranteed usually within the limits provided by parliamentary law.

ECONOMY

The constitution does not favor any economic system over another, although it takes into account nationalized "strategic" industries. Private property is protected, and the freedom to join labor unions is recognized.

RELIGIOUS COMMUNITIES

Burkina Faso is a secular republic. Freedom of religion is assured. There are no reports of interreligious tensions.

MILITARY DEFENSE AND STATE OF EMERGENCY

The president of the republic is the commander in chief of the armed forces. The military is subject to civil rule. Declarations of war and the sending of troops abroad require parliamentary approval.

In a state of emergency, the president takes necessary measures after deliberation in the Council of Ministers. The president may not dissolve the National Assembly in a state of emergency. Prolongation of the state of emergency exceeding 15 days requires parliamentary approval.

AMENDMENTS TO THE CONSTITUTION

Amendments to the constitution may be initiated by either the president, a majority of members of parliament, or a popular petition signed by at least 30,000 voters. The draft amendment is debated first in the National Assembly. Unless three-quarters of the members vote in favor, the draft needs approval in a popular referendum. The republican form of government, the multiparty regime, and the integrity of the state are not subject to amendment.

PRIMARY SOURCES

Constitution in English (extracts). Available online. URL: http://www.chr.up.ac.za/hr_docs/constitutions/docs/Burkina%20FasoC%20(englishsummary)(rev).doc. Accessed on August 21, 2005.

Constitution in French. Available online. URL: http://www.legiburkina.bf/. Accessed on July 25, 2005.

SECONDARY SOURCES

United Nations, "Core Document Forming Part of the Reports of States Parties: Burkina Faso" (HRI/CORE/1/Add.30), 15 July 1993. Available online. URL: http://www.unhchr.ch/tbs/doc.nsf. Accessed on August 1, 2005.

Malte Beyer

BURUNDI

At-a-Glance

OFFICIAL NAME
Republic of Burundi

CAPITAL
Bujumbura

POPULATION
6,231,221 (July 2004 est.)

SIZE
1,074 sq. mi. (27,830 sq. km)

LANGUAGES
Kirundi (national), French (official), Swahili

RELIGIONS
Roman Catholic 62%, other Christian (Protestant) 5%, Muslim 10%, traditional beliefs 23%

NATIONAL OR ETHNIC COMPOSITION
Hutu (Bantu) 85%, Tutsi (Hamitic) 14%, Twa (Pygmy) 1%

DATE OF INDEPENDENCE OR CREATION
July 1, 1962

TYPE OF GOVERNMENT
Semipresidential regime

TYPE OF STATE
Unitary state

TYPE OF LEGISLATURE
Bicameral parliament

DATE OF CONSTITUTION
Interim posttransition constitution promulgated by the president on October 20, 2004; entered in force on November 1, 2004

DATE OF LAST AMENDMENT
No amendment

Burundi is an independent, democratic, and unitary republic that is respectful of its ethnic diversity. The constitution establishes a semipresidential government based on the separation of the executive, legislative, and judicial powers.

After decades of military regimes, in 1993, Melchior Ndadaye became Burundi's first democratically elected president. Unfortunately, this president from the Hutu majority was assassinated in a bloody coup d'état in October, after only four months in power. Burundi then returned to Tutsi-dominated military rule and faced an intense ethnic conflict between Hutu and Tutsi factions, in which hundreds of thousands of Tutsi were killed. In 1998, Burundi troops intervened in the conflict in the Democratic Republic of Congo allegedly to secure the border and destroy the rebel bases operating from that country. On August 28, 2000, the government and the rebels signed the Arusha Accord for Peace and Reconciliation in Burundi, which paved the way for the cessation of hostilities and the start of power sharing in a government of national unity. A new constitution was passed on October 28, 2001, and a transitional government was inaugurated on November 1, 2001, despite the opposition of one of the four rebel groups.

After the Arusha agreement, Major Pierre Buyoya, a former president from the minority Tutsi who had returned to power by yet another coup d'état on July 25, 1996, remained in office as president for the first 18 months of the transition. On April 30, 2003, Domitien Ndayizeye, a Hutu leader, replaced him. On October 20, 2004, the president promulgated a new constitution adopted by parliament in September and October 2004. This constitution, which provides for elections to usher into a new constitutional order, entered into force on November 1, 2004.

CONSTITUTIONAL HISTORY

Urundi existed as an independent kingdom in the 18th century, ruled by the Tutsi minority. It merged with Rwanda in 1884 and became a German colony before passing to Belgium in 1919, after the defeat of Germany during World War I (1914–18). Rwanda-Urundi became a United Nations (UN) trust territory in 1946 and was placed under Belgian administration. Urundi split from Rwanda in 1959. The monarchy was suppressed, and later the Republic of Burundi proclaimed independence from Belgium on July 1, 1962. The 2004 constitution provides that the monarchy may be restored by referendum.

Since independence, Burundi has gone through a vicious circle of military coups d'état and ethnic conflicts between the majority Hutu and the minority Tutsi. Many constitutions that were passed were never enforced. The history of constitutionalism and democracy in the country as yet has been that of failure. The most recent constitution is the transitional constitution of October 28, 2001, which was amended several times prior to its replacement by the interim posttransition constitution inaugurated on November 1, 2004. On its approval by referendum on February 28, 2005, the interim constitution has become the final constitution of Burundi and paved the way for the first posttransition democratic elections in 2005 after a succession of Tutsi-dominated military regimes.

The Republic of Burundi is a member state of the United Nations, the African Union, and several subregional or/and other international organizations.

FORM AND IMPACT OF THE CONSTITUTION

The Constitution of Burundi is the supreme law of the republic. It is written and entrenched and prevails over any other law; any constitutional amendment requires particularly high majorities in both the National Assembly and the Senate. Any law, act, or conduct inconsistent with it is invalid.

BASIC ORGANIZATIONAL STRUCTURE

The Republic of Burundi is a unitary, decentralized state divided into 16 provinces, municipalities, zones, "hills," and other subdivisions as may be determined by law.

LEADING CONSTITUTIONAL PRINCIPLES

The core principle of the republic is government of the people by the people and for the people. Sovereignty is vested in the people, who assume it directly through referendum or indirectly through election of their representatives. Burundi is a pluralistic, unitary, social, democratic, and secular state that is respectful of human rights, constitutionalism, and the rule of law.

Ethnic, religious, and cultural minorities are also protected and have a say in the government. The defense and security corps and the judicial system must protect all Burundians, including the ethnic minorities. National unity and reconciliation are also leading principles of the republic. They are to be restored, preserved, and consolidated.

CONSTITUTIONAL BODIES

The main constitutional bodies are the president, the administration, parliament, and the judiciary.

The President

The president is elected by universal adult suffrage for a five-year term, renewable once only. Exceptionally, the first posttransition president shall be elected by a two-thirds majority of the National Assembly and the Senate sitting as a congress. This provision may be changed when the people decide by referendum. The president is sworn in before parliament and undertakes, among other duties, to combat any ideology of genocide and exclusion, to promote individual and collective human rights, and to safeguard the integrity and independence of the republic. She or he is the head of state and national administration, as well as the symbol of national unity. The president must ensure respect of the constitution; she or he is responsible for the enforcement of national legislation and for the regular functioning of public institutions.

Two vice presidents assist the president. The president appoints the highest civilian and military officers in the republic. Anyone who was president during the transition cannot run for office during the first presidential elections. The bid by President Buyoya and President Ndayizeye to have the relevant constitutional provision amended for them to stand for the presidency has been unsuccessful. However, the debate is not over, and the president may still request the people to decide on this issue in the constitutional referendum.

The Executive Administration

The executive administration consists of the president, two vice presidents, ministers, and vice ministers. It determines and conducts the policy of the nation. The president is the head of government. The vice presidents, who assist the president, are appointed by him or her from parliament and after approval by the National Assembly and the Senate. They must be from different ethnic and political groups. The president appoints the ministers after consulting the vice presidents. The executive administration comprises a maximum of 60 percent Hutu and 40 percent Tutsi ministers and vice ministers. At least 30 percent of its members should be women. The members of the administration are accountable to the president. With the exception of the president elected during the first presidential elections, the president may dissolve parliament. In turn, she or he may be impeached by parliament for high treason. This is a semipresidential system of government reminiscent of that of France.

Parliament

The legislative power is vested in parliament, which also controls the executive authority. Parliament is bicameral, consisting of the National Assembly and the Senate.

The National Assembly

The National Assembly consists of at least 100 deputies; 60 percent of its members must be Hutu and 40 percent Tutsi. Women should constitute 30 percent of the membership, and at least three members should be from the Twa ethnic minority. The members of parliament represent the nation as a whole and are elected by universal direct suffrage for a five-year term. Imperative mandate is prohibited. Their mandate may end with death, resignation, or incompatibility or when the member is sentenced for a criminal offense.

The Senate

The Senate consists of two senators from each province, three from the Twa ethnic minority, and all former heads of state. Of its members 30 percent should be women. In addition to its legislative power, the Senate mediates political conflicts and acts as the "adviser" to the nation.

The Lawmaking Process

Parliament is the main legislative authority in the republic. However, the president and the administration also participate in the lawmaking process. They, along with members of both the National Assembly and the Senate, are entitled to introduce legislation. The president may legislate by decree law with the authorization of parliament or when the latter is on recess. The National Assembly and the Senate must adopt bills with uniform terms. Otherwise, a joint commission is set up to propose a single text to be adopted by the two houses. If the joint commission fails to adopt a single text, the National Assembly has the final say.

The Judiciary

Justice is administered in the name of the people of Burundi. The constitution provides for the independence of the judiciary vis-à-vis the executive and the legislature. The judicial power is mandated to guarantee individual freedoms and fundamental human rights. It is vested in the Supreme Court of Justice, the Constitutional Court, the High Court of Justice, and other courts or tribunals, whether civil or military. Judges are subject to the constitution and the laws that regulate the judiciary.

The Supreme Court of Justice is the highest court in the republic. The Constitutional Court has jurisdiction, among other courts, to decide on the constitutionality of laws and acts having the force of law and to deal with disputes related to legislative and presidential elections. The High Court of Justice, which consists of the Supreme Court of Justice and the Constitutional Court, is competent to judge the highest authorities in the republic, specifically the president, the vice presidents, the president of the National Assembly, and the president of the Senate.

THE ELECTION PROCESS

The constitution provides for universal, equal, secret, regular, free, fair, and direct or indirect suffrage under the authority of an independent and impartial electoral commission. All Burundians over the age of 18, regardless of gender, enjoy all civil and political rights. They are entitled to stand for election and vote in elections.

POLITICAL PARTIES

A multiparty system is guaranteed. Political parties may be created freely according to the law. They are subject to the principles of pluralist democracy, national unity, and sovereignty. Minority parties and ethnic groups are protected and participate in the government. Members of the defense and security corps cannot belong to any party. Article 84 provides for public funding of the parties. There is an explicit role for the opposition.

CITIZENSHIP

Law determines the recognition, acquisition, loss, and resumption of Burundi citizenship. Children born of marriages contracted by Burundians, whether male or female, are equally entitled to citizenship.

FUNDAMENTAL RIGHTS

The constitution refers to the Universal Declaration of Human Rights of 1948, the two International Covenants on Human Rights of 1966, the African Charter on Human and Peoples' Rights of 1981, the Convention on the Elimination of All Forms of Discrimination against Women, and the Convention on the Rights of the Child. Article 19 provides that these international instruments are part and parcel of the constitution.

The Preamble also refers to the Charter of the United Nations and to the Constitutive Act of the African Union. Inspired by the African Charter, the Burundi bill of rights (Title II) provides for fundamental human rights and duties for both the individual and the citizen. Fundamental rights enshrined in this bill of rights include individual and collective rights and freedoms and civil, political, social, and cultural rights. The constitution also provides for duties, including the duty to defend the independence and territorial integrity of Burundi and to contribute to the preservation of democracy and social justice.

Impact and Functions of Fundamental Rights

The bill of rights is the cornerstone of the constitution, which is the supreme law of the republic and should be enforced by the executive, the legislature, and the judiciary. It binds all individuals and organs of the state. The judiciary is the watchdog of fundamental rights. However, institutions such as the National Council for National Unity and Reconciliation and the National Observatory (Commission) for the Prevention and Eradication of Genocide, War Crimes and Crimes against Humanity also have a role to play in the protection and the promotion of human rights in Burundi.

Limitations to Fundamental Rights

Fundamental rights are subject to limitation or derogation. Article 47 is the general limitation clause. It provides that any limitation of a fundamental human right must be governed by law. It must be justified by the need to protect public interest or others' fundamental rights and must be proportionate to its aim. On the other hand, fundamental rights may be suspended in some circumstances, which include a state of war or emergency.

ECONOMY

The constitution protects social and economic rights such as the right to work, protection against unemployment, equitable and satisfactory remuneration, education, secure health, and nondiscrimination against all, including women and the members of ethnic, cultural, and religious minorities. The Burundi economic system can be described as a social market economy, combining aspects of social responsibility with market economy.

RELIGIOUS COMMUNITIES

The Republic of Burundi is a secular state respectful of its ethnic and religious diversity. The constitution prohibits any discrimination based on religion and guarantees the right to freedom of religion. The protection and inclusion of all ethnic, cultural, and religious minorities are among the principles of the republic. Accordingly, there is no state religion. The main religions are Roman Catholic, Protestant, Muslim, and indigenous African.

MILITARY DEFENSE AND STATE OF EMERGENCY

The defense and security corps consists of the national defense force, national police, and national intelligence service. It is mandated to defend the territorial integrity of Burundi; participate in its economic, social, and cultural development; protect persons and their properties; and promote peace, democracy, and national reconciliation. It is bound by the constitution and is subject to the rule of law. It must work in a transparent manner and develop a culture that is not discriminatory, ethnicist, or sexist. Its composition must reflect the desire of all the Burundians to live in peace together and build a democratic and economically prosperous nation. To prevent the recurrence of acts of genocide and coups d'état and to secure balanced representation, no more than 50 percent of the members of the defense and security corps can be from a single ethnic group.

The president is the commander in chief of the defense and security corps. After consulting the executive government, the National Security Council, and the leadership of both the National Assembly and the Senate, the president may declare war or a state of emergency and take necessary measures to restore order or the territorial integrity of the republic. The constitution prohibits any recruitment or participation of child soldiers in wars or armed conflicts.

AMENDMENTS TO THE CONSTITUTION

The introduction of constitutional amendments is concurrently the prerogative of the president, after consulting the administration, and of both the National Assembly and the Senate, which must decide by an absolute majority of members. The president may also submit a constitutional amendment to a referendum. Article 299 of the constitution prohibits any constitutional amendment undermining national unity and reconciliation, territorial integrity, or the democratic and secular character of the republic.

A four-fifths majority in the National Assembly and another two-thirds majority in the Senate are required for a constitutional amendment to be passed by parliament.

PRIMARY SOURCES

Interim Constitution in French. Available online. URL: http//www.abarundi.org/negotiations/arusha1/ burundi_presidence_150904_projet_de_constituti on.html. Accessed on September 5, 2005.
2005 Constitution in French. Available online. URL: http://www.accpuf.org/. Accessed on August 9, 2005.

SECONDARY SOURCES

Christof Heyns, ed., *Human Rights Law in Africa*. Vol. 2. Leiden: Martinus Nijhoff, 2004. Available online. URL: http://www.chr.up.ac.za/. Accessed on July 19, 2005.
F. Reyntjens, "Constitution-Making in Situations of Extreme Crisis: The Case of Rwanda and Burundi." *Journal of African Law* 40, no. 2 (1996): 234–242.
United Nations, "Core Document Forming Part of the Reports of States Parties: Burundi" (HRI/CORE/1/ Add.16/Rev.1), 16 June 1999. Available online. URL: http//www.unhchr.ch/tbs/doc.nsf. Accessed on September 2, 2005.

André Mbata B. Mangu

CAMBODIA

At-a-Glance

OFFICIAL NAME
Kingdom of Cambodia

CAPITAL
Phnom Penh

POPULATION
13,881,427 (July 2006 est.)

SIZE
69,898 sq. mi. (181,035 sq. km)

LANGUAGES
Khmer

RELIGIONS
Theravada Buddhist 95%, other 5%

NATIONAL OR ETHNIC COMPOSITION
Khmer 90%, Vietnamese 5%, Chinese 1%, other 4%

DATE OF INDEPENDENCE OR CREATION
November 9, 1953 (from France)

TYPE OF GOVERNMENT
Parliamentary monarchy

TYPE OF STATE
Unitary state

TYPE OF LEGISLATURE
Bicameral parliament

DATE OF CONSTITUTION
September 24, 1993

DATE OF LAST AMENDMENT
March 4, 1999, additional law to the constitution
July 8, 2004

Cambodia is a parliamentary monarchy with a modern constitution that encompasses democracy, the rule of law, separation of powers, and human rights. A unitary state, the country is structured in 24 provinces and more than 1,600 communes. After the country was ravaged by external and internal warfare, cruel dictatorship, and socialist stagnation, its current constitutional structure was, with the help of the United Nations, implemented in 1993. The impact of the constitution, rule of law, and effective protection of human rights are still to be enhanced, but the end of warfare and ideological confrontation has paved the road for democratic development.

The establishment of a Constitutional Council, a Senate, and a National Audit Authority and the introduction of communal self-government on a democratic basis are some of the institutional steps taken in recent years. The situation is still very dynamic, democracy is volatile, and the rule of law is still more program than reality. However, the progress made in little more than a decade should not be undervalued.

CONSTITUTIONAL HISTORY

Cambodia's proud history is symbolized by the famous ruins of Angkor, which may be the largest historic temple site worldwide; a picture of the main temple at Angkor Wat decorates Cambodia's flag today. Early state building in the area is reported for Funan and later Chenla, but the historical evidence on the size, durability, and state quality of these political systems is sparse. From the eighth to the 13th century C.E., the Khmer Kingdom of Angkor dominated much of the region of Southeast Asia. Social and legal systems were strongly influenced by Indian culture. The structure of the political and constitutional system of this medieval empire has not been verified in every detail, but it essentially was constructed as an absolute monarchy in a highly stratified society, with the king holding political, legislative, and judicial control. However, provincial authorities had some degree of authority in practice, and the theoretical idea of peaceful succession to the throne stands in sharp contrast to a tradition of violent struggle after the death of most kings. In the centuries after the great Angkorian period, the country was under pressure from Siam (Thailand) in the west and Vietnam in the east. Some analysts suggest that the kingdom was at risk of vanishing by the middle of the 19th century when European colonialism changed the course of events.

In 1863, Cambodia was formally under the protection of France, which had recently established its colonial rule in Vietnam. As a "protectorate," Cambodia initially retained more autonomy than neighboring Vietnam. The monarchic principle was not formally violated, and the king stayed in office. Over time, France increasingly interfered in the internal administration. Under threat of removal in 1884, the king accepted substantial reforms, including the abolition of slavery and the installation of French residents in the provincial capitals. A consultative council created in 1913 was in fact an instrument to control the king. French influence on the legal system became especially apparent from the beginning of the 20th century when civil law and criminal law were partly reformed along French lines. However, throughout the colonial period, life in the countryside was only sporadically affected. Perhaps most significant and a basis for major conflicts was the heavy rural tax burden, used for the development of the capital and other prestige projects.

In 1941, the French installed 10-year-old Prince Norodom Sihanouk as king, expecting him to be a compliant puppet. Instead, the young king was an ambitious and charismatic leader. Sihanouk soon defined the sovereignty of Cambodia as a primary policy goal. A short period of independence in the turbulent final phase of World War II (1939–45) was not fully successful; French power was reestablished amid assurances of gradual decolonialization.

In 1947, the first constitution was adopted, following the model of parliamentary monarchy. Pressure from Sihanouk significantly democratized the constitution-making process and the text of the constitution itself. Independence was achieved in 1953. Sihanouk resigned as king in 1955 to lead the country in other formal positions as prime minister and later as head of state within a political system commonly characterized as "guided democracy." Although at first the country developed significantly, Sihanouk eventually failed in his attempt to keep Cambodia out of the Indochinese war. After he allowed North Vietnam to use land and facilities in Cambodia in their war against South Vietnam and the American forces, the United States started attacking eastern parts of Cambodia. In 1970, Sihanouk was ousted from power by a United States–backed regime change led by General Lon Nol.

The Cambodian parliament formally deposed Sihanouk. Monarchy was abolished, and in 1972, a new constitution, which generally followed the model of a presidential democracy, was adopted. The document never really became effective in most of the country as the central government was no longer in control. An intensifying civil war, as well as the war in neighboring Vietnam, set the country on the road to anarchy.

The Communist Khmer Rouge, under their infamous leader Saloth Sar (Pol Pot), in April 1975, seized power in the capital, which along with all other cities was immediately evacuated. The Khmer Rouge installed a literally lawless state called Democratic Kampuchea. Formally, a rudimentary socialist constitution was adopted in 1976, containing only 21 comparatively short articles, but neither the legislature nor the courts provided for in this constitution ever materialized. The constitution itself remained the only law the Khmer Rouge ever formally enacted.

Cambodia was practically transformed into a labor camp; within less than four years, between 1.5 and 2 million people were killed or died of exhaustion, hunger, and disease. When the victims of the preceding civil war are taken into account, Cambodia probably lost about a third of its population during the 1970s. Bringing at least the most responsible surviving leaders of this system to justice is an endeavor that Cambodia finally decided to undertake in cooperation with the United Nations in 2004.

The Vietnamese invasion ended the Khmer Rouge's rule in early 1979. This invasion, which originally was condemned by the Western countries as a breach of international law (and the ousted Khmer Rouge were allowed to represent Cambodia in the United Nations for another decade), at least stopped the "autogenocide" and led life in Cambodia back in the direction of civilization. Politically, the unparalleled, extreme version of "Stone Age communism" of the Khmer Rouge was replaced by a form of government more typical in the contemporaneous Eastern Bloc. The country was again renamed, as the People's Republic of Kampuchea. A new constitutional system shaped along the lines of the Soviet-Vietnamese model was formally adopted in 1981.

After political change in the Soviet Union also led to a pullout of the remaining Vietnamese troops from Cambodia, the transformative process toward democracy and a market economy intensified. In order to end the ongoing civil war with the Khmer Rouge, who were still fighting the government from strongholds in some parts of the country, a multiparty international treaty (Paris Agreements) was brokered in 1991. It was the basis for the United Nations Transitional Authority in Cambodia (UNTAC), which can probably be qualified as the most ambitious democratization project the United Nations had undertaken to that time. The Khmer Rouge soon renewed their guerrilla war, which continued for several more years. However, UNTAC was successful in ensuring basically free and democratic elections of a constitutional assembly. Elections were held and the constitution was adopted in 1993. Despite some justified claims of secrecy in the process, its outcome is a substantially democratic constitution, which regardless of some technical shortcomings has essentially been the basis for the democratic process in Cambodia since then.

Constitutional developments since 1993 may be summarized as a difficult conversion to the routines of democracy and the rule of law. The guerrilla war ended finally with the death of Pol Pot in 1998. Elections were held largely on time in 1998 and 2003. Substantial improvements in the institutional system have been made in recent years. However, a militant overthrow of the government in 1997 and a year-long political deadlock in the aftermath of the 2003 elections are reminders of the volatility of Cambodian democracy. On the other hand, the succession of the king, a challenge that was long feared to have the potential to produce a major crisis, took place in a surprisingly smooth and noncontroversial manner in October 2004.

FORM AND IMPACT OF THE CONSTITUTION

The 1993 Cambodian constitution originally comprised a single written document that encompassed all the typical features of a modern liberal democracy, including a catalogue of human rights. The constitution is, expressly, the supreme law of the land. There are institutional safeguards to guarantee the constitutionality of new laws, and there are rules for amending the constitution, as well as material limits to constitutional amendments. However, because there are still in force many older laws that do not comply with the constitution, and because the courts are not yet effective in systematically enforcing the supremacy of the constitution, the constitution has not yet had a comprehensive impact on the legal system. However, the recently established Constitutional Council has significant powers to enforce the constitution. Furthermore, a codification of major areas of law currently under way may also strengthen the impact of the constitution by replacing many older laws.

A political deadlock after parliamentary elections in 2003 was solved by the adoption the following year of an additional law to the constitution, outside the regular amendment process. The law did win the majorities necessary for an amendment of the constitution, and the Constitutional Council has decided to accept the law on a par with the constitution.

BASIC ORGANIZATIONAL STRUCTURE

At least since the time of French rule, Cambodia has been a unitary state. The current constitution does not address the question of administrative structure in detail but stipulates that the country be divided into provinces and municipalities, each of which is divided into districts (*khan*) and communes (*sangkat*). Details are to be worked out in organic laws. On the provincial and municipal levels, the country is structured into 24 entities with appointed governors as heads of administration. The communal level has been democratized recently with elected communal councils, which have been in charge of local affairs since

2002. Ongoing deconcentration of the formerly centralized structures is a major goal of the current attempts at administrative reform.

LEADING CONSTITUTIONAL PRINCIPLES

The core values of the constitution are pluralistic and liberal democracy, constitutional monarchy, fundamental rights, separation of powers, peace, and the maintenance of the independence and sovereignty of Cambodia. Article 153, limiting amendments of the constitution, seems most appropriate as a description of core values: "liberal and pluralistic democracy and the regime of constitutional monarchy."

One important aspect of Cambodian constitutionalism is the commitment to international values. The constitution itself is a product of an internationally arranged and organized process: The Paris Agreements provided precise guidelines on the content of the constitution. The state's commitment to peace is specified in the constitution extensively, as is the obligation to recognize and respect international human rights (Article 31). The precise status of international law (including human rights) is, however, as in many constitutions, not precisely regulated; this may be one of the important challenges for the Constitutional Council.

CONSTITUTIONAL BODIES

The king, the prime minister and his Council of Ministers, the National Assembly and Senate, the Judiciary, and the Constitutional Council are the central constitutional bodies.

The King

The king is the formal head of state. Whereas Cambodian kings were historically absolute, since the constitution of 1947, the institution has been largely ceremonial. According to the 1993 constitution, the king shall "reign, but not govern." However, the constitution still provides a number of important functions for the king, such as the right to appoint some members to the Constitutional Council and the Senate. As in many countries, the influence of the head of state on politics does not necessarily depend on formal powers but is largely dependent on the personality and style of the officeholder. King Norodom Sihanouk's influence has been commonly acknowledged. His successor, King Norodom Sihamoni, who had not been involved in Cambodian politics before his coronation in October 2004, will have to redefine the role on his own.

The text of the constitution does not expressly provide for the resignation of the king, assuming a lifelong mandate. However, King Norodom Sihanouk declared his resignation on October 7, 2004. On his advice, a Royal Council, as established by the constitution, appointed his son, Norodom Sihamoni, as successor a few days later. Coronation ceremonies took place October 28–30, 2004. Constitutionally, the abolition of the monarchy is explicitly forbidden.

Prime Minister and Council of Ministers

The administration is institutionalized in the Council of Ministers, headed by a prime minister. The current prime minister, Hun Sen, has been leading the country since 1984, with an interval as a "second prime minister" after losing an election in 1993. He is generally considered the undisputed "strongman" of current Cambodian politics. Institutionally, the strength of the office is not immediately evident in the constitution, which gives it the ordinary powers of a chief minister in a parliamentary democracy. However, his power is buttressed by the 1994 Law on the Organization and Functioning of the Council of Ministers. According to this law, the prime minister not only "manages and gives out commands on all activities of the executive in all fields" (Article 9) but is also responsible for the appointment and dismissal of many high-ranking officers in the administration and military.

The Council of Ministers, as assembled by a representative of the winning party (typically the candidate for prime minister), needs a vote of confidence of two-thirds of the National Assembly. This consensus-oriented majority, probably unique within the family of democratic constitutions, makes forming an administration difficult. Cabinet members are constitutionally responsible not only to the prime minister but also to the National Assembly, with the latter having a right to dismiss a cabinet minister (Article 98 of the constitution). The Council of Ministers is currently very large, encompassing one prime minister, seven deputy prime ministers, 15 senior ministers, 28 ministers, 135 secretaries of state, and at least 146 under-secretaries of state.

The Council of Ministers is collectively responsible to the National Assembly. Its workings are regulated by a special law. A special Council of Jurists, established by governmental decree, provides legal expertise to the Council of Ministers and regularly checks its draft legislation.

The National Assembly

The National Assembly is the central legislative organ of the state. Its members (currently 123) are elected by general, direct, free, equal, and secret ballot. Candidates must be nominated by registered political parties. Members of the National Assembly enjoy privileges such as explicit freedom of mandate that includes the ability to prohibit any imperative mandate (Article 77). The member can be removed in case of departure or expulsion from his or her party.

The National Assembly has the usual powers of a legislative organ, including the power to set the state budget. To facilitate practical work, the parliament establishes nine specialized permanent commissions. Members of the oppositional Sam Rainsy Party have been excluded from these commissions since 2004, exclusion that has been criticized as unconstitutional. The constitutional provisions on supervising the administration have not yet been very effective. So far there are no special committees with investigative authority.

The Senate

The Senate was established by constitutional amendment in 1998. The number of senators must not exceed more than half of the members of the National Assembly; it is currently 61. In the first period, the senators were appointed by the king, mostly on the advice of the political parties according to their proportional strength in the National Assembly elections. For future periods, the constitution provides that most of the senators have to be elected.

The powers of the Senate are still fairly limited at this time. Its right to revise laws adopted by the National Assembly is limited by a rigid time frame for the reviewing process. A general Senate responsibility to facilitate relations between the Council of Ministers and the National Assembly is stipulated in the constitution, but the terms are vague and without much practical relevance. However, with a National Assembly much absorbed by party politics, potential for a stronger Senate exists.

The Lawmaking Process

Laws are typically drafted in a ministry, but they can also be introduced in the National Assembly or the Senate. A legal check of ministerial drafts is undertaken by the Council of Jurists. The Council of Ministers finally decides whether a draft is to be sent to the National Assembly. After approval by the National Assembly, the Senate has to review the law, but its objections can be overturned by the assembly. Before the law can be promulgated by a royal decree, there is, in some enumerated cases, a compulsory check for constitutionality by the Constitutional Council. In other cases, the Constitutional Council can be asked by various other bodies to perform that check.

The Judiciary

The formal legal and judicial system of Cambodia is based on the continental European tradition, with some remaining influences of the former socialist system. The "civil law" orientation will be strengthened when a current project to adopt civil and criminal codes is completed. Modernization and reform of the legal and judicial system are currently a political priority in Cambodia. As nearly all qualified lawyers lost their life during the Khmer Rouge regime, and an independent judiciary was not policy in the years of socialist rule, this reform is still a major challenge. Steps have been taken to enhance the quality and neutrality of the work of judges, but salaries are still low and a significant percentage of judges have not had substantial legal training. Overcoming a culture of impunity, which has characterized the legal system for a long time, is as important as ensuring the independence of the judiciary.

The Cambodian court system consists of three tiers: municipal and provincial courts as well as a military court, appellate courts, and finally the Supreme Court. Specialized administrative and commercial courts have not been established yet but are under discussion.

The Constitutional Council

The Constitutional Council, established after significant delays in 1998, is a hybrid institution. It is in part an element of the lawmaking process, but it also fulfils the functions of a real constitutional court. On the request of other bodies including courts, it checks the constitutionality of laws and administrative acts and resolves election disputes. Citizens do not have direct recourse for human rights complaints, but various organs and courts can forward questions to the council.

THE ELECTION PROCESS

All Cambodians from the age of 18 years old have the right to vote in national elections; the right to run in elections is limited to citizens of at least 25 for national elections and 40 for future Senate elections. The National Assembly is elected by free, universal, direct, equal, and secret ballot for a period of five years. According to the election law, candidates are preselected by lists of registered political parties. The system of elections for the Senate has not yet been decided on in detail. Elections to the National Assembly in 1993, 1998, and 2003 took place under massive international scrutiny.

POLITICAL PARTIES

Political parties have had a very strong impact on Cambodian politics and society. The constitution does not define their status, but in 1997 a special law on political parties was enacted. Party membership is necessary to become a lawmaker or government member and to obtain a wide array of positions in the civil service.

The major parties, for the time being, are the former socialist state party the Cambodian Peoples' Party (CCP), the strongest force; the royalist party the National United Front for an Independent, Neutral, Peaceful, and Cooperative Cambodia (FUNCINPEC); and the Sam Rainsy Party (SRP), which is led by and named after an expelled former FUNCINPEC minister. Since democratization in 1993, the country has been governed by a CPP-FUNCINPEC coalition. The Democratic Kampuchea Party, which was the political arm of the Khmer Rouge, was outlawed in 1994.

CITIZENSHIP

The Cambodian constitution frequently talks of Khmer Citizens but does not specify the conditions of citizenship. Khmer citizens cannot be deprived of their nationality and are provided diplomatic protection when residing abroad.

The law on nationality (1996) is, in principle, comparatively generous. Citizenship is acquired either by being a (legitimate or nonlegitimate) child of a Cambodian father or mother or by being born in Cambodia. On request, citizenship is granted after being married and living together with a Cambodian husband or wife for three years or after living in Cambodia for at least seven years under the provisions of the immigration law. In recent times, citizenship has occasionally been offered in gratitude to foreigners who publicly had been sympathetic to Cambodia, most notably to the U.S. movie star Angelina Jolie. Cambodian law does not object to dual citizenship, and, in fact, many members of the country's elite have a second citizenship in France or elsewhere.

FUNDAMENTAL RIGHTS

Fundamental rights are a central element of the constitution. They are embraced in the preamble and stipulated in detail in an entire chapter. This chapter opens with Article 31, which pays explicit respect to the major international human rights treaties to which Cambodia is a party. The precise relevance of these treaties is unclear, beyond an implied obligation to interpret the basic rights of the Cambodian constitution in their light.

The catalogue of rights follows traditional paths with some modern tendencies. The freedom of life explicitly includes the abolition of the death penalty; an attempt of parliament to reintroduce the death penalty for the former leaders of the Khmer Rouge was declared void by the Constitutional Council. The human rights catalogue contains traditional liberal rights, emphasizes equality of men and women, and requires protection from exploitation. There is also an array of "third-generation" rights, including health care and education, which will be difficult to embody in this still very poor country.

Obligations of parents to their children, and vice versa, and citizens' obligations to the state complement the fundamental rights.

Impact and Functions of Fundamental Rights

Fundamental rights are supposed to be a concrete legal standard for all legislation and administrative action, but reality only reflects this in part. Although the courts have authority over administrative decisions, for example, in practice there have been almost no cases in which the constitutionality or legality of such acts has been questioned. For example, demonstrations have been forbidden in Phnom Penh for long periods, though the constitution and a preconstitutional law on demonstrations explicitly guarantee the right to demonstrate. For the time being, it can be said that the direct impact of basic rights lies more in the field of lawmaking than in effective judicial control.

Cambodia is a party to numerous international human rights treaties. It ratified the International Covenant on Civil and Political Rights in 1992 but has until now not signed the first optional protocol to this treaty, which would allow direct individual communications with the Human Rights Committee in Geneva.

Limitations to Fundamental Rights

The constitution envisions law that would define the precise scope of freedoms and by implication their limits. The general understanding accords with the "Asian" approach, which emphasizes not only rights but also duties, and which traditionally accepts as legitimate limitations on rights in the public interest.

Concerns have been raised that the constitution provides most of the basic rights only to "Khmer Citizens" and explicitly bars foreigners from owning land in Cambodia, Article 44. This nonprotection of foreigners may not be in full conformity with international standards; it could also serve as a justification for discrimination against Cambodian citizens not of Khmer ethnicity. However, the constitution explicitly embraces international instruments prohibiting ethnic discrimination and speaks out against such discrimination (Article 31).

From the practical point of view, the human rights situation in Cambodia is checkered. Whereas religious freedom is widely respected and the media and nongovernmental organizations can express critical views, the freedom of peaceful assembly (demonstration) has been completely disregarded by authorities in recent times. Human rights conditions in Cambodia is regularly monitored by international institutions as well as international and national nongovernmental organizations.

ECONOMY

The current constitution contains a whole chapter on economy. Whereas earlier constitutions were strictly socialist, the current one provides for a "market economy system" (Article 56). Private property, freedom of profession, and freedom of trade unions including the right to strike are protected by the constitution. A law on the economic system, as required by the constitution, has not been adopted so far.

In practice, the Cambodian economy has developed below expectations in recent years. Agriculture is dominated by rice production and logging (often illegal), the industrial sector by garment production, and the service industry by tourism. Widespread corruption and an inefficient bureaucracy are major obstacles to development, as the country is considered to be a comparatively expensive and difficult place to start an officially registered business. The need for reform is acknowledged by the government and is especially urgent since Cambodia joined the World Trade Organization in October 2004.

RELIGIOUS COMMUNITIES

According to the constitution, Buddhism is the state religion, but religious freedom is constitutionally guaranteed and practiced. Some Buddhist institutions are supported by the state, and Buddhist leaders are members of the body that decides on the royal succession.

MILITARY DEFENSE AND STATE OF EMERGENCY

Considering Cambodia's recent violent history, it is remarkable that the constitution does not provide many guidelines in this field. A state of emergency can be declared by the king after agreement with the prime minister and the chairs of the National Assembly and the Senate; details are not enumerated. Declaration of war is the prerogative of the king after approval of the National Assembly and the Senate. The king is also the formal commander in chief of the military forces. Khmer citizens have the duty to defend their homeland, but compulsory service has not been practiced in recent years.

The country's commitment to peace is emphasized in the constitution. The preamble foresees Cambodia as a restored "Island of Peace." Articles 53 and 54 prohibit wars of aggression and ban the manufacture, use, and storage of nuclear, chemical, and biological weapons.

AMENDMENTS TO THE CONSTITUTION

Amendments to the constitution require a two-thirds majority vote in the National Assembly. Any amendment affecting the system of liberal and pluralistic democracy and constitutional monarchy is prohibited. As mentioned, in 2004 an "additional law" was promulgated, effectively amending the constitution without following the rules and legalizing similar procedures for the future. Constitutional amendment procedures should be readjusted if effective constitutionalism is to prevail.

PRIMARY SOURCES
Constitution in English. Available online. URL: http://www.cambodian-parliament.org/english/constitution_files/constitution.htm. Accessed on September 9, 2005.

Historical Constitutions: Raoul M. Jennar, *The Cambodian Constitutions (1953–1993)*. Bangkok: White Lotus Pres, 1995.

Constitution in Khmer. Available online. URL: http://www.cambodia.gov.kh/unisql2/egov/khmer/home.view.html. Accessed on September 19, 2005.

SECONDARY SOURCES

Laksiri Fernando, "Khmer Socialism, Human Rights and the UN Intervention." In *East Asia—Human Rights, Nation-Building, Trade,* edited by Alice Tay. Baden-Baden, Germany: Nomos-Verlag, 1999.

Stephen P. Marks, "The New Cambodian Constitution: From Civil War to a Fragile Democracy." *Columbia Human Rights Law Review* 26, no. pp. 45–110 (1994).

Siphana Sok and Denora Sarin, *The Legal System of Cambodia.* Phnom Penh: Cambodian Legal Resources Development Center, 1998.

Jörg Menzel

CAMEROON

At-a-Glance

OFFICIAL NAME
Republic of Cameroon

CAPITAL
Yaoundé

POPULATION
16,063,678 (July 2004 est.)

SIZE
183,568 sq. mi. (475,440 sq. km)

LANGUAGES
English and French (both official), 230 indigenous languages

RELIGIONS
Indigenous beliefs 40%, Christian 40%, Muslim 20%

NATIONAL OR ETHNIC COMPOSITION
Cameroon Highlanders 31%, Equatorial Bantu 19%, Kirdi 11%, Fulani 10%, Northwestern Bantu 8%, Eastern Nigritic 7%, other African 13%, non-African 1%

DATE OF INDEPENDENCE OR CREATION
January 1, 1960; union with southern British Cameroons, October 1, 1961

TYPE OF GOVERNMENT
Constitutional democracy

TYPE OF STATE
Unitary state

TYPE OF LEGISLATURE
Bicameral parliament

DATE OF CONSTITUTION
June 2, 1972

DATE OF LAST AMENDMENT
January 18, 1996

Cameroon is a constitutional democracy based on the rule of law. Clear separation of powers exists among the executive, legislative, and judicial organs of state. Cameroon is a unitary state administratively divided into 10 provinces. The constitution of Cameroon contains a preamble bill of rights, guaranteeing an elaborate list of rights, and incorporating the Universal Declaration of Human Rights, the Charter of the United Nations, and the African Charter on Human and Peoples' Rights. The constitution has, however, failed to take full effect; some of its bodies have not been set up and administrative changes not been implemented. This includes the Constitutional Council, whose main function is to interpret the constitution. Human rights violations, especially on an individual basis, are not effectively remedied on the basis of the constitution. The judiciary is neither strong nor independent.

The president of the republic is head of the administration. The president does not depend on the parliament as the constitution gives the office significant power.

Multiparty elections have only been held since 1992; they have been plagued by irregularities and unfavorably evaluated by independent observers. The political opposition is weak and fragmented.

Religious freedom is guaranteed in the constitution, and church and state are separate. Economically, Cameroon is a market economy. It is politically and economically stable. The military is subject to the civil government in law and in fact.

CONSTITUTIONAL HISTORY

Germany annexed the territory it called Kamerun in 1884. On February 20, 1916, during World War I (1914–18), German troops in the colony surrendered to Britain and France, which split the territory between them. In 1919, the lands were placed under the mandate system of the League of Nations, and in 1945, they became United Nations trust territories. French Cameroun was administered as part of French Equatorial Africa and gained independence on January 1, 1960. British Cameroons consisted of two noncontiguous territories administered as part of Nigeria. The United Nations offered these territories the option of joining either the Federal Republic of Nigeria or the existing Republic of Cameroon.

Northern Cameroons voted to join Nigeria, Southern Cameroons voted to join Cameroon, and on October 1, 1961, the Federal Republic of Cameroon emerged—the previously independent Cameroon became the Federated State of East Cameroon, while Southern Cameroons became the Federated State of West Cameroon.

The federal constitution provided for two federated states, each with a legislature, a court system, and a prime minister. It also provided for federal structures including one state president, a federal legislative body, and a federal court of justice. Article 47(1) expressly prohibited any amendments to the constitution that would run contrary to the nature and purpose of the federation.

On February 11, 1972, 11 days after it was first announced, a referendum produced a suspect 99.9 percent result in favor of ending the federation. Contrary to the constitution, President Ahidjo dissolved the federation by presidential decree and instituted a unitary state; he assumed powers to rule by ordinances and decrees for one year.

The constitution of the new United Republic of Cameroon dissolved all federal structures, including the unique House of Chiefs. Power became heavily centralized with the president, and the one-party state was further consolidated. On February 4, 1984, Paul Biya, who succeeded the founding president Ahidjo in both the ruling party and as head of state, abolished the united republic by decree and restored the original name of Republic of Cameroon.

Cameroon is a member of the Economic and Monetary Community of Central African States (CEMAC).

FORM AND IMPACT OF THE CONSTITUTION

The constitution of Cameroon is written and codified in a single document. In principle, it takes precedence over all other national law. International law must be in accordance with the constitution to be negotiated and ratified by the president of the republic, subject to the authorization of parliament when the law falls within the area of competence of the legislative power.

BASIC ORGANIZATIONAL STRUCTURE

Cameroon is a unitary state divided into 10 provinces, each of which is further parceled into divisions, subdivisions, and districts. There are two English-speaking and eight French-speaking provinces, all of which differ in

geographic area, population, and economic strength. All have identical government powers.

Provinces do not have legislative powers. The administrative hierarchy descends from the provincial governor through the senior divisional officer and the divisional officer. Common law is practiced in English-speaking provinces and civil law in French-speaking provinces. The practice of the former is influenced by the latter. Some areas of law have been unified, such as the penal code in criminal law, but the harmonization process is complete, leaving other areas such as criminal procedure divided.

LEADING CONSTITUTIONAL PRINCIPLES

Cameroon's system of government is a constitutional democracy. The constitution separates the executive, legislative, and judicial powers. In practice, the executive is very strong and influences the legislative and judicial branches of government. The judiciary is independent only in principle.

Cameroon is a decentralized unitary state based on the principles of democracy and the rule of law. Political participation is exercised indirectly through the president of the republic and the parliament or by referendum. Cameroon is a secular state, which guarantees freedom of religion.

CONSTITUTIONAL BODIES

The main bodies provided for in the constitution are the president of the republic; the administration; the parliament, which comprises the National Assembly and the Senate; the Constitutional Council; the Court of Impeachment; the Economic and Social Council; and the judiciary.

The President of the Republic

The president of the republic is the head of state. The president has the power to appoint and dismiss the prime minister, who is the head of the administration, and other members of the administration after consultation with the prime minister.

The president of the republic is elected by direct universal suffrage for a seven-year term and can be reelected once. The president defines government policy.

The Administration

The administration implements policy as defined by the president. It is composed of the prime minister at its head and other members of the administration, who are all appointed and dismissed by the president.

The National Assembly

The National Assembly is the lower of the two houses of parliament. Its 180 members represent the entire nation and are elected by direct, secret, universal suffrage for five years. The primary functions of the National Assembly are to adopt the state budget and to pass laws.

The Senate

The Senate is the upper house of parliament and represents regional and local authorities. Each region is represented by 10 senators, seven of whom are elected by indirect universal suffrage on a regional basis. The other three are appointed by the president of the republic. Their term of office is five years. The Senate was created in the constitutional amendment of 1996 but has not yet been established.

The Lawmaking Process

Bills are drafted either by the president of the republic or by members of parliament (private members' bills). Bills are passed by parliament, which may empower the president of the republic to legislate by way of ordinance for a limited period and for given purposes. Ordinances enter into force on the date of their publication.

Laws are passed by a simple majority of the members of the National Assembly. A bill passed by the National Assembly is immediately forwarded to the president of the Senate by the president of the National Assembly. Within 10 days of receiving the bill, the president of the Senate submits it to the Senate for consideration. A bill declared urgent by the government must be submitted within five days. The Senate may pass or amend the bill.

As the Senate is not yet established, the final bill adopted by the National Assembly is forwarded to the president of the republic for enactment. The president enacts laws passed by parliament within 15 days of their being forwarded to the president, unless he or she requests a second reading or refers the matter to the Constitutional Council (which is also still to be established). If the deadline passes without presidential action, the president of the National Assembly may himself or herself enact the law. Laws are published in the *Official Gazette* of the republic in English and French.

The Constitutional Council

The Constitutional Council is the body with full jurisdiction in all matters pertaining to the interpretation and application of the constitution. Among other powers, it gives final rulings on the constitutionality of laws and the conflict of powers and regulates the functioning of institutions provided for under the constitution.

The Constitutional Council is made up of 11 members appointed by the president of the republic. Three, including the president of the council, are designated by the president of the republic; three by the president of the National Assembly; three by the president of the Senate;

and two by the Higher Judicial Council. They serve for a nonrenewable term of nine years. The Constitutional Council has yet to be established.

The Court of Impeachment

The Court of Impeachment tries the president of the republic for high treason and the prime minister and members of the administration for conspiracy against the security of the state. Its jurisdiction is limited to acts committed in the exercise of their official functions.

The Economic and Social Council

The Economic and Social Council's membership and structure are specified by law. It is meant to combine representatives from associations working in the field of the economy and society.

The Judiciary

The judiciary is independent of the executive and the legislature. The highest court is the Supreme Court of Cameroon, consisting of three benches. The judicial bench mainly rules on appeals arising from judgments rendered in lower courts. The administrative bench rules mainly on disputes of an administrative nature between the state and other public authorities, disputes arising from regional and council elections, as well as appeals from lower courts in administrative cases. The audit bench rules on matters involving public accounts and on appeals arising from lower audit courts.

Until the Constitutional Council is established, its role is performed by the Supreme Court, which has a specially constituted bench for this purpose.

THE ELECTION PROCESS

All Cameroonians over the age of 20 have the right to vote. The vote is equal and secret. Candidates for president must be at least 35 years old; candidates for the Senate must be at least 40 years old. Political parties and groups are required to assist the electorate in making voting decisions.

POLITICAL PARTIES

Cameroon has been a multiparty democracy since 1990. There are approximately 140 political parties, the creation and dissolution of which are subject to decisions of the Ministry of Territorial Administration.

CITIZENSHIP

Cameroonian citizenship is acquired by birth, descent, marriage, or naturalization. A child acquires Cameroonian citizenship if both parents are Cameroonian, irrespective of where the child is born. However, birth within the territory of Cameroon does not automatically confer citizenship, except with regard to a child born of unknown or stateless parents or a child born in Cameroon of foreign parents, at least one of whom was also born in Cameroon.

Cameroonian citizenship by descent is acquired by a child born in wedlock whose father is a citizen of Cameroon, regardless of the country of birth; a child born out of wedlock to a Cameroonian father and foreign mother, if paternity can be established; and a child born out of wedlock to a Cameroonian mother and an unknown or stateless father.

Furthermore, the law permits a foreign woman who marries a citizen of Cameroon to acquire Cameroonian citizenship. Citizenship may also be acquired upon the fulfillment of certain requirements pertaining to residency, age, health, and morality.

The law does not recognize dual citizenship, with the exception of a child born abroad of Cameroonian parents, who may retain the citizenship of the country of birth. However, upon reaching the age of 21, the child must choose Cameroonian citizenship explicitly or lose it.

Citizenship can be lost voluntarily or involuntarily. Voluntary abjuration of Cameroonian citizenship is permitted, upon presentation of proof of new citizenship. Citizenship can be lost involuntarily if a person is employed in the service of a foreign government or voluntarily acquires foreign citizenship. With regard to the latter, the law does not require a Cameroonian woman who marries a foreign citizen to renounce Cameroonian citizenship.

FUNDAMENTAL RIGHTS

The preamble of the constitution strongly asserts fundamental human rights. As well as underscoring adherence to the rights enshrined in the Universal Declaration of Human Rights, the United Nations Charter, and the African Charter on Human and Peoples' Rights, the preamble highlights a number of specific rights for special mention.

The principle of equal rights and obligations under the law forms the basis of the preamble bill of rights. Along with basic rights such as privacy, fair trial, and religious freedom, the constitution mentions the right to development, protection of minorities, and the right to a healthy environment.

In the absence of the Constitutional Council, the enforceability and justiciability of these rights remain untested. Speculation, however, about the status of the bill of rights vis-à-vis the constitution seems to be conclusively settled by Article 65, which states that "the preamble shall be part and parcel of this constitution."

Impact and Functions of Fundamental Rights

In Cameroon, the protection of human rights has not always been a cornerstone of legal thinking. It is only in the last decade that the issue has come to the fore with the creation of the National Commission on Human Rights and Freedoms, the establishment of many nongovernmental organizations for human rights, and the entry into force of the revised constitution in 1996 with its bill of rights. Human rights are now a part of all major political and legal discourse. It is anticipated that once the Constitutional Council is established, rights violations and laws that are incompatible with the ambitious bill of rights will be challenged in court and the constitutional protection of human rights given full effect.

Limitations to Fundamental Rights

Human rights in Cameroon are subject to limitations. Some laws in fact contradict the constitutional protection of human rights. The principle of equality, for example, can be challenged on the basis that sodomy is a crime under the penal code. Also, the constitution provides for only a gradual establishment of new institutions including the Constitutional Council, which in effect delays the full enjoyment of all the rights provided in the constitution.

ECONOMY

The constitution does not provide for a specific economic system. It cites the right of ownership, the right and obligation to work, and the freedom of communication, expression, association, assembly, and trade unionism. Cameroon has a free-market economy.

RELIGIOUS COMMUNITIES

Although Cameroon is a secular state, the constitution guarantees freedom of religion and worship. It further guarantees the neutrality of the state with respect to all religions. Presumably, religions must be treated equally. Both Christian and Muslim holy days are public holidays in Cameroon. In the past, however, Jehovah's Witnesses have seen their basic rights violated as a result of their inability to pay allegiance to the state in contravention of the constitution, which entreats all citizens to contribute to the defense of the fatherland.

MILITARY DEFENSE AND STATE OF EMERGENCY

The president, as commander in chief of the armed forces, ensures the internal and external security of the state. The instrument is the national army, which works with the police and the *gendarmerie* to maintain law and order in peacetime. The president may declare a state of emergency and rule by decree. More seriously, the president may also declare a state of siege if national integrity, sovereignty, or national institutions are threatened. The constitution empowers the president to take any measures deemed necessary to eliminate the threat.

In Cameroon, there is no military service or indeed any kind of national service. All soldiers are professional and serve in the army for life. There are women soldiers. The military is subject to civil government.

AMENDMENTS TO THE CONSTITUTION

Only the president or two-thirds of either house of parliament may propose an amendment to the constitution. To amend the constitution, two-thirds of the members of both houses of parliament must vote in favor of the change. The president also has the right to submit any proposed amendment to a referendum, whereby it can be adopted by a simple majority of the votes cast.

Certain fundamental provisions are not subject to change at all. Article 64 says: "No procedure for the amendment of the constitution affecting the republican form, unity or territorial integrity of the state and of the democratic principles which govern the republic shall be accepted."

PRIMARY SOURCES

Constitution in English. Available online. URL: http://www.idlo.int/texts/leg5518.pdf. Accessed on July 21, 2005.
Constitution in French. Available online. URL: http://www.droit.francophonie.org/doc/html/cm/con/fr/1996/1996dfcmcofr1.html. Accessed on June 12, 2006.

SECONDARY SOURCES

Christof Heyns, ed. *Human Rights Law in Africa.* Vol. 2. Leiden: Martinus Nijhoff, 2004. Available online. URL: http://www.chr.up.ac.za/. Accessed on August 31, 2005.
H. N. A. Enonchong, *Cameroon Constitutional Law.* Yaoundé: CEPER, 1967.
Alain Didier Olinga, "Cameroun: Vers un présidentialise démocratique: Réflexions sur la revision constitution-elle du 23 avril 1991." *Revue Juridique et Politique* 46, no. 4 (1992): 419–429.

Norman Taku

CANADA

At-a-Glance

OFFICIAL NAME
Canada

CAPITAL
Ottawa

POPULATION
32,805,041 (July 2005 est.)

SIZE
3,855,103 sq. mi. (9,984,670 sq. km)

LANGUAGES
English and French (official languages)

RELIGIONS
Roman Catholic 42.6%, Protestant (including United Church 9.5%, Anglican 6.8%, Baptist 2.4%, Lutheran 2%) 23.3%, other Christian 4.4%, Muslim 1.9%, other and unspecified 11.8%, none 16% (2001 census)

NATIONAL OR ETHNIC COMPOSITION
British 28%, French 23%, other European 15%, Amerindian 2%; other, mostly Asian, African, Arab, 6%; mixed background 26%

DATE OF INDEPENDENCE OR CREATION
July 1, 1867

TYPE OF GOVERNMENT
Parliamentary democracy

TYPE OF STATE
Federal state

TYPE OF LEGISLATURE
Bicameral parliament

DATE OF CONSTITUTION
July 1, 1867 (Constitution Act, 1867); April 17, 1982 (Constitution Act, 1982)

DATE OF LAST AMENDMENT
December 6, 2001

Canada is a federal state, a constitutional monarchy, and a parliamentary democracy based on the British constitutional model whereby executive and legislative powers are concentrated rather than clearly separated. There are strong constitutional guarantees for the independence of the judiciary. Canada consists of 10 provinces, three territories, and a federal government. Only since 1982 has the Canadian constitution included a Charter of Rights and Freedoms that guarantees individual and group rights. The constitution is the supreme law of Canada, and any law that is inconsistent with its provisions can be declared of no force or effect by ordinary Canadian courts, including, in the last instance, the Supreme Court of Canada.

In her capacity as Canadian head of state, the British queen is represented by the governor-general on the federal level and the lieutenant governors on the provincial level. However, the functions of the monarch and her representatives are entirely formal and representative. The central political figures are the Canadian prime minister as head of the federal executive government and the provincial premiers as heads of the respective provincial executive governments. The prime minister and provincial premiers can only govern as long as they enjoy the confidence of their respective elected legislative assembly as the representative body of the people. Free, equal, general, and direct elections of the members of the federal House of Commons and provincial legislative assemblies are held approximately every four years.

Religious freedom is guaranteed by the constitution, and the state must remain neutral in religious matters. The constitution does not define the economic system, but the rights and freedoms it guarantees contribute indirectly to the functioning of a market economy.

CONSTITUTIONAL HISTORY

The Canadian federation was created by the British Parliament in 1867 by uniting three North American English colonies that had attained a state of partial internal autonomy: the United Province of Canada (created in 1840 by the fusion of two older provinces: Lower Canada [Quebec] and Upper Canada [Ontario]), New Brunswick, and Nova Scotia. Such a union was considered necessary by the colonies in order to ward off the perceived threat of a military invasion by the United States (Great Britain had helped the Confederate States during the American Civil War) and to respond to important economic problems. A few years earlier, the United States had denounced the Reciprocity Treaty (a free-trade agreement), which had been in force with the Canadian colonies for 12 years. Access by Canadian products to the American market thus became restricted. As a consequence, the Canadian colonies were faced with the necessity to create an economic union among themselves.

Another reason was the need to find a solution to the uneasy relations between the French-speaking Catholic majority of the eastern part of the province of Canada (the former Lower Canada) and the English-speaking Protestant majority of the western part (the former Upper Canada). The entire province had belonged to the colony of New France until the British conquest in 1759. After the conquest, the British had tried to assimilate the French-speaking population in different ways, in particular by uniting Lower and Upper Canada in 1840 in the hope that in a single political entity the French-speaking Canadians would inevitably be assimilated into an English-speaking majority. However, this policy was unsuccessful, and in 1867, United Canada was again divided into two separate provinces, Ontario and Quebec. At that time, French speakers formed the overwhelming majority in Quebec (as they still do) and one-third of the whole population of Canada (this proportion has presently dropped to approximately 24 percent; close to 90 percent of all Canada's francophones now reside in the Province of Quebec).

In 1867, representatives for Canada-West (the future Ontario) favored a unitary state, which would have been controlled by an English-speaking majority. However, representatives for Canada-East (which was to become Quebec) insisted that the future Canadian polity must be a federal union in which francophones would form the majority in at least one of the constituent states and in this way retain the control over their destiny in certain areas considered critical for their particular identity (characterized by the French language, the Catholic religion, and the civil law tradition). The representatives for New Brunswick and Nova Scotia, fearing domination by the more densely populated Upper Canada, also favored a federal union. In the end, a compromise was reached, as the 1867 constitution established a very centralized federation. Many of the centralizing features of the 1867 constitution have since been neutralized, either by political convention or by judicial interpretation of the relevant provisions.

The 1867 constitution was enacted by the imperial parliament as the British North America Act, 1867 (its present title is the Constitution Act, 1867). Out of three preexisting colonies, the constitution created four provinces, Ontario, Quebec, New Brunswick, and Nova Scotia. Six other provinces and three territories were created at later points in time: British Columbia (admitted in 1871), Prince Edward Island (admitted in 1873), Manitoba (created in 1870), Alberta and Saskatchewan (created in 1905), and Newfoundland (admitted in 1949). The three territories are the Northwest Territories (created in 1870), the Yukon (created in 1898), and the Nunavut (created in 1999).

The framers of 1867 wanted the constitution to be similar in principle to that of the United Kingdom. Therefore, no bill of rights was included since such an element of constitutionalism was incompatible with the most important principle of the English constitution, the sovereignty of Parliament. However, certain minimal religious and linguistic minority rights were entrenched. Furthermore, the constitution lacked a complete amending formula because Canada continued to be a British colony, and the British Parliament retained the power to amend the most important parts of the constitution.

During the 60 years that followed its creation, in parallel with the other British "dominions," Canada followed a gradual evolution toward internal, then external autonomy within the British Commonwealth. The culmination was the Statute of Westminster, 1931, adopted by the British Parliament in order to remove the last fetters on the sovereignty of the dominions. However, because the Canadian federal government and the provinces proved unable to agree on a domestic amending formula, the legislative authority of the British Parliament over the Canadian constitution had to be preserved; it could continue to amend the Canadian constitution at the request of Canadian authorities (and only then).

For 50 years, Canadians tried unsuccessfully to "repatriate" the constitution (by taking home the amending formula). As time passed, other contentious issues were added to the debate over the amending formula, making the process ever more difficult. In particular, the francophone majority in the province of Quebec began, from the 1960s on, to claim new legislative powers that it considered necessary for its development as a distinct national group within Canada, as well as a form of constitutional recognition of Quebec's distinct character. It was not long before a segment of Quebec's francophone nationalists turned to more radical demands and formed a political party whose agenda included Quebec's independence from Canada. The Parti Québécois (PQ) won its first election in 1976 and in 1980 held a referendum on "sovereignty-association" (political sovereignty accompanied by an economic union with Canada). However, 60 percent of the voters rejected this option.

Taking advantage of the weakened condition of the Quebec government, the federal government, formed at that time by the Liberal Party, reached an agreement with the nine English-speaking provinces over a constitutional package containing a domestic amending formula, a charter of rights and freedoms, and recognition of the rights of Canada's aboriginal peoples. This package was sent to Westminster and enacted by the British Parliament as the Constitution Act, 1982, in spite of the Quebec government's refusal to assent. A few months later, the Canadian Supreme Court ruled that adopting these far-reaching modifications of the constitution without Quebec's support did not offend any constitutional rule.

In the years after the adoption of the Constitution Act, 1982, a new political situation appeared that seemed more conducive to reconciliation between Quebec and the Rest of Canada (ROC as it has come to be called). A new federal government formed by the Conservative Party rose to power in Ottawa, as well a new government in Quebec formed by the Liberal Party that was opposed to sovereignty for Quebec. After intense negotiations, the federal and 10 provincial governments reached agreement in 1987 on a series of constitutional amendments intended to satisfy Quebec's demands and to convince it to ratify formally the 1982 constitution. However, three years later, the agreement (called the Meech Lake Accord) failed to be ratified by two of the 10 provincial legislatures, frustrating the unanimous consent required under the amending formula. Two years later, another attempt at constitutional reform (the Charlottetown Agreement), aimed this time at satisfying some of English Canada's constitutional concerns as well as Quebec's, also failed. It was decisively rejected in a referendum in Quebec as well as in a majority of the other nine provinces.

Thus, inside a five-year period, two attempts to improve the relations between Quebec and the rest of Canada ultimately failed. This failure contributed to the Liberal Party's defeat and the return to power of the Parti Québécois in the 1994 election. The PQ government subsequently held a second referendum on sovereignty-association in October 1995, which this time yielded very close results: 49.44 percent for sovereignty-association and 50.56 percent against it (with a difference of only approximately 50,000 votes). After the 1995 referendum, the Canadian federal government asked the Supreme Court of Canada for an advisory opinion on the power of a Canadian province to secede. In its 1998 opinion, the court ruled that secession could not be achieved unilaterally but would have to conform to the constitutional amending formula. However, the court also proclaimed the democratic legitimacy of a secession initiative that would be approved by a clear majority vote in Quebec on a clear question and added that such a result would trigger a constitutional obligation of the federal government and the other Canadian provinces to enter into negotiations with the secessionist province.

Finally, in 2003, the Parti Québécois lost the elections and a new provincial government was formed by the Liberal Party. The new government was opposed to secession, and this particular issue has been put to rest for the near future. However, opinion polls show that support for "sovereignty-association" remains stable in public opinion at a 40-to-44 percent level. Therefore, it would be premature to assume that the issue has been resolved or overcome.

FORM AND IMPACT OF THE CONSTITUTION

As is the constitution of the United Kingdom, Canada's constitution is partially written and partially unwritten. The written portion is contained in a number of Canadian and British statutes and orders-in-councils that make up the "Constitution of Canada" in the formal sense. The two most important written instruments are the Constitution Act, 1867, and the Constitution Act, 1982. The older act contains provisions setting out the constitutional organs invested with the executive, legislative, and judicial power at the federal and provincial levels, as well as the distribution of powers between the two levels of government. The newer act consists of the Canadian Charter of Rights and Freedoms, the amending formula, and provisions recognizing aboriginal rights. Most—but not all—of the provisions contained in the formal written constitution can only be amended by recourse to a special amending formula, which requires the approval of the federal authorities and all, or a certain number of, provinces. These "entrenched" provisions have constitutional supremacy and render any inconsistent law of no force or effect. Judicial review of constitutionality, as in the United States, is under the jurisdiction of the ordinary courts rather than the sole jurisdiction of a special constitutional court.

The unwritten portions of the constitution are contained in common law rules and the conventions of the constitution. Constitutional conventions are rules of conduct that are considered binding by political actors but will not be judicially sanctioned by the courts. They typically appear and evolve through precedent and practice, accompanied by a sense of political obligation on behalf of the political actors. Conventions can complement but also contradict the law of the constitution. In Canada, as in the United Kingdom, some of the most fundamental constitutional rules, such as those making up the system of "responsible government," are conventions rather than legal rules. Generally speaking, the role of conventions is to adapt the law of the constitution, some of which has become seriously outdated, to prevailing constitutional values and principles. Thus, the written Canadian constitution still endows the unelected representatives of the monarch with important legal powers, which according to the conventions of the constitution can only be exercised in accordance with the advice of the cabinet and/or the prime minister (or the provincial premier).

The provincial constitutions are also made up of written and unwritten rules. The conventions making up the system of responsible government apply similarly at the provincial level. The written and entrenched portions of the provincial constitutions have no separate existence and are contained in certain provisions of the formal "Constitution of Canada." For instance, the provincial constitutions of the four original provinces form Part V of the Constitution Act, 1867; the constitutions of the provinces created or admitted later are found in the instruments creating or admitting them into Canada.

International treaty law can only be applied by the Canadian courts after transformation into domestic law and thus never has preeminence over domestic Canadian law. International customary law can be applied without transformation but only insofar as it does not contradict domestic law. However, Canadian courts, as far as possible, apply and interpret Canadian law in a way that is compatible with Canada's international legal obligations.

BASIC ORGANIZATIONAL STRUCTURE

Canada is a federation made up of 10 provinces and three territories. In contrast with the provinces, whose autonomy and powers are entrenched in the constitution, the territories are still under federal legislative jurisdiction and enjoy only a nonconstitutional autonomy delegated by the federal parliament. The provinces differ considerably in geographic area, population size, and economic importance. The two geographically central provinces—Quebec and Ontario—together contain over three-fifths of Canada's population. Ontario is the most populous and wealthy province, with almost 30 percent of the population and the largest industrial base. Broadly speaking, each province has the same legislative, administrative, and judicial powers under the constitution. However, certain constitutional provisions apply only to some provinces, thus introducing a measure of asymmetry. For instance, French and English are the official languages at the federal level, but a similar situation exists only in three of the 10 provinces (Quebec, Manitoba, and New Brunswick). Another asymmetry originates from the fact that Quebec is the only province with a guaranteed representation in the Supreme Court of Canada; three of its nine members must be appointed from the Quebec superior courts or bench.

The great majority of legislative powers are exclusively assigned by the 1867 constitution either to the federal parliament or to the provincial legislatures. However, over time, the judicial interpretation of the provisions addressing the division of powers has blurred the lines. This tends to favor overlapping or concurrent jurisdiction in many areas and requires a high degree of cooperation and coordination between the central government and the Canadian provinces, in order to coordinate policies.

With regard to the division of powers, the framers of the 1867 constitution clearly wanted to establish a high degree of centralism. In contrast with those in many other federations, the residual powers were given to the federal

parliament, as well as powers over criminal law and banking, penitentiaries, marriage and divorce, and other areas. The Canadian Parliament was also endowed with all the legislative powers needed to regulate the economy. In particular, the federal commerce power was expressed in an expansive way. Parliament also received all the important taxing and borrowing powers, as well as the power necessary to carry out Canada's treaty obligations even if the matter was otherwise within provincial jurisdiction. Finally, in the opening words of Section 91 of the Constitution Act, 1867, Ottawa was given a general lawmaking authority enabling the national parliament "to make laws for the peace, order and good government of Canada." Indeed, the balance was heavily weighted in favor of the national government.

However, Canada soon evolved toward a much more decentralized condition; one of the main reasons was that the final interpreter of the Canadian constitution was, until 1949, the Judicial Committee of the Privy Council, a court composed of mainly British judges that acted as final court of appeal for countries of the British Empire, and later of the Commonwealth. The Judicial Committee proved very sensitive to provincial rights. Over more than 80 years during which it acted as the court of last resort for Canada, its decisions had the effect of significantly increasing the constitutional position of the provinces. This was done first by removing their subordinate status and elevating them to coordinate status with the central government, and second by giving a restrictive construction to many of the main federal powers. In particular, they limited the federal commerce power and the "peace, order and good government" power and separated the treaty *implementation* power between the Canadian Parliament and the provincial legislatures according to their respective jurisdictions (however, the power to *enter into* treaties is always exercised by the Canadian government, irrespective of the subject matter). They also gave a generous interpretation to the most important provincial power, the power over "property and civil rights," that is, over all private legal relations. In this way, the committee interpreted the highly centralized federal structure set out in the constitution in a decentralizing way, thus frustrating in good part the intentions of the framers.

In 1949, the federal Parliament abolished all appeals to the Judicial Committee. The Supreme Court of Canada, which was now free of the committee's authority, did not reject its precedents wholesale. However, it has progressively expanded federal legislative jurisdiction. In particular, the court has expanded the federal commerce power, the criminal law power, and the "peace, order and good government" power, which gave Ottawa authority over matters of "national dimension." In major decisions, the court ruled that the federal Parliament has the necessary authority to enact legislation designed to sustain and to promote the proper functioning of the Canadian economic union as well as to implement the Canada-U.S. Agreement and North American Free Trade Agreement

(NAFTA). The Supreme Court's vision of federalism appears to be based on considerations of economic efficiency. In the long run, such a vision favors centralization rather than provincial autonomy.

English Canada has generally accepted the Supreme Court's rulings as striking an acceptable balance between the central government and the provinces as the country evolves. By contrast, in Quebec, many people fear that the expansion of federal powers, if continued in the future along the same lines, will endanger Quebec's provincial autonomy. Quebeckers see provincial autonomy as a means to preserve their distinct identity and self-government; hence, they want to protect it against any federal encroachment. English Canadians, on the other hand, conceive of federalism more as a system of dividing powers in the most efficient way between two levels of government; if they can be convinced that administrative or economic efficiency, or national harmonization, requires greater centralization, they often (but not always) accept a weakening of their provincial governments' powers.

However, judicial interpretation of the division of powers is no longer the most important factor in the evolution of Canadian federalism. The balance between centralization and decentralization is increasingly determined by the financial relations between the two levels of government.

The framers of the Constitution Act, 1867, entrusted the federal authorities with the most important jurisdictions and thus assigned them most of the financial resources. They gave the provinces much less financial scope, just enough to meet what was considered to be their lesser responsibilities. However, over the years, an imbalance emerged between the provinces' responsibilities and their financial resources. First, the decisions of the Judicial Committee broadened the jurisdictions of the provinces and narrowed those of the federal government with respect to economics, trade, and social policy. Second, the changed social and economic conditions that appeared in the 1930s rendered provincial responsibilities such as education, health, and welfare much more expensive than they had been. This created a vertical financial imbalance that favors the federal government, which has more power to raise and spend funds. By offering to provide all or part of the funding, and by attaching conditions to the receipt of such money, the federal government has been able to intervene in areas that are constitutionally under exclusive provincial jurisdiction. An estimated 35 percent of all federal spending occurs in these areas.

As in most federations, Canada since 1957 has had a comprehensive system of revenue sharing and fiscal equalization between the richer and poorer regions to ensure that all citizens, wherever they reside, receive comparable services without being subject to excessively different tax rates. The Canadian system is based on federal transfers to the poorer provinces. Currently, eight provinces qualify for equalization—all but Ontario and Alberta.

Except in one instance, the legislative authority of each level of government parallels its executive or administrative authority. However, criminal law is within the exclusive legislative competence of the federal Parliament but is administered by provincial attorneys general and provincial courts.

There is no constitutional basis for municipal or local government autonomy. Municipal entities are regulated by provincial legislation and can be created, abolished, or reorganized at will by the provincial legislatures.

LEADING CONSTITUTIONAL PRINCIPLES

Canada's system of government is a parliamentary democracy based on the British model. There is no strong division of executive and legislative powers. On the contrary, the executive and the legislature are fused; all cabinet members must be members of the elected legislative assembly. In contrast, there exist strong constitutional guarantees of judicial independence.

Canada is a democracy, a federation, and a constitutional monarchy and is based on the rule of law, the independence of the judiciary, and respect for minority rights. The same principles also apply to the provincial political system. Most of these fundamental principles are not expressed in provisions of the constitution but are considered by the courts an implicit part of the constitutional structure.

Canada is a representative democracy. Direct democracy has limited application on the federal as well as on the provincial level. Referenda are held only on the initiative of the federal or provincial government (there is no popular initiative) and are generally only consultative; the result is not usually legally binding on the government and the legislature. The formula for constitutional amendment does not require a referendum, but neither does it prohibit direct consultation of the people. In 1992, a far-reaching constitutional reform project (the Charlottetown Agreement) was submitted to a referendum and rejected. Some scholars are of the opinion that this precedent has formed a constitutional convention requiring the same procedure in the future for any major constitutional reform.

The preamble of the Constitution Act, 1867, proclaims the federal character of Canada and declares that the constitution is to be similar in principle to that of the United Kingdom. This phraseology has been utilized to justify the courts' invocation of implicit constitutional principles when they find it necessary to interpret the written text or fill its gaps. The very brief preamble of the Constitution Act, 1982, proclaims that Canada is founded upon principles that recognize the supremacy of God and the rule of law. The courts have ruled that the reference to God must be given no significance in relation to freedom of conscience and religion guaranteed in the Canadian Charter of Rights and Freedoms.

CONSTITUTIONAL BODIES

The predominant bodies provided for in the constitution are the representatives of the monarch, who were formally invested with the executive power at the federal and provincial levels, and the federal and provincial legislative bodies. However, the formal constitution does not provide for the role of the prime minister (or provincial premiers) or of the cabinet, whose existence and functions depend on unwritten conventions and ordinary legislation. The Supreme Court was created by an ordinary statute adopted by the federal Parliament. Because of the lack of clarity of some provisions in the Constitution Act, 1982, constitutional experts currently disagree on whether this statute has or not been entrenched by implication in the formal constitution in 1982.

The Queen, the Governor-General, and the Lieutenants Governors

The queen is the formal head of state of Canada. Since 1930, the English monarch acts in Canadian matters on the advice of the Canadian federal cabinet, as Canada is an independent country. The powers attributed to the queen are exercised by the governor-general in federal matters and by the lieutenant governors in provincial matters. The governor-general appoints and dismisses the prime minister and other members of the cabinet. He or she summons, adjourns, and dissolves Parliament and gives royal assent to legislation but, by convention, cannot refuse it. The same functions pertain to the lieutenant governors in the provinces. In addition, the governor-general appoints senators and judges of superior provincial courts. The powers of the governor-general and lieutenant governors must be exercised in accordance with constitutional conventions and, in many cases, on the personal advice of the prime minister of Canada (or provincial premier), who is the de facto dominant figure in federal or provincial politics.

The governor-general is appointed and can be removed by the English monarch on advice by the Canadian prime minister. The lieutenant governors are appointed and can be removed by the governor-general. However, the courts have ruled that no subordination of the lieutenant governor to the governor-general exists; both are equally representatives of the Crown.

It is now a constitutional custom to appoint alternatively a French-speaking and an English-speaking governor-general.

The Federal and Provincial Governments

The governor-general at the federal level or the lieutenant governor at the provincial level appoints the prime minister (or provincial premier) and other members of the cabinet according to the conventions of the constitution. They must appoint, as head of the executive government, a person who enjoys the support of a majority of elected members in the federal House of Commons or provincial legislative assembly. Other members of the cabinet are appointed and dismissed on the advice of the prime minister or provincial premier. In most instances, the "first-past-the-post" (or "winner-takes-all") electoral system ensures that a single political party wins an absolute majority. The conventions of the constitution also provide for collective political responsibility of the federal or provincial cabinet before the House of Commons or the provincial legislative assembly. The cabinet must resign or call an election when it can no longer command the support of a majority of elected members.

To become a member of the federal or provincial cabinet, a person must be a member of the House of Commons or of the provincial legislative assembly. The prime minister or provincial premier can also designate a nonelected person but must secure in reasonable time a by-election to give him or her an opportunity to become elected. In case of defeat, the nonelected minister must resign from the cabinet. Exceptionally, senators (who are not elected) can be chosen as ministers in order to ensure cabinet representation for provinces or regions in which the governing party does not have enough elected members.

In Canada, because of the electoral system, a majority administration is the most common outcome. Because a majority administration, combined with a high level of party discipline, can usually dominate the legislature, the executive is in a commanding position, and the role of the federal Parliament and provincial legislatures is somewhat weakened. The situation is significantly different in cases of minority administrations.

The Federal Parliament and Provincial Legislatures

The federal Parliament formally consists of the queen, an upper house called the Senate, and the House of Commons. The members of Parliament and of the provincial legislatures are elected in general, direct, free, equal, and secret elections.

Today, the provincial legislatures are all unicameral and consist of the lieutenant governor and a legislative assembly. Although some provinces initially had bicameral legislatures, all have abolished their upper chamber. To become law, a bill must be adopted by both houses of Parliament (or by the legislative assembly at the provincial level) and receive royal assent, which, by convention of the constitution, cannot be refused.

The members of Parliament and of the provincial legislatures are legally free to vote according to their conscience or to what they perceive to be the wishes of their constituency. However, the level of party discipline is high and members usually follow voting instructions from their party leadership, except in cases in which the government allows a free vote.

The federal House of Commons is composed of 308 members. The maximal duration of a legislature, on the federal as well as on the provincial level, is five years. However, the House of Commons or the provincial legislative assembly can be dissolved during this period by the governor-general or the lieutenant governor on the advice of the prime minister or the provincial premier.

The Senate

Senate reform has been the subject of a great deal of debate and a large number of proposals in the last 30 years. The less populous provinces, particularly in western Canada, have viewed the Senate as an instrument to win more influence in the national political decision-making process. They elect too few members of the House of Commons to wield much influence, compared to the two most populous provinces, Quebec and Ontario. Therefore, they want a Senate modeled on the Australian and American model, with each province represented by an equal number of directly elected senators. This new Senate would have a democratic legitimacy equivalent to that of the House of Commons and thus would be able to exercise comparable powers.

At present, the 105 seats in the Senate are distributed in the following way: Ontario and Quebec, 24 each; New Brunswick and Nova Scotia, 10 each; Prince Edward Island, four; British Columbia, Alberta, Saskatchewan, Manitoba, and Newfoundland, six each; and Yukon, Nunavut, and the Northwest Territories, one each. The four western provinces, with almost 30 percent of the country's population, have only 23 percent of the seats in the Senate. However, equalization of Senate representation for all provinces would also lead to undemocratic results. The six smallest provinces (the four Atlantic provinces, Manitoba, and Saskatchewan) would together hold 60 percent of the Senate seats, while representing only 17 percent of the Canadian population.

At present, senators are appointed by the Canadian prime minister. Appointments are almost always made on the basis of political patronage. Thus, senators represent neither the people nor the governments of the provinces. This lack of legitimacy means that the Senate cannot really exercise the powers with which it is formally endowed and which are almost identical to those of the House of Commons, in legislative matters. In most circumstances, the Senate cannot block or even unduly delay the adoption of bills passed by the House of Commons. Senate reform must thus aim at reestablishing congruence between senators' formal powers and their political capacity to exercise them.

Direct popular election of senators appears to have widespread support. This solution does, however, have serious drawbacks within the context of a Westminster-style parliamentary system that includes responsible government and party discipline. A popularly elected Senate may either be too similar to the House of Commons, which would make it redundant or too different, which could result in a confrontation between the two houses and their mutual neutralization. Either way, the danger would be that party discipline would lead the senators to align along party lines rather than in defense of the interests of the provinces or regions.

The Lawmaking Process

With the exception of revenue bills, laws can be introduced either in the House of Commons or in the Senate, but the overwhelming majority of bills proposed by a member of the cabinet are introduced in the house. The Constitution Act, 1867, requires that revenue bills, which raise taxes or appropriate the receipts, originate in the House of Commons at the recommendation of the governor-general (or of the lieutenant governor in the case of provincial bills). After a constitutional convention, the monarch's representative, at both levels of government, only recommends a revenue bill proposed by a member of the cabinet. This rule severely restricts the capacity of ordinary members of Parliament or of a provincial legislature to propose consequential legislation. More generally, the federal or provincial government controls the agenda of parliamentary business and usually restricts the time dedicated to private members' bills. Thus, the cabinet tends to control the preparation and initiation of legislation strictly.

After a bill has been adopted by the house in which it was introduced, it is sent to the other house and must be adopted on identical terms. The Senate can propose amendments to a bill passed by the House of Commons. However, if the house insists on its adoption without the proposed modifications, the Senate can in practice make no further obstruction. The rare occasions in which the Senate can still exercise a real veto are those instances when the government presents a very controversial proposal late in the legislative term that is not part of the electoral program. In such a case, the Senate can get away with refusing its assent in order to give to the citizens the opportunity to weigh in on the proposal during the election.

After adoption by both houses of Parliament or by the provincial legislative assembly, a bill must also receive royal assent to become an act and go into force. However, the monarch's representative's refusal to assent would be incompatible with the conventions of the constitution.

The Judiciary

Canada's judicial system follows the British model in which ordinary judicial courts have jurisdiction over civil and criminal law, regardless of whether the case is litigated between private parties or between a private party and the state. The first two tiers of courts (courts of first instance and courts of appeal) are under provincial legislative jurisdiction and apply provincial as well as much of federal law. The Supreme Court of Canada, which sits at the apex of the system, is under federal legislative jurisdiction. It acts as a general court of appeal, with jurisdiction over all Canadian law, federal and provincial.

However, purely federal courts with a jurisdiction limited to certain parts of federal law also exist. They are created and endowed with their responsibilities by the federal Parliament. When adopting a particular law, the federal Parliament can choose explicitly to hand jurisdiction over to the provincial courts or to a particular federal court. The most important of the purely federal courts is the Federal Court, which has two divisions, one of first instance and one of appeal. The Federal Court holds exclusive jurisdiction (or in certain cases concurrent jurisdiction with provincial courts) over cases involving "the Crown in right of Canada" (i.e., the federal government). This exclusive jurisdiction also covers certain federal issues such as admiralty, copyright, trademarks, patents, citizenship, and other matters regulated by the federal Parliament. Other purely federal courts include the Canadian Tax Court and military tribunals.

Justices of the Supreme Court of Canada, judges of the purely federal courts, and judges of superior provincial courts are appointed by the federal cabinet. Judges of inferior provincial courts are appointed by the provincial cabinet.

Several provisions of the formal constitution, as well as an implicit principle identified by the courts, guarantee judicial independence and impartiality. These constitutional rules put the courts in a position to define for themselves the conditions that the executive and legislative branches must respect in relation to judicial independence. Such conditions include protection against arbitrary removal, financial security, immunity of judges for actions taken while performing their duties, and institutional autonomy.

Judicial review of constitutionality is part of the jurisdiction of ordinary courts. Before any judicial court, federal or provincial, a litigant can question the constitutionality of any law (statutory or common law) used against him or her by another private party or by the attorney general acting on behalf of the federal or the provincial government. The court must then examine the question and, if it finds the law unconstitutional, declare it not applicable or invalid (the inferior courts can only declare the law inapplicable to the actual case or controversy; the superior courts can invalidate it with general effect). Furthermore, preemptive challenges to the constitutionality of a statute are allowed even before it is applied to a particular person. Finally, absent any legal dispute, the federal government can request an advisory opinion from the Supreme Court on any constitutional question. A provincial government can make the same request to the provincial court of appeal. The provincial courts and the Supreme Court can control the constitutionality of federal and provincial laws, while the purely federal courts can only examine federal laws.

The highest court in Canada is the Supreme Court, composed of nine judges including the chief justice. Under the Supreme Court Act, three of the nine judges must be appointed from the courts of Quebec in order to ensure that there are enough judges educated in the civil law of Quebec to sit on an appeal from Quebec concerning civil law questions (elsewhere in Canada, private law is governed by the common law). By usage, the six other members of the court are appointed by following a regional distribution within English Canada (three judges for Ontario, one for British Columbia, one that rotates among the three Prairie provinces, and one for the four Atlantic provinces). Supreme Court judges are appointed by the federal cabinet. Until recently, there was no requirement of consultation with the provincial governments or of examination of the candidates by members of Parliament. In August 2005, a new appointment process was launched. Provincial ministers of justice, along with leading members of the legal community, will be consulted by the federal minister in order to identify a small number of candidates who will be assessed by an advisory committee consisting of members of the House of Commons, a retired judge, representatives of the provincial ministers of justice, the law societies, and the general public. The committee's role is to appraise the candidates and establish a short list of three names, from which the prime minister makes the final choice.

Except in certain criminal cases, appeals to the Supreme Court exist not of right but by leave; the court must authorize the appeal. Accordingly the court has the liberty to choose those cases it wants to hear and that present a sufficiently important legal interest. The court hears fewer than 100 cases every year, of which approximately 25 percent involve constitutional aspects.

THE ELECTION PROCESS

All Canadian citizens above the age of 18 have both the right to be a candidate in a federal or provincial election and the right to vote in the election. These rights are guaranteed by the Canadian Charter of Rights and Freedoms; any limitations must be reasonable (for example, persons found guilty of electoral fraud can be temporarily deprived of the right to vote or to be elected).

Parliamentary Elections

Members of Parliament and of the legislative assemblies in most provinces are elected through the "first-past-the-post" (or "winner-takes-all") plurality system. Canada is divided into single-member constituencies. Within each, the candidate who receives most votes wins, even if he or she does not obtain an absolute majority. A well-known characteristic of this system is that it results in significant distortions between the votes received by the respective parties and the number of seats they obtain in the legislature. For example, in the federal election of 2000, the governing Liberal Party won 53.5 percent of the seats in the House of Commons with only 40.8 percent of the popular vote.

In the Canadian context, the plurality system also exacerbates electoral regionalism. This electoral system favors political parties with strong regional appeal and disadvantages nationally oriented parties whose support is more evenly spread across the country.

As a consequence, it becomes more difficult to form a federal cabinet representative of all regions, as the governing party may have few or no elected members from some provinces. As a consequence, government policies are often attacked as being unfavorable to unrepresented provinces or regions. Electoral regionalism contributes to the phenomenon of "western alienation," originating in the poor representation of western Canada in the central institutions.

Most provinces also use the "first-past-the-post" electoral system, with some or all of the same consequences and problems. Currently, several provinces have initiated reforms to include some element of proportional representation.

POLITICAL PARTIES

Canada has a pluralistic system of political parties at the federal and provincial levels. The formal Canadian constitution contains no provision concerning political parties. Their existence and role appear only in conventions of the constitution and ordinary federal and provincial legislation.

CITIZENSHIP

The Canadian constitution contains no specific rules on citizenship other than the provision endowing the federal Parliament with legislative jurisdiction over the subject. Of course, federal laws on citizenship must conform to the Canadian Charter of Rights and Freedoms and in particular to Section 15, prohibiting discrimination.

Canadian citizenship is primarily acquired by birth from one Canadian parent (*ius sanguinis*), whether in Canada or abroad, or by birth on Canadian soil (*ius soli*). Citizenship can also be acquired by naturalization three years after a person has been legally admitted as an immigrant. Dual or plural citizenship is allowed under Canadian law.

FUNDAMENTAL RIGHTS

The main constitutional instrument guaranteeing rights and freedoms is the Canadian Charter of Rights and Freedoms, which forms Part I of the Constitution Act, 1982. Certain linguistic and religious minority rights are also included in the Constitution Act, 1867. In addition, all provincial legislatures and the federal Parliament have adopted, in their respective fields of jurisdiction, human rights legislation that possesses a "quasi constitutional" character, giving it a limited kind of primacy over ordinary corresponding provincial or federal legislation.

The Canadian Charter of Rights and Freedoms guarantees the traditional set of human rights and freedoms but does not include economic, social, or cultural rights, such as the right to work or the right to an education. The only provincial Human Rights Act in which such rights can be found is Quebec's Charter of Human Rights and Freedoms.

The Canadian Charter guarantees the following:

- Fundamental freedoms—freedom of conscience and religion; of thought, belief, opinion, and expression, including freedom of the press and other media of communication; freedom of peaceful assembly and freedom of association (Sect. 2)
- Democratic rights—the right to vote and to be a candidate for election (Sect. 3–5)
- Mobility rights—the right to enter, remain in, and leave Canada; the right to move to and to take up residence in any province and to pursue a livelihood in any province (Sect. 6)
- The right to life, liberty, and security of the person and the right to not be deprived thereof except in accordance with the principles of fundamental justice (Sect. 7)
- Legal rights—pertaining to search and seizure, arrest, detention and imprisonment, proceedings in criminal and penal matters, and punishment (Sect. 8–14)
- Equality rights and the prohibition of discrimination, in particular discrimination based on race, national, or ethnic origin, color, religion, sex, age, or mental or physical disability (Sect. 15)
- Linguistic rights, relating to the use of the English and French languages (Sect. 16–23)

Most rights contained in the Canadian Charter are guaranteed to every person within Canadian territorial jurisdiction, irrespective of citizenship. Only democratic rights, mobility rights, and minority language educational rights (the right to have one's children receive their education in the French or English minority language in public schools) are limited to Canadian citizens. Mobility rights inside Canada also apply to permanent residents.

Impact and Functions of Fundamental Rights

Most rights and freedoms guaranteed in the Canadian Charter have a predominantly defensive function against interference by state authorities. The only right that contains an acknowledged positive dimension enabling individuals to claim a specific benefit from public authorities is the right, guaranteed only to Canadian citizens, to have their children receive primary and secondary school instruction in the English or French minority language in facilities provided through public funds.

Under certain conditions, equality rights can be interpreted in such a manner as to oblige the state to make certain benefits available. For example, the Supreme Court of Canada has held that the hearing-impaired are unreasonably discriminated against on the basis of a disability unless they receive the aid of a sign language interpreter (paid out of public funds). Section 27 declares that the charter "shall be interpreted in a manner consistent with the preservation and enhancement of the multicultural heritage of Canadians."

Section 15(2) of the Canadian Charter provides for affirmative action programs with the goal of "the amelioration of conditions of disadvantaged individuals or groups including those that are disadvantaged because of race, national or ethnic origin, color, religion, sex, age or mental or physical disability."

The effectiveness of rights and freedoms is ensured by judicial control of parliamentary legislation and regulations adopted by administrative authorities, which can be struck down or reconstructed by courts if inconsistent with the charter, and by Section 24(1) of the charter, which grants victims of any infringement deriving from state action other than legislation the right to obtain the remedies considered as "appropriate and just in the circumstances" by a court of justice.

All levels of government—federal, provincial, territorial, and municipal—are bound to respect the rights and freedoms guaranteed in the charter in every aspect of their activity. The charter does not, however, bind private persons; it applies only "vertically" (to relations between the state and individuals or private corporate entities) but not "horizontally" (to purely private relations). Nevertheless, if a private individual or corporation fulfills a state function or exercises coercive power delegated by the state, the charter will apply to actions performed within that function or power. In a purely private dispute, any litigant can question the constitutionality of any law relied on by another party.

Unlike the Canadian charter, the provincial and federal Human Rights Acts apply not only "vertically" (to state action) but also "horizontally" (to purely private relations). The great majority of provincial and federal human rights legislation concerns the prohibition of unreasonable discrimination in labor relations and the provision of goods and services to the public. However, Quebec's Charter of Human Rights and Freedoms goes much further by also guaranteeing the traditional array of fundamental rights and freedoms, as well as certain economic, social, and cultural rights.

The Canadian constitution also guarantees certain rights relating to the use of the French and English languages. Some of these guarantees appear in the Canadian Charter and others in the Constitution Act, 1867. Language rights relating to the use of French and English in parliamentary debates and documents, legislation, regulations, and the justice system apply only at the federal level and in three provinces—Quebec, Manitoba, and New Brunswick. Language rights of the same sort, however, are guaranteed by ordinary legislation in Ontario. Section 23 of the Canadian Charter, which applies to all provinces, also guarantees the right of members of francophone mi-norities outside Quebec and of the anglophone minority of Quebec to have their children receive primary and secondary school instruction in the minority language in facilities provided out of public funds, where the number of such children warrants.

Limitations to Fundamental Rights

Section 1 of the Canadian Charter of Rights and Freedoms authorizes only such "reasonable limits" to rights and freedoms as are "prescribed by law" and "can be demonstrably justified in a free and democratic society."

The limitations must be authorized in or under a statute, regulation, or common-law rule made public in advance and capable of being understood by those to whom the legal commandment is addressed. Rules limiting rights and freedoms must be sufficiently "intelligible" (clear and precise). Otherwise, the requirements of legal certainty and predictability would not be respected.

The requirement that limitations be reasonable and justifiable in a free and democratic society has been interpreted by Canadian courts to mean, first, that the legislative objective underlying a limitation must be "pressing and substantial" and, second, that the means chosen to implement that objective must meet a three-tiered proportionality test. To begin, the measures must be carefully designed to achieve the objective in question and rationally connected to that objective. In addition, the means should impair the right in question as little as possible. Finally, there must be proportionality between the effects of the limiting measure and the objective—the more severe the deleterious effects of a measure, the more important the objective must be.

The most unorthodox feature of the Canadian Charter of Rights and Freedoms is Section 33, which permits the federal Parliament and a provincial legislature to override most of the charter's rights and freedoms through ordinary legislation by simply declaring in any act or statute that it "shall operate notwithstanding a provision included in Section 2 or Sections 7 to 15 of this charter." The only rights and freedoms that cannot be overridden are democratic rights, mobility rights, and the rights relating to the use of the English and French languages.

Once a statute contains a "notwithstanding clause," it may no longer be judicially reviewed under the provisions of the charter that are overridden. Such a clause has a five-year time limit, but it can be renewed. The charter's drafters apparently wanted to reconcile the power of the courts to control legislation on the basis of vaguely phrased rights and freedoms with a democratic system under which fundamental choices affecting society should be decided by the elected representatives of the people. The explicit "notwithstanding" clause and the five-year limit were designed to ensure democratic control of any rights limitations.

Until now, the override has never been used by the federal Parliament and only on two occasions by provincial legislatures in English Canada. However, Quebec employed the override in a systematic and deliberate way during the first five years of charter application to protest the imposition of the Constitution Act, 1982.

ECONOMY

No specific economic system is specified in the Canadian constitution. Property rights have been deliberately omitted in the Canadian Charter of Rights and Freedoms as a concession to provincial governments that were worried about the possible misuse of such rights by private economic interests that are eager to limit regulation of their activities. Generally, the Supreme Court of Canada has interpreted the rights and freedoms of the charter as not protecting purely economic rights. For instance, the right to liberty in Section 7 has been held not to include the right to choose one's profession freely. The prohibition of discrimination in Section 15 has been interpreted as protecting only natural persons or groups of natural person, but not corporations or other legal persons.

On the other hand, the Supreme Court has also held that when charged with a penal or criminal offence corporations can defend themselves by invoking any right or freedom of the charter, even rights that are usually considered applicable only to human individuals, such as the liberty of religion. In a much criticized decision, tobacco manufacturers succeeded in having federal regulations prohibiting advertisement for tobacco products struck down as an unreasonable limitation on freedom of commercial expression.

Section 2(d) of the Canadian Charter, guaranteeing freedom of association, has been interpreted as protecting the right to form and belong to a labor union, but not the right to collective bargaining or to strike. Legislation requiring workers to join a union in order to obtain work in a particular workplace or imposing union dues (later spent for political ends) on nonunionized employees has been held to be constitutional.

Finally, the Constitution Act, 1982, contains a provision, Section 36, affirming the commitment of the federal Parliament and provincial legislatures to promote equal opportunities and provide essential public services of reasonable quality to all Canadians. In the same provision, the federal authorities commit themselves to make equalization payments to ensure that provincial governments have sufficient revenues to provide reasonably comparable levels of public services at reasonably comparable levels of taxation. To date, however, it remains unclear whether these commitments are purely political or whether they can be enforced by courts.

RELIGIOUS COMMUNITIES

Freedom of conscience and religion is guaranteed by Section 2(a) of the Canadian Charter of Rights and Freedoms. Although the Canadian constitution contains no express principle of the separation of state and religion, courts have found an implied obligation of religious neutrality for the state in Section 2(a). This principle can be satisfied either by the state's total abstention from furnishing aid to any religion or by aiding of all religions in a comparable and equitable manner. Nonreligious beliefs must be accorded the same protection.

For historic reasons, the Constitution Act, 1867, granted Catholics and mainstream Protestants in some provinces entrenched religious privileges to denominational schools supported by public funding. The Supreme Court of Canada has declared that such privileges, although clearly discriminatory, cannot be challenged because they are recognized in the constitution. However, the United Nations Committee on Human Rights has reached the conclusion that this is not sufficient to justify discrimination that is contrary to the International Covenant on Civil and Political Rights.

On the basis of Section 2(a), Canadian courts have held that religious Catholic or Protestant education in state schools as part of the curriculum is unconstitutional, even if parents can obtain an exemption or alternative instruction in ethics for their children.

MILITARY DEFENSE AND STATE OF EMERGENCY

National defense is a responsibility of the federal government. In Canada, general conscription in times of peace has never existed. The Canadian armed forces consist entirely of professional soldiers.

The Canadian constitution contains no express provision relating to a state of emergency. The courts have found implicit emergency powers for the federal Parliament in the "peace, order and good government" clause of Section 91(1) of the Constitution Act, 1867. Currently, those emergency powers are specified in the federal Emergencies Act, which establishes four categories of emergencies: public welfare, public order, international, and war emergency. To be able to exercise the exceptional powers provided for under the act, the federal government must first declare the existence of an emergency, and the declaration must be debated and confirmed by the federal Parliament. The Canadian Charter of Rights and Freedoms continues to apply during a state of emergency; any limitations of rights and freedoms must be justified under Section 1 of the charter.

AMENDMENTS TO THE CONSTITUTION

Some provisions of the formal Canadian constitution, forming, respectively, the "internal federal constitution" and the "internal provincial constitutions," can be amended by an ordinary statute of the federal Parliament or of the legislature of the interested province. The most important provisions (in particular the Canadian Charter and the division of powers) can only be amended by a set of complex formulas requiring approval by the federal authorities, on the one hand, and a certain number of provinces, on the other. In some cases, all provinces must approve the amendment; in others, only the provinces to which the amendment applies must approve. In most cases, approval is needed by at least two-thirds of the provinces (seven of 10) containing at least 50 percent of the total population.

No constitutional provision has been made expressly immutable, and the Supreme Court of Canada has held that there is no implied immutability. Indeed, even the secession of a province can be achieved by applying the proper amending formula. The court has declared that to admit that any part of the constitution is totally unchangeable would contradict the sovereignty of the Canadian people.

PRIMARY SOURCES

Constitution in English and French. Department of Justice of the Government of Canada. Available online. URL: http://laws.justice.gc.ca/en/index.html. Accessed on August 5, 2005.

SECONDARY SOURCES

Peter W. Hogg, *Constitutional Law of Canada*. Scarborough, Ont.: Thomson Carswell, 2004.
Jacques-Yvan Morin et José Woehrling, *Les constitutions du Canada et du Québec: Du régime français à nos jours*. 2d ed. Montréal: Éditions Thémis, 2004.

José Woehrling

CAPE VERDE

At-a-Glance

OFFICIAL NAME
Republic of Cape Verde

CAPITAL
Cidade da Praia

POPULATION
434,812 (2005 est.)

SIZE
1,557 sq. mi. (4,033 sq. km)

LANGUAGES
Portuguese, Crioulo

RELIGIONS
Roman Catholic (infused with indigenous beliefs)
95%, Protestant 5%

NATIONAL OR ETHNIC COMPOSITION
Cape Verdean (mixture of Portuguese and Africans)

DATE OF INDEPENDENCE OR CREATION
July 5, 1975

TYPE OF GOVERNMENT
Semipresidential democracy with a strong
parliamentary component

TYPE OF STATE
Unitary state

TYPE OF LEGISLATURE
Unicameral parliament

DATE OF CONSTITUTION
September 25, 1992

DATE OF LAST AMENDMENT
November 23, 1999

The Cape Verdean constitution was approved two years after changes in the political system that turned the country from a one-party system to a multiparty democracy. The Movement for Democracy, the party that won the first multiparty elections in the history of Cape Verde, controlled two-thirds of parliament, a sufficient number to approve all the constitutional norms that it wanted to implement. Thus, the new constitution was not based on a wide consensus of political forces.

The constitution establishes a semipresidential system of government in which the people directly elect both the president of the republic and the National Assembly. The president has the power (if highly conditional) to dissolve the parliament, as well as the right of political veto as well as veto for constitutional reasons; those rights make the office a moderator of the system.

The state is based on the rule of law, founded on the principle of human dignity of all persons as well as on the recognition of the inviolability and inalienability of human rights. These rights are assured by the courts, including the Supreme Court of Justice, which functions

temporarily as the Constitutional Court. The constitution includes the principle of separation but interdependence of powers and a clear hierarchy of norms. Cape Verde is a secular state, with separation of state and religions.

CONSTITUTIONAL HISTORY

Cape Verde gained its independence after a struggle for national liberation conducted by the African Party for the Independence of Guinea-Bissau and Cape Verde (PAIGC). After negotiations with the former colonial power Portugal, elections were held for the Constituent Assembly. Only the PAIGC ran for those elections. That party obtained more than 90 percent of all of the votes registered. When independence was proclaimed in 1975, a provisional constitution was adopted, providing for a one-party system and lacking a list of fundamental rights.

In 1980, the first permanent constitutional system was adopted, implementing the so-called system of national revolutionary democracy. The constitution prohibited the formation of other political parties and established a state-centered economy but also provided an important list of fundamental rights.

Constitutional Law 2/III/90 of September 28, 1990, which amended the constitution of 1980, abolished the one-party system in favor of a liberal democracy. The freedom to form political parties was introduced, and the semipresidential system of government was reformed. On January 13, 1991, the first multiparty elections in the history of Cape Verde were held, and on September 25, 1992, the present constitution entered into force.

FORM AND IMPACT OF THE CONSTITUTION

The constitution of Cape Verde is a single written document, made up of 293 articles. It has been revised only twice. The constitution of 1992 has significant impact on the national political life.

BASIC ORGANIZATIONAL STRUCTURE

The Republic of Cape Verde is a unitary state, which comprises 17 municipalities. Each island corresponds to at least one municipality.

LEADING CONSTITUTIONAL PRINCIPLES

Cape Verde is a state based on the rule of law, founded on the principle of human dignity of all persons; it recognizes and guarantees human rights as the foundation of the whole human community as well as of peace and justice.

The state is subject to the constitution. It is founded on democratic legality, and it must respect and assure the respect of the laws. The laws and other acts of the state have legal force only if they are in harmony with the constitution.

The Republic of Cape Verde is based upon the popular will, and it organizes itself according to the principle of the separation and the interdependence of powers. Further basic principles are the existence and autonomy of the local powers and the decentralization of public administration. The people exercise political power through referendum, elections, and other constitutionally established means.

The norms and principles of international law as generally accepted by the international community are part of domestic law. They have a value hierarchically higher than the ordinary laws, but lower than Cape Verdean constitutional law.

CONSTITUTIONAL BODIES

The constitutional organs are the president of the republic, the National Assembly, the administration headed by the prime minister, the courts, and the organs of the local power. The constitution also establishes auxiliary organs, such as the Council of the Republic, the ombudsperson, and the Economic and Social Council.

The executive is twofold, including the president, who is elected for a five-year term, and the prime minister, who is head of the administration and president of the Council of Ministers.

The President of the Republic

The president of the republic is the head of state. The president, on his or her own initiative, has the power to dissolve the National Assembly if there is a serious institutional crisis, if it is required for the regular functioning of democratic institutions, and if the Council of the Republic, an organ that advises and assists the head of state, advises the president to do so.

The president of the republic is the commander in chief of the defense force. The president can veto laws of parliament in a relative veto that can be overruled by parliament. The president can also veto legal acts of the administration in an absolute veto that is definite. The veto can be on either political or constitutional grounds.

The president of the republic, after considering the electoral results, appoints and dismisses the prime minister, appoints and dismisses the ministers and secretaries of state on the recommendation of the prime minister, and presides over meetings of the cabinet when invited by the prime minister. The president of the republic dismisses the administration if there has been a vote of no confidence by the parliament.

The president of the republic has the power to preside over various consultative bodies, such as the Council of the Republic and the High Council for National Defense, and can initiate national referendums. The president appoints two members of the Council of the Republic, the chief justice of the Supreme Court, one associate judge of the Supreme Court, two members of the Supreme Council of Judges, and the general auditor, the general prosecutor, both on the advice of the administration. The president can also revoke and commute penalties in individual cases, with the advice of the administration.

As far as foreign relations are concerned, the president has the power to ratify treaties, appoint and dismiss ambassadors, receive credential letters, and recognize and accredit foreign diplomatic representatives.

The prime minister countersigns the acts of the president of the republic, pursuant to the powers vested in the president and carried out on the recommendation and advice of the administration.

The National Assembly

The National Assembly approves constitutional laws and other laws on all matters, except those that fall within the exclusive power of the administration. The National Assembly approves the program of the administration and the state budget on advice of the administration; it adopts treaties and international agreements, which the president then ratifies; and it examines the general accounts of the state. The assembly can also ask the president of the republic to call a national referendum. Furthermore, the National Assembly authorizes and ratifies the declaration of a state of siege and a state of emergency, authorizes the president of the republic to declare war and make peace, and concedes amnesties and generic pardons to offenders.

The National Assembly can censure the administration or vote its confidence in it. Annually, it holds a debate on the state of the nation and reviews the report on the situation of justice submitted by the Supreme Council of Judges. The assembly elects, by a majority of two-thirds of the members of parliament, the judges of the Constitutional Court, the ombudsperson, the president of the Economic and Social Council, three members of the Supreme Council of Judges, and four members of the Supreme Council of the prosecuting office.

In addition, the National Assembly witnesses the installation and the resignation of the president of the republic, authorizes the absence of the president of the republic from the national territory, and requests penal action against him or her.

The Lawmaking Process

Bills can be initiated by members of parliament, the parliamentary groups, or the administration. The constitution also allows for popular legislative initiative, when signed by at least 10,000 voters. The bills are debated in a first reading general debate and a second reading debate on detail. Voting comprises a vote on the first reading, a vote on the second reading, and a final overall vote. If the assembly so decides, texts approved on the first reading can be submitted to committees for their second reading, subject to the power of the assembly to recall them and to a final overall vote by the assembly. The second reading of some laws that require two-thirds majorities to be passed must be done in plenary session.

The Administration

The administration has the power to define, in meetings of the Council of Ministers, the general guidelines for internal and foreign policy and carries out regular evaluations of policy. The prime minister is the head of the administration with the power to preside over the Council of Ministers, lead and coordinate the general policy of the administration, and orient and coordinate the action of all the ministers. The administration is responsible to parliament.

The Judiciary

Justice is administrated by independent courts. Besides the Constitutional Court, there are the Supreme Court of Justice, judicial courts of first instance in all of the municipalities, the military court of instance, and the audit courts. In addition, the Court of Audit is the supreme organ, which reviews the legality of public expenditures and audits the general accounts.

The Constitutional Court, the jurisdiction of which is temporarily held by the Supreme Court of Justice, has the power to decide questions of a legal and constitutional nature, including the review of the constitutionality and legality of the norms. It also verifies the declaration of physical and mental incapacity of the president of the republic, temporary inability of the president to perform his or her functions, and the resignation or the death of the president. It also exercises jurisdiction in matters related to elections and political organizations.

THE ELECTION PROCESS AND POLITICAL PARTICIPATION

The organs of political power such as the National Assembly, the president of the republic, municipal assemblies, and the mayors are elected by universal, periodic, direct, and secret suffrage. Every citizen, male and female, of 18 or more years of age can vote for the National Assembly and for the president. Every Cape Verdean citizen who has the active right to vote can be elected to parliament, unless he or she is affected by any of the ineligibility established in the constitution or in law. Candidates for member of parliament may run only if nominated by the political parties.

Any citizen of Cape Verdean origin 35 or more years of age can be a candidate for president of the republic. At the time of the submission of his or her candidacy, the candidate must have permanent residence in the country for at least three years. Aliens and stateless persons residing in the country can participate in local elections.

The right of petition, the holding of referendums, and the popular legislative initiative are instruments established in the constitution.

The president fixes the dates for presidential and legislative elections. The administration fixes the dates for local elections.

POLITICAL PARTIES

In Cape Verde, political parties are freely formed without the need for administrative authorization. Only political parties have the power to submit candidatures for legislative elections. In contrast, they have no juridical or public power to submit candidates for presidential elections, but they can support candidates proposed by groups of citizens. In local elections, groups of local citizens have often succeeded against the established political parties.

Currently, there are seven political parties in Cape Verde, four of them are represented in parliament.

CITIZENSHIP

Original citizens of Cape Verde are those persons born in Cape Verde whose father or mother is a Cape Verdean national, those born abroad whose father or mother is a Cape Verdean national and serves the state of Cape Verde abroad, and those born in Cape Verde whose mother and father are stateless persons or have unknown nationality and are ordinarily resident in Cape Verde.

Original citizens of Cape Verde by option and according to a specific declaration are those persons born abroad, whose father, mother, grandfather, or grandmother is a Cape Verdean citizen by birth. Also original citizens by option are those born in Cape Verde whose parents are not Cape Verdean citizens but have been residing in Cape Verde for a continuous period of not less than five years and are not serving their respective states in Cape Verde.

Nonoriginal citizenship can be acquired through certification by a minor whose father or mother has acquired Cape Verdean nationality by adoption, by naturalization subject to an act of government, by marriage, and by economic reasons. Any alien who participates in investment programs, who offers solid guarantees to carry out investments in the country that are capable of increasing job opportunities and contributing significantly to the development of the country, can apply for Cape Verdean citizenship; however, he or she does not acquire political rights.

No Cape Verdean original citizen can be deprived of his or her nationality or of the prerogatives of citizenship. Only an original Cape Verdean citizen can be elected president of the republic.

Cape Verdean citizens may acquire the citizenship of any other country without losing their own.

FUNDAMENTAL RIGHTS

It is enshrined in the constitution that the state shall guarantee the respect for the dignity of all persons and recognize the inviolability and inalienability of human rights as the basis of the whole community, of peace, and of justice. In harmony with this founding principle, the constitution establishes a vast list of fundamental rights and duties.

Title I of Part II of the constitution establishes the general principles relating to fundamental rights and duties; Title II refers to the actual rights, liberties, and guarantees; Title III, to the economic rights and duties; Title IV, to the fundamental duties; and Title V, to family.

Besides the fundamental rights, liberties, and guarantees listed in the constitution, others may be established by laws or by international conventions.

Impact and Functions of Fundamental Rights

The norms referring to fundamental rights shall, in harmony with the provisions established in the constitution, be interpreted and integrated in accordance with the Universal Declaration of Human Rights. It is expressly established in the constitution that the constitutional norms referring to rights, liberties, and guarantees shall be respected and upheld by all public authorities and private persons and are directly applicable.

The state and other public entities are responsible for the actions and omissions of their civil servants, carried out in the exercise of their functions, that violate the rights, liberties, and guarantees of citizens. Civil servants are liable to criminal penalties or disciplinarily action for acts and omissions that result in serious violation of fundamental rights.

Everyone has the right to judicial protection of his or her rights. The right to appeal to the courts for the protection of fundamental rights against actions or omissions of the public powers, after using up all the means of ordinary appeal, is specifically available to all citizens.

Citizens can submit claims regarding the protection of their fundamental rights to the ombudsperson, an independent organ functioning in the National Assembly, which can submit recommendations to the competent organs of political power aimed at the prevention of and reperations for illegalities or injustices.

Limitations of Fundamental Rights

The rights, liberties, and guarantees can be restricted only by law. The restrictive laws cannot reduce the extension and the essential content of the constitutional norms. They are limited to what is necessary to safeguard other protected rights.

ECONOMY

The constitution establishes as general principles economic democracy, conservation of the ecosystem and sustainable development, coexistence of the public and private sectors, and existence of communitarian property. It supports activities that contribute positively to the integration of Cape Verde into the world economy, as well as a series of fundamental norms relating to state planning. The constitution also defines the role of the central bank, the objectives of the fiscal system, the guarantees against unfair taxes, the principle of nonretroactivity of fiscal law, and the basic rules for the elaboration, execution, and control of the state budget.

RELIGIOUS COMMUNITIES

Freedom of conscience, religion, and ceremony is guaranteed. Every citizen has the right to practice or not practice any religion. The churches and religious communities are separated from the state and independent and free in their organization and functioning. Nevertheless, the state considers churches and other religious communities as partners. Protection is assured to places of worship and to religious symbols.

The majority of the Cape Verdean population is of Christian belief, predominantly Roman Catholic.

MILITARY DEFENSE AND STATE OF EMERGENCY

The armed forces are subject to and obey the national organs of sovereignty. Their missions are established in the constitution.

Military service is compulsory; however, the right to conscientious objection is granted. The military remains subordinate to the civil power even during a state of siege or emergency.

The president can declare a state of siege or emergency, in consultation with the administration and authorized by parliament. These situations cannot affect either the constitutional powers and functioning of state organs or the rights and immunities of officeholders. There is a list of fundamental rights that cannot, in any case, be affected by the state of siege or emergency.

AMENDMENTS TO THE CONSTITUTION

The constitution can be amended five years after the date of its last ordinary amendment. The amendments to the constitution shall be adopted by a majority of two-thirds of the members of the National Assembly. The constitution can also be amended at any time by extraordinary amendment, by a majority of four-fifths of the members of parliament. Members of parliament have the initiative of amending the constitution.

The constitution provides certain limits to amendments, including a prohibition of amendment in wartime or under a state of siege or emergency.

PRIMARY SOURCES

1992 Constitution in English. Available online. URL: http://www.idlo.int/texts/leg5523.pdf. Accessed on July 23, 2005.

1999 Constitution in Portuguese. Available online. URL: http://www.stj.cv/constituicao.html. Accessed on August 26, 2005.

SECONDARY SOURCES

Jorge C. Fonseca, *O sistema de Governo na Constituição Cabo-verdiana*. Lisbon: Editorial da Associação Académica da Faculdade de Direito de Lisboa, 1990.

Christof Heyns, ed., *Human Rights Law in Africa*. Vol. 2. Leiden, Netherlands: Martinus Nijhoff, 2004.

Fafali Koudawo, *Cabo Verde, Guiné-Bissau: Da Democracia Revolucionária à Democracia Liberal*. Bissau, Guinea Bissau: Instituto Nacional de Estudos e Pesquisa (INEP), 2001.

Aristides R. Lima, *Estatuto Jurídico-Constitucional do Chefe de Estado*. Praia, Cape Verde: Alfa Communicações, 2004.

———, *Reforma politica em Cabo Verde: Do Paternalismo à Modernização do Estado*. Praia: Grafedito, 1992.

Aristides R. Lima

CENTRAL AFRICAN REPUBLIC

At-a-Glance

OFFICIAL NAME
Central African Republic

CAPITAL
Bangui

POPULATION
4,303,356 (July 2006 est.)

SIZE
240,536 sq. mi. (622, 984 sq. km)

LANGUAGES
French and Sango (official languages), Banda, Gbayi, Zande, Ngbaka

RELIGIONS
Protestant 25%, Roman Catholic 25%, Muslim 15%, indigenous beliefs 35%

NATIONAL OR ETHNIC COMPOSITION
Baya 33%, Banda 27%, Sara 10%, Mandja 13%, Mboum 7%, M'baka 4%, Takoma 4%, other 2%

DATE OF INDEPENDENCE OR CREATION
August 13, 1960

TYPE OF GOVERNMENT
Republic

TYPE OF STATE
Unitary state

TYPE OF LEGISLATURE
Unicameral parliament

DATE OF CONSTITUTION
December 27, 2004

DATE OF LAST AMENDMENT
No amendment

In terms of its constitution, the Central African Republic is a republic based on the principles of democracy, unity, laicism, rule of law, and sovereignty of peoples. There is a clear division among the executive, legislative, and judicial powers, although there is significant overlap of the branches of the government.

The Central African Republic is sparsely populated and landlocked. It was classified in 2002 as one of the world's least developed countries. Some 55 percent of the country's gross domestic product (GDP) is derived from agriculture, with cotton, food crops, coffee, tobacco, and timber as the most important crops. The country is rich in natural resources such as diamonds, gold, uranium, and other minerals, but its transportation and communication networks are limited.

CONSTITUTIONAL HISTORY

The French occupied the region in 1894. In 1958, the territory voted to become an autonomous republic within the French Community, and on August 13, 1960, President Dacko proclaimed the republic's independence from France. In 1965, Colonel Bokassa overthrew President Dacko in a coup.

In 1976, the Central African Republic became the Central African Empire, and Bokassa declared himself emperor. He was overthrown in a coup in 1979. Former president Dacko returned to power, and the country's name reverted to Central African Republic. In 1988, the army deposed Dacko in a coup.

In 1991, President Kolingba announced a move toward parliamentary democracy. In the 1993 elections, Prime Minister Patassé defeated Kolingba. In 1996, the military mutinied, but French troops succeeded in suppressing the uprising. An African peacekeeping force occupied Bangui until relieved by a United Nations (UN) peacekeeping mission in 1998. In 1999, Patassé once more defeated Kolingba in the general election. He survived a coup attempt in 2001, only to succumb finally in March 2003 when General Bozizé deposed his civilian government. Bozizé suspended the constitution, dissolved the National Assembly, and established a transitional government.

Although Bozizé's accession to power was irregular and in conflict with the constitution, the transitional government has been inclusive, attracting tacit support from the people and civil society. Bozizé has tried to promote political reconciliation by appointing people from across the political spectrum, including members of the opposition, to the transitional government. Bozizé has affirmed his commitment to restoring democracy. In March 2004, the National Transitional Council created an independent commission to oversee municipal, parliamentary, and presidential elections which were held in 2005. The new constitution, based on a referendum, came into force on December 27, 2004.

FORM AND IMPACT OF THE CONSTITUTION

The Central African Republic has a single, written constitution. Theoretically, the constitution is supreme since the Constitutional Court has the authority to interpret the constitution and to test the constitutionality of all law. The first chapter of the constitution contains a number of fundamental human rights. Furthermore, the constitution gives formal recognition to the rule of law, stating that every inhabitant of the republic must respect the constitution, laws, and regulations. The republican form of the Central African Republic is entrenched in the constitution and may not be changed.

BASIC ORGANIZATIONAL STRUCTURE

The country is a unitary state. Territorially, it is organized into 16 prefectures and one autonomous commune, 60 sub-prefectures, and 174 communities or municipalities. The capital, Bangui, is administered as a separate community.

LEADING CONSTITUTIONAL PRINCIPLES

The constitutional system is defined by a number of principles: The country is a unitary, democratic republic based on universal adult suffrage, unity, national sovereignty, and human rights. The fundamental principle of the republic is "government of the people, by the people, and for the people." The constitution states that the people of the republic oppose any conquest by civil, military and dictatorial force; seizing power by means of a coup d'état is regarded as a crime against the people.

CONSTITUTIONAL BODIES

The main constitutional bodies are of a strong executive branch (president, prime minister, and Council of Min-isters or cabinet), a weaker legislative branch (unicameral National Assembly), and the judiciary, including the Constitutional Court.

The President

The president is the chief executive, as well as the head of state. The president appoints the prime minister, members of the cabinet (on the advice of the prime minister), and military and civil officials. He or she presides over the High Council of Defense and the High Council of the Judiciary and performs all the usual ceremonial duties assigned to a head of state. The president is elected by direct universal ballot for a term of five years, renewable only once.

The Administration

The administration consists of the prime minister and the Council of Ministers or cabinet. The president appoints the prime minister and the other ministers. The prime minister is accountable to the president and to the National Assembly, presides over the cabinet and various interministerial committees, and conducts and coordinates the functions of the executive branch of government.

The National Assembly

The National Assembly passes legislation, imposes taxes, and controls the executive. Members have a free mandate to vote in the assembly without party instructions. The members are elected by universal adult suffrage to five-year terms.

The Lawmaking Process

The president, ministers, and members of the National Assembly may initiate legislation in parliament.

The Judiciary

The judiciary is independent. However, the president appoints members of the judiciary and presides over the High Council of the Judiciary, which is responsible for developing the careers of judicial officers and protecting judicial independence.

The judiciary comprises the Constitutional Court; Criminal Court; Court of Cassation, which consists of the Criminal Chamber, the Civil and Commercial Chamber, and the Social Chamber; the Council of State, which sits as an administrative court; the Court of Accounts, which judges the accounts and finances of territorial authorities and state-owned enterprises; an ad hoc Tribunal of Conflicts, which deals with jurisdictional disputes; and an ad hoc High Court of Justice, which investigates charges of treason against members of the cabinet and parliament. There are also other courts and tribunals, such as military courts, which try military personnel for crimes committed in the course of duty.

The Constitutional Court

The Constitutional Court consists of nine members who serve for a nonrenewable term of seven years. The Constitutional Court interprets the constitution and has the power to review the constitutionality of all legislation and other laws. If legislation is declared unconstitutional, it is null and void and may not be put into effect.

ELECTION PROCESS AND POLITICAL PARTICIPATION

According to the constitution, universal suffrage is the only legitimate source of political power. National sovereignty belongs to the people, who exercise this power directly through a referendum or indirectly through their representatives. Freedom of expression and opinion, the right to vote, and the right to form associations are guaranteed by the constitution. All citizens who are age 21 or older may vote during elections or a referendum. Political parties may be formed, and they may participate in all political activities.

POLITICAL PARTIES

A number of parties actively participated in the political process and contested elections. Among them were or still are the Alliance for Democracy and Progress (ADP), the Central African Democratic Assembly (RDC), the Civic Forum (FC), the Democratic Forum (FODEM), the Liberal Democratic Party (PLD), the Movement for Democracy and Development (MDD), the Movement for the Liberation of the Central African People (MLPC), the Patriotic Front for Progress (FPP), the People's Union for the Republic (UPR), the National Unity Party (PUN), and the Social Democratic Party (PSD).

CITIZENSHIP

Children born within the territory of the Central African Republic, regardless of the nationality of the parents, are citizens, with the exception of children born to certain diplomatic personnel.

Children of a Central African Republican father born abroad automatically obtain citizenship. Children of a foreign father and a Central African Republican mother born abroad are eligible for citizenship if desired by the parents. However, since the Central African Republic recognizes dual citizenship, children may also retain the citizenship of a foreign father.

A foreign national who marries a citizen of the Central African Republic is automatically eligible for citizenship by registration after the marriage. Citizenship may also be acquired by naturalization if the person has resided in the country for five to seven years.

Citizenship may be lost if it was obtained fraudulently or if the person has committed acts of disloyalty against the government or serious crimes after obtaining citizenship. Voluntary renunciation of Central African Republic citizenship is also permitted by law.

FUNDAMENTAL RIGHTS

The constitution provides for the protection of a wide range of fundamental human rights.

Impact and Functions of Fundamental Rights

The preamble to the constitution refers to the protection and equality of vulnerable groups in society, in accordance with, among other covenants, the Universal Declaration of Human Rights and the African Charter of Human and Peoples' Rights. Chapter 1 deals with the fundamental rights of society. It guarantees the classic civil and political rights, such as liberty; the right to life; the prohibition of torture and inhuman, cruel, degrading, or humiliating punishment; equality regardless of gender, race, ethnic origin, sex, religion, political affiliation, or social status; the inviolability of property; freedom of expression; and freedom of movement. It also protects certain socioeconomic rights, such as access to education, and labor rights, such as the right to work and to strike.

Limitations to Fundamental Rights

The constitution does not contain a general limitation clause to govern fundamental rights. It provides that restrictions may be prescribed by law and that the fundamental rights may only be exercised within the limits of the laws and regulations, including the demands of public order. However, in the absence of a general limitation clause, there are no predetermined standards or "thresholds" against which these limitations of the fundamental rights may be tested.

ECONOMY

The constitution guarantees the right to work, the right to form trade unions, and the freedom of enterprise.

The Central African Republic is a landlocked nation rich in gold, diamonds, and other minerals. Agriculture and forestry are the key elements of the economy. The main export crop is coffee. Other export products include timber, wax, rubber, tobacco, and leather. The country is essentially self-sufficient in terms of food such as maize, groundnuts, rice, millet, cassava, and sesame. Although there is a small livestock industry, its growth is hampered by the presence of tsetse flies as well as marketing problems.

Key industries in the Central African Republic are the mining and oil industries; the diamond industry is important Electricity is provided by a quasi-governmental utility. The manufacturing industry in the country is small and mainly focuses on processing of agricultural and forest products, such as leather and textiles, and on light industry.

The country's landlocked position, its poor transportation system, a largely unskilled workforce, political instability, and poor macroeconomic policies have hampered economic growth in the past. The country was rated 169 of 177 in the United Nations Human Development Index in 2004.

RELIGIOUS COMMUNITIES

The constitution guarantees religious freedom. Any form of religious intolerance or fundamentalism is forbidden, freedom of worship is assured, and everybody is equal before the law, regardless of religious belief.

MILITARY DEFENSE AND STATE OF EMERGENCY

On a very basic level, the defense of the republic is the constitutional duty of the citizens. The official security forces include the army, navy, air force, gendarmerie, national police, Presidential Security Unit, and local police personnel. The president is the supreme commander of the armed forces and presides over the Council of National Defense.

Only the National Assembly may authorize a declaration of war. If the institutions of the state, its independence or territorial integrity, the execution of its international obligations, or the normal functioning of public powers is under immediate and serious threat, the president may, on the advice of the cabinet, the National Assembly, and the president of the Constitutional Court, declare a state of emergency (state of siege or alert) for a period of 15 days. This period may only be extended by an extraordinary session of the National Assembly. During such an emergency, the National Assembly may not be dissolved and the constitution may not be amended.

AMENDMENTS TO THE CONSTITUTION

The president, together with a three-fourths majority of the National Assembly, may propose an amendment to the constitution. Constitutional amendments may be adopted by a three-fourths majority of the members of the National Assembly or as the result of a national referendum. The republican form of the state and its territorial integrity may not be amended.

PRIMARY SOURCES

Constitution in English (extracts). Available online. URL: http://www.chr.up.ac.za/hr_docs/constitutions/docs/CentralAfrican%20Republic%20(english%20summary)%20(rev).doc. Accessed on July 27, 2005.

Constitution in French. Available online. URL: http://www.democratie.francophonie.org/article.php37id_article=1126&id_rubrique=115. Accessed on June 17, 2006.

SECONDARY SOURCES

A. P. Blaustein and G. H. Flanz, eds., *Constitutions of the Countries of the World: Central African Republic.* New York: Oceana, 1999.

Christof Heyns, ed., *Human Rights Law in Africa.* Vol. 2. Leiden, Netherlands: Martinus Nijhoff, 2004.

CountryReports.org. Available online. URL: www.countryreports.org/car.htm. Accessed on August 11, 2005.

European Country of Origin Information Network. Available online. URL: www.ecoi.net. Accessed on August 11, 2005.

Index Mundi. Available online. URL: www.indexmundi.com/central_african_republic/constitution.html. Accessed on August 11, 2005.

U.S. Department of State. Available online. URL: http://www.state.gov/r/pa/ei/bgn/4007.htm. Accessed on July 26, 2005.

Christo Botha

CHAD

At-a-Glance

OFFICIAL NAME
Republic of Chad

CAPITAL
N'Djamena

POPULATION
6,370,609 (2005 est.)

SIZE
495,750 sq. mi. (1,284,000 sq. km)

LANGUAGES
French and Arabic (official), other languages 70% of the population

RELIGIONS
Sunni Muslim 49%, Christian 30%, animist 15%, other 6%

NATIONAL OR ETHNIC COMPOSITION
Arab 15%, Saras 20%, Chadic 18%, and some 200 other ethnic groups

DATE OF INDEPENDENCE OR CREATION
August 11, 1960

TYPE OF GOVERNMENT
Presidential democracy

TYPE OF STATE
Unitary state

TYPE OF LEGISLATURE
Unicameral parliament

DATE OF CONSTITUTION
March 31, 1996

DATE OF LAST AMENDMENT
June 6, 2005

A product of colonial powers, Chad still struggles today with the random character of its boundaries, conflicts produced by multiple ethnic and religious groups, and a clan-based culture that aggravates the problem. Despite another attempt at democratization in 1991–93, the prospects for democracy, the respect of the rule of law, and fundamental rights remain insecure.

The president of the republic is the most important figure in constitutional life. The president controls the government and, through his or her party, the National Assembly. The judiciary is weak and ineffective. Protection of fundamental rights is insufficient. Democratization has nonetheless produced encouraging progress toward a free press and a civil society.

CONSTITUTIONAL HISTORY

The territory known today as Chad was home to ancient civilizations. Its position in an area of contact between the Arabs of Northern Africa and populations of black Af-

rica has produced a history of ethnic and religious conflicts that is still relevant today.

In the late 19th century, a Sudanese slave trader ruled much of the country; he was expelled by a French military expedition in 1900. It was not until 1917 that the whole territory was under French control. It became an autonomous French colony in 1920. The French colonial power did not invest much in the colony. The more arable parts of the south were used for cotton plantations, until recently the country's most important source of foreign currency. After 60 years of French rule, Chad became an independent republic in 1960.

The history of independent Chad is one of successive coups d'état and authoritarian or dictatorial rule, most recently by Hissein Habré, who ruled from 1982 until 1990 when Idriss Déby, a former ally of Habré, ousted him in a military coup. Déby promised democratization and convened a Sovereign National Conference (Conférence Nationale Souveraine) to compose a new pluralistic constitution, which entered into force in 1996. The constitutional amendment of 2005 reduced the prospects of democratic development. Among other changes, the two-term limit for the presidency has been abolished.

FORM AND IMPACT OF THE CONSTITUTION

Chad has a written constitution, enshrining fundamental rights. The constitution is complemented by organic law and takes precedence over ordinary law. International treaties that are in conformity with certain constitutional principles are superior to ordinary laws. The constitution was fully revised by a national conference in 1993.

Despite the hopes raised by this revision, respect for law and the constitution among the authorities remains low, especially respect for fundamental rights. The second chamber of parliament, the Senate, has never been established. After being reelected once in 2001, President Déby proposed a constitutional reform package, which was adopted in a popular referendum in 2005. Among other provisions, it abolishes the two-term limit for the presidency, allowing his reelection in 2006. The constitutional provision for the establishment of a Senate has also been abolished.

Strong ethnic and religious tensions have led to repeated coup attempts. There are irregular regional uprisings against government forces, which are dominated by the Zarghawa ethnic group, to which the president belongs. External crises (currently from the neighboring Sudanese province of Darfur) have also posed a threat to the rule of law. Lack of public resources aggravates these problems.

BASIC ORGANIZATIONAL STRUCTURE

Following the French model, Chad is an "indivisible republic," a unitary state divided into 28 départements. Its constitution provides for decentralization of political power to substate entities (collectivités territoriales décentralisées), such as rural communities, municipalities, departments, and regions. These enjoy constitutionally guaranteed autonomy. Decentralization has not yet been put into practice. Most authority remains with the central government.

LEADING CONSTITUTIONAL PRINCIPLES

Modeled after the French example, Chad is a secular, social republic, one and indivisible. It is founded on the principles of democracy, the rule of law, and justice. The separation of state and religion is affirmed.

Chad's government is a presidential republic with separation of powers. The position of the president of the republic is strong. Parliament is unicameral.

The autonomy of customary and traditional laws is assured within certain limits. Fundamental rights are complemented by a series of civic duties.

CONSTITUTIONAL BODIES

The institutional provisions follow, to a great extent, the French model. The main constitutional bodies are the president of the republic; the cabinet; the legislative branch of government, consisting of the National Assembly; the Constitutional Council; the High Court of Justice; the High Council of Communication; and the Judiciary.

The President of the Republic

The president is the most powerful figure of constitutional life in Chad, enjoying vast powers. The president is also the guardian of the constitution and of the integrity and the sovereignty of the nation and an arbiter in institutional disputes.

The president is directly elected for five years. There is no limit on the number of terms. In order to be eligible to run for president, candidates must be of Chadian descent (both mother and father of Chadian origin), be between 30 and 70 years, and have "good morals." The president may not hold any other office.

The prime minister replaces the president of the republic in cases of absence or incapacity.

The president appoints the prime minister and the cabinet. The president can demand the resignation of the prime minister at any time. The president also appoints senior officials in civil administration and the military.

The constitution provides for the dissolution of the National Assembly by the president but only when the functioning of the institutions is threatened by persistent crises between the executive and the legislative branch of government or when the National Assembly has censured the cabinet twice within one year. The president must then wait at least one year before having the right to dissolve the next elected National Assembly.

The Cabinet

The cabinet is composed of the prime minister and the cabinet ministers. It is appointed by the president after a vote of confidence in the National Assembly and is responsible to the assembly. Holding a cabinet post precludes having any other office in public or private institutions.

The cabinet disposes of a large regulatory power. It has the right of legislative initiative. Members of the cabinet may participate in parliamentary deliberations.

The Legislature

The legislature is formed by the National Assembly, which consists of 155 members. Deputies are elected by universal suffrage for a four-year term with possible reelection. The constitution affirms the principle of representation of the whole nation, not of constituencies. There may be no imperative mandate.

Parliamentary activity is limited to two biannual sessions of 90 days maximum each.

The constitution provides for parliamentary immunity. Reports suggest, however, that the assembly is readily prepared to lift the immunity of opposition members in cases of libel suits against the president.

The National Assembly disposes of the lawmaking power. The division between parliamentary lawmaking power and the executive's regulatory power is determined by a catalogue in the constitution.

Parliament possesses the usual means of controlling the executive. The National Assembly must vote on a motion of censure at the demand of one-tenth of its members.

The Lawmaking Process

Laws may be initiated by either the cabinet or members of parliament. Laws need a favorable vote with simple majority in the National Assembly.

The Constitutional Council

As in France, the control of constitutionality of laws and international treaties is assured by a Constitutional Council. The council is composed of nine members. The term of office is nine years without renewal. One-third of the council is replaced every three years. The members may not be removed during their term of office.

The council is responsible for deciding the constitutionality of laws before their entry into force (promulgation) if presented by the president of the republic, the prime minister, the president of the National Assembly, or one-tenth of the members of the National Assembly. It is also responsible for resolving disputes among the different institutions of the republic.

The High Court of Justice

The High Court of Justice adjudicates charges of high treason against the president of the republic or members of the cabinet. Grave human rights violations, abuse of public funds, corruption, drug trafficking, and grave environmental crimes may be considered analogous to high treason. The High Court is made up of deputies from the National Assembly, members of the Constitutional Council, and members of the Supreme Court.

High Council of Communication

The High Council of Communication is an independent body composed of nine members. Four of them are appointed by state institutions, four of them by professional bodies, and one by the president of the Supreme Court. The council's main tasks are the regulation of the media and the guarantee of press freedoms. In practice, it is largely impotent, as evidenced by its noninvolvement in libel suits by government institutions against the media.

The Judiciary

There is a single jurisdiction for civil, criminal, and administrative affairs. It has three levels: Courts of First Instance, Courts of Appeal, and the Supreme Court. It is formally independent, and the independence of individual judges is constitutionally protected. The judiciary is obligated to ensure respect for fundamental rights.

The judiciary lacks basic resources and competent magistrates. Magistrates have admitted taking bribes for the release of criminal offenders. Flagrant disregard for procedural rights of defendants by police authorities, including extrajudicial executions, has apparently undermined morale within the judiciary.

THE ELECTION PROCESS

Every Chadian citizen of at least 18 years may participate in elections. Elections are universal, direct or indirect, equal, and secret. Elections for the office of the president and the National Assembly are organized in two rounds to ensure majorities.

The Constitutional Council watches over the election procedure. Fraud and vote rigging allegedly characterized the 1996 presidential and 1997 assembly elections; assembly elections were boycotted by several parties.

Following the French model, referenda can be organized on any draft law or international agreement affecting the organization of the state institutions.

POLITICAL PARTIES

Chad is on the way to becoming a multiparty system. The National Assembly is composed of more than five parties. The role of parties as a means of structuring political will is impeded by strong ethnic divisions and clan loyalties. Parties serve the purposes of political leaders rather than being characterized by ideological differences. Opposition in parliament is feeble since two major government parties joined forces.

Political parties can be dissolved at the demand of the minister for the interior by an administrative court.

CITIZENSHIP

Citizenship is acquired by descent from parents who are both Chadian citizens, regardless of the country of birth. If only one parent is a Chadian citizen, the child receives citizenship only if it would be otherwise stateless. Naturalization is possible on the condition of 15 years of residence and good health and morality. Citizenship can be revoked by the president if it is determined that a person committed acts that were not in the interest of Chad.

FUNDAMENTAL RIGHTS

The constitution includes a large catalogue of rights and civic duties. Fundamental rights include civil liberties and social rights, as well as rights to culture and to a safe environment. Civil liberties can be limited by the law in order to protect the rights and liberties of others or to protect public order or good manners.

A National Human Rights Commission was established by law in order to deal with individual claims of fundamental rights violations. It is formally attached to the office of the prime minister, who assures its material resources.

Impact and Functions of Fundamental Rights

Actual respect for fundamental rights is low. Freedom of expression, freedom of assembly, and the rights of criminal suspects are frequently and gravely violated. Extrajudicial executions are a reality. The death penalty, after being suspended for some years, is now applied. Female genital mutilation is now prohibited by law, but little is being done to prevent its common practice. Freedom of the press is respected in principle, and there is some press freedom in the capital, N'Djamena. However, the main source of information for the mostly illiterate rural population is radio, which is controlled by the government. High licensing fees discourage private radio operators. Civil society has developed fairly well over the last 10 years but lives under constant threat of attack.

Human rights associations are currently working hard to bring the former dictator Hissein Habré to trial. They have received some help from the current president, Déby, who overthrew Habré's regime.

Limitations to Fundamental Rights

Social rights, especially education, cannot be guaranteed because of a lack of resources.

ECONOMY

The constitution does not favor any economic system over another. Private property is protected, and the right to join a labor organization is recognized.

RELIGIOUS COMMUNITIES

Chad is a secular republic, and freedom of religion is assured. No one may be treated differently on the basis of his or her religious beliefs. On the other hand, no one may rely on religious beliefs in order to be exempted from obligations that serve the national interest.

Ethnic tensions in the country often have a religious component. Persecutions of religious communities are not infrequent, even by public forces.

MILITARY DEFENSE AND STATE OF EMERGENCY

The president of the republic is the commander in chief of the armed forces. The military submits to civil rule, and the armed forces are not political.

Military service is compulsory. Lacking basic legal restrictions, the army has accepted many underage volunteers.

Declarations of war need parliamentary approval. In a state of emergency, the president, meeting with the cabinet, can take appropriate measures for a period of 15 days. Longer periods need the approval of parliament. Emergency measures must respect the proper functioning of institutions and may not include the dissolution of the assembly. No infringements on the right to life, physical integrity, and fair procedures can be justified as appropriate measures.

AMENDMENTS TO THE CONSTITUTION

Amendments to the constitution may be initiated by either the president, after approval by the cabinet, or members of parliament. A proposed amendment needs a two-thirds majority in the National Assembly and approval in a public referendum for passage. Specifically excluded from amendment are the separation of powers, the secular form of government, fundamental rights, and political pluralism.

PRIMARY SOURCES

Constitution in English. Available online. URL: http://www. chr.up.ac.za/hr_docs/constitutions/docs/ChadC%20 (english%20summary)(rev).doc. Accessed on June 17, 2006.

Constitution in French. Available online. URL: http:// droit.francophonie.org/doc/html/td/con/fr/1996/ 1996dftdcofr1.html. Accessed on August 30, 2005.

SECONDARY SOURCES

Thomas Collelo, ed., *Chad—a Country Study*. Washington, D.C.: Library of Congress, 1988. Available online. URL: http://lcweb2.loc.gov/frd/cs/cshome.html. Accessed on September 21, 2005.

Christof Heyns, ed., *Human Rights Law in Africa*. Vol. 2. Leiden, Netherlands: Martinus Nijhoff, 2004. Available online. URL: http://www.chr.up.ac.za/. Accessed on September 14, 2005.

United Nations, "Core Document Forming Part of the Reports of States Parties: Chad" (HRI/CORE/1/ Add.88), 12 December 1997. Available online. URL: http://www.unhchr.ch/tbs/doc.nsf. Accessed on September 19, 2005.

Malte Beyer

CHILE

At-a-Glance

OFFICIAL NAME
Republic of Chile

CAPITAL
Santiago

POPULATION
15,018,000 (2005 est.)

SIZE
292,260 sq. mi. (756,950 sq. km)

LANGUAGES
Spanish

RELIGIONS
Catholic 89%, Protestant 11%

NATIONAL OR ETHNIC COMPOSITION
White and white-Amerindian 95%, Amerindian 3%,
other 2%

DATE OF INDEPENDENCE OR CREATION
September 18, 1810

TYPE OF GOVERNMENT
Presidential

TYPE OF STATE
Unitary state

TYPE OF LEGISLATURE
Bicameral congress

DATE OF CONSTITUTION
October 24, 1980

DATE OF LAST AMENDMENT
August 19, 2005

Chile is a democratic republic with a presidential system based on the separation of powers that has operated since 1830. The constitution defines Chile as a unitary state, although a considerable part of its administrative organization is decentralized into two territorial levels that enjoy far-reaching autonomy. The constitution guarantees, in Article 19, the protection of classic fundamental rights as well as essential rights recognized through treaties. Article 20 guarantees judicial review of administrative action to anyone whose fundamental rights are infringed.

The president of the republic is the chief of state and is in charge of the government and the administration. The president has the constitutional power to appoint and dismiss the ministers of state, who directly cooperate with the president. Neither the president nor the ministers are politically responsible before the National Congress, although they can be removed by impeachment.

The National Congress provides popular representation in its two branches. The Chamber of Deputies and the Senate are both elected by popular vote in districts of two seats. There is a system of stable parties that tend to operate in two large coalitions when making major political and electoral decisions.

The economic system, after the failure of the state-planned-economy model in the 1970s, is predominately liberal. The liberal principles guiding state economic management are promoted by explicit constitutional norms.

The armed forces are subject to civil power. The commanders in chief of army, navy, and air force are appointed and dismissed by the president and have four-year terms.

CONSTITUTIONAL HISTORY

Chile's constitutional history as an independent state begins with the creation of the first governing body in September 1810. After the destitution and capture of the Spanish king, Ferdinand VII, by the French emperor, Napoléon, a political and military confrontation began throughout the Spanish colonies between those who remained close to the king and Spanish institutions and those who wanted autonomy while maintaining ties to the monarchy.

Between 1810 and 1814, supporters of autonomy controlled the government. Unsure of the direction that events in Spain would take, and with only a scarce majority in favor of separation, it was only possible to elaborate provisional constitutional adjustments. During this period known as Patria Vieja, three major constitutional instruments were approved (1811, 1812, 1814), none of which managed to establish stable institutions. The new rulers tried to persuade the aristocracy of the advantages of independence by creating collective, and therefore weak, government organs.

In 1814, the supporters of the monarchy regained power. Their punitive measures pushed popular sentiment toward independence. Finally, the royalists were defeated in the Battle of Maipú in April 1818.

Chile's independence was formally declared that year. Toward the end of the revolution, power resided in the hands of Bernardo O'Higgins, one of the military leaders of the emancipation movement. The absence of consensus on the form of government and the danger of new attacks from troops loyal to the monarchy motivated O'Higgins to approve a provisional constitution in which the only counterbalance to the executive (headed by the so-called supreme director) was a Senate of five members appointed by the same supreme director.

A new constitution to replace the provisional constitution was approved in 1822. The new constitution extended O'Higgins's term as supreme director for another 10 years, triggering a rapid loss of legitimacy that led to the 1823 constitution. But this document, which tried to create an original system of government, was too complex and was for the most part not applied.

In 1828, liberal political forces won approval for a new constitution that combined popular federal ideas and traditional institutions of liberal constitutionalism with a technical quality not shown by previous texts. Nonetheless, political support declined, and it produced no visible results.

In 1830, the struggle within the governing class between liberals and conservatives ended in military confrontation and the victory of the conservatives at the Battle of Lircay.

The conservative triumph meant that parliamentary rule faded away in favor of an executive with great political power, although the idea of a leader for life was rejected as incompatible with constitutional institutions. The conservatives also favored the idea of a progressive democracy: Political participation could not be implemented at once without an adequate citizen base but should be introduced in a gradual manner.

The 1833 constitution expressed this conservative vision. Its provisions reinforced presidential powers and reduced the powers of congress. The main innovation, however, was more political than legal recognition of the president as a ruler with ample powers, including interference in the elections.

The text of 1833 prevailed until 1925. While it underwent few reforms, its interpretation changed in a radical manner. Three great periods can be distinguished: presidentialism (1833–61), moderate parliamentarism (1861–91), and parliamentarism (1891–1925). During the presidential period, the president's leadership was unquestioned. His mandate was for five years, invariably transformed by reelection into a 10-year term. Presidential interference in the elections for deputies and senators was accepted by the ruling class. The president also benefited from emergency powers.

Toward the middle of the century emerging political parties started to criticize the presidential system. In a gradual but steady manner, congress limited the presidential privileges by way of normative reforms.

In 1861, the constitution was modified to prevent presidential reelection. In addition, the power to manage election results passed to the political parties. At last, the congress found itself in a political position to negotiate on equal terms with the president. Toward the end of 19th century, the growing power of congress became intolerable for the president. In 1891, the president refused to abide by the will of the congress, which in response refused to approve the budget. Congress triumphed in the ensuing civil war, and with it the parliamentary interpretation of the 1833 constitution.

At the beginning of 1891, the superiority of the congress over the president was recognized within the institutional framework of the 1833 constitution. The main change was the liberal use of the vote of no confidence. This generated a rotation of cabinet ministers that followed the luck of the unstable majorities in both chambers. The parliamentary regime failed to deal with deep social problems. Social crisis, suffrage limitations, elitist parties, concentration of wealth, and a slow legislative process wore down the regime.

In 1920, a reformist president, Arturo Alessandri, gained power. In 1925, a constitutional reform explicitly favoring a presidential-type regime won a popular plebiscite, and in September of that year, 1925, the new constitution was promulgated. The document established the central constitutional order that prevails to this day. Throughout this time, congress defended its prerogatives, firmly based on more than 90 years of uninterrupted functioning, complicating the relationship with the president. From the executive perspective, the only solution to the recurring conflicts was to increase the president's powers and to reduce the powers of parliament. In 1943, a constitutional reform reduced the parliamentary initiative on public spending. In 1970, a new constitutional reform limited the powers of the congress in economic issues.

The existing political parties in 1925 were replaced in the second half of the 20th century by radically different political forces. These parties had a rigid ideological base. The new doctrines advocated an ambitious agenda of social transformation.

The replacement of the old traditional parties was manifested during the presidential elections of 1952 and 1958, with the victory of two independent candidates. In 1964, Eduardo Frei Montalva assumed power by a solid majority, heading an administration that proposed deep social changes. Politics began to transform into a battlefield where neither values nor principles were shared but just a few formal rules established by the constitution.

Salvador Allende's triumph in the presidential election of 1970 followed the same path initiated in 1964. President Allende did not benefit from a clear majority in either chamber, and legislative deadlock resulted. Without legislative support, the president began employing alternative means to develop his policies. These actions generated profound political criticism and constitutional problems.

The parliamentary elections of 1973 ratified the existing institutional deadlock. In August 1973, the Chamber of Deputies approved a statement that the president had broken the law. Similar claims had previously been made by the Supreme Court.

In September 1973, the military intervened. The National Congress was closed, and the 1925 constitution was suspended. Political parties were dissolved, and all party activity was forbidden.

The military dictatorship launched repression entailing numerous human rights abuses. According to the National Committee's Truth and Reconciliation Report presented in 1991, nearly 2,300 people were killed by the actions of the state.

In October 1973, the military government began a constitutional reform process; after seven years, a text was finally presented for a plebiscite, which approved the document (although many questioned the legitimacy of a plebiscitary conducted under military rule).

The new constitution reinforced presidential powers in line with the proposals of three previous democratic presidents in 1964, 1969, and 1971 (Alessandri, Frei, and Allende). All provisions linked to political rights remained suspended until 1989. The rest began to take effect in October 1980.

In 1989, following the transition program anticipated in the constitution itself, presidential and parliamentary elections were held. As well, more than 50 constitutional reforms were submitted to a plebiscite, resulting in the approval by an ample popular majority. To many, this second plebiscite constitutes the democratic foundation of the new constitution.

From 1990 to the present, more than 10 additional reforms have been applied to the constitution. Most important were the creation of regional governments (1992) and a national prosecutor's office (1997) and the reform of the Senate, Constitutional Court, and National Security Council (2005).

FORM AND IMPACT OF THE CONSTITUTION

Chile has a strong tradition of written constitutions. Constitutional jurisprudence, however, became important only in recent decades. The constitution states that any person may make a claim to the rights recognized in Article 19 before the Court of Appeals. Recent jurisprudence, together with the regular functioning of the Constitutional Court, has strengthened the standing of the constitutional text.

Laws interpreting the constitution are not frequently passed; when they are, they need the same degree of approval as constitutional amendments themselves, and they require prior approval by the Constitutional Court. The historical background for this requirement are the various indirect modifications made under the constitutions of 1833 and 1925.

The constitution rules above all other legal acts and practices, including those derived from international instruments and treaties. The doctrine of the primacy of international human-rights treaties (born along with the 1989 reform) was overturned by the Constitutional Court in 2001.

Ample consensus supports the courts in matters concerning human rights, even in cases in which judges clearly extended the protection beyond the text. Some other values explicitly protected in the constitution have been more problematic, such as the principles of Catholic morality and liberalism, which reflect the sentiments of a portion of the population.

BASIC ORGANIZATIONAL STRUCTURE

Chile is a unitary state, and its territory is divided in regions. Each of the 13 established regions constitutes an administrative unit, headed by a regional government and defined by the constitution as decentralized. The regional government is made up of an indirectly elected assembly and an executive, the intendant. The president of the republic appoints and dismisses the intendants at will, calling into question the practical extent of decentralization.

The regional budgets are assigned by the central government. The most important budget item is the National Fund for Regional Development, an interterritorial compensatory fund distributed according to preestablished poverty and development indexes. Investments, however, are controlled by fixed rules that prevent the regional governments from developing their own policies.

Each region is divided into provinces with their own governments who help to implement regional policies. A third level of territorial organization is the municipality, which is controlled by a directly elected mayor and council. The municipalities have their own sources of funding (such as local taxes), as well as some assistance from the center (such as the Municipal Common Fund, another interterritorial compensation fund). This allows them a degree of autonomy.

LEADING CONSTITUTIONAL PRINCIPLES

Chile is a democratic and presidential republic. The constitution establishes a clear division of powers, complemented by checks and balances.

Democracy is expressed in direct elections of representative authorities (president, parliamentarians, councils, and mayors) and in plebiscites. The latter can be and have, at times, been called at the local municipal level; moreover, they are available to resolve conflicts between the president and the National Congress during a constitutional reform process.

The leading principles can be found in Chapter 1 of the constitution. The starting point is that all human beings are born free and equal in dignity and rights. Article 1 also recognizes the importance of family as the "basic core" of society, although the scope of this declaration has changed in a radical manner since the approval of a divorce law in 2004. The article includes clauses on the supremacy of the constitution and the rule of law.

CONSTITUTIONAL BODIES

The two political and central representational institutions in the constitutional regime are the president and the National Congress. Alongside these powers are the judiciary and the Constitutional Court and a set of organs with constitutional autonomy (the Central Bank and the Office of the Comptroller General of the Republic).

The President of the Republic

The president of the republic is the head of state and chief of the administration. The president appoints and dismisses the ministers of state.

The president has considerable powers in the legislative process, including the exclusive right to initiate bills on taxes and other major economic issues. The president can also declare a bill urgent, forcing the National Congress to vote on it within 30 days. Furthermore, the president can veto bills; two-thirds of the members of each chamber are needed to override the veto.

On budgetary bills, congress only has the power to reduce expenditures; it cannot increase estimates of revenues. If congress does not vote on the budgetary law proposal within 60 days, the bill enters into force.

These formal powers, in addition to the president's informal influence over the members of congress of his or her own party or coalition, explain the absolute dominance of the executive in the legislative process. Although there are legislative initiatives presented by members of congress, they usually concern minor issues or are not approved.

At the request of the president, the National Congress can delegate the legislative power on certain matters to him or her for a maximal period of a year, during which the president can issues decrees that have the same mandatory force as laws. As any law, however, these decrees can be revised by the Constitutional Court.

The president has the power to initiate constitutional amendments and can veto amendments proposed by congress. Even if congress overrides the veto by a two-thirds majority of the members of each chamber, the president can still call for a plebiscite on the measure.

The president is also in charge of the country's international affairs. The president can appoint ambassadors and representatives to international organizations and has the power to negotiate, approve, and ratify treaties. In general, treaties require the approval of congress, although certain executive agreements can be approved without its support.

The president can appoint and dismiss undersecretaries, intendants, provincial governors, and a long list of high administrative and military positions. It is estimated that there are more than 3,000 positions at the president's exclusive disposal. Important reforms, such as the creation of a Council of High Public Administration and a Civil Service Office, are under discussion in an attempt to guarantee the professional qualifications of top civil servants.

The president appoints directors of various independent agencies. This process usually requires ratification of a majority or two-thirds of the Senate. Such ratification has become an important tool in achieving political balance.

The president serves a single four-year term without immediate reelection, a rule introduced in 2005.

The National Congress

The legislative power belongs to a congress made up of two houses, the Chamber of Deputies and the Senate. The congress has functioned uninterrupted since 1933, with the exception of the 1973–90 period. The chambers participate equally in the legislative process.

The Chamber of Deputies also has control powers over the administration. The most useful are the oral and written questions and investigation committees. The congress, in addition, can impeach the president, ministers, superior court magistrates, and other high authorities, for offenses, violations, or abuses described in the constitution. The guilty party is removed and may not hold public office for five years. Since 1990, there have been 22 impeachment proceedings, more than half of them against judges. The only successful conviction has been that of a justice of the Supreme Court (1993) responsible for delaying a human rights violation trial.

The Lawmaking Process

The 1980 constitution establishes four types of laws, distinct according to matter, quorum needed for approval, and control of constitutionality. These are laws interpreting the constitution, constitutional organic laws, laws of a qualified quorum, and common laws.

Legislation can be initiated by members of congress or by the president, who has exclusive initiative in certain areas such as taxes and major economic issues. Both chambers must consent to a bill. The president can veto a bill, and a veto can only be rejected by a majority of two-thirds of the members of both chambers.

The Judiciary

The judiciary is independent and influential in the interpretation of the constitution. Its power is organized in three levels: the Supreme Court, 16 courts of appeal, and more than 400 courts of first instance. The first instance courts can be used in cases concerning civil, labor, or family law.

The courts of appeal and the Supreme Court have jurisdiction to hear applications for the protection of fundamental rights. These remedies have been an efficient instrument to promote and protect fundamental rights.

The judges of the Supreme Court and the courts of appeal are appointed by the president from a list nominated by the Supreme Court. In the case of Supreme Court judges, the appointment must be ratified by two-thirds of the Senate.

The Constitutional Court

The Constitutional Court has power to determine the constitutionality of a variety of normative (legal) acts: legal dispositions or treaties, regulations, instructions, and decrees. It is composed of 10 judges: three appointed by the Supreme Court, three by the president, two by the Senate, and two by the Chamber (with the Senate's ratification). These justices cannot be impeached, and their decisions cannot be appealed.

This body has consolidated its position as the authorized interpreter of the constitution. However, its overuse as a last resort by defeated parties in the National Congress could diminish its legitimacy.

THE ELECTION PROCESS

All Chileans over the age of 18 and not convicted of certain offenses have the right to vote. To run for deputy, a candidate must be at least 21 years of age, have citizenship and residency, and have completed high school. To run for the Senate or the presidency of the republic, the same requirements apply, except that a candidate must be at least 35 years of age.

Presidential Elections

The president is chosen by a direct vote in two rounds, copied from the French *ballotage* system. If no candidate obtains an absolute majority of the votes cast in the first round, a second round is carried out between the two candidates who received the most first-round votes. Since 1989, only one of three presidential elections has gone to a second round.

Parliamentary Elections

The 120 members of the Chamber of Deputies are elected in 60 districts of two seats each. Each party runs two candidates; the top two vote-getting parties each win a seat—unless one of them receives twice as many votes as the other, in which case it receives both. In the past decade, this rule favored the big parties and discriminated against smaller parties.

The Senate is elected in 19 senatorial districts also of two seats each. The electoral rule is identical to the one for the Chamber of Deputies.

POLITICAL PARTIES

Chile has a mature pluralistic system of political parties. Of the six main parties, five have roots from the first quarter of the 20th century. The profound institutional crisis of 1973 has had a moderating effect on the main leaders of the larger parties.

The electoral system has forced the formation of cohesive electoral coalitions. The parties excluded from the two main blocs lack weight in national politics. The larger of these is the Communist Party, which has received 8 percent of the votes in municipal elections.

Parties that are involved in unconstitutional actions can be dissolved by the Constitutional Court.

CITIZENSHIP

Citizenship is acquired by birth on Chilean territory. The principle of *ius soli* applies as a general rule. Children of a Chilean parent born abroad can also acquire Chilean citizenship under conditions elaborated in the constitution.

FUNDAMENTAL RIGHTS

The Chilean constitution enumerates fundamental rights in Article 19, as an elaboration of the principles of equality and freedom of Article 1. The list recapitulates the contents of earlier constitutions and includes the traditional human rights recognized by conventions and treaties. The 1980 text incorporates social rights, such as the right to health care, education, and social security. The right to live in an environment free of contamination is also recognized. There are at least three types of constitutional proceedings to protect fundamental rights, excluding social rights.

Article 19 begins with the right to life and the mental and physical integrity of the human being. The constitution consigns the question of how to protect unborn life to a law. Any type of abortion is punished by law.

Among the guarantees are freedom of speech, personal honor, inviolability of private communication, freedom of conscience and religion, freedom of work and association, and assembly rights. Equality before the law is established with general and special clauses (equal rights for men and women), as is equality in the exercise of rights. Personal freedom is guaranteed by a detailed clause that regulates the conditions in which it may be deprived.

The right to property has been subject of prolific and expanding jurisprudence.

Impact and Functions of the Fundamental Rights

The fundamental rights recognized by the constitution constitute an effective mandate for all three branches of the government. Private or public figures have effectively used litigation against executive decisions, and the constitutional prior review of bills, as means to protect constitutional rights.

These procedures have been most helpful in protecting classic liberal rights *against* state acts. They are less useful in protecting the social rights cited in the constitution, which can often be fulfilled only by positive actions of the state. This situation has been widely criticized, but it cannot be different in a country that has a developing economy.

Limitations to Fundamental Rights

The constitution authorizes certain limits to enumerated rights but requires that their essential content be respected. The Constitutional Court is responsible for defining the extent of these limits.

ECONOMY

The constitution does not opt explicitly for any particular economic model. Nonetheless, the framers' liberal orientation and their desire to prevent the reappearance of any form of state ownership are clear. The constitution protects the right to develop economic activity and bars the state from entrepreneurial activities, except when authorized by a qualified quorum law.

The influence of international economic integration agreements is limited at the moment. Chile is an associated member of MERCOSUR (Mercado Común del Sur, or Southern Common Market) and recently signed free trade agreements with the United States, the European Union, and South Korea.

RELIGIOUS COMMUNITIES

The constitution guarantees to all persons freedom of conscience and religious expression as well as the free exercise of all religions that are not opposed to morals, good customs, or public order. Religious communities may erect and maintain places of worship and other facilities. Equal rights are enjoyed by all churches and religious communities in terms of their assets; all facilities used exclusively for religious activities are exempt from taxes according to the constitution.

MILITARY DEFENSE AND STATE OF EMERGENCY

In case of war, the president takes over the supreme command of the armed forces. It is the president who declares war, subject to authorization by the National Congress. The president can declare a state of emergency and a state of catastrophe and can declare states of alert and siege with the National Congress's approval.

AMENDMENTS TO THE CONSTITUTION

The amendment process specifies different procedures for different types of norms. Those that refer to fundamental rights require approval of two-thirds of the members of each chamber; others can be approved by a three-fifths vote. The amendment is then sent to the president for approval. If vetoed, it returns to congress, where the president's introduced modifications can be accepted. The congress can also revive the original amendment with a majority of two-thirds of the members of each chamber. The president's only recourse then is to call a plebiscite to resolve the controversy.

Since 1989, more than 10 amendments have been approved.

PRIMARY SOURCES
Constitution in English. Available online. URL: http://confinder.richmond.edu/admin/docs/Chile.pdf. Accessed on June 17, 2006.
Constitution in Spanish. Bureau of Public Affairs, U.S. Department of State. "Background Note and Country Reports on Human Rights Practices and International Religious Freedom Report 2004." Available online. URL: http://www.state.gov/. Accessed on September 26, 2005.

SECONDARY SOURCES
Alejandro Silva Bascuñan, *Tratado de Derecho Constitucional.* 2d ed. Santiago: Editorial Jurídica de Chile, 2003.
Enrique Navarro Beltrán, *Veinte años de la Constitución chilena.* Santiago; Ediar-Conosur, 2001.
Bureau of Public Affairs, U.S. Department of State, "Background Note and Country Reports on Human Rights Practices and International Religious Freedom Report 2004." Available online. URL: http://www.state.gov/. Accessed on September 1, 2005.
José Luis Cea, *Tratado de la Constitución Chilena.* Santiago: Pontificia Universidad Católica de Santiago, 2003.
Enrique Evans de la Cuadra, *Los derechos constitucionales.* Santiago; Editorial Jurídica de Chile, 1999.

Alan Bronfman

CHINA

At-a-Glance

OFFICIAL NAME
People's Republic of China

CAPITAL
Beijing

POPULATION
1,300,000,000, not including Hong Kong, Macau, and Taiwan (January 6, 2005 est.)

SIZE
3,706,581 sq. mi. (9,600,000 sq. km)

LANGUAGES
Chinese

RELIGIONS
Not affiliated 82–86%, Christian 0.77%, Muslim 1.4%, Buddhist 8%, Official Catholic Church 0.4%, Unofficial Vatican-affiliated Catholic Church 0.4–0.8%, Registered Protestant 0.8–1.2%, Protestant House Church 2.4–6.5%

NATIONAL OR ETHNIC COMPOSITION
56 ethnic groups: Han 91.59%, others (including Hui, Mongolians, Tibetans) 8.41%

DATE OF INDEPENDENCE OR CREATION
October 1, 1949

TYPE OF GOVERNMENT
Republic

TYPE OF STATE
Unitary state

TYPE OF LEGISLATURE
National People's Congress

DATE OF CONSTITUTION
December 4, 1982

DATE OF LAST AMENDMENT
March 14, 2004

According to the Chinese constitution, all the power of the People's Republic of China belongs to the people themselves, and the framework by which people exercise their power are the National People's Congress and its local counterparts on every level. The Chinese People's Congress system is different from the parliament in the three-branch government systems found in Western countries because it is a decision-making and executive organization (*yixingheyi*) as well as a legislature.

The National People's Congress is a full-fledged constitutional body with comprehensive power. Not only does it enjoy legislative authority, but it also has the power to create administrative organs and judicial and military machinery on the national level. Moreover, these governing bodies are responsible to and supervised by the National People's Congress.

China is a unitary state. There is but one constitution and one legal system; Hong Kong and Macao, however, enjoy their own independent legal system since returning to China in 1997 and 1999. The division of power between the national and the local governments is in accordance with the principle of unified national leadership with a certain degree of activism on the side of the local government.

The Chinese constitution has recently been playing a more important role in national life. Citizens are paying more attention to their constitutional rights. There has been, however, only one precedent of a court's invoking a provision of the constitution as a source of authority (the Shandong Higher Court, in a ruling approved by the Supreme Court in 1999). There has never been a constitutionality suit in a Chinese court. Only the standing committee of the National People's Congress has the authority to interpret the constitution. It also has the power to review the legitimacy of national and local administrative regulations and of local statutes.

The presidency is part of the supreme state power; it acts with the standing committee of the National People's Congress as head of the state. The major function of the presidency is to represent the country to the outside world. The national executive is the State Council, with the prime minister as its head. The prime minister is accountable to the National People's Congress and its standing committee. The congress representatives are elected indirectly by the voters. No official has ever been elected directly by the people.

The party system in China is a multiparty cooperative system led by the Communist Party. The Communist Party of China is the ruling party; the other parties are auxiliary. The Chinese People's Political Consulting Conference coordinates the various parties under Communist direction.

Religious freedom is granted by the constitution to Chinese citizens. Normal religious activities are protected by the government. Religious organizations and religious affairs cannot be dominated by foreign influences.

The Chinese economy has been a socialist market economy since 1992. The amendments to the constitution of the People's Republic of China, adopted at the First Session of the Eighth National People's Congress on March 29, 1993, specify: "The state practices a socialist market economy. . . . The state shall enhance economic legislation and improve macro-control of the economy. . . . The state shall, in accordance with the law, prohibit disturbance of the socioeconomic order by any organization or individual." In this way, the establishment of a lawful standardized system for guaranteeing the smooth construction of a socialist market economic structure and setting up a lawful order for free and fair market competition have been put on the agenda.

CONSTITUTIONAL HISTORY

China had been a centralized empire since 221 B.C.E. It never evolved ideas of freedom, democracy, and constitutionalism. Constitutions were established in modern China as weapons for saving the country from foreign invaders and as a democratic mask by dictators and not as an instrument to prevent the abuse of government power or to protect human rights.

The idea of a constitution was transplanted from the West. In the face of the high-tech warships and artillery of Western countries, China had to learn the skills to survive attacks by its enemies. The Chinese people gradually understood the real source of Western strength—not sophisticated technology, as they first thought, or the Western political system, as they later believed. It was the culture as a whole that made the West advanced. The constitutional idea was part of the deepening but painful process of "finding the truth from the West."

Constitutional history in modern China can be viewed as a series of texts published by successive governments. More deeply, this history represented a process of continuous study of Western constitutional culture and theory. Implanting the constitutional spirit in Chinese culture is still a tough task in China today.

In the late Qing dynasty (1644–1911), the very existence and legitimacy of the Manchu regime, which had ruled all of China since 1681, were being challenged by democratic revolutionary activity, including assassinations, led by Dr. Sun Yat-sen (1866–1925). At the same time, the Western powers were urging the acceptance of constitutionalism. Foreigners refused to be ruled by Chinese law, which they condemned as cruel, and introduced a special jurisdiction for themselves instead. The need to remove the stigma of this loss of judicial sovereignty fueled the legal transformation of modern China.

The Qing government sent official delegations to the leading powers such as Great Britain, Germany, and Japan to study their constitutions. On the basis of their reports, the government decided to imitate monarchical constitutionalism. In 1908, the Royal Constitutional Outlines (*qinding xianfa dagang*) were published; it was the first constitution ever made in China. As the main goal was to retain power for the royal family, the nine-article constitution amounted to a declaration of the emperor's rights. For example, the first article stipulated that "the Qing emperor rules over the Qing empire forever with everlasting honor." The 14 articles concerning the rights and duties of the subjects existed only as an appendix to the Royal Constitutional Outlines. In 1911, the government issued the 19 Important Credenda (*zhongda xintiao shijiutiao*), a constitutional document with stronger limits on the state but too late to save the dynasty from overthrow that same year.

The revolutionary movement that had begun in the late Qing Empire resulted in the establishment of a modern democratic government by the end of 1911. The revolutionary government promulgated the Governmental Organization Outlines of the Republic of China (*zhonghua minguo linshizhengfu zuzhi dagang*). This document set up a governing structure modeled after the United States; the Chinese provinces declaring independence from the Manchus (who were foreigners from Manchuria) viewed themselves as similar to the American colonial states forming a union in 1776. Four months later, having to yield power to Yuan Shikai (1859–1916), a sophisticated and powerful politician, the acting president, Sun Yat-sen, managed to legislate the Transitional Covenantal Constitution of the Republic of China (*zhonghua minguo linshi yuefa*), which changed the presidential system into a cabinet system. The difference between the presidential system (Dagang) and the cabinet system (Yuefa) mirrored the troubling process of modern Chinese constitutionalism.

Yuan Shikai and powerful regional warlords led post-Qing China through a turbulent era with ceaseless changes of governments. Each new regime promulgated its own constitution as a badge of legitimacy. For example, in October 1923, Caokun assumed the presidency by bribing and intimidating the congress members, and the Constitution of the Republic of China (*zhonghua minguo xianfa*) was immediately published to make this administration appear legal. This document was the first formal constitution as such in China. It restored the cabinet system and made local rule a national policy to appease the warlords.

Chiang Kai-shek succeeded Sun Yat-sen as the leader of a nationalist revolution that put an end to the war-lords' separatist regimes. The new nationalist government took the founding father Sun Yat-sen's political theory as its constitutional foundation. Sun had foreseen that the nationalist revolution would go through three successive stages—the military, the disciplinary, and the constitutional; the Nationalist Party was to lead in the first two periods and return governing power to the people in the third. Sun believed that the people were ignorant and had to be taught to exercise power. Chiang Kai-shek sought to extend the disciplinary period as long as possible, while the Communists challenged it vehemently.

Sun Yat-sen divided the governing power into five, rather than three, branches. In addition to the three familiar in the West, he added the examination power and the supervising power, following traditional Chinese political wisdom. Adhering to this constitutional theory, the Nationalist Party began a comprehensive legislative program in 1928, topped in 1947 with its Constitution of the Republic of China (*zhonghua minguo xianfa*), which is still in effect in Taiwan today. It granted comprehensive rights to the people, but it did not stop Chiang Kai-shek from taking absolute power.

The Nationalists lost power because of their notoriously corrupt government and their failure to defeat the Communists on the battlefields. In 1949, the Communist Party completely abolished the Nationalist legal system without providing a new one to take its place. Instead, the party's ever-changing policies have served to direct the civil and political life of China ever since. The lack of a coherent legal system has still not been rectified.

The Communist Party began issuing constitutional legislation in its revolutionary years. Its first such instrument was the Constitutional Outlines of the China Soviet Republic (*zhonghua suweiai gongheguo xianfa dagang*), adopted in 1931. It declared that power belongs to the working class and the masses. The 1954 constitution of the People's Republic of China (*zhonghua renmin gongheguo xianfa*), issued after the Communist leader Mao Zedong (1893–1976) and his comrades took over power in mainland China in 1949, imitated the 1936 Russian constitution, with a long preamble praising the party's glorious history of winning independence for the Chinese people from feudalism, capitalism, and imperialism. According to this constitution, the sovereign body of China is the People's Congress and its Standing Committee.

The current constitution was adopted in 1982 and had been amended several times, an indication of dramatic changes in the political and economic situations ever since the open door policy initiated by Deng Xiaoping. Dramatic political and economic change has occurred since 1979. Human rights issues loom large as a result of economic growth in an international context. Following a zigzag process, the constitutional amendments by 2004 added formal guarantees for civil rights and private property in a socialist legal framework.

FORM AND IMPACT OF THE CONSTITUTION

China has a written constitution that claims to be the supreme law. Any statute, administrative law, or local by-law is null and void if it is contrary to the constitution. No constitutional body other than the standing Committee of the National People's Congress exists, however, to protect this exalted legal status.

The constitution has undergone drastic changes since its enactment in 1954, in part because the economic system had to be changed repeatedly to adapt to the changing policies of the Communist Party. Besides, the constitution has been regarded as the embodiment of the will of the ruling party, and this will keeps changing. As a convention, amendments originate in the party and are always passed.

The preamble of the constitution says that "the people of all nationalities, all state organs, the armed forces, all political parties and public organizations and all enterprises and institutions in the country must take the Constitution as the basic standard of conduct, and they have the duty to uphold the dignity of the Constitution and ensure its implementation." Everybody has a responsibility, but nobody will take it. Without specifying a procedure to review violations of the constitution, the constitution will remain largely a ceremonial document.

The constitution assigns no special status to international law and treaties.

BASIC ORGANIZATIONAL STRUCTURE

The People's Republic of China is a unitary multinational state composed of 23 provinces, four municipalities directly under the central government, five national autonomous areas, and two special administrative regions (Hong Kong and Macau). Taiwan is declared an inseparable part of China in the constitution. All of these components must follow the leadership of the central government, but they are encouraged to show some originality and initiative. The individual components are granted varying powers by the constitution and the central government.

On the provincial level, there are three different kinds of administrative units. First, 23 ordinary provinces and four municipalities, all with a Han Chinese majority, relate to the central government in accordance with the principle of democratic centralism. They have no autonomous power, but their people's congresses and their standing committees may adopt local regulations, although they all report to the Standing Committee of the National People's Congress, and they must not contravene the constitution, the statutes, and the central administrative rules and regulations.

The second kind of provincial administration is formed by the five national autonomous areas (Inner Mongolia,

Guangxi Zhuang, Ningxia Hui, Xinjiang Uygur, and Ti- bet), established for the formal purpose of "strengthening socialist relations of equality, unity, and mutual assistance among the people of all nationalities." They enjoy more autonomous power than the ordinary provinces in areas such as economic regulation, finances, and culture. For ex- ample, they may "independently administer educational, scientific, cultural, public health, and physical culture affairs in their respective areas, protect and accumulate the cultural heritage of the nationalities and work for the development and flourishing of their cultures" (Article 119). In short, they have power to enact specific regula- tions in light of the political, economic, and cultural char- acteristics of the nationality or nationalities in the areas concerned. However, these regulations must be approved by the Standing Committee of the National People's Con- gress. In addition to the provincial autonomous regions, there are autonomous prefectures and counties.

The third kind of administrative units are special administrative regions, namely, Hong Kong and Macau. They were established to maintain the prosperity and stability of those areas in the light of their history and realities while still achieving national unity and territo- rial integrity. The legal reference is Article 31 of the con- stitution, the principle of "one country, two systems," which means that the socialist system and policies will not be practiced in those regions. The special adminis- trative regions are responsible to the State Council for the record, but they exercise a high degree of autonomy and enjoy executive, legislative, and independent judi- cial power. The central government levies no taxes in those regions.

These two areas each have their own basic law, but the power of interpretation is vested in the Stand- ing Committee of the National People's Congress. The major interest of the central government in Hong Kong and Macau is national sovereignty. The central gov- ernment runs their foreign and defense affairs. It also appoints their chief executives and other principal ex- ecutive officials.

The unitary system of China has its roots in the cen- tralist tradition going back to 221 B.C.E. when Qin Shi- huang (259–210 B.C.E.), the first feudal emperor, united a war-stricken country. "The Great Union" (Dayitong) has been widely accepted as a political and cultural ideal and has become a part of the political psychology of the Chi- nese people. In fact, a powerful central government may better allocate national resources to common economic objectives, but it may also prevent experimental initia- tives on the regional and local levels. Regional autonomy faces a great challenge in a totalitarian, centralized frame- work.

On the other hand, China's history of multitiered ad- ministration also goes back to the Qin Empire (221–206 B.C.E.). Today, provinces and national autonomous areas have their subordinate prefectures and counties, and coun- ties are composed of towns (zhen) and townships (xiang).

The various administrative levels tend to be subor- dinate to the level above in hierarchical fashion. Accord-

ing to the constitution the chief executive on every level is elected and recalled only by the people's congress in that jurisdiction; in fact, the officials are responsible only to their counterparts on the higher level. To this day, no prime minister, governor, or mayor has ever been directly elected by the people in China.

In accordance with the constitution, residents' com- mittees and villagers' committees are established among residents of urban neighborhoods and rural villages and are meant to be mass organizations at the grassroots level. Their chairpersons, vice chairpersons, and members are elected by the residents. They are the only cadres (but not government officials as such) the people have the right to elect directly.

LEADING CONSTITUTIONAL PRINCIPLES

Throughout the history of the People's Republic of China, the formulation of constitutional principles has varied considerably. For example, the 1954 constitution took socialism and democracy as its essential principles. It fo- cused on state or collective ownership. It proclaimed that the state would eradicate exploitation and poverty and build a prosperous and happy socialist country. It upheld the ideology of Marxism-Leninism, purportedly demo- cratic to the masses and dictatorial to the enemy. It has nothing to do with separation of powers and checks and balances.

The current 1982 constitution and its amendments accept such cardinal principles as people's sovereignty and representative democracy. In regard to the distribu- tion of power, this constitution embodies the principle of democratic centralism. The constitution says that the state protects the basic rights of the Chinese citizens and practices the socialist rule of law.

According to the constitution, the National People's Congress is the basis of the political system. "All power in the People's Republic of China belongs to the people. The organs through which the people exercise state power are the National People's Congress and the local people's congresses at different levels" (Article 2).

The National People's Congress and its local counter- parts have been gaining momentum and power in an on- going process of constitutional reform. This has become apparent in cases in which they help the judiciary render justice in particular cases. Such power, however, may also be an excuse for interfering with the judicial process.

According to the principle of democratic centralism, the people create the people's congresses at different levels through general elections. These congresses then install the administrative and judicial organs, which are under the supervision of and are responsible to the congresses. Unified leadership of the central authorities is empha- sized, although the initiative and enthusiasm of the local authorities are encouraged. The people's congresses not only make legislative decisions but are also in charge of putting these decisions into practice. Thus, the people's congresses have in fact both legislative and executive power. The supremacy of the people's congresses over the administrative authorities exists at least in the legal text.

The principle of the socialist rule of law was introduced in the constitution in 1999 as an amendment, which states: "The People's Republic of China [rules] in accordance with the law and build[s] a socialist country of law," and "No organization or individual may enjoy the privilege of being above the Constitution and the law" (Article 5). Nevertheless, the lack of judicial independence has been a stumbling block on the way to the rule of law in China.

A new amendment in 2004, which declares that "the State respects and preserves human rights" (Article 33), can be regarded as another constitutional principle. That language is to some degree a response to Western criticism of China's human rights record. More importantly, China stresses "collective human rights," that is, the rights of the whole people to survive and develop. The language of rights is also checked by an emphasis on the citizen's duties under the constitution.

The current constitution takes "four cardinal principles" as its basic guidelines; they are proclaimed in the preamble and can be found throughout the text. These principles are Marxism-Leninism and the thought of Mao Zedong, the leadership of the Communist Party, the people's democratic dictatorship, and the socialist road. In the amendments of 1999 and 2004, the theory of the former party leader Deng Xiaoping and the idea of the "Three Represents" were added to reflect the changing character of socialist theory. The "Three Represents" are that the Communist Party of China should represent the development trend of advanced productive forces, the orientation of advanced culture, and the fundamental interests of the overwhelming majority of the people in China.

CONSTITUTIONAL BODIES

The national constitutional organs consist of the National People's Congress and its Standing Committee, the president of the People's Republic of China, the State Council and its ministries and commissions, the Central Military Commission, and judicial organs such as the Supreme People's Court and the Supreme People's Procuratorate.

The National People's Congress and Its Standing Committee (the Parliament of China)

The National People's Congress is the highest organ of state power. The legislative power of the state resides in the congress and its Standing Committee. According to the constitution, the congress creates and holds accountable all the other central governing bodies.

The congress exercises the following functions and powers (Article 62): to amend and to enforce the constitution; to enact and amend basic statutes concerning criminal offenses, civil affairs, the state organs, and other matters; to elect the president, the vice president, and other top officials; to approve the national economic and social development plan and its implementation; to approve the state budget and its implementation report; to decide on questions of war and peace; and to exercise such other functions and powers as the highest organ of state power should exercise.

The National People's Congress is composed of deputies elected indirectly through several levels from the various provinces and other high-level administrative divisions and from the armed forces. The approximately 3,000 deputies all serve only part-time during their five-year terms; they convene once a year for less than 20 days. The Standing Committee is the permanent body of the congress and exercises almost all powers when the congress is not in plenary session.

The Standing Committee is elected by the National People's Congress. Its members may not hold any office in any of the administrative, judicial, or other organs of the state. The constitution authorizes the Standing Committee to perform nearly all the functions of the congress, except that its changes to existing laws may not contravene the basic principles of these statutes. It also interprets statutes and supervises the work of the State Council, the central military commission, the Supreme People's Court, and the Supreme People's Procuratorate, among others (Article 67).

The President

The president acts as the head of state and represents the country to the outside world. According to the constitution, citizens who have the right to vote and to run for elections and who have reached the age of 45 are eligible to be president or vice president (Article 79). Both are elected by the National People's Congress. Their terms of office are the same as that of the congress, and they can serve no more than two consecutive terms. In recent years the constitutional convention that the general secretary (head) of the Communist Party has also been the state president has developed.

The State Council

The State Council is the central administration, the executive body of the People's National Congress. It is the highest organ of state administration. The council is composed of the prime minister, the vice prime ministers, state councilors, ministers in charge of ministries or commissions, the auditor general, and the secretary general. The prime minister is nominated by the state president and is formally appointed by the National People's Congress. All the other members of the State Council are nominated by the prime minister and formally appointed by the National People's Congress. Members of the State Council serve five-year terms; the prime minister, vice prime ministers, and state councilors can serve only two consecutive terms.

The prime minister has overall responsibility for the State Council. The ministers have overall responsibility for the ministries or commissions under their charge. The State Council enjoys comprehensive power, from adopting administrative measures to deciding on a declaration of a state of emergency. The State Council can enact administrative rules and regulations, which may not be contravened by any local people's congress or local executive.

Since 1949, the executive branch has played the critical role in the government, especially during the so-called Cultural Revolution (1966–69) when the people's congress system and the judiciary were put aside. With the growing importance of the parliament and the judiciary, the State Council and other executive branches are not as prominent as before, although they still wield huge power without sufficient checks and balances.

The Central Military Commission

The central military commission has the supreme authority in China's military. However, it has not been fully defined in the constitution. It is composed of a chairperson, vice chairpersons, and ordinary members. The National People's Congress elects the chair of the central military commission and, upon nomination by the chairperson, decides on the choice of all other members of the central military commission. The term of office is five years, the same as that of the National People's Congress. The chairperson is responsible to the congress and its Standing Committee.

Historically, the true leadership of the military resides in the Communist Party. The 1982 constitution appears to assign control of the military to the state, but, in fact, the commission shares the same personnel as its counterpart body in the party.

The Lawmaking Process

The legislative power resides in the National People's Congress and its Standing Committee.

The following bodies have the power to propose bills: the presidium of the congress, the Standing Committee, committees of the congress created for a specific issue, the State Council, the central military commission, the Supreme People's Court, the Supreme People's Procuratorate, and any group of 30 congresspersons. The Standing Committee is in charge of the daily routine of legislation. Its law subcommittee does most of the preparation of bills, including writing and editing drafts. A draft usually has to be reviewed at least three times within the Standing Committee before it is submitted to the congress.

According to the 2000 Legislative Law, any governmental bodies may ask the Standing Committee to review any statute or regulation that it believes is unconstitutional or illegal. Similar requests from civil organizations, state-owned enterprises, and private citizens are referred to the law committee and can be assigned to the appropriate ad hoc committee if deemed necessary.

Statutes passed by the National People's Congress or its Standing Committee are promulgated by the state president.

The Judiciary

There are two kinds of judicial organs in China: people's courts and people's procuratorates. By law, judicial organs are independent of the executive, responsible only to the people's congress and the standing committee at the same level. Unfortunately, the judiciary is created by and reports to that congress and thus does not enjoy independence in the sense that the judiciary does in the West.

The common courts are organized into four tiers, corresponding to the respective administrative layers. In addition to the common courts, there are special courts, such as the military and admiralty law courts. The president of the Supreme People's Court is elected by the National People's Congress and serves no more than two consecutive terms. Local chief judges are elected by the local congresses.

According to the People's Courts Organizing Law, all citizens who have the right to vote and to run for election and who have reached the age of 23 are eligible to be judges or presidents of the people's courts. However, a 1993 amendment requests that the judges have professional legal knowledge. The poor qualification of the judiciary has long been a serious problem in China.

According to the constitution, courts are not subject to interference by administrative organs, public organizations, or individuals. But the individual judges have little authority, especially in view of the powers of the judicial committee in every court. The committee reviews any verdict or ruling that the head of the court finds in error in matters of fact or law. The head of the court and the committee can change any ruling they regard as wrong.

The people's congresses have legal power to supervise the work of the courts. In practice, they tend to interfere in particular cases. No judge has power to review the constitutionality of any law or administrative regulation; he or she may only decide whether to apply it in a particular case. When a court's interpretation of law conflicts with the interpretation of a congress, the latter prevails. For example, a judge in a Luoyang court was dismissed at the request of the Henan province people's congress when she ruled a province law invalid because it contradicted a corresponding national law.

Hong Kong and Macau retained their independent legislative and judicial powers after returning to China. However, the Standing Committee of the National People's Congress retains the power to interpret the Hong Kong Basic Law, although local courts can interpret those provisions that are within the limits of the region's autonomy. In 1999, a dispute arose between the Court of

Final Appeal for the region and the Standing Committee. The Standing Committee prevailed, leaving much doubt about Hong Kong judicial independence.

People's procuratorates are state organs for legal supervision. As are the courts, they are appointed by and accountable to the congresses. According to the constitution (Article 35), the courts, procuratorates, and public security organs must coordinate their efforts and check each other to ensure correct and effective enforcement of the law. How their coordination and their checking each other can work at the same time is still a mystery. But one point is certain: that is, that all of these branches are subordinate to the Communist Party's political and law committee of the same level. It is not easy for any of these branches to be independent.

THE ELECTION PROCESS

The constitution prescribes that, except persons deprived of political rights, all citizens who have reached the age of 18 have the right to vote in and to run for elections, regardless of nationality, race, sex, occupation, family background, religious belief, education, property status, or time of residence. The Chinese election system includes the election of the people's congresses at separate levels and the grassroots elections of the village committees.

There are direct and indirect elections for the people's congresses according to their level in the administrative hierarchy. Those at or below the county level are elected directly by their constituencies. The National People's Congress is composed of deputies elected from the high-level territorial divisions and from the armed forces. All the minority nationalities are entitled to appropriate representation. The military has its own election system. The congresses of the high-level divisions are in turn elected by the people's congresses of the next lower level.

While the Election Law takes equality as its principle, the number of deputies is determined by the Standing Committee, and the result is always a poorly balanced representation among different constituencies. Taking the ninth National People's Congress (1998–2003) as an example, one deputy represented 880,000 rural people, while another represented only 220,000 urban people, and a military deputy represented only 10,000 people. The Election Law prescribes the quota distribution principle at the lower levels. As a rule, the urban population has four times the number of deputies in proportion to the rural population.

There are no political campaigns in China. Candidates are nominated by electorates or precincts. Factors such as gender, party affiliation, and nationality weigh heavily in the selection. The qualified candidates are recognized by the election commission of each precinct five days before the election. Private citizens rivaling party officials have difficulties in passing through this stage of the election process. There is no definite rule on whether a candidate may or may not publicly address the constituency, and the voters have little access to the political opinion of the candidates. Large legal gaps give wide leeway to the local election commission or standing committee, which is in charge of the election process at each level. The election commission or the presidium of the people's congress must verify the results at each level. All the costs of elections are paid by the public purse.

POLITICAL PARTIES

A broad, patriotic, united front was one of the key political strategies of the Communist Party of China in the years before it won power and was kept alive as part of the new political structure. The system of multiparty cooperation under the leadership of the Communist Party is emphasized in the preamble of the constitution.

The leading role of the Communist Party, which is not specified in any operative constitutional article, is an omnipresent fact in Chinese political life. It has political, organizational, and intellectual components. Politically, the party's principles and policies guide the state; the constitution itself has been viewed as the legalization of the party's will. Organizationally, the party recommends officials to fill government posts. Intellectually, the party aims to indoctrinate the people with the party's political ideas. Such leadership tends to contradict the constitution's rule of law clause: "All political parties and public organizations . . . must abide by the constitution and the law" (Article 5).

The Chinese People's Political Consultative Conference embodies the party's "united front" policy. It is through this framework that the eight "democratic parties" founded before 1949 participate in politics as associate parties. They are not the party's rivals, and the conference is not a constitutional, but only a "consultative" body.

CITIZENSHIP

There are two ways to acquire Chinese citizenship: by birth and by naturalization. A person can be a Chinese citizen if at least one of his or her parents is a citizen, unless one or both parents settle abroad and the person is born abroad and acquires foreign citizenship as a result. Any person born in China whose parents have no or unknown nationality is also a citizen.

Foreign nationals or stateless persons can be naturalized if they are willing to abide by China's constitution and laws and they are near relatives of Chinese citizens, reside in China, or have other legitimate reasons. A person whose application for naturalization as a Chinese citizen has been approved cannot retain foreign citizenship. China does not recognize dual citizenship.

FUNDAMENTAL RIGHTS

Unlike the earlier Communist Chinese constitutions, the current document places the chapter on fundamental rights and duties before the chapter on the structure of the state. This puts a greater emphasis on civil rights.

In Articles 33 to 50, the constitution provides citizens with a full set of rights. Article 33 promises that all citizens are "equal before the law." An amendment was added in 2004 in response to domestic and international criticism, declaring that "the State respects and preserves human rights." This was the first time that *human rights* entered the constitutional lexicon in China.

Article 34 gives citizens the right to vote in and to run for elections when they have reached the age of 18 (except persons deprived of political rights according to law). Freedom of speech, press, association, and demonstration is provided in Article 35. According to Article 36, freedom of religious belief and "normal" religious activities are protected. Articles 37–40 declare that personal freedom and personal dignity are inviolable and prohibit unlawful search. They guarantee freedom and privacy of correspondence. The right to criticize and to make suggestions to any state organ or official is granted by Article 41, which also grants a right of compensation when citizens suffer losses through infringement of their civil rights by any state organ or official.

Articles 42–47 list the economic, social, and cultural rights, such as the right to work and to rest. Article 45 provides for a social insurance system that gives the right to material assistance from the state and society to old, ill, or disabled citizens, including disabled veterans. The blind, deaf mutes, and other disabled citizens may expect the state and society to help make arrangements for their work, livelihood, and education. The state protects the equal rights and interests of women, and maltreatment of old people, women, and children is prohibited

An amendment in 2004 made the protection of a citizen's lawful private property one of the general principles of the constitution. It is "inviolable." Expropriation or requisition of private property by the state shall take place only if it is in the public interest and in accordance with law and if compensation is provided.

The Chinese constitution provides positive rights. For example, Article 42 says that the state by using various channels creates conditions for employment, strengthens labor protection, improves working conditions, and increases remuneration for work and social benefits. Receiving an education, according to Article 46, is another positive right by which the state promotes the all-around moral, intellectual, and physical development of children and young people.

Fundamental Duties

The enumeration of positive rights appears to be attractive. However, positive rights can be a good excuse for the government to exercise enormous power over society and the economy. In addition, the constitution stresses corresponding duties, which to some degree dim the rosy color of the positive rights. For example, work and education are duties as well as rights. Work is even

characterized as being "the glorious duty of every able-bodied citizen."

Articles 52–56 specify numerous duties, such as safeguarding the unity of the country and its nationalities, abiding by the constitution and the law, keeping state secrets, protecting public property, observing labor discipline and public order, and respecting social ethics. Thus, the constitution sounds like a moral code.

Impact and Functions of Fundamental Rights

The unity of rights and duties is highlighted by the constitution. Every citizen, as Article 33 says, enjoys the rights and at the same time must perform the duties prescribed by the constitution and the law. This makes rights guarantees helpless against their greatest threat, which is state power. It remains to be seen to what extent the fundamental rights clauses in the Chinese constitution can be put into practice, given that they rarely enjoy judicial protections today.

International Human Rights Treaties

Rights in the Chinese constitution are defined mostly in terms of civil rights of citizens, not as general rights of "human beings." International human rights conventions and treaties have no definite legal position in the constitution. Since 1980, China has signed, approved, or joined 14 such conventions created by the United Nations, nine conventions passed by the International Labor Organization, three international humanitarian conventions, and 12 other international conventions and treaties concerning human rights. The Chinese government has expressed reservations against some clauses of these conventions, both some procedural and some substantive. China has also not been willing to be supervised by the international community.

In 1997, China joined the 1966 International Covenant on Economic, Social and Cultural Rights, which was approved by the National People's Congress in 2001, with the reservation of the free union clause. China also joined the 1966 International Covenant on Civil and Political Rights in 1998 but has not yet approved this covenant.

The Chinese government weighs the general human-rights principles in the context of the varying situations of different countries. It also recognizes collective human rights and gives priority to countries' rights to exist and to develop.

Limitations to Fundamental Rights

Citizens of the People's Republic of China, in exercising their freedoms and rights may not infringe upon the interests of the state, of society, of the collective, or upon the lawful freedoms and rights of other citizens (Article 51). Defining those competing interests has been a problem. The rights of citizens are easy prey of "the interests of the collective" when the latter is not clearly defined.

A few rights clauses are given special provisos, which leave the state much room for limiting freedoms. For example, the freedom of religion clause prohibits religious bodies and religious affairs from being subject to any foreign domination. However, it remains unclear what constitutes foreign domination. Similarly, while citizens are guaranteed the right to make complaints against state organs or expose them for violation of the law or dereliction of duty, it is prohibited to invent or to distort facts for the purpose of libel or a false charge (Article 41).

Some rights are effectively curbed by broad adjectives. Freedom of religion is guaranteed for *normal* religious activities; the state protects the *lawful* rights and interests of returned overseas Chinese (Article 50); *lawful* private property is inviolable (Article 13). It is the state that decides what these terms mean. Furthermore, the Chinese constitution has no "limitation-limits" clause; rights may be limited indefinitely, at least in theory. In fact, many statutes and regulations narrow the fundamental rights in the constitution. For example, the Law of Assembly and Demonstration was amended in 1989 by a strict licensing procedure. Freedom of assembly and association depends on approval by the relevant government body and on the confirmation by the civil registration bureau, according to the 1998 Regulation of Social Groups Registration. The 1997 Publishing Regulation provides for prepublication censorship and after-publication punishment.

ECONOMY

Articles 6–18 specify that socialist public ownership of the means of production is the basis of the economic system, that is, ownership by the whole people and collective ownership by the working people. The state-owned economy is established as the leading force in the national economy. Collective ownership by the working people and the lawful rights and interests of urban and rural economic collectives are also protected or encouraged as sectors of the socialist economy.

Mineral resources, waters, forests, mountains, grassland, unreclaimed land, beaches, and other natural resources are owned by the state or by collectives. Land in the cities is owned by the state. Land in the rural and suburban areas is owned by collectives, except those portions that belong to the state.

Amendments to the constitution have been focused on the economic system since 1988. In an amendment that year, private economic activity is permitted within the limits prescribed by law. The right to the use of land may be transferred according to law. The socialist planned economy was dethroned, and the socialist market economy was proclaimed in 1993.

As for private property, the constitution in 1982 tolerated only lawful personal income, savings, homes, and right to inheritance. An amendment in 2004 declared that a citizen's lawful private property is inviolable. The state had long been expropriating and requisitioning land. Now, the state can do so only in the public interest and in accordance with the provisions of law, and compensation is clearly required.

The right to social insurance, social relief, and medical health services was explicitly added to the constitution in the 2004 amendments.

Workers and staff in state-owned enterprises and collective economic organizations may practice democratic management through their congresses, and in other ways in accordance with the law, their unions are branches of the local government-controlled unions. There is no right to strike. On the contrary, heroic socialist labor is to be emulated and promoted, and voluntary labor is encouraged.

RELIGIOUS COMMUNITIES

Freedom of religious belief is guaranteed, but the free exercise of religion is not explicitly recognized. In effect, since religion is a matter of the mind, it is better to keep it in one's mind. Normal religious activities are protected in Article 36; the term *normal* allows activities to be limited by the state. Article 36 specifically prohibits any foreign domination of religious bodies or religious affairs. The historical background, according to the state, is that religion had been used as an instrument of foreign invasion in China.

No one, the article warns, may make use of religion to engage in activities that disrupt public order, impair the health of citizens, or interfere with the educational system. This statement causes religious activities to be viewed as especially dangerous to public order and education.

Religious association is also limited by administrative regulations. The 2005 Regulation on Religious Affairs (*zongjiao shiwu tiaoli*), the first national law on this subject, requires religious bodies and sites to be registered in accordance with the 1998 Regulation on the Registration of Social Associations. Any religious association or site is legal only when licensed by the qualified religious office and civil registration agency. This double-licensing system makes legalization of nonconformist religious bodies difficult. Traditional religions such as Buddhism, Taoism, Islam, Roman Catholicism, and Protestantism are officially recognized. Their adherents were formed into state-backed patriotic organizations to promote the Party's religious policy. Those religious groups that are not affiliated with the government-sanctioned religious bodies face interference and closure by law-enforcement bodies. Space does exist for civil religious activities. It is the highly organized religious groups that are the primary targets of state control.

State-backed religious bodies and sites are encouraged by positioning their leaders in people's congresses and by granting financial aid and tax exemptions. They are in charge of leading their adherents to adapt to socialist society.

MILITARY DEFENSE AND STATE OF EMERGENCY

National defense in China is the task of the armed forces, the constitution states. Article 29 aims to revolutionize, modernize, and regularize the armed forces to strengthen their national defense capability.

Defending the homeland is described by the constitution as the sacred obligation of every citizen, and it is the honorable duty of citizens to perform military service or join the militia in accordance with the law. No conscientious objection is recognized; only the disabled are excused. In addition, those who are deprived of political rights cannot enter the military.

The National Defense Law puts the Communist Party in charge of the armed forces, which include the active duty and reserve corps of the People's Liberation Army, the People's Armed Police Corps, and the militia. The armed forces are given responsibility for strengthening the national defense, resisting aggression, defending the homeland, safeguarding the people's peaceful labor, and participating in national reconstruction.

The armed forces have always played an important role in national political life. They claimed 268 members of 2,985 (8.98 percent) in the National People's Congress of 2004, a rather disproportionate representation.

The Central Military Commission has final say in making military law. It need not report its laws to the Standing Committee of the National People's Congress. Thus, the constitutionality of military law is beyond the power of the National People's Congress.

The constitution and the national defense law both affirm that China adheres to an independent foreign policy as well as to the five principles of mutual respect for sovereignty and territorial integrity, mutual nonaggression, noninterference in internal affairs, equality and mutual benefit, and peaceful coexistence in diplomatic relations and economic and cultural exchange with other countries. This is the basis for China's military relationships with other countries. China proclaims support for the international community in maintaining world and regional peace and in its efforts to resolve international disputes and encourage disarmament.

It is the National People's Congress alone that has the power to make war and peace. The Standing Committee of the National People's Congress also decides whether to call a state of emergency throughout the country or in particular provinces. The State Council has the responsibility to call emergencies in more localized areas. However, the state president officially proclaims a state of emergency or war and issues mobilization orders.

The 1996 Martial Law Act declared that the state shall enforce martial law when insurgents or riots threaten the nation's unity, security, or public order. Every constitutional and legal right can be withdrawn in that circumstance, and personal freedom can be strictly limited.

AMENDMENTS TO THE CONSTITUTION

Frequent amendments characterize China's constitutional history since 1949. The 1982 constitution was a complete rewrite; since then, amendments have become the route to change the document. As of 2004, there had been four changes with a total of 31 amendments. The primary reason there were so many amendments was the dramatic change in the economic system. More than four amendments relate to socialist public ownership. The private sector of the economy is now far more tolerated, and private property has become "inviolable," although it still is not "sacred," as is public property. Compensation has to be given when private property is expropriated by the state.

Human rights have been the subject of some other amendments. In 2004, the state explicitly promised to respect and preserve human rights.

Amending the constitution is not as difficult as the strict procedure might indicate. Every proposed amendment succeeded in recent years. Amendments can be proposed only by the Standing Committee of the National People's Congress or by a group of more than one-fifth of the deputies; a two-thirds majority of all the deputies to the congress is necessary for adoptions.

PRIMARY SOURCES

Constitution in English. Available online. URL: http://www.oefre.unibe.ch/law/icl/ch00000_.html. Accessed on September 2, 2005.

Constitution in Chinese. Available online. URL: http://www.legalinfo.gov.cn/. Accessed on September 27, 2005.

SECONDARY SOURCES

Lin, Feng, *Constitutional Law in China*. Hong Kong: Sweet and Maxwell Asia, 2000.

Thomas Benjamin Ginsburg, "Growing Constitutions Judicial Review in the New Democracies." Ph.D. diss., University of California, Berkeley, 1999.

Guobin Zhu, *The Legal System of the PRC*. Hong Kong: Sweet and Maxwell Asia, 2002.

Wei Luo and Joan Liu, "A Complete Research Guide to the Laws of the People's Republic of China (PRC)." Available online. URL: http://www.llrx.com/features/prc.htm. Accessed on July 20, 2005.

United Nations, "Core Document Forming Part of the Reports of States Parties: China" (HRI/CORE/1/Add.21/Rev.2), 6 November 2001. Available online. URL: http://www.unhchr.ch/tbs/doc.nsf. Accessed on August 12, 2005.

Zhang Shoudong and Zhou Qingfeng

COLOMBIA

At-a-Glance

OFFICIAL NAME
Republic of Colombia

CAPITAL
Bogotá

POPULATION
45,325,261 (2004 est.)

SIZE
44,083 sq. mi. (114,174 sq. km)

LANGUAGES
Spanish

RELIGIONS
Catholic 95%, unaffiliated or other 5%

NATIONAL OR ETHNIC COMPOSITION
Mestizo 58%, white 20%, Mulatto 14%, black 4%,
Indian 1%, other 3%

DATE OF INDEPENDENCE OR CREATION
July 20, 1810

TYPE OF GOVERNMENT
Presidential democracy

TYPE OF STATE
Unitary state

TYPE OF LEGISLATURE
Bicameral parliament

DATE OF CONSTITUTION
July 4, 1991

DATE OF LAST AMENDMENT
July 27, 2005

Colombia's Constitution begins with declaring that the state is founded on the principle of the "Social Rule of Law." Colombia is organized in the form of a unitary republic, decentralized, with autonomy of its territorial entities. It is democratic, participative, and pluralist. Moreover, it is based on the respect for human dignity, on work, on solidarity of the people, and on the primacy of the general interest. The legislative, executive, and judicial powers are clearly separated but collaborate to perform their functions. The National Electoral Council independently supervises the election of government officials. Political decisions can also be made by referendums, popular consultations, and other forms of political participation.

Personal rights hold supremacy within the constitutional order. They must be respected by all authorities, and their protection is guaranteed by the courts, including a Constitutional Court.

Religious freedom is guaranteed, although the presence of a strong Roman Catholic tradition has justified the existence of a treaty with the Holy See.

CONSTITUTIONAL HISTORY

During the Spanish colonial period, the Colombian territory was under the jurisdiction of the Audiencia del Nuevo Reino de Granada (Court of the New Kingdom of Granada), located at the city of Santa Fe from 1549, and later of the Virreinato de la Nueva Granada (Vice Kingdom of the New Granada). The latter was established in 1717, abolished in 1723, and reestablished in 1739.

Between 1763 and 1830, Europe lost a substantial part of its colonies in the Western Hemisphere. The invasion of Spain by the French emperor Napoléon in 1808 produced a legitimacy crisis in Spain and in the American colonies. At first, the new Spanish government was accepted. However, tensions created by the lack of representation of the *criollo* (the descendents of the colonists) part of the population and by excessive taxation led to the declaration of independence on July 20, 1810. A new government was established, and the first constitutions were passed.

In the independence period (1810–19), the provinces issued their own constitutions. This was a time of great naiveté, sometimes called the *patria boba* (dumb nation). The population was divided between those guided by Camilo Torres, who defended federalism, and those who proposed a centralized government, guided by the champion of human rights Antonio Nariño.

The second era of Colombian constitutional history is known as Gran Colombia (1819–30). After winning the Battle of Boyacá on August 7, 1819, Simón Bolívar, the liberator, proclaimed guidelines for the constitutional organization of the state in the Carta de Angostura (Angostura letter). This was the basis for the 1821 constitution. Bolívar declared a dictatorship in 1828. Another constitution was issued in 1830, but it never gained any practical significance; Venezuela and Ecuador had declared their independence, and the Great Colombia was divided.

Nueva Granada (1830–58) was the third constitutional period. An 1832 constitution followed the model of the 1830 text and was moderately centralist. In 1843, a more conservative and centralist constitution was passed. By the end of the 1840s, the Liberal and Conservative Parties had taken shape; they were to become a landmark of Colombian history throughout the following 140 years. Once the Liberal Party entered office, a series of reforms took place: the abolition of monopolies, of Indian reservations, and of slavery. All vestiges of the colonial period were ended. The 1853 constitution had a profederal inclination and emphasized municipal organization.

The next period (1858–86) was marked by federalism—the 1858 constitution, attributed to Florentino González, established a federal state. Tomás Cipriano Mosquera led a successful revolt (1860–62) that resulted in the Pacto de la Unión (Union Pact) of 1861. It was celebrated as a provisional constitution that legitimated Mosquera as president. In 1863, the radically liberal constitution of Rionegro was issued. It did not mention God in its preamble, it abolished the death penalty, and it limited the presidential term to two years. However, the amendment process was so complicated that adjustments became impractical, and the system eventually failed. There were more than 50 provincial and two national civil wars during this period of only 28 years.

The fifth period of Colombian constitutional history (1886 to today) has been characterized by a unitary republic with administrative decentralization. The 1886 constitution, attributed to Miguel Antonio Caro, was a compromise between the moderate factions of the two traditional parties, determined to overcome the crisis of the previous decades. Inspired by the constitutions of 1830 and 1843, it joined political centralism with administrative decentralization. As did the model of Bolívar, it strengthened presidential powers, established Catholicism as the official religion of the country, included economic protection, and created the central bank. After many amendments, the document was replaced in 1991, by which time the old structures were undermined by the difficulty of reform, armed uprisings, an incomplete peace process, and the corruption and violence introduced by the drug cartels.

FORM AND IMPACT OF THE CONSTITUTION

The 1991 constitution has 380 articles and 60 transitory articles. It has been amended 18 times, and further amendments are under consideration.

Foreign relations are to be based on national sovereignty, respect for self-determination and the principles of international law, and the integration of Latin America and the Caribbean. International human rights treaties approved by Congress take precedence over ordinary laws. The treaties and the laws that implement them are reviewed by the Constitutional Court before ratification to make sure they comply with the constitution.

The constitution is the supreme legal document, and all other laws and rules must comply with it. Human rights hold a supreme position; the constitution includes a complete system of procedures for their effective guarantee. The governmental structure is explicitly designed to render service to people.

The values established by the constitution are life, human dignity, coexistence, work, justice, equality, knowledge, liberty, solidarity, peace, and the supremacy of the public interest within a legal, democratic, and participative system that guarantees fairness.

BASIC ORGANIZATIONAL STRUCTURE

Colombia is a politically centralized nation with administrative decentralization and autonomy of territorial entities. The territory is divided into 32 departments and more than 1,100 municipalities with administrative autonomy. The municipalities have popularly elected mayors in charge of rendering public services. The departments have governors, who are also elected popularly and implement and coordinate the policies laid down by the national government.

LEADING CONSTITUTIONAL PRINCIPLES

The first 10 articles of the constitution establish its basic principles. According to constitutional jurisprudence, they have a higher status than the rest of the document and must be complied with by all state authorities. They proclaim Colombia to be a unitary, decentralized republic with autonomy of its territorial entities, democratic, participative, and pluralist. The clause calling for a welfare state has been used by the Constitutional Court to build its interpretation of the entire constitution.

The purpose of the state is to serve the community, promote general prosperity, guarantee duties and rights, enable participation, defend national independence, ensure peaceful coexistence, and maintain justice.

Sovereignty resides with the people. They can adopt decisions directly, through referendums, plebiscites, and popular consults. They can also remove mayors, governors, and national authorities from office.

The nation recognizes the primacy of individual rights and protects the family as a basic institution. The constitution has been called person-oriented, with the human being is at its center.

The principle of responsibility establishes that people are free as long as they do not infringe on the constitution or the law. Public officials also are responsible for the exercise of their functions.

Colombian ethnic and cultural diversity is recognized. This principle is a great advance compared with the previous constitution, which conceived the nation as a homogeneous entity without recognition of the existence of black and indigenous communities.

CONSTITUTIONAL BODIES

The main bodies included in the constitution are the president of the republic; the Congress, which is divided into two chambers: the Senate and the Chamber of Representatives; and the Judiciary. The crucial Constitutional Court impacts the activities of both president and Congress.

The President

The president is the head of state, head of government, supreme administrative authority, and supreme commander of the armed forces. He or she freely appoints and dismisses cabinet ministers, is in charge of the direction of foreign relations, and opens and closes sessions of Congress. The president signs, promulgates, and regulates laws; appoints directors of decentralized service entities; oversees public services; organizes the national credit and national debt; and grants pardons for political crimes.

The president is elected by the citizens for a four-year term by the absolute majority of votes cast in a direct and secret ballot. If none of the candidates obtains a majority in the first round, the two candidates who have the greatest number of votes compete in a second and final round. A president must be Colombian by birth, an active citizen, and at least 30 years old.

A constitutional amendment, approved by Congress in December 2004, allows presidential reelection for only one term. The amendment states that nobody can be elected to the presidential office for more than two terms. Reelection, as allowed by this amendment, can be immediate.

While in office the president may not be prosecuted or judged for any crimes except by the Chamber of Representatives and the Senate.

The Congress

Senators and representatives are elected by the citizens in direct and secret elections for four-year terms. They rep-resent the people and must act according to justice and common well-being.

The Senate is made up of 100 members elected by national vote. An additional two senators are chosen nationally by Indian communities. To be elected as senator one must be Colombian by birth and at least 30 years old. The Chamber of Representatives is elected in territorial districts, two representatives from each department and one more for every additional 250,000 inhabitants in a department. It is made up of approximately 170 representatives. To be elected as a representative one must be a Colombian citizen at least 25 years old.

The Lawmaking Process

One of the main functions of Congress is to make laws. Laws can be initiated by members of Congress, by the administration (through its ministers), or by 5 percent of voting citizens. In addition, the Constitutional Court, the Supreme Judicature Council, the Supreme Justice Court, the Council of State, the National Electoral Council, the attorney general, and the general finance office of the republic may present bills concerning their own their functions to Congress. However, bills related to the national development plan, administrative structure, the budget, the central bank, national credit, and foreign commerce can only be presented by the cabinet.

For a bill to become a law, it must be approved in four debates: first by the permanent committee of the Chamber of Representatives or Senate, then by the full chamber, and then by the commission and chamber in the other house. Finally, it must be signed by the president of the republic. In case of discrepancies between the chambers, a joint committee tries to find a common text, which must be approved by both chambers.

The Judiciary

The judicial branch in Colombia is independent of the executive and the legislature. There are four different jurisdictions. Ordinary jurisdiction has competence over civil, commercial, family, labor, and criminal matters. The highest authority of this branch is the Supreme Court of Justice, inspired by the French system. The administrative jurisdiction, also based on the French model, judges disputes between individuals and state bodies. The highest authority of this branch is the Council of State. The constitutional jurisdiction has powers over the constitutionality of laws and government actions. Cases in the latter category may originate in the other jurisdictions, but the highest appeal is still the Constitutional Court. Finally, the disciplinary jurisdiction judges the conduct of administrative and judicial personnel, as well as lawyers. Its highest authority is the Supreme Judicature Council, Disciplinary Section. The Supreme Judicature Council, Administrative Section, is in charge of the administration of the judiciary.

The magistrates of the Supreme Court of Justice and of the Council of State are elected by the members of those entities from lists presented by the Supreme Judicature

Council, Administrative Section. The magistrates of the Constitutional Court are elected by the Senate, one-third from among groups of three candidates presented by the Supreme Justice Court, another third from groups of three candidates presented by the Council of State, and the last presented by the president of the republic.

The constitutional jurisdiction has made some very important decisions in recent years. For example, it has decided not to impose penalties for possession of personal doses of illegal drugs or for assistance of terminally ill patients in committing suicide.

THE ELECTION PROCESS AND POLITICAL PARTICIPATION

All citizens 18 years old or older have the right and the duty to vote in elections for president of the republic, members of Congress, governors, departmental assemblies, mayors, and city councils. They also have the right to participate in popular referendums, law initiatives, and constitutional amendments.

The National Electoral Council supervises and protects the electoral process. Its members are elected by the Council of State for four-year terms from among groups of candidates presented by political parties. Its composition must reflect the political composition of Congress.

POLITICAL PARTIES

For more than a century, Colombia had a two-party system. The constitution of 1991 gave official status to any party that had at least one member in Congress or that was created with the support of 50,000 signatures. As a result, the country now has a vigorous multiparty system. In fact, observers believe the system is too pluralistic: Because there may be as many as 70 parties active at any given moment, it is difficult for the president to build or hold majority support in Congress.

CITIZENSHIP

Nationals are those who have a Colombian father or mother and who were born in Colombia, or they are children of foreigners, one of whose parents was domiciled in Colombia at the time of birth. People born to Colombians abroad who later move to the country are also nationals.

Colombian nationality can be acquired through adoption. Double nationality is permitted. Nationals gain citizenship when they reach the age of 18.

FUNDAMENTAL RIGHTS

One of the fundamental principles of the constitution is that the rights of human beings have primacy within the constitutional order.

The constitution specifies a full but not limiting list of rights. It incorporates human rights treaties into the national legal system and requires that constitutional rights must be interpreted according to these treaties.

Among the explicit guarantees are the right to life, personal integrity, equality, speech, good name, free movement, information, career choice, legal defense, due process of law, and association. Economic and social rights are also recognized, such as education, health, social security, housing, work, collective bargaining, property, access to property by workers, a healthy environment, and consumer protection.

Impact and Functions of Fundamental Rights

Individual rights are of immediate application. This means that they are directly applicable to all particular and concrete situations and do not need the promulgation of a law to regulate their exercise. They hold a preferential position in the constitutional system, as they can be raised in the context of any subject, and they have specific procedures for their protection.

Regarding equality, the constitution not only establishes equality before the law, with no distinction concerning race, sex, or social condition, but also establishes the state's duty to promote true and material equality in favor of low-income groups. As a result of the *tutela* action, a procedural right in court, fundamental rights have begun to take effect in family, work, education, and religious contexts with an important and significant impact on Colombian society.

At times, judges from the different jurisdictions have disagreed in their interpretations of fundamental rights. However, this sometimes yielded new ways of interpretation and broadened the scope of protected rights.

Limitations to Fundamental Rights

Fundamental rights are not absolute. They are limited by other fundamental rights and by the legal system as such. Their exercise can be regulated by laws. The Constitutional Court has established the principles of rationality and proportion in accepting limits on rights.

In a state of emergency, war, or internal commotion, the president of the republic has the power to promulgate measures with the status of law in order to reestablish order. However, even then human rights and fundamental liberties cannot be limited.

ECONOMY

The state does not control economic activity or private enterprise. There is a free, competitive economic system, with implied rights for the people.

Nevertheless, the *direction* of the economy is under state control. The state controls national resources and land use and owns underground and nonrenewable natural resources. In addition, it rationalizes the economy to achieve a better lifestyle for all inhabitants; to that aim, it influences public and private services and the production, distribution, and consumption of products. The state must intervene to ensure that everyone has access to goods and basic services, especially those with who have income.

Every administration must issue a national development-plan law with public participation. It specifies long-term objectives, priorities of state activity, budgets, and public investment programs. This law takes precedence over other laws but not over the constitution.

The central bank, called Banco de la Republica, is an autonomous legal entity, separate from other branches of state power. It regulates the currency, international exchange rates, and credit. It also issues bills and coins, administers international reserves, acts as bank lender of last resort and banker of banks, and is the fiscal agent of the state. Its board of directors is the monetary, exchange, and credit authority. It has seven members, among them the minister of finance, who acts as president of the board. The manager of the bank is elected by the board and is part of it. The other five members are appointed by the president of the republic for four-year terms that can be extended.

RELIGIOUS COMMUNITIES

The Catholic religion has deep roots in Colombian society. In the past, the state was linked to the Catholic Church, and teaching in schools was provided by religious communities. Currently, the state has an international treaty with the Holy See, called the Concordato. The Catholic Church has acted as an intermediary between the government and various rebel groups and has rendered very valuable services in peace negotiations.

The constitution of 1991 established freedom of religion and equality before the law for religious communities. Freedom of religion is an individual right of all people and is protected through the *tutela* action.

There are small Jewish, Muslim, Protestant, and other Christian communities in Colombia. There are also Indian communities who practice their own ancestral religions.

MILITARY DEFENSE AND STATE OF EMERGENCY

The public force, whose commander in chief is the president of the republic, is composed of the armed forces and the national police. The armed forces have the task of defending the country's sovereignty, independence, territorial integrity, and constitutional order. The national police is an armed body of a civil nature, which has the

tasks of maintaining the necessary conditions for the exercise of the rights and liberties of the public and ensuring that people coexist peacefully.

The minimal age for recruitment to the armed forces is 18. Colombians are considered to have the duty to take up arms when public needs require in order to defend freedom and national institutions.

Active duty service members cannot vote or participate in political party activities, debates, or political movements. They may not assemble without legitimate orders to that effect, and they may not submit petitions, except regarding their own service. Crimes committed by members of the public forces in the course of duty are judged under the military criminal code by military tribunals.

Only the government may produce or import arms, military ammunition, and explosives. People may not carry arms without the permission of the competent authorities. Such permission cannot be extended to political meetings, elections, or public corporation meetings.

The president of the republic, with the signature of all ministers, has the power to declare a state of emergency in case of war, internal commotion, or economic, social, or ecological emergency. In a state of emergency, the administration can issue decrees with the force of law in order to confront the exceptional circumstances and encourage the restoration of normality.

Decrees issued under a state of emergency must be signed by the president and all cabinet ministers. They may only address subjects directly related to the exceptional circumstances; they may not suspend human rights or fundamental freedoms; and they must not interrupt the normal functioning of state bodies. The Constitutional Court reviews the constitutionality of these decrees.

AMENDMENTS TO THE CONSTITUTION

The 1991 constitution had 18 amendments in its first 13 years, one approved by referendum. There are three different ways to amend the constitution. Congress can pass a bill called a Legislative Act. The Legislative Act needs eight debates in Congress, the last four with absolute majority for approval. Such a proposal can be submitted by the administration, 10 members of Congress, 20 percent of the municipality council members or department deputies, or a number of citizens equivalent to 5 percent of those who may vote.

Amendments can also be adopted by a Constituent Assembly. In this procedure, Congress initiates the proposal, approves it by an absolute majority, and presents it to a direct vote by the citizens. This procedure has never been used.

The third method of amending the constitution is by referendum. The proposal can be initiated by the administration, Congress, or 5 percent of all citizens. It must first be passed by an absolute majority in Congress. At least 25 percent of all citizens must participate, and a majority of them must approve. Even then, the amendment can be rescinded by another referendum within six months of its publication. Two recent governments tried to amend the constitution through referendums. The first attempt failed, and only one of 10 articles submitted in the second attempt was approved.

The Constitutional Court, at the request of any citizen, reviews the amendment process to make sure it complies with the constitution. However, it may not address the content of the proposed changes.

PRIMARY SOURCES

Constitution in Spanish. Available online. URL: http://www.georgetown.edu/pdba/Constitutions/Colombia/col91.html. Accessed on September 15, 2005.

SECONDARY SOURCES

David Bushnell, *Making Modern Colombia: A Nation in Spite of Itself.* Berkeley: University of California Press, 1993.

John C. Dugas, *Explaining Democratic Reform in Colombia: The Origins of the 1991 Constitution.* Ann Arbor, Mich.: UMI, 1997.

Jacobo Pérez Escobar, *Derecho Constitucional Colombiano.* Bogotá: Temis S. A., 2003.

Donald L. Herman, *Democracy in Latin America: Colombia and Venezuela.* Westport, Conn.: Praeger, 1988.

Harold José Rizo Otero, *Lecciones de Derecho Constitucional Colombiano.* Bogotá: Temis S. A.

Jaime Vidal Perdomo, *Derecho Constitucional General e Instituciones politicas.* Bogotá: Universidad Externado de Colombia—Universidad Nacional De Colombia, 1996.

Tulio Enrique Tascón, *Derecho Constitucional Colombiano.* Bogotá: Minerva.

Carlos Ariel Sánchez Torres, *Derecho electoral colombiano.* Bogotá: Legis, 2000.

United Nations, "Core Document Forming Part of the Reports of States Parties: Colombia" (HRI/CORE/1/Add.56/Rev.1), 30 June 1997. Available online. URL: http://www.unhchr.ch/tbs/doc.nsf. Accessed on July 16, 2005.

Donna Lee van Cott, "Legal Pluralism in Bolivia and Colombia." *Journal of Latin American Studies* 32 (2000): 207–234.

Juan Manuel Charry Urueña

COMOROS

At-a-Glance

OFFICIAL NAME
Union of the Comoros

CAPITAL
Moroni

POPULATION
671,247 (2005 est.)

SIZE
719 sq. mi. (1,862 sq. km)

LANGUAGES
French (official), Arabic (official), Shikomor

RELIGION
Sunni Muslim 98%, other 2%

NATIONAL OR ETHNIC COMPOSITION
Comorian 96.9%, French 0.33%, other (Swahili, Malagasy, Arabian) 2.77%

DATE OF INDEPENDENCE OR CREATION
July 6, 1975

TYPE OF GOVERNMENT
Parliamentary democracy

TYPE OF STATE
Federal state

TYPE OF LEGISLATURE
Each island has a unicameral legislature, which in turn has representation in the unicameral National Assembly of the Union

DATE OF THE CONSTITUTION
December 23, 2001

DATE OF LAST AMENDMENT
No amendment

The Comorian state, l'Union des Comores, is a parliamentary democracy. It has a federal constitution and a constitution for each of the three main islands.

The constitution is the fundamental law of the country. It guarantees the division of power among the executive, the legislative, and the judiciary, the latter independent of the executive and the legislative.

The federal constitution gives each island significant autonomy over its own financial management and administration. Nevertheless, the union government has supremacy when necessary and relevant. Recent legislation passed by the Assembly of the Union has given the union exclusive authority over matters such as religion, nationality, money, and immigration. The union and islands governments share competence over, among other, internal security, education, health, environment, agriculture, and tourism.

The preamble provides that Islam is a source of inspiration for the government of the union. Islam is thus a state religion, although the constitution states that everyone is equal in rights and duties regardless of religious affiliation.

There is no specific bill of rights within the constitution. However, the preamble guarantees some basic individual human rights such as the right to freedom, to security, and to information.

CONSTITUTIONAL HISTORY

Before French colonization in the middle of the 19th century, Bantu Africans populated the Comoros Islands. They were then invaded by Arab-Persians, followed by Madagascans. The three islands (Grande Comore, Anjouan, and Moheli) were a French protectorate from 1886 onward. In 1912, together with Mayotte, they became a French colony. In 1945, the islands obtained administrative autonomy and, in 1958, became a French overseas territory.

In 1974, Grande Comore, Anjouan, and Moheli opted for independence by referendum. Mayotte decided to remain French. On July 6, 1975, independence was proclaimed for the three Comorian islands. They became the state of Comoros. The Federal Islamic Republic of the Comoros (République fédérale islamique des Comores) was created on October 1, 1978.

In 1997, the population of Anjouan and Moheli rose against the government and asked to be reattached to France. France found the request inadequate and refused.

After several peace conferences and coups d'états, a referendum aiming at ending the political and constitutional crisis was held on December 23, 2001. The referendum marked the formal approval of the new Comorian constitution.

FORM AND IMPACT OF THE CONSTITUTION

The Union of the Comoros has a written constitution, and each of the three islands has its own constitution. The issues concerning the division of powers between the union and the islands have been referred to legislation that was recently passed by the Assembly of the Union. In view of the current political situation, it is also likely that they might be totally changed at any time.

The constitution of the union is the highest law of the country. It takes precedence over any federal law, island constitution, or island law. A constitutional amendment is required before any international treaty provision can enter into force. After such amendment or ratification, the instrument enjoys immediate force and direct effect.

BASIC ORGANIZATIONAL STRUCTURE

The constitution of the union provides that four islands make up the republic: Anjouan, Grande Comore, Mayotte, and Mohéli. In reality, Mayotte remains French territory, and only the three other islands are economically, administratively, and politically part of the union.

The state is organized as a federation. Each island has its own constitution and its own administration headed by a president assisted by cabinet ministers. They are economically and administratively autonomous.

Matters related to religion, currency, external relations, defense, and national symbols are the exclusive responsibility of the union government. The island authorities can rule on any other matter provided that the union does not impose its veto. A veto can be imposed if it is anticipated that the proposed law will jeopardize the interest of the islands and/or the unity of the Union of the Comoros.

LEADING CONSTITUTIONAL PRINCIPLES

The Union of the Comoros is a parliamentary democracy. The constitution guarantees the divisions among the executive, the legislative, and the judiciary. Each of the three institutions has its own system of accountability. The judiciary's independence is guaranteed by the constitution.

The key principles defining the constitutional system are the following: All state bodies must be established by law and be based on democracy; they have to respect the principles of good governance; the Union of the Comoros is a republic; every island can freely administer its own affairs; Islam is a permanent source of inspiration for the government of the union and thus is the religion of the state; the presidency rotates among the islands; the president is elected in a one-round universal suffrage vote every four years; and no authority can limit freedom of movement or relocation or circulation of goods in the territory of the union.

CONSTITUTIONAL BODIES

Provision is made for six constitutional entities: the president, the Assembly of the Union, the Council of the Ulemas, the Economic and Social Council, the judiciary, and the Constitutional Court.

The President of the Union

The president is elected together with two vice presidents by direct universal suffrage for a period of four years. Every four years, the presidency rotates among the islands.

The president is the representative of the state in the international arena. The president is the head of the administration and nominates the cabinet ministers with the assistance of the vice presidents. The president promulgates the laws that have been voted by the Assembly of the Union and defines and leads the administration's policy.

Finally, the president has to present an annual report on the state of the union to the assembly, to the Constitutional Court, and to the assemblies and executives of the islands.

The Assembly of the Union

The assembly is the legislative organ of the union. It votes new laws, amends existing ones, and approves the state budget.

The assembly is composed of 33 delegates elected for five years. The population directly elects 18 of them, and the three island assemblies designate the 15 remaining delegates. The members of the island assemblies are elected by the population of each island.

The Lawmaking Process
Bills can be introduced by the president as well as by the delegates. Bills of laws and amendments introduced by delegates are not accepted if they lead to a diminution of the resources of the union or increase its public tasks.

Laws specified by the constitution as organic laws require a majority of two-thirds of all the members of the assembly. The same applies to financial laws.

The Council of the Ulemas (Le Conseil des Ulémas)

The Council of the Ulemas is one of the two consultative organs created by the constitution. It has the task of assisting the administration of the union and those of the islands on religious matters.

The Economic and Social Council

The Economic and Social Council assists the administration of the union and the islands in economic and social affairs.

The Judiciary

The judiciary is independent of the executive and the legislature. The president of the union, assisted by the High Council of the Magistracy (le Conseil Supérieur de la Magistrature), is responsible for the independence of the judiciary.

On criminal and administrative matters, the Supreme Court (Cour Suprême) is the highest judicial authority of the Comoros. No appeal exists against a decision of the Supreme Court. The Supreme Court also sits as a High Court of Justice (Haute Court de Justice) to try the head of state, a vice president, or any member of the administration in case of high treason.

The Constitutional Court

The Constitutional Court judges the constitutionality of the laws of the union and the islands. It also controls the election and referendum processes and hears electoral litigation. It is also the guardian of human rights, and any individual citizen can appeal to it.

THE ELECTION PROCESS

The constitution provides that all Comorians, male and female, aged 18 and above, who possess full civil and political rights are allowed to vote. All citizens aged 40 and above can be candidates in presidential elections, and those aged 30 and above can be candidates to be members of the Assembly of the Union, provided that they possess full civil and political rights.

POLITICAL PARTIES

The constitution guarantees the existence of a multiparty political system. All parties enjoy freedom of activity provided they respect the rules of democracy and national unity.

CITIZENSHIP

Anybody born to a Comorian parent enjoys Comorian nationality.

FUNDAMENTAL RIGHTS

The preamble of the constitution guarantees a number of fundamental rights and freedoms, especially civil and political rights such as freedom of expression and of association, and the right to a judicial defense. Economic and social rights such as the rights to education and health, to the security of investment, and to private property are also guaranteed.

Impact and Functions of Fundamental Rights

The constitution gives particular consideration to principles and rights contained in international instruments such as the United Nations Charter, the Organization of African Unity (OAU) Charter, the Covenant of the League of Arab States, the Universal Declaration of Human Rights, and the African Charter on Human and People's Rights. It also puts particular emphasis on instruments protecting the rights of the child.

Limitations to Fundamental Rights

The fundamental rights are subject to respect for morality and law and order and to abstention from any act that can be a nuisance to others.

ECONOMY

The constitution makes no specific provision for any economic system. Economic analysts have been reluctant to qualify the Comorian economy as a market economy. Moreover, the political and economic crisis the country is now undergoing does not allow any proper definition of its economic system.

RELIGIOUS COMMUNITIES

The constitution imposes Islam as the national religion, though not in so many words. The preamble states that the people of the Comoros wish to find in Islam the inspiration for the principles and rules governing the union; no other religion is mentioned by name. The constitution also provides for the Council of Ulemas to guide the union and island governments.

Another interesting point is that although the constitution recognizes many international instruments that guarantee freedom of religion, it does not provide for such freedom. Nevertheless, a Christian community is present in the country, and it practices Christianity without any hindrance.

MILITARY DEFENSE AND STATE OF EMERGENCY

External defense is under the authority of the union. The president of the union is the chief of the army and is responsible for the safety of the country against external attacks. Only men can be members of the armed forces.

AMENDMENTS TO THE CONSTITUTION

Only the president of the union and at least one-third of the assembly are allowed to submit changes to the constitution. An amendment is valid if it is approved by two-thirds of the members of the assembly and of the island assemblies or if it wins majority support in a referendum.

No amendment proposing a change to the unity and inviolability of the borders of the union or to the autonomy of the islands is allowed.

The constitution will automatically be amended if Mayotte returns to the sovereignty of the Union of Comoros.

PRIMARY SOURCES

Constitution in French. Available online. URL: http://droit.francophonie.org/doc/html/km/con/fr/2001/2001dfkmcofr1.html. Accessed on August 11, 2005.

SECONDARY SOURCES

Michael Bogdan, "Legal Pluralism in the Comoros and Djibouti." *Nordic Journal of International Law* 69, no. 2 (2000): 195–208.
Helen Chapin Metz, ed. *Comoros: A Country Study.* Washington, D.C.: Library of Congress, 1994. Available online. URL: http://lcweb2.loc.gov/frd/cs/kmtoc.html. Accessed on August 4, 2005.
Martin Ottenheimer and Harriet Ottenheimer, *Historical Dictionary of the Comoro Islands.* Metuchen, N.J.: The Scarecrow Press, 1994.

Mohamed Sanaty

CONGO, DEMOCRATIC REPUBLIC OF THE

At-a-Glance

OFFICIAL NAME
Democratic Republic of the Congo

CAPITAL
Kinshasa

POPULATION
62,660,551 (July 2006 est.)

SIZE
905,400 sq. mi. (2,345,000 sq. km)

LANGUAGES
French (official), Tshiluba, Lingala, Kikongo, Swahili (national)

RELIGIONS
Roman Catholic 50%, Protestant 20%, Kimbanguist 10%, Muslim 10%, traditional beliefs 10%

NATIONAL OR ETHNIC COMPOSITION
Bantu (predominant group with about 300 subnational groups), Tutsi, and Pygmy (minorities)

DATE OF INDEPENDENCE OR CREATION
June 30, 1960

TYPE OF GOVERNMENT
Quasi-presidential

TYPE OF STATE
Quasi-federal state

TYPE OF LEGISLATURE
Bicameral parliament

DATE OF CONSTITUTION
February 18, 2006

DATE OF LAST AMENDMENT
No amendment

During the inter-Congolese Dialogue (ICD) held in Sun City, South Africa, a 204-article constitution was adopted to govern the country during a 24-month transitional period. Based on the all-inclusive agreement signed in Pretoria on December 17, 2002, this constitution was promulgated on April 3, 2003.

The new constitution of the Democratic Republic of the Congo (DRC) was adopted by the transitional parliament on May 13, 2005, and approved by referendum on December 18–19, 2005. It came into force on its promulgation in January 2006. It provides that the Democratic Republic of the Congo is an independent, sovereign, united, indivisible, social, democratic, and secular state, based on the separation of the executive, legislative, and judicial powers, and respectful of human rights and fundamental freedoms. The president is the head of state and presides over the Council of Ministers despite that the prime minister is the head of the executive branch of government. The legislative power is vested in the Parliament, which consists of the National Assembly and the Senate. The Constitutional Court is the highest court in all constitutional matters.

The constitution enshrines the rights of all people in the country, including freedom of religion, and provides for a pluralistic system of political parties. The military is apolitical and subject to the civil government and to the rule of law. They cannot participate in elections either as voters or candidates. The economic system can be described as a social market economy.

CONSTITUTIONAL HISTORY

During the 1884–85 Berlin Conference on the Colonization of Africa, the Congo was allocated to Belgian king Leopold II. It became a Belgian colony in October 1908. The first fundamental law that governed was drafted by the Belgian government, adopted by the Belgian Parliament, and promulgated by the Belgian king even before the

Belgian Congo gained its independence on June 30, 1960. It established a parliamentary regime.

A 1965 coup d'état suspended the Luluabourg Constitution adopted by referendum in 1964 and inaugurated the Second Republic, under which the country was renamed Zaire, in 1971. On May 17, 1997, the country regained its original name, Democratic Republic of the Congo. In 1998, the Congo was confronted with yet another rebellion, aggravated by foreign aggression.

Internal and international pressure to end the conflict resulted in the signing of the Lusaka Agreement in 1999 under the aegis of the Southern African Development Community, the Organization of African Unity (now superseded by the African Union), and the United Nations. This agreement provided for an inter-Congolese dialogue to reconcile the people and leaders of the Congo and to reunite the country under a single government of national unity with a national and integrated army to guarantee the integrity of the country and secure its peoples.

The inter-Congolese Dialogue took place in Sun City, South Africa. The first round of talks in February-April 2002 resulted in an agreement which was rejected by some parties. On December 17, 2002, an all-inclusive agreement was reached in Pretoria, allowing for the inter-Congolese Dialogue to the reconvened in Sun City late in March 2003. The Pretoria Agreement was ratified and served as the basis for the interim constitution adopted on March 31 and promulgated on April 3, 2003. This agreement provided for the formation of a transitional government of national unity. Together with the interim constitution to which it was annexed, it became the basic law during the transition.

In its more than 40 years of independence, the Congo has known more than 32 constitutional documents. This sets a world record of one constitution for every 15 months.

Parliament adopted a new constitution on May 13, 2005. This constitution was approved by referendum held on December 18–19, 2005 and promulgated on February 18, 2006.

FORM AND IMPACT OF THE CONSTITUTION

The new Congolese constitution prevails over any other law or conduct. It is binding on all state organs and must be respected by all people in the republic. It is also entrenched in the sense that it cannot be easily amended.

BASIC ORGANIZATIONAL STRUCTURE

The Democratic Republic of the Congo is a unitary state made up of the capital city of Kinshasa and 25 provinces, which all enjoy legal personality. However, this provision will only come into operation within 36 months following the establishment of the political institutions set by the new constitution. Until then, the republic will consist of Kinshasa and 10 provinces, as provided by the previous constitutions. The capital is granted the status of a province and may be transferred to any other place of the republic by referendum. The provinces are subdivided into a number of entities, some of which are decentralized while some others are not.

The constitution provides for a division of competence between the republic and its provinces. There are areas of exclusive and shared competence. The provinces are administered by their own elected organs. They are also represented in the national administration through the Senate and enjoy a high level of autonomy. The constitution does not determine the nature of the state, whether federal or not. Nevertheless, the autonomy enjoyed by the provinces and the extent to which the central administration may still interfere with provincial matters lead to the argument that the Democratic Republic of the Congo has become a quasi-federal state.

LEADING CONSTITUTIONAL PRINCIPLES

The Congolese system is a quasi-presidential system defined by a number of leading principles: The Congo is a republic; a pluralist, independent, sovereign, united, indivisible, democratic, social, and secular state respectful of human rights, constitutionalism, and the rule of law. The constitution guarantees the independence of the judiciary. Sovereignty belongs to the people who exercise it through referendum and/or elections.

CONSTITUTIONAL BODIES

The constitutional bodies are the president, Parliament consisting of the National Assembly and the Senate, the cabinet, the courts and tribunals, and the Economic and Social Council. Out of the five institutions supporting democracy established under the interim constitution, the new constitution only retains the National Independent Electoral Commission and the High Authority of the Media and Communication. The other institutions are considered dissolved on the establishment of the new Parliament. Nevertheless, the latter may later establish new ones by organic law.

The President

The president is the head of state and represents the nation. He or she is the symbol of national unity and the guarantor of national independence, territorial integrity, sovereignty, and respect for the constitution, treaties, and other international agreements. The president is directly elected by universal adult suffrage for a five-year term renewable only once. He or she appoints the prime minister within and after consultation with the majority party in Parliament. The other members of the cabinet are appointed on a list presented by the prime minister. The president is also the commander in chief of the armed forces and presides over the High Council of Defense.

The Cabinet or Administration

The cabinet consists of the prime minister, ministers, and vice ministers. It may include vice prime ministers and state or delegated ministers. It is led by the prime minister. The cabinet determines the policy of the nation after consulting the president. It is accountable to Parliament.

Parliament

The legislative authority of the republic is vested in Parliament, which is bicameral and consists of the National Assembly and the Senate.

The National Assembly

The National Assembly enacts laws and controls the administration, public enterprises, and public services. Its members are called deputies and represent the nation. They are elected on a direct and universal adult suffrage for a five-year term. They may be reelected and enjoy parliamentary immunities. They may not be prosecuted and/or arrested except in some circumstances and in the conditions prescribed by national legislation. The administration is accountable to Parliament, and both the president and the prime minister may be removed from office by the Constitutional Court seized by Parliament.

On the other hand, the National Assembly may be dissolved by the president after consulting the prime minister and the presidents of both the National Assembly and the Senate when there is a persisting crisis between the National Assembly and the administration or the cabinet. A deputy who resigns from the political party or grouping that nominated him/her during elections ceases to be a member of the National Assembly.

The Senate

The Senate is the second chamber of Parliament. Its members, the senators, are elected by the provincial assemblies for a five-year term, which is renewable. They represent their respective provinces although their mandate is a national one. Former elected presidents are senators for life.

The senators also enjoy parliamentary immunities. As for the deputies, any senator who resigns from the party or political grouping that nominated him or her during elections ceases to be a senator.

The Lawmaking Process

The National Assembly and the Senate constitute the legislative authority during the transition. They must adopt bills in identical terms. Otherwise, a joint commission must be set up to propose a single. If the disagreement persists, the National Assembly decides in the last instance. The president and the administration also participate in the lawmaking process.

The Judiciary

Justice is administered in the name of the people, but judicial decisions are enforced in the name of the president. Article 147 of the constitution provides for the independence of the judiciary. The judiciary is meant to guarantee individual freedoms and fundamental human rights. The judges are subject to the constitution, a special law determines their status.

Courts and tribunals that form the judiciary include the Constitutional Court, the Court of Cassation, the Council of State, the High Military Court, and other civil and military courts and tribunals. The offices of the public prosecutors also belong to the judiciary. The nine-member Constitutional Court is the judge of the constitutionality of laws and other acts having the force of law. It must decide on their conformity to the constitution before their promulgation by the president and may invalidate them in case of inconsistency with the constitution.

It is also competent to interpret the constitution and deals with disputes related to legislative and presidential elections and to referenda. The Constitutional Court is the criminal judge of the president and the prime minister in the conditions prescribed by national legislation.

THE ELECTION PROCESS

Sovereignty belongs to the people, who assume it directly through referendum or elections and indirectly through their representatives. Article 5 entitles all Congolese, male or female, over the age of 18 to stand for elections and vote in the elections.

POLITICAL PARTIES

Political pluralism is guaranteed. Political parties must respect the principles of pluralist democracy, national unity, and sovereignty. The constitution provides for public funding of electoral campaigns and other party activities. Political opposition is recognized. A law determines the rights and duties of the opposition. The creation of a single-party state is considered a crime of high treason.

CITIZENSHIP

A law determines the conditions of recognition, acquisition, loss, and resumption of Congolese citizenship, which cannot be retained concurrently with other citizenship. To address the problem that gave rise to the recent rebellions, the constitution confers the Congolese citizenship on anyone who belongs to any ethnic groups and nationalities that occupied the territory what became known as Democratic Republic of the Congo on independence.

FUNDAMENTAL RIGHTS

The preamble to the constitution refers to the Universal Declaration of Human Rights, the African Charter on Human and Peoples' Rights, and other United Nations and African Union instruments duly ratified by the Congo. Title II of the constitution enshrines individual and collective rights and duties. These rights are civil, political, social, cultural, individual, and even peoples' rights. The constitution also imposes a number of duties on Congolese citizens such as the duty prescribed by Article 63 to defend the nation and its territorial integrity and to oppose any individual or group who would seize power by force or assume it in violation of the constitution.

All national, provincial, local, and customary authorities are also bound to safeguard the unity of the republic and its territorial integrity. Failure to do so would constitute a crime of high treason.

Women's rights and the rights of the elderly and disabled persons are also entrenched in the constitution. The Bill of Rights in binding on all individuals and state organs.

Impact and Functions and Fundamental Rights

Human rights are at the heart of the constitution. Democracy and human rights are intertwined. The constitution was inspired by these principles and cannot be interpreted without reference to international human rights agreements.

Limitations to Fundamental Rights

There is no general limitation clause in the constitution, but rather specific limitations to specific rights. Rights may be limited only to protect the law, public order, and morals. On the other hand, fundamental rights may be suspended in circumstances such as during the declaration of a state of emergency or when the country is aggressed by a foreign power. However, even under these exceptional circumstances, some rights and fundamental principles cannot be derogated from.

These include the right to life; the right to appeal against a judicial decision and to be defended in court; the right to freedom of thought, conscience, and religion; the principle of legality of crimes and sentences; the interdiction of torture and other cruel, inhuman, and degrading treatments; and the prevention of slavery, servitude, and imprisonment for debts.

ECONOMY

A number of constitutional rights relate to the economy, namely the rights to freedom of movement and enterprise, equality before the law and equal protection of the law, freedom of association, and private property; the

obligation of the state to encourage and secure private foreign or national investments; freedom to exercise art, trade, and industry; and prohibition on expropriation of private property, except in the public interest and in accordance with the law.

The Democratic Republic of the Congo is a "social" state that guarantees fundamental rights such as the right to work, protection against unemployment, equitable and satisfactory remuneration, education, health, and nondiscrimination against all people, including women. The Congolese system can be described as a social market economy, combining aspects of social responsibility with market economy.

RELIGIOUS COMMUNITIES

There is no state religion. The Democratic Republic of the Congo is a secular state respectful of all forms of thoughts and beliefs. The right to freedom of thought, conscience, and religion is guaranteed under the law, public order, and morals. A law determines the conditions for the creation of religious associations.

MILITARY DEFENSE AND STATE OF EMERGENCY

The armed forces are distinguished from the police, who are responsible for public order. The armed forces must defend the territorial integrity of the country; participate in the economic, social, and cultural development; and protect persons and their properties, within the limits of the law.

The armed forces are subject to the civil authority and to the president, who is their supreme commandant. The organization of a private militia is a crime of high treason. Education, morality, and balanced representation of all the provinces are key criteria in the recruitment in the army. Any recruitment of persons under the age of 18 or participation by them in wars or armed conflicts is unconstitutional. The president of the republic may declare a state of emergency or siege after consulting the prime minister and the presidents of both the National Assembly and the Senate. He or she then addresses the nation.

The president may also declare war by a decree initiated by the cabinet as advised by the High Council of Defense and with the authorization of both the National Assembly and the Senate.

AMENDMENTS TO THE CONSTITUTION

The president, the National Assembly, the Senate, the cabinet, or at least 100,000 citizens through a petition addressed to one of the two chambers of Parliament may propose constitutional amendments. The National Assembly and the Senate must each decide on an absolute majority vote whether a proposed constitutional amendment is well founded. A constitutional amendment is final after its approval by referendum unless it has been ratified by a three-fifths majority of the National Assembly and the Senate during a joint session. No constitutional amendment may be decided during the state of war, siege, or emergency; when the presidency is vacant or when the National Assembly and the Senate are prevented from seating freely. No constitutional amendment is allowed if it changes the republican form of the state and the representative nature of the government; if it infringes the principle of universal suffrage, the independence of the judiciary, the plurality of political parties and unions; if it changes the number and duration of the terms of office of the president; or if it reduces the fundamental rights and freedoms or the powers vested in the provinces and decentralized territorial entities.

PRIMARY SOURCES

Assemblée Nationale de la République Démocratique du Congo, *Projet de Constitution de la RDC* (2005), in French. Available online. URL: http://www.iss.co.za/AF/profiles/DRCongo/cdreader/bin/constitution13may2005.pdf. Accessed on August 7, 2005.

2003 Interim Constitution in French: *Constitution de la Transition,* Special Issue, *Journal Officiel de la République Démocratique du Congo,* April 5, 2003. Available online. URL: http://www.accpuf.org/cod/constit.htm. Accessed on September 25, 2005.

SECONDARY SOURCES

Christof Heyns, ed., *Human Rights Law in Africa.* Vol. 2. Leiden, Netherlands: Martinus Nijhoff, 2004.
André Mbata B. Mangu, "The Road to Constitutionalism and Democracy in Post-colonial Africa: The Case of the Democratic Republic of Congo." LLD Thesis, University of South Africa, 2002.

André Mbata B. Mangu

CONGO, REPUBLIC OF THE

At-a-Glance

OFFICIAL NAME
Republic of the Congo

CAPITAL
Brazzaville

POPULATION
2,998,040 (2004 est.)

SIZE
132,000 sq. mi. (342,000 sq. km)

LANGUAGES
French (official), Lingala, Kikongo (national)

RELIGIONS
Roman Catholic 35%, other Christian (Protestant, Kimbanguist) 15%, Muslim 2%, traditional beliefs 48%

NATIONAL OR ETHNIC COMPOSITION
Bantu (15 principal groups, including Kongo, Téké, Vili, M'Bochi, and Sangha, and 70 subgroups), and Pygmy (minority group)

DATE OF INDEPENDENCE OR CREATION
August 15, 1960

TYPE OF GOVERNMENT
Presidential

TYPE OF STATE
Unitary state

TYPE OF LEGISLATURE
Bicameral parliament

DATE OF CONSTITUTION
Approved by referendum in January 20, 2002; entered into force in June 2002

DATE OF LAST AMENDMENT
No amendment

The Republic of the Congo is a unitary state with a presidential government based on the separation of the executive, legislative, and judicial powers. An elected president is the head of state and presides over the Council of Ministers. Parliament consists of the National Assembly and the Senate. The Constitutional Court decides on the constitutionality of any law in the republic. The Supreme Court of Justice is the highest court in all other matters.

In 1997, after overthrowing President Pascal Lissouba, who had been democratically elected in terms of the 1992 constitution, the former military and Marxist-Leninist leader General Sassou-Ngusesso set up a forum for national reconciliation, which proposed a new constitution. The latter was adopted by referendum in January 2002 and is now the supreme law of the republic. It provides that the Congo is a sovereign, indivisible, secular, social, and democratic state that guarantees the rights of all people in the country, including their right to reli-

gious freedom. It also establishes a pluralistic system of political parties. The economic system is a social market economy.

The civil service is apolitical. The military is subject to the civil government and the rule of law, although this principle has been regularly violated in the past.

CONSTITUTIONAL HISTORY

The Congo emerged from the Berlin conference of 1884–85 as a French colony. Its first constitution was adopted in 1959 under the French Community. The former French Middle Congo gained its independence from France on August 15, 1960, and became the Republic of the Congo.

The constitution established a parliamentary regime, which shortly fell apart after a series of "revolutions" or coups d'état (1963, 1968, 1977, 1979, and 1997). In 1991, the Congo abandoned its Marxist-Leninist stance and one-party system. A national conference recommended the adoption of a pluralist and democratic constitution. This constitution was approved by referendum in 1992, paving the way for free and fair elections. It provided for a French-modeled semipresidential government. It was suspended in 1997 in still another coup. A forum of national reconciliation was then set up to discuss the nature and duration of the transition. A new constitution that emerged from this forum was approved by referendum on January 20, 2002. The last presidential, local, and legislative elections took place from March to July 2002.

FORM AND IMPACT OF THE CONSTITUTION

The Congolese constitution is a written, supreme, and entrenched constitution. It prevails over any other law in the republic. It is difficult to amend, as special majorities are required in the National Assembly and the Senate.

BASIC ORGANIZATIONAL STRUCTURE

The Republic of the Congo is a unitary state made up of 10 regions dependent on the central government, plus the city of Brazzaville. These regions differ considerably from one another in area and population and have a degree of autonomy.

LEADING CONSTITUTIONAL PRINCIPLES

The Congo is a republic; it is a pluralist, unitary, social, secular, and democratic state respectful of human rights, constitutionalism, and the rule of law under a presidential system of government. The leading principle of the republic is "government of the people by the people and for the people." National sovereignty belongs only to the people, who exercise it through universal adult suffrage, by their elected representatives, or by referendum.

CONSTITUTIONAL BODIES

The constitutional bodies are the president; parliament, which consists of the National Assembly and the Senate, the Supreme Court; the Constitutional Court; the High Court of Justice; the Court of Accounts and Budgetary Discipline; the Economic and Social Council; the Council for Freedom of Communication; the Human Rights Commission; and the mediator of the republic.

The President

The president is elected by universal adult suffrage for a seven-year term that is renewable only once. The president is the head of state and of the administration and presides over the Council of Ministers. As the symbol of national unity, the president must ensure respect for the constitution and the regular functioning of public institutions. The president determines the policy of the nation and guarantees the continuity of the state, national independence, territorial integrity, and respect for international agreements. The president is the keystone and the leading institution of the republic.

There is no prime minister. The ministers are appointed by the president and accountable only to the president, who may dismiss them. They do not form an administration in the true sense of the word. They merely assist the president in the exercise of executive power.

Parliament

The legislative power is vested in parliament, which also controls the executive authority. Parliament consists of the National Assembly and the Senate. The president cannot dissolve parliament. On the other hand, the latter cannot remove the president from office.

The National Assembly

The National Assembly consists of deputies who represent the nation as a whole and are elected by universal adult suffrage for a five-year term. They may be reelected. Imperative mandate is prohibited. Their term of office may also end with death, resignation, incompatibility, or sentencing for criminal offense.

A deputy who resigns from the party or political grouping that nominated him or her during the election ceases to be a deputy. Only the National Assembly or the president may authorize a declaration of war.

The Senate

The Senate consists of senators elected for a six-year term by local councils. In addition to its legislative power, the Senate mediates political conflicts and serves as the adviser to the nation.

As with deputies, any senator who resigns from the party or political grouping that nominated him or her during the election ceases to be a senator.

The Lawmaking Process
The main task of parliament is to enact laws. Constitutional bodies such as the president and the Constitutional Court also take part in the lawmaking process. The president and the members of parliament may concurrently initiate legislation or amend it.

The National Assembly and the Senate must adopt bills in identical terms. Otherwise, the president may request a joint commission to propose a single text to be adopted by the two houses. This final text cannot be amended without presidential authorization. If the joint commission fails to adopt a consensual text, the president may, after a second deliberation by the National Assembly and the Senate, request the National Assembly to decide finally. The president may request parliament to vote a law authorizing the president to legislate by ordinance or decree to implement his or her program of action.

The Judiciary

Justice is administered in the name of the people. The constitution provides for the independence of the judiciary vis-à-vis the executive and the legislature, but the president guarantees this independence and presides over the High Council of the Judiciary.

The judicial power is vested in the Supreme Court and other courts or tribunals. A special law deals with their organization, composition, and functioning. The members of the Supreme Court and magistrates are nominated by the High Council of the Judiciary and appointed by the president.

The judiciary protects individual freedoms and fundamental human rights. Judges are subject to the law in performing their functions, and a law regulates their status.

THE ELECTION PROCESS

All power emanates from the people, who assume it directly through referenda or elections and indirectly through their representatives. Any Congolese citizen over the age of 18 may stand for election and vote in the election.

POLITICAL PARTIES

Title IV of the constitution deals with political parties. Parties must be national and not identify themselves with any ethnic group, region, religion, or belief. They must respect the principles of democracy, national unity, territorial integrity, and national sovereignty, and they must promote fundamental human rights. A law provides for the funding of political parties; foreign funding is outlawed.

CITIZENSHIP

Every Congolese is entitled to Congolese citizenship and may change his or her citizenship under the conditions determined by the law.

FUNDAMENTAL RIGHTS

Fundamental rights and freedoms are enshrined in the constitution, including civil, political, social, economic, and cultural rights. Women's rights, children's rights, and the rights of the elderly and disabled persons are also entrenched. Foreigners are entitled to the same rights and freedoms as nationals as applicable by treaties and laws on condition of reciprocity. Inspired by the African Charter on Human and Peoples' Rights, the constitution also provides for duties of the citizens.

Impact and Functions of Fundamental Rights

The Human Rights Commission is designed to protect and promote human rights and fundamental freedoms. The constitution also stresses that the judiciary is the guardian of the law and fundamental freedoms.

Limitations to Fundamental Rights

Fundamental rights are not absolute. They may be limited by law. There is no general limitation clause but rather internal limitations specific to each right. The limitations should be reasonable and subject to the law. Fundamental rights may be suspended in certain circumstances such as in a case of emergency.

ECONOMY

The constitution does not refer to any economic system, other than stating that the Republic of the Congo is a "social" state. Various explicit freedoms and rights demonstrate that the framers sought to establish a social market economy: freedom of movement, art, trade, and industry; right to private property and inheritance; freedom of association; and right to work, education, and health; nondiscrimination against all, including women and children, and prohibition of expropriation of private property except for public interests and in accordance with the law.

RELIGIOUS COMMUNITIES

There is no state religion; the Republic of the Congo is a secular state. Nevertheless, the constitution guarantees the right to freedom of thought, conscience, and religion. Use of religion for political purposes is outlawed.

MILITARY DEFENSE AND STATE OF EMERGENCY

The public force consists of the national police, gendarmerie, and armed forces. They are apolitical and subject to civilian authority and to the rule of law. They cannot be used for personal interests. A law determines their organization and functioning and the status of their members. It is a breach of criminal law to organize or maintain a private militia, although the incumbent president used militias to return to power.

The president is the chief of the armed forces, also presiding over the Council of Defense. If there is a serious threat to the institutions of the republic, national independence, or territorial integrity, or when international agreements cannot be enforced, the president may take exceptional measures required by the circumstances or proclaim a state of emergency after consulting the presidents of the National Assembly, the Senate, and the Constitutional Court.

AMENDMENTS TO THE CONSTITUTION

The president and the members of parliament may initiate constitutional amendments. Amendments that affect the republican form of the state, its secular character, the terms of office of the president, and human rights are prohibited. An organic law deals with constitutional amendments. Before an amendment is submitted to a referendum or to the National Assembly and the Senate, in which a two-thirds vote is required for approval, the Constitutional Court must declare that the bill is consistent with the constitution.

PRIMARY SOURCES

Constitution in English. Available online. URL: http://www.chr.up.ac.za/hr_docs/constitutions/docs/CongoC%20(english%20summary)(rev).doc. Accessed on June 17, 2006.

Constitution in French: *Constitution de la République du Congo.* Available online. URL: http://www.republique-congo.com/politique/CORPpol3.htm. Accessed on September 11, 2005.

SECONDARY SOURCES

Emmanuel Dieudonné Alakani, "Congo-Brazzaville—faut-il changer la Constitution du 15 mars 1992?" *Revue juridique et politique* 54, no. 3 (2000): 258–264.

Eric Dibas-Franck, "L'acte fondamental du Congo-Brazzaville du 24 octobre 1997." *Revue juridique et politique* 52, no. 3 (1998): 300–308.

United Nations, "Core Document Forming Part of the Reports of States Parties: Congo" (HRI/CORE/1/Add.79), 10 November 1997. Available online. URL: http://www.unhchr.ch/tbs/doc.nsf. Accessed on September 11, 2005.

André Mbata B. Mangu

COSTA RICA

At-a-Glance

OFFICIAL NAME
Republic of Costa Rica

CAPITAL
San José

POPULATION
4,016,173 (2005 est.)

SIZE
19,730 sq. mi. (51,100 sq. km)

LANGUAGES
Spanish (official), with a southwestern Caribbean Creole dialect of English spoken around the Limon area

RELIGIONS
Catholic 69%, Protestant 18%, unaffiliated or other 13%

NATIONAL OR ETHNIC COMPOSITION
European and some mestizo 94%, African origin 3%, Chinese 1%, indigenous 1%, other 1%

DATE OF INDEPENDENCE OR CREATION
September 15, 1821

TYPE OF GOVERNMENT
Mix of presidentialism and parliamentarism

TYPE OF STATE
Centralist state

TYPE OF LEGISLATURE
Unicameral parliament

DATE OF CONSTITUTION
November 7, 1949

DATE OF LAST AMENDMENT
July 15, 2003

Costa Rica is a democratic republic with a mixed government system with elements of presidentialism and parliamentarism. According to the 1949 constitution, the executive power is exercised, on behalf of the people, by the president and the cabinet ministers. The 57 members of the unicameral Legislative Assembly are elected at the same time as the president for a term of four years. The Supreme Electoral Tribunal independently organizes and supervises all acts pertaining to suffrage. The main tasks of the Constitutional Chamber of the Supreme Court of Justice are to protect the fundamental rights established by the constitution and the international legal instruments ratified by Costa Rica and to ensure their full implementation. Costa Rica is divided into seven provinces, which are administered by governors.

The constitution provides for liberal rights as well as for social rights and guarantees. It establishes Roman Catholicism as the state religion but also secures freedom of religion. Costa Rica has no military and maintains only a nonconscripted civil guard with police duties.

CONSTITUTIONAL HISTORY

Christopher Columbus's last voyage to the "New World" in 1502 took him to the shores of Costa Rica (translated "rich coast"). Spanish settlement of Costa Rica started in 1522. Spain administered the region for nearly three centuries as part of the Captaincy General of Guatemala under a military governor. In 1821, the Central American provinces, Costa Rica, Guatemala, Honduras, Nicaragua, and El Salvador, declared independence from Spain and subsequently formed the Central American Federation. Costa Rica ratified its first constitution in 1825. In 1838, the Central American Federation was dissolved, and Costa Rica became a fully independent republic.

The 1871 constitution installed a powerful presidential regime in which the president of the republic concentrated in his hand the main functions of the state, and the congress played a secondary role.

The result of the 1948 presidential election was annulled when the government's candidate, who finished second, refused to accept defeat. The subsequent revolt in favor of the winning oppositional candidate led to an interim regime. The Government Board convened a Constituent Assembly to promulgate a new constitution. The final text of the constitution of November 7, 1949, was the product of compromise among the main political players. It established the separation of powers among the legislative, executive, and judicial branches of government. The Supreme Electoral Tribunal is considered a fourth power. Since 1949, the constitution has been partially amended more than 50 times.

FORM AND IMPACT OF THE CONSTITUTION

Costa Rica has a written constitution, codified in a single document. The Constitución Politica de la República de Costa Rica of November 7, 1949, is the 10th constitution in the country's history.

International treaties play an important role in Costa Rican legislation since Article 7 of the constitution provides that treaties, international agreements, and concordats that have been ratified and approved by the Legislative Assembly are superior to national law. However, any international agreements that affect the territorial integrity or political organization of Costa Rica require the approval of the Legislative Assembly by a vote of not less than three-fourths of its total membership and the approval of two-thirds of the members of a Constitutional Assembly called for the purpose.

BASIC ORGANIZATIONAL STRUCTURE

Costa Rica is divided into seven provinces, which are administered by governors appointed by the president. However, most government agencies have their own administrative organization, which ignores provincial boundaries. Each province is divided into cantons, which again are subdivided into districts. Costa Rica held its first general mayoral election, whereby mayors were elected directly by the voters, in December 2002.

LEADING CONSTITUTIONAL PRINCIPLES

Costa Rica is a free and independent democratic republic. Its system of government is a mixture of presidentialism and parliamentarism with a strong system of constitutional checks and balances. The legislative, executive, and judicial branches are distinct and independent; none of these branches may delegate the exercise of its own functions. Public officials are mere depositaries of authority

and must take an oath to observe and comply with the constitution and the laws.

CONSTITUTIONAL BODIES

The predominant bodies provided for in the Costa Rican constitution are the Legislative Assembly, the president, and the cabinet of ministers. The Supreme Electoral Tribunal and the Office of the Comptroller-General also play important roles.

THE LEGISLATIVE ASSEMBLY

The legislature is the unicameral Legislative Assembly with 57 representatives who represent the whole nation but are elected at provincial level at the same time as the president. The legislature has six standing committees—government and administration, economic affairs, budgetary matters, social affairs, legal affairs, agriculture and natural resources—which are responsible for evaluating proposed laws. The Legislative Assembly has the power to question cabinet ministers and censure them if they are guilty of unconstitutional acts or serious errors. In 1992, the legislature created the Office of the Ombudsperson, which may take cases against the government either on its own initiative or at the request of any third party.

The Lawmaking Process

The initiative for enactment of laws can be taken by any member of the Legislative Assembly or by the executive branch through the cabinet ministers. In order to become a law, any bill of law must be subjected to two debates, obtain the approval of the Legislative Assembly and the sanction of the executive branch, and be published in the *Official Journal*. The Legislative Assembly may also delegate the consideration and passing of bills to permanent commissions, which must reflect on a proportional basis the number of representatives of the constituent political parties.

The President and Cabinet Ministers

The executive power is exercised, on behalf of the people, by the president of the republic and the cabinet ministers in the capacity of subordinate collaborators. The president and the two vice presidents are elected by popular vote; in case no candidate obtains 40 percent of the votes, a second ballot is held. The president may appoint and remove the cabinet ministers.

The Supreme Electoral Tribunal

The organization, direction, and supervision of acts pertaining to suffrage are the exclusive function of the Supreme Electoral Tribunal, which enjoys independence in the performance of its duties. The members of the

Supreme Electoral Tribunal are appointed by the Supreme Court of Justice by a vote of no less than two-thirds of its members.

The Office of the Comptroller-General

The constitutional body in charge of the oversight of public finances is the Office of the Comptroller-General of the republic. This office is an auxiliary to the Legislative Assembly, but it enjoys full functional and administrative independence in the performance of its duties.

The Judiciary

The legal system is based on the Spanish civil-law system. Legislative acts are subject to judicial review by the Supreme Court of Justice. The justices are elected for renewable eight-year terms by the Legislative Assembly.

A Constitutional Chamber of the Supreme Court was established in 1989 in order to guarantee, by means of habeas corpus and *amparo,* the rights and freedoms enshrined in the constitution and the human rights recognized in international law that are in force in Costa Rica. It also monitors the constitutionality of all laws and acts subject to public law. The Constitutional Chamber rules on its own jurisdiction so that constitutional matters are not decided by other courts and that jurisprudence maintains sufficient consistency to safeguard the principle of prompt recourse.

Costa Rica became the first nation to recognize the jurisdiction of the Inter-American Human Rights Court, based in Costa Rica's capital city, San José.

THE ELECTION PROCESS

Costa Rican citizens of at least 18 years of age are eligible to vote. In April 2003, the Supreme Court annulled a constitutional amendment barring presidents from running for reelection enacted by the Legislative Assembly in 1969. Thus former presidents of Costa Rica may run for reelection after they have been out of office for two presidential terms.

POLITICAL PARTIES

An important element introduced by the 1949 constitution was the constitutionalization of political parties. All citizens have the right to organize themselves into parties in order to participate in national politics, provided that such parties have committed themselves in their programs to respect the constitutional order of the republic. In addition, the Electoral Code gives parties a monopoly in nominating candidates for elective positions.

Since the mid-20th century, Costa Rica has had a stable democratic government. The fairness of national elections has been indicated by the fact that almost every four-year period has seen a change in the party winning the presidency. At the 2002 elections, the two main political parties, Social Christian Unity Party (PUSC) and National Liberation Party (PLN), were challenged by the recently formed Citizen Action Party (PAC).

CITIZENSHIP

Costa Rican citizenship may be acquired either by birth or by naturalization. Citizenship by birth includes children born within the territory of the republic to a Costa Rican father or mother as well as children born abroad to a Costa Rican–born father or mother upon registration in the civil register. Children born in Costa Rica to foreign parents and infants of unknown parents who are found in Costa Rica are also Costa Rican by birth. The conditions to become a Costa Rican by naturalization are easier to fulfill for nationals of Central America, Spaniards, and Iberian Americans than for other foreigners.

FUNDAMENTAL RIGHTS

The constitution establishes the basic rights of all persons, without discrimination on grounds of sex, race, national or family origin, language, religion, or political opinion. The right to life is guaranteed, and the death penalty does not exist in the Costa Rican legal system. The constitution also provides for social rights, such as labor as a right of the individual and an obligation to society. Freedom of education and training and due process are guaranteed. Every person also has the right to a healthy and ecologically balanced environment and is therefore entitled to denounce any acts that may infringe this right and claim redress for the damage caused.

Every person has the right to present writs of habeas corpus to guarantee his or her freedom and personal integrity and writs of *amparo* to maintain or reestablish the enjoyment of other rights conferred by the constitution, as well as those of fundamental nature established in international human rights instruments, provided that they are enforceable in Costa Rica.

Impact and Function of Fundamental Rights

While freedom of expression is guaranteed in principle, members of the clergy or secular individuals cannot make political propaganda in any way invoking religious motives or making use of religious beliefs. The Inter-American Court of Human Rights found in July 2004 that the criminal defamation sentence against the Costa Rican journalist Mauricio Herrera Ulloa violated the right to freedom of thought and expression according to Article 13 of the American Convention on Human Rights.

Limitations to Fundamental Rights

Some fundamental rights are limited by law such as the right to freedom of communication. For reasons of public necessity, the Legislative Assembly can impose limitations related to social interest on property.

ECONOMY

The constitution protects the right to private property. However, domestic and foreign property owners have had difficulty in obtaining adequate, timely compensation for lands expropriated for national parks and other purposes. Furthermore, the law grants substantial rights to squatters who invade uncultivated land, regardless of who may hold title to the property.

RELIGIOUS COMMUNITIES

The constitution establishes the Roman Catholic and apostolic religion as the state religion but also provides for freedom of religion. Persons of all denominations freely practice their religion without government interference. In the event of a violation of religious freedom, the victim's remedy is to file a lawsuit with the Constitutional Chamber of the Supreme Court of Justice.

The government does not inhibit the establishment of religious groups through taxation or special licensing requirements. Although religious groups are not required to register as such with the government, all groups must incorporate in order to have legal standing and must have a minimum of 12 members. Religious groups must register with the Department of Justice to conduct any type of fundraising activity.

MILITARY DEFENSE AND STATE OF EMERGENCY

Article 12 of the constitution abolishes the army as a permanent institution. Military forces may only be organized under an international agreement or for the national defense. In either case, they must always be subordinate to the civil power and may not deliberate or make political statements or representations individually or collectively. Costa Rica maintains a nonconscripted civil guard that has police duties. In addition, a professional coast guard was established in 2000.

The constitution provides for three kinds of states of emergency: suspension of constitutional rights and guarantees, authorization to declare a state of national defense and to make peace, and the right to control sections of the budget during periods of legislative recess. The suspension of constitutional rights and guarantees may last a maximum of only 30 days and requires the approval of not less than two-thirds of all members of the Legislative Assembly.

AMENDMENTS TO THE CONSTITUTION

A general amendment to the constitution can only be made by a Constituent Assembly called for this purpose. A law calling such assembly needs a vote of no less than two-thirds of the total membership of the Legislative Assembly but does not require the approval of the executive branch. The Legislative Assembly may also partially amend the constitution in strict compliance with the provisions of Article 195. There have been more than 50 partial amendments to the Costa Rican constitution since it entered into force in 1949.

PRIMARY SOURCES

Constitution in English. Available online. URL: http://www.costaricalaw.com/legalnet/constitutional_law/constitenglish.html. Accessed on August 3, 2005.
Constitution in Spanish. Available online. URL: www.tse.go.cr/Constitucion_cr.doc. Accessed on September 7, 2005.

SECONDARY SOURCES

Robert S. Barker, "Judicial Review in Costa Rica—Evolution and Recent Developments." *Southwestern University Journal of Law and Trade in the Americas* 7, no. 2 (2000): 267–290.
Debevoise and Plimpton, "Amicus Brief in Support of Mauricio Herrera Ulloa and Fernan Vargas Rohrmoser." Available online. URL: http://www.cpj.org/news/2002/Costa19feb04_AmicusBrief.pdf. Accessed on September 24, 2005.
Rubén Hernández, "The Evolution of the Costa Rican Constitutional System." *Jahrbuch des öffentlichen Rechts der Gegenwart* 49 (2001): 535–548.
Miguel González Marcos, "Specialized Constitutional Review in Latin America: Choosing between a Constitutional Chamber and a Constitutional Court," *Verfassung und Recht in Übersee* 36 (2003): 164–205.
Roger A. Peterson, "A Guide to Legal Research in Costa Rica." Available online. URL: http://www.llrx.com/features/costarica.htm. Accessed on August 5, 2005.

Michael Wiener

CÔTE D'IVOIRE

At-a-Glance

OFFICIAL NAME
Republic of Côte d'Ivoire

CAPITAL
Yamoussoukro (official); Abidjan (de facto)

POPULATION
18,100,000 (2003 est.)

SIZE
124,500 sq. mi. (322,500 sq. km)

LANGUAGES
French (official language), five principal native language groups

RELIGIONS
Muslim 35–40%; Christian (Catholic, Protestant, and other) 25–35%; indigenous beliefs 10–20%

NATIONAL OR ETHNIC COMPOSITION
More than 60 ethnic groups in five principal divisions: Akan, Krou, Southern Mande, Northern Mande, Senoufo/Lobi; more than 5 million non-Ivoirian Africans (many from Burkina Faso); 100,000 Lebanese, 20,000 French

DATE OF INDEPENDENCE OR CREATION
August 7, 1960 (from France)

TYPE OF GOVERNMENT
Presidential democracy

TYPE OF STATE
Centralist state

TYPE OF LEGISLATURE
Unicameral parliament

DATE OF CONSTITUTION
July 24, 2000

DATE OF LAST AMENDMENT
No amendment

The Republic of Côte d'Ivoire is a presidential democracy. It is a secular, unitary state made up of 58 departments. The constitution adopted in 2000 provides for a separation of the legislative, executive, and judicial powers. A multiparty system is officially recognized. The president is the dominant figure in Côte d'Ivoire's constitution: the head of state, head of the executive, and commander in chief of the armed forces. The constitution enumerates many fundamental freedoms and rights that the authorities have to protect. The Constitutional Council has jurisdiction over constitutional disputes.

Côte d'Ivoire was unstable in the early years of the 21st century. It was unclear whether or how national reconciliation could succeed.

CONSTITUTIONAL HISTORY

French missionaries landed in what is now Côte d'Ivoire in the early 17th century. In the 19th century, the territories of local kings were placed under a French protectorate.

In 1893, Côte d'Ivoire officially became a French colony. The country became independent on August 7, 1960. The country's first constitution also dates to that year.

Under its first president, Félix Houphouët-Boigny who ruled the country until 1993, Côte d'Ivoire was stable. On Christmas Eve 1999, his successor was overthrown in a military coup. In a referendum in 2000, a new constitution was adopted. Shortly afterward, presidential elections took place; General Guei stopped the counting and declared himself winner. After bloody fighting, he had to flee the country, and his opponent, Gbagbo, was declared president.

A coup attempt in January 2001 failed, but another one in 2002 turned into a prolonged rebellion. The northern part of the country split off and has been controlled by the Patriotic Movement of Côte d'Ivoire ever since. A government of national reconciliation was formed in 2002. However, new fighting occurred at the end of 2004. Peacekeeping missions, the United Nations Operation in Côte d'Ivoire (UNOCI), were deployed to the country from the United Nations as well as peacekeeping missions from the Economic Community of West African States (ECOWAS).

FORM AND IMPACT OF THE CONSTITUTION

The constitution adopted in 2000 has only limited impact. This is due to the ongoing division of the republic into northern and southern segments since the 2002 rebellion and the lack of stability.

The constitution of Côte d'Ivoire is one single document with 133 articles. International treaties, after being ratified and officially published in Côte d'Ivoire, take precedence over national laws. However, ratification of international treaties that are contrary to the relevant provisions of the constitution may take place only after the constitution is amended.

BASIC ORGANIZATIONAL STRUCTURE

The country has a centralist structure. It is divided into 19 regions and 58 departments. At the moment, the official state authorities control only about half of the country.

LEADING CONSTITUTIONAL PRINCIPLES

The constitution provides for a presidential democracy within the framework of division of powers. The people participate in politics by way of referendum and through elections.

According to the constitution, Côte d'Ivoire is a secular, democratic, and social state. Equality of all before the law is to be ensured by the authorities. The constitution also speaks of ethnic, cultural, and religious diversity. The country shall be one and indivisible. The national motto is "Union, Discipline, and Work."

The promotion of regional and subregional integration, with a view to achieving African unity, is one of the commitments listed in the constitution.

CONSTITUTIONAL BODIES

Major constitutional organs are the president of the republic, the executive government, the National Assembly, and the judiciary.

The President of the Republic

The president of the republic is the head of state as well as head of the executive. The president determines the politics of the nation.

The president appoints and dismisses the prime minister and, upon the prime minister's advice, the other members of the executive government. The president also appoints other high civil and military officials. Together with the parliament, the president plays a strong role in the creation of new law. The president of the republic commands the armed forces. The president is elected for a five-year term by the people with the possibility of one reelection.

The Executive Government

The executive government is headed by the prime minister, who is appointed by the president of the republic, as are the cabinet ministers on the advice of the prime minister. The prime minister holds personal responsibility before the president of the republic.

The National Assembly (Assemblée Nationale)

The 225 members of this unicameral parliament are elected for a five-year term through universal suffrage. The National Assembly holds ordinary sessions twice a year. Extraordinary sessions can be held upon request of the president of the republic or the absolute majority of the members of the National Assembly. The mandate of members of parliament is renewable. Each member of parliament is supposed to represent the whole people. The National Assembly of Côte d'Ivoire has the authority to declare a state of war.

The Lawmaking Process

The president of the republic and the members of parliament have the right to initiate legislation. In practice, the president dominates that function. The president has to promulgate a law within 15 days after its transmission from parliament. If the president fails to do so in the given time, the Constitutional Council can declare a law executable. However, the president may call for a second reading of the law. If a two-thirds majority in parliament votes for the draft law in the second reading, the presidential refusal is overridden. Regular laws may be submitted to the Constitutional Council in order to check their compliance with the constitution. Organic law—the law regulating the structure and system of constitutional organs or other law defined as organic by the constitution—must be submitted to the Constitutional Council before promulgation for a ruling on constitutionality.

The constitution provides for an alternative way of creating new law. The president can submit a bill to a national referendum on any question. In case of approval, the president promulgates the law within the 15-day period.

The Judiciary

The legal system is based on French law as well as on customary law. The judiciary is supposed to be independent from the executive and legislative powers. Apart from ordinary jurisdiction with the Supreme Court as highest instance, there is also a Higher Court of Justice. It exclusively deals with crimes committed by cabinet members and high treason by the president of the republic.

Another institution, the Constitutional Council, has to decide whether laws are in accordance with the constitution. Some of its members are selected by the president, others by parliament.

THE ELECTION PROCESS AND POLITICAL PARTICIPATION

The people can participate politically in referendums and elections.

Côte d'Ivoire has universal suffrage for all Ivoirians. The minimal voting age is 18. To be eligible as president of the republic, a candidate has to be between 40 and 75 years of age, Ivoirian by birth, and of Ivoirian descent.

The 225 members of the National Assembly are elected for five-year terms from single-seat constituencies. According to the 2000 Electoral Code, only Ivoirians who have been citizens of the country for at least 10 years and have reached 25 years of age are eligible to serve in the National Assembly.

POLITICAL PARTIES

Côte d'Ivoire has had a pluralistic party system since 1990. There are a few large and numerous smaller parties. Opposition parties boycotted recent major elections. The constitution bars regional, denominational, tribal, ethnic, or racially based parties.

CITIZENSHIP

The concept of *Ivoirity* has been widely discussed since the mid-1990s. *Ivoirity* is described as a set of sociohistorical, geographical, and linguistic data that determine whether a person is an Ivoirian. Such a person is supposed to be born of Ivoirian parents of one of the ethnic groups of Côte d'Ivoire. Because a very high percentage of non-Ivoirians live in the country, the question of who is entitled to citizenship and is eligible to stand for office has been a top political issue for more than a decade.

FUNDAMENTAL RIGHTS

Fundamental freedoms and the rights and duties of the citizen are enumerated in the first title of the constitution. The traditional set of liberal rights is guaranteed. The individual is regarded as sacred and enjoys many rights that the authorities must protect. Ivoirian citizens have the duty to respect the laws and regulations of the republic, to respect public assets, and to protect the environment.

Impact and Functions of Fundamental Rights

The actual impact of the fundamental rights specified in the constitution is very limited. The country is split into a rebel-held north and a south run by the government. The peace process has been fragile over the past years. Torture and summary executions have been reported. Military actions have included alarming attacks against civilians. Violence first broke out between indigenous groups and outsiders and later was aimed at the French in particular and non-African residents in general.

Limitations to Fundamental Rights

The fundamental rights are not unlimited. For instance, deprivation of property may be done for public benefit with compensation. Restrictions to the inviolability of a person's home may be introduced by special law.

ECONOMY

The constitution of Côte d'Ivoire does not favor any specific economic system. However, certain rights set the economic framework. Thus, the right to join trade unions and the right to strike are guaranteed. Every citizen is allowed to engage in free enterprise. Special laws may provide limits to these rights.

RELIGIOUS COMMUNITIES

The republic of Côte d'Ivoire is a secular country. Freedom of all religious opinions is be guaranteed. These provisions reflect the religious reality, as both the Christian (in the south) and Muslim (in the north) religions are widespread, and neither dominates the country.

MILITARY DEFENSE AND STATE OF EMERGENCY

The president is supreme commander of the armed forces and appoints high military personnel. Therefore, the president has a strong position during a state of emergency.

A state of emergency can be decreed at a meeting of the executive government, but it can be prolonged beyond a period of 15 days only with the prior consent of the National Assembly.

AMENDMENTS TO THE CONSTITUTION

A revision of the constitution may be initiated conjointly by the president of the republic and the National Assembly. In most cases, a four-fifths majority of the parliament is required to pass an amendment. In cases of changes that affect the election of the president or the presidential mandate, the proposed revision must be approved in a referendum by an absolute majority of votes cast. No amendment can change the republican or secular form of the state or its territorial integrity.

PRIMARY SOURCES

Constitution in English (extracts). Available online. URL: http://www.chr.up.ac.za/hr_docs/constitutions/docs/CoteD%27ivoire(english%20summary)(rev).doc. Accessed on June 17, 2006.

Constitution in French. Available online. URL: http://www.ethnonet-africa.org/data/ivoir/const2000.htm#proj_const2000. Accessed on September 24, 2005.

SECONDARY SOURCES

Frances Akindès, *The Roots of the Military-Political Crises in Côte d'Ivoire*. Research Report No. 128. Uppsala: Nordiska Afrikainstitutet, 2004.

Lansana Gberie and Prosper Addo, "Challenges of Peace Implementation in Côte d'Ivoire." Available online. URL:http://www.iss.org.za/pubs/Monographs/No105/Contents.html. Accessed on July 21, 2005.

"Pretoria Agreement on the Peace Process in the Côte d'Ivoire (April 2005)." Available online. URL: http://www.iss.org.za/AF/profiles/cotedivoire/ptapax.pdf. Accessed on August 9, 2005.

Hartmut Rank

CROATIA

At-a-Glance

OFFICIAL NAME
Republic of Croatia

CAPITAL
Zagreb

POPULATION
4,496,869 (July 2004 est.)

SIZE
21,831 sq. mi. (56,542 sq. km)

LANGUAGE
Croatian

NATIONAL OR ETHNIC COMPOSITION
Croat 89.6%, Serb 4.5%, Bosniak 0.5%, Hungarian
0.4%, Slovene 0.3%, Czech 0.2%, Roma 0.2%,
Albanian 0.1%, Montenegrin 0.1%, other 4.1% (2001)

DATE OF INDEPENDENCE OR CREATION
June 25, 1991 (from Yugoslavia)

TYPE OF GOVERNMENT
Parliamentary democracy

TYPE OF STATE
Unitary state

TYPE OF LEGISLATURE
Unicameral parliament

DATE OF CONSTITUTION
December 21, 1990

DATE OF LAST AMENDMENT
March 26, 2001

Croatia is a new parliamentary democracy in the process of transitioning toward realization of the rule of law. There is a separation of executive, legislative, and judicial powers. Croatia is a unitary state divided into 21 counties and the capital. There are also local government units. The constitution provides for far-reaching guarantees of human rights and specifically the rights of ethnic minorities. A system of institutions protects against violations of the constitution, including a rather strong constitutional court, an ombudsperson, and an independent judiciary. The constitution is still in the process of implementation, and the rule of law has gradually strengthened during the last decade.

The governmental organization was substantially changed in 2000 and 2001 when the former semipresidential system was replaced by a parliamentary one. The president of the republic is elected directly and participates in important decisions of the government. The prime minister is the central political figure and depends on the confidence of parliament as the representative body of the people. Free, equal, general, and direct elections of the members of parliament are guaranteed. Political parties dominate the political system and sometimes tend to disregard the constitution.

The economic system can be described as transitioning into a market economy. The military is subject to the civil government in terms of law and fact. "Love for peace" is considered one of the fundamental values of the constitution. Religious freedom is guaranteed. State and religious communities are separated.

CONSTITUTIONAL HISTORY

Since the 12th century, Croatia has lived as a part of various compound states in which it struggled to maintain its independence; it was attached to Hungary (1102), the Habsburg monarchy (1527), the Austro-Hungarian Empire (1867), the Kingdom of Yugoslavia (1918), and the Yugoslav federation (1945–91). For many years, large parts of the country were occupied by the Turks, and a military frontier existed along the border with the Ottoman Empire.

In 1945, the communist federation of Yugoslavia was established in order to accommodate a number of nationalities, several of which have at times formed their own nation-states. The 1974 constitution attempted to maintain unity in a confederal constitutional arrangement and to ensure equality to the six republics and two autonomous provinces. This system did not perform well, and together with the collapse of the communist regime, the federation disintegrated in 1991. Croatia defended its independence in the Homeland War against Serbia from 1991 to 1995. It received international recognition on January 15, 1991.

The framers of the 1990 constitution attempted to ensure a peaceful transition to a pluralist political system, rule of law, and a free market economy. During the war and a state of emergency that lasted until 1997, a highly centralized system of presidential dominance developed. This system required constitutional changes after the first change of governmental parties, which occurred in 2000. Parliamentary government was established in order to prevent another such centralization of power. The bicameral system was abandoned in 2001 with the aim of strengthening the position of parliament in relation to the executive. The Republic of Croatia has been a candidate for membership in the European Union since 2004.

FORM AND IMPACT OF THE CONSTITUTION

The 1990 constitution was amended in 1997, 2000, and 2001, and the integral text was published in April 2001. The implementation of the constitution is under way, but it can be qualified as transitional since changes related to the expected membership in the European Union and in the North Atlantic Treaty Organization (NATO) have been under consideration. International law is an integral part of the domestic legal system, even dominant over domestic legislation. Legislation must continually be adjusted to European law.

BASIC ORGANIZATIONAL STRUCTURE

Croatia is a unitary and centralist state. Local government is guaranteed. It is based on 21 counties and more than 400 municipalities and townships. Reform of this system is under consideration.

LEADING CONSTITUTIONAL PRINCIPLES

Certain values are enumerated in the constitution as fundamental and provide a basis for its interpretation: freedom, equal rights, national equality, equality of genders, love of peace, social justice, respect for human rights, inviolability of ownership, conservation of nature and the environment, the rule of law, and a democratic multiparty system.

CONSTITUTIONAL BODIES

The main constitutional bodies are the president, the cabinet of administration, parliament, the Constitutional Court, and the judiciary.

The President of the Republic

The president of the republic represents Croatia at home and abroad. The president also is responsible for the regular and harmonious functioning of the state and its stability. The president is responsible for the defense of the independence and territorial integrity of the republic.

The president is elected directly by the people for a five-year term and can be reelected only once. In order to reduce the role of the president, the prime minister and not the president is the head of government.

The Cabinet

The cabinet is appointed by, and responsible to, the parliamentary majority. The prime minister has the authority to set the administration's policy. In three important areas, the cabinet needs the countersignature of the president of the republic: emergency measures, foreign policy, and control of the security services and the military.

Sabor (Parliament)

The Sabor is a representative body of the people vested with the legislative power. It monitors the executive and can dismiss the cabinet after a vote of no confidence.

Representatives are elected in general, direct, free, equal, and secret balloting. Croatian citizens who live abroad participate in elections. Proportional representation is applied.

The Lawmaking Process

Bills are generally initiated by the cabinet. Legislation related to human rights, elections, state organization, and local government must be passed by the majority of all members of parliament, laws related to ethnic minorities by a two-thirds majority of all representatives.

The Constitutional Court

The Constitutional Court is a fourth branch of government separate from the judiciary. It rules on the constitutionality of legislation and offers protection to individual constitutional rights. The court supervises elections and referenda and rules on the impeachment of the president of the republic for violations of the constitution. It consists of 13 justices elected by parliament for a term of eight years. Justices may be reelected.

The independence of the justices is guaranteed and respected. The court has established and continues to strengthen its role as a watchdog of democracy. Its best-known decision was a 1998 ruling that a reduction of retirement allowances during a state of emergency was unconstitutional. By hearing individual constitutional appeals, the court plays an important role in establishing respect for human rights.

The Judiciary

The judicial power is autonomous and independent. Judges are appointed for life by the State Council of Judiciary. The judiciary has an enormous backlog of cases and is generally considered to be inefficient. It is undergoing serious reconstruction.

The Supreme Court is the highest court; it is expected to ensure uniform application of laws and equal justice to all. The president of the Supreme Court is appointed for a four-year term by parliament at the nomination of the president of the republic on the recommendation of the sitting justices.

THE ELECTION PROCESS

All Croatian citizens over the age of 18 have the right to stand for elections and to vote. Proportional representation is used in both parliamentary and local elections. The president is elected by a majority of voters, in two rounds of balloting if necessary.

POLITICAL PARTIES

Political parties are easy to establish and are numerous. They dominate public life. A political party can be banned by a decision of the Constitutional Court for acting against democratic constitutional order.

CITIZENSHIP

Croatian citizenship is primarily acquired on the basis of place of birth in Croatia. It can also be obtained by naturalization. A great number of Croatian nationals living abroad bear dual citizenship and participate in Croatian elections.

FUNDAMENTAL RIGHTS

The first chapter of the constitution defines human rights. In addition to the traditional set of human rights and civil liberties, it includes a set of social and economic rights, as well as strong, explicit guarantees of the rights of ethnic minorities. Rights pertain to the relationships between citizens and government and between citizens themselves.

The provisions on human rights are binding on the legislature and other branches of government. Legislation concerning human rights requires the approval of a majority of all representatives. Constitutional law relating to the rights of ethnic minorities must be passed by a two-thirds majority. Article 20 provides that anyone who violates human rights and fundamental freedoms shall be held personally responsible and may not be exculpated by the invocation of a superior order.

The people's ombudsperson is authorized to provide extrajudicial protection of human rights.

Impact and Functions of Human Rights

Thanks in part to international attention, human rights and freedoms have been the focus of the struggle to develop and promote the rule of law in Croatia. Generally, it can be said that public awareness of the importance of human rights has risen continuously since the end of the war in 1995. The initially precarious situation has improved under strict monitoring by international organizations, such as the Organization for Security and Co-operation in Europe and the European Union.

Limitations to Fundamental Rights

Freedoms and rights may only be restricted by law and only to protect the freedoms and rights of others, public order, public morality, or health. Every restriction must be proportional to the need for it.

ECONOMY

The constitution, at length, specifies the basic principles of a market economy in order to facilitate a smooth transition to that system. Among these principles are freedom of property, market freedoms, the freedom of occupation and profession, the right to form associations such as trade unions and employer associations, and a prohibition of the abuse of monopolies.

Other principles are aimed at speeding up the development of markets. The rights acquired through the investment of capital cannot be diminished by law or by any other legal act. Foreign investors are guaranteed free transfer and repatriation of profits and of the capital invested.

The republic, declared a social state, is expected to promote the public welfare. Specific social rights, such as the right to work and the right to just remuneration, are also included in Croatian law by virtue of the European Social Charter, which Croatia has signed. Social responsibility is expected to work in combination with market freedom.

In general, the Croatian economic system may be defined as a transitional economy, rapidly developing toward a free market economy, but needing to develop proper instruments of social responsibility that work with market freedoms, as required by the constitution.

RELIGIOUS COMMUNITIES

Freedom of religion and belief includes the equality of religious communities in the country. There is no state religion, but there is a Catholic majority, through whom the Catholic Church has some influence. The constitution demands that public authorities remain strictly neutral in their relations with religious communities and treat them equally.

The importance of religious equality stems from the fact that the most important ethnic minorities are not Catholic. All the communities regulate and administer their affairs independently within the limits of the relevant laws. Religious schools are permitted and assisted by the state.

MILITARY DEFENSE AND STATE OF EMERGENCY

The armed forces protect the sovereignty, independence, and territorial integrity of the republic. They may act beyond Croatia's borders only with a prior decision of parliament, except when performing maneuvers within international defense organizations or when offering humanitarian aid. In case of an emergency, the armed forces may be used to assist the police and other governmental bodies.

During a state of war, the president of the republic may issue decrees with the force of law within the bounds of authority obtained from parliament. If parliament is not in session, the president is authorized to regulate all the issues required by the state of war through decrees with the force of law. In cases of emergency apart from war, the president may, at the proposal of the prime minister and with the countersignature of the prime minister, issue decrees with the force of law.

Not even in the case of an immediate threat to the existence of the state may restrictions be imposed on the application of constitutional provisions concerning the right to life, prohibition of torture, and cruel or degrading treatment or punishment; on the legal definitions of penal offenses and punishments; or on freedom of thought, conscience, and religion.

Parliament exercises civil control over the military and security services. The people's ombudsperson is also authorized to oversee their activities.

Conscientious objection is guaranteed. Croatian conscripts have increasingly tended to request alternative civilian service in social institutions.

AMENDMENTS TO THE CONSTITUTION

The constitution is relatively easy to change. Amendments may be proposed by at least one-fifth of the members of parliament, the president of the republic, or the cabinet. Parliament decides by a majority vote of all the representatives whether to start proceedings. Draft amendments are first approved by a majority vote of all members. Decision to amend the constitution is then made by a two-thirds majority vote of all the members, whereupon the amendment is promulgated by parliament.

Certain aspects of the constitution cannot be amended. Any act that might lead to the renewal of a South Slav state community or of any other Balkan state is explicitly prohibited.

Any other international alliances are also specially regulated. They may be initiated by one-third of the members of parliament, the president of the republic, or the cabinet. They must be first approved by a two-thirds majority vote of all the representatives and ratified in a referendum by a majority vote of the total number of electors in the state.

PRIMARY SOURCES

Constitution in English. Available online. URL: http://www.usud.hr/default.aspx?show=ustav_republikce_hrvatske&m1=27&m2=50&lang=en. Accessed on June 17, 2006.

Ustav Republike Hrvatske in Croatian. *Official Gazette* no. 41 (2001).

The Constitution of the Republic of Croatia, translated by Branko Smerdel and Dunja Marija Vièan. Zagreb: Narodne novine, 2001.

SECONDARY SOURCES

Council of Europe, "The Protection of Fundamental Rights by the Constitutional Court." *Proceedings of the UniDem Seminar Organized in Brionie, Croatia, on September 23–25, 1995, in Cooperation with the Croatian Constitutional Court and with the Support of the European Commission.* Strasbourg: Council of Europe Publishing, 1996.

Smiljko Sokol and Branko Smerdel: *Ustavno pravo [Constitutional law].* Zagreb: Informator, 1998.

Branko Smerdel

CUBA

At-a-Glance

OFFICIAL NAME
Republic of Cuba

CAPITAL
Havana

POPULATION
11,308,764 (July 2004 est.)

SIZE
42,803 sq. mi. (110,860 sq. km)

LANGUAGES
Spanish

RELIGIONS
Non-Catholic, Santeria, and other mixed communities; Roman Catholic; Protestant; Jehovah's Witnesses, Jewish

NATIONAL OR ETHNIC COMPOSITION
Mixed race 51%, white 30%, Afro 18%, Chinese 1%

DATE OF INDEPENDENCE OR CREATION
May 20, 1902
January 1, 1959 (Day of the Revolution's Victory)

TYPE OF GOVERNMENT
State socialism

TYPE OF STATE
Unitary state

TYPE OF LEGISLATURE
Unicameral parliament

DATE OF CONSTITUTION
February 24, 1976

DATE OF LAST AMENDMENT
June 26, 2002 (Agreement V-74)

The Republic of Cuba is a socialist state with a Soviet-style popular democracy based on the principle of legality. It has a unitary government in which the legislative power formally dominates, by constitutional rules, the executive and judicial branches. Organized as a unitary state, Cuba has a strong central government without local autonomy. The economic system is organized on socialist principles of state control.

The head of state is the president of the Council of State, who by the constitution is also the president of the Council of Ministers. The sole president since 1976, when the current constitution was adopted, has been Fidel Castro, who is also first secretary of the Communist Party. The president proposes the members of the Council of Ministers, and the National Assembly of People's Power approves them.

Since changes to the constitution were approved in 1992, free, equal, general, and direct elections of the members of National Assembly of People's Power are guaranteed by the constitution. Candidates are not required to belong to the Communist Party in order to be nominated; however, the election process is closely supervised by the party. Candidates to the Municipal Assembly are proposed directly by the people. The candidates to the other representative organs are proposed by the candidatures commissions, made up of members of the mass organizations, such as the Committees for the Defense of the Revolution, neighborhood committees that enroll most of the adult population.

Religious freedom is guaranteed by the constitution; the state and religious communities are declared to be separated. Clerics may be elected as deputies to the National Assembly of People's Power or as delegates to the other representative organs.

The members of the military can both vote and run for office in general elections. They are considered the same as the people and serve according to the constitution in order to preserve peace. The constitution states that the National Assembly of People's Power can declare war only if the nation is attacked.

CONSTITUTIONAL HISTORY

Before 1492, the island was populated by indigenous people, who were almost exterminated within a few years after Christopher Columbus arrived. In 1868, Cuba declared war against Spain, initiating the war of liberation. At this time in the free territories, four constitutions were approved (1869, 1872, 1895, and 1897). Cuba was a colony of Spain until 1898, when the United States of America intervened in the war of liberation between Cubans and Spain.

In 1901, after a constituent assembly was formed to approve the first free constitution of the new state, the U.S. government imposed an amendment, the Emends Platt, that limited Cuban sovereignty by authorizing the U.S. government to intervene in Cuba in defense of "their properties." In 1902, the republic was established with a presidential system of government, a bicameral parliament as legislative power, and an independent judiciary.

In 1928, women acquired the fundamental right to vote in elections.

A new constitution was approved in 1940. It established a semipresidential government and recognized many fundamental rights, but these fundamental rights were not implemented in fact. In 1952, an army sergeant, Fulgencio Batista, rose to power through a coup d'état and established a new constitution, but in the face of popular opposition and armed rebellion, he restored the previous document later in the decade.

The victory of the revolution led by Fidel Castro occurred on January 1, 1959. The following day, Castro reestablished the 1940 constitution. The revolutionary and provisionary government was headed by the president of the republic, accompanied by the Council of Ministers. This structure was maintained after February 7, 1959, when the Fundamental Law of the Republic was promulgated, replacing the 1940 constitution.

In 1976, a new constitution, establishing Cuba as a socialist state, was adopted and approved in a referendum. With some modifications, this constitution is still operative today. It provided formal equality in voting rights and added new fundamental rights for members of the military forces and citizens.

The new government structure departed from the principle of three separate powers. The constitution states that the National Assembly of People's Power is the supreme power in the republic. It is vested with the power to elect from among its deputies the members of the Council of State, judges of the Supreme Court, and the attorney general of the republic.

The president of the Council of State is both the head of state and government and the commander in chief of the military forces. The president has far-reaching powers during a state of emergency as head of the National Council of Defense. The president chooses the cabinet ministers, who then are appointed by the National Assembly of People's Power or by the Council of State.

The government, headed by the president of the Council of Ministers (who is also the president of the Council of State), is responsible to the legislative organ and may be removed by the National Assembly of People's Power.

FORM AND IMPACT OF THE CONSTITUTION

Cuba has a written constitution, codified in a single document, called the Constitution of the Republic of Cuba, which takes precedence over all other national law. International law must be in accordance with the constitution to be applicable within Cuba, and it must first be given legal form by the Council of State. Articles 10 and 66 establish that the constitution and laws must be strictly observed by all state organs and their leaders, officials, and employees, and that strict observation of the constitution is a duty of all.

The constitution is also considered a source of values. The preamble says that Cuban citizens continue the work and traditions fostered by early independence leaders. It also states that Cuban foreign policy is to be based on fraternal friendship, help, cooperation, and solidarity with the people of the world, especially with those of Latin America and the Caribbean. Article 62 establishes that none of the freedoms recognized for citizens may be exercised against what is established in the constitution or in the laws.

BASIC ORGANIZATIONAL STRUCTURE

The Republic of Cuba is a unitary state, divided into 14 provinces and 169 municipalities. Local communities are entities subordinated to the state, which have no administrative or political autonomy. However, local communities can make their own decisions and pursue initiatives aimed at taking advantage of local resources and potential. To this end, they can mobilize social and mass organizations.

The constitutional reform of 1992 introduced some changes relating to municipalities, recognizing them as the local society that has legal personality and the powers to satisfy the local needs. This resulted in some decentralization in the determination or distribution of the national financial and investment budgets.

Also introduced by the 1992 constitutional reform are the People's Councils, organized in local neighborhoods. Chosen by municipal assemblies, they are the supreme local authority to coordinate and control local economic entities. They also have powers in education and other local services and promote public participation in local programs. In permanent session, they control the administration of the towns.

LEADING CONSTITUTIONAL PRINCIPLES

The Cuban constitutional system defines Cuba as a democracy, a unitary republic, and a socialist state. Article 1 of the constitution says: "Cuba is an organized socialist state of workers, independent and sovereign, with all and for the good of all a united and democratic republic, for the enjoyment of political freedom, social justice, the individual and collective well-being and human solidarity." Direct democracy, whereby people decide relevant issues directly and exercise popular control over administrative activity, is another basic principle.

Articles 9, 11, and 12 of the constitution concern principles of foreign policy: the fight for national independence, the right to self-determination, and the defensive character of the state. The constitution states that the republic "considers wars of aggression and of conquest international crimes [and] recognizes the legitimacy of the struggle for national liberation" (Article 12 Section h). "Power to declare war formally resides in the National Assembly" (Article 75 Section j). The constitution states that Cuba wishes to integrate with Latin American and Caribbean countries in order to reach true independence (Article 12 Section c) and promotes the unity of "Third World countries" confronting the "neocolonialist and imperialist policy which seeks to limit and subordinate the sovereignty of our peoples, and worsen the economic conditions of exploitation and oppression of the underdeveloped nations" (Article 12 Section d).

The protection of the environment and of natural resources is a constitutional principle. The constitution also recognizes the civic duty of contributing to the protection and conservation of water, the atmosphere, the land, the flora, the fauna, and the whole rich potential of nature.

CONSTITUTIONAL BODIES

The predominant bodies provided for in the constitution are the National Assembly of People's Power, the Council of State and Council of Ministers, and their president.

The National Assembly of People's Power

The constitution states that the National Assembly of People's Power is the supreme representative organ of the state. It can amend the constitution and call for a popular referendum. The national assembly is vested with the legislative and constituent power.

The members of the National Assembly of People's Power are directly elected by the people, with one or more deputies elected from each municipality. The assembly has the right to appoint and revoke the executive government of the state. It can make inquiries to the Council of State and Council of Ministers; these inquiries must be answered during the course of the same session or at the following one.

The members of the National Assembly of People's Power generally retain their previous jobs, as they receive no salary for their assembly work, as is generally the case in Cuban representative bodies. The constitution requires them to exercise their duties for the benefit of the people and to remain in contact with their electors and render account of their activities. They can be removed from office at any time. However, no deputy may be arrested or placed on trial without the authorization of the assembly—or the Council of State if the assembly is not in session—except in cases of flagrant offenses.

The assembly consists of 601 deputies. Its period of office, the legislative term, is five years. The deputies are elected by secret ballot from lists presented in each municipality, which have one deputy for each 20,000 inhabitants. These can be voted en bloc or individually by selecting one, two, or three candidates from the list.

The National Assembly of People's Power has two general sessions per year, in June and December, each lasting a few days. At other times, deputies gather in permanent and temporary commissions to work on bills or evaluate ministries' reports. The assembly elects a Council of State from among its members to execute its decisions and to represent the state.

The Council of State

The Council of State is the organ of the National Assembly of People's Power that represents it in the period between its brief sessions. It is elected by the assembly. It enforces the laws and performs other duties assigned by the constitution. It issues decrees that can modify laws; the assembly has the right to ratify or revoke the decrees in later session. The Council of State also gives binding interpretations of existing laws whenever necessary. It decrees general mobilization for the defense of the country and assumes the authority to declare war in the event of aggression or to make peace. It can replace the members of the Council of Ministers when the National Assembly of People's Power is in recess.

The Council of State has the right to pardon criminal offenders. It issues instructions to the office of the attorney general of the republic and to the courts through the governing council of the people's Supreme Court. It can ratify or reject international treaties and can suspend and revoke decisions of the Council of Ministers or provisions of local administrative bodies, if it considers such decisions to be detrimental to the constitution, the laws, or the general interest of the nation.

The Council of Ministers

The Council of Ministers is the highest-ranking executive and administrative organ and constitutes the executive government of the republic. Members of the Council of Ministers are proposed by the president and approved by the National Assembly of People's Power or its Council of State. The Council of Ministers is vested with the powers to organize and conduct the political, economic, cultural, scientific, social, and defense activities approved by the national assembly; to conduct the foreign policy of the republic; to draw up the draft for the state budget and prepare legislative bills; to attend to the national defense; to conduct the administration of the state and to implement laws and decree laws; and to issue decrees of its own.

The cabinet ministers serve for the duration of the assembly term. They must report to the National Assembly of People's Power at least once in a legislative period.

The President of the Council of State and Council of Ministers

The president of the Council of State is also the president of the Council of Ministers. He or she represents the state and the government, controls and supervises the activities of the ministries, proposes the members of the Council of Ministers to the National Assembly of People's Power, exercises the supreme command of the armed forces, and signs decree laws of the Council of State.

The Lawmaking Process

The National Assembly of People's Power passes legislation on the principle of the "unity of power," without the participation of other organs of the state. Bills can be proposed by the deputies of the national assembly or its commissions, the Council of State and the Council of Ministers, the National Committee of Mass Organizations, the Supreme Court and the attorney general (in matters within their jurisdictions), or a group of at least 10,000 citizens who are eligible to vote. The president of the National Assembly of People's Power promulgates the laws and arranges for their publication.

The Judiciary

The judiciary in Cuba is structured independently. However, all judges are elected by the National Assembly of People's Power or by the Council of State when the assembly is not meeting, and the Council of State can issue instructions to the courts through the Governing Council. The People's Supreme Court (Corte Suprema del Pueblo) is the highest court of the system. It is headed by a Governing Council. There are various chambers, divided according to the legal nature of the matter—civil and administrative, criminal, military, special, economic, labor, and state security.

The Governing Council exercises legislative initiative in matters related to the administration of justice and statutory power; it makes decisions and enacts norms that are binding for all courts. It issues binding instructions, on its experience, to establish uniform judicial practice in the interpretation and enforcement of the law.

The Attorney General of the Republic

The office of the attorney general of the republic is a unit subordinate only to the National Assembly of People's Power and the Council of State. It is independent of all other judicial and administrative bodies. It is a unit structured vertically and operates at all levels of the country. According to the constitution, its main objective is to ensure compliance with the law and represent the state in exercising penal authority.

THE ELECTION PROCESS

All Cubans over the age of 16 have both the right to vote in elections and the right to stand for elections to the municipal and provincial assemblies. The right to be elected to the National Assembly of People's Power is gained at the age of 18.

The process of choosing national and provincial assemblies is opened by the Council of State every five years (general process); corresponding municipal elections are held every two and a half years (partial process).

Delegates or deputies of all assemblies elect the president and vice president of those organs. There are no general elections for the executive branch. The head of state is chosen ex officio by the National Assembly of People's Power when it chooses the president of its Council of State. The presidents of provincial and municipal assemblies are ex officio presidents of the corresponding administrative councils.

MASS OR SOCIAL ORGANIZATIONS AND POLITICAL PARTY

Many mass organizations exist in Cuban society, such as the Committee for the Defense of the Revolution (CDR), the Federation of Cuban Women (FMC), the National Association of Small Farmers (ANAP), the Federation of University Students (FEU), the Federation of Students of Intermediate Education (FEEM), and the Central Organization of Cuban Trade Unions (CTC). There are also professional organizations, such as the National Union of Writers and Artists of Cuba (UNEAC), the Union of Journalists of Cuba (UPEC), and the National Union of Cuban Jurists (UNJC).

The constitution establishes that the state recognizes, protects, and stimulates mass organizations because they represent the specific interests of their members and incorporate the people in the task of building and consolidating society (Article 7).

These mass organizations participate in the electoral process. They propose candidates for the provincial and national assemblies, who are then nominated by the municipal assemblies.

As the only legal political party, the Communist Party of Cuba (PCC) constitutes a fundamental element of public life. The constitution acknowledges its role in Article 5. According to the constitution, the PCC is the highest force in the society and the state, which organizes and guides the common effort to achieve the goals of the construction of socialism. Its internal structure must be in accordance with democratic principles, as understood in Marxist-Leninist doctrine, that are established in its statutes. As a social grouping, it relies on membership fees. The PCC does not directly participate in proposing candidates for the electoral process.

Another political organization, the Young Communist League (UJC), undertakes to promote the participation of young people in the construction of socialist society as defined in the constitution (Article 6).

CITIZENSHIP

Cuban citizenship is acquired by birth or by naturalization. By birth, the main principle is the *ius solis,* through which all children born in Cuba are considered Cuban citizens. There are a few exceptions: the children of foreigners who are working for foreign governments or international bodies and the children of other foreign nonpermanent residents in the country. Also considered Cuban citizens are those born abroad, at least one of whose parents is on official assignment from the Cuban state. The principle of *ius sanguinis* is also applied. This means that a child acquires Cuban citizenship if one of his or her parents is a Cuban citizen or a Cuban national who lost citizenship but satisfies a legal requirement, such as having been born in Cuba.

FUNDAMENTAL RIGHTS

Although the constitution defines fundamental rights in Chapter 7, many other rights are regulated in other chapters without legal distinction between them. They all have the same legal status.

The constitution recognizes the traditional, classic set of human rights: freedom of conscience, press, and religion, and the right to property and inheritance, to association and assembly. It also proclaims the right to work; to rest; to social security; to education; to protection, safety, and hygiene at work; and to health protection and care. The inviolability of the home, mail, and freedom is also guaranteed by the constitution.

Cuba's constitution, as do other constitutions, distinguishes between human rights, which apply to every human being, and those fundamental rights reserved for Cubans only. In this last group, one may find the freedom of speech and of the press and the right to vote and to be elected.

In Chapter 6, the constitution establishes the equality of men and women and obligates the state to work toward that goal.

Impact and Functions of Fundamental Rights

Fundamental rights also involve the right to intervene in the direction of the state or to participate in the organs of power. There are in the constitution various provisions that aim at defending fundamental rights.

Article 26 establishes the right to claim and obtain due compensation for any person who suffers damages or injuries that are unjustly caused by a state official or employee while in the performance of his or her public functions. Citizens also have the right to file complaints and send petitions to the authorities and to receive an answer.

Limitations to Fundamental Rights

The Cuban constitution specifies possible limitations to fundamental rights according to the specific needs of the public and for the protection of rights of others. For example, according to Article 62, none of the freedoms recognized for citizens may be exercised contrary to what is established in the constitution and the law or contrary to the existence and objectives of the socialist state, effectively prohibiting all forms of legal dissent and opposition to the government. Article 60 provides for confiscation of property as a punishment. Article 25 authorizes the expropriation of property for the benefit of the public or social interest, with due compensation.

ECONOMY

The economic system is organized on socialist principles of state control: That is, most of the means of production are owned and operated by the government. There are different kinds of property, including state ownership, cooperative ownership, personal ownership, and small farmer's ownership. After 1992, another type of property was recognized, one that allows the establishment of foreign capital in the country, under the form of companies of mixed capital. The state directs and controls foreign trade and organizes enterprises and other economic entities for the administration of socialist property.

RELIGIOUS COMMUNITIES

Freedom of religion or belief, which is guaranteed by the constitution as a human right, is protected by the separation of religion from the state. There is no established state church. All religions must be treated equally. Catholicism, Protestantism, and African religions are practiced in Cuba.

MILITARY DEFENSE AND STATE OF EMERGENCY

The creation and maintenance of armed forces are the responsibility of the government. In Cuba, general conscription requires all men above the age of 16 to perform basic military service. In addition, professional soldiers also serve. Women are allowed to volunteer.

Exceptional situations may be declared in case of war, catastrophe, or natural disaster, and in any other circumstances that affect domestic order, the security of the country, or the stability of the state. The National Assembly of People's Power, or the Council of State when the assembly is not meeting, declares war. The Council of State has responsibility to declare the national mobilization of the population, and the president may declare a state of emergency in case of a natural catastrophe. At this time, the most important military body is the Council of National Defense and, at the local level, the Council of Provincial or Municipality Defense.

AMENDMENTS TO THE CONSTITUTION

The constitution can only be changed if two-thirds of the members of the National Assembly of People's Power vote in favor of an amendment. A popular referendum is required if the change affects the fundamental rights or duties recognized by the constitution or the authority of the National Assembly of People's Power or the Council of State.

There are intangible clauses and fundamental provisions that are not subject to change under any circumstances. Articles 3, 11, and 137 guarantee the continuity of the existing political and social system. These provisions were introduced in the last constitutional reform in 2002.

PRIMARY SOURCES

Constitution in English. Available online. URLs: http://64.2133.164/ref/dis/consC92_e.htm; http://www.embacubalebanon.comlconstite.html#Cap 1. Accessed on September 17, 2005.

Constitution in English and Spanish. Available online. URL: http://www.pdba.georgetown.edu/Constitutions/Cuba/cuba2002.html. Accessed on June 17, 2006.

Constitution of the Republic of Cuba in Spanish. Available online. URL: http://www.cuba.culgobierno/consti.htm. Accessed on September 17, 2005.

SECONDARY SOURCES

Crawford Morrison Bishop, *A Guide to the Law and Legal Literature of Cuba, the Dominican Republic and Haiti.* Washington, D.C.: Library of Congress, 1944.

Rex A. Hudson, *Cuba: A Country Study.* 4th ed. Washington, D.C.: U.S. Government Printing Office, 2002.

Francisco Fernández Segado, "El control de constitucionalidad en Cuba (1901–1952)." In *Revista derecho* 12 no. 1, 205–228.

Lissette Pérez Hernández and Martha Prieto Valdez, *Selección legislativa de derecho constitucional cubano.* La Habana, Félix Varela, 1999.

Juan Valdes, "Notas sobre el sistema politico cubano." In *La Democracia en Cuba y el Diferendo con los Estados Unidos,* edited by Haroldo Dilla. Havana: Centro de Estudios sobre America, 1996.

United Nations, "Core Document Forming Part of the Reports of States Parties: Cuba" (HRI/CORE/IIAdd.84), 13 October 1997. Available online. URL: http://www.unhchr.ch/tbs/doc.nsf. Accessed on June 17, 2006.

Martha Prieto

CYPRUS

At-a-Glance

OFFICIAL NAME
Republic of Cyprus

CAPITAL
Nicosia

POPULATION
790,000 (2005 est.)

SIZE
3,568 sq. mi. (9,240 sq. km)

LANGUAGES
Greek, Turkish

RELIGIONS
Christian Orthodox 83%, Muslim 13%, Maronite
0.6%, Armenian 0.4%, Roman Catholic 0.3%,
unaffiliated or other 2.7%

NATIONAL OR ETHNIC COMPOSITION
Greek 83%, Turkish 13%, other 4%

DATE OF INDEPENDENCE OR CREATION
October 1, 1960

TYPE OF GOVERNMENT
Presidential democracy

TYPE OF STATE
Unitary state

TYPE OF LEGISLATURE
Bicommunal parliament

DATE OF CONSTITUTION
August 16, 1960

DATE OF LAST AMENDMENT
December 28, 1996

The Republic of Cyprus is a presidential democracy based on the rule of law, with a clear division of executive, legislative, and judicial powers. It is a unitary state that comprises two legally recognized communities, the Greek community and the Turkish community. The constitution safeguards human rights in a comprehensive way. It is widely respected by the public authorities; if a violation of the constitution does occur, in individual cases, there are effective remedies enforceable by an independent judiciary. The Supreme Court of Cyprus guarantees that the constitution is respected by all.

The president of the republic is the head of state and has vast executive powers. The president is elected directly by the people and appoints a council of ministers to assist in the exercise of the executive powers. Members of parliament are elected in free, general, and direct elections. A pluralistic system of political parties plays an intense role in political life. Religious freedom is guaranteed, and state and religious communities are separated. The military is subject to the civil government in law and fact.

CONSTITUTIONAL HISTORY

The Republic of Cyprus was established in 1960. The constitutional structure was based on the Zurich and London Agreements of 1959 among Greece, Turkey, and the United Kingdom and was decided without the participation of the people of Cyprus. The Zurich Agreements did not succeed in establishing cooperation between the two communities of the island, and in 1963, there was a constitutional breakdown. Turkish Cypriots vacated their offices in the government, and there followed an outbreak of violence in the island. A United Nations peacekeeping operation entered the island in 1964 and has remained there since.

In 1974, the Republic of Turkey, one of the guarantor powers of the independence, sovereignty, and territorial integrity of Cyprus, invaded the country with its armed forces and occupied the northern part of the island. As a result of the occupation, the Greeks and other Christians of the region fled to the southern part of the island. The

Turks of the southern part of the island were forced to move to the north. In 1983, the Turkish-occupied area declared itself the Turkish Republic of Northern Cyprus, but that entity is recognized only by Turkey.

The Turkish occupation has prevented the Republic of Cyprus from exercising its powers over the occupied territory. A number of constitutional provisions, which refer to the Turkish Cypriot community, are temporarily not in force. Proposals for the solution of the "Cyprus problem" have until now failed. The Republic of Cyprus became a member of the European Union on May 1, 2004.

FORM AND IMPACT OF THE CONSTITUTION

Cyprus has a written constitution, codified in a single document, that takes precedence over all other law. International law takes precedence over all national law as long as it has been ratified by parliament. A doctrine of necessity has been accepted by the Supreme Court of Cyprus so that the House of Representatives may enact laws even contrary to those provisions of the constitution that are temporarily not in force because of the "Cyprus Problem."

BASIC ORGANIZATIONAL STRUCTURE

Cyprus is a unitary state. There is a central government that comprises the two communities of the island. The constitution also provides for two communal chambers, a Greek communal chamber and a Turkish communal chamber, which have legislative powers in educational, cultural, religious, and other matters of a purely communal nature. After the constitutional crisis of 1963, the Greek communal chamber was dissolved, and the Turkish communal chamber does not function. At the present time, all powers belong to the central government.

LEADING CONSTITUTIONAL PRINCIPLES

Cyprus's system of government is a presidential democracy. There is a strong division of the executive, legislative, and judicial powers, based on checks and balances. The judiciary is completely independent. Cyprus is a representative democracy, a unitary state, and a republic and is based on the rule of law. The most unique feature of the constitution is its bicommunal nature; all constitutional organs must comprise members of the two communities. Rule of law has a decisive impact. All state actions impairing the rights of the people must have a basis in parliamentary law. The constitution provides for neutrality of the state toward religions, although there are specific is-

sues of cooperation between the state and major religions, such as family law.

CONSTITUTIONAL BODIES

The predominant bodies provided for in the constitution are the president; the council of ministers; the parliament, called the House of Representatives; and the judiciary, which includes the Supreme Court.

The President

The president is the head of state and represents the republic in all its official functions. He or she belongs to the Greek Cypriot community and is elected for a five-year term directly by universal suffrage and secret ballot. The president appoints and dismisses the members of the council of ministers and has vast executive powers. The constitution also provides for a Turkish Cypriot vice president, who is the vice head of state and has similar powers to the president's. Since the constitutional crisis of 1963, the office of the vice president has remained vacant.

The Council of Ministers

The constitution provides that the council of ministers be composed of seven Greek Cypriots and three Turkish Cypriots, who shall be designated, respectively, by the president and the vice president of the republic. Since the constitutional crisis of 1963, all 10 ministers are Greek Cypriots. An 11th ministry of education and culture has replaced the dissolved Greek Communal Chamber. Ministers are chosen from outside the House of Representatives. The council of ministers exercises the executive power alongside the president.

The House of Representatives

The House of Representatives, with 80 members, exercises the legislative power of the republic. The constitution provides that 70 percent of the representatives shall be elected separately by the members of the Greek Cypriot community and 30 percent separately by the members of the Turkish Cypriot community. Since the constitutional crisis of 1963, the offices of the Turkish Cypriot representatives remain vacant. The representatives are elected for a term of five years in free, general, and direct elections.

The Lawmaking Process

The main duty of the House of Representatives is to pass legislation. The right to introduce bills belongs to the representatives and to ministers. However, bills relating to an increase in budgetary expenses can be introduced only by ministers. Laws are passed by a simple majority vote of the representatives present and voting. Laws become operative on their publication in the official gazette of the republic.

The Judiciary

The judiciary is independent of the executive and legislative bodies and is a powerful factor in both legal and social life. The highest Cypriot court is the Supreme Court of Cyprus, which functions both as the supreme constitutional court and as the supreme appellate court of the republic. Many of the court's decisions have had the highest legal and political impact. The most important decisions relate to the "doctrine of necessity." After the constitutional crisis of 1963 and the Turkish invasion of 1974, it became impossible to follow the most important provisions of the constitution of Cyprus. In order to preserve the republic, the Supreme Court accepted that the executive and the legislature could continue to function despite the absence of the Turkish Cypriot members. The House of Representatives may enact laws, even contrary to those provisions of the constitution that are temporarily not in force because of current conditions. The Supreme Court examines whether the laws can be justified by the situation and whether or not they violate human rights.

THE ELECTION PROCESS

All Cypriots over the age of 18 have the right to vote in elections. Cypriots may not be elected as members of the House of Representatives unless they are at least 25 years old, and they may not stand for president unless they are at least 35 years old.

POLITICAL PARTIES

Cyprus has a pluralistic system of political parties. Political parties are a fundamental element of public life, and their function is an essential element of the constitutional order.

CITIZENSHIP

Cypriot citizenship is acquired by birth, by registration, or by naturalization. A child acquires Cypriot citizenship by birth if one of his or her parents is a Cypriot citizen or if he or she is born in Cyprus. If the child is born abroad, he or she may acquire Cypriot citizenship by registration.

FUNDAMENTAL RIGHTS

The part of the constitution of Cyprus that guarantees fundamental rights and liberties is modeled on the European Convention on Human Rights. However, the provisions of the European Convention have been extended and enlarged in some respects, with a number of social and economic rights added in order to meet the basic requirements of a modern society. The rights are generally guaranteed for every person, but only citizens are protected against extradition or deportation.

Impact and Functions of Fundamental Rights

For Cyprus, human rights are of fundamental importance to legal thinking. Fundamental rights are binding for all public authorities under any circumstances. The courts have the power to declare that any law or action that is contrary to fundamental rights is unconstitutional and invalid.

Limitations to Fundamental Rights

Fundamental rights in Cyprus are not without limits, but no fundamental right may be disregarded completely. The constitution expressly provides that even in those circumstances in which fundamental rights may be limited, such limitations must be prescribed by law. In addition, any limitations to fundamental rights must be reasonably justified and must respect the principle of proportionality.

ECONOMY

The constitution does not specify a specific economic system. However, certain basic decisions by the framers of the constitution provide for a set of conditions that have to be met while structuring the economic system. Among them are the freedom of property, the freedom of occupation or profession, and the right to form associations.

RELIGIOUS COMMUNITIES

Freedom of religion or belief is guaranteed as a human right; it also involves rights for religious communities. There is no official or prevailing religion, and the state does not have an official religion. All religions and creeds in Cyprus deal with their own affairs, without any interference in the affairs of the state. The state has recognized broad discretionary powers in their favor and does not have the right to intervene in their religious affairs. Whenever matters of common interest arise, such as religious education or family matters, the state and the five major religious corporations debate on equal terms. These religions are the Christian Orthodox Church, the Islamic religion, the Maronite Church, the Armenian Church, and the Roman Catholic Church.

MILITARY DEFENSE AND STATE OF EMERGENCY

The constitution provides that the republic shall have an army of 2,000 men, of whom 60 percent shall be Greek

Cypriots and 40 percent shall be Turkish Cypriots. Such an army never came into being. After the constitutional crisis of 1963, the republic created armed forces called the National Guard, which are composed exclusively of Greek Cypriots. Such armed forces are used only for defensive purposes. It is compulsory for all men over the age of 18 to do military service lasting 25 months. In addition, there are professional soldiers who serve for fixed periods or for life.

The military always remains subject to civil government. The constitution provides for the possibility that certain articles may be suspended for the duration of war or other public danger that threatens the life of the republic. Such articles refer to specific fundamental rights; the limitations are in accord with permissible state action under the European Convention on Human Rights.

AMENDMENTS TO THE CONSTITUTION

A significant number of constitutional provisions are considered to be fundamental and are not subject to change. These articles have been incorporated from the Zurich Agreement and concern the essential bicommunal iden-

tity of the constitution. Other articles of the constitution can only be changed if two-thirds of the Greek Cypriot representatives and two-thirds of the Turkish Cypriot representatives vote in favor. Since the constitutional crisis of 1963, these articles can change if two-thirds of the Greek Cypriot representatives vote in favor.

PRIMARY SOURCES

Constitution in English. Available online. URL: http://www.kypros.org/Constitution/English/. Accessed on August 13, 2005.
Constitution in Greek: *To Σύνταγμα της Κυπριακής Δημοκρατίας*. Nicosia: The Press and Information Office, 1960. Available online. URL: http://www.kypros.org/Constitution/Greek/. Accessed on July 30, 2005.

SECONDARY SOURCES

Achilles Emilianides, "The Zurich and London Agreements and the Cyprus Republic." *Mélanges Seferiades*. Athens: Panteion, 1961 vol. II, 629–39.
Criton G. Tornaritis, *Cyprus and Its Constitutional and Other Legal Problems*. Nicosia: The author, 1980.

Achilles Emilianides

CZECH REPUBLIC

At-a-Glance

OFFICIAL NAME
Czech Republic

CAPITAL
Prague

POPULATION
10,230,060 (2005 est.)

SIZE
30,450 sq. mi. (78,866 sq. km)

LANGUAGES
Czech

RELIGIONS
Believers (Catholic 26.9%, Bohemian Brethrens' Protestant Church 1.1%, Czechoslovak Hussite Church 1.0%, Jehovah's Witnesses 0.2%, Christian Orthodox 0.2%) 32.1%, without religion or not specified 67.9%

NATIONAL OR ETHNIC COMPOSITION
Czech 90.4%, Moravian 3.7%, Silesian 0.1%, Slovak 1.9%, other (made up largely of Polish, German, Ukrainian, and Roma) 3.9%

DATE OF INDEPENDENCE OR CREATION
January 1, 1993

TYPE OF GOVERNMENT
Parliamentary democracy

TYPE OF STATE
Unitary state

TYPE OF LEGISLATURE
Bicameral parliament

DATE OF CONSTITUTION
December 16, 1992 (approval) / January 1, 2003 (in force)

DATE OF LAST AMENDMENT
March 1, 2003

The Czech Republic is a young parliamentary democracy. Its democratic reconstruction began after the collapse of the communist regime and the so-called Velvet Revolution. Because of the rich heritage of the interwar period of the First Czechoslovak Republic (1918–38), the newly created republic can carry the torch of its former sovereign tradition.

The Czech Republic is defined by division of legislative, executive, and judicial powers, supplemented with the system of mutual checks and balances. The president of the republic is the head of state. The administration is responsible to the Chamber of Deputies, confidence in which is a necessary condition of its political existence. The Parliament has two chambers; the Senate is the weaker of the two but has some significant powers. The Constitutional Court has relatively strong powers to protect constitutional order and human rights.

The political and economic system is characterized by free competition among political parties, free elections to democratically governed institutions, religious neutrality of the state, and the transition from a communist centralized economy to a market economy. The Czech Republic has been a member of the North Atlantic Treaty Organization (NATO) since 1999 and of the European Union since May 2004.

CONSTITUTIONAL HISTORY

The origins of Czech statehood date to the 10th century C.E. From then until the 13th century, the Přemyslovci princes established a political entity called the Lands of the Czech Crown (or simply Czech Lands) that covered approximately the present territory of the Czech Republic (or its historical parts Bohemia, Moravia, and Silesia). These lands were more or less linked with the history of the Holy Roman Empire (of the German Nation) during the Middle Ages and with the Austrian (1806–67) and Austrian-Hungarian (1867–1918) Monarchy.

There are three main periods in the recent constitutional history of the Czech Republic: the constitutional traditions of the Austrian(-Hungarian) period after 1848, the First Czechoslovak Republic (1918–38), and, in a negative way, the time of the Communist regime (1948–89). The reconstruction of democracy that followed the November events in 1989 (the Velvet Revolution) deepened the crisis between Czechs and Slovaks, and in 1992 the Czechoslovak federation dissolved and two independent states emerged: the Czech Republic and the Slovak Republic.

Political moves after the revolutionary year of 1848 to restrict the absolute monarchy and to establish a constitution were the most important developments in the Austrian monarchy of which the Czech Lands were a part. However, the constitutions that emerged (April 1848, March 1849, February 1861, or December 1867) were imposed by the monarch and were not the result of a democratic process. The establishment of a dual Austrian-Hungarian Monarchy by the constitution of 1867 weakened the position of the Czech Lands.

The territory of Czechoslovakia, created in October 1918 as a result of World War I (1914–18), was made up of the historic Czech Lands, Slovakia, and sub-Carpathian Russia in the east. Formally, it was recognized by several international treaties (e.g., Saint-Germain in 1919 and Trianon the following year) that formed part of the Peace of Versailles that concluded World War I.

The constitutional system of interwar Czechoslovakia was based on the Constitutional Charter of 1920, the first democratic constitution on Czech territory. It was the major source of inspiration for the present Czech constitution. The charter contained the rules of state organization and a list of human rights. As these rights were subject to statutory limitation, they were referred to as "monologues of the legislator." The charter was defined by division of powers, responsibility of the administration to the Chamber of Deputies, and a bicameral parliament. The office of the president of the republic enjoyed great authority, because of the respect held by President T. G. Masaryk.

The underlying principle of Czechoslovakia—and its most problematic issue—was the idea of Czechoslovakism, that is, the existence of the Czechoslovak nation. Nevertheless, Czechoslovakia between the two world wars was one of the most developed economies in the world and formed a democratic island in a region full of destabilized countries. This island of democracy was threatened by the so-called Munich dictate, an agreement among Great Britain, France, Italy, and Germany at the end of September 1938 that resulted in the extinction of the country when German troops created the Protectorate of Bohemia and Moravia in March 1939 and simultaneously declared the puppet Slovak State. In the course of 1940, a provisional government in exile in London was created. The legal nature of the provisional government corresponded to a constitutional state of emergency. Decrees of the president of the republic became the source of law; they were ratified in 1945 by a constitutional act and declared to be law. Decrees of the president regulated not only substantial matters of the state's organization but also some problematic issues such as expatriation of inhabitants of German or Hungarian nationality.

The increasing involvement of the Soviet Union in Central Europe and the increasing influence of the Communist Party within the state were more important than the continuity of the republic and the restoration of the state. The postwar era culminated in the Communist coup d'état in February 1949. The Communist regime underwent its own evolution with constitutions in 1948, 1960, and 1968. However, it was always governed with a mixture of legal and unlawful instruments and practices. The events that followed the Velvet Revolution in 1989 led to the full restoration of democracy in Czechoslovakia. This democratic restoration was accompanied by a deepening crisis between Czechs and Slovaks that resulted in the split up of Czechoslovakia in 1992–93. Entry in NATO in 1999 and in the European Union in 2004 are two milestones of the recent Czech constitutional history.

FORM AND IMPACT OF THE CONSTITUTION

The Czech Republic has a written constitution. The basic constitutional acts are the constitution of the Czech Republic, which was approved at the end of 1992 and went into force on January 1, 1993, and the Charter of Fundamental Rights and Freedoms. This charter was in force at first for the whole of Czechoslovakia and was thereafter promulgated as a constitutional act of the independent Czech Republic. The Constitutional Order as referred to in the 1993 constitution is formed by the sum of constitutional norms; it embraces constitutional acts under the 1993 constitution, the Charter of Fundamental Rights, former constitutional acts concerning state boundaries, and certain constitutional acts regarding the dissolution of the Czechoslovak Federation in 1992. There are also constitutional acts on the security of the Czech Republic, on higher self-governing units, and on the referendum on joining the European Union. Any other statutory or implementation legislation, as well as international treaties, must be in compliance with this constitutional order.

According to Article 10 of the constitution, binding international agreements ratified by the Parliament constitute a part of the legal order. Should an international agreement have a provision contrary to a law, the international agreement is to be applied. From 1993 to 2002, this primacy was confined solely to human rights treaties. Article 10 was amended in 2001 and now includes all international agreements.

BASIC ORGANIZATIONAL STRUCTURE

The Czech Republic is a unitary state in which local and regional governments have limited powers defined by law. Framing public power on three levels of government contributes to greater effectiveness and division of power. The 1993 constitution has embedded the legal existence of municipalities and regions, as provided for in statutory regulations. There are 14 regions charged by law with independent or delegated administrative and legislative powers.

LEADING CONSTITUTIONAL PRINCIPLES

The Czech Republic is a parliamentary democracy with a strong division of the executive, legislative, and judicial powers, supplemented with a system of checks and balances. The constitutional system is characterized by a number of legal principles: The republic is a sovereign, unitary, and democratic law-abiding state, based on respect for the rights and freedoms of all citizens. The state is founded on democratic values and must not be bound either by an exclusive ideology or by a particular religion. Consequently, the Czech Republic is a secular state with very limited cooperation with religious communities. Special attention is paid to human rights and to the principle of the rule of law. The power of the state may be asserted only in defined matters and within the limits set by law and in a manner determined by law. Everybody may do what is not prohibited by law, and nobody may be forced to do what the law does not command.

CONSTITUTIONAL BODIES

The most important constitutional bodies are Parliament, the president of the republic, the administration, and the judiciary, including the Constitutional Court. The constitution also provides for a supreme auditing office, the Czech National Bank, and regional self-government.

Parliament

Parliament consists of two chambers, the Chamber of Deputies and the Senate, but the status of the two chambers is unequal. The Chamber of Deputies plays the predominant role in the legislative process. The administration is responsible to the deputies, who can bestow or withhold confidence, exercise parliamentary inquiry and interpellation (challenging policy), and question ministers. The state budget is also approved only by the Chamber of Deputies. On the other hand, the Senate has exclusive powers to approve candidates for justices of the Constitutional Court and to impeach the president of the republic. Both chambers of Parliament are in permanent session. The Chamber of Deputies can be dissolved by the president of the republic for reasons defined by the constitution. Subsequently, temporary legislative authority vests in the Senate, which cannot be dissolved.

Elections to the Chamber of Deputies follow a system of proportional representation; elections to the Senate take place by the principle of the majority system within electoral districts. The 200 deputies are elected for a term of four years and the 81 senators for a term of six years. One-third of the senators are elected every two years. All representatives exercise their mandate freely and independently.

The Lawmaking Process

Bills are first introduced in the Chamber of Deputies. An initiative for legislation may originate from a deputy, a group of deputies, the Senate as a whole, the administration, or the representative body of a region. The Chamber of Deputies deliberates the bills in three readings. Passage of the bill requires the votes of the majority of voting deputies; a quorum is one-third of all members of the chamber. Subsequently, the bill is submitted to the Senate. The Senate may adopt it, reject it, or return it to the Chamber of Deputies with suggestions for amendment, all within a term of 30 days. The Senate's vote can be overridden in a renewed vote by the Chamber of Deputies with the majority of all members of the chamber. The same majority requirements apply with respect to the president's right to a suspensive veto after a bill passes both chambers.

Any electoral law, or law defining the principles of transactions and contacts between the two chambers, or law containing rules of procedure of the Senate, must be approved by both chambers.

The President of the Republic

The president of the republic is the head of state. He or she is elected at a joint session of both chambers of Parliament for a term of five years. Any citizen who is eligible for election to the Senate may be elected president of the republic. Nobody may be elected president of the republic more than twice in succession. He or she acts for and on behalf of the state with respect to third parties, negotiates and ratifies international treaties in cooperation with the administration, and is the supreme commander of the armed forces.

Some of the president's powers can be exercised only with the approval of the prime minister or of the appropriate member of the administration. These acts are the so-called countersigned acts of the president under Article 63. The president of the republic appoints and recalls the prime minister and other members of the administration and accepts their resignation, convenes sessions of the Chamber of Deputies, and dissolves the Chamber of Deputies. The president appoints justices of the Constitutional Court with prior approval of the Senate, issues pardons and mitigates penalties within the criminal justice system, and exercises a suspensive veto within the legislative process.

The Administration

The supreme executive and political authority of the Czech Republic is the administration. This consists of the prime minister, the deputy prime minister, and other ministers. The administration is accountable to the Chamber of Deputies. The most important expression of this accountability is the rule of confidence. To be in office, the administration needs the confidence of the Chamber of Deputies. The administration helps prepare proposals of laws. In practice, the majority of laws come about at the administration's initiative. This administration's initiative for legislation is exclusive in the case of the state budget bill. The administration is, in general, authorized to enact implementing regulations, not exceeding the limits of the law.

The Judiciary

The independence of the judiciary, of judges and courts, is one of the most important principles for the new Czech democracy. There is a system of general courts on four different levels: the Supreme Court and the Supreme Administrative Court, the High Court, regional courts, and district courts. A judge is appointed for life by the president of the republic with the approval of the prime minister or the minister of justice.

The Constitutional Court is a specialized judicial body charged with the protection of the constitution. It consists of 15 judges who are appointed for a term of office of 10 years by the president of the republic with the approval of the Senate. The jurisdictional powers of the Constitutional Court are enumerated in Article 87 of the constitution. From a practical point of view, the most frequent procedures are those dealing with constitutional complaints of individuals against the public authorities. The decisions of the Constitutional Court declaring laws unconstitutional and void are of foremost importance. The case law of the Constitutional Court, especially in human rights, has had an enormous if indirect impact on the decisions of policymakers.

THE ELECTION PROCESS AND POLITICAL PARTICIPATION

Article 21 of the Charter of Human Rights and Fundamental Freedoms stipulates general conditions for democratic elections. Accordingly, citizens have the right to participate in the administration of public affairs either directly or through free election of their representatives. They also have access to any elective and other public office under equal conditions.

Elections to both chambers of Parliament are held by secret ballot on the basis of universal, equal, and direct suffrage. Every citizen of the Czech Republic who has attained the age of 18 has the right to vote. Every citizen of the Czech Republic who has the right to vote and who has attained the age of 21 may be elected to the Chamber of Deputies. Every citizen of the Czech Republic who has the right to vote and who has attained the age of 40 may be elected to the Senate and to the office of the president of the republic. The same principles as for the election to the Chamber of Deputies apply to the elections to representative bodies of communities and regions.

Article 2, Paragraph 2 stipulates that a constitutional act may allow the people to exercise state power directly. This provision was the legal basis for the referendum on the accession of the Czech Republic to the European Union. Other forms of direct democracy are confined to local plebiscites on local matters.

POLITICAL PARTIES

The political system of the Czech Republic is based on the free and voluntary formation of and free competition between political parties respecting basic democratic precepts. The system of proportional representation prevailing in the majority of election procedures is restricted by some rules that promote improved effectiveness. One is the obligation for parties to pay a deposit in the course of the nomination procedure. Another is the minimum of votes needed to win representation in the Chamber of Deputies—5 percent for individual parties and 10, 15, or 20 percent of the total number of votes for coalitions of parties, respectively.

Political parties can only be banned by a decision of the Supreme Administrative Court. The Constitutional Court has the final say whether the dissolution conforms to constitutional or other laws.

CITIZENSHIP

Acquisition and loss of citizenship of the Czech Republic are delegated by the constitution to statutory laws, except that nobody may be deprived of his or her citizenship against his or her will. Citizenship arises primarily by birth, adoption, determination of paternity, or naturalization. In general, the principle of *ius sanguinis* is applied: That is, a child is a citizen of the Czech Republic if his or her father or mother is a Czech citizen.

State citizenship ceases for three reasons: at the person's own request, by a court's decision, and by acquisition of foreign nationality at one's own and deliberate request.

FUNDAMENTAL RIGHTS
The Basic System of Human Rights and Fundamental Freedoms

Human rights and fundamental freedoms are guaranteed by the constitution and the Charter of Fundamental Rights and Freedoms. International treaties also help guarantee these rights, most importantly the European Convention for the Protection of Human Rights and Fundamental Freedoms of 1950. This convention is one of the most important sources of inspiration for the Czech charter. Other sources are the 1920 Constitutional Charter and a number of contemporary foreign constitutional documents such as the German Basic Law. Human rights are protected by general courts and the Constitutional Court. The protection of human rights and fundamental freedoms is also vested in the office of the public protector of rights, the ombudsperson.

Impact and Functions of Fundamental Rights

The charter distinguishes several groups of rights. There are fundamental human rights and freedoms such as the prohibition of discrimination; the right to life; the right to respect of privacy; the right to personal liberty, to ownership of property, and to freedom of movement and residence; the sanctity of the home; and freedom of thought, conscience, and religious conviction. There are also political rights such as the freedom of expression, the right to associate and to assemble, and the right of petition. Furthermore, there are rights of national and ethnic minorities, and economic, social, and culture rights such as the right to education, the right to free choice of occupation and to participation in a trade union, the right to strike, and the protection of women and children. Finally, there are rights to judicial and other legal protection. The charter and constitution distinguish further between rights that apply to everybody and those reserved for Czech citizens, which apply to some political or social rights.

The primary function of human rights and fundamental freedoms is to create a space of freedom for every individual; that is regarded as their defensive function. However, the state is also obliged to create conditions for implementing these rights and freedoms. The wording of some provisions of the charter and the doctrinal opinions of jurisprudence indicate that some other effects may be derived from or linked with human rights and fundamental freedoms. Nobody denies, for example, that the state has to protect actively some categories of human rights. The direct effect of some special rights among private persons is currently under discussion.

Limitations to Fundamental Rights

The general rule of human rights limitation is spelled out in Article 4 of the charter. Any limits placed on fundamental rights and freedoms must be governed by law under conditions set out by the charter. Any statutory limitation of fundamental rights and freedoms must apply equally to all cases meeting the set conditions. Even when applying limits on rights and freedoms, the government must respect their essentials and substance. Article 41 of the charter stipulates that enumerated rights from the group of economic, social, and cultural rights may be claimed only within the scope of laws implementing them. This means that the margin of application for policy- and lawmakers is broader than in the case of other rights of the charter.

ECONOMY

The constitution of 1993 does not specify any economic system nor contain any guidelines for its establishment. The free market economy is a corollary of transition from communism to democracy. The concrete economic policy of the government is a subject of political competition between political parties. The most important instrument is the state budget act that is approved every year by the Chamber of Deputies. Some essential requirements of economic policy result from membership in the European Union.

RELIGIOUS COMMUNITIES

The law on religion in the Czech Republic is based on the following principles: nonidentification with any ideology or religion, the state's neutrality in religious affairs, equality of religious communities, and constitutionally guaranteed autonomy of religious communities. There is, however, still space for cooperation between the state and religious communities. Therefore, the Czech system of the law on religion ought to be described as institutional separation with cooperative elements.

Religious freedom is protected extensively by Articles 15 and 16 of the Charter of Fundamental Rights and Freedoms. Accordingly, freedom of thought, conscience, and religious conviction is guaranteed. Everyone has the right to change his or her religion or to have no religious conviction at all. Furthermore, everyone has the right to profess freely his or her religion or faith either alone or jointly with others; privately or in public; though religious service, instruction, religious acts, or rituals. Churches and religious communities administer their own affairs. In particular, they appoint their organs and their clergy and establish religious orders and other church institutions independently of organs of the state.

MILITARY DEFENSE AND STATE OF EMERGENCY

The entry of the Czech Republic in NATO in 1999 was a milestone of Czech military and political history. After this accession, the Czech army was reorganized on a professional basis. The president of the republic is formally the commander in chief of the armed forces and appoints and promotes generals, subject to the responsibility of the administration.

Military activities of the Czech army either abroad or on the territory of the Czech Republic are under strong parliamentary control. The parliament may decide to declare a state of war should the Czech Republic be attacked or should international contractual obligations concerning common defense be met. The Parliament must also approve any participation of the Czech Republic in defense systems of an international organization.

Special regulation is envisaged in the Constitutional Act on Security of the Czech Republic for the cases of a nonmilitary state of emergency, such as a natural or technical disaster, or when the sovereignty of the republic is endangered from outside.

AMENDMENTS TO THE CONSTITUTION

According to Article 9, the constitution may be supplemented or amended only by constitutional acts. The provisions that are requisites of a democratic, law-abiding state may not be amended. The approval of a three-fifths majority of all deputies and of a three-fifths majority of voting senators is required to pass a constitutional act. From 1993 to 2004, there were only five important amendments of the constitution. The presidential right of suspensive veto does not apply to constitutional acts.

PRIMARY SOURCES
1993 Constitution in English. Available online. URL: http://www.psp.cz/cgi-bin/eng/docs/laws/constitution.html. Accessed on September 14, 2005.
Charter of Fundamental Rights and Freedoms in English. Available online. URL: http://www.psp.cz/cgi-bin/eng/docs/laws/listina.html. Accessed on July 19, 2005.

SECONDARY SOURCES
Aleš Gerloch, Jiři Hřebejk, and Vladimir Zoubek, *Ústavní systém České republiky: Základy Českého ústavního práva.* 4th ed. Prague: Prospektrum. 2002.
Richard Potz, Brigitte Schinkele, Karl Schwarz, Eva M. Synek, and Wolfgang Wieshaider, eds., *Recht und Religion in Mittel- und Osteuropa.* Band 2, *Tschechien* [*Law and religion in Central and Eastern Europe.* Vol. 2, Czech Republic]. Vienna: WUV Universitätsverlag, 2004.

Stepan Hulka

DENMARK

At-a-Glance

OFFICIAL NAME
Kingdom of Denmark

CAPITAL
Copenhagen

POPULATION
Denmark: 5,330,000; Faroe Islands: 43,678;
Greenland: 56,124 (2005 est.)

SIZE
Denmark: 16,639 sq. mi. (43,096 sq. km), Faroe
Islands: 540 sq. mi. (1,399 sq. km), Greenland:
836,330 sq. mi. (2,166,086 sq. km)

LANGUAGES
Danish, Faroes, and Greenlandic

RELIGIONS
Folk Church 84%, Roman Catholic 3.6%, Jehovah's
Witnesses 1.5%, Pentecostal Movement 0.5%, Baptist
Community 0.5%, Jewish Community 0.3% (43 other
registered religious communities, apart from Muslim
communities)

NATIONAL OR ETHNIC COMPOSITION
Danish (including Faroe Islanders and Greenlanders)
91.9%, other (largely made up of other Nordic,
Turkish, German, Bosnian, Iraqi, Lebanese, Pakistani,
Somalian) 8.1%

DATE OF INDEPENDENCE OR CREATION
About 950 C.E.

TYPE OF GOVERNMENT
Parliamentary democracy and monarchy

TYPE OF STATE
Centralist state

TYPE OF LEGISLATURE
Unicameral parliament

DATE OF CONSTITUTION
June 5, 1849

DATE OF LAST AMENDMENT
June 5, 1953

Denmark is a parliamentary democracy based upon the rule of law with a clear division of executive, legislative, and judicial powers. It is organized as one state consisting of the mainland European territories bordering Germany and the territories of the Faroe Islands and Greenland in the northern part of the Atlantic, which have a special constitutional position with home rule.

The monarch is formally the head of state but has mostly representative functions. The central political figure is the prime minister as head of the government. Free, equal, general, and direct elections of the members of the parliament are guaranteed. A pluralistic system of political parties has great political impact.

Religious freedom is guaranteed. State and the religious communities other than the Folk Church are separated. The Folk Church, however, has a position as part of the state. The military is subject to the government and parliament.

CONSTITUTIONAL HISTORY

Denmark as a political entity emerged in northern Europe from the 10th century onward. The word *Denmark* (Tanmarker) is known since at least 950 C.E. Denmark has been an autonomous country ever since and is thus one of the oldest states in Europe. It has been a monarchy from its earliest beginnings. The first known kings were Gorm, who died in 958, and his son, Harald I, who died in about 985. The kings were elected by the house of carls, later by the noble knights, on the provincial land stings, the regional assemblies for legislation and jurisdiction. Until 1660, Denmark was legally an elective rather than a hereditary monarchy, but the kings were normally chosen from the old royal dynasty. From 1448, the descendents of Gorm and Harald were succeeded by the related descendents of the house of Oldenburg, which kept the throne until 1863 when descendents from the related house of

Glücksburg took over. The current monarch, Queen Margrethe II, belongs to the Glücksburgian house.

In 1661, the electoral monarchy was changed into a hereditary and absolute monarchy. Danish absolutism (1660–1848) was based upon a written constitution called Lex Regia, proclaimed by King Frederik III (1648–70) in 1665. The constitution had the character of a fundamental or basic law that was difficult to change. It expounded upon the king's sovereignty and his royal rights or prerogatives and prescribed succession rules. The Lex Regia was inspired by political philosophers of the time, among them the French philosopher Jean Bodin.

As a consequence of the revolutionary movements in Europe and especially of political developments in Prussia, provincial consultative assemblies were instituted in 1831 and 1834 in Denmark and in the Duchies of Schleswig and Holstein. Only 3 percent of the population had the right to vote in these provincial assemblies, but they managed to strengthen personal freedoms and property rights, as well as important preparatory work toward a new constitution and the transition to a parliamentary regime.

The new constitution of 1849 (called Danmarks Riges Grundlov) instituted a parliamentary regime, which it styled a restricted monarchical government, but the royal power remained hereditary. The new constitution was based upon the principle of division of the executive, legislative, and judicial powers. Formally, the legislative power was vested with both the king and the parliament, while the king had the executive power alone. However, the king could not act alone, only together with a minister who had to countersign his decisions.

The new constitution gave only 14 percent of the population the right to vote—males above the age of 30 with an independent household could vote for or be elected to the first chamber, the Folketinget, and only males above the age of 40 with a certain income could vote for or be elected to the second chamber, the Landstinget. The parliament, Rigsdagen, was bicameral until 1953.

The ties between Denmark and the Duchies of Schleswig and Holstein created frictions with Prussia when a new common constitution was issued for Denmark and the two duchies in 1854. In 1863, Schleswig and Denmark gained a common constitution. This was contrary to international agreements and caused a war with Prussia and Austria, which Denmark lost in 1864. Denmark had to surrender the duchies to Prussia.

A rather conservative revised constitution, which caused internal political problems, was created in 1866. The government constantly faced majority opposition in Folketinget, which declined to pass the budgets, forcing the administration to rule with the help of provisional acts.

In 1901, the king accepted the "principle of parliamentarism" by which the administration is chosen by the majority of Folketinget and does not remain in office if it loses the support of the majority of the Folketinget. This principle had the character of a constitutional custom until it was formalized by the amendment of 1953 when it was codified in Article 15.

With the amendment of 1915, women and servants received the right to vote and to be elected to both chambers. This amendment was not put into effect until 1918, however, because of World War I (1914–18). The peace treaty allowed the population in the duchies to vote in favor of a reunion with Denmark. Part of Northern Schleswig voted for reunion, and a special amendment to the constitution was passed in 1920.

After World War II (1939–45) and the judicial purge of collaborators and traitors, preparations for a new amendment were made to accommodate new demands: female succession to the throne, a lower voting age, more opportunities for referenda, a change into a unicameral parliament, transfer of limited sovereignty to international organizations, and the institution of an ombudsperson for the control of the administration. These amendments were all accepted, and the new constitution, which is still in force, was approved in 1953.

The constitution is valid for all parts of Denmark's realm. Denmark, the Faroe Islands, and Greenland from a constitutional point of view are one entity, comprising three equal parts. There is not and never was legal uniformity in the three parts. The Faroe Islands was included in the 1849 constitution and was given local self-government in the Act on Home Rule of 1948. Greenland was a colony until 1953 and was given self-government in the Act on Home Rule of 1978. In practice, there no longer exists a constitutional unity but a constitutional community of the realm. The governments of the Faroe Islands and Greenland are, with the cooperation of the Danish government, working for complete independence from the constitutional community. It is legally uncertain whether a formal, constitutional amendment will be necessary to complete this process.

Denmark is a member state of the European Union and a member of the North Atlantic Treaty Organization (NATO).

FORM AND IMPACT OF THE CONSTITUTION

Denmark has a written constitution, codified in a single document called the Basic Law (Grundloven), which takes precedence over all other national law. The Basic Law permits that certain powers exercised by the authorities of the Danish realm may in a limited way be placed in the hands of international authorities such as the European Union. The law of the European Union may have precedence over the Danish constitution in certain subjects as long as it does not contradict the basic principles of the Danish constitution.

The Danish constitution has survived great social changes and political storms in its 150-year history. The catalogue of fundamental civil rights in the constitution of 1953 was only slightly influenced by the United Nations Declaration of Human Rights of 1948 and the European Convention on Human Rights of 1950.

BASIC ORGANIZATIONAL STRUCTURE

The realm of Denmark is one state with different territories: Denmark, the Faroe Islands, and Greenland. The Basic Law covers all three territories, each with its own legal system, but it contains no claims of legal unity of the whole kingdom. In separate agreements with the Faroe Islands and Greenland, the Danish government has made preparations for the two territories to leave this community of the realm in order to be independent sovereign states when they themselves feel strong enough.

The Faroe parliament (Lagtinget) and government (Landsstyret) exercise sovereignty in certain special matters. The extent of sovereignty is expected to increase over the years until complete self-government is achieved. Greenland achieved self-government under similar conditions. The local authorities have legislative and executive powers but until now no judicial ones. The Danish authorities also rule in matters of the realm such as foreign policy and police. Neither the Faroe Islands nor Greenland is a member of the European Union. Greenland was a member from 1973 onward but left the European Communities in 1985. Local municipal communities in Denmark are entities incorporated by the state, whose role is guaranteed in the constitution. They make their own decisions on quite a number of issues. Citizens of the local communities elect mayors and other members of local political boards. The system is currently under reorganization into a smaller number of regional communities and local municipalities in order to provide for bigger and stronger entities.

LEADING CONSTITUTIONAL PRINCIPLES

Denmark's system of government is a parliamentary democracy. There is a clear division of the executive, legislative, and judicial powers. Denmark has no special constitutional court. The Supreme Court is supposed to deal with all types of legal problems, including constitutional issues. A special court, Rigsretten, decides cases against single ministers concerning their discharge of official duties after they are charged by the government or Folketinget.

The Danish constitution is defined by several leading principles: Denmark is a democracy and a monarchy. It is also a social state and is based upon the rule of law, which is not expressed directly but is presupposed indirectly.

Political participation is shaped as an indirect, representative democracy. Direct democracy by means of referendum is possible but is rather rare in practice. There are two forms of referendum: a decisive referendum and a voluntary decisive referendum. Majority decisions of Folketinget may be put to a voluntary decisive referendum, as occurred in 1992 and 1993 concerning the Edinburgh-Maastricht treaty of the European Union because this treaty concerned a question of surrendering Danish sovereignty.

The principle of monarchy is "restricted." The power of the monarch is limited by the three branches of government; the principle of monarchy means only that Denmark shall not be a republic.

CONSTITUTIONAL BODIES

The four bodies are the monarch, the cabinet or administration, the Folketinget or parliament, and the courts.

The Monarch

The monarch appoints and dismisses the prime minister after taking counsel from the political parties represented in Folketinget. The person nominated by the parties representing a majority in parliament is appointed. The monarch has the highest authority in state affairs, but it is executed through the ministers of the government. The monarch promulgates the laws that are countersigned by the relevant minister or ministers. The monarch represents Denmark in international affairs and formally appoints and dismisses civil servants. The monarch has the right to pardon or to grant amnesty to criminal offenders. Yet, the king does not have political importance or influence; the office is largely symbolic.

The royal power is inherited by male and female descendants according to the rules in the Act on Succession to the Throne of 1953. Before his or her accession to office, the monarch must tender a solemn written assurance in the Council Meeting of Ministers of State to keep the Basic Law unbreakable.

The monarch is free from legal liability; the ministers of the cabinet are responsible for all action of the administration. The monarch's person is sacrosanct; therefore, he or she must receive respect and veneration.

The Cabinet

The cabinet consists of all ministers under the leadership of the prime minister. The cabinet serves for the legislative period of Folketinget, unless dismissed during the term via a vote of no confidence. The ministers function in two special bodies: the Council Meeting of Ministers of State with the king, in which royal decrees are ratified through countersigning, and the weekly Meeting of Ministers, in which the practical work is done. The individual ministers head the various ministries or departments of government.

Folketinget

Folketinget consists of 179 delegates, 175 from Denmark, two from the Faroe Islands, and two from Greenland. Its term of office is four years. The delegates are elected in general, direct, free, equal, and secret elections. The members of Folketinget have the right to put questions to the administration and to any minister who can be called to appear before parliament.

The members have a parliamentary privilege to ensure their independence. They are protected against legal actions or other negative consequences arising from their voting or statements in parliament. Only with permission of Folketinget can a member be subjected to any criminal prosecution, be arrested, or have his or her freedom limited.

The Lawmaking Process

The main duty of Folketinget is to pass legislation. This is done in cooperation with the executive government, which normally introduces the draft bills. Individual members of parliament, alone or as a group from one party or from several parties, may introduce a bill, which is then called a private bill.

A bill has to be passed three times in plenary meetings of the assembly, after which it is sent for the royal assent and countersignature of the appropriate minister. A minority of 60 members of Folketinget may try to have expropriations bills repealed by summoning a referendum.

The Judiciary

The judiciary in Denmark is independent of the executive and legislative branches. There are ordinary lower and higher courts for civil and criminal cases and different courts for special issues: the Tax Tribunal, the Labor Tribunal, and the Maritime and Commercial Court, among others. The Supreme Court is the highest court of appeal. All complaints concerning constitutional questions can be taken before the Supreme Court as well.

Rigsretten is a special court for cases against ministers. It consists of up to 15 judges from the Supreme Court and a corresponding number of persons from outside parliament but chosen by Folketinget. There have been five cases since 1849. The last one concerned a minister of justice, tried in 1995 for his implementation of a law related to reuniting families of Tamil refugees.

THE ELECTION PROCESS

All Danes over the age of 18 have both the right to stand for election and the right to vote in the elections. The election system for parliament consists of two separate votes: election by proportional representation and elections in multimember constituencies (a winner-takes-all majority vote). A political party must win at least one seat in a Folketinget multimember constituency and at least 2 percent of all votes in order to sit in the house. In 2004, eight parties were represented in Folketinget.

POLITICAL PARTIES

Denmark has a pluralistic system of political parties. Political parties are private associations that are primarily self-financing, relying on membership fees, donations, and additional financing from private or public funds. The Basic Law does not expressly mention the existence of political parties; they are presupposed in the internal bylaws of Folketinget. A political party may be banned from exercising freedom of association if the purpose of the party is illegal. The dissolution of an association requires an act of Folketinget or a court decision.

CITIZENSHIP

Danish citizenship is primarily acquired by birth or by naturalization through a special law.

FUNDAMENTAL RIGHTS

The Basic Law expresses the liberal natural-law philosophy of the 1840s. The civil rights or liberties in the first constitution concerned the relation of the individuals to the state. The basic rights are personal freedom and freedom of property, trade, speech, association, assembly, and religion. However, there also was a right to social support. The 1953 constitution was somewhat influenced by the United Nations' Declaration of Human Rights of 1948 and the European Convention on Human Rights of 1950, at least concerning social and economic rights and the right to education.

Civil rights are part of Chapter 8 of the constitution, which also regulates the right to self-government for municipalities; the abolition of all privileges attached to title, nobility, and rank; and the duty for every man to do his military service.

The Danish constitution guarantees the traditional classic set of human rights that express democratic respect for the individual. Social human rights are somewhat underrepresented. For example, the Basic Law does not include an equal treatment clause for women.

Impact and Functions of Fundamental Rights

The human rights guaranteed in the Basic Law apply only to the relations between individuals and the state. International standards of human rights have been observed more seriously by government authorities in the last decade. The Basic Law does not distinguish between fundamental rights for Danes and human rights that apply to every human being.

The European Convention on Human Rights was incorporated as part of Danish legislation in 1992, but it is not part of the constitution. There has been discussion about whether the Danish courts should follow the decisions of the European Court of Human Rights in Strasbourg concerning the interpretation of human rights and central legal concepts if this interpretation differs from the Danish legal and legislative tradition.

The constitution also guarantees due process. The state must provide appropriate organizational and procedural structures to ensure the prompt and effective protection of fundamental rights.

Limitations to Fundamental Rights

The fundamental rights in the Danish constitution have some limits according to specific needs of public and individual interests. Public encroachment on the fundamental freedoms concerning the security of life and property must follow the due process of law. This necessitates a limitation of the general power of legislation for Folketinget.

If freedom of speech, assembly, or association is abused to undermine the democratic constitutional order, these rights may be put aside. The decision is made by the courts or, in case of illegal assemblies, by the police.

The economic, social, and cultural freedoms included in the constitution do not have the character of special guarantees that limit the legislative power. Instead, they are programmatic goals meant to guide legislation in those areas.

ECONOMY

The Danish constitution does not specify any particular economic system. However, fundamental rights do protect the right to property and the choice of one's profession, general personal freedom, and the freedom to form associations for any legal purpose, including economic and industrial.

The Danish economic system can be described as a social market economy, which combines aspects of social responsibility with market freedom.

RELIGIOUS COMMUNITIES

Freedom of religion involves rights for the religious communities. Before 1849, the Danish Church was a state church; the Evangelical-Lutheran Confession was the only accepted religion in the Absolutist Constitution of 1665. The constitution of 1849 changed the status of the church into a Folk Church, the "people's church" for the majority of the population, and promised that the Folk Church would have its own constitution in order to be autonomous. This promise has not yet been fulfilled.

The Folk Church has a special legal status as a state agency in combination with the Ministry of Ecclesiastical Affairs and Folketinget but with local self-government through parish councils. The constitution declares the Evangelical-Lutheran Church to be the Folk Church and calls for it to be funded by the state. All other churches and religious communities are, from a legal point of view, private associations, which receive no state funding different from that of other private or public utility associations.

MILITARY DEFENSE AND STATE OF EMERGENCY

Apart from defending the Danish realm or Danish armed forces against a military attack, the government cannot use military forces against any foreign state without the consent of Folketinget.

In Denmark, general conscription requires all men above the age of 18 to perform basic military service for four months. In addition, there are professional soldiers who serve for fixed periods. Women can volunteer but are not required to serve.

Conscientious objectors can file a petition to be excluded from military service. If their petition is granted, they are obliged to do alternative service in civil institutions.

AMENDMENTS TO THE CONSTITUTION

The Basic Law is particularly difficult to change. If Folketinget accepts a draft of amendments, there must be a general election. If the new elected Folketinget passes the bill without new amendments, it must be presented to the electors within six months in a direct referendum. If a majority of the voters and at least 40 percent of the total entitled voters vote in favor of the amendment, the draft becomes part of the Basic Law when it has received the royal assent and the ministerial countersignature.

PRIMARY SOURCES
Constitution in English: *The Constitutional Act of Denmark of June 5, 1953.* Available online. URL: http://www.folketinget.dk/pdf/constitution.pdf. Accessed on July 18, 2005.
Constitution in Danish: *Danmarks Riges Grundlov.* Available online. URL: http://www.grundloven.dk/. Accessed on September 11, 2005.

SECONDARY SOURCES
Inger Dübeck, "State and Church in Denmark." In *State and Church in the European Union,* edited by Gerhard Robbers, 37–56. Baden-Baden: Nomos, 1996.
P. Germer, *The Danish Constitution 150 Years.* Copenhagen: The Royal Danish Ministry of Foreign Affairs, 1999.
Henrik Zahle, ed., *Danmarks Riges Grundlov med Kommentarer.* Copenhagen: Jurist- og Økonomforbundets Forlag, 1999.
J. A. Jensen, "The Danish Ombudsman Institution." *European Public Law* 4, no. 3 (1998): 285–389.
———, "Constitutional Law, Denmark." *European Public Law* 10, no. 2 (1998): 375–389.

Inger Dübeck

DJIBOUTI

At-a-Glance

OFFICIAL NAME
Republic of Djibouti

CAPITAL
Djibouti

POPULATION
476,703 (2005 est.)

SIZE
8,880 sq. mi. (23,000 sq. km)

LANGUAGES
French (official), Arabic (official), Somali, Afar

RELIGIONS
Sunni Muslim 99%, Christian 1%

NATIONAL OR ETHNIC COMPOSITION
Somali 60%, Afar 35%, other (French, Arab,
Ethiopian, and Italian) 5%

DATE OF INDEPENDENCE OR CREATION
June 27, 1977

TYPE OF GOVERNMENT
Presidential democracy

TYPE OF STATE
Unitary state

TYPE OF LEGISLATURE
Unicameral parliament

DATE OF CONSTITUTION
September 4, 1992

DATE OF LAST AMENDMENT
February 2, 2006

The Republic of Djibouti is a presidential democracy. According to the constitution, the institutions of the republic are the executive power, the legislative power, and the judicial power. Organized as a unitary state, Djibouti is made up of five districts or cercles.

The constitution provides for far-reaching guarantees of human rights. The state has the obligation to respect and protect them.

The president is the powerful head of both state and administration. The president appoints the prime minister and the cabinet ministers, which are all responsible to the president. Universal, equal, and secret elections are guaranteed. Multiparty elections began in 1992.

The constitution, while declaring Islam to be the state religion, provides for freedom of religion. The economic system can be described as a social market economy. The president of the republic is the head of the armed forces.

CONSTITUTIONAL HISTORY

Djibouti is located at a strategic geographic location at the mouth of the Red Sea. By the year 1862, even before the Suez Canal was opened (1869), France had purchased the anchorage of Obock. Treaties with the sultans of Tadjoura and Gobaad were exchanged. By 1896, the area now comprising the Republic of Djibouti was known as French Somaliland. With a constitutional referendum in 1958, the region opted to join the French community as an overseas territory (1967). This act entitled the region to representation by one deputy and one senator in the French parliament. The name of the region was changed to the French Territory of Afars and Issas. The Afar and the Issa people have strong connections with Ethiopia and Somalia, respectively.

The Issa community strongly favored full independence.

After an overwhelming referendum in favor of independence, the territory became independent on June 27, 1977. Hassan Gouled Aptidon, a senior Issa politician and leader of a unified political movement (Popular African League for Independence [LPA]), became the first president of the republic of Djibouti. He was reelected, unopposed, to a second term in 1987 and to a third term in 1993.

Aptidon's longtime adviser, Ismail Omar Guelleh, won the election to succeed him in 1999. For the first time since independence, no group boycotted the elections.

The 1981 constitution had established a single-party system, which was replaced in 1992 with a multiparty system with a maximum of four political parties. The restriction on the number of parties was lifted only in 2002.

Located in a region of conflict, Djibouti generally pursued a policy of neutrality. It signed separate treaties of friendship and cooperation with Ethiopia, Somalia, Kenya, and Sudan (1981). Internally, it faced a civil war between the predominantly Afar rebel group, the Front for the Restoration of Unity and Democracy (FRUD), and the government from 1991 until 1994. Peace accords were signed in 2001.

Djibouti today is a member of the Arab League and the African Union (AU).

FORM AND IMPACT OF THE CONSTITUTION

Djibouti has a written constitution. The short document consists of 93 articles. Any international pact that contradicts the constitution may not be ratified until the constitution is amended appropriately.

BASIC ORGANIZATIONAL STRUCTURE

Djibouti is a unitary state, made up of five districts called *cercles*.

LEADING CONSTITUTIONAL PRINCIPLES

Djibouti's system of government is a presidential democracy. The institutions of the republic are the executive power, the legislative power, and the judicial power. According to the constitution, the judiciary is independent.

The Djibouti constitutional system is defined by a number of leading principles in Article 1: The state of Djibouti shall be a democratic sovereign republic, one and indivisible. It shall ensure the equality of all citizens before the law, without distinction as to origin, race, sex, or religion. It shall respect all beliefs. Its motto shall be "Unity, Equality, and Peace." Its principle shall be government of the people, by the people, and for the people. Political participation is exercised through representatives and by way of referendum.

CONSTITUTIONAL BODIES

The authority of the state is exercised by the president of the republic and the cabinet (prime minister and cabinet ministers), the National Assembly, and the judicial power, including the Constitutional Council.

The President

The president is both the head of state and head of the executive branch of government. The powerful president designates and can dismiss the prime minister. On the advice of the prime minister, the president also appoints the other cabinet ministers and presides over the Council of Ministers. The president may delegate certain functions to the prime minister or the cabinet ministers, who all are responsible to the president. It is the president who determines and directs the policy of the nation. The president has regulatory powers and must ensure the execution of decisions of the courts.

The president is elected for a six-year term and can be reelected only once. When the office of the president falls vacant, the president of the Supreme Court assumes power as the head of state for a minimum of 20 days and a maximum of 35 days, during which a new president is elected.

The National Assembly (Assemblée Nationale)

Parliament is the legislative body. Its period of office is five years. The number of deputies is determined by an organic law.

The Lawmaking Process

Both the president and the deputies have the right to initiate legislation. The National Assembly generally passes laws by simple majority. The laws that the constitution characterizes as organic (e.g., on the number of deputies, the Constitution Council, and the High Court of Justice) need an absolute majority of members of the national assembly to pass. These laws and the assembly's rules of procedure must be submitted before adoption to the Constitutional Council, which rules on their constitutionality.

The president may, after consultation with the president of the National Assembly and the president of the Constitutional Council, submit any bill to a referendum.

The president promulgates the laws adopted by the National Assembly within 15 days of their transmission, having the right, however, to request a second reading by the assembly. The president notifies the Constitutional Council when considering whether a law is contrary to the constitution. A provision that has been declared unconstitutional may not be promulgated.

The Judiciary

The constitution provides for an independent judiciary. However, in practice, the judiciary has not always been independent of the executive.

The judiciary, based on the French civil law system, is composed of a lower court, appeals courts, and a Supreme Court as the highest ordinary court. The Constitutional Tribunal deals exclusively with constitutional disputes. Laws may be referred to the Constitutional Council before their promulgation by the president, the president of the National Assembly, or 10 deputies within a certain period.

Legislative provisions relating to the fundamental rights of any person may be referred to the Constitutional Council in connection with proceedings that are under way before a court. A provision found unconstitutional on the basis of this article shall cease to be applicable and may no longer be applied in proceedings.

Decisions of the Constitutional Council are binding and may not be appealed. They must be recognized by the executive and juridical authorities and by all people and legal entities.

THE ELECTION PROCESS

All Djiboutians above the age of 18 have the right to vote in the elections. The constitution provides for universal, equal, and secret suffrage.

Parliamentary Elections

Deputies are elected from five multimember constituencies. Voters have only one vote, and the party that wins the most votes takes all the seats in the district (party block vote). All Djiboutians above the age of 23 have the right to stand for elections.

Presidential Elections

The president is elected by direct suffrage and majority vote. If an absolute majority is not obtained on the first ballot, there is a second round open only to the two candidates who have received the greatest number of votes. Candidates for the presidency must be presented by a regularly constituted political party and represented by at least 25 members of parliament.

POLITICAL PARTIES

Djibouti has had a pluralistic system of political parties since 1992. The restriction on the number of parties was lifted in 2002. The following year, eight parties contested the elections in two broad coalitions. The ruling coalition for the presidential majority secured all of the parliamentary seats.

CITIZENSHIP

Birth within the territory of Djibouti does not automatically confer citizenship. A child whose father is a Djiboutian citizen has Djibouti citizenship. The same applies to a child born in Djibouti to a Djibouti mother and an unknown father.

FUNDAMENTAL RIGHTS

The constitution defines fundamental rights and duties in Title II, where it lists the traditional set of liberal rights and civil liberties. Taking the sanctity of the individual as its starting point, it goes on to an equal treatment clause and a right against arbitrary detention. The document also cites the duty of Djiboutian citizens to defend the nation and the integrity of the republic.

Impact and Functions of Fundamental Rights

Djibouti acceded to both the International Covenant on Civil and Political Rights and the Covenant on Economic, Social and Cultural Rights in 2003. According to human rights reports, the government has in practice restricted some rights.

Limitations to Fundamental Rights

Fundamental rights are not without limits in the constitution. For example, the right to property may be restricted in the case of "public necessity" and subject to the prior payment of just compensation. The inviolability of the home may be restricted in the interest of a "common danger." However, no fundamental right may be disregarded completely.

ECONOMY

The Djibouti constitution does not specify an economic system. It recognizes the right to property, the right to strike, and the right to form associations and trade unions. Taken as a whole, the Djibouti economic system can be described as a social market economy.

RELIGIOUS COMMUNITIES

While Islam is declared to be the state religion, the constitution protects freedom of religion as a fundamental right.

MILITARY DEFENSE AND STATE OF EMERGENCY

The president is the guarantor of national security as the supreme commander of the armed forces, who appoints the military personnel.

When the institutions of the republic, the independence of the nation, the integrity of its territory, or the fulfillment of its international commitments is "threatened in a grave and immediate manner" and when the regular functioning of the governmental authorities is interrupted, the president may, after consulting the president of the National Assembly and the president of the Constitutional Council and informing the nation in a message, "take any measure" that may reestablish the regular functioning of the government and ensure the protection of the nation.

Martial law and states of emergency shall be decreed in a meeting of the Council of Ministers. Prolongation of martial law or a state of emergency beyond 15 days may not be authorized without the prior consent of the National Assembly.

AMENDMENTS TO THE CONSTITUTION

The president and the deputies have the right to propose an amendment. The constitution can be changed if the majority of the members of the national assembly vote in favor, and if the amendment is approved in a referendum, by a simple majority of the votes cast. To propose an amendment, at least one-third of the members of the national assembly must sign any parliamentary bill for amendment. The president may dispense with the referendum requirement, provided that the assembly approves it by a two-thirds majority of all members.

Certain fundamental provisions are not subject to change. Article 88 reads: "No amendment procedure may be undertaken if it calls in question the existence of the state or jeopardizes the integrity of the territory, the re-publican form of government or the pluralist character of Djiboutian democracy."

PRIMARY SOURCES

Constitution in English (extracts): Christof Heyns, ed. *Human Rights Law in Africa,* Vol. 2. Leiden, Netherlands: Martinus Nijhoff, 2004. Available online. URL: http://www.chr.up.ac.za/hr_docs/constitutions/docs/DjiboutiC%20(english%20summary)(rev).doc. Accessed on June 17, 2006.

Constitution in French (authentic text): "Constitution de Djibouti." *Journal Officiel de la République de Djibouti.* Available online. URL: http://droit.francophonie.org/doc/html/dj/con/fr/1992/1992dfdjcofr1.html. Accessed on July 17, 2005.

Last amendment: http://www.presidence.dj/jo/2006/loi134pr06.htm.

SECONDARY SOURCES

A. P. Blaustein and G. H. Flanz, *Constitutions of the Countries of the World.* Dobbs Ferry, N.Y.: Oceana, 1971.

Bureau of Public Affairs, U.S. Department of State, "Background Notes and Country Reports on Human Rights Practices and International Religious Freedom Report 2004." Available online. URL: http://www.state.gov/. Accessed on September 5, 2005.

United Nations Development Programme (UNDP), "POGAR—an Information Portal Dedicated to Development and Governance in the Arab World." Available online. URL: http://www.undp-pogar.org/. Accessed on September 25, 2005.

Michael Rahe

DOMINICA

At-a-Glance

OFFICIAL NAME
Commonwealth of Dominica

CAPITAL
Roseau

POPULATION
69,278 (2005 est.)

SIZE
290 sq. mi. (751 sq. km)

LANGUAGES
English, French patois, Cocoy (English dialect)

RELIGIONS
Roman Catholic 77%, Protestant (Methodist 5%,
Pentecostal 3%, Seventh-Day Adventist 3%, Baptist
2%, other 2%) 15%, none 2%, other 6%

NATIONAL OR ETHNIC COMPOSITION
Black 91.0%, Mulatto and Creole 6%, Caribbean
Indian 1.5%, small white minority

DATE OF INDEPENDENCE OR CREATION
November 3, 1978

TYPE OF GOVERNMENT
Parliamentary democracy

TYPE OF STATE
Unitary state

TYPE OF LEGISLATURE
Unicameral parliament

DATE OF CONSTITUTION
July 25, 1978

DATE OF LAST AMENDMENT
1984

Dominica gained independence in 1978 after being ruled by the British since the 1700s. Since then, it has been an independent republic within the British Commonwealth. Dominica is a full and participating member of the Caribbean Community (CARICOM).

The preamble to the constitution professes faith in fundamental rights and freedoms, respect for the principles of social justice, and belief in a democratic society and the rule of law. The government generally respects fundamental rights and freedoms. The president is head of state, and the prime minister is head of the executive government. The parliament is for the most part elected through popular vote in free, equal, and direct elections. To some extent it is appointed.

Religious freedom is guaranteed. The economic system can be described as an agrarian, market-based economy.

CONSTITUTIONAL HISTORY

The island of Dominica's indigenous Arawak people were expelled or exterminated by the Carib in the 14th century. In 1635, France claimed Dominica. Shortly thereafter, French missionaries became the first European inhabitants of the island. Carib incursions continued, however, and in 1660, the French and British agreed that Dominica should be abandoned. The island was officially neutral for the next century, but rival expeditions of British and French foresters were harvesting timber by the beginning of the 18th century.

In 1763, the British established a legislative assembly, representing only the white population. In 1831, reflecting a liberalization of official British racial attitudes, political and social rights were also conferred on free non-whites.

In 1865, the colonial office replaced the elective assembly with a new type of assembly—half the members were elected and half appointed. In 1871, Dominica became part of the Leeward Island Federation. Crown Colony government, however, was reestablished in 1896. In the first half of the 20th century, Dominica was transferred from the Leeward Island Administration to be governed as part of the Windward Islands until 1958 when it joined the West Indies Federation.

After the federation dissolved, Dominica became an associated state of the United Kingdom on February 27, 1967, when it formally took responsibility for its internal affairs. On November 3, 1978, the Commonwealth of Dominica was granted independence by the United Kingdom.

FORM AND IMPACT OF THE CONSTITUTION

Dominica has a written constitution, codified in one main document and three separate schedules to the constitution. The constitution is held as the supreme law of Dominica and prevails over other legal provisions. The constitution establishes and defines the powers and authority of the main instruments of the state.

BASIC ORGANIZATIONAL STRUCTURE

The island is a unitary state, divided into 10 parishes with their own governments. Furthermore, there are also special town governments.

LEADING CONSTITUTIONAL PRINCIPLES

Dominica is a democratic parliamentary republic, and its legal system is based on English common law. The judiciary is independent, and the rule of law is manifested in the preamble of the constitution and enhanced by the court's subordination to the Eastern Caribbean Supreme Court.

CONSTITUTIONAL BODIES

The constitution defines the following bodies for Dominica: the president as head of state, a cabinet of ministers headed by the prime minister, and a unicameral parliament. There is also a parliament commissioner.

The President

The president is the head of state. He or she is elected by parliament for a five-year term and can be reelected.

Executive authority is vested in the president, but in exercising most of the executive functions, the president is required to act in accordance with the advice of the cabinet or a minister acting under the general authority of the cabinet.

The Parliament

The parliament consists of the president and the House of Assembly, the legislative body of Dominica. The House of Assembly has 30 members. Of these, 21 are elected for a five-year term in single-seat constituencies and nine are appointed senators. In practice, five senators are appointed by the prime minister, four by the opposition leader.

The Prime Minister and the Cabinet

The president appoints the leader of the majority party in parliament to be prime minister and also appoints, on the prime minister's recommendation, members of the parliament from the ruling party to be cabinet ministers. There should be no more than three ministers from among the appointed senators. The cabinet advises the president in the governing function and is responsible to the parliament for any advice given to the president and for every action taken by a cabinet minister in the execution of the office. The prime minister and cabinet can be removed by parliament in a no-confidence vote.

The Parliament Commissioner

The parliament commissioner is not an elected member of the parliament and is appointed by the president for a term of five years. The duties of the parliament commissioner are to investigate any action, decision, or recommendation made by any department or authority of the administration that seemed to be a result of faulty administration or injustice, not including proceedings in a court.

The Lawmaking Process

Lawmaking powers are vested in the parliament. The House of Assembly passes bills that the president assents to and afterward are published in the official gazette as laws.

The Judiciary

Dominica has a multilevel judicial system commencing with the Lower Court or Magistrate's Court. This is the first level of recourse for violators of the country's laws. The Supreme Court serves as the second level in this system. Appeals may be made to the Eastern Caribbean States Supreme Court, which consists of a Court of Appeal and a High Court, the third level in Dominica's court structure. As a last resort, in the event of an unsuccessful appeal, individuals have recourse to the Judicial Committee of the Privy Council in London, in which decisions of the Supreme Court may be reviewed for a final ruling.

THE ELECTION PROCESS

Universal adult suffrage was introduced in 1951. The electoral system is patterned on the British Westminster system. All Dominicans above the age of 18 have the right to vote in elections. They have the right to stand for elections at the age of 21.

POLITICAL PARTIES

The constitution allows for any citizen of the country who is 18 years of age or over and who is literate and not bankrupt to organize and take part in political activity. The constitution does not make any provisions for political parties, nor is their formation required for participation in elections. The freedom of assembly and association is, nonetheless, named in Section 1 of the constitution's first chapter as a protected right. Candidates may, therefore, stand for election either in association with a party or as independents.

CITIZENSHIP

Citizenship is defined in Chapter 7 of the constitution. Upon the date of independence, November 3, 1978, citizenship was granted to citizens of the United Kingdom and Colonies (UKC) who were born, naturalized, or registered in Dominica. A person born in the territory of Dominica after November 3, 1978, regardless of the nationality of the parents, is also granted citizenship, as well as a child born abroad, before or after independence, at least one of whose parents is a citizen or was eligible for citizenship at the time of independence. It is also possible to request citizenship for those foreigners or Commonwealth citizens who have resided in Dominica for seven years or who are married to a citizen of Dominica, either living or deceased. This request is subject to the approval of the administration. Dual citizenship is recognized. A bill to allow the purchase of citizenship is under discussion.

FUNDAMENTAL RIGHTS

The constitution's first chapter deals with fundamental rights and freedoms. The constitution guarantees a set of liberal human rights and civil liberties but does not address economic and social rights beyond a general statement in the preamble. The combination of an independent press, an effective judiciary, and a functioning democratic political system is designed to ensure respect for civil liberties.

Impact and Functions of Fundamental Rights

As all laws that are contrary to the constitution are void, all laws that violate fundamental rights or freedoms as specified in the constitution are also invalid. Any person who alleges violation of his or her human rights has the right under the constitution to apply to the High Court for redress.

Inheritance laws do not fully recognize women's rights. When a husband dies without a will, the wife cannot inherit his property, although she may continue to inhabit their home. There are no provisions mandating equal pay for equal work for men and women in private-sector jobs. Although sexual harassment and domestic violence are common, there is no family court that specifically deals with domestic violence issues.

Limitations to Fundamental Rights

The fundamental rights specified in Chapter 1 of the constitution are subject to limitations that ensure that the enjoyment of the rights and freedoms by any person does not prejudice the rights and freedoms of others or the public interest.

ECONOMY

The country has always had a primarily agrarian, market-based economy. The government began a comprehensive restructuring of the economy in 2003—including elimination of price controls, privatization of the state banana company, and tax increases. The government has also tried to develop offshore banking businesses.

RELIGIOUS COMMUNITIES

The constitution provides for freedom of religion. The predominant religion is Christianity, and the Roman Catholic faith claims over 70 percent of the population. The government is secular and does not interfere with an individual's right to worship, but it maintains a close relationship with the Christian churches.

MILITARY DEFENSE AND STATE OF EMERGENCY

The Dominica Defense Force was disbanded in 1981 after being implicated in attempts by the supporters of a former prime minister to overthrow the government. Since then, the military of Dominica has consisted of the Commonwealth of Dominica Police Force (including the Special Service Unit and the Coast Guard) as the only security force.

The office of the prime minister oversees the Dominican police, and civilian authority maintains effective control over the security forces.

AMENDMENTS TO THE CONSTITUTION

There are various provisions concerning alterations or amendments to the constitution. The core provisions of the constitution can only be changed by a vote of three-quarters of the members of parliament. An interval of 90 days and a public referendum with a majority of votes cast are necessary before the bill is allowed to be passed to the president for presidential assent. Other provisions can be changed by the votes of two-thirds of the members of parliament.

PRIMARY SOURCES

Constitution in English. Available online. URL: http://www.pdba.georgetown.edu/Constitutions/Dominica/dominica78.html. Accessed on August 22, 2005.

SECONDARY SOURCES

Associated States: The Dominica Constitution Order 1967. London: H.M.S.O., 1967 (legal textbook).

Bureau of Public Affairs, U.S. Department of State, "Background Note and Country Reports on Human Rights Practices and International Religious Freedom Report 2004." Available online. URL: http://www.state.gov/. Accessed on August 20, 2005.

Dominica: The Commonwealth of Dominica Constitution Order, 1978. London: H.M.S.O., 1978.

Bettina Bojarra

DOMINICAN REPUBLIC

At-a-Glance

OFFICIAL NAME
Dominican Republic

CAPITAL
Santo Domingo de Guzmán

POPULATION
8.95 million (July 2005 est.)

SIZE
18,704 sq. mi. (48,442 sq. km)

LANGUAGES
Spanish

RELIGIONS
Roman Catholic 95%, other 5%

NATIONAL OR ETHNIC COMPOSITION
European descent 16%, African descent 11%,
Mixed 73%

DATE OF INDEPENDENCE OR CREATION
February 27, 1844 (from Haiti)

TYPE OF GOVERNMENT
Presidential republic

TYPE OF STATE
Unitary state

TYPE OF LEGISLATURE
Bicameral parliament

DATE OF CONSTITUTION
November 28, 1966

DATE OF LAST AMENDMENT
July 25, 2002

The Dominican Republic is a presidential republic. The executive, legislative, and judicial powers are clearly divided. The constitution provides for safeguards against military rule. The Dominican Republic is organized as a unitary state with 31 provinces and a national district. The constitution provides for a set of traditional liberal as well as social rights.

The president is the head of the public administration, who exercises the executive powers with the help of secretaries of state he or she appoints. The parliament is called the National Congress; it comprises a Chamber of Deputies and a Senate. Members of both chambers are elected by direct and universal suffrage for a four-year term. Elections are free and universal and are multiparty.

Freedom of religion is guaranteed. There is no official state religion. No specific economic system is favored by the constitution. The military is subject to the civil government.

CONSTITUTIONAL HISTORY

The Dominican Republic is situated on the central and eastern part of the island of Hispaniola, as well as on a number of adjacent islands. It was Hispaniola where Columbus first touched down on American soil in 1492 C.E. Within a few decades, the Spaniards had reduced the native population to a marginal group, while ever more African slaves were taken to the island.

The Haitians were the first on the island to free themselves from their French colonists. In the early 19th century, they conquered all of Hispaniola. In 1844, Juan Pablo Duarte liberated the eastern part from the Haitians and founded the Dominican Republic. From 1861 until 1865, the Dominicans once more voluntarily became part of the Spanish Empire. The Dominicans speak of that time as of the "restoration." After years of disorder, the republic was occupied from 1916 until 1924 by the United States. For three decades, the dictator Rafael Trujillo ruled over the country. In the 1960s, several military coups took place. In 1966, Joaquín Balaguer was elected president in free elections. Since that year, the current constitution has been in force. The Dominican Republic has seen many peaceful changes of elected presidents since then. The constitution has been amended several times, most recently in 2002.

FORM AND IMPACT OF THE CONSTITUTION

The constitution of the Dominican Republic consists of one single document with 122 articles. It is a stable constitution existing for almost four decades. Previously the Dominican Republic had seen 29 constitutions in a 150-year period.

The constitution is the most important law. Any law, decree, resolution, or regulation contrary to it is void. The same is true of decisions made during an intervention of the armed forces (Article 99), once the emergency has ended. Norms of international law are recognized and applied by the Dominican Republic.

BASIC ORGANIZATIONAL STRUCTURE

The Dominican Republic is a presidential democracy. It is composed of 31 provinces and a National District. Each province is run by a civil governor appointed by the central executive power.

LEADING CONSTITUTIONAL PRINCIPLES

The constitution allows for a separation of the executive, legislative, and judicial powers. They are independent of each other, and they cannot delegate any of their powers. Key principles are enumerated in Article 4: The Dominican Republic is essentially civil, republican, democratic, and representative.

CONSTITUTIONAL BODIES

The most important constitutional bodies are the president of the republic and the vice president, the secretaries of state, the National Congress of the republic composed of the Chamber of Deputies and the Senate, and the Supreme Court.

The President of the Republic

The president of the republic is the head of the public administration as well as the supreme commander of the armed forces. The president has the power to appoint and remove the secretaries of state. He or she is also the president of the National Council of the Magistrature and thus has influence in appointing judges of the several levels of court up to the Supreme Court. The president also may declare a state of siege or national emergency if the National Congress is not in session.

To become president, a candidate must be Dominican by birth and have attained the age of 30. Most importantly, a candidate must not have been in active military or police service for at least one year before the election. Reelection to a second consecutive term is no longer possible since the 1994 amendment to the constitution.

Jointly with the president, every four years a vice president is elected in the same manner and on the same conditions. The vice president exercises the executive power during the president's incapacity.

The Secretaries of State

Secretaries of state must have attained the age of 25 years and have acquired Dominican nationality at least 10 years before taking office. It is their task to conduct the business of public administration.

The Congress of the Republic

The parliament of the Dominican Republic—the National Congress—comprises two chambers. Both senators and members of the Chamber of Deputies are elected by direct suffrage for four years. A senator represents one province. The number of deputies per province is proportional to its population but in no case fewer than two. Among the many functions of congress are levying taxes, approving the statement of revenue collection, adopting the budget, and creating new provinces.

Both chambers together convene as the National Assembly, which meets at least twice a year, to receive the message of the president of the republic or to examine the president's election.

The Lawmaking Process

The right to initiate legislation lies with the senators and deputies as well as with the president. In addition, the Supreme Court and the central electoral board have the right of initiative in specific matters. A bill has to pass two discussions in one chamber and then pass the other chamber before it is sent to the president. The president may reject the bill, but if a majority of two-thirds of the initiating chamber votes for the bill, the president then must promulgate the law.

The Judicial Power

The judicial power is vested in the Supreme Court, at least nine courts of appeal, lands courts, courts of first instance, and justices of the peace. The legal system resembles the French system. Judges cannot be removed until their terms expire.

THE ELECTION PROCESS AND POLITICAL PARTICIPATION

Voting is personal, free, and secret. Members of the armed forces and the police are not allowed to exercise their voting rights.

POLITICAL PARTIES

The constitution does not set criteria for the organization of political parties, but parties must conform to the principles of the constitution. There are several major as well as minor parties in the country. Many of them rely more on the personalities of candidates than on a political orientation.

CITIZENSHIP

Dominican nationality can be obtained through birth on the territory of the Dominican Republic or by birth abroad of a Dominican father or mother. Dual nationality is possible since the 1994 amendment of the constitution.

FUNDAMENTAL RIGHTS

In the second section of the constitution, individual and social rights and duties are defined. The effective protection of these rights is recognized as the principal aim of the state. The constitution provides for social as well as for liberal rights.

The Dominican Republic has abolished the death penalty. Individual security is one of the rights that find comprehensive protection in the constitution.

The constitution mandates free elementary and secondary education. It considers the formation of strong families to be of "high social interest."

Impact and Functions of Fundamental Rights

There is no specific mechanism for individuals to enforce their rights against the state. Therefore, some of the rights have the nature of intentions that may be difficult to realize.

Limitations to Fundamental Rights

The rights enumerated in the constitution are not without limits. For example, some may be limited by respect for public order, good morals, or national security. Although the constitution guarantees the right to own property, it also considers the breakup of large landholdings to be an interest of society.

In practical terms, the Dominican Republic has been criticized for a poor human rights record. Among the serious problems reported are extrajudicial killings by the police, the forceful expulsion of Haitian and Dominican-Haitian migrants, and weak discipline among members of the police force.

ECONOMY

The constitution does not specify an economic system. Still, some basic rights set a framework for economic development: the right to own property, freedom of association and of assembly, and freedom of enterprise, commerce, and industry. Special regulations for the frontier area are embodied in the constitution, as this territory is considered to be of supreme and permanent national interest.

RELIGIOUS COMMUNITIES

Freedom of conscience and worship is guaranteed by the constitution. There is no official state religion. However, Roman Catholicism is the predominant religion in the Dominican Republic, and the Roman Catholic Church benefits from some tax exemptions and other special privileges. Bible reading became obligatory in public schools in 2000.

MILITARY DEFENSE AND STATE OF EMERGENCY

Service in the Armed Forces of the Dominican Republic is voluntary. The armed forces are expected to remain apolitical and obedient to the civil authorities. Active military personnel do not have the right to vote.

A state of national emergency can be declared by the National Congress. If congress is not in session, the president of the republic may do the same. During a state of emergency, the exercise of individual rights may be suspended.

AMENDMENTS TO THE CONSTITUTION

A proposal for an amendment to the constitution requires the support of one-third of the membership of both chambers of the National Congress. A meeting of the National Assembly is then ordered. During the voting on the proposed amendment, more than half of the membership of both chambers of the National Congress has to be present. A two-thirds majority is necessary for the proposed amendments to pass.

PRIMARY SOURCES

Constitution in English: Gisbert H. Flanz, *Constitutions of the Countries of the World, Dominican Republic*. Dobbs Ferry, N.Y.: Oceana, September 1996.
Constitution in Spanish. Available online. URL: www.pdba.georgetown.edu/Constitutions/DomRep/domrep02.html. Accessed on June 17, 2006.

SECONDARY SOURCES

Emelio Betances, *State and Society in the Dominican Republic*. Boulder, Colo.: Westview Press, 1995.

U.S. Department of State, "Country Report on Human Right Practices 2001." Available online. URL: http://www.state.gov/g/drl/rls/hrrpt/2001/wha/8345.htm. Accessed on September 27, 2005.
Philip Young, *The Dominican Republic: Stabilization, Reform and Growth*. Washington, D.C.: The International Monetary Fund, 2001.

Hartmut Rank

EAST TIMOR

At-a-Glance

OFFICIAL NAME
The Democratic Republic of East Timor

CAPITAL
Dili

POPULATION
800,000 (2005 est.)

SIZE
5,794 sq. mi. (15,007 sq. km)

LANGUAGES
Tetum and Portuguese (official); Bahasa Indonesian and English (working languages in the public service); 16 other indigenous languages, including Galole, Mambae, and Kemak

RELIGIONS
Roman Catholic 92%, Protestant 3%, Muslim 1.7%, Hindu 0.3%, Buddhist 0,1%, Animist 2.9%; some degree of animist belief in formal religions

NATIONAL OR ETHNIC COMPOSITION
Austronesian (Malayo-Polynesian), Papuan, small Chinese minority

DATE OF INDEPENDENCE OR CREATION
May 20, 2002 (date of international recognition of independence from Indonesia)
November 28, 1976 (proclamation of independence prior to annexation by Indonesia)

TYPE OF GOVERNMENT
Parliamentary democracy (emerging)

TYPE OF STATE
Unitary state

TYPE OF LEGISLATURE
Unicameral parliament

DATE OF CONSTITUTION
March 22, 2002

DATE OF LAST AMENDMENT
No amendment

After 450 years of continuous foreign occupation, the Democratic Republic of East Timor achieved independence in 2002. This made it the first new nation of the millennium. The drafting and adoption of East Timor's first constitution were an important task for this fledgling democracy. The nation's long and, at times, violent struggle for independence is recognized in the opening words of the constitution. It states that the constitution "represents a heart-felt tribute to all martyrs of the Motherland." It is to be a nation under the rule of law "where respect for the constitution, for the laws and for democratically elected institutions constitute its unquestionable foundation."

East Timor is a democratic republic with a president as head of state and a prime minister who leads a parliamentary system of government. The constitution has an extensive section devoted to fundamental rights. Religious freedom is guaranteed, and the contribution of the Catholic Church to national liberation is acknowledged.

Given East Timor's history of occupation and bloodshed and its lack of experience in governance, one of the main difficulties facing the young nation is its ability to build effective legal and administrative institutions in keeping with the requirements of the constitution.

CONSTITUTIONAL HISTORY

In early times, the island of Timor was made up of a number of local kingdoms, each under the control of a king or chief, known as the Liural. The system of customary law emanating from the authority of the Liural continues to have significance today, especially in the villages.

In 1520, the island became a colony of Portugal, and in 1860, the island was divided into East and West Timor. West Timor was part of the Dutch East Indies until 1950, when it became Indonesian. The constitution of Portugal applied to East Timor, which was categorized from 1952 as an overseas province of Portugal.

In 1974, a leftist coup in Portugal resulted in Portuguese withdrawal from East Timor. This was in line with Portugal's policy of immediate decolonization of all overseas territories. While the debate on the country's future was occurring, civil war broke out. A referendum was held in March 1975 to determine this question. Full independence for East Timor, supported by Frente Revolucionária de Timor-Leste Independente, or Revolutionary Front for an Independent East Timor (Fretilin), obtained 55 percent of the vote. Fretilin declared itself the legitimate government of East Timor on November 28, 1975. The current constitution recognizes this date as marking East Timor's proclamation of independence.

Indonesian troops mounted a full invasion of East Timor toward the end of 1975, which led to the formal annexation of East Timor as the 27th province of Indonesia. President Suharto signed the Bill of Integration on July 17, 1976, and the constitution of Indonesia was imposed on the island. The struggle for independence continued. In 1999, the new Indonesian president, B. J. Habibie, agreed to another referendum. The United Nations formed the United Nations Assistance Mission to East Timor (UN-AMET) to conduct a fair referendum. An overwhelming percentage of Timorese (78 percent) voted for full independence. Violence erupted once more. The United Nations (UN) Security Council authorized a multinational peace enforcement mission in East Timor (INTERFET) to restore peace and security and to facilitate humanitarian relief efforts. The United Nations also established the UN Transitional Administration in East Timor (UNTAET) to assist the transition to independence.

In August 2001, East Timor held its first democratic elections to establish the initial 88-member constituent assembly. This assembly was responsible for drafting and adopting the first constitution of independent East Timor. The constitution was approved by the assembly on March 22, 2002.

FORM AND IMPACT OF THE CONSTITUTION

East Timor has a written constitution contained in a single document. The state is subject to the constitution and all laws and government actions must comply with it.

The constitution recognizes the traditional norms and customs of East Timor, provided that they are not contrary to the constitution or to any legislation dealing specifically with customary law.

The general and customary principles of international law apply, and the provisions of international conventions, treaties, and agreements apply once they are approved and ratified by the government.

BASIC ORGANIZATIONAL STRUCTURE

East Timor is a unitary state. There are a national administration, national parliament, and judicial system. The country is divided into 13 administrative divisions.

LEADING CONSTITUTIONAL PRINCIPLES

East Timor's system of government is a parliamentary democracy. The president is the head of state, and the prime minister is the head of the administration. The constitution acknowledges the doctrine of the separation of powers and the equality of all before the law.

CONSTITUTIONAL BODIES

The main constitutional organs are the president; the national parliament; the Council of State; the administration, which includes the prime minister; and the judiciary.

The President

The president of the republic is the head of state and the symbol and guarantor of national independence and unity. The president is elected for a five-year term of office, and the term can be renewed only once. The president cannot hold any other public office or undertake private work during the term of office.

The National Parliament

The National Parliament is a unicameral body with legislative, supervisory, and political decision-making power. Its members are elected by universal suffrage and hold office for five-year terms. Although there were 88 elected members in the first national parliament, the constitution provides that thereafter there must be a minimum of 52 and a maximum of 65 members.

When parliament is in recess or has been dissolved, a standing committee of parliament fulfills many of its functions. This committee also has a range of other duties: It coordinates the activities of parliamentary committees, convenes and organizes parliamentary sessions, gives consent to trips taken by the president, conducts relations with other parliaments or institutions in other countries, and authorizes the declaration of a state of siege or state of emergency.

The Lawmaking Process

The national parliament can pass bills on the basic issues of domestic and foreign policy. These become law when approved by the president. Also, parliament can authorize the administration to make laws on a range of matters. The administration has exclusive lawmaking power on matters concerning its own organization, functions, and management of the state. The prime minister and the relevant minister sign these into law.

The Council of State

The Council of State is a political advisory body to the president. It comprises the current president and former presidents, the Speaker of parliament, the prime minister, five citizens elected by parliament, and five citizens appointed by the president. The Council of State advises the president and gives its opinion on major issues, including the declaration of war and peace, dismissal of the administration, and dissolution of parliament.

The Administration

The administration is responsible for policy in the nation and the way the country is administered. It consists of the prime minister, the ministers, and secretaries of state. The members of the administration, other than the prime minister, are nominated by the prime minister and are appointed by the president. The administration is accountable to the president and to parliament. It must act in accordance with the constitution and the law.

Once appointed, the administration has 30 days in which to develop its program, which must set out its aims and objectives and the actions to be taken. The program has to be approved by the Council of Ministers and then submitted to the National Parliament. Parliament can debate the program for up to five days before approving or rejecting it. If a program is rejected for a second consecutive time, the administration is dismissed.

The Prime Minister

The prime minister oversees the way the country is administered. The prime minister chairs the Council of Ministers and coordinates the activities of the ministers. The prime minister is chosen by the political party or the coalition of parties that holds the majority of seats in the parliament. Power to dismiss the prime minister lies with the president, who is required first to consult the Council of State. The grounds for dismissal are set out in the constitution and include a vote of no confidence by an absolute majority of the members of the parliament.

The Judiciary

The constitution states that the courts and judges must be independent of the government. The highest court is the Supreme Court of Justice. It can deal with all legal, elec-toral, and constitutional matters. However, as this court has not yet been established, the Court of Appeal, which was set up under the UNTAET regulations, continues as the highest court. Regulations require appeals to be heard by a panel of three judges. One must be an East Timorese, and the other two must be international. Because of a lack of available judges, the Court of Appeal did not sit until June 2003. UNTAET regulations also established four district courts as court of original jurisdiction for civil and criminal cases. A special panel for serious crimes was established in 2000 to hear cases involving genocide, war crimes, and crimes against humanity.

The constitution also provides for two other categories of courts to be established: one for administrative and tax matters, the other the military court.

The Superior Council of the Judiciary was established to ensure the independence of the judiciary and to oversee the courts. The council has the task of appointing, transferring, and promoting judges.

THE ELECTION PROCESS

All citizens over the age of 17 are able to vote and to be elected in national elections.

POLITICAL PARTIES

East Timor has a pluralistic system of political parties. The constitution honors the Fretelin Party for its role in bringing about the nation's independence.

CITIZENSHIP

Citizenship is acquired by being born in East Timor. Once he or she reaches 17 years old, a child born to a foreign mother or father can declare his or her will to become an East Timorese national. A child born outside the country to an East Timorese parent can also acquire citizenship.

FUNDAMENTAL RIGHTS

Given the human-rights violations that occurred during the period of occupation, it was seen as important that the new independent East Timor prioritize the protection of human rights. Fundamental rights are to be interpreted in accordance with the Universal Declaration of Human Rights.

Part II of the constitution sets out the fundamental rights, duties, freedoms, and guarantees in the constitution. The first title establishes the general principles of equality and universality. The second title specifies personal rights and freedoms, including the right to a fair trial, due process, freedom of expression, freedom of association, freedom of the press, and the right to political participation. Title III covers economic, social, and cultural rights and duties, including the right to work, right to strike, right to health and medical care, right to housing, and right to education. Section 61 grants the right to a humane, healthy, and ecologically balanced environment and imposes a duty on the state to protect the environment.

Impact and Functions of Fundamental Rights

Given the new nation's economic difficulties, its lack of experience, and its scarcity of trained personnel, including lawyers and judges, many of these fundamental rights cannot realistically be implemented until some time in the future. For example, the guarantees relating to criminal proceedings, detention, and due process cannot be met until there are the facilities and trained staff to ensure compliance with the constitutional protections. The same limitation applies to the economic and social guarantees.

Limitations to Fundamental Rights

The fundamental rights provisions can be suspended during a state of siege or state of emergency. The declaration of siege or emergency must list the rights that are to be suspended. Even during a state of siege, certain rights cannot be denied. These include the right to life, nonretroactivity of criminal law, freedom of conscience and religion, and the right not to be subject to torture, slavery, or cruel, inhumane, or degrading treatment.

ECONOMY

Section 138 of the constitution states that the economy is to be based on a combination of community forums with free initiative and business management. There is to be a coexistence of public, private, cooperative, and social sectors in ownership of the means of production.

The reality is that East Timor is one of the world's poorest nations. Much of its infrastructure was destroyed by the antiindependence militias and Indonesian troops prior to independence. The economy remains heavily dependent on foreign aid and international financing. Potential investors are wary as East Timor lacks the fundamental institutions of a market economy.

RELIGIOUS COMMUNITIES

Freedom of conscience, religion, worship, and teaching of any religion is guaranteed in the constitution. No one can be persecuted or discriminated against because of his or her religion. The state respects the different religious denominations and will promote cooperation between them.

There is no state church. The constitution does acknowledge that the Catholic Church of East Timor has always been able to "take on the suffering of the people with dignity, placing itself on their side in the defense of their most fundamental rights."

MILITARY DEFENSE AND STATE OF EMERGENCY

The constitution provides that the defense force must be made up exclusively of national citizens. Its role is to guarantee independence, maintain the territory, and ensure the security of the people against external aggression. Internal security is the responsibility of the police force. The military is not permitted to intervene in political matters. There is a consultative body, the Superior Council for Defense and Security, that advises the president on matters of defense and security.

There is no conscription. Both men and women can serve in the defense force.

The administration can propose a declaration of a state of siege or a state of emergency, with the authorization of parliament. Such a state cannot last for more than 30 days unless renewed. Circumstances that allow for a state of emergency or siege include aggression by a foreign force, serious disturbance to the democratic constitutional order, and public disaster. Suspension of fundament rights and freedoms may occur.

AMENDMENTS TO THE CONSTITUTION

Review of the constitution can begin six years after it has entered into force. It also can be revised at any time with the support of a four-fifths majority of the members of parliament. The constitution sets out a list of matters that cannot be revised. These include the separation of powers, independence of the courts, fundamental rights and freedoms, and the election process.

Any amendment that follows a review must be passed by two-thirds of the parliament.

PRIMARY SOURCES
Constitution in English. Available online. URLs: http://www.elaw.org/resources/text.asp?ID=/065. Accessed on June 17, 2006.
Constitution in Portuguese. Available online. URL: http://etan.org/etanpdf/pdf2/constfnpt.pdf. Accessed on August 4, 2005.
Constitution in Tetum and Bahasa Indonesian. Available online. URL: http://www.uni-tries.de/~ievr/constitutions/worldconstitutions.htm. Accessed on June 17, 2006.

SECONDARY SOURCES

Hilary Charlesworth, "The Constitution of East Timor May 20, 2002." *International Journal of Constitutional Law,* 1, no. 2 (April 2003): 325–334.

"The Government of East Timor (Timor Leste)." Available online. URL: www.timor-leste.gov.tl/. Accessed on June 17, 2006.

"The Judicial System Monitoring Program for East Timor." Available online. URL: http://www.jsmp.minihub. org/new/reportsindex.htm. Accessed on August 2, 2005.

David Wurfel, "Constitution for a New State: Political Context and Possible Problems in East Timor." *Portuguese Studies Review* 11, no. 1 (2003): 103–121.

Ann Black

ECUADOR

At-a-Glance

OFFICIAL NAME
Republic of Ecuador

CAPITAL
Quito

POPULATION
13,212,742 (July 2004 est.)

SIZE
109,483 sq. mi. (283,560 sq. km)

LANGUAGES
Spanish (official), Quechua, Shuar, and other
indigenous languages (recognized)

RELIGIONS
Roman Catholic 95%, other 5%

NATIONAL OR ETHNIC COMPOSITION
Mestizo (mixed Amerindian and white) 65%,
Amerindian or indigenous 25%, Spanish and other
7%, Afro-Ecuadorian or black 3%

DATE OF INDEPENDENCE OR CREATION
May 24, 1822

TYPE OF GOVERNMENT
Republican presidential system

TYPE OF STATE
Unitary state

TYPE OF LEGISLATURE
Unicameral congress

DATE OF CONSTITUTION
August 10, 1998

DATE OF LAST AMENDMENT
May 2, 2002

Ecuador is a democracy based on a constitutionally guaranteed rule of law, with a clear division of powers, although a precise, stable division has not yet been delineated. The current constitution recognizes and guarantees ample human rights, but they are only discretionarily respected by the authorities and seldom enforced by the judiciary.

After a long period of military regimes, Ecuador has been struggling during the last 25 years to construct the basis of a real democracy. Political and economic interest groups have designed and redesigned the political system to suit their particular interests and control of all sectors of government. In fact, Ecuador has had more than 17 constitutions over the years, as well as numerous amendments.

The president is both the chief of state and head of the executive administration; however, the current electoral system does not necessarily provide for a strong representation of the president's party in the National Congress.

Successive constitutional reforms have diminished the power of congress, thereby inducing parties to choose less and less qualified people to run on their lists. In addition, the many political parties, although deemed desirable in a democracy, often negatively impact the ability of the political sector in Ecuador to reach any long-term agreements. As a consequence, there is little effective governance in Ecuador.

CONSTITUTIONAL HISTORY

The Royal Audience of Quito (Real Audiencia de Quito) was established in 1563 as an administrative dependency of the Spanish Crown; it included the territory of present-day Ecuador. Political instability characterized the colonial period; it was primarily due to the numerous changes of jurisdiction to which the Royal Audience of Quito was subjected. Economic decline marked the second half of the 18th century. Historians attribute the fall of the colonial system to various factors, including the decrease of silver production in Potosí (now Bolivia), a substantial decline in textile production in Quito due to legal restrictions limiting their export to other colonies, and the fact that the social elites had attained control over the local economy and were eager to attain political control.

Independence, which was sought between the end of the 18th century and the early decades of the 19th century, was inspired by a number of external factors, one of which was the French Revolution. The first attempt at independence in the region took place in Quito on August 10, 1809; however, the effort did not receive the support of the other territories and resulted in the slaughter of about 100 revolutionaries by Spanish troops. Independence was finally attained in 1822. Later the three most important cities, Quito, Guayaquil, and Cuenca, were incorporated into Grand Colombia, the project of the Venezuelan independence leader Simón Bolívar, to unite the territories of South America into one country. The project failed, and Ecuador was created as a separate republic by local elites on May 13, 1830.

A constitutional assembly enacted the first constitution of the nation on September 11, 1830, when the state was named the Republic of Ecuador. It was a country without a national identity, incorporating three distinct geographical regions with very little in common, as well as a very large indigenous population completely dominated by social elites of Spaniards, descendants of Spanish colonists, and mestizo (mixed Amerindian and Spaniard). This reality very much influenced the content and philosophy of the first constitution as well as many of the subsequent ones.

The constitution called for the separation of powers into three branches of government. Catholicism was recognized as the only religion accepted and protected by the state, thus eliminating by government sanction any other faith.

The current constitution took effect on August 10, 1998, after presidential and parliamentary elections had been held.

FORM AND IMPACT OF THE CONSTITUTION

Ecuador has a written constitution, codified in a single document, that takes precedence over all other national law. International law must be in accordance with the constitution in order to be applicable within Ecuador; once an international instrument is duly ratified, it has the same status as a constitutional norm. The constitution of Ecuador gained more clout in 1996 when a Constitutional Court was created and given the power of judicial review of the constitutionality of all laws and administrative acts of all branches of government.

BASIC ORGANIZATIONAL STRUCTURE

Ecuador is a unitary republic made up of 24 regional departments called provinces, including the Galápagos Islands. Although defined as a republican presidential system with a strong central government, Ecuador is characterized by decentralized provincial and local governments. Provinces differ considerably in geographical area, population size, and economic strength and are themselves divided into municipalities. All municipalities have equal rights and responsibilities; the law provides that the central government may confer increased responsibilities to municipalities that demonstrate sufficient financial and administrative capacity.

LEADING CONSTITUTIONAL PRINCIPLES

Ecuador's system of government is a presidential democracy that abides by the rule of law. The constitution provides for a clear division of powers based on checks and balances, but in practice, the country is still struggling to implement such a system. The independence of the justice system has been an important goal; for some seven years up to December 2004, a certain degree of stability was attained in the judicial system. Unfortunately, that month, congress, with the support of the ruling party, unconstitutionally removed the entire Supreme Court and unlawfully appointed a new group of magistrates. The previous month, they had done the same to members of the Constitutional Court and the Electoral Tribunal. These events have produced the most import institutional crisis of the last two decades. Popular uprisings in the capital forced the president to resign and leave the country in 2005. Since then, a new president has been confirmed and a semblance of stability returned.

CONSTITUTIONAL BODIES

According to the 1998 constitution, the most important government institutions are the president, head of the executive, and the National Congress as the legislative power; as well as the institutions of the judicial system, which include the judiciary, the Constitutional Court, the prosecutor general, the attorney general, the comptroller general, and the Commission of Civil Control of Corruption. Other important institutions are the Superintendencies of Banks, Companies, and Telecommunications.

The constitution contains a number of contradictions regarding the functions assigned to the different institutions that are part of the justice system. The specific attributes, faculties, responsibilities, and interrelations of the entities are not clearly defined and even overlap. Given the constitution's highly political nature, reform of its problematic aspects has become an almost impossible task. Such reforms affect the balance of power among the executive, legislative, and judicial branches of government and among diverse social and political interests.

The President

The president of the republic exercises the executive powers as head of the state and of the executive administration. The president is elected for a term of four years. Any candidate for the presidency must be Ecuadorian by birth, enjoy all political rights, and be at least 35 years of age. The spouse, father, children, or brothers of the president in office may not run for the presidency; the vice president may run only after having resigned from office. The president and the vice president are elected by majority vote in a universal, direct, equal, and secret balloting process. The president appoints and dismisses the ministers of state.

The National Congress

The legislative power is vested in the National Congress, the parliament. Members of the national congress are elected for a term of four years. They are obliged to comply with a Code of Ethics adopted by congress. In case of violation of this code, they can be sanctioned by a majority vote of the members of congress. Sanction can include loss of membership.

The Lawmaking Process
The lawmaking process is vested in the National Congress. Bills in general need to be approved by the majority of members present.

There is a Commission for Legislation and Codification made up of seven members who are elected by the national congress but may not be members of congress. The commission prepares and drafts bills and publishes laws that have been passed.

The Judiciary

The judiciary is made up of the Supreme Court of Justice, regular courts, and tribunals. A National Council of the Judiciary manages the internal administration of the judiciary. Justices of the peace are charged with resolving conflicts between individuals and neighbors by arbitration and mediation. The judiciary is independent and is subject only to the constitution and the law.

THE ELECTION PROCESS AND POLITICAL PARTICIPATION

Any Ecuadorian citizen of at least 18 years of age can vote and is eligible to run in the elections. The process for the election and removal of the president, vice president, con-

gressional representatives, and other officials is described in the constitution and detailed in various laws and regulations. The constitution also establishes a Constitutional Tribunal, which approves and registers political parties, organizes and controls the electoral process, and adjudicates all matters related to the electoral system.

In Ecuador, any citizen can run for office without the endorsement of a political party. Even candidates for congress who have party backing may, once elected, distance themselves from their party or political movement without losing their seat. These two facts have harmed the efficient functioning of congress.

POLITICAL PARTIES

The system of multiple political parties that exists in Ecuador impacts the ability of the political sector to reach long-term agreements. The decision-making process is characterized by extreme posturing and strategic positioning, making achievement of consensus almost impossible.

CITIZENSHIP

The current constitution has made great strides in clarifying and defining the concept of citizenship by recognizing that all persons born in Ecuador are citizens who have constitutional rights, regardless of their age. Political rights are granted to citizens at the age of 18, whereas civil rights are granted to any person at birth.

FUNDAMENTAL RIGHTS

Fundamental rights and the mechanisms to uphold them were broadly and thoroughly incorporated into the constitution enacted in 1998. This area of constitutional development is considered the most important achievement of the 1997 Constitutional Assembly.

Impact and Functions of Fundamental Rights

Notwithstanding the importance given to fundamental rights in the 1998 constitution, the chapter defining the Constitutional Court was not changed. In the end, the Constitutional Tribunal has been extremely ineffective in responding to petitions that have been filed in both the quantity and the quality of its rulings.

ECONOMY

Ecuador's economic system is described in the constitution as a social market economy, but, in practice, it is a neoliberal economic system. The instability resulting from continuous economic crises and the increase in social conflicts between 1997 and 2000 have led to a progressive loss of public support for representative democracy. In the year 2000, the financial system of Ecuador underwent bankruptcy, leading to the political decision to adopt the American dollar as the only local currency. This process, known as dollarization, was adopted de facto and has yet to be incorporated into the constitution, which continues to recognize the *sucre* as the official currency of Ecuador.

RELIGIOUS COMMUNITIES

The 1945 constitution (and the constitutions of 1979 and 1998) firmly established freedom of religion and the separation of church and state.

MILITARY DEFENSE AND STATE OF EMERGENCY

The military falls under the jurisdiction of the civil government, and the president is the official commander in chief of all military forces. Although the military cannot, under the constitution, act unilaterally, at many times of political instability, it has acted on its own, often becoming the arbiter of democracy.

A state of emergency can be declared only by the president and only in cases of external aggression, imminent war, grave internal unrest, or natural disasters. Once a state of emergency has been declared, the president must notify congress within 48 hours of its declaration, at which time congress can nullify the president's declaration if it finds insufficient justification. Under a state of emergency, the president can suspend some fundamental rights, such as freedom of speech, sanctity of the home, right to privacy in postal or electronic communications, right to public assembly, and freedom of movement within the national territory.

Military service continues to be compulsory for all men. Those who declare themselves to be conscientious objectors can, instead, choose to perform an assigned social service to the community.

AMENDMENTS TO THE CONSTITUTION

Several constitutional reforms were introduced in the past decade, mainly in 1992, 1995, 1997, and 1998. Since the implementing legislation for one amendment has not always been enacted before another was adopted, in 1998, a new procedure for reform of the constitution that makes the process much more rigorous and difficult was approved. The new procedure mandates two discussions of the text by congress to take place one year apart, followed by a two-thirds majority vote, for approval. At this point, the president can still exercise the power to veto the proposed reform.

PRIMARY SOURCES
Constitution in Spanish. Available online. URL: http://www.georgetown.edu/pdba/Constitutions/Ecuador/ecuador.html. Accessed on August 18, 2005.

SECONDARY SOURCES
Valeria Merino Dirani, *Avances en el Proceso de Reforma Judicial desde que se Preparo la Primera Estrategia Integral en 1995*. Quito: Corporación Latinoamericana para el Desarrollo, 2000.

Dennis Michael Hanratty, *Ecuador—a Country Study*. Washington, D.C.: U.S. Government Printing Office.

Oswaldo Hurtado Larrea, *Gobernabilidad y Reforma Constitucional*. Quito: Corporación Editora Nacional, 1993.

Enrique Ayala Mora, *Los Partidos Políticos en el Ecuador*. Quito: Ediciones la Tierra, 1989.

———, "El Derecho Ecuatoriano y el Aporte Indígena." In *Revista Aportes Andinos* Quito: Universidad Andina Simón Bolívar.

Santiago Andrade Ubidia, Julio César Trujillo, and Roberto Viciano Pastor, *La Estructura; Constitucional del Estado Ecuatoriano*. Serie Estudios Jurídicos Volume 24. Quito: Corporación Editora Nacional, 2004.

Valeria Merino Dirani

EGYPT

At-a-Glance

OFFICIAL NAME
Arab Republic of Egypt

CAPITAL
Cairo

POPULATION
77,505,756 (2005 est.)

SIZE
395,793 sq. mi. (1,025,100 sq. km)

LANGUAGES
Arabic

RELIGIONS
Muslim 94%, Christian (Orthodox, Catholic, Protestant) and other 6%

NATIONAL OR ETHNIC COMPOSITION
Egyptian, Bedouin, and Berber 99%; Greek, Nubian, Armenian, other European (primarily Italian and French) 1%

DATE OF INDEPENDENCE OR CREATION
February 28, 1922 (from United Kingdom)

TYPE OF GOVERNMENT
Republic, based on mixed parliamentary and presidential systems

TYPE OF STATE
Centralist state

TYPE OF LEGISLATURE
Bicameral parliament

DATE OF CONSTITUTION
September 11, 1971

DATE OF LAST AMENDMENT
May 25, 2005

Egypt is a hybrid of parliamentary and presidential forms of government that endows the president with a wide variety of executive and legislative powers. It is a centralist state, divided into governorates that enjoy very little autonomy. The constitution provides for far-reaching guarantees of both generations of human rights, liberal and social. A rather powerful and quite independent constitutional court is in charge of reviewing the conformity of laws and administrative regulations with the provisions of the constitution.

The head of state is the president, who dominates the entire field of political activity. The head of government enjoys limited internal influence. Members of the lower chamber of parliament are elected, but there have been frequent allegations of fraudulent electoral practices. Pluralism is guaranteed by the constitution, but political parties must be registered and very few have any real influence.

Egypt is an Islamic state, and the principles of the Sharia are to be the main source of legislation, according to the constitution. The constitution also states that the economic system is socialist, but in practice, Egypt is moving more and more toward a market economy and privatization. The military plays an important though informal role in politics, and all presidents so far have been from the armed forces. A state of emergency was proclaimed in 1981 and has not been lifted since.

CONSTITUTIONAL HISTORY

Egypt, home of one of world's earliest civilizations, became a province of the Ottoman Empire in 1516. After the failure of the French campaign led by Napoléon Bonaparte (1798–1801), Muhammad Ali, leader of the Albanian contingent of the Ottoman army, became viceroy of Egypt (1805). He and his successors started the country on the road to modernization.

Starting in 1841, succession to the viceroyalty became hereditary to the oldest surviving male in the Muhammad

Ali family. Given the title of khedive in 1867, they gradually expanded their prerogatives at the expense of the Ottoman sultan and reformed the administrative, legal, and political systems on the European model. In 1866, an Assembly of Delegates was established. Its functions were merely consultative at first, but its establishment marked the beginning of parliamentary life in Egypt. In 1878, Khedive Ismail established a Council of Ministers and entrusted them with some of his executive powers.

A Fundamental Law, adopted in 1882, provided for a parliamentary system with a cabinet responsible to the assembly but with the power to dissolve it. The same year, Egypt was occupied by British troops, and the Fundamental Law was abrogated. An Organic Law was adopted in 1883 that gave only consultative powers to the representative bodies, except in the imposition of new direct taxes, in which its opinion was binding. The Organic Law was amended in 1912 to give members of the legislative assembly the right to interrogate cabinet ministers. It was amended again one year later to create a new representative assembly with increased legislative powers, which met for a permanent annual session and whose proceedings were open to the public. In 1914, Egypt became a British Protectorate and was detached from the Ottoman Empire.

The representative assembly was soon suspended, never to be restored. In 1922, the British abolished the Protectorate and unilaterally proclaimed Egypt's independence, recognizing Sultan Fuad I as king of Egypt. England, however, maintained its own military forces in the country and reserved four questions for future negotiations, namely, the defense of the country, the security of communications of the British Empire, the protection of foreign interests and minorities, and the status of the Sudan. This was a formal independence but not a real one as the British still intervened in Egyptian internal affairs.

In 1923, the first Egyptian constitution was adopted. It set up a parliamentary system of government with a separation of powers, though the king retained extensive executive and legislative powers. Its second section contained an extensive list of civil and political rights, such as freedom of expression, freedom of association, freedom of religion, and independence of the judiciary. The 1923 constitution was abolished in 1930 and replaced by a new one that strengthened the powers of the monarchy. The 1930 constitution was abrogated in 1934, and the 1923 constitution was reinstated the following year; it remained in force until 1952. This was a so-called liberal era characterized by governmental instability. Few cabinets and parliaments completed their constitutional term. The majority party itself (Wafd) did not rule for more than seven and a half years of the 28-year era. The autocratic monarch suspended the constitution several times. Egypt did, however, gain experience with democratic institutions and practices such as political parties, separation of powers, elected assemblies, constitutional protection of human rights, and a fully developed judiciary, all in a country still under foreign military occupation.

In 1936, the Treaty of Independence and Honor, which called on Britain to limit its military presence in the Suez Canal zone and asked for negotiations to end the capitulation system, was signed. The latter was a series of privileges, originally granted by the Ottoman sultan to European heads of state, according to which foreigners were placed under the extraterritorial jurisdiction of their consular courts, which applied their own national laws.

During this period, the judiciary took major steps toward independence. In 1948, the two-year old Council of State, an administrative court, ruled itself competent to exercise judicial review of legislation in the course of deciding a case submitted to it and to refrain from enforcing a law found unconstitutional. In 1952, the Court of Cassation (final appeal) decided to follow the example of the Council of State. After this precedent, Egyptian courts at all levels began to exercise judicial review of legislation. This decentralized review, however, led to legal instability and contradictory decisions among judges since the ruling of a particular court had no binding effect on other courts.

On July 23, 1952, a coup d'état by young army officers overthrew the king and ushered in the July Revolution. On December 10, the constitution of 1923 was abrogated. A three-year transitional period was declared to last until January 16, 1956, during which the Revolution Command Council, consisting of Free Officers, ruled under martial law. A constitutional proclamation of February 10, 1953, organized the basic structure of the transitional government, which was characterized by a strong concentration of power. On June 18, 1953, another proclamation abolished the monarchy and made Egypt a republic.

A new constitution was finally adopted in 1956 and submitted to a referendum after a first draft, deemed too liberal, was rejected in 1955. For the first time, citizens enjoyed not only civil and political rights but also social and economic ones. Candidates to parliamentary elections had to be selected by the one party, the National Union. Women were given political rights for the first time in the history of the country by a law of 1956.

After the union between Egypt and Syria in 1958, a constitution was adopted for the newly created United Arab Republic. After the union was dissolved in 1961, a constitutional declaration was issued in 1962 to organize the structure of the state until another constitution could be adopted. It centralized all powers in the hands of the president. A provisional constitution was adopted in 1964 and submitted to referendum, designed to last until a permanent constitution could be drawn up. The official denomination of the state remained United Arab Republic, though it now applied to Egypt alone. It contained first- and second-generation (liberal and social) rights. In a departure, the new constitution established the principle that half the assemblies' representatives must be workers and peasants.

A 1969 law decree created a Supreme Court entrusted with the exclusive power of judicial review in constitutional issues. Its members served three-year terms and were appointed directly by the president of the republic, who could also discharge them. After the death of Nasser in 1970, Anwar al-Sadat acceded to power and ordered the parliament to draft a new constitution. The text was adopted on September 11, 1971, by a referendum. The official denomination of the state became Arab Republic of Egypt. The constitution reflected different trends: the socialist values, one-party system (until the amendment of 1980), and Arab nationalism inherited from the Nasser era, juxtaposed with liberal democracy and Islam. It accorded the president far-reaching powers.

FORM AND IMPACT OF THE CONSTITUTION

Egypt's constitution is codified in a single document that is considered to be at the apex of the hierarchy of domestic norms (laws and regulations). International treaties, duly ratified, have "the force of law," meaning that the constitution and most recent laws enjoy a higher rank. The Supreme Constitutional Court, established in 1979, is the guardian of the constitution.

According to Article 2, as amended in 1980, the principles of the Islamic Sharia are the main source of legislation (and no longer *a* main source of legislation, as was stated in 1971). The Supreme Constitutional Court has refused to interpret this provision as giving supraconstitutional value to the Islamic Sharia. First of all, it has ruled that the 1980 amendment has no retroactive effect; the court considers itself incompetent to review the conformity to Article 2 of laws adopted before 1980. In addition, the court believes that only certain principles of the Islamic Sharia can have precedence over domestic laws: those that are from identified sources and have a precise meaning that all religious scholars have always accepted.

BASIC ORGANIZATIONAL STRUCTURE

Egypt is a centralist state with a strong centralization of power. All the main institutions and judicial bodies are based in Cairo, the capital. The territory is divided into 26 governorates headed by governors appointed by the president of the republic. Local councils at the governorate and district levels are elected but enjoy very little power. The decision-making process does not really rely on the principle of public participation.

LEADING CONSTITUTIONAL PRINCIPLES

Egypt is defined as a socialist democracy, based on an alliance of the working forces of the people (Article 1) and an Islamic state (Article 2), based on popular sovereignty (Article 3) and the rule of law (Article 64). Its system of government has elements of both parliamentary and presidential systems. The constitution of 1971 retains strong presidential powers and strengthens the dominant position of the president under exceptional circumstances (Article 74). Article 68 states that no administrative act or decision is immune from appeal to a court. The constitution, for the first time, makes the principles of the Sharia the main source of legislation.

Political participation can be exercised through elections to the parliamentary assemblies, and the people may be consulted directly through referendums in certain cases, such as after a motion of no confidence or during the dissolution of the People's Assembly. This option, however, is rarely used. Workers and peasants must constitute at least 50 percent of parliamentary bodies. Political participation is low.

In practice, the system of checks and balances provided for by the constitution did not lead to a real balance of powers between the executive and the legislative. Only the judiciary, and particularly the Supreme Constitutional Court and the State Council, has succeeded in putting limits on executive power.

CONSTITUTIONAL BODIES

The constitution provides for a president of the republic; an administration consisting of a prime minister and cabinet ministers; a bicameral parliament made of the People's Assembly and, since 1980, a Consultative Assembly; and a judiciary, including a Constitutional Court in charge of reviewing the constitutionality of laws and administrative regulations.

The President of the Republic

The president of the republic is the main figure in the current Egyptian political system. Since the constitutional amendment of 2005, the president is elected by direct secret ballot for a six-year term. Since the amendment of 1980, the president can serve unlimited successive terms. The president must be born to Egyptian parents and be at least 40 years of age.

The constitution gives the president of the republic a wide range of executive and legislative powers. The president appoints and dismisses the prime minister and the cabinet ministers, convokes the cabinet, and presides over its meetings. The president issues regulations for implementing the laws, makes all military and civil appointments, concludes treaties, is the chief of the army, declares war, grants amnesty, and can also proclaim a state of emergency.

The president also has the right to propose and promulgate laws. The president can veto a bill adopted by the People's Assembly; if the deputies approve it again with a two-thirds majority, the president is required to promulgate it. It is the president who dissolves the People's Assembly in case of necessity and after a referendum and who can also call a referendum on any important matter deemed to affect the supreme interests of the country. The president can pass legislation by decree laws when special circumstances require urgent measures or after a delegation of powers by the People's Assembly or on the president's own initiative. The president is not accountable to the parliament.

The Administration

The administration (cabinet) consists of the prime minister and other ministers, all appointed and dismissed by the president of the republic. Ministers must be Egyptians, no less than 35 years old. They may be members of the People's Assembly.

The cabinet, with the president, determines the general policy of the state; directs, coordinates, and follows up the work of the ministries; issues administrative regulations; and prepares draft laws and the draft general budget. Ministers are individually and collectively responsible before the People's Assembly.

As a result of the far-reaching powers of the president, the role of the prime minister is secondary, mainly one of coordination and confined to domestic policy. Some ministers have continuously held office for more than 20 years.

The People's Assembly

The People's Assembly is made up of 454 members who serve for a five-year term. They are elected in a general and direct balloting process from two-member districts. At least half of the members must be workers or peasants. Ten members are nominated by the president of the republic. The assembly meets for about seven months a year.

Each member of the assembly has the right to propose laws. The People's Assembly also monitors the work of the administration through questions, interpellations (challenging of government actions), fact-finding committees, and withdrawal of confidence from any cabinet minister. A motion of no confidence may be adopted by a majority of the members of the assembly upon an initiative of one-tenth of them. The president of the republic may approve the assembly's decision and decide to put the subject to a referendum. If the result is in support of the assembly, the cabinet resigns. If the referendum is in favor of the administration, the assembly is considered dissolved.

Membership in the assembly may not be revoked except on specific grounds such as loss of one of the conditions of membership, loss of the member's status as a worker or peasant if he or she was elected as such, loss of confidence, or violation of the mandate. The decision to lift a deputy's immunity must be made by a two-thirds majority of the members. The delegates may not be subject to criminal prosecution without the permission of the assembly except if the member is arrested in the course of committing a crime.

The People's Assembly is dominated by the regime's political party, as the opposition is underrepresented. The assembly exercises no real control of the actions of the executive branch. Cabinet-proposed bills are not rejected or even subject to serious amendments by deputies.

The Consultative Assembly

Established in 1980 after amendment of the constitution, the Consultative Assembly can be regarded as the second chamber of the parliament. It is composed of 264 members, two-thirds of whom are elected by direct secret public balloting and one-third appointed by the president of the republic. Half must be workers and peasants. No one can be member of both the People's Assembly and the Consultative Assembly. The term of office is six years, and half of the members are renewed every three years.

This assembly must be consulted on, among other matters, proposals for the amendment of the constitution, draft laws complementary to the constitution, most important treaties, and draft laws referred to it by the president of the republic. It has no power to monitor the government's work, and ministers are not responsible before it. The assembly can be dissolved by the president of the republic in case of necessity.

The Lawmaking Process

Both the president of the republic and members of the parliament have the right to initiate laws. Draft laws are submitted to one of the 19 permanent committees of the People's Assembly before they are submitted to the assembly and approved by a majority of all members. The laws are promulgated by the president, who has the right of veto. If the People's Assembly approves the draft law again after the veto, the president must promulgate it. Laws passed are published in the *Official Gazette*. In practice, most laws are government-sponsored bills and are adopted with little debate by a large presidential majority.

The Judiciary

The judiciary in Egypt is constitutionally independent of the executive and legislative powers. It follows the civil-law model, with an administrative justice separate from the civil and criminal one. The State Council controls administrative action with regard to laws and regulations, and another set of courts is competent in civil, commercial, and criminal matters as well as for questions regarding personal status. Each set of courts is headed by a supreme court that can rule on points of law only.

The constitution of 1971 was the first Egyptian one to establish a constitutional court in charge of reviewing the constitutionality of laws and administrative regulations. Its justices are nominated through a process of co-optation, and they serve until they retire. Cases can be taken before the Supreme Constitutional Court by a court or by a party to a court case. The rulings of the constitutional court are binding upon all public authorities and persons. This court has proved to be very active and has developed a jurisprudence supporting the protection of human rights.

The judiciary as a whole is a powerful actor in legal and political life. In many sensitive cases, it has been a real counterpower to the other two branches and a major force in fostering democracy and human rights. This may explain why so many exceptional courts have been set up: to remove the ordinary judiciary from politically sensitive cases. State security courts as well as military courts have been given wide-range jurisdiction during states of emergency. They issue rulings without appeal, after summary procedures.

THE ELECTION PROCESS

Since 1956, all Egyptians over the age of 18, men and women, have the right to vote in elections. Naturalized citizens must wait five years after obtaining nationality to vote. Only Egyptians over 30, born to an Egyptian father, who have completed military service or been exempted and are literate can stand for elections. In 2000, the State Council decided that binationals were not allowed to run for office.

Parliamentary Elections

At one time, Egypt followed proportional representation and a party list system, but this was declared unconstitutional by the Supreme Constitutional Court in 1987 and 1990 because independent candidates could not run for elections. The country has thus resumed elections of individuals by a two-round majority vote. Two candidates, one of whom necessarily is a worker or a peasant, are elected in each of the 222 constituencies. The People's Assembly is the only authority competent to decide upon the validity of the mandate of its members.

Since another decision of the Supreme Constitutional Court in 2000, judges are empowered to oversee elections in all polling stations. Judicial supervision inside the polling stations has helped curtail numerous fraudulent practices of the past. However, judges can still not prevent intimidation and exclusion of voters outside the polls.

Presidential Elections

Since 2005, the constitution provides that the president is popularly elected by direct secret ballot. This reform gives political parties that have five years of existence the opportunity to nominate their leaders as presidential candidates, if the party won a minimum of 5 percent of seats in both houses of parliament. Independent candidates need the combined support of 250 members of the People's Assembly, the Consultative Assembly, and Municipal Councils. In case none of the candidates wins an absolute majority in the first round, a second round of elections between the two top candidates is held.

POLITICAL PARTIES

All political parties were dissolved in 1953 by the Revolution Command Council, and a one-party system was established. Only in 1976 was a multiparty system reinstituted in Egypt. In 1980, the constitution was amended to recognize the multiparty principle. This pluralistic system is limited by a law of 1977 that regulates the formation of parties. Political parties have to meet certain vague and general conditions and be licensed by a special committee in order to operate. This Political Party Committee is headed by the Speaker of the Consultative Assembly and is composed of ministers and members close to the ruling party. The committee can also decide to freeze or dissolve a party. Its rulings can be appealed before a special circuit of the State Council.

In practice, since the reestablishment of a multiparty system, only four political parties have been licensed by the Political Party Committee, all of them after 2000. Other parties have been granted recognition by the judiciary on appeal. The activities of about one-third of the 21 existing parties have been frozen by the committee, mostly because of internal turmoil. The ruling party is the National Democratic Party, led by the president of the republic. The Muslim Brotherhood is not recognized as a political party on the grounds that the 1977 law prohibited parties organized on religious lines. Muslims Brothers nevertheless compete in elections as independent candidates or through alliances with recognized parties. In practice, political parties cannot be considered a dynamic democratic force in Egypt.

CITIZENSHIP

Egyptian citizenship is primarily acquired by birth to an Egyptian father. Until 2004, having an Egyptian mother was not sufficient to confer Egyptian nationality unless the father was unknown or stateless. Under national and international pressure, however, the law was finally amended in June 2004 to allow all Egyptian mothers to transmit their nationality to their children. Nationality can also be granted under certain conditions to foreigners who have resided in Egypt for at least 10 years.

FUNDAMENTAL RIGHTS

The Egyptian constitution devotes Part 3 to public freedoms, rights, and duties, whereby civil and political rights are protected. Among these are the principle of equality, individual freedom, and protection of the rights of detainees; freedom of religion, of expression, of the press, of movement, of assembly, and of association; the principle that crimes and penalties must be defined by law; and the presumption of innocence.

The constitution explicitly guarantees economic, social, and cultural rights in Part 2, Basic Components of Society. Chapter 1 sets forth the social and moral components of society, Chapter 2 its economic constituents. Among the rights guaranteed are the right to work, to health insurance services, to pensions, and to education.

Some human rights provisions are also found in other parts of the constitution. For example, the multiparty system is guaranteed in Part 1, The State and the independence of the judiciary in Part 4, Sovereignty of the Law.

Most of the rights stated in the constitution (e.g., the principle of equality, inviolability of private life, or freedom of movement) apply to "all citizens," meaning Egyptians only. Other rights (e.g., protection against arbitrary arrest or the rights of detainees) apply to "any person," including foreigners.

Impact and Functions of Fundamental Rights

Most fundamental rights guaranteed by the Egyptian constitution were already protected by previous constitutions. First-generation rights (liberal rights) already existed under the constitutions of the monarchy, and second-generation ones (social rights) appeared at the Nasser era, mostly in the 1964 constitution.

The 1971 constitution defines some "positive discrimination" (affirmative action) measures, such as allotting workers and peasants at least half the seats in all representative bodies. This provision is often criticized as contradictory to the principle of equality.

Some provisions also establish duties for citizens. These include defending the homeland, safeguarding national unity and keeping state secrets, safeguarding social gains, working, paying taxes, and participating in public life.

Limitations to Fundamental Rights

The Egyptian constitution specifies possible limitations on fundamental rights. No criteria are specified for limiting rights in general; such limitations are prescribed on a case-by-case basis. Freedom of expression or freedom of assembly, for instance, shall be exercised "within the limits of the law." No rights are stated as never to be limited.

The Supreme Constitutional Court has ruled that no law can deprive any right of its core content. Only limitations necessary for the exercise of the right shall be allowed, and those limitations shall themselves be limited by the principle of proportionality (the limitation should be appropriate to the specific need).

ECONOMY

According to the constitution, Egypt is a socialist state, and socialist gains have to be protected. Public ownership is sacred, and its protection and consolidation are the duty of every citizen. These provisions are a heritage of the Nasser era.

However, since the Sadat era, Egypt has been moving toward an economic system based on capitalism, liberalization of the economy, and privatization of the public sector. One of the objectives of this new policy is to attract foreign investments.

The constitution protects private property, the right to work, and the right to form associations and trade unions. It also guarantees the social function of property. Some economic rights have been inherited from the Nasser era, such as popular control over the means of production or the right of participation of workers in companies' management and profits.

RELIGIOUS COMMUNITIES

Freedom of religion is guaranteed by the constitution, which also guarantees the principle of equality of all citizens and forbids discrimination on the basis of religion. However, the constitutional text also declares that Egypt is an Islamic state. The norms of the Islamic Sharia still influence the personal status law, but most other branches of law have been secularized.

Fourteen non-Muslim communities are recognized in Egypt. Most of them are Christian: Orthodox (four different communities), Catholic (seven different communities), and Protestants. The Jewish community is divided into two parts. Each community has power to legislate its own personal status law, although courts dealing with these issues have been unified since 1956. Islamic Sharia, as codified by Egyptian law, is applied whenever the two parties to a personal status dispute are not members of the same religious community.

A Muslim man can marry a Christian or a Jewish wife, but a Muslim woman cannot marry anyone but a Muslim. Muslims cannot convert to another religion.

MILITARY DEFENSE AND STATE OF EMERGENCY

The president of the republic is the supreme commander of the armed forces and has the authority to declare war, with the approval of the People's Assembly. No organization or group may establish military or semimilitary formations such as private militias. According to the constitution (Article 58), the defense of the homeland and its territory is a sacred duty, and conscription is compulsory. All men between 18 and 30 years of age are liable for military service. Conscripts serve three years of active duty. College graduates serve only 12 months. Sons who do not have brothers and family breadwinners are eligible for exemptions. Women can volunteer for the armed forces to perform administrative tasks. Conscientious objection is not allowed.

The constitution of 1971 authorizes the president of the republic to proclaim a state of emergency for a limited period but must notify the People's Assembly within 15 days for their approval. A state of emergency was proclaimed on October 6, 1981, the day President Sadat was assassinated. It has remained in force since. It gives the president of the republic far-reaching powers and places restrictions on many constitutionally guaranteed rights. Special courts have also been established to adjudicate crimes against the internal or external security of the state. The president can refer ordinary crimes to such courts. They judge without appeal, but their decisions can be challenged by the president within 15 days.

The president may also refer to military courts civilians accused of any crimes proscribed by the penal code or any other law. These courts have been used to try Islamists.

AMENDMENTS TO THE CONSTITUTION

Article 189 of the constitution sets out a special and complex amendment procedure. First, the president or one-third of the People's Assembly initiates the procedure. The assembly then approves the principle of the amendment by a majority vote of its members. After two months it resumes deliberation; if the amendment is approved by a two-thirds majority, it is referred to the people for a referendum.

The constitution was amended twice. In 1980, the amendments ended the two-term limits for the president (Article 77); created a multiparty system by ending the exclusive constitutional status of the Arab Socialist Union (Article 5); made Islamic principles *the* principal source of legislation and not *a* principal source of legislation (Article 2); created the Consultative Assembly and a Supreme Press Council to authorize licenses to newspapers and to oversee distribution of foreign publications in the country (Part 7); changed Egypt from "a democratic socialist state" to "a socialist democratic state" (Article 1); and, finally, obliged the state to "narrow the gap between incomes" instead of to "suppress class distinctions in society (Article 4)."

In 2005, Article 76 of the constitution was amended to allow multicandidate presidential elections. The very restrictive conditions set for candidacy, however, make it extremely difficult for independent and even party candidates to run.

PRIMARY SOURCES

Constitution in English (as amended in 2005). Available online. URL: http://www.parliament.gov.eg/EPA/en/Levels.jsp?levelid=6&levelno=1&parentlevel=0. Accessed on June 17, 2006.

Constitution in Arabic. Available online. URL: http://www.parliament.gov.eg/EPA/ar/Levels.jsp?levelid=3&levelno=1&parentlevel=0. Accessed on June 17, 2006.

SECONDARY SOURCES

Kevin Boyle and Adel O. Sherif Adel Omar, eds., *Human Rights and Democracy: The Role of the Supreme Constitutional Court of Egypt.* CIMEL Book Series, no. 3. The Hague/London/Boston: Kluwer Law International, 1996.

Eberhard Kienle, *A Grand Delusion: Democracy and Economic Reform in Egypt.* London and New York: I. B. Tauris, 2001.

Nathalie Bernard-Maugiron

EL SALVADOR

At-a-Glance

OFFICIAL NAME
Republic of El Salvador

CAPITAL
San Salvador

POPULATION
6,704,932 (2005 est.)

SIZE
8,124 sq. mi. (21,040 sq. km)

LANGUAGES
Spanish, Nahua (among some Amerindians)

RELIGIONS
Roman Catholic 83%, other 17%

NATIONAL OR ETHNIC COMPOSITION
Mestizo 90%, white 9%, Amerindian 1%

DATE OF INDEPENDENCE OR CREATION
September 15, 1821

TYPE OF GOVERNMENT
Presidential democracy

TYPE OF STATE
Unitary state

TYPE OF LEGISLATURE
Unicameral assembly

DATE OF CONSTITUTION
December 20, 1983

DATE OF LAST AMENDMENT
October 15, 2003

El Salvador's system of government is a presidential democracy. The basic branches of the government are the legislature, the executive, and the judiciary.

El Salvador is a unitary state made up of 14 departments. The country has experimented with various constitutional reforms, of which the most relevant is the one adopted in the peace treaties of January 16, 1992, which put an end to the 12 years of internal armed conflict.

The strong president is both the chief of state and the head of the executive branch of government, although the president cannot be elected for a consecutive second term.

According to the constitution, there is a pluralistic system of political parties; in fact, there are two major parties. The traditional set of liberal human rights and civil liberties is constitutionally guaranteed. During the 12-year civil war, human rights violations by both the government security forces and left-wing guerrillas were rampant.

The constitution provides for freedom of religion and specifically recognizes the Roman Catholic Church. After the peace agreements, the constitution was amended to prohibit the military from playing an internal security role except under extraordinary circumstances.

CONSTITUTIONAL HISTORY

The Republic of El Salvador, which became independent of the Spanish Crown in 1821, has had 12 constitutions to today. The first was implemented in 1824 when the country formed part of the Federation of Central American States. In 1841, El Salvador adopted an independence constitution after the breakup of the federation.

A series of failed constitutions followed, most lasting for only a few years. In 1886, the country adopted a constitution that can be regarded as a cornerstone of the constitutional development of El Salvador. It was drafted by a national constituent congress that was strongly influenced by the idea of natural law; it took a highly defined and developed liberal approach.

After decades of constitutional stability, two more constitutions were introduced, in 1939 and 1944. However, in 1945, the 1886 constitution was reintroduced, with certain amendments.

After World War II (1939–45), the international community was restructured by the rise of new international organizations with a humanist and democratic approach, as typified by the 1948 Universal Declaration of Human Rights. This development was reflected in El Salvador's 1950 constitution, adopted by the historically important constituent assembly. The new document was characterized by a profound social approach and by the preeminence that it gave to the human person. Another constitution was adopted in 1962.

After increasing clashes between the Marxist coalition guerrilla movement of the Farabundo Martí Liberation Front (FMLN) on the one hand and El Salvadoran armed forces (ESAF) and rightist death squads on the other, a full-scale civil war broke out and lasted for 12 years (1980–92). One of the most infamous death-squad assassinations was the murder of the archbishop of San Salvador, Óscar Romero, in 1980. Romero had publicly urged the U.S. government not to provide military support to the El Salvadoran government. A constituent assembly elected during the conflict adopted the current 1983 constitution of the republic.

On January 16, 1992, the government of El Salvador and the FMLN signed the Peace Accords that ended one of the most painful chapters in the history of El Salvador.

In the past, the plethora of new or reformed constitutions had often been imposed as a result of military or civil-military coups d'état, with no regard for the amendment procedures of the existing constitutions. The reforms introduced as part of the negotiations to end the armed conflict of the 1980s were implemented in a legal, constitutional fashion. These amendments, adopted in 1991, 1992, and 1995, constituted a precedent not only in the field of constitutional law of El Salvador but also in the field of comparative constitutional law in general. For the first time, internal peace treaties became a source of constitutional law.

In recent years, as other amendments have arisen to deal with a variety of matters, they too were adopted by parliament at two consecutive ordinary legislative periods, the only procedure allowed by the current constitution for amending the constitution.

To sum up, it is widely believed that the key moments in El Salvador's constitutional history reflected the dramatic changes in the country's economic, political, and social circumstances at three crucial eras. The 1886 constitution established the basis for the liberal, individualistic approach in politics; it was a product of the influential natural law trend in philosophy and stressed individual and property rights. The 1950 constitution was influenced by the social movements of the postwar era, by the development of public international law, and by the adoption of the 1948 Universal Declaration of Human Rights, of which El Salvador was one of the 48 original signatory states. The document recognizes economic, social, and cultural rights and the social responsibility of the state. In the last decade of the 20th century, reforms were adopted as a product of a political treaty between the government and a guerrilla group. These changes transformed the functions of the organs and institutions of the state, limiting deeply rooted institutions such as the police and the armed forces and creating new institutions to help protect human rights.

It is widely believed that the current constitution, while closely reflecting the country's history, suffers from important gaps and deficiencies that require immediate revision and extensive adjustments. The most important constitutional challenges for the country are to complete the democratic transformation and to meet the needs imposed by regional and international integration and globalization, which impact group rights. Some observers argue that a new constitution must provide a constituent assembly path to amendments, to end the monopoly on constitutional reform currently held by the party-dominated legislature.

FORM AND IMPACT OF THE CONSTITUTION

El Salvador has a written constitution, consisting of 11 titles and 274 articles that take precedence over all other national law. International treaties that enter into force in accordance with their own provisions and the constitution become laws of the republic.

BASIC ORGANIZATIONAL STRUCTURE

El Salvador is a unitary state made up of 14 departments called *departamentos* that exercise some limited governmental powers.

LEADING CONSTITUTIONAL PRINCIPLES

El Salvador's system of government is a presidential democracy. There is a division of the executive, legislative, and judicial powers. According to the constitution, the judiciary is independent. El Salvador is a sovereign state. Sovereignty is vested in the people, who exercise it within the limits specified in the constitution. The form of government is republican, democratic, and representative.

CONSTITUTIONAL BODIES

The main constitutional bodies provided for in the constitution are the president, the vice president and the cabinet ministers, the unicameral parliament, and the Supreme Court.

The President

The strong president is both chief of state and head of the executive branch of government. The president cannot be elected for a consecutive second term.

The Administration

The executive branch of the government is further made up of the vice president of the republic, the ministers and deputy ministers of state, and their subordinate officials. Each minister (and one or more deputy ministers) is assigned one of the secretariats of state, which control the various sectors of the administration. The ministers are selected by the president as chief executive.

Parliament (Asamblea Legislativa)

Legislative power is vested in the Legislative Assembly, a unicameral parliament consisting of 84 members. The parliament has the power to levy taxes, to ratify treaties, and to approve the budget. The assembly also has the power to declare war, ratify peace treaties, and grant amnesty for political offenses or ordinary crimes.

The Lawmaking Process

Legislation may be introduced by deputies, the president, the ministers, and the Supreme Court. A presidential veto may be overridden by a two-thirds vote of the Legislative Assembly.

The Judiciary

The judicial power is exercised by the courts. The highest court is the Supreme Court; second instance chambers, first instance courts, and justices of peace complete the judicial hierarchy.

The Supreme Court is itself divided into four chambers: civil, penal, constitutional, and administrative. While the civil and penal chambers deal with appeals, the other chambers deal with original cases related to constitutional guarantees for the protection of civil rights, habeas corpus, and fair administrative procedures.

THE ELECTION PROCESS

Every Salvadorian citizen over the age of 18 has the right to vote in the elections. Voting is compulsory.

Presidential Elections

The president and the vice president are both elected for a five-year term. The president is directly elected by a majority of the people; if no candidate receives more than 50 percent of the votes in the first round, a second round runoff is required.

Parliamentary Elections

Members of the assembly serve for a three-year term. The electoral law provides for a system of proportional representation. Twenty of the 84 deputies are elected on the basis of a single national constituency; the other 64 are elected in 14 multimember constituencies. Every Salvadoran citizen at 25 years of age has the right to stand for elections.

POLITICAL PARTIES

El Salvador has a pluralistic system of political parties. In practice, it is a two-party system; it is extremely difficult for anyone to achieve electoral success under the banner of any other party.

CITIZENSHIP

Salvadoran citizenship is primarily acquired by place of birth: A child acquires Salvadoran citizenship if born in El Salvador, regardless of the citizenship of the mother or father. A child born abroad acquires Salvadoran citizenship if one parent is a Salvadoran citizen. El Salvador recognizes a special citizenship designation for natives of other Central American states.

FUNDAMENTAL RIGHTS

The constitution guarantees the traditional set of liberal human rights and civil liberties. For example, Article 2 states that every person has the right to life, physical and moral integrity, liberty, safety, work, property and possession, and protection in maintaining and defending these rights.

The constitution states that all persons are equal before the law. It prohibits discrimination based on nationality, race, sex, or religion.

Impact and Functions of Fundamental Rights

The rights established in the International Covenant on Civil and Political Rights are included in the constitution and further developed in subsidiary legislation. The constitutional rights laws of El Salvador are characterized by the influence of both current liberal thought and the natural law philosophy of the 19th century. In the past, the oligarchial powers in the country, relying on the armed forces, also influenced the rights regime in order to defend their economic and political interests. More recently, the constitution has been influenced by emerging post–civil-war democratic developments.

During the 12-year civil war, human rights violations by both the government security forces and left-wing guerrillas were rampant. The peace accords established a

Truth Commission under United Nations (UN) auspices to investigate the most serious cases. The commission recommended judicial reform and removal of human rights violators from government and military posts.

According to the 1993 Law of National Reconciliation (Legislative Decree No. 147), a blanket amnesty was granted to all persons responsible for perpetrating violence during the civil war, with the notable exception of those responsible for the killing of Archbishop Romero in 1980.

Limitations to Fundamental Rights

The right to free expression is only guaranteed as long as it "does not subvert the public order." The right to the free exercise of religion is guaranteed as long as it is exercised within the boundaries of "morality and public order." Further rights may be suspended in a state of emergency.

ECONOMY

Title 5 defines the outlines of the economic order. Private property is guaranteed, and its social function is recognized. Taken as a whole, the Salvadoran economic system can be described as a social market economy. It combines aspects of social responsibility with market freedom.

RELIGIOUS COMMUNITIES

The constitution provides for freedom of religion but also specifically recognizes the Roman Catholic Church, which is granted a legal status.

MILITARY DEFENSE AND STATE OF EMERGENCY

According to the constitution, military service is compulsory for all Salvadorans between 18 and 30 years of age. In practice, military service has been voluntary since the end of the armed conflict in 1992.

The legislative and the executive branch both have authority to issue a decree suspending certain constitutional guarantees in the event of war, invasion, rebellion, sedition, catastrophe, epidemic or other general disaster, or serious disturbances of the public order. The maximal period for which constitutional guarantees can be suspended is 30 days. The legislature and the ministers are mandated to restore constitutional guarantees as soon as the special circumstances giving rise to their suspension have ceased to exist.

After the peace agreements, the constitution was amended to prohibit the military from playing an internal security role, except under extraordinary circumstances. The civilian police force, created to replace the discredited public security forces, deployed its first officers in 1993.

AMENDMENTS TO THE CONSTITUTION

Initial approval of an amendment requires a simple majority vote in parliament. However, it must be ratified by a two-thirds majority in the next elected assembly.

PRIMARY SOURCES

1983 Constitution in Spanish. Available online. URL: http://www.georgetown.edu/pdba/Constitutions/ElSal/elsalvador.html. Accessed on August 21, 2005.

SECONDARY SOURCES

Bureau of Public Affairs, U.S. Department of State. "Background Notes and Country Reports on Human Rights Practices and International Religious Freedom Report 2004." Available online. URL: http://www.state.gov/. Accessed on August 13, 2005.

Richard A. Haggarty, *El Salvador—a Country Study.* Washington, D.C.: Federal Research Division, Library of Congress, 1988. Available online. URL: http://lcweb2.loc.gov/frd/cs/Avtoc.html. Accessed on June 17, 2006.

United Nations, "Core Document Forming Part of the Reports of States Parties: El Salvador" (HRI/CORE/1/Add.34/Rev.1), 5 August 1996. Available online. URL: http://www.unhchr.ch/. Accessed on August 28, 2005.

Florentín Meléndez

EQUATORIAL GUINEA

At-a-Glance

OFFICIAL NAME
Republic of Equatorial Guinea

CAPITAL
Malabo

POPULATION
523,000 (July 2004 est.)

SIZE
10,830 sq. mi. (28,050 sq. km)

LANGUAGES
Spanish, French (official languages), aboriginal languages

RELIGIONS
Roman Catholic 87%, Protestant 5%, animist 5%, other (including Muslims and atheists) 3%, in practice many traditional beliefs

NATIONAL OR ETHNIC COMPOSITION
Fang 85%, Bubi 10%, other (consisting of Annobonese, Ndowe, Bisio, others) 5%

DATE OF INDEPENDENCE OR CREATION
October 12, 1968 (from Spain)

TYPE OF GOVERNMENT
Constitutional democracy

TYPE OF STATE
Centralist state

TYPE OF LEGISLATURE
Unicameral parliament

DATE OF CONSTITUTION
November 17, 1991

DATE OF LAST AMENDMENT
January 17, 1998

The Republic of Equatorial Guinea is a presidential democracy. According to the constitution, there is separation among the three branches of government: the executive, the legislative, and the judicial. Organized as a unitary state, Equatorial Guinea is made up of both a mainland region and an island region. The two regions are subdivided into seven provinces.

The president is the predominant figure in the Equatoguinean constitution. This powerful head of state, who has vast authority, is also head of the administration. Furthermore, the president is supreme commander of the armed forces.

Universal, equal, and secret elections are guaranteed. Multipartism, however, was introduced only in 1991.

The constitution provides for liberal as well as social rights. The state has the obligation to respect and protect them. Freedom of religion is guaranteed by the constitution. The economic system with its strong public sector is gradually opening up to private actors.

CONSTITUTIONAL HISTORY

Equatorial Guinea is one of the smallest countries on the African continent. It consists of five inhabited islands and a mainland portion at the Atlantic coast of Central Africa. In 1471, the island of Bioko was discovered by the Portuguese. In 1778, Spain took over control of the island in exchange for territory in South America. As for the mainland territories, they were placed under Spanish rule in 1900 after some territorial disputes. These territories were known then as Spanish Guinea. In 1963, the Equatoguineans were granted limited autonomy. They were also allocated a few representatives to the Spanish parliament.

After pressure from the United Nations, Spain promised to grant independence to Equatorial Guinea. In a referendum held on August 11, 1968, the majority of Equatoguineans voted in favor of the new constitution. The country became independent on October 12, 1968.

The first president, Francisco Macias Nguema, took the title of president for life. Major parts of the constitution were neglected, and huge violations of human rights were reported, including mass killings, slavery, and expulsions. Macias Nguema's rule was ended in a military coup by his nephew, Teodoro Obiang Nguema Mbasogo, in 1979. Obiang Nguema was reelected in 1989, in 1996, and in 2002.

A new constitution took effect in 1982. The current constitution was approved by a national referendum in 1991 and amended in 1995.

FORM AND IMPACT OF THE CONSTITUTION

Equatorial Guinea has a written constitution. It is one single document of 104 articles. It is the fundamental law, and no other law can be contrary to it. Some adjustments to the 1991 constitution were made in 1995. According to the constitution, the parliament has 80 members. However, since the last parliamentary elections in 2004, it has de facto consisted of 100 members.

In a special procedure, the Constitutional Court can declare international treaties unconstitutional.

BASIC ORGANIZATIONAL STRUCTURE

Equatorial Guinea is a centralist state. The country is subdivided into regions, provinces, districts, and municipalities. The mainland region is often called Rio Muni; it has four provinces. The insular or island region consists of three regions. The capital, Malabo, is situated on Bioko island.

LEADING CONSTITUTIONAL PRINCIPLES

The constitution provides for a presidential democracy system of government. The executive, legislative, and judicial powers are separated.

Equatorial Guinea's constitutional system is defined by the following principles: It is a republican, unitary, social, and democratic state. Unity, peace, justice, freedom, and equality are called supreme values.

There is a certain stress on the principle of national unity. This term appears many times in the constitution. Accordingly, political parties must operate nationwide and may not be based on specific districts or municipalities. These provisions were probably designed to counteract localist movements for separation and self-determination, such as movements advocating the separation of the islands from the mainland.

According to the constitution, another key value in Equatoguinean society is the traditional African family.

That expression can be found twice in the preamble and in many other articles of the constitution.

CONSTITUTIONAL BODIES

The constitution names the following major constitutional bodies: the president of the republic, the Council of Ministers, the Chamber of People's Representatives and the judiciary with a special constitutional court. Among them, the president is the predominant figure.

The President of the Republic

The president of the republic is the head of state. In addition to this representative function, the constitution allocates vast powers to the office. The president determines the policies of the nation and can make laws by presidential decree. He or she appoints and dismisses the prime minister as well as many other high civilian and military officials and has the right to dissolve parliament. The president commands the armed forces and may declare war and peace. Under special circumstances, the president may even suspend the constitution for three months—or longer, if necessary. Furthermore, the president may negotiate and ratify international treaties. When parliament does not adopt a general budget, it is the president who has the right to institute the budget bill.

The president is elected for a seven-year term directly by the people, with the possibility of multiple reelections. The current president has been ruling the country since 1979. The presidency ends with resignation, death, permanent physical or mental disability, or expiration of the term of office.

The Council of Ministers

The Council of Ministers executes the policies determined by the president. It consists of the prime minister, cabinet ministers, and deputy ministers. Many of its decisions must be approved by either the president or the parliament or both. The prime minister coordinates government activities in areas other than foreign affairs, national defense, and security.

The prime minister is appointed by the president of the republic. The other members of the Council of Ministers are appointed by the prime minister. The members of the Council of Ministers are not individually but jointly responsible.

The Chamber of People's Representatives (Cámara de Representantes del Pueblo)

The 80 members of this unicameral parliament are elected for a five-year term through universal suffrage. The Chamber of People's Representatives is the legislative body in

Equatorial Guinea, but its power is limited. It meets in ordinary two-month sessions only twice a year, in March and September. Extraordinary sessions can be held at the request of the president of the republic or three-quarters of the members of parliament.

Between the two sessions, the president of the republic is authorized by the Chamber of People's Representatives to enact statutory orders. The president may order the dissolution of the Chamber of People's Representatives and call for new elections.

The Lawmaking Process

There are two ways to create new laws in Equatorial Guinea. When parliament is not in session, law is made by presidential decrees, which enter into force upon release. When parliament is in session, it can vote draft laws submitted to it by the administration or from within the assembly. The president can veto the draft law and request additional hearings in parliament. When the president believes a draft violates the constitution, he or she can refer it to the Constitutional Court. Laws that have been adopted by parliament are then promulgated by the president.

The Judiciary

The court system can be described as a combination of traditional, civil, and military justice. It is based on Spanish civil law as well as on tribal custom, and it often operates in an ad hoc manner. The judiciary is formally independent of the other powers; however, the president of the republic appoints all the judges of the Constitutional Court and the Supreme Court, as well as the attorney general.

The Constitutional Court deals with disputes of constitutional bodies and has the authority to declare international treaties and other laws unconstitutional. It has five members, each serving a seven-year term. Supreme Court judges, on the other hand, serve five-year terms.

THE ELECTION PROCESS AND POLITICAL PARTICIPATION

Suffrage is universal and the minimal voting age is 18. A candidate for the presidency must be Equatoguinean by birth and have lived in the country for at least five years and must be neither younger than 40 nor older than 75 years of age. To be elected, the candidate needs the relative majority of votes cast through direct, equal, secret, and universal suffrage.

Members of the Chamber of People's Representatives are elected for five-year terms by proportional representation in multimember constituencies. Parliament used to have 80 members, but since the 2004 elections, that number has changed to 100.

POLITICAL PARTIES

One-party rule formally ended in 1991. However, in practice, many opposition parties regularly boycott major elections.

The constitution recognizes multipartism in Article 1, which considers parties as the vehicle for the popular will and as the basis for political participation. Thus, the prime minister must be a member of the political party that has the majority of seats in parliament. Parties may not be based on tribe, religion, ethnicity, gender, locality, social condition, or profession.

CITIZENSHIP

Citizenship can be acquired by birth on Equatoguinean territory or by birth to at least one Equatoguinean parent.

FUNDAMENTAL RIGHTS

Fundamental rights and duties are enumerated in the first part of the constitution. The document lists a large number of liberal rights, as well as some social rights. Thus, work is a right. Primary education is obligatory and free. Labor and the family are to be protected. The constitution also contains judicial rights, such as the right to be presumed innocent until found guilty.

Impact and Functions of Fundamental Rights

The constitution reaffirms the country's attachment to the principles in the 1948 Universal Declaration of Human Rights and other international agreements. However, United Nations and U.S. State Department reports list grave shortcomings in protection of human rights. Certain laws and regulations severely restrict political rights. Thus, the authorities have extensive power to restrict media activities. Numerous irregularities, such as evidence of torture, were reported by observers in a 2002 case against some 150 people, including leaders of three opposition parties, accused of attempting a military coup.

Limitations to Fundamental Rights

No fundamental rights named in the constitution's second chapter may be exercised in a manner that infringes upon other people's fundamental rights or other principles stated in the constitution such as human dignity or democracy.

ECONOMY

The constitution of Equatorial Guinea does not favor a specific economic system. However, it does cite the principles of free exchange of goods and services and freedom of enterprise. The constitution also contains a list of resources and services that are reserved to the public sector. Since 1991, stronger efforts to promote the private sector have been made. In the 1990s, oil exports increased substantially.

RELIGIOUS COMMUNITIES

The constitution guarantees freedom of religion and worship. Religious organizations have to be formally registered with the Ministry of Justice and Religion before their activities are allowed. Religious study is required in schools. Though the state is formally separated from religion, a 1992 law includes an explicit preference for the Roman Catholic Church. Usually, a mass is held as part of major public ceremonial acts.

MILITARY DEFENSE AND STATE OF EMERGENCY

In a state of emergency, the president, who also commands the armed forces, clearly dominates.
    Military service is obligatory for all.

AMENDMENTS TO THE CONSTITUTION

The constitution may only be changed via a popular referendum, which is held upon request of the president or of the majority of parliament. The constitution may not be changed during a vacancy of the presidency. No amendment can change the republican and democratic system or the principles of unity and territorial integrity.

PRIMARY SOURCES

Constitution in English. Available online. URL: http://www.ceiba-guinea-ecuatorial.org/guineeangl/nvelle_const.htm. Accessed on July 28, 2005.
Constitution in Spanish. Available online. URL: http://www.ceiba-guinea-ecuatorial.org/guineees/nvelle_const.htm. Accessed on August 3, 2005.
Constitution in French. Available online. URL: http://www.ceiba-guinea-ecuatorial.org/guineefr/nvelle_const.htm. Accessed on July 24, 2005.

SECONDARY SOURCES

United Nations, "Report on the Human Rights Situation in the Republic of Equatorial Guinea, Special Rapporteur of the Commission on Human Rights" (esp.: E/CN.4/1994/56; E/CN.4/1995/68; E/CN.4/1996/67/Add.1; E/CN.4/2003/65/Add.1). Available online. URL: http://unbisnet.un.org/. Accessed on September 26, 2005.
U.S. Department of State, *Country Report on Human Rights Practices: Equatorial Guinea*. Washington, D.C.: U.S. Government Printing Office, 2003.
Geoffrey Woods, "Business and Politics in a Criminal State: The Case of Equatorial Guinea" *African Affairs* (2004): 547–567.

Hartmut Rank

ERITREA

At-a-Glance

OFFICIAL NAME
State of Eritrea

CAPITAL
Asmara

POPULATION
4,561,599 (July 2005 est.)

SIZE
46,842 sq. mi. (121,320 sq. km)

LANGUAGES
Tigrinya, Arabic, English, Tigre, Bilen, Kunama, Saho, Nara, Italian, Afar, Hidarb

RELIGIONS
Christian, Muslim, and animist (very small number of Kunama ethnic group)

NATIONAL OR ETHNIC COMPOSITION
Tigrinya 50%, Tigre and Kunama 40%, Saho 3%, Afar 4%, other (Hidareb, Nara, Bilen, and Reshaida) 3%

DATE OF INDEPENDENCE OR CREATION
May 24, 1991 (de facto), May 24, 1993 (de jure)

TYPE OF GOVERNMENT
Constitutional democracy

TYPE OF STATE
Unitary state

TYPE OF LEGISLATURE
Unicameral parliament

DATE OF CONSTITUTION
May 23, 1997

DATE OF LAST AMENDMENT
No amendment

Eritrea obtained independence in fact from Ethiopia after a 30-year armed struggle on May 24, 1991, and formal independence on May 24, 1993. The 1997 constitution expressly states that Eritrea adheres to constitutional supremacy. The guiding principles are the rule of law, social justice, and democracy. The separation of powers of the executive, legislative, and judiciary is clearly stated. Eritrea is a secular and unitary state divided into units of local government. Currently, it is divided into six local governments. The 1997 constitution has not yet entered into effect.

The president is the head of state and head of government. The president is selected from among the members of the National Assembly, the legislative body.

According to the 1997 constitution, the members of the National Assembly are directly elected by the people. Fundamental freedoms, rights, and duties are guaranteed and safeguarded under the constitution.

The defense forces owe allegiance to and must obey the constitution and the constitutional government.

CONSTITUTIONAL HISTORY

Eritrea is a newly emerged nation in the horn of Africa. The Ottoman Empire, Egypt, Italy, Great Britain, and Ethiopia have all colonized Eritrea, which has been under the sway of colonialism since the 16th century. In 1517, the coastal regions of Eritrea fell under the rule of the Ottoman Empire. At about the same time, kingdoms from present-day Ethiopia and Sudan fought over the rest of the country.

In 1823, Egyptian forces encroached on the Gash Barka or Western Lowland area of Eritrea; by 1840, they controlled the region. In 1872, the Egyptians displaced the Turks and ruled the Eritrean Red Sea coast. During the period of 1872–82, Eritrea was under the colonial rule of Egypt. The Ottoman Empire and Egypt mainly occupied the coastal area of Eritrea and hardly influenced the legal system.

In 1882, Italy occupied the port of Assa, and by 1889 conquered all of Eritrea. In 1890, the Italian king, Umberto

I, officially declared Eritrea an Italian colony. A formal judicial system was established. However, there was no trace of constitution making or constitutional litigation during the Italian colonial period. Native Eritreans were subject to discrimination based on race and color, and the rights to movement, education, and freedom of expression were extremely limited.

A British Military Administration ruled Eritrea between 1941 and 1952. During that period, the Italian laws were applicable with some modification, based on English laws imposed by British administrators. The British introduced political reform, expanded education, and abolished racially discriminatory laws. The Eritrean people for the first time were officially permitted to form political parties. However, they were denied the right to make their own constitution and to decide their destiny.

In 1950, the Eritrean case was taken before the General Assembly of the United Nations to determine the destiny of the Eritrean people. The General Assembly decided to support a federation between Eritrea and Ethiopia. In 1952, this simulated "federation" was proclaimed. In the same year, the democratic constitution of Eritrea was ratified. The 1952 constitution included civil and political rights, the separation of powers, formation of political parties, freedom of expression, and other democratic principles. In contrast, the Ethiopian constitution at the time was based on absolute monarchy. The emperor was compelled to pass a new constitution in 1955 providing for a constitutional monarchy.

On September 1, 1961, the Eritrean Liberation Front (ELF), a guerrilla organization, was established. For the next 30 years, the ELF and later the Eritrean People Liberation Front (EPLF) fought a bitter armed struggle against Ethiopia. In 1994, at the third congress of the EPLF, a National Charter for Eritrea was adopted. The six basic goals stated in the National Charter were national harmony, political democracy, economic and social development, social justice, cultural revival, and regional and international cooperation. It further listed six basic principles: national unity, active participation of the people, decisive role of the human factor, relationship between national and social struggle (struggle for social justice), self-reliance, and a strong relationship between people and leadership.

In 1995, a Constitutional Commission was established to draft a constitution for the State of Eritrea. A document was drafted within two years, and a Constituent Assembly ratified it on May 23, 1997. This constitution has not yet entered into force.

FORM AND IMPACT OF THE CONSTITUTION

Eritrea has a written constitution that is codified in a single document. It is the supreme law of the land; any law or act that contradicts it is null and void.

International laws or agreements are signed by the president and must be ratified by the National Assembly as laws. They become applicable in the legal system of Eritrea after being published in the *Gazette of Eritrean Law* or any other legally recognized gazette in Eritrea.

BASIC ORGANIZATIONAL STRUCTURE

Eritrea is a unitary state divided into units of local governments. The local governments differ in geographic area, ethnic composition, population, and economic strength. However, they all have the same rights, duties, and powers.

LEADING CONSTITUTIONAL PRINCIPLES

The form of the Eritrean government is unique. It is a mix of the presidential, parliamentary, and hybrid forms of governments. As in many presidential systems, the president is the head of state and chief commander of the armed forces as well as head of the administration. However, the president is chosen from among the members of the National Assembly, just as prime ministers are in parliamentary systems. Other ministers may be selected from within or outside the members of the National Assembly; that is, a member of the executive can continue to be a member of the legislature, as in a hybrid systems.

CONSTITUTIONAL BODIES

The basic bodies of the constitution are the parliament, known as the National Assembly; the president, aided by a cabinet; and the judiciary.

The National Assembly

The National Assembly of Eritrea is a single-chamber parliament. Its members are the representatives of the Eritrean people. According to the 1997 constitution, they are elected in general, direct, free, universal, fair, and secret suffrage. The members of the National Assembly have the powers and duties of legislation, control of executive or administrative bodies, hearing of citizens' complaints, and approval of appointments to important public offices such as the presidency. The term of parliament is five years. It may extend its term by vote of not less than two-thirds for a period of six months in a state of emergency. The immunity of a member of the National Assembly may be lifted only if he or she is apprehended while committing a crime.

The Lawmaking Process

The National Assembly is the sole legislative body. However, it may delegate its authority to legislate to any other person or organization. The delegation must be duly authorized and proclaimed in a law that is passed by parliament. The constitution expressly states that only the National Assembly has the power to enact tax laws, approve the national budget, ratify international agreements by law, approve government borrowing, and approve the declaration of peace, war, or emergency. The president must approve legislation passed by parliament within one month and has no veto power. The president continues to serve as a member of the National Assembly; hence, he or she can oppose, support, or abstain on a bill before parliament.

The President

The president is the head of state and government and the commander in chief of the armed forces. He or she is elected for a five-year term and can be reelected only once. The president is elected from among the members of the National Assembly by an absolute majority. A candidate for the office of the president must be a citizen of Eritrea by birth.

The president must ensure respect for the constitution, integrity of the state, efficiency of management, the interest and safety of all citizens, and enjoyment of fundamental freedom and rights of citizens. With the approval of the National Assembly, the president has the power to appoint and dismiss ministers and to appoint commissioners, the auditor-general, the governor of the National Bank, the chief justice of the Supreme Court, and other persons specified by the constitution. The president also has the power to grant pardon or amnesty, establish and dissolve ministries and departments, and preside over and coordinate meetings of the cabinet.

The Judiciary

The courts, in exercising their judicial power, are free of the direction and control of any person or authority. The highest court of Eritrea is the Supreme Court. It has sole jurisdiction to interpret the constitution and the constitutionality of any law or acts of the government or individual. It also has sole jurisdiction to hear and adjudicate charges against an impeached president and appeals from lower courts. A law will determine the cases that can be appealed before the Supreme Court. A law will also determine the tenure and number of justices of the Supreme Court.

Under the constitution, the Judicial Service Commission proposes the appointment of the Supreme Court justices to the president. It also recommends the recruitment, terms, and conditions of service of judges. The Supreme Court is not yet established.

THE ELECTION PROCESS AND POLITICAL PARTICIPATION

All Eritrean citizens 18 years of age or older have the right to vote. The constitution states that the National Assembly shall enact electoral laws that will determine the qualifications and election of the members of the National Assembly. So far, an electoral law is drafted but not yet duly proclaimed; it states that a candidate must be 21 years old by Election Day.

POLITICAL PARTIES

Every citizen has the right to form organizations for political, social, economic, and cultural ends. The constitution and the National Charter for Eritrea expressly proclaim a pluralistic political system in Eritrea. A Proclamation on the Formation of Political Parties and Organizations is drafted but not yet duly proclaimed.

CITIZENSHIP

The constitution states that the National Assembly shall enact laws to regulate citizenship. Currently, the Eritrean Nationality Proclamation of 1992 governs citizenship in Eritrea. It states that citizenship is attained through descent or origin, by birth if the descent of the person born in Eritrea cannot be tracked, and by naturalization.

FUNDAMENTAL RIGHTS

Chapter 3 of the constitution specifies fundamental freedoms, rights, and duties. The constitution in principle guarantees civil, political, and socioeconomic rights. The civil and political rights are enforceable provisions, while socioeconomic rights refer to national objectives and directive principles. The enforcement of socioeconomic and cultural rights is subject to qualifications, such as the "the state shall strive," "use all available resource," "shall encourage," and "shall endeavor." The fundamental freedoms, rights, and duties apply in disputes between state and individuals as well as between individuals.

Limitations to Human Rights and Fundamental Freedoms

Fundamental freedoms, rights, and duties may be limited. The constitution has a general limitation clause and specifies limitations within each specific right. The limitations apply to both the state and individuals.

The general limitation clause states that the fundamental freedoms and rights guaranteed in the constitution may be limited in the interest of national security, public safety, economic well-being of the country, health or morals, prevention of public disorder, and protection of the rights and freedoms of others. Any limitation of the fundamental freedoms and rights guaranteed in the constitution must be consistent with the principles of democracy and justice, must be of general application, and may not negate the essential content of the rights and freedoms in question. The law that limits any fundamental freedoms and rights must be duly proclaimed and specify the authority for the enshrined limitation.

There are certain fundamental rights that may not be limited under the general limitation clause, such as equality before the law, right to life and liberty, right to human dignity, proscription of ex-post-facto criminal punishment, writ of habeas corpus, presumption of innocence, and freedom of thought, conscience, and belief.

The fundamental freedoms and rights can be suspended during a state of emergency. The president can declare the state of emergency when war, external invasion, civil disorder, or natural disaster threatens the state. The declaration of the state of emergency must be approved by a two-thirds majority of the members of the National Assembly.

ECONOMY

The constitution of Eritrea does not expressly specify the economic system. However, economic policy must take into account the citizens' rights to social justice, the needs of economic development, and balance and sustainability in development. It must also take into consideration the right to property, freedom of occupation or profession, and the right of association for economic ends.

RELIGIOUS COMMUNITIES

Eritrea is a secular state. The constitution guarantees the right to freedom of thought, conscience, and belief of any person. It safeguards the freedom to practice and manifest any religion. There is no state-sponsored church or mosque.

MILITARY DEFENSE AND STATE OF EMERGENCY

The defense and security forces of Eritrea owe allegiance to and obey the constitution. They are accountable to the law. The constitution stipulates that the defense and security forces are an integral part of society and must be productive and respectful to the people. They are dependent on the people and subject to the civil government.

All citizens are obliged to fulfill national service. The National Service Proclamation states that every citizen below 40 years of age is obliged to perform national service of 18 months. The medical board can certify individuals as unfit to serve. Those so certified are obliged to perform the 18-month service in social and governmental institutions.

AMENDMENTS TO THE CONSTITUTION

The constitution of Eritrea is difficult to amend. The president or 50 percent of all the members of the National Assembly can initiate a proposal for the amendment of any provision. For its passage, the proposal requires a three-quarters majority vote of the members of the National Assembly, followed by a one-year deliberation period. After the end of the one-year deliberation, the National Assembly can approve the amendment with a four-fifths majority of its members.

PRIMARY SOURCES
Constitution in English. Available online. URLs: http://www.nitesoft.com/eccm/Constitution_TOC.htm; http://www.ucis.unc.edu/programs/eritrea%20journal/constitution.pdf. Accessed on July 31, 2005.

SECONDARY SOURCES
The Eritrean People's Liberation Front (EPLF), *A National Charter for Eritrea.* Asmara: Adulis Printing Press, 1994.

Establishment of the Constitutional Commission, Proclamation No. 55/1994, *Gazette of Eritrean Laws* 4, no. 3 (15 March 1994). Asmara: The Government of Eritrea.

Richard A. Rosen, "Constitutional Process, Constitutionalism and the Eritrean Experience." *North Carolina Journal of International Law and Commercial Regulation* 24, no. 2 (winter 1999): 263–311.

Bereket Habtes Selassie, "Democracy and the Role of Parliament under the Eritrean Constitution." *North Carolina Journal of International Law and Commercial Regulation* 24, no. 2 (winter 1999): 227–261.

"The Constitution of Eritrea," Ratified by the Constituent Assembly on May 23, 1997. In *North Carolina Journal of International Law and Commercial Regulation* 24 (1999) 2, 417–449. Chapel Hill, N. C.: University of North Carolina School of Law.

Muluberhan Berhe Hagos

ESTONIA

At-a-Glance

OFFICIAL NAME
Republic of Estonia

CAPITAL
Tallinn

POPULATION
1,324,333 (July 2006 est.)

SIZE
17,462 sq. mi. (45,227 sq. km)

LANGUAGES
Estonian, Russian

RELIGIONS
Christian churches (Evangelical Lutheran 11%,
Christian Orthodox 10%; smaller communities
of Roman Catholics, Baptists, Methodists) 23%;
Muslims, Buddhists, Jews, and others; large
unaffiliated segment of the population

NATIONAL OR ETHNIC COMPOSITION
Estonian 67.9%, Russian 25.6%, Ukrainian 2.1%,
Belorussian 1.3%, Finn 0.9%, other 2.2%

DATE OF INDEPENDENCE OR CREATION
February 24, 1918 (from Soviet Union: August 20,
1991)

TYPE OF GOVERNMENT
Parliamentary democracy

TYPE OF STATE
Unitary state

TYPE OF LEGISLATURE
Unicameral parliament

DATE OF CONSTITUTION
June 28, 1992

DATE OF LAST AMENDMENT
September 14, 2003

Estonia is a politically unitary state. The division of territory into administrative units is established by law—there are currently 15 units. The Estonian system of government is a parliamentary democracy. There is a strong division of the executive, legislative, and judicial powers, based on checks and balances.

The predominant bodies provided for in the constitution are the parliament, called Riigikogu; the president of the republic; the administration; the legal chancellor; and the courts. The Republic of Estonia shapes and develops its statehood on the basis of the principles of social justice, democracy, and the rule of law. Fundamental rights and freedoms form an inherent and central part of the Estonian national legal order.

The Estonian constitution expressly protects freedom of religion for individuals and religious communities. There is no state church, but cooperation between state and religious communities has been accepted in the limits of law.

The national defense of Estonia is conducted on the principles of civilian control, consonant with the demo-cratic organization of the state. By the constitution, Estonia is obliged to protect internal and external peace.

CONSTITUTIONAL HISTORY

The independent Republic of Estonia was born in the aftermath of World War I (1914–18) when it broke away from the Russian Empire. The Proclamation of Independence was followed by the War of Independence in 1918–20.

The first Estonian constitution (ratified in June 1920) was influenced by the liberal thinking prevalent in Europe after the First World War. The 1920 constitution emphasized the principle of a state based on the rule of law. One of its essential components was the acknowledgment of the fundamental rights of the person. As a result, it was one of the most democratic constitutions in Europe of its time.

The 1930s saw significant political changes in Estonia, characterized by the centralization of the state administration, the concentration of power, a decline of democracy, and the expansion of state control. The second Estonian constitution (1938) introduced a number of amendments on fundamental rights. It stated a new philosophy, according to which the legal rights and duties of an individual emanated from his or her status as a member of a commonwealth. This change reflected the more collectivist orientation of the era.

The outbreak of World War Two disturbed the peaceful development of the country, which was subsequently occupied by the Soviet Union (1940–41, 1944–91) and Nazi Germany (1941–44). After the war, Estonia was formally annexed to the Soviet Union.

A resurgence of Estonian national identity began in the late 1980s, leading to independence in 1991. The constitution of Estonia that entered into force in 1992 is, in a number of ways, a compilation of aspects of Estonia's previous constitutions. It has maintained the democratic spirit of the 1920 constitution, with some added mechanisms to maintain the balance of power of the state. In drafting the document, great attention was paid to fundamental rights. International treaties, the European Convention on Human Rights, and constitutions of other democratic states were taken as models. The constitution of the Federal Republic of Germany has had the greatest influence on the Estonian constitution.

FORM AND IMPACT OF THE CONSTITUTION

Estonia has a written constitution, codified in a single document. The Estonian constitution is named as a Põhiseadus (Basic Law). It has precedence over all other national law. Universally recognized principles and norms of international law are an inseparable part of the Estonian legal system. They are superior in force to national legislation and binding on the exercise of legislative, administrative, and judicial powers. In short, the hierarchy of laws stands as follows: (1) constitution, (2) international law, (3) laws enacted by parliament, (4) administrative regulations adopted by the executive branch including local governments, (5) administrative decisions made by the executive branch including local governments. Estonia joined the European Union on May 1, 2004. The law of the European Union takes precedence over Estonian law, as long as it does not contradict the Estonian constitution's basic principles.

BASIC ORGANIZATIONAL STRUCTURE

Estonia is a politically unitary state with 15 territorial administrative units. All local issues are resolved and regulated by local governments, which operate independently and in accordance with the law. Obligations may be imposed upon local governments only in accordance with the law

or with the agreement of the local government. All permanent residents, regardless of citizenship, are eligible to vote in local elections. The constitution provides for another type of government, also with a large degree of autonomy and cultural self-government, or ethnic minorities.

LEADING CONSTITUTIONAL PRINCIPLES

The Estonian system of government is a parliamentary democracy. There is a strong division of the executive, legislative, and judicial powers, based on checks and balances.

The Republic of Estonia shapes and develops its statehood on the basis of the principles of social justice, democracy, and the rule of law. Fundamental rights and freedoms form an inherent and central part of the Estonian national legal order. Estonia is an independent and sovereign democratic republic wherein the supreme power of the state is vested in the people. The constitution has established the principle of legal reservation, pursuant to which an administration is entitled to take action only if the law empowers it to do so.

There is no state church in Estonia. The cooperation between state and religious communities has been accepted within the limits of law.

CONSTITUTIONAL BODIES

The dominant bodies provided for in the constitution are the parliament, called Riigikogu; the president of the republic; the administration; and the judiciary. The constitution also provides for a Bank of Estonia, independent of the government, which operates as the bank of issue; an office of the legal chancellor, whose task is also to be ombudsperson; and the office of the auditor general.

The Parliament

According to the constitution, the supreme power of the state is vested in the people. The people exercise this supreme power in the elections for the Riigikogu by citizens who have the right to vote. The parliament has three main functions: legislation, monitoring of the activities of the executive power, and representation. It has 101 members and is elected for a period of four years.

The Lawmaking Process

Lawmaking is the main task of parliament. In order to pass an ordinary act, a simple majority of members in attendance is required. Article 104 of the constitution lists certain types of laws that can be passed and amended only by a majority of the membership of the Riigikogu. Bills passed by the Riigikogu are presented to the president of the republic for proclamation. The president may use the right of veto and return the bill to the Riigikogu. If the

Riigikogu does not amend it, the president has the right to ask the Supreme Court to declare it unconstitutional. After a bill is proclaimed as law, it is published in the *Riigi Teataja*, the state gazette.

The President of the Republic

The president has mainly representative functions, but the office has a number of executive powers. The president may veto a parliamentary bill and have it sent back for revision, and the president's signature is required for appointment of the ministers of the government. The president is also empowered to present the parliament with nominees for several higher offices.

The president is the supreme commander of the armed forces. He or she is elected for a five-year term by the parliament. If a sufficient majority of votes is not forthcoming, the president is elected by an electoral college, which consists of representatives of local governments and members of parliament.

The Administration

The executive power of the state—the administration or cabinet—consists of a prime minister and other ministers. It is responsible to parliament. Parliament appoints the prime minister and can withdraw its support from the administration. In turn, the administration can dismiss the Riigikogu with the consent of the president and call for new elections if the Riigikogu expresses no confidence in the government.

The Judiciary

The court system is divided into three levels: county and city courts, circuit courts of appeal, and the Supreme Court, which also functions as the Constitutional Court. The Estonian judicial system is based primarily on the German model, especially in the field of civil law, in which there are direct historical links. The courts are independent; judges are appointed for life and may not take up any other appointed public offices.

The Legal Chancellor

The legal chancellor ensures that state agencies guarantee the constitutional rights of individual and reviews the conformity of legislation and executive acts, including those of local governments, with the constitution and the laws. The chancellor also serves as ombudsperson; he or she is independent in all activities.

THE ELECTION PROCESS AND POLITICAL PARTICIPATION

Every Estonian citizen who has attained 18 years of age by the day of the elections has the right to vote (with the exception of those who have been divested of legal competence by a court). Every Estonian citizen 21 or older who is entitled to vote has a right to stand for elections to the parliament. All permanent residents over 18 years old, regardless of citizenship, are eligible to vote in municipal elections.

The electoral system is based on proportional representation by party lists. The Riigikogu is elected for four years. Local governments are elected for three-year terms. Local government also is elected for a term of four years.

POLITICAL PARTIES

Estonia has a pluralistic system of political parties. The multiparty system is a basic structure of the constitutional order, and the political parties are a fundamental element of public life. Political parties whose aims or activities are directed to violent change of the Estonian constitutional system or otherwise violate a criminal law are prohibited. The termination, suspension, or penalization of political parties can only be done by a court in cases in which the law has been violated.

CITIZENSHIP

Estonian citizenship is primarily acquired by birth. This means that a child acquires Estonian citizenship if one of his or her parents is an Estonian citizen. It is of no relevance where a child is born. Any person who as a minor lost his or her Estonian citizenship has the right to have it restored.

FUNDAMENTAL RIGHTS

The constitution defines fundamental rights, liberties, and duties in Chapter II, immediately after the seven general provisions listed in Chapter I. The prominence of fundamental rights indicates the society's person-centered attitude.

The catalogue of fundamental rights and liberties includes both liberal rights and social rights. One of the main principles of the constitution postulates the equality of Estonian citizens and citizens of foreign states as well as stateless persons. The constitution has extended fundamental rights to legal persons (i.e., organizations) insofar as these rights are in accordance with the general aims of legal persons and with the nature of such rights.

The rights and freedoms set out in the catalogue of fundamental rights do not preclude other rights and freedoms that arise from the spirit of the constitution or are in accordance therewith, and conform to the principle of human dignity and of a state based on social justice, democracy, and the rule of law.

Impact and Functions of Fundamental Rights

The Republic of Estonia shapes and develops its statehood on the basis of the principles of social justice, democracy, and the rule of law; therefore, fundamental rights and freedoms form an inherent part of the Estonian national legal order. The basic rights of the Estonian constitution have a subjective character in that they grant claims to individuals. Basic rights have fully binding force. The fundamental rights apply in the relation of the individual and the state and have effect among private persons. The fundamental rights affect all areas of the law.

Limitations to Fundamental Rights

The constitution contains four general limitation clauses; Article 11, however, is the central and most important one: "Rights and liberties may be restricted only in accordance with the constitution. Restrictions may be implemented only insofar as they are necessary in a democratic society, and their imposition may not distort the nature of the rights and liberties." Thus, every case of restriction of rights and liberties has to be justified and pass the test of proportionality—the limitation must be proportional to the need. Article 19(2) constitutionalizes the common-sense idea that in exercising their rights and liberties, all persons must respect and consider the rights and liberties of others and observe the law.

ECONOMY

Estonia's annexation by the Soviet Union in 1940 resulted in a forced transformation of its economy from a typical market economy similar to that of neighboring Scandinavian countries to a part of the Soviet centrally planned system. After regaining independence, the primary objective was the development of a Western-oriented economic system.

The transition to a market economy started at the beginning of the 1990s. Estonia is known for its radical free-market policies, liberal trade and tax policies, and stable currency, thanks to the comprehensive reforms that have characterized the Estonian economy since 1991.

Nevertheless, the Estonian constitution does not specify any particular economic system. It does defines the country as a social state. This aspect of the constitution has gradually gained more attention.

The constitution creates the legal preconditions for protection of property rights and economic freedom. Property of all persons, physical or legal persons, is inviolable and equally protected by law.

RELIGIOUS COMMUNITIES

There is no state church in Estonia. The separation of state and church has not been interpreted strictly in practice. A certain degree of cooperation between state and church (religious communities) has been accepted.

Both religious individuals and religious communities enjoy freedom of religion under Article 40 of the constitution and other constitutional provisions. Autonomy of religious communities also entails the right to self-administration in accordance with their own internal laws and prescriptions.

MILITARY DEFENSE AND STATE OF EMERGENCY

The Estonian defense forces and national defense are subject to civil control by parliament, the president of the republic, and the administration. The highest leader of the national defense is the president of the republic, advised by the National Defense Council. In addition to defense obligations, the defense forces provide assistance to civilian authorities in cases of national emergency.

The constitution of the Republic of Estonia requires compulsory military service for all physically and mentally healthy male citizens. Women can volunteer. The duration of the compulsory military service is eight or 11 months, depending on the education and the position assigned by the Defense Forces to the conscript. In accordance with Article 124(2) of the constitution, any person who refuses service in the defense forces for religious or ethical reasons is obliged to participate in alternative service. The compulsory alternative service is 16 months.

AMENDMENTS TO THE CONSTITUTION

Amendments to the constitution may be offered by one-fifth of the members of parliament or by the president of the republic. Amendments to Chapter I (General Provisions) or Chapter XV (Amendments to the Constitution) may be made only by referendum. The constitution may be amended by referendum, by two successive parliaments, or by parliament in one session in matters of urgency. For example, the change in the terms of local government councils was made by parliament as a matter of urgency.

A proposal to consider a draft law to amend the constitution as a matter of urgency has to win a four-fifths majority. In such a case, the law to amend the constitution has to be adopted by a two-thirds majority of the members of parliament. An amendment to the constitution in relation to accession to the European Union was adopted by a referendum held on September 14, 2003. The law to amend the constitution must be proclaimed by the president of the republic.

PRIMARY SOURCES
Constitution in English. Available online. URL: http://www.riik.ee/en/eestiriik.html. Accessed on June 17, 2006.

Constitution in Estonian: *Eesti Vabariigi Põhiseadus.* Tallinn: Eesti Vabariigi Riigikantselei, 1993.

SECONDARY SOURCES

Kalle Merusk, Raul Narits, *Estonia, International Encyclopedia of Laws.* Vol. 29. The Hague: Kluwer Law International, 1998.

Raul Narits, "The Republic of Estonia Constitution on the Concept and Value of Law." *Iuridica International* 1 (2002): 10–16. Available online. URL: http://www.juridica.ee/index_en.php. Accessed on September 9, 2005.

Joachim Sanden, "Methods of Interpreting the Constitution: Estonia's Way in an Increasingly Integrated Europe." *Iuridica International* 1 (2003): 128–139. Available online. URL: http://www.juridica.ee/index_en.php. Accessed on August 24, 2005.

Merilin Kiviorg

ETHIOPIA

At-a-Glance

OFFICIAL NAME
Federal Democratic Republic of Ethiopia

CAPITAL
Addis Ababa

POPULATION
67,851,281 (2004 est.)

SIZE
425,000 sq. mi. (1,100,756 sq. km)

LANGUAGES
Amharic (official), Oromiffa, Tigrigna, Sidama, Afar, Somali, Guragigna, Arabic, English

RELIGIONS
Ethiopian Orthodox Christian 45%, Muslim 40–45%, Protestant 5% (2005 est.)

NATIONAL OR ETHNIC COMPOSITION
Oromo 35%, Amhara 30%, Tigre 6.3%, Somali 6%, Sidama 6%, Gurage 4%, Wolaita 4%, Afar 2%, other nationalities 6.7%

DATE OF INDEPENDENCE OR CREATION
An independent Ethiopian state has existed since early times

TYPE OF GOVERNMENT
Parliamentary democracy

TYPE OF STATE
Federal state

TYPE OF LEGISLATURE
Bicameral parliament

DATE OF CONSTITUTION
December 8, 1994

DATE OF LAST AMENDMENT
No amendment

Ethiopia is a parliamentary democracy, with a federal multiparty system of government. The federal government powers are divided into the legislative, executive, and judicial branches. The president of the Federal Democratic Republic of Ethiopia is the head of state, but this function is mostly representation. The highest executive powers rest in the prime minister and the Council of Ministers. The House of People's Representatives is the federal lawmaking organ. The constitution further provides for an independent judiciary.

The constitution specifically recognizes fundamental human rights and freedoms. It also provides that all laws, customary practices, and decisions that contravene its provisions are of no effect. However, certain unconstitutional practices and laws have yet to be replaced to fill in the gaps of the law.

The constitution clearly stipulates that the state and religion are separate. The economic system can be described as a market economy. The armed forces are obliged at all times to obey and respect the constitution.

CONSTITUTIONAL HISTORY

Ethiopia existed as a state since pre-Christian times. The earliest records of Ethiopian constitutional history go back to 500 B.C.E.

Important legal documents existed in traditional Ethiopia, such as the Fetha Negest (a codex of law providing for secular and religious legal provisions), Kibre Negest (which colorfully weaves the legend of the Solomonic dynasty to serve certain politicoreligious needs of the time), and Serate Mengist (which includes administrative and protocol directives useful to the constitutional process). However, there was no written constitution in the modern sense of the term.

The Ge'ez literary language developed during the first century C.E. when the Axumite Empire was converting to Christianity; both processes were important to the constitutional history of Ethiopia. The advent of Islam before the end of the first millennium also had an impact. The warlike Oromo people of the 16th century, with their effective socioeconomic system and powerful warfare, had a major impact on medieval Ethiopia.

The first written constitution was promulgated by Emperor Haile Selassie I in 1931. It was the result of a strong need to modernize and to convince the world of Ethiopia's modernization. The main internal goal of the constitution, which was modeled after the 1898 Meiji Constitution of Japan, was to make the monarchy the superpower vis-à-vis the church and nobility.

Ethiopia's international standing did improve. In 1945, it became a founding member of the United Nations and, in 1962, the headquarters of the Organization of African Unity in Addis Ababa.

The constitution, however, was not found adequate to internal needs despite a revision in 1955. In 1973, the emperor appointed a Constitutional Commission to review the constitution, but the changes they recommended did not have much impact. In September 1974, the Derg overthrew the emperor and established a military regime with socialism as the guiding ideology. *Derg* means committee and is a short name for the committee of military officers, which then ruled the country. While the takeover was originally peaceful, it soon turned violent, and many years of civil war ensued.

A new constitution promulgated in 1987 emphasized human rights; the regime did not follow through in practice. In July 1991, the Tigrean People's Liberation Front overthrew the Derg and established a transitional government based on a Transitional Charter. The charter was replaced by the 1994 constitution, which provides for a parliamentary democracy and incorporates fundamental rights and freedoms.

FORM AND IMPACT OF THE CONSTITUTION

Ethiopia has a written constitution, codified in a single document that is the supreme law of the land. All international agreements ratified by Ethiopia are an integral part of the law of the land. Any other law, customary practice, or decision that contravenes the constitution is considered to be of no effect. However, many laws still need to be amended or replaced to conform to the constitution.

BASIC ORGANIZATIONAL STRUCTURE

Ethiopia is a federal state, which comprises a federal government and member states or regions. Presently, there are nine member states and two special city administrations that are treated as states. The constitution recognizes the right of other nations, nationalities, and peoples (ethnic groups) within Ethiopia to establish their own states, and it provides a process by which they can exercise this right.

The states of the Federal Democratic Republic of Ethiopia have legislative, executive, and judicial competence. All states have their own constitutions, which enjoy legal supremacy. The legislature, called State Council, is always the supreme political body. The state governor, called president, nominates his or her cabinet from among the council or from without and seeks approval by the council. The president is a member of the council by virtue of popular elections every five years. However, the president is not the Speaker of the State Council at the same time. All powers not given expressly to the federal government alone or concurrently to the federal government and the states are reserved to the states. In practice, the states depend on the federal economy.

The state constitution now recognizes a zonal government, which is an intermediary between the states and the local government unit, called Wereda.

LEADING CONSTITUTIONAL PRINCIPLES

Ethiopia is a parliamentary democracy, which provides for the division of powers into the legislative, executive, and judiciary. It is a federal state and a republic based on the rule of law. The constitution further provides for a multiparty system of government.

One unusual and important feature of the constitution is its ethnolinguistic components, which reflect Ethiopian society. The nations, nationalities, and peoples of Ethiopia form the sovereign power of the country. The constitution even recognizes the right to secession, which is considered the ultimate expression of the right to self-determination.

Yet another feature of the constitution is the right to ownership of rural and urban land, which is exclusively vested in the state and in the peoples of Ethiopia. With regard to language policy, the constitution provides for the equality of Ethiopian languages and for their practical application in government. The constitution further provides clearly that the state and religion are separate.

CONSTITUTIONAL BODIES

The federal government is composed of the legislative, executive, and judicial institutions and powers. The bodies established to exercise these powers at the federal level are the two federal houses; the president; the administration, including a prime minister and Council of Ministers; and the Federal Supreme Court.

The Federal Houses

The legislative institutions of the federal government are the two federal houses, known as the House of People's Representatives and the House of Federation. The House of People's Representatives is the highest authority of the federal government. It is responsible directly to the people. The members are elected for a five-year term on the basis of universal suffrage by direct, free, and fair elections held by secret ballot. The constitution further provides that minority nationalities and peoples shall have "at least 20 seats" in a house whose members shall not exceed 550 seats. The most important function of the House of People's Representatives is to issue laws. The House of People's Representatives nominates the president and shares power with the House of Federation to elect him or her.

The House of Federation, on the other hand, is composed of each nation, nationality, and people of Ethiopia. The members are elected for a five-year term through direct or indirect election, depending on the decision of the councils of member states. Larger nations have greater representation; each nation, nationality, and people is represented by at least one member and by one additional member for every 1 million of its population.

One of the main powers of the House of Federation is to interpret the constitution. The Council of Constitutional Inquiry calls issues of constitutional interpretation to the attention of the House of Federation. The council is an advisory body made up of 11 persons composed of the chief justice and vice-chief justice of the Federal Supreme Court, six legal experts nominated by the House of People's Representatives and appointed by the president of the republic, and three persons designated by the House of Federation from among its members. When an issue of constitutional interpretation is submitted to the council, the latter has the power either to remand the case to the concerned court if it finds that there is no need for constitutional interpretation or to submit its recommendations to the House of Federation for a final decision. A dissatisfied party may appeal the decision of the council to the House of Federation.

The President

The House of People's Representatives has the duty of nominating a candidate for president of the republic. The nominee is elected president at a joint session of the two houses, if supported by a two-thirds majority vote. The president of the republic is the head of state and serves a six-year term. He or she cannot be elected for more than two terms. The most important duty of the president is symbolic representation of the nation.

The Federal Administration

The head of the government is the prime minister, who together with the Council of Ministers has the highest executive powers. The prime minister is elected from among the members of the House of People's Representatives for five years. The minister is the chief executive, the chair of the Council of Ministers, and the commander in chief of the armed forces. Members of the Council of Ministers are nominated by the prime minister and appointed by the House of People's Representatives. The council is accountable to both the prime minister and the House of People's Representatives.

The Lawmaking Process

A draft proclamation may be submitted by a member of either the House of People's Representatives or the Council of Ministers. The plenary considers a committee's proposal and, after debating it, votes to approve, amend, or disapprove the draft law. The approved draft proclamation is then sent to the president for signature and published in the official gazette. If the president does not sign the law within 15 days, it takes effect without his or her signature.

The Judiciary

The constitution provides for an independent judiciary. The Federal Supreme Court is the highest court. The two other courts of the federal government, the Federal High Court and the Federal First Instance Court, may be established countrywide or partially by a two-thirds decision of the Council of People's Representatives, if and when deemed necessary, but they have not yet been created.

THE ELECTION PROCESS

Every Ethiopian has the right to vote and be elected on the attainment of 18 years of age.

POLITICAL PARTIES

The constitution provides for a multiparty system. Every Ethiopian has the right to be a member according to his or her own will of a political organization.

CITIZENSHIP

Ethiopian nationality is primarily acquired by birth. That is, any person either of whose parent is Ethiopian can be an Ethiopian national. Foreign nationals may acquire Ethiopian nationality according to ordinary law.

FUNDAMENTAL RIGHTS AND FREEDOMS

The constitution categorizes fundamental rights into human and democratic rights without giving any further explanation. It recognizes that human rights and freedoms are inviolable and inalienable. All federal and state legislative, executive, and judicial organs at all levels are bound to respect and enforce these rights. The constitution provides for the establishment of a human rights commission and an ombudsperson.

The right to equality is provided in Article 25, which guarantees equality before the law and effective protection without discrimination on any grounds. Article 41 enumerates the constitutionally recognized economic, social, and cultural rights, while Articles 43 and 44 provide for the right to development and a clean environment, respectively.

Impact and Functions of Fundamental Rights

The constitution provides that fundamental rights and freedoms shall be interpreted in accordance with the principles of the Universal Declaration of Human Rights, international covenants on human rights, and international instruments adopted by Ethiopia. All international agreements ratified by Ethiopia, including international human rights instruments, are an integral part of the law of the land.

Limitations to Fundamental Rights

Fundamental rights may be limited in the interest of public convenience, protection of democratic rights, public morality, and peace. Fundamental rights may also be limited or even suspended in case of a state of emergency. The Council of Ministers may not, however, suspend or limit the rights to equality; the right to protection against cruel, inhuman, or degrading treatment or punishment; the right of nations, nationalities, and peoples to self-determination, including the right to secession; and the right of nations, nationalities, and peoples to speak, write, and develop their own language and to express, develop, and promote their culture and preserve their history.

ECONOMY

The Ethiopian constitution does not provide for a specific economic system. Every Ethiopian citizen has the right to own private property. However, the constitution specifically provides that land is a common property of the nations, nationalities, and peoples of Ethiopia and is not subject to sale or other means of exchange.

The constitution binds the government to formulate national policies to ensure equal opportunity and equitable distribution of wealth and resources among all Ethiopians.

RELIGION

Freedom of religion and belief is recognized as a fundamental human right. The constitution specifically pro- vides that the state and religion are separate and that there shall be no state religion. Education must also be provided without any religious influence.

MILITARY DEFENSE AND STATE OF EMERGENCY

The constitution requires that the composition of the national armed forces should reflect an equitable representation of the nations, nationalities, and peoples of Ethiopia. The armed forces defend the country and carry out any other responsibilities during a state of emergency, as detailed in the constitution. The minister of defense must be a civilian. The Ethiopian constitution does not provide for mandatory military service.

AMENDMENTS TO THE CONSTITUTION

A formal request for an amendment to the constitution may be made by either the regional or federal legislative bodies. If a regional legislative body has taken the initiative, one-third of the state councils must support the proposal. At the federal level, either of the federal houses may submit a proposal by a two-thirds majority vote.

The constitution provides for stricter requirements for amending provisions dealing with fundamental rights and freedoms. For such an amendment, the federal houses must each support the proposal by a majority vote of two-thirds, in addition to a support by a majority vote of all state councils. On the other hand, amendment of other constitutional provisions requires a two-thirds majority vote in a joint meeting of the federal houses, in addition to support from two-thirds of the states.

PRIMARY SOURCES
The Constitution in Amharic and English, December 8, 1994. Available online. URL: http://www.ethiopianembassy. org/constitution.pdf. Accessed on September 4, 2005.

SECONDARY SOURCES
Fasil Nahum, *Constitution for a Nation of Nations: The Ethiopian Prospect.* Asmara, Eritrea: Red Sea Press, 1997.
Tsegaye Regassa, "State Constitutions in Federal Ethiopia: A Preliminary Observation—A Summary for the Conference on 'Subnational Constitutions and Federalism: Design and Reform' from March 22–27, 2004 in Bellagio, Italy." Available online. URL: http:// camlaw.rutgers.edu/statecon/subpapers/regassa.pdf.

Rakeb Messele Aberra

FIJI ISLANDS

At-a-Glance

OFFICIAL NAME
Republic of the Fiji Islands

CAPITAL
Suva

SIZE OF POPULATION
833,000 (2005 est.)

SIZE OF COUNTRY
7,054 sq. mi. (18,270 sq. km)

LANGUAGES
English, Fijian, and Hindustani

RELIGIONS
Christian (Methodist 37%, Roman Catholic 9%) 52%,
Hindu 38%, Muslim 8%, other 2%
Fijians are mainly Christian; Indians are primarily
Hindu with a Muslim minority.

NATIONAL OR ETHNIC COMPOSITION
Fijian 51%, Fijian Indian 43%, European, other
Pacific Islander, Chinese, and mixed race 6%

DATE OF INDEPENDENCE OR CREATION
1970 (Independence Day is second Monday of
October)

TYPE OF GOVERNMENT
Parliamentary democracy

TYPE OF STATE
Sovereign democratic republic

TYPE OF LEGISLATURE
Bicameral parliament

DATE OF CONSTITUTION
July 10, 1997, in force July 27, 1998

DATE OF LAST AMENDMENT
Constitution Amendment Act 1998

Fiji Islands is a sovereign democratic republic and a member of the Commonwealth. It was granted independence by Great Britain in 1970; after time, a constitution was enacted. In 1990, after two military coups in 1987, a new constitution entered into force. The current constitution was enacted in 1997.

The constitution establishes a British Westminster-style system of parliamentary democracy with a separation of powers. Executive power is vested in the president as head of state, acting on the advice of the prime minister and cabinet. The Bose Levu Vakaturaga (Great Council of Chiefs) has an advisory role and, in practice, wields substantial power. There are separate electoral rolls for different ethnic groups and one open roll. A certain number of seats are reserved for each group, the largest number reserved for Fijian candidates. The constitution contains a bill or rights and establishes a human-rights commission. The military is subject to civil authority in law but in the past has taken independent action. The status of the constitution is fragile, and some of its provision have been ignored during recent and past conflicts.

CONSTITUTIONAL HISTORY

In 1865, the indigenous kingdoms on Fiji Islands formed the Confederacy of Independent Kingdoms of Viti, and the country's first constitution was drawn up and signed by seven paramount chiefs. The arrangement collapsed in 1867, and in 1874, Fiji was ceded to Great Britain as a colony. In 1966, Fiji was granted self-government. The country became independent within the Commonwealth of Nations in 1970, as part of the decolonization process. The constitution was appended to the Fiji Independence Order 1970 (U.K.). In 1987, a military coup was led by Sitiveni Rabuka, who objected to Indian domination in government. Fiji became the Republic of Fiji. In late 1987, a civilian government was formed. In 1990, a new constitution, which weighted government representation in favor of Fijians, was put in force. In 1992, Rabuka became prime minister. In 1997, a new Constitution of the Republic of the Fiji Islands, designed to balance the demands of the two major ethnic groups, was introduced.

In May 2000, the Indo-Fijian prime minister and members of Parliament were taken hostage during a session of Parliament in a civilian-led coup. In the same month, an interim military government was formed and revoked the constitution. In July, it established an interim civilian government. In November 2000, the Court of Appeal upheld a challenge to the validity of the civilian government and ruled that the 1997 constitution remained the supreme law of Fiji. The Interim Civilian Government refused to stand down and was confirmed in place by elections held in September 2001.

FORM AND IMPACT OF THE CONSTITUTION

The written constitution is contained in a single document, which is the supreme law. The constitution contains a "compact"—not enforceable in court—that attempts to balance the competing interests of different ethnic groups with principles of freedom and equality. In interpreting the constitution, the courts are to have regard for international law that is applicable to human rights.

The safeguards provided by the constitution proved ineffective in 2000 when the legitimate government was overthrown and its provisions were bypassed. The current government has also shown a willingness to ignore the constitution. Contrary to the power-sharing provisions in the constitution, the prime minister has refused to allow the next largest party, led by the deposed prime minister, a seat in cabinet. A declaration by the Court of Appeal that this is unconstitutional has been ignored.

BASIC ORGANIZATIONAL STRUCTURE

The constitution establishes a central form of government. Regional government is not dealt with in the constitution but is established by legislation on a divisional basis with separate councils for urban areas.

LEADING CONSTITUTIONAL PRINCIPLES

The constitution establishes a Westminster-style system of parliamentary democracy. There is a division of powers among the executive, legislature, and judiciary. The rule of law is enshrined in the constitution but has not prevailed in recent times when ethnic divisions have proved more powerful than national allegiance. Government is responsible to Parliament.

The 1997 constitution removed the preexisting constitutional arrangements that gave indigenous Fijians control of Parliament but still reserves the largest number of parliamentary seats for Fijians. The constitution provides that Parliament must introduce social justice and affirmative action programs designed to give disadvantaged groups equal access to education and training, land and housing, commerce, and all services of the state.

The constitution establishes a code of conduct for constitutional and statutory officeholders. The code seeks to maintain the integrity of public officers by, for example, preventing conflicts between private interests and public duties. It also establishes the office of ombudsperson to investigate complaints about administrative actions by public authorities or officers.

CONSTITUTIONAL BODIES

The most important bodies provided for in the constitution are the president, the prime minister and cabinet, the House of Representatives, the Senate, the Bose Levu Vakaturaga (Great Council of Chiefs), and the judiciary.

The President

Executive authority of the state is vested in the president, who generally acts on the advice of cabinet. The president's role is largely honorific, but there are some powers that may be exercised on his or her own judgment. The president is appointed by the Bose Levu Vakaturaga, after consultation with the prime minister, for a term of five years. Candidates must be citizens who have had a distinguished career in some aspect of national or international life, whether in the public or private sector, and must by qualified to be a candidate for election to the House of Representatives.

The president holds office for five years and is eligible for reappointment for one further term of five years. The president may be removed from office for inability to perform the functions of office or for misbehavior. Removal is by the Bose Levu Vakaturaga after investigation by a tribunal or, in case of incapacity, a medical board established by the chief justice at the request of the prime minister.

The Prime Minister

The prime minister is appointed by the president on the basis of majority support in the House of Representatives. The president may dismiss the prime minister only if the government lacks the confidence of the House of Representatives. The 1997 constitution abolished the requirement that the prime minister must be an indigenous Fijian.

Ministers and Cabinet

The president appoints and dismisses ministers from among the members of the House of Representatives or Senate on the advice of the prime minister. Ministers have such titles, portfolios, and responsibilities as the prime minister determines from time to time. The prime minister must establish a multiparty cabinet reflecting, as far as possible, the strength of the parties represented in the House of Representatives. More particularly, the prime minister must invite all parties whose membership in the House of Representatives comprises at least 10 percent of the total membership of the house to be represented in the cabinet in proportion to their numbers in the house. The Court of Appeal has declared the current prime minister to be in contravention of this duty to establish a multiparty cabinet. The cabinet is collectively responsible, and a minister is individually responsible to the House of Representatives.

The House of Representatives

There are 71 members of the House of Representatives, elected for a five-year term in single-seat constituencies. There are 23 seats reserved for Fijians, 19 for Indians, one for the Rotuman, and three for other ethnic groups. Twenty-five seats are open to all members of the community. The house is divided into five committees, which are responsible for scrutinizing government administration and examining bills and subordinate legislation.

Senate

The Senate consists of 32 members, appointed by the president on the advice of the Bose Levu Vakaturaga (14 members); the prime minister (nine members); the leader of the opposition (eight members); and the Council of Rotuma (one member). The term of the Senate expires at the same time as that of the House of Representatives unless it is dissolved earlier.

Bose Levu Vakaturaga

The constitution maintains the existence of the Bose Levu Vakaturaga, which was established by the Fijian Affairs Act of 1978, Cap 120. Its membership, functions, operations, and procedures are as prescribed from time to time by or under that act. It is the highest assembly of traditional chiefs and meets at least once a year. Functions of the Bose Levu Vakaturaga include advising the president, making recommendations for the benefit of the Fijian people, and considering draft legislation relating to Fijians.

The Lawmaking Process
The power to make laws vests in a parliament consisting of the president, the House of Representatives, and the Senate. Bills originate in the House of Representatives and must normally pass through both houses and obtain the president's assent.

The Judiciary

Judicial power is vested in the High Court, the Court of Appeal, the Supreme Court, and in any other courts created by law. These include magistrates' courts and a Family Court. The judges are independent of the legislature and the executive.

The common law is developed by the judiciary. In interpreting the constitution, the courts must have regard to the values based on freedom and equality that underlie a democratic society. They must also have regard to the principles of government set out in the compact.

THE ELECTION PROCESS AND POLITICAL PARTICIPATION

All Fiji citizens over the age of 21 and residing in Fiji for two years prior to application are entitled to register to vote. There are five separate rolls of voters: one for Fijians, one for Indians, one for Rotumans, one for other ethnic groups, and an open roll. Only a person who is entitled to register to vote may be nominated as a candidate for election to the House of Representatives. Candidates stand for election by voters on a specific roll and nomination must be by a person registered to vote on that roll.

Elections must be held at least every five years. Voting is compulsory for registered voters. The right to vote and to be a candidate in free and fair elections is a principle of government, set out in the compact.

POLITICAL PARTIES

Fiji Islands has a pluralistic system of political parties. Currently, 10 parties have representatives in the House of Representatives. The right to form and join political parties is a principle of government, set out in the compact.

CITIZENSHIP

Citizenship is acquired by birth in the Fiji Islands, registration, or naturalization. Application for registration may be made by a child born outside the Fiji Islands if either parent is a citizen, by a former citizen who renounces foreign citizenship, or by an adult who marries a citizen and is present in the country for three of five preceding application. Naturalization requires residence in Fiji Islands for five of 10 years preceding application.

FUNDAMENTAL RIGHTS

The constitution of Fiji Islands incorporates a bill of rights. Exceptions to these rights are described in detail. Exceptions include laws that enshrine customary land or fishing rights and chiefly titles or ranks, which prevail over the right to equality.

The constitution expressly states that human rights provisions bind only "the legislative, executive and judicial branches of government" and persons holding public office. It specifically provides that constitutional interpretation is to take account of developments in the understanding of the content and promotion of particular human rights.

The constitution also establishes a human rights commission to educate the public about the nature and content of the bill of rights and to make recommendations to the government about matters affecting compliance with human rights provisions.

Impact and Functions of Fundamental Rights

Human rights provisions are at times in conflict with customary law and practices, which are still strong in the Fiji Islands. In particular, the right to equality conflicts with traditional status and patriarchy. This condition has been recognized in the constitution, which validates laws made for the governance of indigenous communities or for the application of customs to questions relating to land, fishing rights, and chiefly rank, even if they discriminate on the grounds of race or ethnic origin.

Superior courts in the Fiji Islands have generally enforced the fundamental rights provisions, but government has, on occasion, shown itself willing to flout both the provisions and the judgments of the courts enforcing them.

ECONOMY

The constitution does not specify an economic system. However, the compact states that the equitable sharing of economic and commercial power is a principle of government to ensure that all communities benefit from economic progress.

RELIGIOUS COMMUNITIES

Freedom of conscience, religion, and belief is protected by the bill of rights. The right to practice religion freely is also a principle of government, set out in the compact.

Religion and the state are theoretically separate, but the constitution contains an acknowledgment that worship and reverence of God should be the source of good government and leadership. In practice, the Methodist Church is a powerful body.

MILITARY DEFENSE AND STATE OF EMERGENCY

The Fiji Islands military forces are governed by the constitution. The president is the commander in chief and appoints a commander, on the advice of the minister, to exercise military executive command. The commander is responsible for appointments to the forces, disciplinary action, and removal of members. There is no conscription.

Emergency powers are exercised by the president, acting on the advice of the cabinet and subject to limitations imposed by the constitution. On proclaiming a state of emergency, the president must summon the House of Representatives to meet. The house may disallow the proclamation.

AMENDMENTS TO THE CONSTITUTION

A bill for the alteration of the constitution must normally be passed by both houses after being read three times in each and passed by a majority of at least two-thirds of the members of each house on the second and third readings. An interval of at least 60 days must elapse between the second and third readings in the House of Representatives, and each reading must be preceded by full opportunity for debate. The third reading in the House of Representatives must not take place until the relevant standing committee has reported on the bill. These procedures may be bypassed in the case of a bill that is certified by the prime minister to be an urgent measure, pursuant to a resolution passed by at least 53 members of the house. In such cases, the amending bill may be passed by a majority of at least 53 members of the house on its third reading. A bill to alter the distribution of reserved seats in parliament requires a special majority.

PRIMARY SOURCES
Constitution in English. Available online. URL: http://www.paclii.org/fj/legis/num_act/ca1997268/. Accessed on August 30, 2005.

SECONDARY SOURCES
Jennifer Corrin Care, Teresa Newton, and Donald Paterson, Chapter 5. In *Introduction to South Pacific Law*. London: Cavendish Press, 1999.

John Nonggor, "Fiji." In *South Pacific Island Legal Systems*, edited by Michael Ntumy, 26–74. Honolulu: University of Hawaii Press, 1993.

Jennifer Corrin Care

FINLAND

At-a-Glance

OFFICIAL NAME
The Republic of Finland

CAPITAL
Helsinki

POPULATION
5,214,512 (July 2004 est.)

SIZE
130,559 sq. mi. (338,145 sq. km)

LANGUAGES
Finnish and Swedish (national languages), Sami (semiofficial language), Romani and Russian (traditional minority languages, subject to limited positive measures)

RELIGIONS
Evangelical Lutheran 84.2%, no religious affiliation 13.5%, Russian Orthodox 1.1%, other 1.2%

NATIONAL OR ETHNIC COMPOSITION
Finnish speakers 92.0%, Swedish speakers 5.6%, small Sami and Russian-speaking minorities

DATE OF INDEPENDENCE OR CREATION
Province of Sweden until 1809, thereafter autonomous grand duchy within the Russian Empire until 1917, declaration of independence December 6, 1917

TYPE OF GOVERNMENT
Parliamentary democracy

TYPE OF STATE
Unitary state

TYPE OF LEGISLATURE
Unicameral parliament

DATE OF CONSTITUTION
March 1, 2000

DATE OF LAST AMENDMENT
No amendment

Finland is a liberal welfare state. Its constitution is based on democracy, the rule of law, and respect for fundamental rights. It is a unitary state with a republican form of government. Since March 1, 2000, a new constitution is in force. Its Chapter 2 on fundamental rights protects a wide catalogue of fundamental rights, including minority rights and economic and social rights. The practical relevance of the constitution is relatively high in the spheres of legislative power, the operation of the judiciary, and the control of legality.

CONSTITUTIONAL HISTORY

Finland was a province of Sweden until 1809, subject to Swedish constitutional documents. In 1809, and after a war with Russia, Sweden ceded its eastern territories to the Russian Empire. Within the Russian Empire these territories became the autonomous grand duchy of Finland. The representatives of the Four Estates (the nobility, the clergy, the bourgeoisie, and the peasants) were called to the town Porvoo, where Czar Alexander I gave a solemn declaration to respect the religion, the laws, and "the constitution" of Finland. This declaration by the emperor was the starting point for the emergence of Finland as a separate nation and finally, in 1917, as an independent state. While a grand duchy within the Russian Empire, Finland enjoyed considerable autonomy. The Russian Empire was represented through an appointed governor-general, but Finland was nevertheless governed under the Swedish Form of Government Act of 1772 and other Swedish constitutional documents. As a result of this legal framework, Lutheranism was the official religion, and administrative officials and judges had to be Swedish—now interpreted as

Finnish—citizens. Legislative power was exercised jointly by the Four Estates and the monarch. The monarch was now interpreted to refer to the Russian emperor in his capacity of grand duke, and the Four Estates were now interpreted as constituted within the borders of Finland.

Until 1863, the provisions of the Swedish constitution pertaining to the legislative assembly were not relevant in practice, as Swedish laws, supplemented by administrative regulations, were sufficient for running the country, and no new legislation was required. Gradually, however, changes in the economy caused legislation to lag behind. Finally, conditions for revitalizing the legislative assembly ripened; the assembly was called to session by the emperor in 1863 and regularly thereafter.

During the Russian period of 1809–1917, efforts were made to replace the 18th-century Swedish constitutional documents with new ones written specifically for Finland. These efforts were successful in relation to the internal operation of the legislative assembly, which was totally reformed in 1869. Finally, in 1906, this process led to the adoption of a Parliament Act, establishing a unicameral Parliament elected through universal suffrage and replacing the traditional framework of legislative power exercised by the Four Estates. In addition, a separate enactment, of constitutional rank, was adopted in 1905, affording protection to freedom of expression, assembly, and association as fundamental rights.

After the February 1917 revolution in Russia, Finland was on a course to full sovereignty as an independent state. In July 1917, Parliament proclaimed itself sovereign, but it was only after the Bolshevik revolution that an actual declaration of independence was adopted on December 6, 1917. After the Bolsheviks accepted the declaration on December 31, 1917, as Lenin's gesture to demonstrate compliance with the principle of self-determination of peoples, other states recognized the independence of Finland.

After a period of civil war and unrest, a new Constitutional Act was adopted in 1919. This document was largely based on earlier drafts prepared during the Russian period. In the formulation of the final text, the most important controversy concerned the choice between a monarchy and a republic. Largely because of external developments, namely, the defeat of Germany in World War I (1914–18), the decision to invite a German prince to be king was reversed. The Constitutional Act was adapted to include a compromise, a republican form of government with strong and independent presidential powers. In 1928, a new Parliament Act was adopted to replace the 1906.

Between 1919 and 1999, the constitution was subject to several dozen amendments, including gradual reductions in presidential powers, streamlining of the legislative process, and introduction of new institutions into the existing framework. In the fundamental rights reform of 1995, the 1919 narrow catalogue of constitutional rights was replaced with a modern framework heavily influenced by international human rights treaties.

As of March 1, 2000, Finland has a new constitution (Finnish, Suomen Perustuslaki; Swedish, Finlands Grundlag). Although the new constitution builds on the tradition of earlier constitutional documents and the piecemeal amendments made to them, it also includes new elements that establish it as a modern constitutional document of a European parliamentary democracy.

Finland has been a member state of the European Union since 1995.

FORM AND IMPACT OF THE CONSTITUTION

The adoption of a single constitution is a departure from the older tradition in which several enactments with constitutional status existed and operated side by side. While the preceding constitutional instruments were subject to frequent amendment, the new uniform constitution is expected to remain more stable.

International treaties must be separately ratified by Parliament and formally incorporated within Finnish law. All important international treaties, including most human-rights treaties, are formally a part of the Finnish legal order.

One of the first clauses in the constitution, Section 1, Subsection 3, proclaims that Finland works for international cooperation to protect peace and human rights and to develop society. International human-rights norms enjoy semiconstitutional status in various references within the document.

Although the impact of the constitution has been comparatively high in Finland, Finnish courts did not have a mandate to rule on the constitutionality of Parliament's laws until 2000.

BASIC ORGANIZATIONAL STRUCTURE

Finland is a unitary republic, although the autonomous Åland Islands add a dimension of federalism to its organizational structure. The central and regional structures of administration are under the authority of the national government. Local administration is based on self-governing municipalities with their own elected bodies and powers of taxation. Municipalities may form cooperative bodies with one another, thus creating additional regional structures based on self-government.

LEADING CONSTITUTIONAL PRINCIPLES

Chapter 1 of the constitution, entitled Fundamental Provisions, spells out many central constitutional principles.

Finland is sovereign and a republic. The inviolability of human dignity, the freedom and rights of the individual, and the promotion of justice in society are three fundamental values of the constitution. Finland is a liberal welfare state. The principle of internationalism prescribes that Finland participates in joint international efforts to protect peace and human rights and to develop society.

The constitution reflects the principles of democracy, representation through Parliament, and the rule of law. The reference to "the people" in the constitution reflects the idea of a unitary state based on the unity of its people. Nevertheless, the constitution affirms the status of the Sami "as an indigenous people" and uses the expression "Finnish-speaking and Swedish-speaking populations" when addressing the status of the two national languages. Furthermore, the constitution upholds the special status of the Åland Islands, the population of which exercises a high degree of autonomy, including legislative powers, on the basis of the 1991 Autonomy Act. The act cannot be amended without the consent of the Åland Islands legislature.

The constitution incorporates the principles of parliamentarism and the separation of powers. As a logical consequence, it also affirms the principle of the independence of the judiciary.

The Swedish Form of Government Act of 1772 incorporated Christianity as a fundamental constitutional value. While the 2000 constitution of Finland derives its continuity from the 1772 act, the ties between the Finnish state and the Protestant (Lutheran) Church have gradually loosened to the point that religious neutrality is now a constitutional principle.

CONSTITUTIONAL BODIES

The predominant constitutional bodies are Parliament, the Constitutional Law Committee of Parliament, the president and the cabinet, the judiciary, the ombudsperson, and the chancellor of justice.

Parliament

In 1906, Finland became the first country in Europe to introduce universal suffrage for men and women and the first in the world also to accept women as representatives. As did the contemporaneous 1906 Parliament Act, the new 2000 constitution prescribes a unicameral parliament (Finnish, Eduskunta; Swedish, Riksdagen) with 200 members, elected through universal suffrage. Parliamentary elections are based on proportional representation, and the term of Parliament is four years. Parliament exercises legislative power and determines the state budget.

The cabinet, headed by the prime minister, operates at all times under a requirement of confidence of Parliament, which is explicitly tested whenever a new cabinet is appointed. After its appointment, the cabinet must submit its program to a vote of confidence in Parliament.

Parliament may at any time express its nonconfidence in the cabinet, or in an individual minister. Thereafter the president is obligated to dismiss the cabinet or the minister, even if no request is made.

The Constitutional Law Committee of Parliament

One of the traditional, distinctive features of the Finnish constitution is a developed system of preview that evaluates the constitutionality of new legislation. Several actors participate in this preview. The Supreme Court and the Supreme Administrative Court may play a role when the president, before her or his decision to confirm an act adopted by Parliament, seeks an opinion from either or both of these courts. However, the key player in the system of preview is the Constitutional Law Committee of Parliament (Finnish, Eduskunnan perustuslakivaliokunta; Swedish, Riksdagens grundlagsutskott). It has a unique role in protecting constitutional rights, other constitutional provisions, and international human rights treaties.

When questions arise as to the compatibility of a bill with the constitution or with Finland's international human rights obligations, the matter is sent to this committee for an opinion. Composed of politicians, the body receives legal advice from constitutional law experts, typically university professors. The opinions of the committee are generally understood as binding. The committee also rules, with legally binding authority, when the Speaker of Parliament refuses to allow voting on a proposal that she or he considers unconstitutional and the plenary contests the Speaker's decision.

The President and the Cabinet

Traditionally, Finland belonged, together with France, to the category of presidential democracies in which an elected head of state exercised real powers apart from the requirement of parliamentary confidence. In Finland, the president of the republic (Finnish, Tasavallan presidentti; Swedish, Republikens president) used to have rather broad powers in international relations, legislation, and appointment of state officials, as well as power to dissolve Parliament.

Throughout the 1980s and 1990s, amendments gradually moved the system in a more parliamentary direction, and the new constitution moves this transformation further. The role of the prime minister and the cabinet (Finnish, Valtioneuvosto; Swedish, Statsrådet; literal English translation, Council of State) is now central. Given that the cabinet must at all times enjoy the political confidence of Parliament, Finland in effect now has a parliamentary type of government.

Under the new constitution, the president "informs Parliament of the nominee for prime minister" after a process of political negotiation. Thereafter, Parliament elects either the nominee or, through a complicated procedure, another person as prime minister and the president makes the formal appointment to office. The president is constitutionally bound to accept Parliament's choice.

The president is elected by the people through direct elections. If none of the candidates receives a majority of the votes cast, the two candidates who received the most votes compete in a second round. The president must in practice cooperate with the cabinet. All her or his important decisions depend on the presence, preparation, and cooperation of the cabinet. In addition, the chancellor of justice and the parliamentary ombudsperson have the duty to monitor the lawfulness of decisions by the president. The cabinet has the right, and the duty, not to implement unlawful presidential decisions.

The constitution provides that foreign policy is directed by the president of the republic, but even in this field, she or he must act in cooperation with the cabinet. The president makes decisions "in a meeting with the cabinet on the basis of proposals for decisions put forward by the cabinet" (Section 58, Subsection 1). In case of disagreement between the president and the cabinet, the opinion of the latter is decisive in presenting a bill to Parliament, whereas other matters are referred to the cabinet for new preparation.

According to a specific clause in the constitution, Finland's participation in the European Union is in the hands of Parliament and the cabinet. Nevertheless, because of the close linkage between European Union matters and foreign policy and the general role of the president in matters of foreign policy, the president has often participated in meetings of the European Council, with the authorization of the cabinet.

The prime minister has the power to propose early elections, but the president thereafter makes the official decision.

The president, the cabinet, and the ministries all have powers to issue decrees or regulations in their areas of competence. However, the constitution explicitly gives Parliament sole power to issue regulations concerning the rights and obligations of private individuals and other areas that the constitution considers of a legislative nature. The interpretation of this clause has been quite strict. All substantive regulation that affects constitutionally guaranteed fundamental rights must be done in the form of an act of Parliament.

The Lawmaking Process

Constitutionally, individual members of Parliament have equal rights to introduce legislation, but in practice almost all bills are introduced by the cabinet. Such bills and legislative motions by members of Parliament are always sent to one of the standing committees of Parliament, whose report serves as basis for decisions in two plenary readings. In the first reading, each section and subsection of a draft law is approved separately and, if needed, voted upon. In the second reading, which at the earliest takes place on the third day after the conclusion of the first reading, Parliament decides whether to accept the proposal as a whole.

An act adopted by Parliament is submitted to the president for confirmation. If it is not confirmed within three months, it is returned to Parliament for reconsideration. If Parliament again adopts the law without material alterations, it enters into force without presidential confirmation.

The Judiciary

Finland has two parallel sets of courts, ordinary courts that deal with civil and criminal matters and administrative courts. Administrative decisions are subject to appeal, either before a regional administrative court or directly to the Supreme Administrative Court (Finnish, Korkein hallinto-oikeus; Swedish, Högsta förvaltningsdomstolen). The Supreme Court (Finnish, Korkein oikeus; Swedish, Högsta domstolen) is the highest court of appeal in civil and criminal cases. Both supreme courts may handle constitutional issues.

The constitution guarantees the independence of the judiciary. The president appoints tenured judges through a procedure regulated by an act of Parliament; in practice, the judiciary itself takes part in the selection process.

Traditionally, the role of the Finnish judiciary has not been predominant in the protection of the constitution. However, in the 2000 constitution, an explicit provision was introduced according to which a court shall give priority to the constitution in cases in which the application of an act of Parliament would be in "manifest conflict" with the constitution.

The Ombudsperson and the Chancellor of Justice

The parliamentary ombudsperson (Finnish, Eduskunnan oikeusasiamies; Swedish, Riksdagens justitieombudsman) and the chancellor of justice (Finnish, Oikeuskansleri; Swedish, Justitiekansler) play important roles in protecting the rule of law. The former is elected by Parliament, the latter appointed by the president. Both receive complaints from individuals and report annually to Parliament. Both may issue reprimands, propose legislative action, or order criminal charges against any person for unlawful conduct in the exercise of public authority. The chancellor of justice has a special responsibility to oversee the lawfulness of the operation of the cabinet and the president. The ombudsperson, in turn, has in practice a more prominent role in examining complaints from individuals. A distinctive feature of the Finnish system is that the ombudsperson's supervision also extends to the exercise of judicial power.

Charges of unlawful conduct in office against cabinet ministers, the chancellor of justice, the parliamentary ombudsperson, or judges of the two highest courts are dealt with by the High Court of Impeachment (Finnish, Valtakunnanoikeus; Swedish, Riksrätten). The same court also deals with charges against the president in cases of treason, high treason, or a crime against humanity.

Municipal Self-Government

Municipal self-government is protected by the constitution. Although the forms of municipal self-government are determined by an act of Parliament, the constitution secures the right of municipalities to levy municipal taxes and protects municipalities against the executive power by prescribing that only Parliament can establish responsibilities of the municipalities.

The self-government of the Swedish-speaking, demilitarized, and culturally distinctive Åland Islands also enjoys constitutional protection. The arrangement is regulated in a 1991 act, which can be changed only through the constitutional amendment process and only with the consent of the Åland Islands Legislative Assembly.

The constitution also recognizes the linguistic and cultural autonomy of the Sami, the indigenous people of the north. It also grants a certain autonomy to universities and to the Evangelical Lutheran Church.

THE ELECTION PROCESS AND POLITICAL PARTICIPATION

The minimal age for voting is 18 years. Only citizens of Finland are allowed to vote in parliamentary or presidential elections, but no other earlier restrictions remain. For instance, prisoners and persons in mental health institutions are entitled to vote. Foreigners permanently residing in Finland have the right to vote in municipal elections.

Parliamentary elections are based on proportional representation. Of the 200 seats, one is reserved for the Åland Islands, while the remaining 199 are allotted among the 15 electoral districts in proportion to their populations. The parties draw up lists of candidates in each district; the voter casts his or her ballot not for the party but for an individual candidate. The total number of votes cast for a party's candidates in a district decides the number of candidates from the list who are elected The number of votes each candidate receives decides his or her rank on the party list.

This system gives an advantage to the larger political parties. Since party totals are not consolidated on a national basis, a party could win 3 or 4 percent of the vote in every one of the 15 districts (and even a higher percentage in districts with fewer candidates) and still fail to win a single seat in Parliament.

Everyone who can vote and who is not under legal guardianship can be a candidate in parliamentary elections, apart from military officers and certain other officeholders: the chancellor of justice, the parliamentary ombudsperson, a justice of the Supreme Court or the Supreme Administrative Court, and the prosecutor-general.

The rules regarding the right to vote in the presidential elections follow the rules for parliamentary elections. The president's term of office is six years, with only two consecutive terms allowed. If none of the candidates receives a majority of the votes cast, a second round is held between the two leading candidates.

The president must be a native-born Finnish citizen. To nominate a candidate for president, a party must have won at least one member of Parliament in the most recent parliamentary elections. Any group of 20,000 voters may also nominate a presidential candidate.

Municipal council elections are held every four years. The elections are based on the same principles as parliamentary elections. A citizen of another European Union member state is entitled to vote in the elections for the European Parliament provided that the person has reached the age of 18 not later than the day of the election, that his or her municipality of residence is Finland, and that the person has not lost the right to vote in European elections in the country of which he or she is a citizen.

The constitution allows Parliament to present consultative referendums to the voters. Such a referendum was held before Parliament decided to join the European Union.

POLITICAL PARTIES

There are currently eight political parties represented in Parliament. The state provides funding to the parties in proportion to the number of seats they have in Parliament. Political parties operate both under the 1989 Associations Act and under a separate 1969 Act on Political Parties. If an association wishes to be included in the list of registered political parties, it must collect 5,000 signed declarations of support by persons who are entitled to vote in parliamentary elections. A registered political party loses this status if it does not win at least one seat in Parliament in two consecutive elections. If it wishes to run again, it must once again collect 5,000 membership cards. Once registered, a party may nominate candidates in all parts of the country, irrespective of where its members reside.

A political party can be dissolved by a judicial decision through the application of the relevant provisions of the Associations Act. Largely because of earlier constitutional provisions that made it difficult to carry out a legislative program with only a narrow majority in Parliament, Finland has developed a political culture of broad coalitions. For instance, it is not unthinkable that the political Right (the Coalition Party), the Left (the Social Democratic Party and the Left Alliance), and certain centrist forces (the Green Party and the Swedish People's Party) share governmental power. The three major political parties are the Center Party, the Social Democratic Party, and the Coalition Party. Usually, one of these is in opposition and two cooperate in the cabinet, together with some of the smaller parties.

CITIZENSHIP

The starting point for the rules on citizenship is *ius sanguinis:* Everyone born of two Finnish parents, of a Finnish mother, or of a Finnish father married to the child's mother becomes a Finnish citizen. In addition, a child born in Finland of any parents who does not become a citizen of another country becomes a Finnish citizen. A foreigner may be granted Finnish citizenship after living in Finland for at least six years. The applicant must have satisfactory oral and written skills in either Finnish or Swedish or analogous skills in sign language. The 2003 Citizenship Act makes dual nationality more easily obtained than the previous one.

As a rule, the constitution since 1995 guarantees constitutional rights irrespective of Finnish citizenship, with the exceptions of freedom of movement across borders and voting rights in national elections. The president of the republic must be a native-born Finnish citizen, and all members of the cabinet must be Finnish citizens. In addition, certain public offices may be reserved to Finnish citizens by an act of Parliament. Only Finnish citizens have a duty to participate in national defense.

FUNDAMENTAL RIGHTS

The constitutional protection of fundamental rights includes both the traditional civil and political rights and economic, social, cultural, and environmental rights. The constitution guarantees rights such as equality and nondiscrimination; the right to life, personal liberty, and integrity; and the right to private life, honor, home, data protection, confidentiality of communication, freedom of religion and conscience, freedom of expression, assembly and association, and protection of property. Also protected is the right to education, minority linguistic rights, the right of minorities to enjoy and develop their own culture, the right to work and the freedom to engage in commercial activity, the right to indispensable subsistence and care, the right to social security and services, the right to housing, and environmental rights and responsibilities. Finland formally incorporates all major human rights treaties in its domestic law.

The Finnish constitution's emphasis on minority rights and the bilinguality of the nation make it distinctive. Finnish and Swedish are the two national languages, and certain individual rights arise from that fact. The Sami, as an indigenous people, as well as the Roma and other groups, have the right to maintain and develop their own language and culture. The Sami have the right to use the Sami language in their dealings with administrative and judicial authorities in matters that emanate from within the so-called Sami homeland (the three northernmost municipalities and a large part of the Sodankylä municipality). In this sense, Sami can be described as a third official language.

Impact and Functions of Fundamental Rights

Constitutional rights are binding with respect to any exercise of public authority, whether legislative, administrative, judicial, or municipal. Furthermore, it is a con-

stitutional duty of all public authorities "to guarantee" the realization of constitutional rights and human rights. This rule forms a constitutional basis for the indirect horizontal effect of constitutional rights: They are not immediately binding on private subjects, but the public authorities must secure that fundamental rights are not violated by private subjects.

Since 1995, the Finnish courts have begun actively to enforce certain of the economic and social rights provisions of the constitution. The Supreme Administrative Court has, on some occasions, based its ruling in social assistance cases on the constitution, which prescribes an individual right to social assistance for those in need. In another ruling, the same court referred to the minority rights clause as grounds to pay proper attention to the higher clothing costs of a Roma woman in determining her right to social assistance. One of the most important Finnish cases in the field of economic and social rights concerned a municipality's having a legal obligation to arrange an opportunity for a long-term-unemployed person to work for six months. As the municipality had failed to comply with this duty, it was ordered to pay damages.

Limitations to Fundamental Rights

There is no uniform procedure in the constitution related to restrictions on fundamental rights, apart from derogations (limitations) during a state of emergency. Some of the rights clauses specifically allow Parliament to pass restrictions. For example, Parliament may pass laws barring people from leaving the country during legal proceedings or as a way to escape punishment or to avoid the duty of national defense.

No restriction that extends to the core of a constitutional right may be made through an ordinary act of Parliament. Restrictions must comply with the requirement of proportionality—a restriction may not extend further than what is justified, taking into account the weight of the societal interest in relation to the right being restricted.

ECONOMY

Since World War II, Finland has developed itself as a Nordic welfare state while upholding the constitutional protection of the right of private property. Everyone has the right to earn his or her livelihood by the employment, occupation, or commercial activity of his or her choice. The provision has been interpreted as setting constitutional limits to licensing requirements for businesses.

The idea of a welfare state has been constitutionalized. Everyone is guaranteed the right to basic subsistence in the event of unemployment, illness, and disability and during old age as well as at the birth of a child or the loss of a provider. The clause has been understood as barring any moves toward a totally insurance-based system of social security. For example, the constitution guarantees a basic-subsistence-level old-age pension for persons who were never gainfully occupied and secures that unemployed persons receive unemployment benefits until they either obtain work or become eligible for another form of basic-subsistence-level support.

RELIGIOUS COMMUNITIES

Although freedom of religion is one of the fundamental rights protected by the constitution, historically the Evangelical Lutheran Church has been in the position of a state church. Since the time that Finland was an autonomous part of the Russian Empire, the Orthodox Christian Church has also enjoyed official status through specific legislation. Gradual steps have been taken toward religious neutrality of the state, and the 2000 constitution reflects this development. The old connection between the Lutheran Church and the constitution remains visible, however.

The constitution notes that the Church Act governs the organization and administration of the Evangelical Lutheran Church. The special legislative procedure for changing this act is set forth in the act itself.

Both the Lutheran and Orthodox Churches receive tax revenues through the state, which collects church taxes from the members of these communities. In addition, they enjoy a certain percentage of taxes paid by juridical persons, such as business corporations. Other religious communities depend on voluntary contributions by their members.

The 2003 Freedom of Religion Act removed certain restrictions that previously governed the establishment of new religious communities. Religious communities are recognized as a special category of juridical persons, different from ordinary associations governed by the Associations Act.

The rules on religious education in public schools have been amended. Schools still teach the religion of the majority of the pupils of a school—in practice always Lutheran Christianity—but no longer with the aim of strengthening the belief of the pupils, only of providing knowledge of the religion. Nevertheless, pupils who do not belong to the Evangelical Lutheran Church are fully exempted from this education. Pupils thus exempted receive teaching in their own religion, either in the school or within their community or in ethics.

MILITARY DEFENSE AND STATE OF EMERGENCY

The president decides on matters of war and peace with the consent of Parliament. He or she also decides, on the proposal of the cabinet, whether to mobilize the defense forces. If Parliament is not in session at that moment, it is summoned at once. Thus, civilian state organs retain power during armed conflict.

The president of the republic is the commander in chief of the defense forces. However, on the proposal of the cabinet, the president may relinquish this task to another Finnish citizen, that is, to a military officer. The primacy of civilian rule is reflected in the fact that the president appoints the officers of the defense forces.

Finland retains conscription as the foundation of its system of defense. Every Finnish citizen is obligated to participate or assist in national defense, as provided by law. The Conscription Act of 1950 prescribes mandatory military service for men. Women may perform voluntary military service. Persons who have the right of domicile of the Åland Islands are exempt from conscription.

The constitution provides for the right to exemption, on grounds of conscience. The term of the alternative civilian service is 395 days, compared with either 180, 270, or 362 days for regular military service.

The constitution allows for certain derogations (limitations) of constitutional rights in situations of emergency. Such derogations must be temporary, necessary, and compatible with Finland's international obligations concerning human rights. Rights that according to international law are nonderogable, such as the right to life, the prohibition against torture and any other form of inhuman treatment, and the requirements of legality and nonretroactivity of criminal law, are also nonderogable under the constitution. Derogations to derogable rights are permitted only in the case of an armed attack against Finland or similar emergency.

AMENDMENTS TO THE CONSTITUTION

There are two alternative methods for amending the constitution. An ordinary amendment proposal, once passed by a majority of the votes cast in Parliament, is left in abeyance until a new Parliament is elected. It then requires a second vote, this time with a majority of two-thirds of the votes cast. Alternatively, Parliament may, by five-sixths of the votes cast, declare an amendment proposal to be urgent. It can then be adopted by the usual two-thirds vote. As referendums are only of consultative nature, they do not play a role in the procedure for amending the constitution.

Finnish constitutional law provides for exceptive enactments—laws that contradict the constitution and can only be passed by using the same procedures required for amending the constitution. This kind of law was developed when the country was an autonomous grand duchy within the Russian Empire (1809–1917). The old pre-1809 Swedish constitution was still in effect, and there was no way to amend it, other than by exceptive enactments. After independence, the institution continued to be used, this time to amend the 1919 Constitution Act. The special procedure has been used more than 1,000 times, and many of the exceptions are permanent in nature. However, since the fundamental rights reform of 1995 and the adoption of the new constitution in 1999, there has been a strong tendency to avoid the use of exceptive enactments. The new constitution states that any such exception must be of a "limited" nature.

Exceptive enactments have been used to incorporate international treaties that are in conflict with the constitution. For example, Finland's membership in the European Union was decided by a majority of two-thirds in Parliament, without the need to amend the constitution itself.

PRIMARY SOURCES

Constitution in English. Available online. URL: http://www.om.fi/uploads/54begu60narbnv_1.pdf. Accessed on September 5, 2005. (The official text of the constitution was published in Finnish and Swedish in the statute collection, Suomen Säädöskokoelma, No. 731 of 1999. The text has been reprinted in English, Finnish, and Swedish.)

Suomen Perustuslaki. Helsinki, 2000.
Finlands Grundlag. Helsinki, 2000.
Electronic versions can be obtained at the Web site of the Ministry of Justice (Finnish, Swedish, Sami, English, German, French, Spanish). Available online. URL: http://www.om.fi/21910.htm. Accessed on August 20, 2005.

SECONDARY SOURCES

Jaakko Nousiainen, "The Finnish System of Government: From a Mixed Constitution to Parliamentarism." Available online. URL: http://www.om.fi/3344.htm. Accessed on September 28, 2005.
Martin Scheinin, "Constitutional Law and Human Rights." In *An Introduction to Finnish Law,* edited by Juha Pöyhönen. Helsinki: Kauppakaari, 2002: 31–57.

Martin Scheinin

FRANCE

At-a-Glance

OFFICIAL NAME
French Republic

CAPITAL
Paris

POPULATION
61,005,600 including overseas territories (2005 est.)

SIZE
342,686 sq. mi. (551,500 sq. km)

LANGUAGES
French

RELIGIONS
Catholic 83–88%, Muslim 5–10%, Protestant 2%,
Jewish 1%, unaffiliated or other 4%

NATIONAL OR ETHNIC COMPOSITION
French 97.65%, Portuguese 0.92%, Algerian 0.88%,
Italian 0.32%, Belgian 0.11%, German 0.12%

DATE OF INDEPENDENCE OR CREATION
Clovis (481–511 C.E.), king of the Franks

TYPE OF GOVERNMENT
Semipresidential

TYPE OF STATE
Decentralized unitary state

TYPE OF LEGISLATURE
Bicameral parliament

DATE OF CONSTITUTION
October 4, 1958

DATE OF LAST AMENDMENT
March 1, 2005

France is a parliamentary and presidential democracy based on the rule of law, with a clear division between the executive and legislative powers. There also is a judiciary authority. France has been a unitary state; decentralization has increased since the constitutional law of March 28, 2003. The constitution guarantees human rights, per the 1789 Declaration of the Rights of Man and of the Citizen, which has constitutional force. The constitution must be respected by the public authorities. The Constitutional Council ensures this respect, although individuals cannot appeal to it. The council has seen its role strengthened since the 1970s, although it is still not a true Supreme Court.

The president is head of state but also exercises important executive powers. The prime minister's powers depend largely on the will of the president. In a period of "cohabitation" (when the president and the prime minister belong to opposing political sides), the prime minister makes use of all the powers attributed to this office by the constitution. In this case, the prime minister and not the president directs the politics of the nation.

The prime minister is responsible only to the Assemblée Nationale, the Parliament, and not to the president. In practice, the system is developing from a semipresidential one to a parliamentary government. The elections for Parliament are by secret, free, equal, general, and direct ballot, contested by multiple political parties.

Religious freedom is guaranteed, and church and state are separated. The economic system can be described as a market economy with a certain degree of government intervention that is becoming blurred under the influence of European integration. The military is by law and in fact subordinate to civil government.

France is a member of the United Nations and a permanent member of its Security Council. It also is member of the North Atlantic Treaty Organization (NATO).

CONSTITUTIONAL HISTORY

France is a political entity that emerged gradually in history. In the fifth century C.E., the Franks, a Germanic tribe, settled in the territories of today's France. The Frankish king, Charles the Great, or Charlemagne (742–814), established a European empire, which was divided in the 843 Treaty of Verdun. The western part of the Frankish realm (Francia occidentalis) eventually became France.

After the decline of Charles's dynasty, Hugh Capet became king of France in 987. The monarchy rapidly became hereditary, but in the beginning, the Capetian dynasty remained weak against powerful feudal lords. Soon, however, the Capetian monarchy became stronger by securing the help of the church and by progressively enlarging its property. Philippe IV the Fair defended the independence of the Crown against the pope and convoked the first Estates General (1302), the representative body of the nobility. The growth of Capetian power was, however, halted in its progress by the Hundred Years' War (1337–1453).

In the 16th century, religious wars between Catholics and Calvinists produced new crises. King Henry IV reestablished religious peace by the 1598 Edict of Nantes and restored royal authority. The Frondes, a series of civil disturbances that lasted from 1648 to 1653, were suppressed by King Louis XIII, who, assisted by Cardinal Richelieu, established an absolutist monarchy. His successor, King Louis XIV, was the absolute ruler of France.

Enlightenment philosophy combined with bad harvests and financial crises forced King Louis XVI to convoke the Estates General in 1789. This resulted in the French Revolution and the end of the *ancien régime*, as the traditional monarchy was called. The Declaration of the Rights of Man and the Citizen was proclaimed in 1789. From then on, there were no more subjects, only citizens. Jews and Protestants became citizens with equal rights. Feudal rights were abolished on August 4, 1789, and civil equality was proclaimed. The constitution of September 3, 1791, introduced a constitutional monarchy, in which the king had only limited powers. In 1792, a decree abolished the monarchy altogether and proclaimed Year I of the Republic. From then on, and particularly during the 19th century, France experienced long years of constitutional instability.

The constitution of the Year I (June 24, 1793) was inspired by democracy and decentralization; it was, however, never implemented. The leading revolutionary, Robespierre, presided over the Reign of Terror that lasted until 1794. A new constitution passed in 1795 only lasted until 1799, when General Napoléon Bonaparte took power in a coup d'état and imposed the 1799 constitution. Strengthened by military victories, Napoléon transformed the regime into an empire through the 1804 constitution, which was ratified by plebiscite. The empire centralized administration and introduced an important series of laws (Civil Code, Penal Code, etc.) that are extant today. Military defeats led to Napoléon's fall in 1815.

The Restoration (1814–30) saw the birth of a parliamentary regime. The 1814 Constitutional Charter, imposed by King Louis XVIII, established a monarchy checked by parliament. The Charter of 1830, negotiated between the king and parliament, installed the July Monarchy (1830–48). It instituted a parliamentary monarchy founded on national sovereignty. The 1848 revolution put an end to this regime. A provisional government convoked a constituent assembly that adopted the 1848 constitution, forming the Second Republic.

After a coup d'état in 1851, the princely president, Louis-Napoléon Bonaparte, won the support of the French people to adopt a constitution in 1852 that installed the Second Empire. Defeat in the Franco-Prussian War of 1870 put an end to this empire.

After a transition period, the Third Republic gradually took shape. The constitutional laws of 1873–75 organized a parliamentary regime. The Third Republic passed laws that strengthened public freedoms: freedom of the press, freedom of assembly and of association, union rights, separation of church and state, and secular and compulsory education.

After liberation from German occupation in World War II (1939–45), the Fourth Republic was established. Voting rights for women were acknowledged in 1944 by an ordinance of General de Gaulle. The 1946 constitution opened with a preamble affirming the principles of the Declaration of 1789, as well as proclaiming new economic and social rights, especially the recognition of the right to strike.

The Algerian crisis that marked the end of French colonialism caused the fall of the Fourth Republic. The new 1958 constitution founded the Fifth Republic. Created under the inspiration of General de Gaulle, it revived the authority of the executive and especially of the president of the republic.

The French republic is a founding member of the European Union. It participates in the process of European integration and tries to develop peace, stability, and prosperity all over the world. France, along with the other member states, transfers a degree of sovereignty to the union, whose law has increasing impact on its member states.

FORM AND IMPACT OF THE CONSTITUTION

France has a written constitution—the Constitution of October 4, 1958, or Constitution of the Fifth Republic. It incorporates the preamble of the 1946 Constitution of the Fourth Republic as well as the 1789 Human Rights Declaration. These different texts have constitutional force and are ranked above ordinary laws. International law must be in conformity with the constitution in order to be applicable in France. European law also prevails over ordinary laws. If European law is in contradiction with the constitution, the constitution must be amended to make it applicable.

The French constitution is binding on all the branches of state power, and it is the source of fundamental principles of constitutional value. In principle, laws must be in conformity with the constitution, but appeals to the Constitutional Council, which can declare laws unconstitutional, were limited in the past. Since 1971, the Constitutional Council has bit by bit confirmed its jurisdiction and has developed a certain number of fundamental principles that pervade all branches of law. It particularly monitors respect for fundamental rights.

BASIC ORGANIZATIONAL STRUCTURES

France is a decentralized unitary state. It is divided into regions, departments, *arrondissements,* cantons, and communities. The regions, departments, and communities are territorial entities whose existence and powers are recognized by the constitution. The entities are very different in size and population. Until recently their structure was uniform (apart from that of the overseas territories), but recent constitutional amendments have given them room for greater diversity.

A strong centralism has been characteristic of France since the days of the Capetian monarchy. The movement toward decentralization did not really begin until the 1960s, and the process has not been finalized because problems remain. Among these problems is the insufficient financial autonomy of the local communities, despite some progress, at least on paper. Another problem is that the size of the regions is very unequal; many of them are considerably smaller than the European average: There are more than 36,700 communities for a population of just above 60 million.

LEADING CONSTITUTIONAL PRINCIPLES

The French system of government is midway between a parliamentary and a presidential regime. The Fifth Republic of 1958 was meant to be a rationalized parliamentary system. However, the introduction in 1962 of presidential elections by universal suffrage and the operational style of President de Gaulle made it more like a presidential system.

There is a division between the executive and the legislative powers with a certain predominance of the executive. The independence of the judicial power was strengthened by a number of constitutional reforms, as were the powers of the Constitutional Council.

The French constitutional system is based on a number of constitutional principles: France is a democracy, a decentralized unitary state, a republic, a state with strong social security and the rule of law. The preamble of the constitution of October 27, 1946, carried over into the constitution of 1958, proclaims a certain number of social rights: the right to strike, union rights, the right to work and to vocational training, health protection, and rights

of workers in old age. It recognizes the equal rights of women and proclaims that "every human being without difference of race, religion or belief, has inalienable and holy rights." The right to asylum is recognized.

France is a representative democracy. The people elect representatives to Parliament who decide on political questions. Direct democracy, whereby the people decide directly, exists on the national level.

The principle of republican government is underlined in Article 89 of the constitution, which states that "the republican form of government shall not be the object of an amendment." Freedoms are guaranteed by the constitution as well as by the Constitutional Council.

The basic structural principles are found in Article 1: "France shall be an indivisible, secular, democratic, and social republic. It shall ensure the equality of all citizens before the law, without distinction of origin, race or religion. It shall respect all beliefs."

The republic participates in the European communities and in the European Union and agrees to transfer those powers necessary for the establishment of a European economic and monetary union.

CONSTITUTIONAL BODIES

The main organs of the constitution are the president of the republic; the executive administration, consisting of a prime minister and Council of Ministers; the Parliament, in which the National Assembly is largely predominant (the Senate, which represents the territorial entities, has a clearly less important role); and the judiciary, which includes the Constitutional Council.

The President of the Republic

The president of the republic is the head of state. According to Article 8, the president has the power to nominate the prime minister. Political practice allows the president to depose the prime minister if the two are members of the same political camp. The president does not have this power during periods of "cohabitation" in which they belong to rival camps.

The president of the republic must ensure that the constitution is observed. The president is the guarantor of national independence, territorial integrity, and observance of treaties.

The president is elected for a period of five years by direct and universal suffrage and can be reelected indefinitely. The president approves legislation. He or she has 15 days either to sign a law, submit it to the Constitutional Council for review, or demand a second reading of the law; the latter course is rarely taken. The president can refuse to sign ordinances; this sometimes does occur in periods of cohabitation.

The president represents France in international affairs alone in normal political times, together with the prime minister in periods of cohabitation. The president presides over the Council of Ministers and signs its decrees, accredits ambassadors, is commander in chief of the armed forces, and has the right of pardon. The president guarantees the independence of the judiciary.

These powers depend on countersignature—they can only be exercised if the prime minister approves. Other important powers of the president do not depend on countersignature. These powers differentiate the French president from heads of state in other parliamentary democracies. Besides appointing the prime minister, the president has the power to dissolve the National Assembly, has full powers in case of emergency, and has access to the Constitutional Council, three of whose members he or she appoints. The president may also, on a proposal of the Council of Ministers or on a joint motion of the two chambers of the legislature, submit to a referendum any bill that deals with certain topics, such as the organization of public authorities.

The president cannot be charged with criminal offenses while in office except high treason, which is defined in the constitution. In that case, both chambers of the legislature must approve identical charges by a majority vote of their members. In case of vacancy of the office, the president of the Senate exercises the president's functions. Past presidents belong to the Constitutional Council for life.

The Executive Administration

According to Article 20 of the constitution, the administration (prime minister and cabinet) determines and conducts the policy of the nation. It is in charge of the executive and the armed forces. The prime minister directs its actions. In exceptional cases, the prime minister can also represent the president of the republic in presiding over the Council of Ministers if there are both an explicit delegation and a fixed agenda.

The prime minister is responsible for national defense, ensures the execution of the law, and appoints civil and military officers except those appointed by the head of state. The prime minister can delegate certain of these powers to cabinet ministers.

When the two heads of the executive belong to the same political camp, the president can replace the prime minister, who thus appears as a lieutenant or chief of staff charged with implementation of policy. In this system, the prime minister can be removed by the president as well as by the National Assembly. In practice, the risk of being replaced is small because there has almost always been a stable political majority and the prime minister is usually the leader of that bloc. In a period of cohabitation, however, the president and the prime minister are political adversaries. The prime minister conducts a policy in opposition to that of the president, except, usually in matters of foreign affairs and defense.

In times of cohabitation, the president cannot remove the prime minister, who is in that case responsible only to the National Assembly. In fact, in such a situation, the president has to choose the prime minister from among the opposition. The cabinet ministers are appointed by the president of the republic on the advice of the prime minister. They can be removed in the same way. Below the cabinet ministers are secretaries of state. Their number varies between 30 and 40, depending on the administration.

The constitution allows for cabinet responsibility to the president, but it only institutionalizes its responsibility to the National Assembly. Article 49 requires the prime minister to present the administration's program before the National Assembly, which can vote its confidence by a simple majority. The same article gives the assembly the power of censure. A censure motion can be proposed by one-tenth of the members. After a reflection period of 48 hours, members can adopt the motion by an absolute majority. The administration can also test its political strength by offering its own "provoked motion of censure." If a motion of censure passes, the administration must resign.

Ministers cannot simultaneously serve in Parliament and engage in any other professional activity. A member of Parliament who becomes a cabinet minister is replaced by his or her alternate.

The National Assembly

The National Assembly is the central representative organ of the people on the national level. As a legislative body, it cooperates with other constitutional organs, in particular with the Senate, which represents the local communities. The National Assembly can express its confidence in the administration or can remove it by a vote of censure. Assembly members have the right to pose oral or written questions to the administration. Commissions of inquiry about the functioning of the administration can be installed.

Votes in the assembly are generally taken by the simple majority of the members present. However, certain decisions need an absolute majority, such as the first two rounds in the election of the assembly president or a motion of censure. Decisions of particular importance require a stronger majority of three-fifths or, alternatively, a national referendum.

Members of Parliament are not legally obligated to follow the instructions of their political party; they are only bound by their conscience. They are also not bound by their electors: "All imperative mandate is void" (Article 27). Each member is seen to represent the whole nation and not just the constituency where he or she was elected. In practice, the members depend on their parties in ways that narrow their maneuvering space, especially if they wish to be nominated in future elections.

The members of Parliament enjoy certain rights, to ensure their independence. No member can be searched, questioned, arrested, imprisoned, or sentenced because of opinions expressed or votes casts in exercising his or her functions. No member is subject to criminal or correctional sanctions, arrests, or any other deprivation of liberty except under the authorization of the office of the assembly of which he or she is a member—unless the member is caught in a criminal act. Detention, prosecution, or any measures depriving of liberty or limiting liberty of a member of Parliament are suspended for the duration of his or her sessions if the assembly so requires.

The National Assembly consists of 577 deputies. The normal duration of the legislative period is five years, but it may be dissolved before that time. The deputies are elected by universal, direct, free, equal, and secret suffrage. The deputies receive substantial remuneration in addition to funds for expenses and payment of parliamentary assistants and a secretariat. Parliament assembles for one ordinary session each year, beginning the first working day of October and ending the last working day of June. The president of the republic can convoke an extraordinary session at the request of the prime minister or the majority of members of the National Assembly. The members of the administration have the right to address either chamber. The sessions of the two assemblies are public.

The Lawmaking Process

The right to initiate a bill belongs to the members of Parliament and to the prime minister. In practice, the majority of adopted laws have their origin as bills of law submitted by the cabinet.

Article 37 deals with regulations, which do not belong to the field of law. The administration can also issue ordinances when Parliament authorizes it to do so.

A bill of law is debated in the chamber where it was introduced, using the text drawn up by the administration. The other chamber debates the text passed by the originating chamber. In principle, texts are sent to one of the six permanent committees. The two chambers must agree on an identical text. In case of disagreement, the prime minister calls a mixed commission of seven deputies and seven senators. If this commission does not reach a compromise, the administration can ask the National Assembly to decide definitively. However, there is a special regime for organic laws—those that expand upon the constitution. Organic laws require a period of reflection of 15 days, and they must be submitted for review by the Constitutional Council (submission is optional for ordinary laws). Once adopted, the law must be signed by the prime minister and by the cabinet ministers concerned. The president of the republic has 15 days to publish them.

The Senate

The Senate represents the territorial entities of the republic. French residents abroad are also represented by the Senate. The Senate is called an Upper Chamber and has fewer powers than the National Assembly. It cannot remove the administration. Even in legislation, the prime minister can give the last say to the National Assembly, which can pass a law without the consent of the Senate. Originally created to assist the president of the republic and his or her assembly majority, it has often found itself in the opposition. The two chambers are equal in their powers to amend the constitution: Constitutional amendments require the consent of the Senate, except if passed by national referendum.

The Senate is elected in a universal and indirect ballot. The senators, therefore, are not elected directly by the people. The electoral body is essentially composed of locally elected representatives.

The Judiciary

It is the president of the republic who guarantees the constitution, with the help of the Superior Council of Magistracy. The latter is made up of two branches, one comprising judges, the other public prosecutors.

For historical reasons, there are two branches of jurisdiction in France: the administrative jurisdiction, which rules on administrative matters, and the judicial branch, which resolves litigation between private individuals and cases submitted by the public authorities to the Superior Council of the Magistracy. The administrative branch comprises the first instance administrative tribunals, the administrative appeal courts, and in final resort the Council of State. The judicial branch consists of first instance cantonal courts and district courts, courts of appeal, and in final resorts the Court of Cassation. There are specialized jurisdictions as well: labor courts, commercial courts, and, in penal matters, police tribunals for offenses, and special courts for crimes and misdemeanors.

The 1958 constitution established a Constitutional Council. It is not a true supreme court, but its decisions are not subject to any further legal remedy. The decisions of the Constitutional Council are binding for all public authorities. The council has nine members with a term of nine years that cannot be renewed. Every three years one-third of the members are replaced. Three members are appointed by the president of the republic, three by the president of the National Assembly, and three by the president of the Senate. Former presidents of the republic are members for life. The president of the Constitutional Council is appointed by the president of the republic and has the decisive vote in case of ties.

The Constitutional Council above all decides on the constitutionality of laws. Laws can be submitted to the court before their promulgation by the president of the republic, the prime minister, the president of the National Assembly, the president of the Senate, 60 deputies, or 60 senators. The council has one month to make a decision, eight days in case of urgency. A provision declared unconstitutional must not be promulgated or applied.

The jurisprudence of the Constitutional Council has gradually consolidated. In the early days of the Fifth Republic, the council exercised great restraint because of a French tradition hostile to constitutional control. More recently it has become a defender of public freedoms by giving constitutional force to the principled language of the preamble to the constitution.

The Constitutional Council functions also as an election court for presidential and parliamentary elections and referendums.

THE ELECTION PROCESS AND POLITICAL PARTICIPATION

Every French citizen above the age of 18 years has the right to vote. He or she can lose this right for a limited period because of certain crimes or misdemeanors, for example, electoral fraud. One can stand for election at age 18 in general or age 23 for deputies to the National Assembly and the president of the republic.

The citizens of the European Union have the right to vote and be elected in local elections in the member state where they reside.

Referendums can be initiated by the president on the recommendation of the cabinet on matters that affect the functioning of government institutions. Referendums are also possible on alterations of French territory and on amendments of the constitution.

Parliamentary Elections

The deputies are elected by universal, direct majority suffrage. The costs of the electoral campaign are partially reimbursed under certain conditions, as long as the candidate submits full accounts. Each political party that receives public aid must also offer an equal number of women and men candidates, with no less deviation than 2 percent. If the deviation is higher, the public aid is reduced.

Senators are elected by indirect universal suffrage. Candidates must reach the age of at least 35 years.

POLITICAL PARTIES

France has always enjoyed a large number of political parties competing for votes. The constitution recognizes political parties in Article 4 as contributing to the exercise of suffrage. They emerge and exercise their activities freely, as long as they respect national sovereignty and democracy. There is a system of public financing of political parties, based largely on the number of votes obtained in assembly elections, on condition of their being obtained in at least 50 constituencies.

Political parties under the Fifth Republic are organized in a system of two great coalitions, one on the Right and one on the Left, alternating in power. On the Right are the Union for a Popular Movement (UMP) and the Union for French Democracy (UDF), and on the Left the Socialist Party (PS), the Communist Party (PC), and the environmentalists (Les Verts). The extreme Right (National Front) and the extreme Left (Workers Fight; Revolutionary Communist League) also represent a sizable number of voters.

CITIZENSHIP

French citizenship is acquired by birth and based on the principle of *ius sanguinis*. This means that a child acquires French citizenship if one of his or her parents is a French national, even if he or she is not born in France. *Ius soli* also applies: Children born in France whose parents are not French can become French on application.

FUNDAMENTAL RIGHTS

The 1958 constitution does not directly contain a catalogue of fundamental rights, but its preamble refers to the 1789 Human Rights Declaration and to the preamble of the 1946 constitution. Both have constitutional rank, as the Constitutional Council recognized in its landmark decision of July 16, 1971. The preamble of the 1946 constitution enumerates the political, economic, and social principles "particularly necessary in our times," such as the right to strike and union rights. The 1789 Declaration of the Rights of Man and the Citizen expresses traditional principles such as individual freedom, equality before the law, nonretroactivity of penal laws, and the right of property (inviolable and sacred). The 1789 principles are sometimes in opposition to the socially inspired principles of 1946. It is up to the Constitutional Council to reconcile the two.

A certain number of rights and freedoms are guaranteed in the 1958 constitution itself. Article 1 covers equality before the law, secularity of the republic, and freedom of conscience; Article 3, the right to suffrage and equal access to electoral mandates; and Article 4, freedom of speech and of political party activities. Article 66 states that "no one shall be arbitrarily detained. The judicial authority, guardian of individual liberty, shall ensure the observance of this principle as provided by statute." Article 72 guarantees self-government of territorial entities.

Impact and Functions of Fundamental Rights

The continuous emergence of principles and rights expressed in successive constitutional texts (for example, the 1789 Declaration of the Rights of Man and Citizen and the Preamble to the 1946 constitution) has led to the application of a number of rules by the Constitutional Council in evaluating the constitutionality of laws. These rules form the constitution in a larger sense.

The Constitutional Council has also recognized the constitutional rank of a number of public freedoms adopted as ordinary law under the Third Republic. A landmark 1971 decision applied this principle to freedom of association; the council understood these laws to be an essential part of the republican system. It has formed a list of such principles in the process of its jurisdiction.

Some critics consider the list to be somewhat arbitrary and speak of a "government of unelected judges."

The Constitutional Council has also developed certain constitutional objectives that define the reach and the limits of certain rights. For example, the protection of the public order is a constitutional objective that allows limits on the right to strike. Also, the right of a person to have decent housing is an objective that can override the principle of self-administration of territorial entities when local communities are forced to finance dwellings. The constitutional law of public freedoms has an impact on legislation in other fields of law, such as criminal or civil law.

While applying the law an ordinary judge is bound by the interpretation given by the Constitutional Council. The legislator and the executive are also obliged to respect the jurisprudence of the council and have in fact developed self-restraint to prevent negative rulings.

Limitations to Fundamental Rights

The fundamental rights recognized by the constitution are not without limits. The freedom of one person ends where the freedom of another begins. The needs of the public can also serve as a limit. Article 16 of the 1958 constitution allows the president of the republic to exercise full powers in case of emergency when there is a grave and immediate threat to the institutions of the republic, the integrity of the territory, national independence, or the international obligations of France.

Finally, certain freedoms are limited by other freedoms or powers that can oppose them. The jurisdiction of the Constitutional Council aims at reconciling these different freedoms such as the right to property with the power of expropriation.

ECONOMY

The French constitution does not impose any particular economic system. However, the 1789 declaration that has constitutional rank supports certain economic principles. Its Article 2 states: "The aim of all political association is the preservation of the natural and imprescriptible rights of man. These rights are liberty, property, security, and resistance to oppression." Article 17 states: "Since property is an inviolable and sacred right, no one shall be deprived thereof except where public necessity, legally determined, shall clearly demand it, and then only on condition that the owner shall have been previously and equitably indemnified."

On the other hand, the 1946 preamble, which also has constitutional rank, proclaims economic and social principles that can be contrary to the right of property. It recognizes that everybody has the duty to work and the right to obtain employment (which in practice is far from fulfilled, with more than 2 million unemployed in the early 21st century). It also recognizes union rights and the right to strike and gives every worker the right to participate through his or her representatives in the collective determination of working conditions and the running of enterprises. Furthermore, "Any property or undertaking which, in the course of its business, possesses or acquires the characteristics of a national public service or a de facto monopoly, shall come under collective ownership." Expropriations therefore are possible, though they must not endanger the right of property. In its jurisprudence, the Constitutional Council has been careful to uphold a just balance.

The 1946 preamble also recognizes the right to health, to material security, to rest, and to free time. Every human being who is not able to work has the right to receive sustenance from the community.

The liberalism of 1789 is thus strongly tempered by the social and workers' rights recognized in 1946. However, the state-directed economy that existed after World War II has been liberalized under the influence of European integration and the principle of free and equal competition.

RELIGIOUS COMMUNITIES

Freedom of religion and belief is guaranteed by the constitution. Article 10 of the 1789 declaration specifies that "no one shall be disquieted on account of his opinions, including his religious views, provided their manifestation does not disturb the public order established by law."

Article 1 of the 1958 constitution says that "France shall be an indivisible, secular, democratic, and social Republic. It shall ensure the equality of all citizens before the law, without distinction of origin, race or religion. It shall respect all beliefs. It shall be organized on a decentralized basis."

The laïcité (secular nature) of the republic was enshrined in the law of separation between church and state of December 9, 1905. It is associated with the principle of equality of all citizens without distinction in relation to religion and liberty of conscience. This principle has again become highly topical with a 2004 law prohibiting wearing of Muslim headscarves in public schools.

Despite the principle of separation between church and state, there are areas in which the two cooperate, for example, in optional religious instruction in public schools by school chaplains. Private religious schools, often Catholic, can negotiate the provision of public services.

Church buildings constructed before the separation of church and state belong to the local communities (churches) or to the state (cathedrals) with the duty to maintain them. Religious structures built after that date must be maintained by those churches themselves.

The minister of the interior is also in charge of the state-owned churches and maintains relations with the authorities of the chief religions. Recently, the minister of the interior has taken steps to implement a national institution for the Muslim religion to foster integration into the state and society.

The main religious groups are Catholics, Protestants, Christian Orthodox, Jewish, Muslim, and Buddhist. A growing number of people declare themselves to be atheists.

MILITARY DEFENSE AND STATE OF EMERGENCY

Article 15 of the constitution states that the president of the republic is the commander in chief of the armed forces, a role established by the practice of the first president, General de Gaulle. The president chairs the higher councils and committees of national defense. The High Council of Defense is composed of persons charged with advising the president. The Committee of Defense comprises the relevant cabinet ministers.

The power to appoint the most important military officials lies with the president according to Article 13. The president can proclaim a state of war, which allows the suspension of certain freedoms and the temporary transfer of the power to uphold public order to the armed forces.

Article 21 assigns the prime minister responsibility for national defense. Nevertheless, the domain of defense, as that of diplomacy, appears to be reserved in practice to the president. For example, the abolition of compulsory military service in February 1996 was a presidential decision that was supported by the administration. Since that date, the armed forces have become progressively professionalized. The head of state is in charge of nuclear weapons.

France is a member of the North Atlantic Treaty Organization (NATO). Its armed forces participate in peacekeeping operations all over the world, increasingly within the framework of the United Nations.

The president can declare a state of emergency after consultation with the two chambers, the prime minister, and the Constitutional Council and inform the nation by a message. The president cannot dissolve the National Assembly and must consult the Constitutional Council about every measure taken. However, the presidential powers in this case are without true control, as the Constitutional Council does not specifically control the application of the relevant Article 16.

The proclamation of a state of war, which transfers powers to a military authority, can suspend the exercise of certain freedoms, but this has never been established. The state of emergency can also lead to restrictions on public freedoms, but the civil authorities retain their powers over the police.

AMENDMENTS TO THE CONSTITUTION

The constitution of the Fifth Republic is a supple document that has been frequently amended in recent years. Article 89 states that an amendment needs the consent of both chambers of Parliament. Afterward, the text is normally presented to a referendum. However, the president can bypass this step and ask the two chambers to meet in joint session, when they can finalize the amendment by three-fifth of the votes cast.

With the exception of the amendment of October 2, 2002, all recent amendments have been adopted by the latter procedure. In 1962, General de Gaulle used the referendum procedure to amend the constitution to permit the election of the president of the republic by universal and direct suffrage. On the other hand, he avoided that procedure when pressing for regionalization and Senate reform.

Article 89 expresses three limits to amendments: First, no amendment may damage territorial integrity. Second, the office of the president of the republic cannot be eliminated. Finally, Article 89 holds sacred the republican form of government. Historically that provision was intended to bar the reintroduction of monarchy. Under the Fifth Republic, it is seen as a safeguard against dictatorship.

PRIMARY SOURCES
Constitution in English. Available online. URL: http://www.assemblee-nationale.fr/english/8ab.asp. Accessed on August 10, 2005.
Constitution in French. Available online. URLs: http://www.conseil-constitutionnel.fr/textes/constit.htm; http://www.legifrance.gouv.fr/. Accessed on September 28, 2005.

SECONDARY SOURCES
John Bell, *French Constitutional Law*. New York: Oxford University Press, 1992.
Stéphane Cottin and Jérôme Rabenou, "Researching French Law." Available online. URL: http://www.llrx.com/features/french.htm. Accessed on June 17, 2006.
Institute of Global Law of the University College London with Translated Statutes and Legal News. Available online. URL: http://www.ucl.ac.uk/laws/global_law/index.htm. Accessed on September 15, 2005.
United Nations, "Core Document Forming Part of the Reports of States Parties: France" (HRI/CORE/1/Add.17/Rev.1), 7 October 1996. Available online. URL: http://www.unhchr.ch/tbs/doc.nsf. Accessed on September 20, 2005.

Jean Pierre Lay